ATHWART HISTORY

ATHWART HISTORY

Half a Century of Polemics, Animadversions, and Illuminations

A William F. Buckley Jr. Omnibus

Edited by Linda Bridges & Roger Kimball

With a Preface by George F. Will

Introduction by Roger Kimball

Encounter Books 𝑒 New York · London

First American edition published in 2010 by Encounter Books,
an activity of Encounter for Culture and Education, Inc.,
a nonprofit, tax exempt corporation.
Encounter Books website address: www.encounterbooks.com

Manufactured in the United States and printed on
acid-free paper. The paper used in this publication meets
the minimum requirements of ANSI/NISO Z39.48-1992
(R 1997) (*Permanence of Paper*).

FIRST AMERICAN EDITION

LIBRARY OF CONGRESS CATALOGING-IN-PUBLICATION DATA

Buckley, William F. (William Frank), 1925–2008.
Athwart history: half a century of polemics, animadversions, and illuminations:
a William F. Buckley, Jr., omnibus/edited by Linda Bridges & Roger Kimball.
p. cm.
Includes bibliographical references and index.
ISBN-13: 978-1-59403-379-7 (hardcover: alk. paper)
ISBN-10: 1-59403-379-X (hardcover: alk. paper) 1. Conservatism—
United States. 2. United States—Politics and government.
I. Bridges, Linda. II. Kimball, Roger, 1953– III. Title.
JC573.2.U6B83 2010
320.52092—dc22
2010015310

10 9 8 7 6 5 4 3 2 1

CONTENTS

PREFACE

George F. Will

The most important intellectual development of the nineteenth century was that history became History—a proper noun. Hitherto it had been the narrative of the human story, sometimes grand and inspiriting, sometimes mundane, sometimes seemingly a tale told by an idiot, full of sound and fury, signifying nothing. But always history had been understood as a drama driven by human choices, with perhaps an occasional intervention from God, or the gods.

Then came the nineteenth century's invention of historicism. The idea has had many advocates and manifestations, but one man made it a world-shaking fixation, especially for intellectuals. Karl Marx argued that there are iron laws that govern the unfolding of history, driving it to a destination that can be known, and hastened, by the discerning few, who deserve to be the leaders of the undiscerning. Those who lack the key of theory cannot unlock History's secret. They are unable to pierce the veil of mere appearance. They are in the grip of false consciousness. Although they fancy themselves the masters of their fate, they are actually mere play-things of events, a.k.a. History.

The most important intellectual event of the twentieth century was the revolt against the idea that vast, impersonal forces make a mockery of the illusion that we make meaningful choices about how we shall live. Those who led this uprising in defense of life's moral seriousness decided to stand athwart history—make that History—and tell it to stop thinking that it is at the wheel of the world. And *that* is why what William F. Buckley Jr. did five years after midcentury mattered so much.

When he, in effect, rolled up that first copy of *National Review* and swatted History on its upturned nose, he was saying: You are not all that you have been cracked up to be. Yes, Buckley said, there are political tendencies, and very strong ones, in Western societies. But tendencies tend to be resistible, so let the resistance begin.

And let it begin with the high spirits and sense of fun that should accompany a quickened sense that humanity has emancipated itself from fear of all determinisms. If there is a common thread in Buckley's writings, it is the compatibility of seriousness, even occasional indignation, with an unfailing sense of merriment about the pleasures of intellectual combat.

One of Buckley's first tasks, however, was to convert conservatism from a mere sensibility and a literary phenomenon into a political force. For that, he needed a horse to ride. Appropriately, he found one in cowboy country.

Arizona's junior senator, Barry Goldwater, was, in the felicitous phrase of Richard Rovere, a commentator prominent in the 1950s and 1960s, a "cheerful malcontent." He was not an intellectual, but he knew that politics without the ballast of ideas is a lighter-than-air balloon that will be blown about by gusts of wind. Goldwater's 1964 presidential campaign was, as the title of a book on it declared, a "magnificent catastrophe." But it was catastrophic only in the short run and only because he lost forty-four states. It was magnificent because it was an insurrection against the conventional wisdom about the narrow limits within which political debate supposedly had to take place.

Sixteen years later, the seeds sown by Goldwater's candidacy came to fruition, making possible—no, mandatory—the following conclusion: Buckley was America's political Johnny Appleseed. Without Buckley, there would have been no *National Review*; without *NR*, there would have been no coming into existence, and coming together, of the forces that captured the Republican Party and nominated Goldwater. Without that nomination, the presidency of Ronald Reagan probably would not have happened. Therefore, Buckley was the most consequential political controversialist since Thomas Paine.

Buckley was, of course, much more than that, because his tastes and interests were so catholic. Yes, the pun is intended.

Actually, it sometimes seemed that Buckley considered conducting political arguments, narrowly understood, a duty to be done in order to gather a readership for other, more interesting and often more important subjects, such as the health of the culture and of the religious impulse that must, Buckley thought, sustain any durable and defensible culture. But politics, broadly and properly understood, concerns how humanity should live in its social dimension. Which means it concerns *everything*. So, although it might have mortified him to think so, Buckley really was merely—merely!—a political commentator, even when he wandered far afield from the mundane matters of elections and stuff.

Those elections that once seemed so momentous have now receded from memory, and we can now see what made Buckley such a history-making figure: He helped to unmake History, thereby reviving history as a truly human drama. He asserted, and then proved, that a few determined men and women, equipped with sound ideas, could put paid to all ideas of determinism. They could choose to command history to halt, step back, and turn right.

It did. It had no choice.

INTRODUCTION

Roger Kimball

" **O**f making many books," we read in *Ecclesiastes*, "there is no end." I do not believe that sage found the prospect cheering, either. But for William F. Buckley Jr., the making of many books was an ineluctable part of life. He started young, in his mid-twenties, with *God and Man at Yale* (1951), and he was busy finishing *The Reagan I Knew* (2008) when he died, age 82, sitting in the closest thing to a saddle most writers possess: at his desk in his study in Stamford, Connecticut, the morning of February 27, 2008. In between came fifty-odd other books: collections of essays and columns, monographs, travelogues, memoirs literary, political, and religious, not to mention some twenty novels.

Of making many books, in short, Bill Buckley was a modern master. At some point in the *Entwicklung*, Bill's son, Christopher, had a copy of each of his father's books rebound, and presented him with the imposing uniform set as a gift. I do not know if every subsequent book made it to the binder and found its place of honor in that bookcase set aside in the Buckley homestead for the WFB *œuvre*. I suspect a few late volumes were missing. But I could never glimpse that monument to literary productivity without a sense of awe tinged with envy, feelings that were augmented when I considered that making books was merely one arrow in the Buckley quiver. Other arrows included *National Review*, the magazine that Bill founded in 1955, and which he molded during his long editorship into America's foremost conservative journal of opinion. There was also *Firing Line*, the public-affairs television show that he started in 1966 and over which he presided for thirty-odd years, providing the most intelligent and entertaining forum for the exchange of ideas and exhibition of eccentricity in the history of television.

Author, entrepreneurial editor, television personality: we must also add Bill Buckley, public speaker and polemicist. For many years, Bill traversed the country, indeed the world, purveying the urbane gospel of enlightened conservatism at college campuses, think tanks, centers of commerce, and other conclaves public and private. At one point, he was averaging seventy events a year. That's seven-zero. I pause to remind you, Dear Reader, that a year contains but fifty-two weeks. And let's not forget Bill's syndicated column (thrice weekly for more than thirty years; twice weekly from 1994 on), the countless articles for *NR* and a galaxy of other magazines from— well, from *The New Criterion* to *Playboy*: how's that for range? Then there were the avocations. Bill skied. He sailed across the Atlantic, across the Pacific, to Canada, to Bermuda. He played the piano and harpsichord, not just in the privacy of his living room but with symphony orchestras before hundreds. In his spare time, he ran for mayor of New York City and, along the way, rescued American conservatism from irrelevance and crack-pottery.

If you have read this far, it is likely that you already know something about William F. Buckley Jr., and if you know something about William F. Buckley Jr., it is likely you know that our title, *Athwart History*, comes from the famous publisher's statement introducing the inaugural issue of *National Review*, November 19, 1955. "*National Review* is out of place," that bulletin informed readers, "in the sense that the United Nations and the League of Women Voters and the *New York Times* and Henry Steele Commager are *in* place. It is out of place because, in its maturity, literate America rejected conservatism in favor of radical social experimentation." The brash new magazine had arrived with its brash young editor to cast a cold and inquisitive light upon that presumption. The magazine "stands athwart history," Bill announced, "yelling Stop, at a time when no one is inclined to do so, or to have much patience with those who so urge it."

Take a look at that inaugural statement: it appears below, on pages 6–8. It was written more than fifty years ago. But I suspect that you will find, as I did on re-reading it, that it has preternaturally contemporary relevance. "Radical social experimentation"; "the inroads that relativism has made on the American soul"; "the intransigence of the liberals, who run this country." If those yelling Stop! in 1955 were "out of place," how much more out of place now, in 2010, when what Bill called "the relationship of the state to the individual" in the United States is poised to undergo its most thoroughgoing transformation in history?

Is this overstated? Ponder (for starters) these phrases: "stimulus package," "cap and trade," "spread the wealth around," "nationalized health care." Just before the 2008 election, Barack Obama declared to his acolytes that he was only a few days away from "fundamentally transforming the United States of America." If you didn't believe him then—if you thought that talk of "fundamentally transforming" the country was mere hustings hyperbole—perhaps the last year and a half will have convinced you otherwise. Ideas, Bill observed in that editorial, "rule the world." What ideas? Liberty for one. The United States was "conceived in liberty," as Lincoln put it. The idea of individual freedom was the country's cynosure, its guiding principle. By 1955, that principle had been insidiously undermined by the well-intentioned dispensations of "literate America," intoxicated as it was by "radical social experimentation." Think of it: In 1955, Bill Buckley, not yet thirty, argued that "There never was an age of conformity quite like this one." And today? Looking back, we understand that the dampening spirit of conformity and the assault on freedom were then in their infancy. They have suddenly come of age. The question is not whether Bill's inaugural bulletin is still pertinent. It could hardly be more so. The question is whether those "uncorroded by a cynical contempt for human freedom" will command the wit, rhetoric, and moral courage to stand athwart tomorrow whispering, confiding, explaining—sometimes even yelling Stop!—in order that freedom might have an opportunity to prevail.

That is the sort of question I found myself asking frequently as Linda Bridges and I sifted through the Buckley œuvre to arrive at the contents of this capacious volume. The most recent piece ("Inside Obama"), written just a few weeks before Bill's death, is a vigorous and canny reflection on candidate Obama's "mischievous" suggestion that increased government intervention in our lives would increase the chance that "every American child" would benefit from the riches produced by the mighty engine of American capitalism. It was, Bill observed, a mendacious suggestion, a false promise that would "foster frustration and stimulate disillusion." The earliest piece, which opens the volume, dates from the summer of 1951. In it, Bill, invoking Friedrich von Hayek's *Road to Serfdom* (then only seven years old), limned two critical dangers facing American liberty: the external threat of Communist imperialism and the homegrown threat of "government paternalism." The fall of the Soviet colossus signaled not the end but the dissipation of the former threat, its distribution over a more amorphous field of action. The threat of government paternalism is today more patent than ever. Indeed, reading through these essays, I was often brought up short by a sense of historical foreshortening: Bill was writing in

1957 or 1967 or 1977, but his essays read as if they were written yesterday, or possibly this morning. Environmentalism. The oil crisis. The Religious Right. States' rights. Reforming health care. Immigration, illegal and the other kind. The future of Social Security. Israel. Irresponsible accusations of racism. The Supreme Court. Iran and the bomb. "Why We Need a Black President in 1980" (written in 1970). The substance as well as the subject might have been taken from what is happening now, today.

In part, no doubt, the contemporaneous feel of so much that Bill wrote is explained by another passage from *Ecclesiastes*: "There is nothing new under the sun." But there was also Bill's unerring instinct for the pertinent. When he wrote about a matter of public interest, he went for, and generally hit upon, the jugular. I do not mean only that he deployed the successful debater's trick of touching on spots that were sore or weak. Bill was an able debater, and was plenty adept at ferreting out and exposing his opponents' weaknesses, evasions, ambiguities, enthymemes, and unwarranted presumptions. But he also had a conspicuous talent for getting to the heart of a matter. And so whether his subject was environmentalism, school choice, race relations, religious observances, foreign policy, or encroaching statism, what he wrote was likely to touch upon what was central and enduring. That is one of the benefits of conservatism: embracing the permanent, one may be unfashionable, but one is never out of date. Literature, said Ezra Pound, is news that stays news. I have met few people better informed about public affairs than Bill Buckley. But his mastery of the day's ephemera was only a prelude to his embrace of the principles that underlay the controversies.

Like Athena, Bill seems to have sprung forth fully armed. He was barely graduated from Yale when he published *God and Man at Yale*. The book catapulted its twenty-five-year-old author to an atmosphere of hostile notoriety from which, despite Bill's later acceptance by the world of high society, he never completely descended. It is difficult at this distance to recreate the stir—no, the tornado—that book precipitated. Remember the apoplexy that *The Closing of the American Mind* occasioned in the late 1980s? My, how the left-wing academic establishment loved (and continues to love) to hate that book! Double that enmity, treble it: that will give you some sense of the hostility that engulfed *God and Man at Yale*. Bill's opening credo that "the duel between Christianity and atheism is the most important in the world" was simply not to be borne. His codicil—"I further believe that the struggle between individualism [i.e., conservatism] and collectivism is the same struggle reproduced on another level"—elevated disbelief into rage. The liberal establishment, Dwight Macdonald observed at the time, "reacted with all of the grace and agility of an elephant cornered by a mouse." McGeorge Bundy pronounced anathema upon the book in *The Atlantic Monthly*. The (then) well-known Yale philosopher T. M. Greene deployed the word "fascist" three times in as many sentences. "What more," Professor Greene asked, "could Hitler, Mussolini, or Stalin ask for?" Well, as Bill observed in his response, "they asked for, and got, a great deal more."

In retrospect, the reaction to *Gamay* (as the book was nicknamed by the Beaujolais-minded publisher) is partly amusing, partly frightening. The amusing part arises from the elephant-cornered-by-mouse aspect Dwight Macdonald mentioned. The frightening part comes when you realize how contemporary Bill's travails seem. Professor Greene went on to pontificate that

> What is required is more not less tolerance—not the tolerance of indifference, but the tolerance of honest respect for divergent convictions and the determination of all that such divergent opinions be heard without administrative censorship. I try my best in the classroom to expound and defend my faith, when it is relevant, as honestly and persuasively as I can. But I can do so only because many of my colleagues are expounding and defending their contrasting faiths, or skepticism, as openly and honestly as I am mine.

Sound familiar? But this, Bill rightly noted, is "*ne plus ultra* relativism, idiot nihilism." No ethical code requires "honest respect" for *every* divergent opinion. "Eating people is wrong," as Flanders and Swann put it, and you needn't be Aristotle to extend the list of things unworthy of toleration no matter what a "divergent opinion" might dictate. "Complete moral tolerance," as James Fitzjames Stephen noted in *Liberty, Equality, Fraternity* (1873), "is possible only when men have become completely indifferent to each other—that is to say, when society is at an end." Besides, Professor Greene's aria about tolerance would have been sweeter—or at least ostensibly more plausible—had he deigned to practice what he preached. "An honest respect by him for my divergent conviction," Bill wrote, "would have been an arresting application at once of his theoretical and his charitable convictions."

The nerve that Bill struck with *God and Man at Yale* is still smarting; indeed, it is throbbing uncontrollably, as anyone can attest who has contemplated the discrepancy between proclamations of "diversity" on campuses and the practice there of enforcing a politically correct orthodoxy on any contentious subject. The bottom line: There is plenty of room for "diversity," so long as you embrace the left-liberal dogma. Diverge from that dogma and you will find that the rhetoric of diversity has been replaced by talk of "prejudice," "hate speech," and the entire lexicon of liberal denunciation.

Pascal once apologized to one of his correspondents for writing him so long a letter: "*Je n'ai fait celle-ci plus longue que parce que je n'ai pas eu le loisir de la faire plus courte.*" *Athwart History* is indisputably a long book. Perhaps, had Linda Bridges and I had another six months, we might have trimmed it by another hundred pages or so and still preserved its essential character. Readers anxiously contemplating the book's bulk should know that it was at one point considerably larger. After assembling a working draft, we realized that we were competing in girth with the Calcutta phone book—the unexpurgated version—and we set about ruthlessly trimming, excerpting, pruning, removing repetitions, redundancies, and anything we felt was both inessential and insufficiently charming. Our aim was to provide a companion volume to Bill's last big anthology, *Miles Gone By* (2004), the "literary autobiography" made up of essays that include Bill as an actor or subject.

Every life can be characterized by one or two governing attitudes. Perhaps the word that best characterizes Bill is "relish." The depth and variousness of *Miles Gone By* reflect the depth and variousness of its author's pleasures. It is a cheerful book, a convivial book, somehow a youthful book, though Bill was no youngster when it was published.

Emerson, who wasn't wrong about everything, devoted a book to Representative Men, men who epitomized some essential quality: Shakespeare; or, the Poet; Napoleon; or, the Man of the World; Goethe; or, the Writer. Bill Buckley is, in Emerson's sense, a Representative Man. One cannot quite imagine Emerson getting his mind around a character like William F. Buckley Jr. But if one can conjure up a less gaseous redaction of Emerson, one may suppose him writing an essay called Buckley; or, the Conservative.

I hasten to add that by "conservative" I do not mean any narrow partisan affiliation. Yes, yes, Bill was known above all as a conservative: the man who did as much as anyone to make American conservatism respectable. That's all very well, but unfortunately the term "conservative" (like its opposite number, "liberal") has degenerated into an epithet, positive or negative depending on the communion of the person who wields it, but virtually without content.

Being conservative may commit one to certain political positions or moral dogmas. But it also, and perhaps more importantly, disposes one to a certain attitude toward life. Walter Bagehot touched upon one essential aspect of the conservative disposition when, in writing of Walter Scott, he observed that "the essence of Toryism is enjoyment." Whatever else it is, *Miles Gone By* is an affidavit of enjoyment: a record of, an homage to, a life greatly, and gratefully, enjoyed. Part of Bill's conservatism is his Catholicism. Our secular age is unfriendly to Catholics, to religion generally, but the irony is that secularists are often less jubilantly worldly than their Jewish and Christian compatriots. "God made the world and saw that it was good." That bulletin from Genesis might have provided an epigraph for *Miles Gone By*.

Athwart History contains its share of kindred allegro pieces, especially in the section called "Grace Notes." But our chief aim was to reintroduce the public to the serious, sinewy, occasionally pugnacious side of Bill Buckley. Nearly half of the pieces collected here are appearing between hard covers for the first time. Many others appeared in books that are now out of print. A large proportion of the pieces deal with matters of urgent public concern. Not a few tackle basic questions of political philosophy.

It would be pleasant to claim credit for the idea of *Athwart History*, but that honor belongs to Charles Kesler, editor of *The Claremont Review* and an old friend of Bill's. On the morning of April 4, 2008, some 2,500 people filled St. Patrick's Cathedral in New York to pay their last respects to Bill Buckley. "If I'm still famous," Bill had told his son a few years earlier, "try to convince the Cardinal to do the service at St. Patrick's. If I'm not, just tuck me away in Stamford." Friends and admirers had streamed in from all over the country to be at the memorial Mass. Bill was still famous. That afternoon, *National Review* sponsored a panel discussion at the Princeton Club in New York to talk about Bill's legacy and achievement. The discussion was moderated by Jay Nordlinger, then *NR*'s Managing Editor, and included talks by me, Charles Kesler, *National Review*'s Editor, Rich Lowry, and the author and syndicated columnist George Will. In the course of his remarks, Charles pointed out that much of Bill's more trenchant work was out of print. What was needed, he said, was a collection that represented the intellectual Bill Buckley, Buckley the polemicist, controversialist, and thinker.

That is what we have endeavored to provide in *Athwart History*, throwing in for good measure a large handful of essays that demonstrate something of the range of Bill's interests and avocations. The pieces come from a very wide variety of sources. We have followed some general "house rules" but have not attempted to impose absolute stylistic uniformity, a bootless task given the diversity of the literary macédoine we have assembled. We list the provenance and date after each essay; where a date only appears, the provenance was Bill's syndicated column.

Athwart History ends with some of Bill's reflections on a virtue little practiced these days: gratitude. It seems appropriate that I should conclude this introduction on the same note. Thanks, then, to George Will, Bill's friend and comrade-in-arms, for his gracious preface; to Stefan Beck for his assiduous work in helping to track down and digitize many of the pieces that appear in *Athwart History*; and to Linda Bridges, Bill's longtime assistant and former Managing Editor of *National Review*, for her gargantuan labors in preparing this book. I am deeply grateful to them all for their help in making *Athwart History* a reality.

RK
Norwalk, CT
May 2010

POLITICS IN PRINCIPLE

Too Much to Take

W e conservatives have suffered a great deal. Twenty years of political impotence; two score years of intellectual inertia; abusive speeches, articles, columns, and books that, piled on top of one another, would tower arrogantly over the gates of Heaven—all this our dwindling cadre has borne, and withal patiently. But I, for one, am now suffering from a sprained back.

For in the last year or so, confident no doubt that there is little left to be said with respect to how this country ought to be run, our restless and expansive collectivists have wandered afield, this time to ravish us in the inner sanctity of our boudoirs: *They are now telling us how we conservatives ought to act*, and, in the course of it all, *what "conservatism" really is!*

This last has become a lively pastime for the "liberals," as they are called (though they are a far cry from classical liberals). It was most brazenly touched off, as far as I know, in the early spring of 1950 by Arthur Schlesinger Jr., who wrote for the *New York Times* Sunday magazine an article titled "Needed: An Intelligent Opposition," or some such thing. The ink wasn't dry when Herbert Agar tackled the same subject for *Harper's*, in which he outlined carefully what conservatives ought to think, say, and do. Chester Bowles and Henry Steele Commager and scores of others have carried the banner forward in their headlong rush to save conservatism from the abysses in which it will flounder if the conservatives are left to their own resources. They tell us we must refashion our thinking "if we wish to serve our country." (Or, better still, to avoid provincialism, "if we wish to serve the world.")

Their arguments all follow a pattern: "Look, gentlemen, why don't you face up to the fact that a social revolution has occurred in the United States in the last several decades. No jeremiads, no melancholy post-mortems are going to change this. Social Security, farm parities, progressive income taxes, irredeemable paper currency, a large and entrenched bureaucracy, withering state borders, powerful unions—all these are here to stay. Why not acknowledge them and formulate a *constructive* alternative to the Democratic platform, an alternative that will accept the foregoing reforms and focus, accordingly, on some new, intelligent *casus belli*—such as, for example, administrative procedure, efficient management, and the like. Yours are *negative* policies. You're always *against* this or that; you seldom come forward with original and constructive legislation of your own. As firm believers in democracy, we liberals believe there ought to be more than one political party; but the way it's been going, what we have in fact amounts to just one party, because you don't seem to learn, your quadrennial embarrassments notwithstanding, that your reactionary program is unacceptable."

~

Incredibly, this approach electrifies many conservatives and leaves them impressed and agog. It must be the force of habit that causes so many individualists to resign themselves to the invincibility of "liberal" dicta. For it is these counsels that are molding the thinking of many elements of the Republican Party, nominally the "opposition party."

Witness the popularity of Harold Stassen with the Young Republican Club in 1948; the clamor of so many "conservatives" for a "progressive" Republican Party; the happy, burgeoning group of Eastern progressives and their increasing power in the Senate. See the emergence of the *New York Herald Tribune*, that unbelievably unprincipled and opportunistic news-sheet, as the spokesman for New Republicanism. Surely, if the metamorphosis of the conservative opposition continues in this direction, it won't be long before we have satisfied Arthur Schlesinger Jr. of our patriotism. And this seems to be the most ambitious goal of many good Republicans.

How is it, I'd like to know, that so many of us heed and even solicit the counsel of our sworn enemies, the collectivists? To begin with, what reason have we to believe that they are acting in good faith when they spell out to us a platform which, they insist, might woo the American people away from their demigods, the Democrats? I should as soon believe that Schlesinger, Agar, et al., are altruistically concerned over the prosperity of Republicanism as I would that the Soviet Union is interested in nourishing democracy.

What so many Republicans have been guilelessly willing to interpret as benevolent and detached advice on how they ought to conduct themselves is in fact something else: It is nothing more than a typical symptom of the liberals' obsessive desire to distend bipartisanship—as it has been applied, for example, to foreign policy—to all other issues as well. It is a well-calculated maneuver to *destroy*, rather than to construct, an intelligent and meaningful opposition.

This is in the collectivist tradition. Deviations are as heinous to the New Dealer as they are to the Stalinist. But for a few minor embellishments, the demagoguery of a Walter Reuther or a Charlie Michelson is as intolerant of the opposition as that of a Gromyko or an Ehrenburg; and it is natural that this be so. For after all, socialism scorns competition. It follows naturally that competition at the most crucial echelon—national policy—should appear most appalling to the statists, and that they should, accordingly, focus their best energies to the end of proscribing any significant policy alternatives at this level.

An additional reason explains the collectivist anxiety for homogeneity in national policy. While the American individualist hearkens always to 150 million human beings, who ought not be impeded from harboring and implementing 150 million convictions and policies, the collectivists' concern is with one policy, the State's policy. And there is only one State. Their stakes are therefore high, for it's win the State or lose the battle. Since the statists have never been squeamish about their methods, it is only natural that they should exploit every potential ally; and a most valuable ally has always been the conservative, whose demonstrated gullibility makes him easy prey.

And how do they camouflage these raw tactics? Advice from collectivists to individualists is automatically suspect. So, they tag their concern for a flourishing opposition as stemming from their solicitude for the democratic fabric of our institutions, which presupposes the existence of at least two political parties. This way they can destroy the opposition in the name of "democracy," which leaves them feeling clean all over.

~

It's not too early—and not too late, let's hope—to anticipate the forthcoming caucuses, primaries, and the lot, that will crystallize in the early summer of next year into a Republican Party platform. Shall we be able to conduct ourselves without reference to the Schlesinger-Agar book on Political Behavior and Policy Formation? Dare we risk the displeasure of the liberals by adopting a platform which, on the domestic level at least, rings forth with a clear alternative to, and an equally clear denunciation of, the collectivism of the Democrats?

Several questions are posed here. The first is, Can the Republicans win if they publicly decry the "social revolution" which we are enjoined to respect as a *fait accompli*? The second, of course, is, Do we care about winning if we don't do just that?

One thing we know: In the past we have temporized with collectivism and we have lost. And after the campaigns were over, we were left not with the exhilaration and pride of having done our best to restore freedom, but with the sickening humiliation of having failed to seduce the American people because we were pitted against a more glib, a more extravagant, a more experienced gigolo.

Assuming, then, that we shall campaign in behalf of what we feel in our hearts and minds to be in the best interests of the American people, will our program appear to be a negative one? Most certainly it will. For it will call for the *abolition* of federal power and control wherever possible. It will call for the abolition of farm, school, and housing subsidies, Social Security, government loans and financing, pork barreling, special privileges, and much more that is "negative."

All such legislation continues to imply that the State can better administer social power, that the central government knows better than the people, acting individually or through their local governments, how best to spend the people's money. If we are guilty of "negativism" in calling for the pruning of State power, then at least we have honorable bedfellows in our constitutional fathers.

~

Friedrich von Hayek stated in *The Road to Serfdom* that the line that separated individualism from collectivism is clear-cut. Those of us who believe this to be so ought to acknowledge that line and give the American people an opportunity to step to one side of it or to the other. To that end, I respectfully sketch out the following thoughts as a possible basis for a preamble to the Republican Party's 1952 platform:

"The American people are engaged in two wars—the one against Russian imperialism, the other against government paternalism. Only history will tell whether Joseph Stalin or Franklin Roosevelt will have wrought greater damage to individual freedom in the United States.

"Our task today is to cast off defiantly the influence of both offenders. Our foreign policy must aim at the destruction of Soviet power; and our domestic aim is the dissolution of the bureaucracy consistent with waging an effective fight against Stalinism. Both struggles must be won, or neither is worth winning."

As for the hoots and cries from the Schlesingers, let them come. After all, *their* program still has a ways to go before they can shut us up forcibly.

—*Human Events*, July 18, 1951

Standing Athwart History

There is, we like to think, solid reason for rejoicing. Prodigious efforts, by many people, are responsible for *National Review*. But since it will be the policy of this magazine to reject the hypodermic approach to world affairs, we may as well start out at once, and admit that the joy is not unconfined.

Let's face it: Unlike Vienna, it seems altogether possible that did *National Review* not exist, no one would have invented it. The launching of a conservative weekly journal of opinion in a country widely assumed to be a bastion of conservatism at first glance looks like a work of supererogation, rather like publishing a royalist weekly within the walls of Buckingham Palace. It is not that, of course; if *National Review* is superfluous, it is so for very different reasons: It stands athwart history, yelling Stop, at a time when no one is inclined to do so, or to have much patience with those who so urge it.

National Review is out of place, in the sense that the United Nations and the League of Women Voters and the *New York Times* and Henry Steele Commager are *in* place. It is out of place because, in its maturity, literate America rejected conservatism in favor of radical social experimentation. Instead of covetously consolidating its premises, the United States seems tormented by its tradition of fixed postulates having to do with the meaning of existence, with the relationship of the state to the individual, of the individual to his neighbor, so clearly enunciated in the enabling documents of our Republic.

"I happen to prefer champagne to ditchwater," said the benign old wrecker of the ordered society, Oliver Wendell Holmes, "but there is no reason to suppose that the cosmos does." We have come around to Mr. Holmes's view, so much so that we feel gentlemanly doubts when asserting the superiority of capitalism to socialism, of republicanism to centralism, of champagne to ditchwater—of anything to anything. (How curious that one of the doubts one is *not* permitted is whether, at the margin, Mr. Holmes was a useful citizen.) The inroads that relativism has made on the American soul are not so easily evident. One must recently have lived on or close to a college campus to have a vivid intimation of what has happened. It is there that we see how a number of energetic social innovators, plugging their grand designs, succeeded over the years in capturing the liberal intellectual imagination. And since ideas rule the world, the ideologues, having won over the intellectual class, simply walked in and started to run things.

Run just about *everything*. There never was an age of conformity quite like this one, or a camaraderie quite like the liberals'. Drop a little itching powder in Jimmy Wechsler's bath and before he has scratched himself for the third time, Arthur Schlesinger will have denounced you in a dozen books and speeches, Archibald MacLeish will have written ten heroic cantos about our age of terror, *Harper's* will have published them, and everyone in sight will have been nominated for a Freedom Award. Conservatives in this country—at least those who have not made their peace with the New Deal, and there is serious question whether there are others—are nonlicensed nonconformists; and this is dangerous business in a liberal world, as every editor of this magazine can readily show by pointing to his scars. Radical conservatives in this country have an interesting time of it, for when they are not being suppressed or mutilated by the liberals, they are being ignored or humiliated by a great many of those of the well-fed Right, whose ignorance and amorality have never been exaggerated for the same reason that one cannot exaggerate infinity.

There are, thank Heaven, the exceptions. There are those of generous impulse and a sincere desire to encourage a responsible dissent from the liberal orthodoxy. And there are those who recognize that when all is said and done, the marketplace depends for a license to operate freely on the men who issue licenses—on the politicians. They recognize, therefore, that efficient getting and spending is itself impossible except in an atmosphere that encourages efficient getting and spending. And in back of all political institutions there are moral and philosophical concepts, implicit or defined. Our political economy and our high-energy industry run on large, general principles, on ideas—not by day-to-day guesswork, expedients, and improvisations. Ideas have to go into exchange to become or remain operative; and the medium of such exchange is the printed word. A vigorous and incorruptible journal of conservative opinion is—dare we say it?—as necessary to better living as chemistry.

We begin publishing, then, with a considerable stock of experience with the irresponsible Right, and a despair of the intransigence of the liberals, who run this country; and all this in a world dominated by the jubilant singlemindedness of the practicing Communist, with his inside track to History. All this would not appear to augur well for *National Review*. Yet we start with a considerable—and considered—optimism.

After all, we crashed through. More than 120 investors made this magazine possible, and more than fifty men and women of small means invested less than $1,000 apiece in it. Two men and one woman, all three with overwhelming personal and public commitments, worked round the clock to make publication possible. A score of professional writers pledged their devoted attention to its needs, and hundreds of thoughtful men and women gave evidence that the appearance of such a journal as we have in mind would profoundly affect their lives.

Our own views, as expressed in a memorandum drafted a year ago, and directed to our investors, are set forth in an adjacent column. We have nothing to offer but the best that is in us. That, a thousand liberals who read this sentiment will say with relief, is clearly not enough! It isn't enough. But it is at this point that we steal the march. For we offer, besides ourselves, a position that has not grown old under the weight of a gigantic, parasitic bureaucracy, a position untempered by the doctoral dissertations of a generation of Ph.D.s in social architecture, unattenuated by a thousand vulgar promises to a thousand different pressure groups, uncorroded by a cynical contempt for human freedom. And that, ladies and gentlemen, leaves us just about the hottest thing in town.

—*National Review*, November 19, 1955

Liberal Presumption

Halfway through the second term of Franklin Roosevelt, New Deal brain-trusters began to worry about mounting public concern with the soaring national debt. In those days, the size of the debt was on everyone's mind; indeed, Franklin Roosevelt had won a landslide victory in 1932 on a platform that contained the pledge to hack away at a debt which, even under the frugal Mr. Hoover, was thought to have grown to menacing size. At just that moment, an insight came to the rescue. Economists throughout the land were electrified by an alluring theory of debt that had grown out of the new, nationalistic economics of John Maynard Keynes. The ghost of the National Debt was finally laid! To depict the intoxicating political effect of the discovery, the artist of the *Washington Times-Herald* drew for the front page of his paper a memorable cartoon. In the center, seated on a throne, was a jubilant FDR, cigarette holder tilted almost vertically, grinning from ear to ear. Dancing about him in a circle, hands clasped, his ecstatic brain-trusters sang together the magical incantation, the great emancipating formula: "WE OWE IT TO OURSELVES!"

In five talismanic words the planners had disposed of the problem of deficit spending. Anyone, thenceforward, who worried about an increase in the national debt was simply ignorant of a central insight of modem economics: What do we care how much we—the government—owe, so long as we owe it to ourselves?

There is no room in a brief discussion of the root economic assumptions of liberalism for technical commentary on such economic *tours de force* as the one about the national debt. I am drawn to the *Times-Herald*'s amusing cartoon, and its symbolic significance. A root assumption of the liberal ideology is that, intellectually, man has come to dominate the economic elements, and that we need only will it, in order to have fair weather all the time. The occasional relapses—for instance the recession of the winter of 1957–58—are due not so much to absence of economic expertise, as to the inexpertness of Republican technicians. An inexpertness traceable, primarily, to their bewitchment by the antique superstitions.

The accelerability of economic development by force of will (a premise of President Truman's Point Four Program) is an article of faith for leading liberal spokesmen. Mr. Walter Reuther is fond of observing that the years 1953 to 1958 (recognize?) were years of an "under-utilization of productive resources"; that had the rate of growth gone forward "dynamically," the gross national product would have been "*$140 billion* higher over this period." Though Mr. Reuther relies heavily on a demonology, he does not take the pains to motivate the desire of "big business," "vested interests," "warmongers," and "reactionary politicians" to depress the level of economic activity—at their own expense. One would think no one would work more assiduously than a businessman to implement Mr. Reuther's economic schemes, were it demonstrable that they would raise the national income as dramatically as Mr. Reuther contends.

The point is that economics—which to be sure has always had an uneasy time of it asserting its autonomy as a social science—has become the pliant servant of ideology. For all one knows, Mr. Reuther seriously believes that the implementation of his political program would have the salutary economic consequences he describes. But one thing is sure, that even if the program could be demonstrated *not* to have such economic consequences, Mr. Reuther would not modify his politics, any more than the economic stupidity of the collective farm has modified Mao Tse-tung's enthusiasm for it. If ideology calls for a $15-billion program of public health, the assumption is that the $15 billion are there—somewhere. It becomes pettifoggery and obstructionism to maintain that the money is *not* "there": in the sense of being readily available and uncommitted. It is reactionary to insist that to produce the money it becomes necessary either to raise the level of economic production and thus increase tax revenues, to raise existing taxes, or to inflate the money into existence. Such demurrals, it is easy to see by examining the rhetoric of the heavy spenders, are inadmissible. *What is important is the public-health program.*

The salient economic assumptions of liberalism are socialist. They center on the notion that the economic ass can be driven to Point A most speedily by the judicious use of carrot-and-stick, an approach that supersedes the traditional notion of conservatives and classical liberals that we are not to begin with dealing with asses, and that Point A cannot possibly, in a free society, be presumed to be the desired objective of tens of millions of individual human beings.

The liberal sees no moral problem whatever in divesting the people of that portion of their property necessary to finance the projects certified by ideology as beneficial to the Whole. Mr. J. K. Galbraith wages total war against any putative right of the individual to decide for himself how to allocate his resources. The typical liberal will go to considerable pains to avoid having to say, in as many words, that the people don't know what's good for them (the people are not to be thus affronted); and so the new line is that the people, in expressing themselves in the marketplace, are not expressing their own views, but bending to the will of Madison Avenue. "The conventional wisdom," Mr. Galbraith writes in *The Affluent Society*, "holds that the community . . . makes a decision as to how much it will devote to its public services . . . [that the] people decide how much of their private income and goods they will surrender in order to have public services of which they are in greater need. . . . It will be obvious, however, that this view depends on the notion of independently determined consumer wants. . . . But . . . the consumer makes no such choice. He is subject to the forces of advertising and emulation by which production creates its own demand. Advertising operates exclusively, and emulation mainly, . . . on behalf of privately produced goods and services." And then there is the notorious ingratitude of man, toward the nobleman who has the courage to tell him what he really wants. "The scientist or engineer or advertising man who devotes himself to developing a new carburetor, cleanser, or depilatory for which the public recognizes no need and will feel none until an advertising campaign arouses it, is one of the valued members of our society. A politician or a public servant who dreams up a new public service is a wastrel. Few public offenses are more reprehensible." I do not know the name of, and hence am not in a position to lionize, any carburetor maker, nor do I know the name of a single maker of depilatories (though I am grateful to them all), and surely all the Henry Fords of history do not command the public adulation of a Franklin Roosevelt. No, Mr. Galbraith, it is more nearly the other way round: The scientist who develops a new cleanser is likely to find that there is little he can expect in the way of public recognition; and that the financial gain he thought he was entitled to has been pre-empted—somebody got there first, namely, the politician or public servant, who, scoring yet another public success, has just sold the people yet another public service that has to be paid for.

The liberals' answer? Tax, to preserve the "social balance." And take public spending out of the hands of the people. Institutionalize your tax system. To avoid having to make the difficult public case for public expenditures year after year we might devise a "system of taxation which automatically makes a *pro rata* share of increasing income available to public authority for public purposes."

There once was a moral problem involved in taxation.

No longer. On the contrary, it is clear that to the extent morality figures at all in taxation, it is as an affirmative imperative. It is morally *necessary* to take from the rich, and not merely to give to the poor. If there were no poor, it would still be necessary to take from the rich, egalitarianism being a primary goal of the liberal ideology. In the past generation the concept of private property metamorphosed from a right to an instrumental convenience—a long journey from when Aristotle listed "possession" as the tenth "predicament" of the human being. Theodore Morgan, in his widely used freshman economics text, *Income and Employment*, writes about the corollary of private property, freedom of enterprise: "Probably majority opinion agrees with our own national policy," says Morgan, "that the right of a man to engage in business for himself is not a basic freedom, like freedom from fear[!], and want[!], freedom of speech and of worship."

And so the way is cleared to set up the problem: Either the individual disposes of his surplus funds, in which case you have stagnation, chaos, dissipation, incoherence, synthesized desires; or else a central intelligence disposes of it, in which case you have order, progress, social balance, coherence. Looked at in this way, the problem ceases to be, "Can the people afford to look after their own health, build their own schools, buy their own homes?" and becomes, "Does it not make more sense for political governors to allocate the people's resources as between doctors, schools, and homes, to impose order upon the chaotic and capricious allocation of dollars when left to their owners to spend?"

It is not easy to understand the liberals' fear, manifested at so many levels—most recently and most conspicuously in the concerted liberal opposition to right-to-work laws in the individual states—of the voluntary approach to society. Their case is not built on the administrative need for 100 percent cooperation. It does not matter that a program of federal Social Security might work just as well if enrollment in it were voluntary. If it *were* voluntary, a presumptive majority would still subscribe (I say that because a law that is on the books in a democratic society is presumed to have the majority's support); and, that being so, the secession of a minority would not alter the economic balances the program presupposes.

But as with joining a union, membership must be compulsory. The reasons are sometimes given that the individual cannot be trusted to set aside savings toward his old age, and a government cannot very well address the delinquent when he arrives, destitute, at old age, as the ant addressed the grasshopper, refusing him sustenance in the name of abstract justice. But has any liberal suggested that in deference to the ideal of free choice an individual be exempted from membership in the Social Security program if he *has* taken substitute measures to look after his old age, through the use of private pension schemes, investment, or insurance programs?

Although they represent only 10 percent of the whole, and are constantly defending themselves against the attacks of secularists and levelers, the private grammar and secondary schools in this country flourish, and operate under the voluntarist dispensation. "Education" is compulsory. Educational facilities are publicly provided. But those who elect to do so, and can afford to, may seek out private educational facilities. The arrangement is a very ancient one, and is secured by the prescriptive sanction of the public. But private schools remain an anomaly of the planned society; they are "divisive" and "undemocratic"—in the words of Dr. James Conant, who spoke in 1951 as president of the most venerable private educational institution in the land, Harvard University—and so are subject to indirect and direct harassments. The former consist primarily in steeply progressive income taxes; the latter, in such measures as educational antidiscrimination laws and petty refusals to provide milk and buses, under the pretext that to do so would make the authors of the First Amendment roll about in their graves. "The American people are so enamored of equality," Tocqueville wrote, "that they would rather be equal in slavery than unequal in freedom."

The call by liberalism to conformity with its economic dispensations does not grow out of the economic requirements of modern life; but rather out of liberalism's total appetite for power. The root assumptions of liberal economic theory are that there is no serious economic problem; that in any case economic considerations cannot be permitted to stand in the way of "progress"; that, economically speaking, the people are merely gatherers of money which it is the right and duty of a central intelligence to distribute.

—Excerpt from *Up from Liberalism*, 1959

The Conservative Alternative

. . . an essay such as this is far more important for what it destroys—or to speak more accurately, for the destruction which it crystallizes, since the ultimate enemy of myth is circumstance—than for what it creates. This is sharply at odds with the conventional wisdom. The latter sets great store by what it calls constructive criticism. And it reserves its scorn for what it is likely to term a purely destructive or negative position. In this, as so often, it manifests a sound instinct for self-preservation.
—*J. K. Galbraith*, The Affluent Society

Up where from liberalism? There is no conservative political manifesto which, as we make our faltering way, we can consult, confident that it will point a sure finger in the direction of the good society. Indeed, sometimes the conservative needle appears to be jumping about as on a disoriented compass. My professional life is lived in an office battered by every pressure of contemporary conservatism. Some of the importunities upon a decent American conservatism are outrageous, or appear so to me, at any rate (*"We should have high tariffs because the farmers have high subsidies, and they shouldn't, by the way"*). Some are pathological (*"Alaska is being prepared as a mammoth concentration camp for pro-McCarthyites"*). Some are deeply mystical (*"The state can do no good."* My answer: It can arrest Communists, can't it?); some, ambitiously spiritual (*"Conservatism has no extrinsic significance except in relation to religion"*). Some urge the schematization of conservatism (*"What passes for conservatism these days is nothing more than sentimentality and nostalgia. Let us give it structure"*), or the opposite (*"Beware the ideologization of conservatism"*).

Still, for all the confusion and contradiction, I venture to say it is possible to talk about "the conservative position" and mean something by it. At the political level, conservatives are bound together for the most part by negative response to liberalism; but altogether too much is made of that fact. Negative action is not necessarily of negative value. Political freedom's principal value is negative in character. The people are politically stirred principally by the necessity for negative affirmations. Cincinnatus was a farmer before he took up his sword, and went back to farming after wielding some highly negative strokes upon the pates of those who sought to make positive changes in his way of life.

The weakness of American conservatives does not reduce neatly to the fact that some want tariffs, others not. Dr. J. Robert Oppenheimer was much taken during the 1950s by what goes by the name of "complementarity," a notion having to do with revised relationships in the far reaches of philosophical thought, where "opposites" come under a single compass, and fuse into workable philosophical and physical unities. No doubt physicist Oppenheimer was sticking an irreverent finger into the higher chemistry of metaphysics: but his theory, like the Hegelian synthesis, served to remind us that there is almost always conceivable the vantage point from which the seemingly incongruous, the apparently contradictory, can be viewed in harmony. A navigator for whom two lighthouses can mark extreme points of danger relative to his present position knows that if he goes back and makes a wholly different approach, the two lighthouses will fuse together to form a single object to the vision, confirming the safety of his position. They are then said to be "in range."

There is a point from which opposition to the Social Security laws and a devout belief in social stability are in range; as also a determined resistance to the spread of world Communism—and a belief in political non-interventionism; a disgust with the results of modern education—and sympathy for the individual educational requirements of the individual child; a sympathetic understanding of the spiritual essence of human existence—and a desire to delimit religious influence in political affairs; a patriotic concern for the nation and its culture—and a genuine respect for the integrity and differences of other peoples' cultures; a militant concern for the Negro—and a belief in decentralized political power even though, on account of it, the Negro is sometimes victimized; a respect for the omnicompetence of the free marketplace—and the knowledge of the necessity for occupational interposition. There is a position from which these views are "in range"; and that is the position, generally speaking, where conservatives now find themselves on the political chart. Our most serious challenge is to restore principles—the right principles; the principles liberalism has abused, forsaken, and replaced with "principles" that have merely a methodological content. Our challenge is to restore principles to public affairs.

What was once a healthy American pragmatism has deteriorated into a wayward relativism. It is one thing to make the allowances to reality that reality imposes, to take advantage of the current when the current moves in your direction, while riding at anchor at ebb tide. But it is something else to run before political or historical impulses merely because fractious winds begin to blow, and to dismiss resistance as foolish, or as perverse idealism. And it is supremely wrong, intellectually and morally, to abandon the norms by which it becomes possible, viewing a trend, to pass judgment upon it; without which judgment we cannot know whether to yield, or to fight.

Are we to fight the machine? Can conservatism assimilate it? Whittaker Chambers once wrote me that "the rock-core of the Conservative Position can be held realistically only if Conservatism will accommodate itself to the needs and hopes of the masses—needs and hopes which, like the masses themselves, are the product of machines."

It is true that the masses have asserted themselves, all over the world; have revolted, the Spanish political philosopher José Ortega y Gasset said, perceiving the revolutionary quality of the cultural convulsion. The question: How can conservatism accommodate revolution? Can the revolutionary essence be extravasated and be made to diffuse harmlessly in the network of capillaries that rushes forward to accommodate its explosive force? Will the revolt of the masses moderate when the lower class has risen, when science has extirpated misery, and the machine has abolished poverty? Not if the machines themselves are irreconcilable, as Mr. Chambers seemed to suggest when he wrote that ". . . of course, our fight is with machines," adding: "A conservatism that cannot face the facts of the machine and mass production, and its consequences in government and politics, is foredoomed to futility and petulance. A conservatism that allows for them has an eleventh-hour chance of rallying what is sound in the West."

What forms must this accommodation take? "The welfare state" is the non-Communist answer one mostly hears. It is necessary, we are told, to comprehend the interdependence of life in an industrial society, and the social consequences of any action by a single part of it on other parts. Let the steelworkers go on strike, and sparkplug salesmen will in due course be out of work. There must be laws to mitigate the helplessness of the individual link in the industrial chain that the machine has built.

What can conservatism do? Must it come to terms with these realities? "To live is to maneuver [Mr. Chambers continued]. The choices of maneuver are now visibly narrow. In the matter of social security, for example, the masses of Americans, like the Russian peasants in 1918, are signing the peace with their feet. I worked the hay load last night against the coming rain—by headlights, long after dark. I know the farmer's case for the machine and for the factory. And I know, like the cut of hay-bale cords in my hands, that a conservatism that cannot find room in its folds for these actualities is a conservatism that is not a political force, or even a twitch: it has become a literary whimsy."

Indeed. The machine must be accepted, and conservatives must not live by programs that were written as if the machine did not exist, or could be made to go away; that is the proper kind of realism. The big question is whether the essential planks of conservatism were anachronized by the machine; the big answer is that they were not. "Those who remain in the world, if they will not surrender on its terms, must maneuver within its terms [wrote Mr. Chambers]. That is what conservatives must decide: how much to give in order to survive at all; how much to give in order not to give up the basic principles. And, of course, that results in a dance along a precipice. Many will drop over, and, always, the cliff-dancers will hear the screaming curses of those who fall, or be numbed by the sullen silence of those, nobler souls perhaps, who will not join in the dance." We cliff-dancers, resolved not to withdraw into a petulant solitude, or let ourselves fall over the cliff into liberalism, must do what maneuvering we can, and come up with a conservative program that speaks to our time.

It is the chronic failure of liberalism that it obliges circumstance—because it has an inadequate discriminatory apparatus that might cause it to take any other course. There are unemployed in Harlan County? *Rush them aid.* New Yorkers do not want to pay the cost of subways? *Get someone else to pay it.* Farmers do not want to leave the land? *Let them till it; then buy and destroy the produce.* Labor unions demand the closed shop? *It is theirs.* Inflation goes forward in all industrial societies? *We will have continued inflation.* Communism is in control behind the Iron Curtain? *Coexist with it.* The tidal wave of industrialism will sweep in the welfare state? *Pull down the sea walls.*

Conservatism must insist that while the will of man is limited in what it can do, it can do enough to make over the face of the world; and that the question that must always be before us is: What shape should the world take, given modern realities? How can technology hope to invalidate conservatism? Freedom, individuality, the sense of community, the sanctity of the family, the supremacy of the conscience, the spiritual view of life—can these verities be transmuted by the advent of tractors and adding machines? These have had a smashing social effect upon us, to be sure. They have created a vortex into which we are being drawn as if irresistibly; but that, surely, is because the principles by which we might have made anchor have not been used, not because of their insufficiency or proven inadaptability.

"Technology has succeeded in extracting just about the last bit of taste from a loaf of bread," columnist Murray Kempton once told me spiritedly. "And when we get peacetime use of atomic energy, we'll succeed in getting *all* the taste out!" How can one put the problem more plainly? I assume by now Mrs. Kempton has gone to the archives, dusted off an ancient volume, and learned how to bake homemade bread. And lo! the bread turns out to be as easy to make as before, it tastes as good as before, and the machine age did not need to be roasted at an *auto-da-fé* to make it all possible. A conservative solution to *that* problem. But when the atom does to politics what it threatens to bread, what *then* is the solution? Can one make homemade freedom, under the eyes of an omnipotent state that has no notion of, or tolerance for, the flavor of freedom?

Freedom and order and community and justice in an age of technology: that is the contemporary challenge of political conservatism. How to do it, how to live with mechanical harvesters and without socialized agriculture. The direction we must travel requires a broadmindedness that, in the modulated age, strikes us as antiquarian, even callous. As I write there is mass suffering in Harlan County, Kentucky, where coal mining has become unprofitable, and a whole community is desolate. The liberal solution is: immediate and sustained federal subsidies. The conservative, breasting the emotional surf, will begin by saying that it was many years ago foreseeable that coal mining in Harlan County was becoming unprofitable, and that the humane course would have been to face up to that reality by permitting the marketplace, through the exertion of economic pressures of mounting intensity, to require resettlement. That was not done for the coal miners (they were shielded from reality by a combination of state and union aid), any more than it is now being done for marginal farmers; so that we are face to face with an acute emergency for which there is admittedly no thinkable alternative to immediate relief—if necessary (though it is not) by the federal government; otherwise by the surrounding communities, or the state of Kentucky. But arrangements for relief having been made, what then? Will the grandsons of the Harlan County coal miners be mining coal, to be sold to the government at a pegged price, all this to spare today's coal miners the ordeal of looking for other occupations?

The Hoover Commission on government reorganization unearthed several years ago a little rope factory in Boston, Massachusetts, which had been established by the federal government during the Civil War to manufacture the textile specialties the Southern blockade had caused to be temporarily scarce. There it was, ninety years after Appomattox, grinding out the same specialties, which are bought by the government and then sold at considerable loss. "Liquidate the plant," the Hoover Commission was getting ready to recommend. Whereupon a most influential Massachusetts senator, Mr. John F. Kennedy, interceded. "You cannot," he informed a member of the commission, "do so heinous a thing. The plant employs 136 persons, whose only skill is in making this specialty."

"Very well then," said the spokesman for the commission, anxious to cooperate. "Suppose we recommend to the government that the factory retain in employment every single present employee until he quits, retires, or dies—but on the understanding that none of them is to be replaced. That way we can at least look forward to the eventual liquidation of the plant. Otherwise, there will be 136 people making useless specialties generations hence; an unreasonable legacy of the Civil War."

The senator was unappeased. What a commotion the proposal would cause in the textile-specialty enclave in Boston! The solution, he warned the commission, was intolerable, and he would resist it with all his prodigious political might.

The relationship of forces being what it is, the factory continues to operate at full force.

To be sure, a great nation can indulge its little extravagances; but a long enough series of little extravagances can add up to a stagnating if not a crippling economic overhead. What is disturbing about the incident involving the Civil War factory is first the sheer stupidity of the thing, second the easy victory of liberal sentimentalism over reason. Subsidies are the form that modern circuses tend to take, and, as ever, the people are unaware that it is they who pay for the circuses.

But closing down the useless factories—a general war on featherbedding—is the correct thing to do, if it is correct to cherish the flavor of freedom and economic sanity. There is a sophisticated argument that has to do with the conceivable economic beneficences of pyramid building, and of hiring men to throw rocks out into the sea. But even these proposals, when advanced rhetorically by Lord Keynes, were meliorative and temporary in concept: The idea was to put the men to work *until* the regenerative juices of the economy had started flowing. Now we wake to the fact that along the line we abandoned our agreement to abide, as a general rule, by the determinations of the marketplace. We once believed that useless textile workers and useless coal miners and useless farmers—and useless carriage makers and Pony Expressmen—should search out other means of employment.

There is the dawning realization that, under the economics of illusion, pyramid building is becoming a major economic enterprise in America, which has set advanced liberals to finding more persuasive ways to dispose of the time of the textile-specialty workers. And their solution—*vide* Galbraith—is great social enterprises: roads, schools, slum clearance, national parks. The thesis of the Affluent Society is that simple. We have (1) an earned surplus, (2) unemployment, (3) "social imbalance" (i.e., too many cars, not enough roads; too much carbon monoxide, not enough air purification; too many children, not enough classrooms). So let the government (1) take over the extra money, (2) use it to hire the unemployed, and (3) set them to restoring the social balance i.e., to building parks, schools, roads.

The program prescribed by Mr. Galbraith is unacceptable, conservatives would maintain. Deal highhandedly as he would have us do with the mechanisms of the marketplace, and the mechanisms will bind. Pre-empt the surplus of the people, and surpluses will dwindle. Direct politically the economic activity of a nation, and the economy will lose its capacity for that infinite responsiveness to individual tastes that gives concrete expression to the individual will in material matters. Centralize the political function, and you will lose touch with reality, for the reality is an intimate and individualized relationship between individuals and those among whom they live; and the abstractions of wide-screen social draftsmen will not substitute for it. Stifle the economic sovereignty of the individual by spending his dollars for him, and you stifle his freedom. Socialize the individual's surplus, and you socialize his spirit and creativeness; you cannot paint the *Mona Lisa* by assigning one dab each to a thousand painters.

Conservatives do not deny that technology poses enormous problems; they insist only that the answers of liberalism create worse problems than those they set out to solve. Conservatives cannot be blind, or give the appearance of being blind, to the dismaying spectacle of unemployment, or any other kind of suffering. But conservatives can insist that the statist solution to the problem is inadmissible. It is not the single conservative's responsibility or right to draft a concrete program—merely to suggest the principles that should frame it.

What then *is* the indicated course of action? It is to maintain and wherever possible enhance the freedom of the individual to acquire property and dispose of that property in ways that he decides on. To deal with unemployment by eliminating monopoly unionism, featherbedding, and inflexibilities in the labor market, and be prepared, where residual unemployment persists, to cope with it locally, placing the political and humanitarian responsibility on the lowest feasible political unit. Boston can surely find a way to employ gainfully its 136 textile specialists—and its way would be very different, predictably, from Kentucky's with the coal miners; and let them be different. Let the two localities experiment with different solutions, and let the natural desire of the individual for more goods, and better education, and more leisure, find satisfaction in individual encounters with the marketplace, in the growth of private schools, in the myriad economic and charitable activities which, because they took root in the individual imagination and impulse, take organic form. And then let us see whether we are better off than we would be living by decisions made between nine and five in Washington office rooms, where the oligarchs of the Affluent Society sit, allocating complaints and solutions to communities represented by pins on the map.

Is that a program? Call it a No-Program, if you will, but adopt it for your very own. I will not cede more power to the state. I will not willingly cede more power to anyone, not to the state, not to General Motors, not to the CIO. I will hoard my power like a miser, resisting every effort to drain it away from me. I will then use *my* power as *I* see fit. I mean to live my life an obedient man, but obedient to God, subservient to the wisdom of my ancestors; never to the authority of political truths arrived at yesterday at the voting booth. That is a program of sorts, is it not?

It is certainly program enough to keep conservatives busy, and liberals at bay. And the nation free.

—Excerpt from *Up from Liberalism,* 1959

The Politics of Beauty

It is a thesis of the literature of protest against the way physical America is shaping up that external harmony is necessary for the repose of the soul. I

suppose I am not absolutely certain that this is so, but I do know that it is
so for some people (for instance myself), though not necessarily for those
people who, according to fashion's book, are the most to be admired in
the human race. These last include the inner-directed types of whom the
absentminded professor is the most widely caricatured example, who are
generally oblivious to external surroundings. And there are the hard intellectuals, whose physical life is mostly spent inside the cavernous libraries,
and whose intellectual life is in the mind; who could not care less whether
one, two, or a dozen trees grow in Brooklyn.

One's own experience counts greatly. Mine, during my childhood, was
a continuing confrontation with beauty. I do not know whether I'd have
recognized it as such, or even whether I'd have thought back about it as
such, except that my father was constantly calling attention to it, wherever
we were—and that was, on account of the travels on which his work took
him, all over the place. He had lived, after college, in Mexico, and intended
to settle there and would have, except that he backed the wrong revolution,
which was easy enough for a political activist to do, since during the period
there was almost always an incumbent revolution. So he left, escorted to
the border by armed guard, in 1921, and took with him the plans for a
beautiful house and garden he had just begun to build in Tampico and
on which he had lavished infinite attention. He bought a large house in
Sharon, drawn to the little town in northwest Connecticut for the simple
reason of its extraordinary beauty. We went to Paris, and Switzerland, and
London, for protracted stays when I was a boy, but kept popping back to
Sharon, where we settled more or less permanently during the Thirties,
spending winters in Camden, South Carolina, where my father undertook
the rehabilitation of a derelict antebellum house which is surrounded now,
the fruit of his diligent supervision, with whole terraces of flowers, red and
white and lavender. I remember one spring my older brothers and sisters
giving vent to their underworld amusement because a red azalea had had
the nerve to raise its head smack in the middle of a bed of white azaleas,
quite against my father's orders, which no vertebrate had ever been known
to defy.

But such acts of insubordination were rare even among the flowers, the
shrubs, and the trees, which performed prodigies under his direction. In
Sharon we lived among many acres of green, on a property called Great Elm,
after a tree of noble girth and stature, which was reputed to be the largest
elm in Connecticut, and in whose irenic shade a treaty with the Indians was
said to have been concluded shortly before the Revolutionary War. The town
itself was—is—an elongated rectangle; in those days it had rows of majestic

elms going the length of it, and extending a mile or more to the south. The Garden Club of Connecticut once classified Sharon as, after Litchfield, the most beautiful town in Connecticut; and it was a source of constant pleasure to my father, who loved it even as he loved the trees on his own property, which he looked after with pride and loving care. The Dutch-elm disease struck Sharon before he died, and one of the first casualties was the great elm, and we all knew the pain he experienced on account of its loss because, when the time for fortitude came, as when there was a death or illness in the family, he fell into a preternatural silence; and the decision was made to cut the tree down. But he saved the trunk, which stands even now about twenty feet high, to remind observers, by its enormous waistline, of the splendor of its maturity. All those elms, the whiteness of the town, the coordinated vision, did, I think, communicate something to our lawless brood, indeed so much so that several of my brothers and sisters, though it is infinitely inconvenient for them to do so, continue to live there; and I do not think this is merely a matter of desiring to live in the place where one grew up. For one thing, their background was cosmopolitan; for another, they have most of them continued to care very deeply about the elms and the shrubs and the flowers, and the stillness; and about the town itself, which continues to look as if it were hewn out of a single, pleasant dream. They have, I think, come by that repose of the soul about which we hear more and more, as related to one's surroundings.

~

During the Thirties my mother was active in the Dutchess County Garden Study Club, whose principal effort was to guard the Hudson River against the irruptions of billboarders who had designs on its banks for large and garish announcements of their magical contributions to modern commerce. After an extensive war, the Garden Club won; and I remember cheering the victory against Coca-Cola even when I was too young to be permitted to drink it, though I may merely have been acting as echo chamber for my father's enthusiasm. At about the same time, without any notice whatever, all of a sudden a large billboard sprang to life about a mile and a half north of Sharon, interrupting the theretofore uninterrupted stretch of New England landscape that coaxed the tourist up toward the Berkshires. On seeing it my father was seized with indignation, which he communicated to us at dinner. Activists that my older brothers and sisters were, they promptly volunteered to go out and burn the sign down. My father's allegiances were in conflict. On the one hand he had himself once been a revolutionary, or rather counterrevolutionary, who, as a young man, undertook nothing less than the replacement of the order of things in all of Mexico. On the other hand, he was a conservative who believed in law and order. The dialectic did not yield altogether convincing results: We were to do no such thing. *However*, he said, if the town of Sharon itself rose in popular uprising against the billboard, and marched against it, our sympathies would clearly be on the side of Sharon rather than on the side of BBD&O or whoever the villain was.

So, in loose application of the Machiavellian law that insurrections, in order to be justified, must be successful, we were to wait for the day when insurrection galvanized the whole of the population. We sulked at the enforced inactivity, in part because we had an anarchic streak within us, in part because we felt it would be a fine way to demonstrate our admiration for our father to proceed on our own initiative, at our own risk, to do his implicit bidding.

As often happens in such situations, we ended up doing the thing halfway, and ignobly. Caught up in the post-Depression exuberance of 1939, the owner of the local soda fountain and cigar store abutting the local post office hoisted a spectacular Coca-Cola sign above his building, an unnecessary piece of exhibitionism, considering that there was only one other place in all of Sharon to go if you wanted to buy Coca-Cola at the fountain. We stole there late one night, with mops and a bucket of white paint, and streaked the sign into unrecognition, a venture in beautification that we found especially easy to perform inasmuch as the gentleman in question was the town's premier grouch, and, quite coincidentally, we supposed, Republican lord of all he surveyed. The next day a horrible communal silence fell on the town, as the question was moot whether the omnipotent Republican would call in the National Guard to detect the malefactors or whether he would submit to the implicit censure of the community, always assuming the expression had indeed been the community's. He did neither. He merely, within a matter of days, hoisted a fresh sign; whereupon, after a council of war, we reasoned that, unlike Hercules, we were not equipped to cut off Hydra's head. So he won; but a demonstration of sorts had been made. I now no longer feel I can theoretically defend what I had a hand in doing at age thirteen; but, come to think of it, the sign is no longer there. Neither, on the other hand, is the old Republican, though I cannot quite remember whether he went off to his reward having first renounced Coca-Cola.

~

I am, then, myself committed to the notion that attractive external surroundings can mean a great deal, and to the corollary that something
ought to be done about it: just how and just what being, of course, the
question. Next in order of consideration is the question, *Who knows what
is beautiful?* Perhaps it boils down to the easier questions, *Who will decide
what is beautiful?* That, after all, is merely a matter of political arrangement. The Congress of the United States, for instance, is absolutely in
charge of deciding what is beautiful and what isn't in respect to its own
quarters. Sam Rayburn was in charge of the Congress of the United States
at the time the plans were drawn for a new House office building, and
so it came about that the sovereign legislature of the United States, representing all the people, devised and constructed a building not merely
lacking in beauty, but positively drunk in its featurelessness, $86 million
worth of white neoclassical blah.

The thing was, presumably, designed by an architect, which therefore raises the other question, *Is there an expertise in beauty?* To which the
answer of course is, yes and no; yes in that some people's eyes are better
than other people's; no in the sense that there is continuing disagreement
on just whose eyes are operatively better. And this, in turn, makes insufficient the recommendation of Mr. Daniel Patrick Moynihan, a very fashionable intellectual who also happens to be very bright, that the architectural
"profession" form a lobby. "There wasn't a special interest in America that
didn't have a hunk of [the highway] bill except the architects," he observed
at one of our regular conferences of disgust over the deteriorating face
of America, enjoining the architects to become "a lobby." Why not? The
most beautiful buildings in the world are designed by architects. But so are
the ugliest buildings in the world, and it isn't that the beautiful buildings
are beautiful because they are free of the pressures of the marketplace,
though those pressures do figure, often for the worse, in certain types of
buildings.

Disagreements about architecture—and indeed about all art—are often
written about as if they were being fought between the beautiful spirits and
the Philistines, which is all very well until the moment comes when we
are asked to distinguish between the two in such a way as is aesthetically,
or politically, acceptable. The monster that rises over Grand Central Station in New York City is despised by Norman Mailer and adored by August
Heckscher. Heckscher is In, culture-wise; indeed he was JFK's number-one
on-duty aesthete. And Mailer is concededly erratic; but he is in very steady
company in his dislike of the Pan Am Building, and, quite apart from that,
greatly respected for the occasional jewel that washes in with the flotsam

and jetsam that inundates us from his ongoing collision with the world he lives in. The most galvanizing words recently uttered on the matter of saving America the Beautiful came from President Johnson, whose superb French cook, inherited from JFK, recently resigned in despair after the superordination of a dietitian from Austin, Texas, who ordered him to serve beets with cream on them at affairs of state. Can a man who thus misorders his own kitchen be trusted to design the Acropolis?

It is not safe, in a word, to assume that great and beautiful buildings are automatically what happen when you allocate more money to be spent on great and beautiful buildings—even when you give the money to those among our highest political authorities who bloviate most regularly on the subject of the beautiful life. To say that taste differs is not to concede, to be sure, that all tastes are equally defensible. It is merely to say that the demonstration of the poorer and the better taste is not easy to make, that it often cannot be done merely by a blackboard demonstration whose at-onceness overwhelms the Philistine, but depends on a lengthening perspective; the kind of thing that over a period of several hundred years came absolutely to establish that Westminster Abbey and Chartres, both built about the same time, were respectively a catastrophe and a thing so sublime as might have been designed by God Himself. There weren't any art critics in the thirteenth century who attended cathedral openings, but it isn't necessary, in order to make the point, that there should have been. The "finest" available designers and craftsmen were called together at about the same time to construct the two elysian cathedrals. They did their best, and there is no reason to believe that a talented designer doing his best doesn't, during the period of his absorption with his fancy, proceed with as much conviction—and as much of a right to his conviction—as the critic. If a well-trained architect can act on a defective impulse, so can a well-trained critic. It is time that gradually erodes the dross, settling the impression, and making possible the universal judgment. When Johann Sebastian Bach died, the obituarists acclaimed him as a choirmaster and organist, and his son Carl Philipp Emanuel as the composer. Obviously this is not an argument against all public buildings. Familiarity breeds contempt, a Cambridge debater argued before the First War, opposing the maximization of contact between His Majesty's and the Kaiser's subjects. "True," his opponent observed, "but a lack of familiarity breeds nothing at all."

Well, then, if we cannot necessarily expect beautiful buildings to arise from an act of political will, can we hope for better luck from Authority in city planning? Edward Durell Stone remarks that most of the cities of the world intended to be spectacularly beautiful—Leningrad, Paris, Washington—were designed by the assertion of central authority. Louis Napoleon hired Haussmann to redesign Paris in 1853, and the result was certainly smashing. The czars recognized that the Russian talent was not for visual beauty, and so when St. Petersburg was to be made, Peter the Great called in a Frenchman; and behold the result. Washington, says Stone, was conceived as a "white city," and even that elementary conceptual commitment gave it what character, what beauty it has. It is a pity that more cities aren't thus conceived, i.e., that there isn't a master planner around, with a first-rate sensitivity for the natural character of the place and the people, to require a kind of loose-footed uniformity, which is nothing more than a respect for harmony. A spontaneous cultural homogeneity is an adequate substitute. It isn't always a master planner who is responsible for beautiful cities. Charleston, South Carolina, has that harmony, and it is a joy forever. On one of its main streets there sits, interrupting the tall white-wood pleasure, a squalid concrete two-story office building in Modern-Austere that looks like a raised cement fill, and could only have been built (a) by someone who hated Charleston, or (b) by an institute for the blind, intending to interrupt the prevailing reverie so as to compel attention to the plight of the less fortunate. Salamanca, of course, has it to perfection—the special yellow, everywhere, that turns to gold when the sun is on the horizon—and only the anarchist will resent the municipal coordination that made it so.

It is, of course, a tricky business to regulate, in behalf of an overarching aesthetic idea, what a man may build on his own plot of land; but even so, I'd be for taking that risk, and, I shall argue, libertarian theory would accommodate the requirement provided that titles were devised and exchanged with the impediments clearly prescribed. Thus the idea is widely accepted that if you buy a lot that is not zoned for business, you may not transact business on that lot; and there are no persuasive squawks, addressed either to the civil-liberties unions or to the natural law, to deny the municipality the right to zone. What about the extension of the zoning right to regulate a building's façade? It is a dangerous business, because the doctrine of congruity, fanatically extended, very well might have the effect of discouraging those elegant variations which, expressing a disciplined individuality, sometimes give birth to the flowering of an idea, and even to breathtaking mutations. But the rewards of running the risk can be very great, whether in a small town like Litchfield, Connecticut, a medium-sized town like Charleston, or a very large town like Paris. The British critic Ian Nairn, recoiling from the typical American city, says that although "chaos occasionally is good fun and essential, chaos all the time is just chaos"; and, pleading for relief from the "chaos of non-relation, probably worse in America than anywhere else," he reminds us as so many others have done that "townscape depends on two things, relationship and identity." In places like Litchfield and Charleston and Paris, one can walk about and know what it is that Nairn means when he promises skeptics that a walk in a properly expressive town "can be as refreshing and exhilarating as Scotch-on-the-rocks after a hot, tiring day."

～

Having acknowledged that something should be done about the problem, we need to ask what, concretely. What are the theoretical problems, and what are the practical problems? The first have to do with the role of the government; the second, with the capacity of the community to rise to the challenge.

As regards the first, I fear greatly that it is only a matter of time before some president will think to declare a War against Ugliness. He may very well be a president who couldn't care less about ugliness, but who is desperate for programs by which to confer Democratic benefits on his people. When that happens, theoretical arguments will rage, even as, less conspicuously, they rage at this moment, for instance on the question of what are the rights of the collectivity over the individual. Some hard thought should be given to that problem and the sooner the better, and herewith a modest and, I hope, heuristic contribution.

The role of our various governments, local, state, and federal, ought to remain primarily negative. Governments are as a rule better at reeling off prohibitions than fancying themselves as creative artists. I have mentioned the overarching problem: How is the government going to decide what is beautiful; will the Library of Congress send down a memo on the matter? And secondly, don't we need to understand that the kind of organic beauty we most greatly need to encourage in our towns and cities can issue only from the genes of the community. Infusions of federal money and federal bureaucrats tend, as Jane Jacobs has amply demonstrated in her book on the life and death of the great American cities, to upset the glandular balances of individual neighborhoods; and the baby is deformed.

In some areas, the federal government has intruded probably forever. One never quite understands, in retrospect, why the federal government had to get into some of the acts, but so it happened. As regards highway building, for instance, the program arose like Venus from the Cyprian seas ordaining that henceforth the government would pay 90 percent of the cost of building interstate highways. That, of course, gave the federal government a little leverage, which it sought to exercise, by happy accident, for the common good—by offering a bribe (an extra one-half of 1 percent of gasoline taxes) to those states that would agree to ban billboards along the highways. Only seven states have qualified for that subsidy.

The pressure from the billboarders in the other states was overwhelming. They used every weapon, including theory. Now here is something that needs to be done: some first-class theorizing in behalf of the aesthetic order. The cynic will doubt that this is of any material importance, and the cynic will be wrong, because ours isn't an altogether pragmatic community (if it were, the Commies, for instance, would long since have been exiled, or jailed, or something); it is very much theory-oriented. We brood, and I think it is good that we should do so, over the niceties of such questions as whether the individual has the quote right unquote to post billboards on quote his unquote land. Granted that human beings will produce fancy theoretical justifications at the clink of a nickel. But grant, also, that those justifications are effective weapons, and that we have been delinquent in failing to shoot down presumptuous theory with better theory.

It is true that the billboarders survive primarily through political pressures and manipulations. But, draped in theoretical mantle, they seduce a not inconsiderable number of people who are convinced by the private-property argument. Robert Moses, who has been fighting the billboarders for almost thirty years, tells us it is "dirty fighting, with eye-gouging, rabbit-punching, bone-breaking, mayhem, and no holds barred." At the level to which he refers, nothing will do but the mobilization of the aesthetic conscience followed by irresistible political counterpressure. But meanwhile the billboarders must be stripped of their theoretical armor. This one oughtn't to be difficult. Other problems are much more difficult, such as those that need to be attacked before we can pave the way for a harmonious architecture. Here the individual can say, with some plausibility, that his is an undisputed right to build a house exactly along the lines chosen by his own potty little self—on the grounds, *tout court,* that he has the sovereign right to define the specifications of his own enjoyment. A very intricate case needs to be developed, wooing public acceptance, to knock down that argument; and I myself believe it can be done. "The quarrel between the individual's right to design his own home and the neighborhood's right to architectural unity can only be solved," a philosophical friend of mine has argued, "by an existential dialectic. If the community desires architectural harmony, it must win the argument by the exercise of power."

But the billboarders, I should think, are more readily disrobed. The display of hortatory commercial slogans is not covered by the same set of arguments used by the anarchical housebuilder—because the billboards are manifestly not directed at himself, but rather at others who pass by. As such the billboards are acts of aggression against which the public is entitled, as a matter of privacy, to be protected. If a homeowner desires to construct a huge Coca-Cola sign facing his own house rather than the public highway, in order to remind him, every time he looks out his window, that the time has come to pause and be refreshed, he certainly should be left free to do so. But if he wants to face the sign toward us, that is something else, and the big-name libertarian theorists should go to work demolishing the billboarders' abuse of the argument of private property.

As regards the maintenance of the natural beauty of great parts of the nation, the weight of the argument is, once again, on the side of the public. The present secretary of the interior, Mr. Stewart Udall, is, I think it fair to say, as aggressive a champion of the necessity to maintain oases of natural beauty as anyone who ever held high federal office. Sometimes, to be sure, he does leave the impression that he resents any private dwelling at all, on the grounds that it is liable to get in the way of a meandering buffalo. But his occasional excesses, unlike those of some of his own coadjutors, are tolerable in an age that very much needs to be reminded of the factor of beauty, natural and man-made. Mr. Udall has launched a great land-acquisition program, attempting to husband the natural parks to the use of the public. I must depart from the company of those conservatives who are always resenting the acreage owned by the government, always provided said government does not go hog wild, and that the great reservations continue—as some city parks, for instance, do not—to be dedicated to the enjoyment of the public (42,500,000 people visited one or another of our national parks during the last year, which suggests Udall must be doing something right). The withholding of land, to be retained in its supernal beauty, is a legitimate function of government, as Adam Smith was among the first to observe.

I would greatly welcome an exhaustive theoretical justification of an extension of the present zoning ideas. As they stand, they are after all widely accepted. Most towns and cities, as I have noted, have zoning laws; and some—for instance, New York City—use the power to discourage, for instance, the obnoxious ziggurat with its mechanical terraces. But Mrs. Jane Jacobs has pointed out that the mere acquisition of power is not by any means a solution to the problem. New York City conferred powers upon itself beginning in 1916, and subsequently did much, by the use of those powers, to damage the potential of New York for beauty. Circumspect use of power is supremely important, with a heavy respect for those domiciliary prejudices which are indispensable to beauty, preserving their individuation, without which relationships are utterly lifeless. The practical problem with cities is infinitely complex, in large part because of the transient population—it takes a while before an individual is incorporated into a city. Suburbanization has greatly increased the difficulties. Since 1945 our cities have grown hardly at all—but the suburban communities have increased in size by almost 70 percent. The result has been to leave the cities at the mercy of the awful urban-renewal programs.

Still, progress can be made, block by block, area by area; and the theoretical problems having been chased at least to the point where a respectful and considerate attention for theoretical differences is exhausted, the question will finally arise—my friend's existential dialectic—Will we, or won't we, do something about it? And at this point one needs, in a democratic society, to depend on the community.

~

The community. It is cursed by indifference. That indifference is perhaps exaggerated, but it is most certainly there. "Indifference," sighs Herbert Read, "is endemic . . . a disease which has spread through our whole civilization, and which is a symptom of a lowered vitality. The sensibilities are dulled and the average human being no longer cares to feel the keen edge of life, to have freshness in vision or zest and savor in the senses."

Mr. Read is very largely correct, but it is demoralizing to take his conclusions as an absolute judgment on the current state of mind, because if one does, one faces a dilemma. It is, very simply, that the only way to do anything about the problem of natural beauty and architectural harmony is to do so athwart the people's indifference; indeed, by extension, athwart their will.

At this point a word should be said about the Very Gloomy. The point can be made, as with Mr. Udall, that their exaggerations are galvanizing. But the opposite point can also be made, that their gloom is so total as to invoke not the impulse to reform, but the impulse to despair.

Herewith Miss Marya Mannes on her especial irk:

"Cans. Beer cans. Glinting on the verges of a million miles of roadways, lying in scrub, grass, dirt, leaves, sand, mud, but never hidden. Piels, Rheingold,

Ballantine, Schaefer, Schlitz, shining in the sun or picked up by moon or the beams of headlights at night, washed by rain or flattened by wheels, but never dulled, never buried, never destroyed. Here is the mark of the savages, the testament of wasters, the stain of prosperity." And her climax: "*Slowly the wasters and despoilers are impoverishing our land, our nature, and our beauty, so that there will not be one beach, one hill, one lane, one meadow, one forest free from the debris of man and the stigma of his improvidence.*" Now: Does that kind of thing make you want to give up beer cans, or does it make you wonder whether Miss Mannes has, as regards beer cans, the same kind of problem that the fellow had who went to the psychiatrist and kept brushing the mosquitoes off his arms and legs?

Or there is the crushed poet, an anonymous employee of the Department of the Interior, who comes up with the grisliest metaphor of the season in, no less, an official publication of DepInt:

"The shift of our Nation from a predominantly rural to an urban population *has made a sinister sandwich of much of our land, buttering our soil with concrete and asphalt, piling people on people, and then hanging a pall of polluted air over all.*" And, not to be outdone by Miss Mannes, he reaches his own immolation: "*If current trends continue unchecked, in another generation a trash pile or piece of junk will be within a stone's throw of any person standing anywhere on the American continent.*" Surely before that happens the hungry cosmos will have gulped down the sinister sandwich and eliminated all of our worries?

Another kind of criticism, more subtle but equally enervating, is that of *el fastidioso*, the kind of man who, because Shakespeare ever wrote, can't bring himself to see anything good in John Cheever; can't listen to an Appalachian folk song because the organ tones of Johann Sebastian Bach crowd his ear. Listen to Edward Durell Stone:

"*Compared with us, the Italians are impoverished. They hold body and soul together with a few strands of spaghetti and are not pampered by creature comforts. But you hear opera on every street corner and people walk among fabulous things of beauty. Verdi, Titian, Michelangelo are spoken of with reverence by the taxi drivers and the waiters. They are more concerned with the well-being of the spirit than with material well-being. I once flew from Venice to Akron, Ohio, and when I landed and looked about me, I decided that the so-called poor people of Italy were a lot better off.*" Ho hum. The "so-called poor people" of Italy happen to be very poor indeed, and a lot of them express their reverence for life by voting the Communist ticket at election time, and prefer the Beatles to Verdi. And anyway, genius is genius precisely because it is not normative, but unique. To compare Venice to Akron is not only stupid, but outrageously irrelevant, the cant millenarianism which makes so many of our cultural critics, like so many of our political critics, so very profoundly boring.

~

In fact, things can be done. In fact, things are being done. Not nearly enough, but enough to permit, to admit, hope.

In southern California a group of merchants and housewives, unsubsidized by the federal government and, I daresay, unread in Miss Mannes or in the literature of the Department of the Interior, have undertaken a program—they call it Los Angeles Beautiful, and let us not raise our noses; what would you call it?—which is doing what it can, where it can. "When we started out," the executive director, Mr. Fred Chase, commented to a *Newsweek* reporter, "my old friends thought I'd changed my sex or something. But we've shown everybody." The program is being emulated in more than two hundred southern-California communities.

"'Plant-a-tree,'" *Newsweek* reports, is among LAB's projects. "Converting abandoned trolley-car strips into landscaped traffic islands, sponsoring horticultural experiments to determine which plants have the highest resistance to auto-exhaust fumes; and promoting a 'plant-a-tree' campaign in the downtown area. A neighboring group, the Pasadena Beautiful Foundation, recently helped remove all but a few billboards from the main thoroughfares and persuaded the city to adopt 'sight-nuisance' and sign-control ordinances."

Individuals and private associations can begin the work, and then enthusiasm can catch on.

At a formal level, it is not easy to devise the means by which to inculcate the appreciation of beauty. To some it comes naturally; for others it is intellectually received. I remember with great affection a chauffeur-companion of my childhood, a refugee from Russia—he was of course a nobleman, full of flossy ancestry, and married to Tolstoy's niece—who, finding himself impoverished in Paris between the wars, took a job as a bus driver on the condition that he be assigned the route to Chartres, so that he might adore it every day. How do you create such men as a class? As a nation? Nobody knows. I do believe that it is correct to make the effort, i.e., not to leave such matters to fate. If I were a teacher I do not know what techniques I would use, beyond attempting to stimulate a mere interest in the question. Perhaps I would try showing the children slides of various buildings, and asking, "Is this ugly? Is this beautiful?" and bringing down a cane upon the knuckles of the blockhead who grunted the wrong answer. I would do so with due recognition of the hazard of my undertaking, because my own knuckles are constantly being rapped, as for instance when I go and see some of the work of our most prestigious artists and architects. . . . Still, I would take the risk, in behalf of the idea that a regard for beauty, an inquisitiveness about it, can be communicated, even as I learned about it merely by sensing the pleasure in my father's soul as he walked among his azaleas or along the streets of the beautiful villages and cities of the world.

Another doomsayer, with, however, restraint in his voice: "For some of our mountains at present will only support trees, but not so very long ago trees fit for the roofs of vast buildings were felled there and the rafters are still in existence. They were also many other lofty cultivated trees which provided unlimited fodder for beasts. Besides, the soil gets the benefit of the yearly 'water from Zeus,' which was not lost, as it is today, by running off a barren ground to the sea." Plato, on the despoliation of Attica.

—*Esquire*, July 1966

The New Conservatism

The question is asked, What is the new conservatism? Because it is supposed (correctly) that it is, in some respects at least, different from the "old" conservatism. Let me see, ten years ago? Conservatives in America rallied in their disapproval of the invitation to Nikita Khrushchev to visit the United States, attaching to that visit a symbolic significance which, indeed, it had, notwithstanding the violent reversals in U.S.-Soviet relations during the next three years, in which Khrushchev successively (1) withdrew his reciprocal invitation to Eisenhower, on the grounds that the U-2 so greatly offended him; (2) constructed the Berlin Wall; and (3) sent missiles to Cuba with which to threaten us. But the trend had set in, and when, in June 1967, Kosygin came over to the U.N. and popped down to New Jersey to visit with President Johnson, there wasn't a picketer in sight.

The incident is revealing not only for reteaching us what is after all obvious, that that which arouses public protest can quickly become routine, and routinely accepted. It teaches us that some issues are forever snapped by merely turning the symbolic switch. What appeared so very wrong to some people was the notion of a state visit by the active leader of the most highly organized totalitarian force in history. But the moment that visit was consummated, it would become all but impossible to restore the *status quo ante*; so that the return to chastity became, in a way, pointless: once deflowered, that is it; one moves on. And conservatives, who continue to be, loosely speaking, the most orthodox anti-Communists in America, look for new forms through which to express themselves. The Soviet Union does not let too much time go by without giving them cause, though every time it becomes a little tougher, on account of the general attrition of anti-Communism and the great symbolic rupture of 1959. Thus when the invasion of Czechoslovakia took place, the editorial chastisements were just a little perfunctory, rather like what one would write about Belsen a year after beholding Buchenwald. *Sub specie aeternitatis* they are equally horrifying: the rape of Hungary, as we used to call it, and that of Czechoslovakia. But somewhere along the line the word had gone out, and its force was not lost on conservatives, that it had become vulgar to raise one's voice against the Communists. So that when we did so in the summer of 1968, it was like an unscripted cadenza, the climax of which was Richard Nixon's suggestion that perhaps this was not the ideal climate in which to vest our confidence in an anti-proliferation treaty. Six months later President Nixon routinely sent the treaty on through for ratification, with an explanation as to why things were different now from what they were in August, which nobody could quite recall.

What does all of this do to the new conservatives? It drives them back, even as domestic developments drive them back, toward different, if not exactly more basic, positions.

The next major battle was over the Anti-Ballistic Missile treaty. Leave alone the scientific dispute, which, after all, is neatly consigned to irrelevance by the observation that if the one group of scientists is correct, we have lost $5 billion; if the other is correct, we might lose 30 million lives. The anti-Communism of the old conservatives was one part evangelistic. It held that we had an obligation to help those who could not help themselves, to fend off the juggernaut. There was talk, even, of rolling back the Iron Curtain—the liberation rhetoric of the early Fifties. But the principal strength of anti-Communism was less evangelistic than self-affirmative. Anti-Communism was a means of saying not only that we disliked Stalin, but also that we liked the opposite of Stalin: represented, roughly speaking, by—us.

The debate on the ABM treaty was joined, at one level, by the true conservatives and the true—call them what you will—doubters, perhaps, is the least provocative designation. The new conservatives are reduced to insisting that the defense of their country is worth it at any cost—and we speak now not of the lousy $5 billion, but of one thousand hydrogen bombs aimed at the enemy that finally threatens our survival. This was at the heart of the debate. During the four or five years preceding it, doubts had been cast about America which raised questions never raised before outside the camps of armed ideology. Who, let us say, listening to every public utterance during that period by the Reverend William Sloane Coffin or Dr. Benjamin Spock—not to say the typical contributor to *The New York Review of Books*—could conclude that in order to save what we have, we are justified in slaughtering 100 million Russians? What we have is (ask the Kerner Commission) a country deeply and passionately committed to racism; a country (ask Seymour Melman) altogether dominated by the military-industrial complex; the world's principal agent of violence and savagery (ask Martin Luther King); the apogee of materialism and hypocrisy (ask Herbert Marcuse). Why would anyone go to such lengths as conceivably might be required to defend such a nation as that? A velleity to survive is one thing. An atomic war is another.

I see it as the historical role of the new conservatives not to abandon their traditional concerns, but to accept the necessity of gut affirmations respecting America's way of doing things, some of which were traditionally espoused by the liberals and the progressives, whose contemporary uncertainty about them (Messrs. Wicker and Reston of the *New York Times* have several times, for instance, shown themselves sympathetic to the use of force by Negro militants) imposes special burdens on the conservatives. For instance:

1. *The democratic process.* This was never considered by the conservatives as a principal responsibility of theirs. There were enough bards of democracy floating about, even ideologists of democracy, even imperialists of democracy. So that for years conservatives thought it better to ask questions about what it was that democracy had ushered in, rather than join in the chorus that made of the democratic process itself the venerable thing.

It is a little different now; because order has been challenged, and the conservatives have always believed in the blessings of order. It was (primarily) the conservatives who observed that Lyndon Johnson had been elected president by the democratic process, and that under the circumstances, pending his repudiation, he had rights that were his to exercise. The new conservatives have had to stress the democratic process at other levels. It is not exactly a democracy that designates who will be the president and the governors of Harvard University, but there is a feel of democracy there. Some of the governors are directly elected by the relevant constituency—the alumni of Harvard. Those who are not so elected, but are designated by the incumbents, cannot in fact be so offensive to the alumni body as to cause it to mutiny—Harvard is rich but not that rich. So that conservatives find themselves defending the rights of the authorities of Harvard, over against the mobocratic demands of students and faculty who wish to leapfrog the authorities so as to have their way, instantly.

2. *And due process.* The meticulous cousin of the democratic process, due process was looked at cynically by many conservatives as a means, along with the Constitution's commerce clause, by which the federal government managed whatever intervention in human affairs appealed to it at the time. Thus due process was used by the Supreme Court to revolutionize criminal prosecutions, even as the Court had used the commerce clause to defend Congress's right, via its authority over interstate commerce, to set the rate of pay of elevator operators. The abuse of due process was rampant; but how valuable due process becomes, up against Marcusean furies. Thus the new conservatives, though perhaps historically bitter at what due process can be made to do at the hands of abstractionists and ideological profiteers, find themselves fighting especially hard for its survival. The guillotine is sharpened for many victims. Not alone those who have been raised over us by the exercise of democratic authority— the Lyndon Johnsons, the Richard Daleys, the Nathan Puseys—but also the prosperous owners of Dow Chemical (merchants of death; take away what they have) and the little Jewish delicatessen owner in Harlem (racist exploiter; vandalize him out of existence).

3. *Upward mobility.* Over the years the social democrats were thought of as the principal enthusiasts for it because of their programs which were essentially egalitarian, redistributionist. The conservatives insisted (quite rightly) that upward mobility was precisely what the free-market system most generously contributed to, and they had the figures to prove it. But having said as much, the conservatives left it (quite naturally) to human resources, up against the system, to take advantage of the opportunities to rise. Many, many millions did so. But now the need for that mobility is more acute than ever, so much so that the new conservatives are giving

the free marketplace something of a hand—for instance, by preferential hiring of Negroes. That is helpful. More helpful, I think most of them would agree, is a concerted assault on institutional barriers to the rise of the poor. So? Repeal minimum-wage laws. Destroy anti-black discrimination in the labor unions. Ease the progressive feature of the income tax. Adopt an altogether different attitude toward those whom Mr. Roger Starr so acutely isolates as the "disorganized poor," in contrast to the transient poor.

Here, then, is an order of concerns for the new conservatives, which by no means suggests the abandonment, let alone the theoretical repudiation, of some of our other concerns. (One of these days I'd like to find out just who *did* promote Peress.) But the historical responsibility of the conservatives is altogether clear: It is to defend what is best in America. At all costs. Against any enemy, foreign or domestic.

—New York Times Almanac, April 1969

Impeach the Speech, Not the President

I listened to President Nixon's speech at the faculty club of Stanford University. At the dinner were a dozen professors and a dozen students, and we sat at our places in the private dining hall and trained our eyes on the portable TV. There is no television regularly available at the faculty club of Stanford University, but when it was suggested that one be brought in, that was done and the dinner postponed without demurral. Nelson Algren once said that he was so removed from matters of the day that he would not even step out onto his own stoop to witness the wedding of the man in the gray flannel suit to Marjorie Morningstar. My guess is that Algren was standing by at 9 P.M., E.D.T., as much on attention as were the professors and students at Stanford, who knew that the speech would be a historic occasion, if not in exactly the same sense that Richard Nixon is given to suggesting that history follows him about with a Polaroid camera, lest history miss something.

I don't know quite why we all assumed the speech would last only a few minutes, but we did. Restiveness set in when Mr. Nixon was done with Watergate, whereafter he enjoined us to meditate on matters other than Watergate; to remind ourselves, for example, that the chancellor of the Republic of West Germany would be visiting with the president the very next day, in the very room from which he was addressing us, in order to discuss matters of great international concern. Going into emotional overdrive, the president divulged the inscription he had written in his inaugural memento to the members of his staff. Here, his psychological sense of his audience proved astonishingly malfunctional. On January 20 he had written to his subordinates, he said, that there were 1,461 days left in his administration. Today, he said, looking directly at us, an audience skeptical of his representation and surfeited by his techniques, there were only 1,361 days left in his administration. It was as if the coach, seeking to encourage his long-distance runners after they had started on a twenty-mile cross-country course, had bellowed out, "*Come on, team! Only 19 miles left!*" Then there were the distracting verbal slips, as when he announced with great dignity that he would give all his "intention" to the problems at hand, suddenly sounding less like a self-assured president who 174 days ago was elected by the biggest landslide of the century than like the befuddled CBS executive conscripted to microphone duty during the recent strike, sweating out the weather forecast and announcing that tomorrow there would be "mosterly easterly winds." When, looking up again into the camera, the president said, "Two wrongs do not make . . ." a muted but fatalistic plea escaped me, as if to the headsman whose stroke is already committed, "*No! Don't!*" But it was ineluctable, and we were informed that two wrongs do not make a right; and then finally the president asked the blessing of God on each and every one of us, and it crossed my mind that, on this occasion, we had truly earned it.

I was accordingly astonished and confused by the judgment of almost all those present, who pronounced it, in varying degrees, an effective speech. Oh, of course they didn't mean that *they* thought it was effective; they meant that the people *out there* would think it was wonderful—the heroic denials, the piety, the patriotism, the statesmanship. The theme was set by older members of the faculty, graduates of the Checkers speech, which they had thought quite awful, only to wake up the next morning to discover that it had moved the entire nation. I myself had thought the Checkers speech extremely good and had not been surprised in the least that it had the intended effect. But I thought this one quite unmitigatedly awful; and probably ineffective. There was no immediate way of discovering which assessment was correct, and Mr. Nixon did not, this time, help us out. It would have been inappropriate, under the circumstances, for Mr. Nixon to suggest that telegrams be sent direct to the White House by those who supported him; and humiliating to suggest that they be sent to the White House in care of Price Waterhouse.

The rhetoric apart, I thought the speech mortally flawed by low analytical cunning. Mr. Nixon sought to construct an august scaffolding for himself, whence to preside over the restoration of the public rectitude. Instead, he produced a spindle, on which he impaled himself. The structure of the speech compresses into a single sentence: "*Although it is clearly unreasonable that I as president—laboring full-time to bring peace to our generation and to combat inflation and to make it safe to walk the streets at night—should be held responsible for the excesses and minor illegalities of the entire executive and political staffs, nevertheless, because I am that kind of man, I do accept responsibility, and I commence my discharge of it here tonight by firing two innocent men.*"

Three days later, the president calmly informed the executive that conversations with him could not be divulged to anyone or anybody, and that no conversations with third persons about conversations with him could be divulged to anyone or anybody. The president's new counsel subsequently made an effort to fix the exact meaning of executive privilege, but, as of this writing, he has failed to clarify the question of just how the privilege will be used. It is accordingly not clear what was the meaning of Mr. Nixon's assumption of responsibility for Watergate, the more so since he neglected to describe what penalties or humiliations he had exposed himself to by the act of assuming responsibility. The president did not say that if the Senate committee, having looked into Watergate, concluded that he had knowledge of the affair before he communicated that knowledge to the public, or to the Justice Department, he would resign. Or that, relinquishing executive privilege, he would now undertake to convince the Senate of his innocence; or even that he would accept, contritely, if the evidence militated against him, a motion of censure. He said, in effect: "I am, for the purposes of exorbitant propriety, accepting academic responsibility for Watergate, but I shall proceed so to shelter myself as to make it all but impossible to prove that I am in fact responsible."

～

Arguing passionately against those who opposed the projected Constitution of the United States—publicists who had been busily stoking the suspicions of wary republicans who had so recently fought their way free of the fetters of King George—Alexander Hamilton wrote (*Federalist*, 67) that the detractors of the proposed presidency, "calculating upon the aversion of the people to monarchy, . . . have endeavored to enlist all their jealousies and apprehensions in opposition to the intended President of the United States; not merely as the embryo, but as the full-grown progeny of that detested parent." He polemicized against the caricature his opponents had drawn. The president, he wrote, "has been shown to us with the diadem sparkling on his brow and the imperial purple flowing in his train. He has been seated on a throne surrounded with minions and mistresses, giving audience to the envoys of foreign potentates, in all the supercilious pomp of majesty."

Don't you understand, said Hamilton (*Federalist*, 69), pleadingly—striving to train the public's attention on the differences between an American president and an English king—"The President of the United States would be an officer elected by the people for *four* years; the King of Great Britain is a perpetual and *hereditary* prince. The one would be amenable to personal punishment and disgrace; the person of the other is sacred and inviolable."

It has not worked out that way. The president of the United States is much, much less than "amenable" to personal punishment. John Stuart Mill warned against American provisions for the selection of the chief executive. Not only would a president popularly elected prove less "eminent" than a parliamentary leader of a party, Mill said, but he would be less easily disciplined. Early in the American experience, this proved so, though exactly why, the fiercely republican founders were unwilling to acknowledge, sensitive as they were to the notion that the president had *ex officio* acquired some of the spangles of the sovereign. Before very long it had become plain that the American arrangement, having taken hold, had, however tacitly, made appropriate institutional assertions.

So that while in Europe and Latin America, under constitutional monarchs and parliamentary republics, governments came and went, the American presidency proved miraculously stable. In England not long ago, the government survived by the slimmest margin under the stress of a single prevarication by John Profumo, the gentleman whose girlfriend was also involved with the Soviet naval attaché. In American history, there was the single impeachment proceeding, against Andrew Johnson, initiated in post–Civil War circumstances by the same ugly energies that beheaded

Charles I, and it failed in the Senate, thanks to the grandeur of a single member. In due course it was quietly acknowledged that, having wedded the offices of chief of state and chief of government, America was restrained from punctiliously meting out Punishment and Disgrace on its presidents; restrained by the awful fear of the unknown, unspecifiable consequences of regicide. It is one thing to replace the government of Anthony Eden with the government of Harold Macmillan, or the government of Harold Macmillan with that of Alec Douglas-Home—the kind of thing the English can do without the piano player's missing a note. It is another thing, to elevate the vice president by removing the president. The vice-presidential successor is confidently anointed in America only by popular election or by the assassin's removal of the legitimate president. After Andrew Johnson, resistance to impeachment as an available remedy grew as the office of the presidency grew, in due course investing in the incumbent something of the inviolability Hamilton overconfidently assured the rustic republican community our presidents would never acquire. The paraphernalia of the modern executive—the Transylvanian epaulets, the buglers' "Hail to the Chief," the presidential seal extending, yea, even unto Lyndon Johnson's Levi's, the Oval Room's solemnity, which eschews only incense—all this gives sensory confirmation to the reality, which is that the American presidency is a republican production of the sovereign. Those who believe that Richard Nixon has introduced a unique isolation to the presidency have not read the sad and bracing book by George Reedy deploring the isolation of Lyndon Johnson, whom he served, and of presidents in general. The evolution of the presidency slowly, but no less certainly, transformed the office and presented the Republic with an unwritten qualification. It is this: You must not impeach and remove a president *merely for the purpose of punishing him.* The Constitution, to be sure, speaks of the impeachment procedure as available against a president found guilty of "high crimes and misdemeanors," but the phrase in question was probably accepted at Philadelphia either because it was legal boilerplate (misdemeanors, after all, include a trivial misuse of the mailing frank, or the misuse of Air Force One for political purposes—it is inconceivable that a president goes a week without committing a legal misdemeanor), or as a sop to those whom, fearing the inchoate despot, Alexander Hamilton sought to reassure. It is not seriously suggested, this side of Ralph Nader—who has taken to rejecting presidents as matter-of-factly as the ignition system of a Ford car—that a president should be impeached for a misdemeanor. "Nothing but [such crimes as] are dangerous to the safety of the state, and which palpably disqualify and make unfit an incumbent to remain in the office of

President, can justify the application of this clause," Senator Garrett Davis said in the Senate during the debate over Andrew Johnson.

What is it that constitutes a high crime, of an impeachable character? When Judge Sirica imposed the breathcatchingly severe sentences on the Watergate conspirators, he was generally understood to be engaged in putting pressure on the defendants to talk. One of them, James McCord, did, and since then there have been developments in the Watergate case every day.

But one wonders what Judge Sirica would have done on the day he set aside, seven days after the original sentencing, to review those sentences, if the defendants had clung to the story that they alone were involved in initiating and executing the Watergate affair. Would he have confirmed his sentence of thirty-five years in jail against, say, Howard Hunt?

Judges generally weigh two factors in arriving at an appropriate sentence. They inquire into the motive of the wrongdoer, and into his record.

It is generally the case that the motive of a wrongdoer is personal, the gratification of greed, jealousy, or lust. Howard Hunt cannot be reasonably suspected of desiring for his own purposes a record of the conversations of Democratic strategist Lawrence O'Brien or the psychiatric record of Daniel Ellsberg (though the break-in at the psychiatrist's office was unknown to Judge Sirica when he handed down his sentence). Hunt was never (nor were any of his confederates) a burglar-for-hire, available in the Yellow Pages of the underground. For one thing, at $106 per day, which is the consultant's fee he was paid when he became involved with the White House, the pay is simply insufficient for someone of his background doing work that risky. No self-respecting burglar with any experience at all comes that low, especially when the work is irregular. Hunt, like the others, knew he was engaged in an illegal enterprise—obviously—but in an enterprise he just as obviously must have believed was justified by higher purposes. Having spent more than twenty years with the CIA, he knew that the techniques of espionage are routinely employed for political purposes adjudged by the sponsoring government to be justified. He understood, moreover, that the profession of the espionage agent is, however soft-spokenly, acknowledged as a part of the necessary enterprise of national sovereignty, particularly in an age of great-power tension.

As for a conventional criminal record, he simply had none. It is not established that he ever double-parked his car. The men he recruited as mechanics were deeply committed to the anti-Castro movement, had no criminal records, and would not—so far as one is able to judge—have been in the least bit attracted to conventional criminal careers.

One must assume that Hunt was enlisted by the use of arguments that had a plausible ring for an inflamed patriot, and a compelling ring, perhaps, to an inflamed patriot who was merely being asked to employ techniques of a profession he had practiced for two decades.

What kind of arguments might his recruiter have used? Let us attempt to imagine them as they might have been laid on by an advocate both convinced and convincing. Probably such a man stressed, to begin with, a *particular* need, the need to discover who in the White House—who *wherever*—was feeding intimate details of secret policy meetings to the press, most specifically to Jack Anderson, whose transcriptions of the minutes of the National Security Council meeting that considered America's role during the India-Pakistan war were sensational, in that they not only made headlines in papers all over the world, but also affected the policy decisions of the warring states and, indirectly, the policies of the standby major powers. The chill that continues between India and the United States grew less out of any objective act of the United States during the war than out of the damage to the Indian national pride caused by the revelations of Jack Anderson. At all costs, the man must be found, our recruiter can almost be heard to say.

"However"—he might have gone on—"you cannot expect much help from the Establishment, because Jack Anderson is the kind of person who is not nowadays being reproached for doing that kind of thing. Far from it: he got the Pulitzer Prize for doing it. Don't you see, Howard? That is the attitude today of people who should know better but don't. Their hostility to this country and to its institutions is their first attachment. Did you see how they flocked to Dan Ellsberg when he admitted stealing our documents and giving them to the *Post* and the *Times?* They made a hero out of that bastard overnight, Howard. He's on trial now, and he has a pinko lawyer aching all over Hollywood for him, and he's going to get him off, and other little Ellsbergs will spring up all over the place, because they'll be saying there's no such thing as a national secret. The People—get that, the People, Howard, the kind of talk they use at Berkeley to justify burning down the joint—have a right to know. Wish to God they'd agree that the people have the right to a functioning government. They won't have a functioning government for very long if that madman George McGovern gets elected, that's for sure. Now let's discuss a practical problem. . . ."

I, for one, would have no difficulty whatever in imagining such an amplification coming from the lips of someone who happened to be in the Oval Office at the moment when, say, Anderson's column on Bangladesh was published, or when Jack Anderson was given the Pulitzer Prize.

Perhaps it is easy for me to understand its happening because if someone had on the same occasions bothered to record my own mutterings, they would not have been significantly different, except that my commentary goes out quite safely in newspaper columns and on television, and is prettily laced with brooding historical references to a lowering American antinomianism. Is it so reckless to say that a lawless counterculture is likely to beget a lawless *counter*-counterculture—to say this at the level of prediction, rather than of judgment?

Of course Hunt shouldn't have done it, and of course he should be punished. But the national attention is fixed now on whether the man in the chain of command who gave rise to such thoughts—volatilized by his subordinates into such galvanizing language as caused Bernard Barker, Frank Sturgis, and the others to believe that by breaking into that office in the Watergate they were in their own small way pressing the war against Fidel Castro—did, by attempting to provide executive cover for his servants' servants, commit an impeachable crime.

Most of the critics who parlay Watergate into impeachment belong in the pulpit or in the academy, not in Congress. Congress, which has always been potentially supreme—it can deny jurisdiction to the Supreme Court and funds to the executive, and it can impeach the lot of them—is ultimately responsible for the stability of the nation. Under certain circumstances, the stability of the nation could require the removal of the president. But there is the lapidary distinction: The purpose cannot be to punish the president, only to effect his removal. This is the distinction that threatens to be drowned out in the fury of the current debate. They are still saying—even so august a conservative as Senator Barry Goldwater—that if Richard Nixon is "proven" to be guilty of having foreknowledge of Watergate, or guilty (which is worse) of attempting to obstruct justice, then he must be removed in deference to the office of the presidency. In deference to the office of the presidency, he must not be removed. Censured, yes; humiliated, yes. But to remove a president is to remove the sovereign. To remove him is to punish the citizenry who benefit from the national stability. The general point is underscored by the concrete point—the public is greatly divided on the fitness of Spiro Agnew to serve. That there are many Americans who would prefer Agnew to Nixon is not in point. There are many Americans who would not, and the narrow question must be framed around the primary question of whether the ascendancy of Agnew, the indispensable corollary to the deposition of Nixon, is justified. That is the way to put the argument *a posteriori*, for those who shrink from the abstract approach.

The moral question is whether the democratist idea of the same punishment for the same crime, no matter the station of the transgressor, is historically secure. Plainly it is not, and a meticulous constitutionalist could run his finger over American presidential history and come up with cogent arguments for impeaching presidents long since honorably buried whose crimes against the spirit of the Constitution were far removed from the chicken-thieving of Watergate; and yet they were left alone, Jefferson to suspend the Constitution in order to purchase Louisiana, Lincoln to override the Bill of Rights in order to wage war, Roosevelt to do his best to vitiate the judiciary by packing the Supreme Court.

Impeachment is a technical resource available against the president who becomes, or threatens to become, Caligula. Useful and usable against the despot, or the madman. Richard Nixon is neither. Assuming that every insinuation against him and his staff were proved to be true, it does not add up to Nixon as despot, or even to Nixon as madman, or even to Nixon as a plausible national threat to individual freedom by virtue of his exercises in managerial tyranny.

But there is a delicate corollary to the presumptive nonimpeachability of the president. The collision of two standards, not easily reconcilable, made for the bafflement, and the pathos, of the Richard Nixon of the April 30 speech. We hear much of the American tradition that a man is innocent until proved guilty. The distinction is correct in law, but has always been abstractionist as regards what it actually expects of a community toward an unconvicted defendant whom it believes to be guilty in plain fact.

We have now the extraordinary finding of the Gallup poll—that even before Nixon delivered his address on April 30, 40 percent of the American people thought him to have had foreknowledge of Watergate. The Stanford intellectuals' knowledge of the mind and heart of the booboisie notwithstanding, the television address had the astonishing effect of increasing, rather than diminishing, the number of Americans who believed that Nixon was not telling the truth.

The ethos, in America, demands almost fetishistically ("And ye shall know the truth, and the truth shall make you free") the whole truth. So here was the president, asking the people to accept as truth that which half of them did not believe. And here was the president trickily declining to furnish the data on the basis of which they might accept his accounting. It is better not to provoke the Puritan conscience of America at all than, having done so, to frustrate the mechanism by which it could arrive at a solemn judgment on the matter. This was Richard Nixon's great error of April 30. He asserted his innocence, then quickly maneuvered to inhibit the executive from cooperating fully with investigating bodies that sought to document that innocence. Thus he activated the Puritan conscience, which, after so much foreplay, is not easily denied.

Far better the blur, the vagueness, a formalistic contrition, the subliminal appeal to a postulated incorruptibility of the institution of the presidency. Granted such a speech would have confirmed many in their suspicion of Nixon's personal guilt, even as the evasiveness of Senator Edward Kennedy after Chappaquiddick confirmed the belief of many in his guilt. But that way, the skeptical minority—or majority—could, with Nixon as with Kennedy, proceed to other business, acknowledging that Nixon is flawed after all and must be watched but that, after all, life has to go on; and, after all, Nixon has his strengths, even as Kennedy does, and the personal humiliation of their ordeals is probably enough punishment to shrive them—in this world, at least; which is the only world we govern. For which, among so many other things, we truly have God to thank.

—*New York Times Magazine*, May 10, 1973

Marx Is Dead

Although it is likely that more academic and philosophical attention has been devoted in the last fifty years to the flowering of Marxist thought than to life under Marxism, it is astonishing how little thought is given to the great residual paradox. It is expressed in the antipodal manifestos of our time. The first is the voice of Solzhenitsyn—a single voice to be sure, but it is the voice of baptized humanity. What he said is that there is probably not one believing Marxist in Moscow. The contrary voice is the voice of—the Politburo: a great assembly of lords secular, disposing of three thousand silos armed with hydrogen bombs, and the world's greatest army, navy, and submarine force, commanding the greatest empire since Rome's. They are fighting for the most penetrable idiocies in the history of superstition; and yet on and on they go.

What would the Soviet Union be, if you stripped it of its ideological pretensions? There are three typhonic vectors in the postwar world. One of them is nationalism. The second—related—is anti-imperialism. The third is Marxist imperialism. Although every nation represented in the

United Nations, ourselves included, will vote against imperialism, very nearly as many (subtract a dozen) regularly vote to ratify the Soviet Union's de facto imperialism. Although every nation will swear out a blood oath against tyranny, the majority will back tyranny—as long as it is done in the holy name of Marx. Find yourself any old country, impoverished, agricultural, illiterate: by rigorous definition laid down by Marx himself, lacking the constituent parts to pass over into Communism. But you need only require that the prevailing tyrant declare himself to be a Marxist, and the propaganda war is half won. If Samora Machel of Mozambique had said everything he has said, done everything he has done, but announced that he was just a good old-fashioned bourgeois despot, he'd have been the target of universal obloquy from the beginning, in 1975. He has only to say that he is a Marxist, and he is accounted blessed among the ignorant, and the cynical, of this world. The question arises: Why doesn't the West take better advantage of the palpable superstitions? The obvious differences apart, Karl Marx was no more reliable a prophet than was the Reverend Jim Jones. Karl Marx was a genius, an uncannily resourceful manipulator of world history who shoved everything he knew, thought, and devised into a Ouija board from whose movements he decocted universal laws. He had his following, during the late phases of the Industrial Revolution. But he was discredited by historical experience longer ago than the Wizard of Oz: and still, great grown people sit around, declare themselves to be Marxists, and make excuses for Gulag and Afghanistan.

The Republican candidate for president of the United States should declare himself devoted absolutely to the total atomization of the Marxist myth. He doesn't need to conscript thinkers-for-hire. The thinking has been done. The research has been done. History is there begging to be used as witness before the court of the people. The demonstration, at a private level, has been done by the poets, historians, and martyrs of our time. It requires only that it become an official crusade, one to which we will attach ourselves as vigorously as if we were spreading the word of how to extirpate smallpox from the fetid corners of the world.

In this effort we can exploit the technology of communications. The Voice of America? Hell, the voice of humanity. If we undertake a systematic, devoted, evangelical effort to instruct the people of the world that the Soviet Union is animated not by a salvific ideology, but by a reactionary desire to kill and torture, intimidate and exploit others, for the benefit of its own recidivist national appetites for imperialism—we will have done, by peaceful means, what is so long overdue. We will have buried Marx, and Marxism, in that common grave in which he belongs, together with such recent historical figures as Jim Jones, or such ancient historical impostors as Lucifer.

—January 24, 1980

The Call of Public Service

As the crowds move into Washington and the crowds move out of Washington, there are sounds of weeping and of laughing. It is one thing to weep because you no longer have access to the rampart o'er which you watched, and indeed there is no reason to do so because the enemy overcame. To wish to remain in Washington for the purpose of keeping the barbarians at bay is one thing. To wish to be there in order to govern is another. The differences are worth reflecting upon.

I know people (not a lot) who go around saying things like, "Public service is the great opportunity in life." Those who feel this are of two kinds, and the distinction is critical. The person who devotes himself to public service defined as missionary work in Burma, or Red Cross work in Somalia, or any of the hundred different activities that can be done in a community to help those who need help, is the public servant who is truly admirable.

It is a pity that one so seldom hears about this type of person. Oh, maybe the woman who founded the Red Cross (what was her name?), or the man who began the Jesuit order. Mostly they are anonymous men and women, and their gratification is in serving their fellow men and their God.

But "giving your life to public service" these days is generally intended to describe an ambition to serve in political office. Recently it was recalled that Tip O'Neill was asked what was it that, having left Washington, where he had served as speaker of the House, he missed most. He replied without hesitation: "Power."

Power. That is the great aphrodisiac. Granted, our legislators get pretty fair pay these days. But back before the Reform Acts in Great Britain, there was no pay to speak of for members of the House of Commons. But there were long lines of men who wished to "serve" the public.

It is arresting to remind oneself that, as often as not, those men in public service are engaged in doing great disservice: Until 1807 the British continued to authorize the trade in slaves. The dissenter may think me too categorical in saying so, but I nonetheless say that I deeply wish that Lyndon Johnson had gone in for real estate instead of government.

At the extreme, of course, there are the forthright tyrannies. These are, except in situations of anarchy—such as Somalia's—brief in duration. Usually there is organized government behind the concentrated ugliness of power. I note that of the 220 million people killed during the twentieth century, 155 million of them were killed by their own governments. The Nazis killed more Germans than did the Allies. Ask how many Germans were killed by Hitler, Russians by Stalin, Chinese by Mao, and one quickly gets the idea.

That is the harsh end of government. At the softer end, you have the governor who attempts to do something beneficent for his subjects but ends by doing them a disservice. The national debt is the accumulated excess of government spending over government income. The deficit has risen in America to the point where, counting in all forms of taxes, Americans work full time for federal and state governments until May 5, when they begin to work for themselves. One hundred twenty-four days.

Enthusiasts for government will list the benefits of government: free schooling, health care, the lot. Well, the slavemasters also provided food, lodging, and medical care. Government is of course necessary, but in a season where the Religious Left (the happy designation of Fran Liebowitz, referring to the aggregations that surrounded Bill Clinton when he was inaugurated as president) is in a delirium of enthusiasm about what the new government is going to do for us, it pays to remind ourselves that we are in the hands of men and women who love power. They mainline on it.

What can we do today for the American citizen? ("The government can do something for the people only in proportion as it can do something to the people." —T. Jefferson.) How can we get more taxes from him? What next can we forbid him to do? Require him to do?

The joy of the cadet entering West Point to do public service is a wholly understandable phenomenon. He is there to do as he is told, in defense of the policies his country devises. But it pays to remember that the "defense policies" of many countries in many centuries have made of a nation's armies primarily shooting squads, because the men who command those armies are mostly predators.

Our governors are, for the most part, the enemy. The government, John Adams wrote, "turns every contingency into an excuse for enhancing power in itself." That was almost two hundred years ago. How right he was. Our enemy, the state.

—January 28, 1993

POLITICS IN PRACTICE

The Party and the Deep Blue Sea

Two thousand words are mine to give "an appraisal of the Republican Party as it is today, what it stands for, and what changes might be expected if it were swept into office next year." In a word, it is in sorry shape; it stands, though with overtones of reluctance, for a continued transfer of social power into the hands of the State; changes would be few, and yet such changes as there would be are desirable.

Albert Jay Nock once wrote in *Our Enemy, the State* that the average American is the most unphilosophical of persons; that "Mr. Jefferson Brick, General Choke and the Honourable Elijah Pogrom made a first-class job of indoctrinating their countrymen with the idea that a philosophy is wholly unnecessary, and that a concern with the theory of things is effeminate and unbecoming." Mr. Nock sums up American political adolescence by suggesting that Michel Chevalier properly tagged us, even though he wrote a hundred years ago, as having the "morale of an army on the march."

As witness to this, of course, is our lack of purposive, three-dimensional thinking about the nature of the State. Reflecting this void, our two major political parties have painfully constructed an ephemeral battle line dividing two almost identical streams of superficial thought about the proper role of the State in a free society. It is perhaps due in part to our frantic preoccupation with the trivia that separate the 1952 Republican from the 1952 Democrat that we do tragically little thinking about the genus State, which many of us still believe, along with Herbert Spencer, to be "begotten of aggression and by aggression," and which many of us still regard, along with Henry Mencken, as "the common enemy of all well-disposed, industrious, and decent men."

Thus, the most striking feature of the coming elections, and certainly the one that will most puzzle future students of our history, is that in 1952 no American citizen had an opportunity forthrightly to reject the ideology of the Leviathan State. The pretensions of the Republican Party to offering a significant alternative to statism are palpably unconvincing.

They are not, of course, to be measured by Republican compliance with the extensive and productive tax laws that are needed to support a vigorous anti-Communist foreign policy. The indices of the Republican attitude toward a free society are seen in far less spectacular items than foreign aid to Africa or a $50-billion defense budget, and yet they are seen in far more meaningful terms. For the "opposition" party today countenances all the important hallmarks of political and economic centralization: managed currency, egalitarian fiscal policies, federal minimum-wage laws, federal Social Security, federal subsidization of favored classes, institutions, and special interests, and the withering away of boundaries between the states.

The question that hotly follows is why. Why does the opposition party refuse to offer a genuine opposition? At this juncture the statists leap to their favorite answer to the query. They tell us that the anarchistic, uncivilized, uncharitable rugged individualism associated with the pre-Roosevelt era has been forever discredited by the American people. The social revolution of the New Deal is a *fait accompli* and no political party could rally any enthusiasm in 1952 for a genuinely anti-statist program.

My own diagnosis does not totally contradict this one. To begin with, I see the issue primarily as one of freedom or non-freedom. To the extent that a fraction of the individual's time, which we will for convenience equate with his earnings, is *a priori* mortgaged to the government and against his will, then he is to that same extent not free. Since there is no money except the individual's money, and since his money represents his labor or his savings or the product of his tools, the assessment of that money by the State represents a direct levy on that individual's freedom. If it is true, as the liberals would have it, that the Republican Party could not evoke any support for a program that calls for extracting from the individual *only* that money necessary to carry on the minimum functions of government (loosely, defense, courts, and conservation), then it must follow that the American people no longer value maximum individual freedom.

Now this may well be the case. Most human beings respond to education, and freedom has been depreciated in the nation's schools for some years now. The responsibility of the State to regulate and nourish individual lives us not only acknowledged, but eloquently and insistently affirmed by an increasing number of the most efficacious of influence-molders: the teachers.

And yet, there has been no dramatic showdown. There is no tangible proof that the Republican Party would indeed fail to win over the people to a platform of freedom. And even if it should fail, it would have succeeded in alerting the people to the fact that there still exists, in theory at least, an alternative to State paternalism. And this would seem to be a noble enough and a traditional service for a political party whose birth and early success grew out of its refusal to condone human slavery.

∼

There is perhaps a more decisive reason why the Republican Party will not seriously oppose the Democrats, and here we return to the indictment of Mr. Nock against the American people. It may be that because we exhibit the morale of an army on the march it is a fair deduction that we cannot understand the nature of the State, the irreconcilability between individual freedom and State-sponsored security; and perhaps because of this endemic inability to see things as they are, we feel that we can have our cake and eat it too.

Perhaps our plight is even worse than our inability to think through the implications of federal Social Security, the implications of Big Government. Perhaps our trouble is that we don't think about it *at all*. There is disturbing evidence that this is our number-one national problem, and one which the Republican Party, at least, is doing very little to alleviate, for it refuses even to raise the issue.

The objection arises that such apathy hardly squares with the widespread tension and excitement—even today, more than half a year before the national elections—over which of the two parties will wield the mace after next November. After all, the nation's editors and columnists are greeting the pre-election season the way a bridge club would the divorce of its president. They linger over tidbit details, they fabricate and circularize them, and they dress them up in all sorts of fanciful costumes as they solemnly contemplate (a) who will be nominated, and (b) who will win.

But the sense of such activity is gone when the spotlight refuses to train on political platforms, focusing instead on political personalities. National politics have become so remote, so unresponsive, that the basic and all-important unit of society—the individual—feels powerless to assert himself, even assuming he wished to do so.

The result, of course, is a battle for power waged by towering political personalities who are bored by issues, who are afraid to stand or fall on competing political ideologies. There is no more flamboyant example of this than the suggestion by Senator Claude Pepper, at the Democratic Convention of 1948, that Eisenhower be nominated by acclamation and that he be allowed to write his own platform!

Given, then, our preoccupation with species as against genus, it is perhaps inevitable that the forthcoming election, no matter who wins it, will make little difference to the azimuth of our national parade.

∼

The most important issue of the day, it is time to admit it, is survival. Here there is apparently some confusion in the ranks of conservatives, and hard thinking is in order for them. The thus-far invincible aggressiveness of the Soviet Union does or does not constitute a threat to the security of the United States, and we have got to decide which. If it does, we shall have to rearrange, sensibly, our battle plans; and this means that we have got to accept Big Government for the duration—for neither an offensive nor a defensive war can be waged, given our present government skills, except through the instrument of a totalitarian bureaucracy within our shores. The question is raised: Does it make a great deal of difference if we lose our freedom to a Georgian bandit or to a Missouri ignoramus? The question is a good one.

Still and all, our chances of ultimate victory against an indigenous bureaucracy are far greater than they could ever be against one controlled from abroad, one that would be nourished and protected by a worldwide Communist monolith. Thus, many conservatives, and many Republicans, have got to think this problem through. And if they deem Soviet power a menace to our freedom (as I happen to), they will have to support large armies and air forces, atomic energy, central intelligence, war-production boards, and the attendant centralization of power in Washington—even with Truman at the reins of it all.

This, of course, does not argue that there should be bipartisanship in the means of foreign policy, resignation to excessive government waste and dishonesty, or, especially, any diminution of our effort to alert the American people to the horrors of welfarism. That campaign can never end, and we cannot repeat too often Jefferson's infallible axiom: "The government can do something *for* the people only in proportion as it can do something *to* the people"—adding, out of the insight garnered from a turbulent and revealing post-Jeffersonian chapter in world history, "and it most certainly will do something *to* the people."

We must repeat this truism as often as Roosevelt repeated his promises to keep us out of war. Only then might the people believe it.

But with the publication of Senator Taft's book on foreign policy, few people harbor any suspicions that a Republican administration would refuse vigorously to prosecute an effective and single-minded anti-Soviet foreign policy. Thus, on the most important tactical issue of the day, the qualifications of the Republicans and the Democrats are roughly even, except that the odds are slightly in favor of the party that would not be hamstrung by obstinate and unreasoned allegiance to policies and figures responsible for blatant errors of the past.

The second issue of the campaign, the strategic issue, will not be raised, as I have indicated. Ideally, the Republican platform should acknowledge a domestic enemy, the State. The Republicans will unquestionably indulge again in their unprepossessing litany about the desirability of individualism and the evils of collectivism. And indeed, even desultory opposition to at least the most adventurous demands of the Fair Deal makes the GOP, in my mind, the sounder national choice.

Yet, assuming a Republican victory, there is little reason to hope to hold the government even where it is; any such hope is fast dissipated if we review the party's record of assimilating, one by one, the articles of the New Deal. The history of the GOP over the past fifteen years gives evidence of disheartening, though unsuccessful, opportunism. What were once the most dramatic and bitterly contested innovations of the New Deal—the cited managed currency, egalitarian tax policies, minimum-wage laws, civil-rights legislation, labor monopolies, and Social Security—now seem to be indelibly sketched into the "opposition" platform.

It appears to be the new historic destiny of the Republican Party to accept the Democratic platform, less a token constant. To that end, for example, Truman calls for national health measures and for the Brannan plan to guarantee farmers' income, and the Republicans oppose them. But there is no indication that the organic relationship between the two parties is due for a change. In 1956 we may well see the Republican platform approving the health and farm measures, but violently disputing the Democrats' call for national ownership of steel, railroads, and coal. The election of 1980 may well be fought over the issue whether any American has the right to criticize the party in power; and the Big Issue of 1984 might center on whether there shall be an election in 1988.

~

To conclude, a sensible attitude toward the Republican Party (for those who don't feel they have to "be with history" if history is leading them into an abyss) would be to insist that it declare for substantive policy alternatives, to reflect the passions of that unknown but perhaps formidable number of persons who want to vote for the free marketplace but don't know where to go to do it.

Thus, the Republican Party should repudiate the inroads that have been made over the past years into individual freedom. But since the Republican Party will do no such thing, or at least gives no evidence that it contemplates doing any such thing, the election loses much of its interest and all its claims to be an exercise in political democracy. Still and all, reason calls for Republican victory—if only to record a lack of faith in Harry Truman, suspicion of accelerated statism, and the clean and human desire to see new names and faces in the headlines every morning.

—*Commonweal, January 25, 1952*

Reflections on Election Eve

I do not know by how many votes Dwight Eisenhower will be re-elected. But I suspect that if one were to subtract from his total the votes of those who are for him purely on grounds of relative merit—that is to say, the votes of those who feel that though he is the better of the two, he is a bad thing—he would lose the election. Many who will vote for him would insist on putting their feelings more exactly, by saying Eisenhower is the *less bad* of the two candidates. If Eisenhower is due to get his marginal support from those who are dissatisfied with him, but are more dissatisfied with Adlai Stevenson, it becomes highly relevant to understand the nature of the differences between him and his adversary.

What about the men themselves? I happen to think that if Adlai Stevenson and Dwight Eisenhower were each given a South Sea island over which to preside as absolute monarch, life in one island would not differ significantly, in internal affairs, from life in the other; in foreign affairs, the two kingdoms would also be similar, maintaining, I should guess, a most fraternal relationship, what with exchange students, intermarriage, golf tournaments, and much else dedicated to inter-island understanding. I do not believe that society-shaking or world-shaking ideas would spontaneously generate in either man's mind. Mr. Eisenhower is not fascinated by social abstractions, and the evidence is that Mr. Stevenson, when left alone, was not victimized by them. But it is not enough to explore the minds of the two candidates. They are both tied to circumstances.

~

Up until the campaign began, there were no substantive differences of opinion between the controlling factions of the two parties. In foreign policy, the mood was "bipartisan." On the most explosive domestic issue—the Supreme Court's intervention in the South—the parties were as one. On the regulation of the economy, both were committed to the notion that the responsibility for the nation's economic metabolism is the state's. In behalf of the welfare of the people, both tended to more and more federal activity; one party would emphasize the need for immediate action in one field, the other would stress another field; the Democratic Party tended to justify its position by an appeal to abstractions—to the "rights of minority groups," to "equality, to "parity," to "social justice"— while the Republicans, with a whiggish contempt for ideology, used a different vocabulary, the indigenous vocabulary of pragmatism. But the movement was in the same direction.

The concessions made by Republicans to those who oppose the growth of the state were episodic, and seemed almost wayward. The return of the tidelands, the encouragement of private development of nuclear power, the abolition of price controls, the rejection in the Far West of federal power projects, rendered some of those hungry for the least recognition sublimely happy, and eternally grateful, as an aging coquette is grateful to the man-about-town who, every now and then, will pause in making the rounds to blow her a flirtatious kiss. Others reacted differently: The Eisenhower program calls for a net increase in government—what with the expansion of Social Security, the call for gigantic federal expenditures on highways and schools, the impudently counterfeit soil-bank program, and the rest of it. Yet that is not the measure of the Republican Party's relapse into the collectivist approach to social problems. The measure is not in its very own statist innovations or expansions, but in the easy and wholehearted acceptance of all that came before, of the great statist legacy of the New Deal.

But during a national campaign, the compulsion quite naturally arises to find a justification for so unsettling an interruption in the national life. That is generally done by stressing one's differences with one's opponent. And if the differences are so minor as to make the stressing of them appear precious or contrived, why the tendency is to create genuine differences. It is, of course, up to the challenger to identify those differences. In Stevenson's case it was easy, for he had only to lend an ear to the left-wing ideologues who are always buzzing about him. He had merely to let Walter Reuther dictate, and Arthur Schlesinger verbalize, the specifications of the New America into which he was born to lead us; or to let the vociferous Oppenheimer faction among the atom scientists suggest arresting and glamorous means of mitigating the horrors of war.

So Adlai Stevenson succeeded in reawakening the interest of the Left in his cause. But, in the process, he awakened, as was inevitable, the interest of the disgusted Right in the banner of his opponent. It was not necessary for Mr. Eisenhower actually to move to the right, to scrap his program in favor of a genuinely conservative one. All he had to do was hold his ground. Whereupon the program of the Republicans, which is essentially one of measured socialism, looks wonderfully appealing to the conservative by contrast with that of the Democrats. So, gradually, the conservative shakes off his long-nurtured determination to repay the affronts of the last four years by withholding his vote on election day and, galvanized finally, he goes off to the polls—cursing, more often than not, those who stayed at home.

What happened is that the injunction that it is necessary to vote for the better of two choices once again took on relevance, the parties being finally distinguishable, one from the other. It does not matter that experience teaches that the threat is largely illusory. The compulsion to differ is generally satisfied by rhetorical offerings. Still, during a campaign, an encounter with the people takes place; and sometimes the people, feeling like Tantalus, get hold of their tormentor and make him come through.

～

The argument by relative merit is wonderfully persuasive. In some cases it is, I think, conclusive. If one master will enslave me ninety days a year, a second only eighty-nine, if I may choose between them and must choose one, I shall unhesitatingly, all else being equal, elect to serve under the latter; and I should find no difficulty whatever defending my choice. My reasoning becomes inadequate, and perilously so, only when, in my zeal to stress the relative merit of the less exacting master, I find myself speaking approvingly, even enthusiastically about him. When that happens, there is danger to mind and morals.

The danger posed by the Republican Party of today lies bare-breasted in its universal emblem, I Like Ike. It should read, I Prefer Ike.

For on what political or philosophical basis can one approve of Eisenhower? It is not as if he were consciously and actively engaged in doing everything that can be done, given the political realities, in behalf of freedom and order, hating half of what he has to do, but offering it up in return for keeping the reins of power from those who would hasten the demise of our nation. No, General Eisenhower thoroughly approves of and believes in what he does. He does not proclaim—because he does not believe it—that we live in a world that has been seduced by false prophets, or that there lies ahead the task of re-educating a lost generation. He does not say—because he does not believe it—that freedom is intrinsically desirable, that equality is not of this world, that rights have correlative duties, that government must be limited and decentralized. All these things and much, much more, Eisenhower does not say; for he does not believe.

By that standard, the greatest enemies of an honorable Republican Party are its philosophers, its bards, its Arthur Larsons. They devote their time not to establishing the relative merit of Eisenhower's party, but to insisting on its intrinsic worth. Some of its prophets tend to find it more worthy the further it goes in the wrong direction. Paul Hoffman, chairman of the Fund for the Republic, will write, and write jubilantly, that the Republican Party has traveled further, under General Eisenhower, than it had gone in the previous fifty years. Even so, General Eisenhower will himself say; for the Republican Party is in league with the future.

The tendency to justify that which is, is ancient, and, alas, irrepressible. Voltaire mocked the notion that this is the best of all possible worlds, but he did not seriously shake the durable conviction that it is, from which follows the temptation to accept as tolerable any evil if it is widely enough practiced—widely enough, that is to say, to become worldly. Would President Eisenhower and Prime Minister Eden have gone to Geneva to exchange libations with tyrants and slaughterers if those tyrants and slaughterers had tyrannized over, or slaughtered, hundreds of men, rather than hundreds of thousands? Would they go—or deputize anyone to go—to Nairobi to talk amicably with leaders of the Mau Mau?

Ours is an age in which decent persons are disposed to shrug aside sexual perversion because Kinsey has established the frequency with which it is practiced, in which gentle and civilized statesmen tolerate and mingle with Communists because they inhabit one half the globe, and in which principled men and women, who all their lives have sworn by axioms of government that Progressive Moderation explicitly repudiates, now, *because* Progressive Moderation has become the order of the day, Like Ike.

Let those who prefer Eisenhower, whom the campaign seems to have rendered preferable, vote for him, if they are convinced no other course of action holds out any practical hope. But let them for heaven's sake not join in the festivities.

—*National Review*, November 3, 1956

What of Tomorrow?

Mr. Stewart Alsop reports that the Democratic Party is desperate. Or, in his own words, "absolutely desperate." Not for the reasons advanced last summer by Democratic orators and jobseekers, who bemoaned America's march down the road to perdition under the Republican banner, but for exactly the opposite reason: The Republicans are doing just what the Democrats would themselves do were they in power. And this leaves the Democrats without an issue. "The Eisenhower Administration," Mr. Alsop notes, "in fact has now consciously accepted the basic thesis of the dominant wing of the Democratic Party—that the Federal government is responsible for the general welfare. . . . Four years ago, when the Eisenhower Administration took office with a domestic program which differed in no important respect from the program of the late Senator Taft, such a flat, unequivocal acceptance of the basic thesis of the welfare state would have been considered a major heresy."

It is no longer so considered, nor should it be, is the burden of the remainder of Mr. Alsop's column; and on this point the overwhelming majority of the nation's conservatives, who four years ago cursed the welfare state and today curse *National Review* and others who contend that they were right the first time, are agreed.

National Review has often drawn political and economic conclusions from the relentless march of the Eisenhower administration to statism, and we will not go over the ground again here. We wish to say a word, only a word, about the philosophical implications of the relapse into relativism of Mr. Alsop and the conservative community. Our position is that heresy is heresy, yesterday, today, and tomorrow, and that the nature of heresy is not changed by the passage of time, by automation, by the farm vote, by George Gallup, or by anybody or anything else.

Those who four years ago opposed political and economic centralization as constrictive of individual freedom and damaging to the economy were eternally, not transiently, right. In our time, relativism has triumphed. It is a strange and accommodating god. Under it the same people, saying much the same thing, glide with the same party from one set of postulates over to a totally contradictory set—without giving it a second thought. Under relativism we can drift into rigid socialism of a kind Marx himself would not have had the perversity to quarrel with. For those who, in such an age, will show themselves nostalgic for the age of Eisenhower, there will be epithets of "Reactionary! Unreconstructible! Paleolithic!"—the same epithets directed, these days, at those who say Taft was right, and Eisenhower dead, dead wrong.

—*National Review*, March 2, 1957

National Review and the 1960 Election

As in 1956, there are today conservatives who do not intend to vote the Republican presidential ticket, for much the same reason they gave then: For intelligent Americans, a higher political mission than merely electing Republican candidates to office is the liberation of the party mechanism from the control of the liberals, and this can be done only by repudiating the liberal standardbearer. So it was held in 1956, and so it is being held today by perfectly responsible men: men who are not motivated, as is so often supposed, merely by a vindictive disappointment with Nixon. They have a view of history different from that of those conservatives who say simply, Vote Republican, and who fight hard within the Republican Party to direct Nixon and Congress on a rightward course, for the alternative is Kennedy, Reuther, and the Harvard ideologues; and that alternative is intolerable.

In 1956 *National Review* offered this distinction, which is perhaps worth repeating. The argument by relative merit—the argument that one must vote for the lesser of two evils—is very persuasive and within limits conclusive. The trouble is the dynamics of politics do not in fact allow us to go that far and no further. Before we know it, the lesser of two evils is transmuted into a positive good—and from that moment on, we are morally and philosophically adrift. Politics—yes, yes, yes—is the art of the possible; but the ideal, if not possible, is surely more nearly realizable than recent political leadership would indicate. "The danger posed by the Republican Party of today," we wrote in 1956, "lies bare-breasted in its universal emblem, I Like Ike. It should read, I prefer Ike."

Who likes Nixon's Republicanism? We don't. But that does not mean that as individuals we can't vote for Nixon for president, just as most though not all the editors of *National Review* voted in 1956 for Eisenhower. That didn't mean we let up the fire: Indeed, we had to go out in shifts, to leave one editor firing the machine gun at Ike, while another dashed out and voted for him. We must not confuse the verities with the political situation, but we must not, either, lose our vision of the good society merely because, year after year, it fails to materialize.

The arguments are familiar: *In the United States, political parties are not ideological or class parties. They are loose coalitions of varied interests, each of which tries to exercise what power it can within the party. Conservatism, as put forward, say, in Senator Goldwater's* The Conscience of a Conservative, *is a force within the Republican Party. (It is, for that matter, also a force within the Democratic Party.) Nixon is less the leader of a different force within the Republican Party than he is an amalgamator of all the forces. He is, if not the leader, the deputy of the centrist force that has prevailed since the fateful first ballot in the convention at Chicago in 1952. Still another force, further left in many respects, in other respects conservative and nationalistic, is Rockefeller's—and there are others; the lines are unclear. Among the forces there is constant tension. But it is to the advantage of every one of them to work together at election time to keep a common roof over their heads.*

That is a perfectly rational analysis for a conservative to make. It is defensible historically and theoretically.

An opposing view holds: *What is at stake in the next few years is of such consequence as to render irrelevant copybook maxims about the two-party system, coalitions of interest, and so on. Our attention must be given to the supreme problem. We are losing the war to the Soviet Union and we are losing our freedoms at home; and there is no prospect of liberating the Republican Party from the faction that now controls it, so long as the party enjoys executive power. Consequently we must break the old rules, defeat Nixon, and hope that we may succeed during the next four years in developing a true and effective opposition to the left-Democratic president—of the kind mobilized so successfully in the last years of Mr. Truman's administration by Senator Taft. By going into opposition we can hope to paralyze the Left, and unload those leaders who, by their deficient understanding, are hastening the victory of socialism, here and abroad.*

That, too, is a rational position for a conservative.

National Review was not founded to make practical politics. Our job is to think, and to write; and occasionally to mediate. We are tablet keepers. For almost five years we have chronicled the shortcomings of the present administration. And we are ready for either President Nixon or President Kennedy; our bomb shelters are in good order. Our job today is surely to remind ardent members of the conservative community that equally well-instructed persons can differ on matters of political tactic, and that it is profoundly wrong for one faction to anathematize the other over such differences. We do not intend to exhort our readers in a particular line of political action. We have exhaustively explored the illusions of liberalism, which dominate Mr. Kennedy and influence Mr. Nixon. We hope the country is as strong as Mr. Nixon says it is and Mr. Kennedy says it can be. It will have to be just that strong to survive the years to come, whichever one of them comes to power.

—*National Review*, October 22, 1960

So Long, Ike

The American people will do anything for a good man. Dwight Eisenhower is manifestly that. And if it had been he running for president last year, he'd have reduced Jack Kennedy to political dust in six speeches, syntax or no syntax. Indeed, no one could have run against Ike and beaten him. It is not that the people were satisfied with his stewardship, but that they know politics is a grubby, cynical business, the meaning of which they cannot hope to penetrate—so vote for the man you trust. And such a man, to his eternal credit, is Dwight Eisenhower. A man one can trust to do the good, according to his lights.

And yet it must be said, what a miserable president he was! Said regretfully: for it is painful to use such language about so good a man. But if St. Francis of Assisi had been made president of the Chase Manhattan Bank, he too would have made a miserable president. Our enthusiasm for

Francis might cause us to say the Chase Manhattan Bank was not worthy of him, and the failure was really the institution's, not the saint's. Let us agree that the world is not worthy of Dwight Eisenhower. But the world is as it is, and Dwight Eisenhower served as one of its princes, and the world paid him no heed. None at all. And the world is worse off, by far, than when he came to power, sustained by the sentimental faith of millions of people, who thought that his goodness would irradiate out to the cynical reaches of our darkening globe, and renew in the hearts of the great malefactors the spirit of goodness.

As it happened, Eisenhower, when he was not the laughingstock of the troublemakers, was the explicit object of their contempt. Nikita Khrushchev, to whom he tendered a civility St. Francis might have shrunk from showing to a rabid dog, responded with violence and disdain. With surpassing skill, Khrushchev turned to the advantage of the Communist Revolution the lethargy, indecision, and ignorance of the goodhearted man Providence inflicted on the West. The Communists had the measure of Dwight Eisenhower, the man who could not—by his own admission—hold his own against Marshal Zhukov when they used to argue together, as military commanders in Berlin, the relative merits of Communism and freedom.

It was Dwight Eisenhower who concluded in Korea not merely an unwise treaty, but a strategically indefensible peace which has left us, as one of its legacies, the present bitterness of Laos. It was Eisenhower who stood impotently by and let Hungary go, the effective certification by the West of Communism's enduring right to its postwar conquests; he who stood by while Red China consolidated its hold over the wretched masses of Asia; he who instituted those pernicious circumlocutions that go by the name of "cultural" and "economic" exchange. He, indeed, who invited Khrushchev to come over here to test, at first hand, the moral idiocy of the leadership of the West.

At home, radiant with good will, he failed. Under Eisenhower the forces that gnaw at the strength of our country grew stronger—the bureaucratic parasites, the labor-union monopolists, the centralizers. He resisted some of the more radical impulses of the totalists, but his resistance was so theoretically anemic as to leave us disarmed. When the time came to defend ourselves against those who would push us further toward socialism, all we had to offer was the mechanical reincarnation of Mr. Eisenhower's Progressive Moderation, Richard Nixon. Oh Lord!

Let him have peace, even though he has brought neither peace nor hope to the millions of slaves around the world to whom he once spoke of liberation. Let him have peace, even though our own soldiers—we think of the RB-47 fliers who are captive in Soviet prisons—are abandoned. Even though there is less peace at home than there was eight years ago. (Under Eisenhower, James Hoffa and Earl Warren held sway.) Let him have peace in Gettysburg, and fade away in the illusion that the world responded to his goodness, that those cheering crowds in Karachi and Bonn, London and Manila, were the reciprocal of his loftiness. We pray he will never realize what a total, desperate failure he was, compared with what he might have been. We would not wish to visit so bitter a perception on any man, let alone a good man.

—*National Review*, January 14, 1961

The Decline of Mr. Kennedy?

A recent public-opinion poll discloses that Mr. Kennedy's popularity has slipped precipitously. If the finding is correct, it is the most exhilarating datum since Plato's proof that even an illiterate slave boy could be taught to understand a complicated theorem of Pythagoras. There is apparently hope for the human race after all. I intend no personal slight to our leader, for whom I wish a long and happy life. But I do feel it is high testimony to democratic perspicacity that the feeling should finally obtrude into the consciousness of the public that notwithstanding the gentleman's personal virtues and his devout enjoyment of the perquisites of high office, the simple fact is that he has no apparent qualifications for an office the successful discharge of which has everything to do with your and my hopes, dreams, and ambitions, for ourselves and our children.

A few weeks ago a British magazine published a devastating full-page cartoon of a monster machine bursting over with technological gargoyles—pipes, valves, spouts, indicators, bells, keyboards, switches—each of them named after some emblematic human sore—"The Negro Problem," "The Vietnam Problem," "The Berlin Wall," "Castro Cuba," "Gold Flow," etc.—and across the whole of the apparatus the license plate: "The Kennedy Machine." "It's wonderful," one awed spectator remarks to another on beholding it. "But what does it do?"

The word is indeed getting about: The fabulous Kennedy Machine, designed to cope with all the problems that beset mankind, is stalled. The delirious self-assurance, all that youthful energy, all those teeming Harvard brains have fueled it, and it has throbbed away now for three years, nearly; yet nothing, but nothing, important has been accomplished. And the reason why is this: Mr. Kennedy has no grip on reality, no communicable vision of the purposes of his administration. The grandiose rhetoric with which he reassures and galvanizes his constituents every time one of the meters on the machine registers a complaint is beginning to fall flat as the people discern the gruesome truth: that this efficient and likeable young man hasn't the least idea how to maneuver through the greatest crisis in world history.

The concrete indictment of Mr. Kennedy is painfully easy to make. It was he who funked the challenge of the Bay of Pigs, who stood by while the Wall was raised in Berlin, who concluded the unworkable arrangements in Laos, who is the prisoner of monopoly labor unions, who fails to staunch the flow of gold from our bleeding Republic, who sits by acquiescently while the central bureaucracy leeches more and more of the power and freedom of the individual. But I suspect it is not the concrete failures that have caused the diminution in his popularity. It is something else. There is something about the slickness of his total performance that is cloying. The months go by and the problems are not solved, and yet one has the feeling of radiant self-satisfaction within the White House. I believe that any man who would address the public and confess his temporary incapacity to deal with the nation's problems, citing great historical obstructions outside his power to cope with, would earn the patience of the people. But that is not Mr. Kennedy's mode. He is surrounded by vain sycophants who seek to transmute his dismaying record into one great, endless, triumphal parade. The word is rodomontade: a vain, blustering self-righteousness. Lean on it too hard, and you will collapse on the rigidities of reality—for so long, at least, as self-government works. If Mr. Kennedy were to give the impression that he is genuinely and even obsessively concerned with the great lesions on the commonweal, we might show him the patience due to a faltering but determined doctor. Instead, though the patient grows worse, the doctor gambols about the world proclaiming the soundness of his patient's health, and his own magical curative powers.

This is a tough world. Anyone who wanted a serene life, Trotsky reminded us, picked the wrong century to be born in. There are no instant solutions to any problem. But Mr. Kennedy's failure is to admit to the seriousness of these problems. The problem of a Communist state encysted in the womb of our hemisphere is, let us admit it, a problem: yet Mr. Kennedy has no solution for it whatsoever. The problem of the overhead of life in a technological society burdened down by monopoly unions and hedonistic state welfarism is a problem—but its existence never crosses the complacent lips of President Kennedy. Our president emerges as the ultimate man in the gray flannel suit: the great accommodator, the weathervane on perfect ball bearings—soul-free, immune from any of the frictions of reality.

The image of total composure is politically reassuring, but only for so long as the people continue in their drugged state. How would they respond to a totally different figure? A man in shirtsleeves with furrowed brow, whose heart beats in audible anxiety over the elements that are tossing the world about in remorseless fury? Let such a man arise and say: Give me the tiller and let me hurl back imprecations at the gale, howl for howl. Such a man, I think, we sorely need, and if he arises, and is recognized, democracy will be vindicated.

—July 13, 1963

The Case for Goldwater

The pollsters, as we all know by now, were wrong in California. They said that Rockefeller would win, and Rockefeller lost. As the Communist press might put it, Rockefeller came in second, while Goldwater was next to last. The pollsters have defended themselves by insisting that they were absolutely correct as of the moment they wrote, but that a last-minute upsurge for Goldwater, the scale of which they could not reasonably have been expected to foretell, gave him the surprise victory.

I accept as more plausible an alternative explanation that should equally assuage the pollsters' professional pride. It is this: that a great many Californians who had every intention of voting for Goldwater, and subsequently did so, informed the pollsters either that they intended to vote for Rockefeller, or that they didn't yet know how they would vote.

What happened, I have become convinced, is that a large number of voters were ashamed to confess, even in the semiprivacy of an interview with a visiting statistician, that they intended to vote for Goldwater. They were ashamed because the moralists of our community had made it plain that they considered that a vote for Goldwater was an evil act.

Many Americans, contrary to legend, are unaggressive in their politics. For every Goldwater man who is willing to proclaim his allegiance by pasting a Goldwater sticker on the bumper of his car, there are three who, when the question of politics is raised, sit still and smile, and say nothing, and go out the next day and vote for Goldwater.

Anyone who doubts the intensity of Establishment opinion on the subject should sample the hysterical prose of Walter Lippmann: "He [Goldwater] would repeal the progressive income tax, a measure so extreme that it would dismantle the national defense and destroy the credit of the United States." Or Murray Kempton's burst of frenzy: "The effect of his nomination will be to bring us all down to the foul rag-and-bone shop of the heart." Or, sit for a while and meditate the lead letter in a recent issue of the *New York Times*: "If the people choose Goldwater, then it would seem the nation was hardly worth saving after all."

Let Goldwater's enemies take their choice. Either (1) something is drastically wrong with the majority of Americans who participated in Republican primaries and gave Goldwater a larger popular vote than the Democrats gave John Kennedy four years earlier; or (2) something is drastically wrong with the judgment of Goldwater's critics. I timidly suggest that somebody is out of step.

Something is there, it seems to me, that seems to prevent the critics from seeing reality: An imperative of some sort is working to hobgoblinize Goldwater and all his works. They look at him, they hear him say that we must stand firm against the threat of the Soviet Union—and they then report breathlessly that they have just seen Dr. Strangelove in the flesh (*Manchester Guardian*). They hear him say that America must try to distinguish between those poor who are helpless, and those poor who are freeloaders—and they report having seen a man who Hates People (*The New Republic*). They hear him say that the Social Security program should provide for voluntary participation in it—and they accuse him of planning to stop payment on checks going out to old people (Rockefeller).

What is happening to the eyes and ears of American observers? Consider Joseph Alsop, who takes himself very seriously and expects that every dutiful American will do no less. Last March he informed his readership: "No serious Republican politician, even the most Neanderthal type, any longer takes Goldwater seriously." Nobody except the overwhelming majority of the delegates to the San Francisco Convention.

And even then Alsop wasn't quite done: "The real question is why he was taken seriously for so long. On this point, many big businessmen, and, one must add, many big newspapers and magazines, have much to answer for."

What does Alsop have to answer for? What does Rockefeller have to answer for? What does the foreign press have to answer for?

I mean, now that Goldwater has the Republican nomination sewn up, contrary to all their predictions? Will they feel the necessity now to put aside the nightmare world they live in, and admit that there is a case for Goldwater that appeals not merely to the ideologically besotted, to the kooks and cranks, to the warmongers and neurotics and racists; but to levelheaded housewives, cautious businessmen, proud Negroes, bright intellectuals, learned lawyers, peaceloving priests?

The case for Goldwater, under the great weight of existing distortions, needs primarily to be stated in negative terms. There is an ironic congruity here—because the prescriptions for a good life are themselves stated mostly in negative terms (Thou shalt not murder, covet thy neighbor's wife, etc.), as also for civil freedom (Congress shall make no law abridging the freedoms of religion, speech, assembly, etc.).

The Points for Goldwater

1. Goldwater does not intend to provoke a nuclear war, having, among other reasons, nothing much to gain from one, other than premature retirement. His strategy has been consistently based on the assumption that it is weakness, not strength; indecisiveness, not determination, that bring on wars and threats of war. We fought in Korea—because we had been weak, and indecisive, in making Far Eastern policy. We almost had to fight a war over Cuba—because we had been weak and fumbling in asserting our interests there. We are fighting a war in South Vietnam—because we refused, ten years ago and subsequently, to be firm and consistent.

2. Goldwater does not desire to impoverish this country, nor would the domestic reforms he proposes have any such effect; rather they would have the opposite effect, of liberating a latent energy the country has not recently shown, of "getting the country moving again," to quote another politician who was dissatisfied with America's gait. Goldwater's approach, unlike Kennedy's, is based on faith in the creativity of the American people, rather than on fiscal sleights of hand. He views the nation as bound down increasingly by the sclerotic effects of inordinate taxation, labor-union monopolies, government, and regulatory bureaucracies.

3. Goldwater does *not* intend to diminish the rights of any minority groups—but neither does he desire to diminish the rights of majority groups. It is not a right of a Negro child to be bused from one section of the city, where there are schools in operation, into another; nor is it a civic duty of a white child to consent to be bused from one to another section of the city, for anyone's sake. It does not advance John's rights to diminish James's. The concept of helping the Negro to achieve his freedom by diminishing the white man's freedom to exercise his, Goldwater rejects; and in so doing, I believe, stands out as the overarching custodian of American freedoms. Little will have been gained if, on the day when the American Negro finally considers himself emancipated, he looks about him and observes that he has graduated into a totalitarian society, which, in its anxiety to forward the cause of the Negro, reached down and met him halfway in servitude.

4. Goldwater does not intend to eliminate the Supreme Court (as if he could!), but he is clearly out of sympathy with the legal philosophy of its narrow majority, which seems to view the Constitution of the United States as an instrument for the imposition of a sort of radical, secular, rootless egalitarianism. The Warren Court's animus against (a) religion (*Engle* v. *Vitale*), (b) traditional republican practices (*Baker* v. *Carr*), and (c) anti-Communist legislation (*Watkins, Jenkins*) threatens (1) the spiritual mainsprings of the country, (2) traditional ways of diffusing political power within a state, and (3) the legislative supremacy of the Congress and the ability of the Justice Department and the courts to act against our domestic enemies. Goldwater is a symbol of opposition to the "aggressive tendencies of the Warren Court" (the words are Professor Edward Corwin's), an obstacle to the ambitions of the Warren Court to become a "third legislative chamber" (the words are Justice Learned Hand's).

5. I think, too, that much of the senator's popularity derives, paradoxically, from his apparently suicidal political behavior. In 1960 the learned Richard Rovere devoted himself at some length in his column for *The New Yorker* to explaining patiently just why it was politically impossible for Goldwater to get anywhere. Don't you understand, said the understanding author, that Goldwater *systematically* alienates, one after another, the great blocs of voters in this country? Don't you understand that when he talks about unions, he alienates organized labor? That when he talks about Social Security, he loses the old folks? That when he talks about foreign policy he alienates the pacifists and the intellectuals? That when he talks about civil rights, he alienates minority groups? That when he talks about

agricultural subsidies, he alienates the farmers? Who is left? asked Rovere rhetorically.

The GOP's Great Majority

Who is left, apparently, is the great majority of the Republican Party—who include labor-union members, old people, peace-lovers, professors, Jews, Negroes, Poles, Irishmen, farmers, and who actually hope in a few months to surface as a majority of the American people. They are drawn to a man who would not hesitate to say to Walter Reuther that he is helping to wreck the economy; to Castro that he must dismantle his aggressive machinery; to Mao that our Air Force says he is not going to take over Taiwan; to Nasser that our aid will stop unless he calls off his agents who are seeking to destroy the peace of the Middle East; to Martin Luther King that he is going too far.

A man who would stop fawning upon the neo-states in Africa that visit impudencies upon us; who would not hesitate to inform the United Nations that it often behaves with scandalous irresponsibility; who, in his relations with the people of the free world, might just succeed in convincing them, once the static of the foreign press was penetrated, that they are dealing with an honest and reliable anti-Communist who would not, during his tenure, let more walls be erected across the faith and honor of our commitments; who would conclude no Yaltas, find no fancy excuses for permitting a Communist revolutionary to occupy additional areas within the Western hemisphere. And, finally, a president who, in speaking to the people of the United States, could say, "Ask not what your country can do for you—ask what you can do for your country," and mean it.

—*Newsday*, July 11, 1964

Bobby for King

Bobby, Bobby, everywhere. It drives a man to drink. Open the paper, and there he is. A marvel of industry, a brooding omnipresence, the determining factor (it is said) in the nomination of Mayor High in Florida for the governorship, deeply involved in Oregon, and in Kentucky, and in a dozen other states, stitching together a heliocentric alliance of disciples. No one, so far, dares say him nay, not even the government of South Africa, which is, if not exactly about to welcome him there, at least about to tolerate his coming there to propose a civil-rights bill, or whatever it is he plans to do, to the cheers, predictably, of the whole world.

In New York State, Senator Kennedy recently served notice on great big grown men who aspire for the Democratic nomination for governor that unless they would accompany him in a sort of political fashion show about the state, he would decline to endorse the winner. Faced with this insurmountable threat, they dutifully appeared for classes at the appointed hour and time, and the seminar began at Cornell University. Franklin Delano Roosevelt Jr. was among them, and the redoubtable Frank O'Connor, president of the City Council of New York City, who rode into office with several hundred thousand votes more than John Lindsay himself received last fall, but whose prowess isn't such as to embolden him to advise Bobby that he will seek the Democratic nomination in his own way and that he is much too busy to do bumps and grinds around the state under the choreographical direction of Robert F. Kennedy.

Most recently Senator Kennedy resolved to challenge the nomination of a judge designated by the regular Democrats in Manhattan for the important office of surrogate. The Republicans, rather surprisingly, decided to endorse the same man. But Senator Kennedy, no doubt influenced by howls from local editorial writers deploring the alleged incapacity of the Democratic-Republican designee, announced his backing of another judge, who will run on a Reform Democratic ticket. (Bobby doesn't go for hack judges, unless nominated by Teddy for the District Court.) Meanwhile, the Liberal Party in New York is committed to a third candidate, and the Conservative Party to a fourth. So that, not inconceivably, it will be Bobby's candidate against the field. If he wins this one, he will emerge as invincible as Caesar returning victorious from Gaul.

Herewith a constructive suggestion. Why not a constitutional amendment—or, just as good, an edict from Earl Warren—instituting a monarchy and designating Bobby as the first incumbent?

The rules should declare that all successors must be lineal descendants of Joseph P. Kennedy. But—mark this—the rules should not stipulate that the successor must be the first-born son of the king. Anyone directly descended from the founding father would qualify. The advantages are that this would give scope to the competitive political instincts of the Kennedys.

Upon the death or retirement of the incumbent, all qualified Kennedys, male and female, would put forward their claims; perhaps they all could appear at seminars around the country, at which they would stress their qualifications for the throne. A great national election could be held to decide which Kennedy would succeed. The new king or queen would then take office for his or her lifetime and preside over the country as chief of state, while the practical affairs of the government could be administered by an elected president or prime minister.

John Adams remarked that the Constitution was badly mistaken in forbidding American citizens to receive titles of nobility, since such titles are a relatively innocent way of sating human ambitions, the dread substitute for nobility being power over other men. Think of the trouble we would be saved! It would be beneath the royal dignity to specify what should be the procedures by which mere governors of New York should advertise their qualifications, let alone who should be the next surrogate judge of Manhattan. And the adulation all good subjects owe to their sovereign would come more easily than that which goes to a mere politician, whose earthly concerns tend to stain the purity of his radiant presence.

—June 2, 1966

What George Wallace Means to Me

When, early this year, *Human Events* released its poll on George Wallace, conservative-watchers were astonished. The poll had been shrewdly conceived, and reported not on the views of the general reader but on those of more than a hundred "conservative writers, politicians, and organization heads—most of the leading names in American conservatism." "*Do you believe Mr. Wallace to be a fiscal conservative?*" No, 51 percent. (Yes, 30 percent.) "*Will Mr. Wallace's candidacy help or hurt the election of conservatives running for the House and Senate?*" Hurt, 69 percent. (Help, 14 percent.) "*Will the effect of Mr. Wallace's candidacy be to strengthen or to hurt the conservative movement in America?*" Hurt, 74 percent. (Strengthen, 16 percent.) "*How would you vote in the 1968 general election, given the following possibilities?*" Nixon, 79 percent; Johnson, 5 percent; Wallace, 8 percent. (Reagan, 78 percent; Johnson, 9 percent; Wallace, 3 percent.) (Rockefeller, 43 percent; Johnson, 12 percent; Wallace, 23 percent.) "*Do you believe Mr.*

Wallace is knowingly conducting a campaign that is calculated to appeal to racial prejudices?" Yes, 68 percent. (No, 25 percent.)

The figures greatly surprised those who believed (many still do) that Wallace is the answer to conservative prayers; who wondered therefore at the apparent ingratitude of conservative leaders. Or was it that their opposition is purely tactical? Is it merely because conservatives, though they do not really object to George Wallace, far from it, do object (the thinking members among them) to the *effect* his candidacy is likely to have on the candidacy of Richard Nixon, who is the closest thing to a conservative running for president who also has a chance to make it?

Researchers so inclined can carefully study Wallace's personal and political background for replies to the question: Do we have here a sure-enough conservative? The findings are at least confusing. Twenty years ago, George Wallace refused to join Strom Thurmond's famous defection from the Democratic Convention in protest against Hubert Humphrey's civil-rights plank. During that period, and for a while after that, Wallace was an avowed "Folsomite," i.e., a backer of the enormous pretensions of Kissing Jim Folsom, the Alabama governor who thought himself presidential material, served as a *Henry* Wallace delegate at the 1944 Democratic Convention, and had taken the governorship of Alabama—in the words of the London *Economist*—"on the most liberal platform ever offered in Alabama." Wallace later broke with Folsom, for reasons irrelevant to this narrative; but he was still down as a strong believer in federal welfare programs, he backed John Kennedy in 1956 and 1960, and, as governor, he tripled Alabama's bonded indebtedness. Then, of course, came the famous encounter of 1963, where it all officially began.

Now, other public officials publicly resented the use of force as an instrument of integration before Wallace and after him; and yet, we are concerned nowadays with Wallace. What happened after the federal marshals forced Governor Wallace to step aside from the door he was blocking in order to make way for a Negro boy and a Negro girl, who were thereupon registered as students at the University of Alabama, was that history and George Wallace embarked upon an elaborate courtship, to which each contributed about equally, so that now they have quite a thing going.

For his part, Wallace began diligently to cultivate a race-free rhetoric. "I have never said anything unkind about a Negro anywhere," Wallace has said, like Mark Antony addressing the Romans on his devotion to Brutus. He then went on to perfect analytical and rhetorical techniques that (a) stimulate discontents where discontents are latent, (b) aggravate them where they are already overt, and (c) galvanize his listeners into a hot desire to hurl their bodies (never ever their minds) in the path of the federal juggernaut.

For its part, history gave us Lyndon Johnson and his enormous appetite for dominating the affairs of America at every level. And gave us, too, the paralysis of action that grew out of Johnson's failure to reckon on the relative weakness of his own resources (the conservatives would put it that way) or on the relative strength of other people's inertia (as the liberals would prefer). Thus, the war in Vietnam stalled, as did, at home, the war against poverty and the urban ghetto.

Now listen to George Wallace: "*I respect the right of dissent all right*"— note that the formality, what one might call the liberal amenities, has been complied with (I don't have anything against niggers)—"*but anybody who undertakes to give aid to the Vietcong is engaged in treason*"—not that treason is (as indeed it ought to be) a devil-word; and note how useful it is rhetorically, handled thus gravely. "*That's the way I see it*"—a touch of modesty; but shrewdly programmed, to suggest the, er, triumph of innocence in a sick-slick world. "*I'd order the Justice Department to proceed against*"—now watch how the tone changes, so as to introduce true American Resolution—"*these bastards, indict 'em, try 'em. And if any judges tried to say it isn't* legally *treason because we aren't formally at war, I'd get some new judges.*"

There it is. American conservatives are the most distressed of all, not so much because they despise what Wallace says as because they despise what they know to be his venture in political profiteering on grave mutual concerns: just as the responsible Left, in the Thirties, wept tears over the exploitation of their genuine concerns by such as Huey Long. What's more, even the veneer breaks down at the organizational level. Wallace admits, among his official electors, such as Gerald L. K. Smith, the consecrated anti-Semite, and Leander Perez, the devoted anti-Negro. Nobody knows exactly how he will distribute his hurt. During the primaries in 1964 Wallace made his big points among Democrats. But then he was running only among Democrats in the primaries. In November, he will hurt the Republicans most in the South, where they will lose electoral votes to him; but in the North, the Humphrey Democrats will lose, who might otherwise have counted on votes that now will go to a man whose mode reflects frustrations readily intellectualizable by other Americans, who know that something is wrong, and arrive, by careful and morally responsible reasoning, at conclusions similar to Wallace's.

His mode is crude, but hardly unique. He said once about a federal judge who was his classmate at college, but now found himself an adversary in one of those legal brawls Wallace is always caught up in, that the judge was "an integrating, carpetbagging, scalawagging, race-mixing, bald-faced liar." That is the kind of assault, if you change the political coordinates and clean it up a little, that some thoroughbred liberals—e.g., Emanuel Celler and Martin Luther King Jr. and George Meany—were making on Goldwater in 1964, when they saw him as somehow in the tradition of Adolf Hitler.

What are we left with? The coarsening of distinctions, certainly. Polarization, just as certainly. But also the disintegrating penetration of Big Daddy Government. Those conservatives who take sly pleasure from Wallace's techniques should reflect that that kind of thing is doable against anybody at all; doable for instance by the Folsomite Wallace of yesteryear, who roared his approval of his candidate's attack on the "Wall Street Gotrocks," "the damned decency crowd," and "them Hoover Republicans." Those who see in Wallace the end of the world should reflect on the great political movements of the past twenty years. Strom Thurmond, in 1948, led the movement against civil rights. Today, firmly incorporated into a Republican Party that is pledged to defend civil rights, he leads, in effect, the fight against Wallace, who has taken Thurmond' s old position in the South.

That, and reflect also on this: The Wallace candidacy for North, South, East, and West is, among other things, a great national reaction against the ravenous appetites of an overweening Federal Government seeking to craft for us a great society, never mind the disposition of those who are to benefit from it. Not inconceivably, we will be better off for the irruption. Wallace is to one position what Eugene McCarthy is to another. The country rejected (quite wisely) Eugene McCarthy, but the Democrats learned from him. The country will reject (quite wisely) George Wallace, but Democrats and Republicans alike stand to learn from the experience.

—*Look*, October 29, 1968

Why We Need a Black President in 1980

When they used to ask Bobby Kennedy about the FBI calling one morning in the pre-dawn hours at the homes of the steel executives his brother the president was harassing, he would say, "I know you won't believe it, but it happens to be true: I simply did not know the calls were being made. I was attorney general, but I wasn't consulted." I ran for mayor of New York City a few years ago, and the headline in the *New York Herald Tribune* the day after I introduced my running mates was "BUCKLEY HAS A 'BALANCED TICKET': /MARKEY, MRS. GUNNING—ALL IRISH." The professionals rocked with mirth when I subsequently announced that I hadn't known that Mrs. Gunning was Irish and hadn't known even that she was Catholic. I was stung by the criticism of my naïveté and tried to turn it to my advantage later in the campaign by observing that those who sought a religiously balanced ticket or an ethnically balanced ticket were, after all, the ethnically self-conscious and hence the opportunists of discord and of totemic political practices. And I was right—am right—but I am talking out-of-this-world, where, ideally, politics has nothing to do. In this world it is different—especially different, in my judgment, where the Negro is concerned, for reasons which, insofar as they are obvious, are, for that reason, painful to relate, yet relevant to the objective at hand, which is the election of a Negro (no, not any Negro) as president of the United States in 1980 (or thereabouts).

High political office in America (and in most other places) tends, after all, to carry social distinction, and it is for this reason that some Americans, who might have been otherwise inclined if purely political considerations had been consulted, voted for John Kennedy in 1960. Not merely Catholics, who desired to see the decertification of the legend that no Catholic could be elected president; but others who also wished to see broken a religious barrier which they believed generically unhealthy and (in some cases) practically inconvenient: for instance, the Jews, some of whom believed that the election of JFK would more easily remove, by collateral action, impediments to the election of a Jewish president than would a direct assault by a Jewish candidate against Fort Bigotry. It seems to me that this was in fact the case, that the election of Kennedy had this reassuring general effect. And, of course, what happens, when people are reassured, is that they tend to become less ambitious in that particular direction. Thus when Abraham Beame, running for mayor of New York in 1965, was urged on the voters by his friends as potentially the first Jewish mayor of New York, the old ethnocentric juices somehow didn't stir, and the defections among Jewish voters caused the election of a WASP. A grand gesture: The Jewish community had, in effect, transcended race and religion, at least as determinative in a mayoralty election. One senses that the accomplishments of the Jew in America are so pronounced that he disdains now the presidency, not because the presidency is small potatoes, but because the achievement of it is unlikely to add anything to the sense the American Jew now has of being In. Such a certification—election to the presidency—would nowadays strike most American Jews as a redundant affirmation of their importance, of their qualification to serve. In 1957, breaking all tradition—most markedly Bolshevik tradition—Khrushchev, as head of state, wrote a casual letter to the *New Statesman*. Banner headlines. A few weeks later the unpredictable Khrushchev wrote yet another letter to the *New Statesman*, which of course published it; under the lackadaisical banner, this time, "KHRUSHCHEV WRITES AGAIN."

It isn't so with the American Negro. He has not won a dozen Nobel Prizes or crowded Groton graduates out of Harvard or coached us in the mysteries of atom splitting. The debate will continue on the question of whether his gifts are genetically other than those of the Caucasian or only apparently other for reasons of training or environment. I do not myself believe that the final scientific adjudication of that debate will prove to be particularly important, except perhaps in a narrow pedagogical sense. George Washington was less "intelligent" than Albert Einstein, an obvious way of making a point which is nonetheless subtle. But the American Negro needs the kind of reassurance that Einstein did not need. It is the reassurance that he can move into the reaches of reservations from which he has grown up thinking that Americans whose skins are black are permanently excluded.

There are reasons for urging that final achievement (the black president) which are more important than merely buying the reassurance of American Negroes. These reasons are a form not exactly of white expiation, though I would not dismiss this as a factor in any corporate effort to elect a black president. They are a form of white self-assurance. The outstanding charge against America is hypocrisy. It is greatly exaggerated, beyond even the exaggeration that always marks the distance between national practice and national ideal. But where the Negroes are concerned, the practice of inequality directly belies the vision of equality of opportunity, so that the election of Negro public officials (yes, *because* they are Negro) is a considerable tonic for the white soul.

It helps, though it is not enough, to "encourage" the careers of a Sugar Ray Robinson, a Duke Ellington, a Martin Luther King. But such as they will not need, in the 1970s, any particular help, inasmuch as their talents pull them up as inexorably as an escalator. The area in which the Negro needs helps is increasingly the area in which raw talent is not mechanically measured. It is not necessary to experience the goodwill of a predominantly white community in order to confirm that Joe Louis is a better boxer than Max Schmeling. But it is only the white community that can, e.g., express itself—as an act of faith—that it is preferable to elect Carl Stokes as mayor of Cleveland than Seth Taft.

I have had some experience with the black militants, and they are as attractive as I would imagine the Red Guards from the People's Republic of China to be, as attractive as the Aryans who cheered along the drive of Adolf Hitler for racial purity. These militants receive much attention, as indeed they should: They bamboozle a lot of Americans, most typically those Americans who are happiest believing the worst about America. But they remain a very small minority of their people, for reasons that reconfirm the health and sanity of the large body of Negroes, for whom they presume to speak. The issue of the next decade will be over the question: Who will attract the attention of the majority of the American Negroes? Will it be the Rap Browns—the misanthropic bitter-enders, whose satisfaction issues out of the politics of implacability; who cherish and fondle the statistics of white intransigence even as Herbert Marcuse is happy only in finding confirmation of the organic corruption which is the center of his social theology (Marcuse, the perfect Calvinist!)—or the civilized Negroes? A great unpublicized phenomenon is the arrival in America of a class of young Negro leaders who work in the ghettos, in economic cooperatives, in straightforward social work, who are arguing that progress is possible within the System. They are harassed by the demagogy of the racists who say that America cannot make way for the Negroes. But they nevertheless survive—and they proliferate. You can find them (some of them will make it a point to be just a little bit rude, just for the record) in Cleveland, struggling to do something for Hough; in Detroit, learning the politics of adjustment, throwing their weight around in economic and political maneuvers; in San Francisco, deeply involved in trying to spread an understanding of the role of education as the instrument of liberation; in Los Angeles, calmly (if not openly) countering the witch doctors and practicing a tough-minded idealism (the top people in Watts are brilliant, ingenious, tough, graceful, irresistible).

It is from the ranks of these young men, now thirty, thirty-five, forty years old, that I can imagine someone rising, in the next decade, to national prominence as a presidential candidate. When it happens, I think that it is quite possible that he will be greeted gladly by those who, having satisfied themselves that the point they are about to make will not be at the expense of the survival of the Republic, will join in a quite general enthusiasm over his election as president of the United States; who will celebrate his achievement of the highest office in the world as a personal celebration, as a celebration of the ideals of a country which by this act alone would reassert its idealism—shrugging off, as is America's way, by practical accomplishment the chains of cynicism and despair which the detractors and the cynics wear so gladly, singing their songs of hopelessness. How shall we sing the Lord's song in a strange land? the prophet asked. Whittaker Chambers wrote twenty years ago of the Negro people that they have been the most man-despised and God-obsessed people in the history of the world, that on coming to this strange land they had struck their tuning fork, and the sorrow songs, the spirituals, were born. But the sorrow songs are of another age, describing another spiritual plight. "Jes' call me Prez-i-dent Jones," they sing now in the Bahamas, where they have elected their own "Prez-i-dent." It will be even better when "President" Jones is elected by others, who, seeking to alleviate the sorrow of the few, alleviate the burden of the many.

—*Look,* January 13, 1970

McGovern and the National Mood

They are saying (Scotty Reston is saying; ergo, They are saying) that George McGovern might actually become the president of the United States. The reasoning is simple-complex. To begin with, nothing is happening the way it ought to have happened. Three months ago it was not thought by any professional that Ed Muskie could be stopped. Ed Muskie! As well nominate Harold Stassen, at this point. And what did he do to earn such sudden, permanent obloquy? Nothing at all, just act normal. Moral of the season: Act abnormal.

That is what George McGovern has for the most part been doing. Going left left left, presumably alienating the people in the middle, who are supposed to be indispensable to a true victory. Upsetting the labor-union leaders, defying the bosses, ignoring the great social issue of busing, saying things like, "I still think Henry Wallace was right," a statement of such breathtaking perversity as to render George Romney's famous self-disqualifier about having been brainwashed positively unnoticeable by contrast.

But it doesn't stop McGovern. Nothing stops McGovern. I doubt if McGovern would lose a primary if he said that on second thought he wishes the Arabs would take over Israel. Or has he said it already, and nobody noticed?

So—they are saying—who knows? Are the American people just being perverse, backing a nice man to whom it would be thought risky to entrust a college seminar? What then if you add the balls Richard Nixon is juggling, one of which he might drop? Suppose that in October the North Vietnamese topple the Thieu government, by military or political pressure? Or that unemployment and inflation begin to gnaw deeply? Or that the dollar is sold down humiliatingly? There are other possibilities, of the sort that would undo Mr. Nixon, and crystallize the national mood, which seems to be saying: Better not to bear the ills we have, than to shrink from others we know not of.

I do not doubt that Vietnam is hugely responsible for the general frustration. Subtract from consideration of it, for the moment, the cost in human life: the human agony. Think of it only, if you can, as a national enterprise. It is as if we had launched an Apollo missile to the moon every month for the last seven years, and every one of them had failed, though they cost a billion dollars each and the scientists kept telling us that the next one would surely work, and the president proclaimed that confidence in American technology absolutely required that we proceed.

The reversal of our supersonic-transport program is not unrelated to the national mood—that lack of self-confidence which is the principal psychological hangover from the Vietnam War, and I for one wish that we had never entered Indochina, rather than conduct ourselves as we have conducted ourselves there. There are those who believe that disillusion with the Cold War was inevitable, that it would have come to us via some other instruction, some other defeat. Perhaps.

Meanwhile, it has become thinkable that someone will be elected president who quite clearly desires second-class international status for the United States. There is no reason growing purely out of pride why we could not be happy as a second-class nation. The pride of a Swiss is at least the equal of the pride of an American.

But for America to become a second-class power would mean that the world would belong to the Soviet Union, and, in our day, a world that is dominated by the Soviet Union would be a world intolerably bitter to first-class spirits. First-class spirits such as America has pre-eminently nurtured, with our concern for freedom, for the individual, for the underdog, for national sovereignty. There are those ready to give all of that up provided the government will send them a check every week and pay the medical bills and take away H. L. Hunt's money.

Indeed anything can happen, and a lot of it certainly will if the McGovern phenomenon goes on. And though by orthodox analysis the Republicans are entitled to cheer every McGovern primary victory as edging the incumbent further and further along the road to a landslide victory, they'd better watch it. The Gadarene swine, as Mr. Muggeridge observes, are frisky.

—May 24, 1972

Nixon and Resignation

I propose, on completion of these words, to march them over to a printer, shrink them to penny-postcard size, and, wordlessly, hand them out to elevator men, Hollywood stars, and corporation presidents who ask me, as everyone is asked these days, the one question: "Mr. Buckley, do you think Nixon will resign?"

If there were time, I would answer roughly as follows:

There are several Nixons.

The first Nixon is the one that comes most readily to mind. About him the cliché is: He will never quit. It is uncharacteristic of him. He is a determined, stubborn man who fought most of his adult life to be president of the United States. He likes being president. He likes the power of the presidency, the usufructs of the presidency, and the romance of the presidency. You won't drive that man out of the White House until the limousine pulls up to the door on Inauguration Day, 1977.

That is Nixon One. Nixon Two is the political realist. He is the man who can coolly survey the political situation and draw the necessary conclusions, when there are necessary conclusions. It was that Nixon who, having expended himself at the Republican Governors' Conference in Denver in 1964 trying to organize a Stop Goldwater movement, recognized it wouldn't work. Then, unlike the hapless William Scranton, who went on to try to stop Goldwater and ended by looking like Harold Stassen, Nixon Two drew back, recognized Goldwater wasn't going to make it, and— supported Goldwater lustily. That single decision brought him the Republican nomination in 1968. Otherwise it would have gone to—Reagan; yes, Reagan. And Nixon knew that. This Nixon, the political realist, is capable of judging whether there is going to be impeachment plus conviction, and of either (a) acting to try to abort the case against him by hard political maneuvering; or (b) accepting the inevitable and resigning. He has not at this moment concluded that the political reality is that he will be deposed.

Then there is Nixon Three. Nixon Three is a withdrawn, moody, introspective man who revels in a pain that is often self-inflicted. It is a Nixon who works even harder than necessary to get the good grade, or to qualify for the football team, or memorize the name of the ward leader. It is the Nixon who will make himself stay up all night before deciding on a vice-presidential running mate, not so much because he is thereby better equipped to pick the right man, but because he likes to be able to say, "I stayed up all night worrying about this one."

It is the Nixon who blurts out in the prepared speech that he will continue to work "sixteen to twenty hours a day, seven days a week," for his country. The Nixon who feels that all the proper people in the East resent him because he did not go to an Ivy League college and that therefore he will hew to the Rotarian company with which he feels comfortable.

This Nixon feels that he is fated to suffer, must suffer; that suffering is good and that strength comes through adversity. This is the Nixon whose mind begins now to turn to the ultimate suffering: resignation. If, for the man on the make, power is an aphrodisiac, for the man facing the end, martyrdom is orgasmic. There is no other explanation for the smile on the face of St. Sebastian as the archers bent their bows.

And then, if you can stand it, there is Nixon Four. This is Nixon the human being. This week's New York Times Magazine has a million-page rehearsal of the entire Watergate business. One's eyes fasten on a single sentence. "He [Nixon] even deducted $1.24 in finance charges from Garfinckel's Department Store." Nixon Four could prevail over Nixon One for reasons entirely human. Shylock spoke for the Jewish race: He might as well have spoken for Nixon when he said, "Hath not a Jew eyes? Hath not a Jew hands, organs, dimensions, senses, affections, passions? Fed with the same food, hurt with the same weapons, subject to the same diseases, healed by the same means, warmed and cooled by the same winter and summer, as a Christian is? If you prick us, do we not bleed? If you tickle us, do we not laugh? If you poison us, do we not die?"

And—the final line—"And if you wrong us, shall we not revenge?"

Nixon Four is visible walking the sands of San Clemente and riding economy class in the little jet and answering questions about did he deduct $1.24 for finance charges from Garfinckel's. When Nixon Four and

Nixon Three, espying a joint opportunity, fuse their vision, then Nixon will resign, not only with honor, but with pleasure.

—January 14, 1974

The End of the GOP?

At lunch the other day I was startled to hear a specialist in Republican Party affairs give it as his judgment that not inconceivably the Republican Party would die in about three years. "Here's what would do it," he explained to his two guests. "First, a tremendous defeat in the congressional elections this fall. Next, in 1976, a catastrophic defeat at every level—presidential, congressional, and local." After that, he said, in the ruins of 1977, the commanding position of the organized party would be lost, and ambitious conservatives would look for another label. It would be not unlike the end of the Whig Party in the mid-1850s.

As an obliging Providence so often arranges things, not an hour after hearing this analysis my eyes ran over the latest issue of the official Republican Fight Sheet, called *First Monday*. The central message was from Congressman John Rhodes, the minority leader of the U.S. House of Representatives. Mr. Rhodes is on Cloud Nine. He grants, looking ahead to the elections of this fall, that there are things out there to worry about, mostly on account of Watergate. But, he tells us, there isn't all that much to be worried about, for two reasons. The first is that the GOP was in no way responsible for Watergate. So the public won't blame the Republicans in general.

And then, "Secondly, I am of the opinion that our Watergate-inspired difficulties will actually make us stronger as a party in the long run. That is because Watergate has caused many of us to re-examine our party's great principles."

I shall try it. I shall walk the streets, and accost the first pensive face I see. "Sir, excuse me, but could it be that Watergate is causing you to re-examine your party's great principles?"

Poor Mr. Rhodes, playing Knute Rockne to the Republican Party. The trouble is that, in the forward inertia of his pep talk, he *has* to go on. Who says A must say B. Who says that we are fondling our party's great principles has to say what they are. Here is how he copes with the problem:

"We recall that it was the GOP that helped provide America with a sense of racial justice through the wisdom of Abraham Lincoln. We recall that the GOP helped to provide America with a sense of global purpose at the turn of the century through the vision and energy of Theodore Roosevelt. We recall that the GOP helped provide America with a sense of balance and security through the leadership of Dwight Eisenhower. From Taft, to Dirksen, to Goldwater, the Republican Party has supplied the nation with sensible and effective direction at key points in our history."

Somehow, one cannot quite conceive these words coming from the mouth of King Henry V and stirring the troops to prodigies at Agincourt. They are unlikely to stir the voters at the polling places.

The fact of the matter is that in recent years—and this goes back to General Eisenhower—the Republican Party, insofar as it is a party that causes the political blood to heat up with excitement, and voters to swear fidelity to it by their grandmother's grave, is the party that is there to defeat a George McGovern from time to time.

In between, it behaves as if it should apologize to the voters for having done so. Free health, huge deficits, inflation, kissing conferences with the Communists, military weakness, subsidies for string quartets, revenue sharing in place of tax reduction . . .

If my friend's predictions come to pass, they will blame it on Watergate. But Watergate was a transfusion of sick blood into anemic blood, and if we go down, the pathologists will tell us, in the course of time, that it was the latter condition that did it, not that silly little infection which a healthy body could have thrown off laughingly in weeks.

—January 26, 1974

Ford and the Impossible

There is a lot of talk, some of it loose, about President Ford and the conservatives, and how he has lost them, once and for all, by his economic program. Concerning which, a few observations:

1. To say that one knows how a bad situation might have been prevented, or even to say that one knows how a bad situation might be set right, is not to say that an American chief executive can, or even should, attempt the logical plan. An example would be the stalemate in South Vietnam back in 1965–66. There were competent generals then saying: You can't win this war in this way. The alternative was the devastation of Hanoi, cutting off the Ho Chi Minh trail in Laos, and blockading Haiphong. As the months went on and we didn't do this, it became progressively harder to do; and, finally, psychologically and even militarily unthinkable.

It was so with the Berlin Wall. It might have been struck down as illegal on the day after it was erected in 1961. What wouldn't have worked is for President Kennedy to announce that each day the United States Marines would dislodge one brick, leaving Berlin without a trace of the Wall on the 25th anniversary of its erection. It is so with the economic mess brought on by four Democratic Congresses, one Democratic president, one Republican president, and a generation of liberal economists.

2. But it does pay, however unthinkable it may be to make the appropriate recommendations, to remind ourselves of what would in *fact* work. The atomization of Hanoi would in *fact* have worked to end North Vietnamese obduracy. It isn't something we would have done or should, at that point, have done. But the term "unthinkable" here is best used as a metaphor. We should precisely force ourselves to *think* what exactly it is that would cure a situation, however disposed we are to reject that cure. It would cure the evils we now suffer from if we inflicted upon ourselves a commensurate austerity. I say commensurate, because there is some relation—these are figures entered as much in the ledger books of the saints as in those of the statisticians—between overindulgence, and the requisite underindulgence. If, for eight years, a nation's people have voted themselves a couple of hundred billion dollars of services which they didn't pay for, then—using rough figures—they owe themselves a couple of hundred billion dollars of austerity.

3. How is austerity here defined? Let us be entirely direct about it, not at the expense of oversimplification, but in quest of oversimplification. If the budget were slashed by, say, fifty billion per year, four years from now we'd be back in the registrar's good books. But what would be the means of doing this, and the tactical effect?

4. The federal government would have to withdraw substantially from its role as subsidizer of social services. This it should do in any case, in respect of the thirty-one states of the Union whose own resources are

above the national average. Pull out of education, health, construction; let such subsidizing as needs to be done be done in behalf of the nineteen poorer states.

5. Now, this will cause widespread unemployment without offsetting compensation. Benefits would need to be raised locally, by the individual states, and the cost of them would be palpable, because local taxes always are. The result would be a great crack in the wage-price structure. People would be willing to go back to work for a dollar and a half an hour, but lo! they would discover very quickly that they were earning a living wage.

∼

That all this should sound like a parable is a measure of how far we have slouched toward the superstition that the universal enjoyment of plenty is primarily a problem in political-economic manipulation. For Gerald Ford to come forward and recommend what actually should be done would be as shocking as if a voice from the heavens were suddenly to startle the world by reciting the Ten Commandments, and promising hellfire for those who failed to heed them, or failed to repent that failure. A generation of mankind would be swept away.

And that, children, is why Gerald Ford cannot be expected to commit orthodoxy. He would be committing suicide.

—January 20, 1975

The Polish Joke

You can hardly blame Carter for opportunizing on President Ford's startling liberation of Poland during their debate on foreign policy, but the roles of the Democratic and the Republican candidates have become almost impossibly confused by the gaffe. After all, it is the Republicans who have traditionally done the most (however insufficient) to keep alive the hope of the liberation of Eastern Europe. The Democrats tend to be associated with a foreign policy of permanent acquiescence in the coloni-

zation by the Communists of any part of the world with the single exception of Israel.

A political party that, through Senator Frank Church and his committee
set up to investigate the CIA, threatened congressional mutiny when the
executive tried to help Portugal and Italy stave off the Communists is not
going to lie down for anything in Eastern Europe that tends to threaten
their policy of appeasement at any cost. But as a purely political matter,
Ford is now on the defensive.

What Mr. Ford said is, frankly, inexplicable—notwithstanding the explanations he and his aides have attempted. It is as if Ford had said, during
a general discussion of the great rivers of the world and the problems of
flood control: "Fortunately, the Mississippi River doesn't flow through the
United States."

Everybody looks up, and someone finally says, "You do mean the *Amazon*
doesn't flow through the United States, don't you Mr. President?"

And he says, "No, I mean the Mississippi. M-i-s-s-i-s-s-i-p-p-i."

There is simply no accounting for it. The notion that what Mr. Ford
intended to say was not that Poland was autonomous and independent,
but that the United States does not recognize the satellization of Poland by
the Soviet Union as a permanent arrangement, is simply not validated by
what Mr. Ford in fact said in answer to Mr. Frankel's chivalrous question
designed to straighten Mr. Ford out. President Ford said, "Each of those
countries [Yugoslavia, Rumania, Poland] *is* independent, autonomous; it
has its own territorial integrity, and the United States does not concede
that those countries *are* under the domination of the Soviet Union."

Now an explanation for this statement (the last contender for the presidency to make such a statement about Eastern Europe was Henry Wallace,
some of whose speeches were written for him by Communist agents, the
others being incoherent) is beyond the grasp of normal men of tidy deduc-
tive habits. The pernicious aspect of the slip is the damage it did to the
whole post–Kansas City image of Ford as an impressively competent chief
executive.

There is a television series running that features someone called a
Bionic Man. He is reconstructed from an airplane wreck, or something
of the sort, and after umpteen operations by ambitious doctors, runs now
faster than a gazelle, lifts weights heavier than a crane could lift, sees further than a telescope—a miracle of scientific reconstruction. But imagine
if, somewhere along the way, the Bionic Man, sitting by the fireside, discussing poetry with his staff, suddenly reached down, picked up the cocker

spaniel, and ate it. Curses! the scientists say. We forgot to program him not to eat dogs!

Mr. Carter is trying to give out the notion that the White House staff that has so successfully programmed President Ford forgot to tell him that, in 1945, we lost Poland. Unhappily, Mr. Ford made it easy for his opponent. Those who desire the truth must settle for a kind of transliteral confidence. Mr. Ford is not a specialist in verbal precision or rhetorical inflection, and is certainly not at home with the subjunctive mood. One is required to conclude that he meant to convey something else—he is, after all, a bright man. But he faces difficulties now, yet again, of a very broad character, which afflictions he was successfully pulling away from before he committed the ultimate Polish joke.

—October 14, 1976

Buckley on Buckley

It is being said broadly that the Senate race in New York between James Buckley and Daniel Patrick Moynihan is shaping up as a classic confrontation between traditional conservative and traditional liberal lines, and it's true. The contest, moreover, has been described as the second most important of this fall, after the presidential contest; and that also is true. Except for my biological involvement, I'd have written more frequently about it, precisely because of its symbolic importance. Under the circumstances, I shall write only this one time. These observations I have to make or else die of uremic poisoning.

Moynihan has one of the liveliest minds in the nation. He is always rethinking those propositions the ideologues cultivate about the time their skin clears and never again bother to test against experience. That is how Moynihan became an exciting teacher and writer. The concessions he has made, in his race for the Senate, are dismaying. Take his current speeches, homogenize them, and bless us if he does not sound like Eleanor Roosevelt. That's an awful way to go, and the Senate really isn't worth it.

Here, drastically truncated, is what Moynihan and Senator James Buckley are saying:

Moynihan: Buckley is a reactionary, frightened by FDR as a child.

Buckley: It isn't reactionary to take stock of what is happening to this country under the dispensation of the doctrine that the federal government should handle all our problems.

Moynihan: I believe that the federal government should work for us, not against us.

Buckley: So do I. And a government works much better for the people in many situations by staying out of their way rather than interfering actively in their lives. There is a role for government, but the statist's presumption in favor of government ends us up busing children to alien schools, telling old people how many days they can spend with their children, and instructing half the population that they can look forward to spending half their time working for the government.

Moynihan: As a senator from New York, I would labor to bring every last penny of federal money into New York.

Buckley: As a senator from New York, I have labored to get every last penny to New York which is New York's due. As a United States senator I could not in good conscience rob other states—assuming that were possible—for the benefit of such New York lobbyists as the welfare lobby. United States senators are not sent off to Washington with letters of marque and reprisal for use against the other forty-nine states in the Union.

Actually, all of it is really there, in these words. James Buckley is an ideologist only in the sense that Thomas Jefferson was ("The government can do something for the people only in proportion as it can do something to the people"). He is suspicious of government only as John Adams cautioned us to be ("The government turns every contingency into an excuse for enhancing power in itself."). He is a liberal not in the recent mechanical tradition of Moynihan but in the more venerable tradition of Woodrow Wilson ("The history of liberalism is the history of man's efforts to restrain government").

It was the independent-mindedness of James Buckley that brought him to call for the resignation of President Nixon when it had become clear that his continuation in office damaged the country. For this, Senator Buckley suffered every bit as much as Mr. Moynihan did a few years ago for using the phrase "benign neglect." Senator Buckley is rated, even by those who disapprove of some of his policies, as an outstanding member of the Senate. Jack Anderson rates him among the top ten senators.

The voters of New York have the opportunity on election day to accomplish two highly desirable things. Vote to maintain an independent conservative of demonstrated ability, intelligence, and integrity in the Senate. And vote to return Daniel Patrick Moynihan to Harvard, where, liberated from the constraints of ideological politics, he will be free once again to shed his grace on all of us.

—October 21, 1976

Run, Jesse, Run

Integral—but absolutely integral—to the success of the Reverend Jesse Jackson is his idiom. Without it, his heroic up-from-slavery posture simply evaporates. H. L. Mencken once wrote that the Latin recited by the priest was essential to the apparent sublimation of the liturgical process. Unless the priest is incanting in an exotic tongue, uttering strange and progressively hypnotic sounds, the mind of the communicant inevitably focuses on a middle-aged man, his armpits asweat under the encumbering vestments, who if he had not elected to receive Holy Orders would probably be clerking at a grocery store or tending bar. The image is Mencken's, who lost few opportunities to make sport of religion. But the insight is universal: The style is the man, is another way of putting it.

Listen. "*We're movin' on up!*"—uttered slowly, just a hint of mounting excitement.

"*At the '72 convention, George McGovern was the nominee. . . . Reubin Askew was the keynoter. . . . I was just fightin' for a seat in the hall. And I beat 'em in New Hampshire!*"

Pause for a moment.

Suppose that he had said, "We're moving up," instead of, "We're movin' on up." Why, the whole image drains. As if Gary Cooper, having peered over the boulder and viewed the approaching Indians, had reported back to his beleaguered colleagues, "I estimate there are two dozen of them, armed with rifles, and that the probability is they will charge us some time before sundown." No, no, no!

"*There's a lot of them out there, I figure, maybe twenny, twenny-five. Got guns. They'll pro'bly come on in befoh the sun sets.*" That's more like it.

"Movin' on up." The anaphora: the rhetorical device whose effect is achieved by repeating the initial phrase of a sequence. For maximum effect, it is run quickly after the termination of the preceding sentence, as in:

"*I have a dream today.*

"*I have a dream* that one day the state of Alabama, whose governor's lips are presently dripping with the words of interposition and nullification, will be transformed . . .

"*I have a dream today.*

"*I have a dream* that one day every valley shall be exalted. . . .

"*I have a dream.*"

"*Movin' on up. Alan Cranston, a powerful senator from California,* and I beat him!

"*Fritz Hollings.* [Long pause.] *When he was governor of South Carolina, I couldn't use the bathroom in the state capitol.* I beat Fritz Hollings! *We're movin' on up.*

"*John Glenn was up there orbiting the earth when I was scufflin' for dimes down here. Now he is gone,* and I'm still in the race. *We're movin' on up.*"

And then the triumphant bugles sound. The gates of paradise open: "*I am at the apex of the triangle.* And that is the very opposite of blacks being taken for granted by the Democrats or written off by the Republicans!"

~

Ratiocination is subversive in revival meetings. If the American people were tomorrow given the choice of McGovern versus Jackson, Askew versus Jackson, Cranston versus Jackson, Hollings versus Jackson, or Glenn versus Jackson, the score would be Jackson, 0. So that Jackson is left, really, without a point to make. And certainly without any claim to having advanced the evolution of Martin Luther King's dream, which was that white and black Americans would in due course mix as if differences in the color of their skins were irrelevant. Jesse Jackson is engaged in attempting to do quite the opposite. His success is measured precisely by the extent to which he can persuade the black community that just as he, Jackson, is primarily a black man, they are primarily black men and black women, and that therefore their ethnic bond is the chain that binds them together above all other kinships, attenuated, that they share with their neighbors.

This exuberant tribalism makes for flash-flood victories (27 percent of the vote in Virginia, that kind of thing). But the flash-flood victories (remember, George Wallace actually won the primaries in Maryland and North Carolina in 1972) don't really add up to very much, not if such victories tug against orderly inertial thought. And that is a good thing, because we should not wish any political movement to succeed that says of a Jew or of a Protestant or of an Italian or of a Hispanic that he is primarily that, secondarily other things. When John F. Kennedy became the first Catholic elected president, he managed this by persuading the American people that his being a Catholic affected not at all his qualifications to serve as a disinterested chief executive. If Jack Kennedy's bellowed stand had been that he stood at the apex of a triangle in which he represented Catholic interests in America, he would not have gone on to carry Boston.

Jesse Jackson is a remarkable figure. But his strengths are primarily theatrical. He strains, for the most part, athwart the American tradition of progress. That tradition is extraracial. The tradition does not enjoin Jews from helping other Jews, Italians from helping other Italians. In *Beyond the Melting Pot*, sociologists Nathan Glazer and Daniel Patrick Moynihan remarked that 95 percent of the commercial business done by Chinese Americans in New York went to other Chinese Americans. Now, here they remarked an interesting disparity: Negro Americans (as they were then called) patronized primarily white businessmen (the exceptions: beauticians and morticians). If Jesse Jackson were aiming at cultivating pride in the black American of the kind that results in fraternal commercial camaraderie—in creating a demand for more black businessmen, more black professionals—Jesse would be moving with tradition. And this he began to do a dozen years ago with Operation PUSH. That was when he was speaking out about how black Americans need not stand out as athletes: Let them stand out also as mathematicians and as doctors; but lo, this requires homework, and great, extra-athletic application. In recent years, however, Jesse Jackson has sold out to the old political dream. The dream that suggests that the state is the witch doctor with the keys to prosperity.

~

Up to a point, the state can be the effective ally of the oppressed. A convulsive effort, enlisting the police powers of the state, was required to liberate black people from slavery; another statist effort, a hundred years later, to give black people the vote and spare them the humiliation of Jim Crow. But now, even though there are residual prejudices, of course—as there are against Catholics and Jews, Italians and Mexicans—there is no Fortress

America, calculated to exclude blacks from any position of prominence. To suggest otherwise—which is exactly what Jesse Jackson continually suggests (the Reagan administration is "racist")—is to mobilize an army behind an objective that either is unclear (What, assuming President Jackson were inaugurated, would he do for blacks?) or, where it is clear, is un-American (blacks cannot, by virtue of being black, deprive nonblacks of their own rights and opportunities).

Jesse Jackson is a man of transient fixations. For a while he seemed to be concerned exclusively with 1.6 million Palestinian refugees. This at a time when there were 2 million refugees in Africa. He never acknowledged the 350,000 Ethiopians in the Sudan, the 125,000 Angolans in Zaïre, the 134,000 Burundians in Tanzania, the 200,000 Ethiopians in Somalia, the refugees in Cyprus, or Pakistan, the Cambodians in Thailand, the Burmese in Bangladesh.

No, it was the Palestinians, even as now it is South African black victims he wishes to organize our foreign policy around, not Nicaraguan victims, or Chinese victims, or Afghan victims, let alone Russian victims. "Let's build houses, not bombs," he says, which is flower-child cant, like saying, Let's have fiddlers on the streets, not policemen. He is given to the most grating verbal rhetorical disjunctions in contemporary language. ("We're going from the outhouse to the White House." "They've got dope in their veins rather than hope in their brains.") But he knows how to turn them on. He is the biggest political aphrodisiac since Martin Luther King Jr.

He will, of course, be a major production at the convention in San Francisco. The Democratic professionals desire only this, that he not lead a third party. If he decides to do so, it will be ostensibly for the sake of showing how massive the black vote can be, and how critical in critical states. But in order to document this, it will be necessary to document that the black vote is an instrument at the disposal of a "black leader," and this is unhealthy. I so referred to him once, in a public exchange, and was rebuked. "Do you refer to Ronald Reagan as a white leader?" No, I said. "Because Reagan does not seek to be a white leader." But though Jesse Jackson talks about rainbows and extraracial brotherhood, he is in the business of consolidating black America, and that isn't good, not for blacks, not for America. It is good only for Jesse, who is primarily engaged in kingpinmanship.

What else is he engaged in? He was asked this recently. He replied: "We . . . found this widespread dissatisfaction among members of the rainbow—women, Hispanics, blacks, Asians, young people, handicapped people, peace activists, environmentalists. We determined that the way to institutionalize the concerns of the rejected people was to forge an alliance."

Well, women, to the extent that they are dissatisfied, aren't going to look to Jesse for relief. Hispanics, by order of U.S. courts, are receiving free schooling even if they are illegally in the country. Asians who are mad at America are mad over our failure to abide by commitments in Vietnam that Jesse deplores were ever made. Young people, if they have complaints beyond those that young people organically have, can complain about the high overhead of life, much of it owing to Social Security payments to their retired grandparents. Handicapped people are literally causing the streets to be repaved. Peace activists are free to hawk their wares everywhere except in those countries that threaten the peace, and the environmentalists not long ago succeeded in getting the secretary of the interior fired.

What Jesse Jackson needs is what he is bound in due course to get: a dose of realism, after all the noise subsides.

Jesse, run! Jesse, run!

Where?

He's movin' on up—and one day he will scale the mountain and there have a view of reality. Reality is progress achieved by hard work, faith, self-reliance. Not by camp-following with political medicine men.

—*Penthouse*, July 1984

George Bush, Reborn

Those of us who, following the caucus vote in Iowa, declared it too early to count George Bush out are drawn to emphasize different points now that Mr. Bush has all but secured the Republican nomination. And the principal point to make is that George Bush is publicly seen as being most awfully boring.

Along with practically everybody else, I have reflected on what happens to vice presidents, most acutely having lived through what was seen as the public decomposition of Hubert Humphrey. In 1968, Humphrey was widely scorned by the left intelligentsia for the sin of having kept company with Lyndon Johnson, whom said intelligentsia loathed above all living creatures and most dead creatures. But others, too, lost faith in him. It seemed impossible that this political springhead, this gusher of liberal idealism, of spontaneity and effervescence, should have acquired so flat a dimension. Would Winston Churchill have become a wallflower if he had been an American vice president? There are those who tell you that not only is there an appearance of etiolation among those who serve as vice president—it actually happens to you.

I doubt this to be true and have the directest evidence of it. The story, worth careful attention for reasons staid and wonderful, is this. On a particular day in the winter of 1970 I found myself seated at lunch next to Senator Stuart Symington. I asked him whether he had tuned in the night before on Walter Cronkite's CBS interview with former President Lyndon Johnson.

Not only had he done so, said Mr. Symington, he had done so in the company of Hubert Humphrey.

Oh? And what, I asked—who would not have asked?—had been Hubert Humphrey's reaction to what LBJ had said about why Humphrey had lost the election to Richard Nixon? Johnson had said to Cronkite that Humphrey lost because of the speech he delivered in Denver, in which he expressed reservations about the way in which we had committed ourselves in Vietnam.

How did he take it? Senator Symington howled. He then said, Hubert said to me after the broadcast: Stu, I really wish I was president right now. Because if I was, I would order a division of U.S. Marines to lift Cleopatra's Needle from London, fly it to Texas, and stick it up the --- of Lyndon Johnson.

~

George Bush faces two problems: the first internal, the second external. Already the kinds of forces that urged Thomas E. Dewey in 1948 to be bland (the most memorable sentence of Dewey's campaign: "The future lies before us") are at work on Bush, encouraging whatever it is within him that seeks out the prudent alternative. The day before Super Tuesday, reporter David Hoffman of the *Washington Post* was writing of complaints from the field of Bush's somnolent appearances. Hoffman described Mr. Bush in Springfield, Missouri, reviewing the World's Fishing Fair. Bush's only comment: "I'll tell you something. If this country ever loses its interest in sports or ever loses its interest in fishing, we got real trouble, and I don't think that's going to ever happen." I mean, a couple of months of fishing fairs, and the people would vote for Ralph Nader.

George Bush has to turn whatever switches only he can turn within himself to permit to come out of hiding the personality that his old friends and acquaintances (I have known him since 1948) are familiar with.

The second release can only be sprung by Ronald Reagan.

There are broad alternative avenues open to a president in the years ahead, and Mr. Bush should on his own, for his own account, advise us which appeal to him the most. The most important question to answer is: How are we going to guard against the decomposition of our alliance in Europe? The second is: How are we going to cultivate the most valuable of all American resources, which is the latent vitality of conservative impulses to self-help, industry, patriotism, honor, and the integrity of the family?

This is not to suggest that President Reagan will not be giving his own speeches, touching on these subjects. But Mr. Bush ought to be permitted to enunciate what distinctive policies he would pursue after his inauguration. There should be a freshness of approach in these that attracts a following of its own and that energizes the enthusiasm of a somewhat reluctant conservative constituency.

Mr. Bush will never successfully compete with the Great Communicator. Accordingly, he should seek out a style of his own. But he can do this confidently only after assurances from the president that he will not misinterpret a decision to strike out on his own as an act of parricide. Bush should not be understood as seeking to slay his father, whom he properly reveres. But he should be seen as preparing to leave his father's house, prepared to inhabit his own.

—March 10, 1988

Oh My God!

What makes some Americans so mad at Bill Clinton is his glib falsifications. It gets bad when, after hearing a speech from a president, you feel you want to shut your eyes and maybe recite the multiplication tables or say the alphabet or drop an ashtray on the floor to check out gravity. The performance of the president the other night can only be described as fetid.

This was so in matters small and large. Anyone with the least respect for the requirements of formal logic should not declare in one paragraph, "No more something for nothing," and in the very next paragraph, "I'm especially proud that this time the federal government has been fighting alongside the people" in mitigating the Mississippi floods.

1. The victims of the flood are getting something for nothing.

2. What does Clinton mean by saying "this time" the federal government is getting into the relief business? Who was it helped the victims of the hurricane in Florida and the earthquake in San Francisco? Santa Claus?

"We've been given the politics of abandonment—" The listener wonders what that is, exactly. Well, Clinton tells you right there and then, and the next morning you see it in print: "cutting taxes on the well-off and asking nothing of them in return, either, while raising taxes on the middle class to pay more for the same government, instead of investing in our jobs and our future."

That sentence reconstructs history as densely as any one sentence written by Stalin or Goebbels.

The basic 1981 tax law (Kemp-Roth) cut taxes not only on the well-off but uniformly, across the board. The 1982 tax law (TEFRA) had primarily to do with corporations. The 1986 act reduced taxes at all levels, but imposed on the wealthy class the forfeiture of a number of traditional shelters. Six million taxpayers were relieved of any tax whatever. In 1985 the tax code was indexed, relieving the middle class of bumping into higher rates of taxation by the legislative authority of the diminished dollar.

The 1981 and 1986 acts were approved by every member of the Senate Finance Committee, with one exception; and the final vote was overwhelmingly in favor, and included Senator Edward Kennedy. Reconcile these facts with Clinton's paragraph, and you can do Rubik's Cube for a living.

"The second principle of this plan is fairness: Those who have the most contribute the most. As this chart shows, we asked the well-off to pay their fair share, requiring that at least 80 percent of the new tax burden fall on those making more than $200,000 a year."

Does our Rhodes scholar know the difference between "fair" and "expedient"? Would it be "fair" to take the top ten seeded golfers and add ten strokes each to their score? Is it "fair" to impose 80 percent of a proposed $250-billion tax load on fewer than one million Americans—who as things stand are already paying 27 percent of all federal taxes?

We are supposed to have equal treatment under the law, the same laws for rich and poor. The invasive practices of the progressive tax violate the basic commitment of the Fourteenth Amendment, but the use of language by Clinton corrupts thought.

He can't stop making them, the demagogic asides about the rich: "I will not balance the budget on the backs of older Americans while protecting the wealthy." Who asked him to?

The deceptions frame the entire speech. "For the last several years, our economy has failed to generate jobs." Why didn't he have the grace to say that under Reagan our economy produced 18 million jobs?

"They"—the Republicans—"practice partisanship when we need progress. They call for delay when we've been waiting for twelve years." Waiting for what for twelve years? Waiting for a Democratic Senate? But we've had one for ten of the last twelve years. Waiting for a Democratic House? We've had one for twelve of the last twelve years. Waiting for a "fair" tax bill? But the four tax bills passed during the last twelve years were overwhelmingly subscribed to by Democratic legislators. What can Clinton be talking about?

The answer is: His fixation. The current jury rig by which the federal government continues to extend its powers to regulate our activity, and to commandeer the use and misuse of language.

—August 5, 1993

Frightened by Pat Robertson?

A few weeks ago I participated in a two-hour television debate defending the proposition that the Religious Right does not represent any threat to the liberty of America. I was satisfied, after the exchange was over, that the critics on the other side were primarily concerned with the question of the separation of church and state. By which I mean that their fears of the Religious Right seemed hypothetical and ever so abstract.

I remember forty years ago when it was fashionable to suppose that Senator Joseph McCarthy threatened the Bill of Rights and maybe even the balance of nature. In the middle of the putative reign of terror, Professor John Roche, who was steadfastly opposed to McCarthy and who just a few years later would serve as chairman of Americans for Democratic Action, a militantly liberal front, enraged the anti-McCarthy forces by answering a reporter who asked him whether he was afraid of McCarthy by saying: "My fear of McCarthy is 23rd on my list of fears. No. 22 is my fear of being eaten alive by piranhas; No. 24 is my fear of college presidents."

That didn't seem very loyal to the forces who insisted that McCarthy was about to close down American liberties.

What surprised me in the fortnight after the televised debate was the volume of letters from people who seem to have a most extraordinary fear of Pat Robertson. He is the dominant figure in the evangelical Right, formerly a minister. He ran for the Republican presidential nomination in 1988, and before doing so, resigned his ministry. He continues now, as a layman, attempting to mobilize the Christian Right specifically.

One very bright young man wrote to tell me that Pat Robertson had driven him and others he knew into the arms of the Democratic Party.

This seems, to begin with, an odd way to do battle with Pat Robertson, if one is an anti-Robertson conservative. But let that pass, and ponder two questions: (1) Why are people so very much afraid of Pat Robertson? and (2) Why is Pat Robertson so very much exercised?

I wrote to one correspondent to say that as far as I could tell, if Robertson were to wake up and discover that he was omnipotent, and therefore wrote into law every proposal that makes up the program of the Christian Right, America would be in no way different from the country I lived in until I was approximately thirty.

In those days, true, you couldn't go to the movies to see a *Deep Throat*, but that was not a stifling imposition. Pornography had to be bought from dirty old men, who are the people best fitted to serve that purpose. You couldn't find a liquor store open on Sunday, which represented whatever you want to call the hardship of laying in enough booze on Saturday to last you until Monday.

What else? Well, you couldn't get a legal abortion. But up until very close to *Roe* v. *Wade* there was a pretty wide popular consensus against abortion, and one has to suppose that the primary reason the choicers don't want to repeal *Roe* v. *Wade* is that they don't quite trust the American voters to authorize abortion on demand, if the power were to be returned to them. But of course there were a lot of illegal abortions, well over a half million per year.

If American freedom is to be measured by that one index—does the American woman have the right to abort?—then Pat Robertson's America would not be free. But we should be prepared to summon historical perspectives before denouncing as unfree the America that existed until 1973, the year in which the Supreme Court discovered a right of privacy that extended to the right to extinguish unborn life.

OK, now why is Pat Robertson so exercised? Well, one reason is that there has been, in the period we are talking about (the last twenty-five years), a 500 percent increase in crime. When more than six hundred people are murdered every day, a lot of people are losing their freedom pretty definitively. When ten times that many are robbed or mutilated or raped, then we have lost a right of privacy much older than that which authorizes abortion: the primary right over your own body (*habeas corpus*). That right becomes ever more tenuous as the chances increase that a marauder will invade your body with a bullet, a knife, a baseball bat, or a genital organ.

And during that period, we have seen a 400 percent increase in illegitimate births, children consigned to the absence of the father in the home.

So, other than the Sunday blue laws, what are we left with? The need to order *Lady Chatterley's Lover* from some dusky address—a privation, though one wouldn't think of it as major.

It is difficult to know just why people find this so frightening. As it happens, there is no prospect that Pat Robertson is going to be able to implement his entire program. But if he did, we'd be reduced to those liberties we enjoyed right through the 1950s, and in those days we could be young and gay without substantial fears, as far as I can remember.

—October 2, 1993

Who Loses if Clinton Wins

Everybody is trying to figure it out. Approximately 57 percent of the voters believe that:

(a) Bill and Hillary Rodham Clinton have been hiding things;

(b) their most intimate associates from days gone by either commit suicide, resign, or get indicted and, some of them, convicted;

(c) back when Clinton was governor, he did shady things with campaign contributions;

(d) Hillary knew about all this and personally profited from legerdemain done on the futures market;

(e) the White House knew that confidential FBI reports were being brought in for unlicensed purposes; and

(f) Clinton almost certainly has oversexed neurons and underdeveloped self-control.

Approximately 57 percent then say that they will vote for him for re-election.

The pundits pore over these figures and seek refuge in the complicated character of the stories being examined. Vince Foster's papers . . . the billing records . . . the savings-and-loan in Little Rock, Arkansas . . . the convictions of former Clinton associates . . . the trial of the next echelon of associates.

Too complicated, it is said, and too boring. In fact, I agree. I am bored by it.

If every one of the enumerated charges here listed was established (about some there is no doubt: Foster did commit suicide and Jim and Susan McDougal were convicted), I for one would not deprive Clinton of my vote if I approved his policies and the means by which he pursues them.

Those who believe that past American presidents or candidates are comparatively blameless bring to mind the statement of the professor from MIT, a member of the commission dispatched to survey whether in 1966 the elections held in South Vietnam were fair. Well, said the professor on returning to Cambridge, in answer to the question put to him by a reporter, "I would say yes, the elections over there were fair, just as fair as in Massachusetts."

True, Bob Dole hasn't comparable problems with his own past. If Solomon had the only vote, he would find for the challenger, not the incumbent.

What does hurt is the Elmer Gantry factor. Lyndon Johnson didn't really have Clinton's problem in part because everyone simply took it for granted that Landslide Lyndon was a political swinger—that's the way it works in Texas, most of the voters said to themselves. Everyone who cared to know such things knew that LBJ had made millions by exploiting his position to get from the Federal Communications Commission a television monopoly in Austin, Texas. How many people cared to punish him? Not many.

But Johnson was not a sanctimonious type. He would burp into the microphone and exhibit his gallbladder scar and affix the presidential seal to his cowboy boots.

Clinton attempts an entirely different vision of himself. He is the fresh idealist, the young scholar who turned to politics because of his attachment to such activity as a means of doing good for his fellow man.

It is for this reason that the accumulation of character traffic-accidents catches attention. What then begins to make the blood run hot is his characterizations of others.

On Sunday, peacefully watching *60 Minutes*, which told us that the last Mexican president's brother had a character problem inasmuch as he stole $300 million, viewers were treated to an ad sponsored by the committee to re-elect President Clinton. The message disclosed that it was Clinton who was single-handedly protecting Medicare, preserving scholarships and tax deductions for college education, and maintaining the school-lunch program—who was, in short, frustrating Republican designs on the aged, the sick, the hungry, and the afflicted.

Sure, if a stickler had been around to make a few distinctions, the ad would have collapsed from the weight of its horse manure. (The Republican alternative to the administration's Medicare program was to trim the projected growth by 4 percent.)

Clinton's programmers do not mention, nor will they, that at the rate at which entitlements are increasing, everybody will be broke sometime soon after the turn of the century. Nor would they bring up such a datum alongside Clinton's ringing declaration in his State of the Union address that the age of big government is over.

What an American president says is most definitely a clue to his character, as set against what that president does and what that president countenances. A close study of Clinton in office needs none of the material rushing in from Arkansas, the congressional investigations, the FBI, the Justice Department, or Eleanor Roosevelt. His own record should dislodge the 57 percent.

If it does not, this voter would hazard the guess that the re-election of Bill Clinton would not be a catastrophic setback for the United States, but it would gravely damage the pretensions of enlightened democracy.

—June 25, 1996

Rip Van Winkle Reviews the Scene

Crossing Eurasia on a train from Beijing to Moscow is an unusual experi-ence, for most of the reasons one would suppose. But what this traveler neglected to anticipate was twelve days without one whisper of news of the world.

If on arriving in Moscow the passengers had been told that Vice Presi-dent Al Gore had resigned from office after confessing to having shot Vin-cent Foster, and that Princess Di had announced her betrothal to John F. Kennedy Jr., we'd have accepted the news with the dumb fatalism of those who come to terms with the vicissitudes of exile.

So what does one do after such a period of alienation? One reads. Everything in sight. And discovers that the Dayton Accords are the fruit-less enterprise predicted, that John F. Kennedy Jr. did in fact get married, though not to Princess Di, and that candidate Bob Dole is slipping out of sight. Why is this?

What are they going to debate about? says rejected debater Ross Perot, thumping his fist on the table and unleashing a battery of lawyers. A gen-eration ago, candidate George Wallace told the voters that there wasn't "a dime's worth of difference" between candidates Richard Nixon and Hubert Humphrey. Thereafter, the GOP tidied up its philosophical house under Ronald Reagan, but slippage resumed under Bush.

In and out of Nixon-Ford-Reagan-Bush all those years was Bob Dole, and President Clinton does what he can to suggest that Dole has flexible views on such matters as taxes and drug laws and the rest.

Dole's reach for the hard position of tax reduction seems not to have aroused either excitement or confidence. The poll figures haven't moved, except for the spurt that coincided with the naming of Jack Kemp as his running mate and the exhilaration of the four narcissistic days of the San Diego convention.

And the *Wall Street Journal* conducted a poll: "Do you think your taxes will go down, will go up, or will stay about the same if Bill Clinton is re-elected or if Bob Dole is elected?"

Thirty-six percent say up with a Clinton victory.

Thirty-three percent say up with a Dole victory.

The figures tell it all about what voters conclude after listening to politicians make promises. Clinton promised in 1992 to reduce taxes, but he didn't—he raised them. Are the voters mad at him on that account? No, the voters aren't mad at Clinton over anything. With *one* exception. They would not like it if they thought Clinton was a liberal. It's OK for him to say that he is in the tradition of Jefferson, Jackson, Roosevelt, Truman, and Kennedy. But it would not be OK for him to say he was a liberal.

And Clinton is greatly aware of that danger and goes to thunderous lengths to guard against it. Adulterer, OK; tax cheat, OK; drug user, OK; draft dodger, OK.

Liberal, never!

"President [Clinton] came to town a liberal; he's still a liberal," said Dole last week. "The only thing that stopped him in his tracks was electing a Republican Congress in 1994."

The reporters, of course, questioned Clinton on the point later the same day in the White House.

"There's a real problem with that," Clinton began. "One is my record, my record as governor, my record as president." How, he asked, could anybody say that he was a liberal given that he reduced the deficit, supported the death penalty, and overhauled the welfare system? Sure, he and Bob Dole had "different tax plans, but I don't think that that qualifies me as a closet liberal."

There it is. The term liberal lies bloodied on the floor.

But liberalism lives. The percentage of the gross domestic product spent by the federal government (excluding for defense) has risen, the tax on the incremental dollar has risen, the hand of the government regulates everything except the security of unborn children; and poor Bob Dole struggles to make himself heard.

Of course there are differences, and of course it is true that Clinton is a liberal. But the voters are manifestly unimpressed with the differences, with one enormous exception, which is women.

If white men only were to vote (the *Wall Street Journal* does not relay the figures for blacks or Hispanics), Dole would sink Clinton, 51 percent to 37 percent. If only white women voted, Clinton would sink Dole, 53 percent to 35 percent. Women aged 35 to 49 appear to detest poor Bob Dole (60 to 28). We must be grateful that lesbian marriages will be childless.

So what will the psephologists say after hard study given to these figures? That Clinton always had a way with the ladies? What else?

—September 24, 1996

How Much Do We Like W?

The off-the-record meeting of twenty right-wing editors, writers, and diverse others had an agenda. It was to inquire how enthusiastically should American conservatives labor for the election of George W. Bush.

There was unanimity on one point, that the alternative was not to be risked. Years ago, some conservatives argued against voting for Richard Nixon when he was running against John F. Kennedy. The reasoning was that the positions handed down to candidate Nixon by President Eisenhower, whom he had served as vice president, were adulterated stuff, and that a conservative movement that sought ambitious ideological reorientation should pass on Nixon, and wait four years for someone (Goldwater?) more enticing.

The principal concern of conservatives, back in 1960, was over Eisenhower's wobbly Cold War policies. He had not risen to the challenge posed by the Soviet repression of the freedom fighters in Hungary, and meanwhile had undermined the British attempt to recapture control of the Suez Canal; and he had proved ineffectual in hand-to-hand diplomacy with Khrushchev. Other arguments had to do with the wholesale acceptance of New Deal welfare policies.

The emphasis today isn't on foreign policy because there is no worldwide threat against which to mobilize. It is, rather, on the domestic front, with emphasis on the Supreme Court's self-ordination as a super-legislature. Then there are all those pressure points on the ideological profile. What was Bush's reaction to the Supreme Court's decision denying the right to legislate against partial-birth abortion?

Anemic, one observer acknowledged. Yes, he said the right thing, but not in any way that rallied the troops on the question whether the Supreme Court's arrogant decision amounts to an assault on the balance of powers.

And—a second demurral—George W. is against affirmative action, but he declines to back any one of the three state measures that ask for plebiscitary action against quota-making. In his own state, he tolerates an admixture of sorts that bypasses resolute thought. What the Bush program calls for is guaranteeing admission to choice state universities for the top 10 percent of every high-school graduating class, never mind the relative standing of the schools. On the voucher alternative to failing schools, he is on the right side inferentially, but once again, he has not rallied the nation, or tried to do so.

One participant noted resignedly that the incremental advance of welfarism—in recent weeks all but agreed upon in the matter of drugs for the elderly—is an organic aspect of affluence. Welfarism was a bad idea when Bismarck thought it up in the 1880s, and his great-great grandchildren are prolonging it at the advent of the twenty-first century. But it is best evaluated by asking how great are the inroads on the private sector.

The call for help to the elderly on the problem of drug costs can be seen as an expression of economic abundance. What the United States can afford to do, Nicaragua cannot. *Quod licet Jovi, non licet bovi*—the gods can get away with extravagances earthlings can't. Bush's resistance to the Gore plan is formalistic. We're going to get, not free drugs, because nothing of course is free, but drugs that somebody else pays for.

The most arresting contribution involved, interestingly, the identification of George W. with—well, the manly virtues. He is a man's man, and, as such, a woman's man. His career and his pursuits underline an intuitive understanding of a division of duties. This means that men should not affect to be other than men.

In contrast, Mr. Gore is a man who seems to deplore his manhood, so concerned is he for the composite human being, part male, part female, one-quarter Asian, one-third African-American, and one-tenth gay.

There is a trace of indifference to the intellectual and artistic life discernible in W.'s circumlocutory responses to questions on matters like which book has he most recently read. But there is, one participant stressed, a rudimentary cultural intelligence there, of the kind that acknowledges and, as required, defers to those whose primary interest is the life of the mind. He may be indifferent to ballet, but he is not a Philistine.

How does it add up? One participant remembers a cartoon in *The New Yorker* in an election year involving Dwight Eisenhower. The diehard, facing the ballot box, remarks, "I like Ike, period."

The consensus at our meeting was: Conservatives should work hard for the election of George W. Bush, but when the election is over, they should start counting their silver.

—July 11, 2000

Fathoming Kerry

The voters in Massachusetts honor, and should, the heroism of John Kerry in Vietnam. What some voters will want to dwell upon is not Kerry, acknowledged hero in Vietnam, but Kerry, analyst of the Vietnam chapter in U.S. history.

When he returned from Vietnam and formed his committee to oppose the war, he went further than to renounce a military and geostrategic operation. In his famous testimony to the congressional committee, he used the kind of language about the architects of that war that he uses now about President Bush. He told Congress, in 1971, that he felt the call to "one last mission, to search out and destroy the last vestige of this barbaric war, to pacify our hearts, to conquer the hate and fear that have driven this country these last ten years and more, so that when, thirty years from now, our brothers go down the street without a leg, without an arm, or a face, and small boys ask why, we will be able to say, 'Vietnam!' and not mean a desert, not a filthy obscene memory, but the place where America finally turned and where soldiers like us helped it in the turning."

The voters are entitled to ask, "In what way did America 'turn'?" And to ask further, "If the U.S. role in Vietnam was barbaric, our motivations hate and fear, why, thirty-one years later, did John Kerry vote for war in Iraq?" Howard Dean is plainspoken on the question of U.S. guilt. He declares that we had no justifiable reason to go to war in Iraq, and yet Kerry voted to authorize President Bush to go to war. What will he say to veterans of the Iraq war? What he said to veterans of the Vietnam War was, "We cannot consider ourselves America's 'best men' when we are ashamed of and hated for what we were called on to do in Southeast Asia."

Mr. Bush, in his State of the Union address, did not say that our concern for freedom was the single reason we went to Iraq, but he did say that the deposition of Saddam Hussein was a huge humanitarian blessing. Speaking of Vietnam, Lieutenant Kerry testified, "To attempt to justify the loss of one American life in Vietnam, Cambodia, or Laos by linking such loss to the preservation of freedom . . . is . . . the height of criminal hypocrisy, and it is that kind of hypocrisy which we feel has torn this country apart."

The differences between Iraq and Vietnam are considerable, but what they have in common is insufficiently remarked. Our goal in Vietnam was to continue to press the doctrine of containment. We didn't hesitate to emphasize the difference between life under Communism, and life elsewhere. In Iraq, we entered the war to press for a strategic goal, the disarmament of Saddam lest he export his tyranny. And we have not hesitated to emphasize the difference between life under Saddam, and life elsewhere. What threatens in Iraq is an immobilization brought on by terrorist insurgents, and the possibility of civil war if the insurgency is not contained.

Is candidate Kerry declaring that the veteran is the representative of U.S. dishonor and hypocrisy? When will he say that the Iraq war "turned" America, as he pronounced the Vietnam War to have turned America?

Already, candidate Kerry has voted in the direction of retreat, when he refused to approve the supplementary appropriations requested by President Bush. If, when summer comes, the Iraqi engagement is still equivocal, will he treat it as he did Vietnam, as the embodiment of U.S. hate and fear and hypocrisy? Isn't the voter entitled to wonder about the reliability of a President Kerry who deemed past U.S. commitments transitory, en route to becoming dishonorable?

A problem with presidential candidacies is their pursuit of trendy popularity. Kerry tasted deep of this when he paraded before Congress in 1971, condemning the judgment and integrity of three U.S. presidents who had argued the importance of resisting the Communists in Vietnam. And now Kerry has his eyes on a sitting president who with the backing of seventy-seven senators, including John Kerry, set out to disarm Saddam Hussein by force. Does anyone doubt that if the Iraqi insurgency had been quelled six months ago, candidate Kerry would have applauded the leadership of the president he is so consumed to replace?

—January 23, 2004

A Special Odium

The virulence of the anti-Bush movement feeds on itself, and is fed by bad news. The most copious source of this is the Mideast. The mode of execution of helicopter engineer Paul Johnson had the effect the terrorists wanted. The announcement that he would be killed, followed quickly by the execution, followed by the posting on the Internet of photos of the event, had the desired effect.

It may help to recall that beheadings were conventional within living memory. They were the standard means of capital punishment in France, for instance, up until World War II. Even so, the sanguinary exercise chills the mind, and we are asked, however indirectly, to blame Bush for it, as for practically everything else going sour in the world.

A broad search of anti-Bush websites suggests the scope of festering animosity toward Bush. We have, e.g., BartCop, described by a compendium of websites as "Dedicated to hammering Bush and right-wing hypocrisy." The Smirking Chimp gives "news, rants, activism and other things anti-Bush," while the utilitarian Wage Slave Journal gives the George W. Bush Scorecard of Evil. BushAndCheneySuck.com is modestly "dedicated to licking Bush in 2000 and beyond."

That last brings to mind the temper of dissenters in the period of Franklin Roosevelt. It was a take-it-to-bed relief, after the disastrous defeat of Landon in 1936, that at least the two-term convention established by George Washington would mean an end to FDR's presidency in 1940; but of course he decided to run for a third term. Then Pearl Harbor happened, and there was distraction in the critical community, which paused to fight a war. By the time 1944 came around, re-electing FDR had become something of a routine, and the world went on.

As it will in 2005, with the re-election of George W. Bush?

History tends to reassure us on this point. Elections have assimilated American dissent since 1860. The mark of democracy is submission to the majority. But this time around, if the current figures hold, the rupture will be deepened. As of yesterday, the polls were showing Kerry, 48; Bush, 44; Nader, 6. The first two of these data are not striking; a seesaw between the two principal candidates happens frequently. The Nader factor is troubling, however, because if Bush defeats Kerry by a margin smaller than the nick taken by Nader, the anti-Bush community will think itself robbed again. It happened to us, they will be saying, when Gore had the popular vote and we lost by a judicial caprice. Now, if Nader is responsible for a fresh loss, we have to wonder about the reliability of democratic practices.

The kind of people who generate BushAndCheneySuck.com don't make up dissent at an institutional level. If Bush wins, even on account of the Nader factor, it is not likely that the U.S. will stampede for a constitutional convention jettisoning the Electoral College. Such an amendment couldn't get by the states that would be disfranchised on account of it.

But there is a special odium at large in the matter of Bush. It will seek to release itself by a rabid campaign against him. But there will need to be a tranquilizing factor in the campaign. If, for instance, Bush handles Kerry confidently and dispositively in the debates, that could provide a sense of democratic vindication. If progress in Iraq under native rule pivots the scene slightly, but substantially, toward stability, Bush could legitimately profit.

In the absence of such developments, the anti-Bush diehards are headed for a disillusionment likely to affect the democratic culture. What matters, in democratic elections, is not only submission to the majority, but also civil relations.

Nobody from the world of BartCop is going to end up loving Bush himself, but everyone has to gain from a lowering of voices. This isn't going to happen until after November 2, a long four months away.

—June 22, 2004

Great Cheer in Boston

There's something especially appealing about the hero who is safely back home after a risqué experience. Bill Clinton knows this and knows how to arrange his resilient face to show just that strain of I-know-you-caught-me-out-but-I-love-you-anyway. The crowd could not have made its enthusiasm more palpable unless they had put him on their shoulders, marched to the White House, and plopped him down in the Oval Office.

Clinton knows he was naughty, but naughty is exactly the right word for a peccadillo. "Some of [the public] who thought I was a good president didn't think I was a good man," he told Tom Brokaw. But that's other people, he was saying in effect on Monday night in Boston. True love survives these things, and the lightly chastened hero is stronger and braver than ever.

I expect that a similar phenomenon happened, flared, and went to a happy sleep with Teresa Heinz Kerry. For as many hours as interest could possibly be sustained (about three) we heard her engaged in exchanges graduating in asperity, ending when she said to the persistent interrogator that he could "shove it." All public bystanders with microphones or computers at hand stood still. Had a scandal been born? An event? A mini-event? The latter, and within twenty-four hours she had become the heroine of the exchange. You can't bully Teresa Heinz Kerry, they said. She could toss back an epithet—and top it off with a million dollars if she chose. A few such things help enormously with the awful stolidity of her husband's speeches.

Though this is written before Senator Kerry's acceptance speech. If reports are correct, nothing in political prose has been so burnished. We hear that the manuscript is everywhere the senator goes, and he looks at it, corrects it, adds to it, subtracts from it, ten times every day.

And on top of that, we learn, he has practiced his delivery. A friend related to me that a friend of his had served as advance man for Teddy Kennedy at the San Francisco Convention in 1984, and that he had had to listen to the senator's forty-five-minute speech five times, delivered in full and at full volume. This was the speech in which Teddy denounced every Republican thought, word, and deed under the incumbent administration. If I had been there I'd have asked the poor young advance man whether the speaker paused at every point where applause was reasonably expected. If it had been a presidential State of the Union address, such pauses would consume about as much time as the speech itself. "And I am telling you that the voters of America will not put up with this any longer!"

Thinking back, how long would you guess the applause for that line lasted, at the convention center in San Francisco, in 1984? The speech was deafening, and it had a resonant life in the state of Minnesota, which was the only state, four months later, that voted against Ronald Reagan, pursuant to the urging of convention speaker Kennedy.

It won't be so this time, because in 1984 Ronald Reagan had a great deal going for him. The Democrats don't have Ronald Reagan, but they have Ronald Reagan Jr., who has become a Democratic picador. The party of John Kerry can eat hungrily off Iraq. There was no Iraq in 1984 to bedevil Ronald Reagan. The economy back then was going forward in long strides. This time around it is less resolute, and jobs are certainly being lost to outsourcing. The cost of medicine troubles much of the population, and much of the population is living longer. There is the sense in Boston of a president, George W. Bush, whose title is unclear. The picador even said that Al Gore had actually won the Florida vote, which is not true—after the Supreme Court ruling, a neutral inquiry conducted by USA Today and the Miami Herald established that Bush had won the vote in Florida.

Mr. Bush is not going to win as triumphantly as Ronald Reagan, but the cheers for Bill Clinton on Monday aren't going to foretell the national mood on November 2. They are enlivening in Boston, but the day will surely come, as so often in the past, when the cheering has to stop.

—July 27, 2004

Inside Obama

In the small hours the morning after the Iowa caucuses, a tough-minded friend e-mailed me (he didn't want to wake me at 3 A.M., he wrote, merely to record what was going through his mind after the tumultuous victory). "I must say," he wrote, "I liked Barack a lot less after his flagrantly ranty speech about how the real evil in America is (a) the drug companies and (b) the oil companies. That is, the industries that keep us (a) alive and (b) warm."

There is a lot of what we used to write off as "reductionism" in that sentence. But there is also that wholesome impulse to search for a more comprehensive reading of Barack Obama.

Everybody knows Obama has gone further than merely to denounce oil and drug profits. What is it, concretely, that he wants?

One needs to disqualify a few of the candidate's postures, and this applies also to other candidates, of both parties. However demanding the formal requirement, as for the preacher to recall the deceased's name at the funeral, one must attempt to set aside, or to catnap while they go on, the common rhetorical denominators. Nobody, at this stage, is going to favor aggressive military action. The politicians therefore make it clear that such appropriations as they support for the military are for beefing up our self-defense. Kindly do not muddy this proposition by interjecting that, sometimes, self-defense is best done through pre-emptive military initiatives.

So Obama will struggle for peace and a resilient military. On this point, he will disagree only retroactively in the matter of Iraq. So, in understanding Obama, one reaches for concrete policy differences, and here is one that attracts attention: "I simply believe that those of us who have benefited most from this new economy can best afford to shoulder the obligations of ensuring that every American child has a chance for that same success."

Such words bring cheers, because what we are doing is applauding the singular successes of the speaker. But the cavil here is that they must be understood as singular. There is every reason in the world to declare that one wishes for the entire next generation that they come in speaking with the lucidity of Abraham Lincoln and showing the enterprise of Bill Gates. What is wrong is to stimulate the illusion that such things are possible.

One reason for the spectacular success of Barack Obama is the accumulation of burdens he faced and overcame. His father was black, the family destitute; early life was a struggle in Hawaii and Indonesia.

What does it take to transform that into acceptance by Columbia University? OK, it seems that affirmative action leaned a heavy shoulder on the admissions-office door. But wait! Obama was then accepted by Harvard Law School and—finally—he was elected president of the *Harvard Law Review*. There is no reason to suppose that the admissions people, or his colleagues on the *Review*, said, Whoa! Here's a guy homely enough in looks, and cosmopolitan enough in background, he might become a presidential candidate!

The successes thundered in, a show-stopping oration to the Democratic National Convention in 2004, and then election to the U.S. Senate and steady movement (excepting in New Hampshire) toward his eminence today, which is difficult to match.

But to suggest to his listeners that any active intervention by the government would increase the "chance for that same success" for "every American child" is mischievous. To imply that such careers are open to most people, let alone every American child, is to foster frustration, and to stimulate disillusion.

In 1948, when Senator Robert Taft announced that he was seeking the GOP presidential nomination, a reporter asked his wife, "Mrs. Taft, do you consider your husband a common man?"

She turned on him and said: "Oh no, he is not that at all. He was first in his class at Yale College, and first in his class at Harvard Law School. I think it would be wrong to present a common man as a representative of the people of Ohio."

Robert Taft was not to be likened to the common man, and neither is Barack Obama, who can do a great deal urging the younger generation to emulate what he, Obama, did in working to be educated, and mastering the law, and of course expressing gratitude to free American institutions that recognize and encourage advancement. But it is not unimportant to remind the voters of that generation that there is nothing, nothing that the state can do to replicate Obama's success for a million others.

—January 11, 2008

DEALING WITH THE COMMUNIST WORLD

Dean Acheson's Record

The Pattern of Responsibility, edited by McGeorge Bundy from the record of Secretary of State Dean Acheson (Boston: Houghton Mifflin, $4.00)

It is time the critics of Dean Acheson made certain concessions to his admirers. Because as long as they don't, the Big Issues of Acheson's record will be beclouded by outraged affirmations of certain skills of Acheson which are undeniable. So let it stand out indisputably that none of us questions (a) the occasional splendor of Acheson's rhetoric, (b) the eloquence or the abundance of his periodic indictments of Communism, (c) his mastery of parliamentary technique, (d) the effectiveness of his dialectic, and perhaps even (e) the nobility of his intentions. We insist, only, that he be recognized for what he is despite it all: a monumental and tragic failure as secretary of state.

The world abounds in intelligent and articulate men, and opposition to Communism is a very low common denominator among them. In the circumstances, one of our great national problems is not so much to select statesmen with these attributes, which is an easy enough task, but to unearth a man who is not only bright, clever, and democratic, but also *effective* and *perspicacious* and *adjustable*; and no volume or volumes by McGeorge Bundy or anyone else can hope to deflect from the shoulders of Dean Acheson major responsibility, after Truman, for the woeful, abysmal failure of the free world to counter the Communist menace.

Yet Bundy is very aggressive about all this. He states in his preface that "on almost every big issue [Acheson] has been at once right, energetic, and skillful." He then catalogues, primarily by quoting at enervating length from Mr. Acheson's public statements, the standard list of postwar administration countermeasures to Soviet imperialism. They are, briefly, the stand of the United States in the United Nations on the evacuation of Soviet troops from Iran; the promulgation of the Truman Doctrine for Greece; the Marshall Plan; the Berlin airlift; the North Atlantic Treaty; the Korean War. Many of these took place before the appointment of Acheson in January of 1949, yet he is identified with most of them because he gave them his support first as under secretary of state and then as a private lawyer.

Now, each of these anti-Communist measures, with an exception or two, is controversial at least to the extent that the question arises whether it was best exploited, or most shrewdly designed, or most carefully selected from among alternative measures to enhance the strategic position of the free world as against the Soviet Union. For example, was the airlift the most fruitful means of countering brazen Russian aggression in Berlin? Was the administration or the constitution of the Marshall Plan as effective as it might have been? Has our behavior in Korea been intelligent, and has it worked maximum damage, militarily, economically, politically, and psychologically, to the Soviet Union?

~

It was foredestined, of course, that the United States would eventually take some measures to hinder the march of Communism. A government that refused to adopt an anti-Communist foreign policy, however adulterated, would have had about as much popular support as the Progressive Party rallied in 1948. So it must be kept in mind that *something* was bound to be done. The question then becomes, Did Acheson do the minimum, the maximum, or something in between? It is this that Mr. Bundy simply doesn't talk about.

Notwithstanding, time and time and time again Mr. Bundy refers to what he calls "central ideas," "central positions," "central problems," "central questions"; but he never harnesses the vast data at his disposal in any such sensible way as to examine the central issue of Acheson's career as policymaker. If he had, the reader would have been confronted by two naked facts from which to launch his analysis: (a) Acheson is identified as the supporter and the formulator of American foreign policy from 1945 to the present, and (b) over the same period (and to the tune of a despoiled treasury, a hundred thousand casualties, and fancy rhetoric) the free world, led by the United States, traversed a very long path—from easy dominance over nine-tenths of the world's population, to a cringing and uncertain defense of a little over one-half of the globe.

Such a framework for judging Acheson would unquestionably strike Mr. Bundy as founded upon a hoary cliché—discounting, as it is predictable that he would, the fact that more often than not a statement becomes a cliché because of its nagging and persistent identification with the truth. And the truth is that under Acheson, who fastidiously prepared the way by sacrificing hundreds of millions of free men to the reign of the hammer and sickle, we now face the Communists at point-blank range.

Although it would seem sufficient totally to discount Acheson as a moral man of reliable judgment by citing his defense as recently as a year ago of the Yalta treaty, it is reasonable to be patient and observe Acheson's record, so enthusiastically presented by Bundy, in a few specific and crucial instances:

1. *China.* Bundy makes a great deal of the cost of saving China, and not very much of the fact that the expenditure of money has never seriously depressed Truman or Acheson, and that China received less aid than Greece. But Greece and China are *different*, Acheson repeatedly states. Quite true; but they have a decisive similarity in that the integrity of both is vital to the United States, and both are targets of Soviet imperialism. But the 80th Congress voted less money for China than the president requested, Bundy retorts. True, but neither the president nor the secretary of state (and they are the makers of foreign policy) put the situation to Congress as realistically as it was their obligation to do. Neither dramatized the impending tragedy in China as they were both in a position to do; neither made a serious issue of the niggardliness of the appropriation that was forthcoming; nor was the appropriated money delivered to China with the dispatch that was so urgent in 1948. (See Freda Utley's *The China Story*.)

And that isn't all: thousands of words have flowed out of Acheson's mouth to the effect that he has always been anxious to convince the Chinese people that the American government would not interfere with domestic Chinese problems. I submit that the Chinese people were anxious for quite contrary affirmations, affirmations that the American people would *indeed* interfere in China to preserve the outlines of the Open Door Policy, and to guard China against national serfdom to a power hostile to civilization itself. I submit that such assurances were precisely and urgently called for, and that the absence of them contributed far more substantially to the disintegration of the Nationalist armies than any inadequacies of Chiang's administration. After all, national pride, which it was the alleged purpose of Mr. Acheson to salvage by his preposterous ostrichism, did not prevent the puppet armies of Mao Tse-tung from overrunning China, and their dependence on a foreign power was no secret to anyone except American intellectuals.

2. *Loyalty and security in the State Department.* Bundy unconscionably passes over the wealth of incriminating material amassed by the McCarran Committee, and satisfies himself on occasion after occasion with relying upon such categorical (and palpably false) pronouncements of Acheson

as that "there are no disloyal men in the State Department," or words to that effect. An example of Bundy's Tydings-like technique: The *Far Eastern Survey* (an official publication of the Institute of Pacific Relations) did not toe the Communist Party line, as Alfred Kohlberg insisted in 1944 that it did. For proof of it, see the fact that the IPR voted in 1947 by 1,163 to 66 that it did not!

3. *The firing of General MacArthur.* This controversy is treated with appalling legerdemain. MacArthur's analyses and recommendations (with which this writer does not happen to agree) are oversimplified to the point of travesty.

There are other examples of the lengths to which Bundy has had to go to make a case for Mr. Acheson. Since even the most contrived presentation and the most artful rhetorical flourishes are inadequate to sidestep the conclusion we must draw about our foreign policy in the light of our situation today as opposed to our situation six years ago, much of Bundy's case rests on the premise that, things being as they are, we are better off than we would have been without Acheson. We are certainly better off than we would have been had we, let us say, invited Andrei Gromyko to superintend our foreign policy. For this, I suppose, we should be in some measure grateful to Mr. Acheson as also to Mr. Bundy for bringing it to mind. But some of us don't feel that one-step-above-pro-Communism is good enough; and for that reason we ask, again and insistently, why it is that, since our product, freedom, is supposed to be more marketable than the Soviet Union's, and why, since we started off in undisputed control of all the elements necessary to successful salesmanship, the people of the world are buying slavery? If it is true that we are as well off as we could be in the circumstances, then it must be true that malicious little gremlins, infatuated with Marxism, are in the saddle, capriciously manipulating our destiny.

Mr. Bundy has done a man's job in the defense of his idol. Unfortunately, a man's job is not enough to assuage the feelings of a people who after four years of bloody sacrifices were allowed only a short respite before being called upon anew to subsidize the fateful errors of our leaders. The ominous importance of this dull, misleading, improvised book is found not in what it says, but in what it symbolizes, for Mr. Bundy states in his preface that he will "take a chance with history and bet that Mr. Acheson will be listed fifty years from now among the best of our American Secretaries of State."

The odds, as a matter of fact, are with him. Not because he can depend upon a detached posthumous tribunal to vindicate Dean Acheson, but because he will have far more formidable future allies to take up his mantle when he puts it down. He will be able to count on an emerging American class: the domesticators of history, for whom the job of canonizing Acheson will be routine—to be squeezed in somewhere between exalting Franklin Roosevelt and Harry Truman.

—*The Freeman*, March 10, 1952

A Dilemma of Conservatives

America's beleaguered conservatives have kept so busy surviving that they have paid scant attention to an enormous fissure in their ranks. To date, rather than fight their way out of the dilemma, they have simply ignored it; thus when the time comes (as it so frequently does these days) to make common cause via manifestos and resolutions, they lean on murky and generalized language: anything to avoid a direct—and therefore divisive—answer to the question: What are we going to do about the Soviet Union?

All conservatives are anti-Marxists—by definition. In consequence, American conservatives spontaneously unite against Communism, here and abroad. They support movements calculated to uproot, expose, and incapacitate American Communists and fellow-travelers; further, they recognize that the home base of imperialistic Communism is the Soviet Union, and that we must arm against the eventuality of a direct attack upon our sovereignty by Russia and her satellites.

At this point, however, Conservative A will say vastly different things from Conservative B. The "containment" conservatives believe that while it is certainly true that the Soviet Union aspires to rule the world, it cannot possibly do so, given elementary vigilance on our part. They frequently recall what happened when the Greeks, the Romans, the Turks, and the Nazis spread their power too thin. It is axiomatic, they sometimes seem to be saying, that one nation cannot rule the world by force. So long as we will to survive, we shall survive. By maintaining an adequate military machine, conceived as retaliatory in nature, the United States can withstand and repel any direct onslaught.

And even apart from the pull of history, they continue, which teaches us that there are political laws that delimit the area that any single power can subjugate and patrol, the inexorable laws of economics are on our side. In the long term, the society that is not organized around the free marketplace cannot successfully compete with the society that is. Our gravest danger, these men say, is that by engaging in wars, by overdoing national defense, by appropriating billions for our summer allies, by debasing our currency through deficit finance and internal socialism, by surrendering our sovereignty, piecemeal, to world organizations, we are debilitating ourselves internally, and may do so to the point where we shall have dissipated our natural advantages over the police state. When this happens, we shall have lost both the will and the strength to survive. We shall then either succumb to the Soviet Union by default, or else we shall totalitarianize ourselves to a point where life in the United States would be undistinguishable from life in the Soviet Union, save possibly for an enduring folkway or two.

"It may make a difference to me whether we are ruled by Russian dictators or American dictators," a prominent editor recently told me, "but what difference would it make to my grandchildren?" These are the solemn thoughts that run through the minds of the modus-vivendi conservatives.

To which the liberation or interventionist conservatives answer substantially as follows:

Forget the plight of the enslaved peoples who are spending out their tortured lives under the Soviet yoke. And forget what a policy of containment implies in terms of the conscience of the West. Let us discuss our position only in terms of what will conduce to the well-being of the United States. It is the survival of the United States that is at stake.

The liberationist then goes on to insist that his brethren have dangerously underestimated (a) the physical strength of the Soviet Union, (b) the dedication, the cunning, and the resourcefulness of her leaders, (c) the allure of Communism for millions of people, and (d) the durability of the socialist police state.

There is no need, here, to spell out the morbid arguments advanced by these men. They are familiar to everyone. We are reminded of the dazzling military and diplomatic successes of the Communists, and of the long strides the Soviet Union is making toward technological equality, if not—at least in the field of arms—pre-eminence. They conclude, therefore, that militarily the Soviet Union poses a direct physical threat to the United States.

If so, can we come to terms? Is a modus vivendi possible? An answer to this question must be based primarily on a study of the assumptions of the

Soviet Union and those of the United States. Such a study, the liberation-ists insist, indicates not, as we sometimes hear, that we are headed toward a climax, but that we are in a period of climax which will end in decisive victory for us or for the Communists. The events of the past generation have polarized the entire world to the point where there is no third power that can preside over a modus vivendi. All political happenings, every-where in the world, bear on our power struggle with the Soviet Union. One side cannot get weaker except that the other will get, relatively, stronger. And neither side, barring capitulation in substantive matters, can adopt any measures that will appreciably abate the tensions inherent in such dia-metrically opposed views about the nature of man and society.

A representative of the liberation group recently remarked that the his-torical forces that are wagging the human mind have attained such domi-nance that even the plenipotentiaries of the day are relatively helpless. If Malenkov were to summon his ministers of state, and announce that he had decided to disband the Cominform, release all political prisoners, and conclude a genuine peace with the free world, he would be either executed or committed to an insane asylum. It is ironic that some of the conclusions to which our toughest anti-Communists are driven lean so heavily on a methodology that animates the Communist movement itself: historical determinism.

As to the effect that a program of militant action, aimed at the destruc-tion of the Soviets, would have on freedom in this country, the liberation conservative has no smooth words to disguise the fact that only the State can direct a war, or execute a foreign policy. To some extent, then, any totalitarian and imperialistic power that grows to the point where it must be reckoned with by free countries wins at least a partial victory. For to beat the Soviet Union we must, to an extent, imitate the Soviet Union. We must, for example, conscript an army of sorts, and conscription entails the supreme denial of individual freedom. We must tax the people to support that army, and to support the bureaucracy without which, alas, a nation cannot mobilize.

But, they maintain, there is in the long run less danger involved in mobilizing with a view to achieving a certain objective as fast as feasible than in adapting ourselves to a perpetual state of mobilization of the kind we would need to have if we were to aim at an uneasy modus vivendi. For if we are to think in terms of a more or less permanent three-million-man armed force, and of 25 or 30 percent of our income paid over to the govern-ment to sustain it, we must think in terms of institutionalizing native des-potism. The mere fact that two generations have grown up and got used to the Sixteenth Amendment itself points to the difficulties in repealing it. Two generations of conscription would almost surely lead to universal and perpetual military training. And two generations of steeply progressive and exhaustive taxation, and of a mammoth bureaucracy, would mean that readjustment to private property and limited government would be nothing short of revolutionary.

It is a pity that yet one more difference will divide the waning conservative movement in the United States. But the issue is there, and ultimately it will separate us.

—*The Freeman*, August 1954

Who Says They Didn't Die in Vain?

Buried almost out of sight on election day last week was the answer suggested by Senator William Knowland to the Soviet Union's massacre of Hungary. Senator Knowland called for: (1) A worldwide condemnation of the Soviet Union as an aggressor. (2) The expulsion of the Soviet Union from the United Nations. (3) The application of economic sanctions against the Soviet Union and its allies. (4) Withdrawal of diplomatic recognition of the Soviet Union. And 5) the organization of an international, volunteer military "crusade for freedom," dedicated to driving the troops of the Soviet Union from Hungary.

Senator Knowland's was one voice, but it sang out above the American political chorus that met this most grievous affront on humanity with extensive and wordy requiems, and nothing, literally nothing, more. Is Senator Knowland the only man in American politics who grasps the fact that the Communist mind is not reached by appeals to reason, or his heart touched by appeals to compassion; that even a lead editorial in the *New York Times* will not deter the Soviet Union from its absorbing preoccupation with stamping out freedom wherever in the world it presumes to exist? Tens of thousands of Hungarian martyrs have died in vain, it appears, for in the Western mind, and in the Western stomach, there is not the resolution or the will to resist; over their graves, there is nothing being pledged but parliamentary expressions of distaste; as to deeds, there are none. There is only submission.

The editors of *National Review* wish a national moratorium could be declared on verbal and written criticism of Communism and Communists. We wish that every politician, every orator, every editorial writer, every preacher would, one morning, stop deploring any act of the Soviet Union, or aspect of Communism. In the sudden stillness, we would realize how empty has been our "opposition" to Communism, for in that stillness we would hear, in dreadful clarity, only the bustling wheels of normalcy, and know the absence of any meaningful act of resistance; and, without the solace of our rhetoric, we might be ashamed.

—*National Review,* November 17, 1956

Mr. K's Manners—and Ours

It is *not* wise to shrug a shoulder and say, Oh well, Khrushchev is off on one of those bellicose tantrums, and there is nothing much to do about it but wait till he gets over it. Last week Khrushchev called the president of the United States an imbecile, and said of the man who will very likely be the next president of the United States that "demagoguery, adventurism, and madness have never been so completely represented in one man as in Richard Nixon." Chancellor Adenauer is "a lunatic," who should be "taken away by guards" to a sanatorium.

The president's response has been characteristically irenic. A few others, in his behalf, have given the American people a little emotional satisfaction. Senator Keating volunteered the insight that "Khrushchev is the King Kong of international politics"; the editorial writers have dutifully reproached Mr. Khrushchev for his extravagances—and: the essential relationships remain unchanged. For we are all supposed to be quite accustomed to the debauching of norms, diplomatic, political, and philosophical, a precondition of Life with the Soviet Union.

We read recently that in his memoirs Colonel Rudolf Hoess, the brute extraordinary who commanded the concentration camp at Auschwitz, wrote quite calmly about the atrocities he oversaw. So easy is it, apparently, to get caught up in his singsong that before long it becomes almost necessary to remind oneself, every time one turns the page, that gas ovens are *not* for Jews to burn in. By the same token, one needs to remind oneself daily that the president of the United States is *not* for Khrushchev to abuse—in terms more vulgar, more wrenching, more debasing than any used throughout history between heads of state. But we cease to remind ourselves of this, and thereby we ourselves contribute to the evanescence of the norms. The results are evident. It is inconceivable, but for the license we have given Soviet leaders to set an example, that a swaggering Cuban caudillo should resort to the rhetoric of total abuse that Castro has been directing at our great country and its magistrates.

National Review gave warning last September when, caught up in sentimentalisms of liberal diplomacy, the president invited Khrushchev to this country. We warned that it would be difficult in the months to come, when Khrushchev raised his mask again to show his native face, as it was inevitable that he should, to re-evoke a proper civilized response to such a man. Having once, knowing what we did about him, regaled him all over the land, we could not ever again recapture the innocence with which, for so many years, we affirmed implicitly our judgment on the leader of the Communist world: Unfit to be a guest in America.

Now we are at a loss to find a vocabulary suitable to express our resentment at Cuba's inviting Khrushchev for a state visit. If the United States can do it, as an opponent of the Soviet Union, why not Cuba, as a friend? That is the logic of the Cuban man in the street, and it is not easy for us to cope with it. We have, in a word, by dropping the norms in the cause of coexistence, cast ourselves out to sea without a lifeline. We are publicly committed to the notions (a) that Khrushchev wants peace; (b) that bargaining with Khrushchev is defensible, even imperative diplomacy; (c) that Khrushchev should get out of his Kremlin and visit the nations of the world, as a mellowing experience; (d) that Khrushchev's desire to disarm is, notwithstanding the routine rodomontade, quite serious, and that therefore our meetings in Geneva and in the United Nations are profitable. And then, within the space of two weeks, it becomes (a) necessary for the president of the United States to call Khrushchev a liar, as Mr. Eisenhower did in denying that he had at Camp David expressed concern at the prospect of a united Germany; (b) evident by the turnabout at Geneva that twenty months of painful negotiation were absolutely without meaning; and (c) necessary to stand by impotently while Khrushchev makes plans to visit his new little colony in the Caribbean.

But, thank God, the norms are still there, if we will only search them out, and be brave enough to confess that our failure to observe them was aberrational; and affirm that we have learned our lesson. As evidence of our new realism, we should answer this latest onslaught of degrading and deliberately insulting barbarism by (a) recalling our ambassadors from the

slave states; (b) suspending diplomatic relationships and all current negotiations with the enemy; (c) ending the program of cultural exchange; (d)
halting the trade-expansion program; and (e) announcing, looking south,
that the United States will impose an immediate diplomatic and economic
boycott on any country in this hemisphere that permits Khrushchev to set
foot on its soil.

—*National Review*, June 18, 1960

"I Got My Job through the *New York Times*"

It is very much as in the early months of 1950, when, having chased the
last remnants of the opposition off the mainland, Mao Tse-tung, wild with
ideological lust, surveyed his kingdom, and threw himself into the job of
Communizing his people. He chopped off many more heads than Fidel
Castro has had so far to do in Cuba, and there are no doubt differences
between Mao and Fidel, as there are between China and Cuba; but then
as now, as the public slowly awoke to the meaning of what had happened,
the apologists for the revolutionary forces began to retreat in increasing
horror from their sometime enthusiasm. Those who had told us again and
again that the Red Chinese were primarily agrarian reformers began to
fade away, only to reappear, many of them, before congressional committees, which asked them the same questions they are now beginning to ask
the propagandists for Castro, questions to which we desperately need the
answers, now as then: *Who betrayed China? Who betrayed Cuba? Who—in
the process—betrayed the United States?*

There is no longer any defensible defense of the regime of Mao Tse-
tung. But here and there, there are pockets of loyalty to Castro. There is
a Fair Play for Cuba Committee, which may or may not be dominated by
fellow-travelers, but which certainly has among its supporters some men
who are not fellow-travelers, men whose faith in Castro is livelier, alas,
than freedom is in Cuba. The leader of pro-Castro opinion in the United
States is Herbert L. Matthews, a member of the editorial staff of the *New
York Times*. He did more than any other single man to bring Fidel Castro to
power. It could be said—with a little license—that Matthews was to Castro
what Owen Lattimore was to Red China, and that the *New York Times* was

Matthews's Institute of Pacific Relations: stressing this important difference, that no one has publicly developed against Matthews anything like
the evidence subsequently turned up against Lattimore tending to show,
in the words of a Senate investigating committee, that Lattimore was "a
conscious, articulate instrument of the Soviet conspiracy."

~

Herbert Matthews met Castro in February of 1957. To make contact with
him—as he tells the story—he had to get in touch with the Fidelista underground in Havana; drive all one night, five hundred miles across the length
of the island, using his wife as cover; and ride a jeep through tortuous dirt-
road detours to avoid the patrols and roadblocks that an angry Fulgencio
Batista had posted all about the Sierra Maestra mountains in the eastern
tip of the island, to try to break the back of the little resistance group that
two months earlier had landed, eighty-two strong, in Oriente Province in a
diesel cutter from Mexico, pledged to "liberate" Cuba or perish.

Matthews climbed up muddy slopes, swam across an icy river, ducked
behind trees, ate soda crackers, and slept on the ground: and then, in the
early morning hours, Fidel Castro came. In whispers, he talked for three
hours about his plans for Cuba.

To put it mildly, Matthews was overwhelmed. From that moment on he
appears to have lost all critical judgment. He became—always consistent
with being a writer for the *New York Times*, which imposes certain inhibitions—the number-one unbearded enthusiast for Fidel Castro.

Castro, he told the world in a series of three articles that made journalistic and indeed international history, is a big, brave, strong, relentless,
dedicated, tough idealist. His unswerving aim is to bring to Cuba "liberty, democracy, and social justice." There is seething discontent with the
dictator Batista, corrupt and degenerate after nearly twenty-five years of
exercising power; hated by most Cubans for having installed himself as
president by military coup in March of 1952, after a period of excile in
the United States; become, now, a terrorist and a torturer. Fidel Castro is
the "flaming symbol" of resistance. The fires of social justice that drive
Castro on, that cause him to bear incredible hardships, playing against
impossible odds, with the single end in mind of bringing freedom to his
people—these are fires that warm the hearthsides of freedom and decency
all over the land: and they will prevail. . . .

Is Castro's movement touched by Communism? Matthews dismissed
the rhetorical question with scorn. Castro's movement "is democratic,

therefore anti-Communist." And, flatly, "*There is no Communism to speak of in Fidel Castro's 26th of July Movement.*"

The impact of these articles was subsequently recognized even by the *New York Times* itself, normally bashful about celebrating its achievements. When, almost two years later, Batista fell, the *Times* permitted itself to record jubilantly: "When a correspondent of *The New York Times* returned from Señor Castro's hideout [from that point on, by the way, Señor Castro was elevated by the *Times* to "Dr." Castro] . . . the rebel leader attained a new level of importance on the Cuban scene. Nor was the embarrassed government ever able to diminish Fidel Castro's repute again."

~

Foreign correspondents have been very much mistaken before. Foreign correspondents who work for the *New York Times* are no exception, as anyone knows who will attempt to reconcile Soviet history and accounts of the same filed over the years by, e.g., Walter Duranty and Harrison Salisbury; who will, in a word, attempt the impossible. It is bad enough that Herbert Matthews was hypnotized by Fidel Castro, but it was a calamity that Matthews succeeded in hypnotizing so many other people in crucial positions of power on the subject of Castro. "When I was Ambassador to Cuba," Mr. Earl E. T. Smith complained to the Senate Subcommittee on Internal Security last August, "I . . . sometimes made the remark in my own Embassy that Mr. Matthews was more familiar with State Department thinking regarding Cuba than I was."

As ambassador assigned to Havana in June of 1957, Mr. Smith had been the representative of the United States government in Cuba during the seventeen crucial months that brought Castro to power, and he used just that word: Matthews's articles on Castro, he told the senators, had "hypnotized" the State Department. Even as early as the summer of 1957, when Smith took over the ambassadorship from Arthur Gardner, the influence of Matthews was established—only a few months after the interview with Castro in his hideout. Ambassador Gardner had met with stony resistance every time he attempted to pass on to his superiors the information he had about the nature of the Castro movement, which he was convinced—correctly, it proved—was shot through with Marxism. Gardner made himself such a nuisance that he was replaced; and his successor was instructed by Mr. William Wieland of the State Department, in charge of the Caribbean desk, to cap his month's briefing on the Cuban situation by consulting

Herbert L. Matthews. Matthews told Smith that Batista was in all probability through. Castro, he said, was the man to back.

Smith went to Havana determined to do what he could, within the
limits of propriety, to ease Batista out of the way. Batista pledged to hold
elections in November 1958 and turn the presidency over to his successor
in March 1959. The question in Smith's mind was whether he would last
that long. Within two months after arriving in Cuba, Mr. Smith sincerely
hoped he would; for he became convinced, he told the Senate committee,
that the principal danger to the United States lay not in the survival of
Batista for a year or so, but in the rise to power of Fidel Castro, who was
almost certainly a revolutionary Marxist. Abundant evidence was available
that he had made "Marxist statements" in Costa Rica, in Mexico, and in
Colombia; and that, dating back to his college days, he had been a revolu-
tionist and a terrorist. Smith had even heard—and had passed the report
along—that while in Colombia, Castro had had a hand in the assassination
of two nuns and a priest.

But even if Castro wasn't then pro-Communist, Smith said, his closest
associates were, and this was positively documented with respect to his
brother Raúl (now head of Cuba's armed forces) and Ernesto "Che" Gue-
vara (boss of the Cuban economy).

But the ambassador's warnings were to no avail. During the succeeding
seventeen months, Herbert Matthews continued to write glowing accounts
of the Robin Hood of the Sierra Maestra, predicting the downfall of Batista
and the ascendancy of the 26th of July Movement. Others got into the
act. The influential Foreign Policy Association's *Bulletin* for April 1, 1957,
carried an article by Matthews on Cuba, followed by a list of "Reading
Suggestions" prepared by the editors. Among them: "The best source of
contemporary information of a general nature is probably the files of *The
New York Times*, which published three uncensored articles on Cuba by
Herbert Matthews on Feb. 24, 25, 26, 1957." The State Department went
along. "Herbert Matthews . . . is the leading Latin American editorial writer
for *The New York Times*." "Obviously," said Ambassador Smith, "the State
Department would like to have the support of *The New York Times*."

"*Each month the situation deteriorates*," Matthews exulted on June 16,
1957, a theme he elaborated in further dispatches in the succeeding months.
Looking back at these reports one can only say: How right Mr. Matthews was.
Batista *was* losing, and Castro *was* gaining. But reporter Matthews neglected
to give all the reasons why, just as he consistently neglected to report on the
lurid background of Fidel Castro and some of his associates. The increasing
helplessness of Batista was the result primarily of the crystallization of U.S.

support for Castro. During those months a fascinating dialectic went on. Matthews would write that American prestige was sinking in Cuba—on account of the aid the United States government was giving to Batista. Our ambassador in Havana meanwhile complained and complained to the State Department of the demoralization of the Batista government—on account of our failure to provide Batista with the aid to which, under the terms of a series of agreements, we were bound by law and precedent to give him so long as we continued to recognize his government.

Matthews's forces proved much stronger than our ambassador's. An important segment of the press, influential members of Congress, and the Castro apparatus in Washington and New York hammered away at the State Department, urging it to desert Batista. At first the department stalled. When Castro kidnapped forty-seven American servicemen in June 1958, the U.S. government eagerly seized on the opportunity to hold up the shipment of fifteen training planes that Batista was lawfully importing. "In accordance with instructions from the State Department," Smith testified, "I informed Batista that delivery would be suspended, because we feared some harm might come to the kidnapped Americans." Having yielded to blackmail, the U.S. government then continued to refuse to deliver the airplanes—even after Castro had been prevailed upon to turn the soldiers free. Batista's forces were becoming seriously demoralized by the growing aloofness of the U.S. government, even while Castro was getting, the ex-ambassador went on to say, illicitly exported shipments of arms "almost every night" from his friends in the United States. By November it was clear that Batista's days were numbered. On December 17, Ambassador Smith received orders from the State Department to advise Batista that he could no longer exercise power, not even pending the institution of the new president a few months later—whom the United States would not back in any case, since he had been fraudulently elected and didn't have the support of the Cuban people. Two weeks later, Batista fled.

The next morning, on the first day of the new year, 1959, Mr. Roy Rubottom, assistant secretary of state for inter-American affairs, announced that there was "no evidence" that "Castro is under Communist influence." Clearly he had paid no attention to his own ambassador to Cuba. As clearly, he read the *New York Times*.

~

During the 1960 campaign, both Mr. Kennedy and Mr. Nixon expended a considerable amount of rhetoric on the subject of Cuba. For they knew that the birth, right up against the Florida peninsula, of what is now officially classified by the government (under the terms of the Dirksen-Douglas amendment to the Mutual Security Act) as "Communist" territory is a development that has deeply disturbed the American people. They want to know who, or what, was the Frankenstein who created the monster.

Mr. Kennedy blasted Mr. Nixon on the grounds that Castro and Castroism had come about as a reaction against America's tolerance of right-wing dictators—a familiar line, advanced by those who sincerely feel it is an American obligation to purify internal Latin American politics. But Mr. Kennedy was not convincing to those who remembered that in May, shortly before his nomination, he had said publicly that in two respects he backed completely the foreign policy of Mr. Eisenhower, "one of these being Cuba."

Mr. Nixon, on the other hand, pointed proudly to the disappearance of a half-dozen military dictators during the Eisenhower years. He seemed to be suggesting that although the president continued officially to beam at the leader of every nation we formally recognized—as protocol dictated—actually, if you looked closely, you would observe that he was bouncing up and down on a great bellows, which blew upon, and toppled one by one, the first rank of Latin American badmen. Beyond that Mr. Nixon did not go. He did not express a detailed curiosity about the loss of Cuba to Fidel Castro. Indeed, both candidates gave the impression that, like the State Department, *obviously* they wanted to stay on the right side of the *New York Times*. But the candidates whetted the public interest, and it is likely that the Senate Internal Security Subcommittee will pursue its investigation into the strange hold of Herbert Matthews, and the Matthews doctrine, on the men who make our foreign policy.

∼

What will they learn about Mr. Matthews himself? That he is a scholarly, subtle man who makes and continues to make supercolossal mistakes in judgment, but whose loyalty to his misjudgments renders him a stubborn propagandist and an easy mark for ideologues on the make. So well known is he as doyen of utopian activists that when in June of 1959 a Nicaraguan rebel launched a revolt, he wired the news of it direct to Herbert Matthews at the *New York Times*—much as, a few years ago, a debutante on the make might have wired the news of her engagement to Walter Winchell. Matthews was once, to use his own phrase, an "enthusiastic admirer of Fascism." He turned away from fascism while in Spain covering the civil war, where he took up the cause of the Popular Front with the same ferocious partisanship that earlier he had shown for Mussolini's Italy, and later he was to show for Castro's Cuba. His Spanish passion is not yet expended. Mr. Matthews wrote a book in 1957 recommitting himself to the Good Guys/Bad Guys reading of a war fought by democrats and Communists against traditionalists and fascists. Always he writes with considerable sweep, and he loves to prophesy. His two most striking predictions of 1944 were that the "Franco regime is tottering" and that the disbanding of Russia's Comintern the year before was "the final indication that the Russia of 1943 and 1944 does not care to support revolutionary movements to bring about Communist states in other countries."

He has not proved over the years to be an astute judge of how to deal with Russia. "All they [the Russians] want is security," he wrote in *Collier's* in 1945. "By refusing to share the secret of the atomic bomb we are fostering Russian suspicions. . . . One can understand how they feel about our recognition of Franco, our seizure of Pacific bases, our exclusive policy in Japan, our Red-baiting press, and our America-firsters. We have set up a vicious circle of mutual distrust and fear." And he is not an enthusiast for the free-enterprise system, preferring the doctrinaire socialism of postwar Britain: ". . . while Britain slowly struggles toward economic order, sanity, and strength," he wrote in 1946, "the British experiment will be an example [for the U.S.] to follow."

The payoff came when. on July 15, 1959, Herbert Matthews wrote a front-page dispatch from Havana insisting that Castro was neither a Communist, nor "under Communist influence," nor even a dupe of Communism. Moreover, he added, there are "no Communists in positions of control." Indeed, Castro continued to be "decidedly anti-Communist." That dispatch was so brazen a contradiction of the facts that the *Times* reluctantly pulled him away from Cuba, as one might pull a man away from marijuana. Since then, he has not had one by-lined story on Cuba.

That is almost two years ago. Since then, he has continued to affirm his belief in the purity of the 26th of July Movement—but mostly in the arcane journals of the specialists (e.g., the *Hispanic American Report*), and in lectures before important audiences. The fault, he says, is ours, for antagonizing Castro and "forcing him" to take his present hard line. One might as well argue that the Jews, by protesting the confiscation of their property and the insults heaped upon them, *forced* Hitler into genocide. And in any case, Mr. Matthews's analysis never accounted for the compulsiveness with which Cuba turned to Communism, beginning almost immediately after Castro took power.

Now and then Mr. Matthews invites attention to the fact that everyone, *save himself,* is out of step. "In my thirty years on *The New York Times*," he told the American Society of Newspapermen last April, "I have never seen a big story so misunderstood, so badly handled, and so misrepresented as the Cuban Revolution." Those words are, as a matter of fact, exactly true: and the fault was that of the *New York Times.*

The Senate subcommittee may want to know more about Matthews, and may want especially to know whether the Senate is to expect to have the honor of ratifying his appointment as Consultant Extraordinary to the State Department. Certainly it will want to examine the major premises of Matthews's position on Cuba. For it is a position that extends beyond the question of Castro, and one that is shared by many Americans, some of whom are influential with the new president. That position holds, in effect, that the United States *should* interfere, adroitly to be sure, in the internal affairs of nondemocratic Latin American nations. Matthews urged exactly that in the summer of 1958, by proposing that the United States arbitrate the differences between Batista and Castro. To have done such a thing would have been a clear reversal of United States policy—though we might rather have done that than what we did: namely, pull the rug out from under Batista, and turn the entire country over to Castro.

Another article in the Matthews position is that democracy and only democracy distinguishes the good society. Granted, he is perfectly satisfied with the kind of "democracy" that is practiced in Mexico, where everyone votes, and one party always wins; but it bears discussion whether "democracy" is the first objective of American foreign policy in Latin America, or whether it is subsidiary to other concerns, including our own national interest, and, for the Latin Americans, internal stability, economic viability, and nonpolitical freedoms. (Probably the highest per capita incidence of violent deaths in any country this side of the Soviet Union has been in chaotic Colombia, a "democracy.")

Another question is whether the United States can continue, in all good conscience, to encourage Americans to invest in Latin America. Our investments there are over $7 billion—making American capital the largest single job creator in Latin America. But the Matthews position on foreign investment consists, as far as one can make out, in encouraging (a) American investment in general, and (b) those governments that seize, nationalize, or tax to death that investment in particular. He has not, at least in any of his conspicuous writings, deplored Cuba's blithe confiscation of $800 million of American property. Symbolically, the new Kennedy administration must answer the question why, the more offensive Fidel Castro seemed to this country, the madder we got at General Trujillo.

—*The American Legion Magazine*, March 1961

An Answer on Berlin

The Kennedy team should constantly be making clear that the present arrangements in Berlin are by no means ideal, and that we are quite prepared to talk about modifying them, provided it is understood that no modification will be made unilaterally. This precisely is the time when a vigorous international horsetrader, taking advantage of the looseness of the situation caused by Mr. Khrushchev's insistence on changing the status of Berlin, would mount a vigorous campaign calling for the incorporation of all Berlin into a single city administered by an all-German government, Adenauer's or Ulbricht's, according as the people of Berlin voted at a special election. Or, if deeper waters yet are to be disturbed, why not seize the opportunity to call for the integration of all of Germany on the same basis?

These are not goals one could expect to accomplish, but they dispose the scenery in such a way as to permit us to maneuver. The best way to keep Berlin free is to discuss liberating East Germany. The best way to keep Red China out of the United Nations is to discuss whether or not the Polish government should be thrown out. The wars we fight are largely the wars of diplomatic maneuver, and it is dismaying under the circumstances that we should be so clubfooted as to refuse, in the high purpose of national security and freedom for our allies, to dance. What's the matter with us, are we 4-F?

Why shouldn't the United States call upon the United Nations to take up the matter of Berlin as a threat to international peace? And having got the General Assembly together, why shouldn't Kennedy and his team go to work on the delegates—as diligently as if they were delegates at a Democratic convention—clubbing them with their own clichés about democracy and self-rule, and force a vote (it could be done) calling for free elections? The Soviet Union would rant, and Khrushchev's cries would reverberate throughout the history of outrage; and (at the very least) West Berlin would stay free. If it is postulated that Khrushchev will not be deterred by any psychological force whatever, why then we are no longer talking about diplomacy, but about a general war. We must be ready to fight such a war, but we must not let any means go by which can secure us our goals and give us peace besides.

—*National Review,* July 15, 1961

Dead-Red

Many arguments are nowadays posed, and opinions influenced, by gaudy references to the extent of the devastation that would ensue upon a thermonuclear exchange in a third world war. I have heard lecturer after lecturer describe in macrocosmic terms, almost as if they took pleasure in depicting all that gore, the meaning for the United States of a thermonuclear attack on us by, say, one hundred ten-megaton Soviet missiles. I can hear the words of a man who spoke last week: ". . . at least a hundred million dead . . . starvation and contamination for most of the rest of the population . . . reduction of our economy to a primitive level . . ." I shall spare you more, especially the description of the physical appearance of an incinerated child in Hiroshima. There are few things more gruesome.

Still I ask: what actually is the relevance of all that talk?—which is used primarily by pacifists and collaborators and those who plead for disarmament at any price. We know the meaning of violent death intuitively, do we not? Even so we are committed, as individuals, as a nation, and as a civilization, to the proposition that death is the price one must be *prepared* to pay to oppose certain kinds of threats. Granted, if there were a war today, there would be more deaths—far more deaths—than were caused by yesterday's war. But what is the meaning of that statistic to the individual dead man? None—he knows not whether he died alone, or in company with a hundred million others. What is the meaning of it for the survivor? None that goes beyond that abysmal grief of personal loss, experienced well before the nuclear age by, for instance, the frontiersman's wife whose husband and children were massacred by the Indians. An individual human being can sustain only so much grief, and then bereavement becomes redundant. If my wife, son, mother, brothers, and sisters are killed, I have little capacity left to grieve over the loss of my college roommate's uncle. What, then, is the meaning of that statistic for civilization? Civilization has no feelings, and knows not pain: It is we, the dead and the survivors, who feel the loss or advancement of civilization. And here we come to the nub of the question.

What we are asked by those who devote their energies to describing the effects of nuclear war to consider, then, when you analyze it, is less human suffering than the loss to humankind of so many of those things that lived on and on even when generation after generation of human beings died: the intangible things—the sense of community, and of nationhood—and the tangible things—the cathedral at Chartres, the museum at the Prado, the White House, the Vatican, the Bodleian Library. It is, I think, more the sense of these losses than the concern for human life that hard analysis discovers lying beneath the unreasoned hysteria of many of our contemporaries: and indeed, when we contemplate shattering, say, the stained-glass windows of Chartres, we know that unlike the extinction of human life, we are contemplating extinguishing something which, because it was not afflicted with mortality, might otherwise have gone on and on, to refresh and console the people, right through empires risen and fallen, barbarians repulsed or submitted to, the appearance and disappearance of the 100th French Republic.

And yet that is a pagan's analysis. Because human life, even though it cannot last beyond a few score years, is more valuable than all the perdurable treasures of the earth. It is necessary, when we listen to a Norman Cousins or a Steve Allen or a Sidney Lens or a Bertrand Russell or a Kenneth Tynan going on and on about the horrors and scale of nuclear death, to force ourselves to face explicitly what we know intuitively. And that is this: that if it is right that a single man is prepared to die for a just cause, it is right that an entire civilization be prepared to die for a just cause. In contemporary terms it can scarcely be disputed that if ever a cause was just, this one is, for the enemy combines the ruthlessness and savagery of Genghis Khan with the fiendish scientific efficiency of an IBM machine. As we have seen, the collective bereavement is not more than the sum of individual bereavements and cannot therefore, in human terms, outweigh in quality or in intensity the pain that has always been felt, throughout the history of the world, by individuals who did not place mere survival as their highest value. It is important to plumb these arguments, so as to escape the net of those facile little clichés which reduce complex issues to disjunctive jingles. Better Dead than Red is an inaccurate statement of the American position, listing, as it does, non-exclusive alternatives. Properly stated it is: Better the *chance* of being dead than the certainty of being Red. And if we die? We die.

—November 10, 1962

Who Won in Cuba?

Somebody has dissented from the prevailing felicity. "You there, what is your name, sir?" the reporter asked the pedestrian.

"Fernando Castillas."

"Where do you live, sir?"

"Miami."

"What are your comments about the dramatic events of last week?"

"I say it was another Bay of Pigs."

Could this be possible, notwithstanding the tumult of self-congratulations? It may be harder for an American than for an exiled Cuban to adopt this point of view, yet it is my very own, and here is my reasoning.

After the fiasco of the Bay of Pigs, President Kennedy, speaking at the National Press Club, pledged that if Cuba were to arm itself with offensive weapons, the United States would move—alone, if necessary. Who in the United States—who, except of course the Left far gone in crackpottery—doubted that this was a minimal guarantee? *Obviously* we would move against a Cuba armed with atomic warheads sufficient to pulverize American cities. The great debate over the next year and a half was not over what we would do about a Cuba armed offensively, but over what we would do about a Cuban slave state that sits deep in American waters taking its day-to-day orders from a foreign power dedicated to subverting our government and every free government in Latin America?

It was generally deplored, after the Bay of Pigs landing, that the president had not taken the unique opportunity, then and there, when the Cuban air force had a mere seven airplanes, to wipe Castro off the face of the map and liberate Cuba. In the next months, before the offensive weapons were positively identified, the debate was over whether the United States could continue to tolerate a Communist Cuba: which sunders the basic unanimity of the hemisphere in its collective stand against Communism; serves as a base for hemispheric subversion, and is the bone in the throat of anti-Communists from Tierra del Fuego to Hudson's Bay. And then, two months ago, Khrushchev announced ostentatiously that he was sending war matériel to Cuba, proclaiming that the Monroe Doctrine was dead. The pressures mounted heavily on Mr. Kennedy to do something to prove the Monroe Doctrine was still alive. He resisted. He went so far as to denounce Senator Homer Capehart's desire to "send other people's sons to war" (a dishonorable piece of demagogy: Is the president implying that a senator of the United States—or a citizen of the United States, for that matter—has no right to take a position on American security policy unless he has a son in the Marines? How old is John F. Kennedy Jr.?)

Finally, the president revealed that the offensive weapons *were* there, and went immediately into action—as who could have doubted that he would? He quickly got from Khrushchev (as was easily predictable, once Khrushchev saw that Kennedy meant it) the promise of dismantlement. The reason Khrushchev acted fast was to avoid an invasion of Cuba by the United States. For if he had tarried, Kennedy, having declared the bases to be intolerable, would have had to move against them militarily: and Castro would have been deposed.

What Khrushchev cares about primarily is the Communist regime in Cuba—not the lousy missiles, which were useful as instruments of terror, but hardly of critical value to him so long as the United States maintains its power to retaliate against the Soviet Union and inflict upon it insupportable damage. What Khrushchev clearly wants is a foot in the hemispheric door, whence to pursue the Cold War by political and psychological means, which is how the Communists have been pursuing the war 95 percent of the time since 1945. He wasn't going to give up the Communist pearl of the Antilles, you could be sure. And so he jockeyed with Kennedy, and succeeded in getting from Kennedy himself "guarantees against an invasion of Cuba"!

That means, in words of one syllable, that John F. Kennedy, 35th president of the United States, has formally given our bitterest enemy a pledge that we will enforce the non-enforcement of the Monroe Doctrine: that Khrushchev is free to keep Cuba enslaved till kingdom come; and, by logical deduction, that Khrushchev has the right to enslave any other nation in Latin America, without military let or hindrance from the United States. How can it be maintained that we have won a great victory when Khrushchev is, in October, ahead of where he was in May?

—*National Review Bulletin*, November 13, 1962

A Day in Laos, and an Evening

SAIGON—Pity the poor Laotians, however depleted your reserves of pity. There aren't very many of them, just over two and one-half million; they are very very poor, earning per capita $50 per year, which the United States practically doubles with its various projects in Laos, military, economic, and social. The country is split right down the middle, with the eastern half dominated by North Vietnamese soldiers who use it as a conveyor belt to feed the war against South Vietnam. The war costs the Laotians, on a typical day, thirteen soldiers dead. Multiply that by one hundred, and you have an idea what would be a comparable loss to the United States—1,300 dead per day.

Probably Laos will survive or not depending on whether South Vietnam survives. Souvanna Phouma, the prime minister, told the visitor sadly, philosophically, that for so long as that war continues, Laos is definitely in danger, because the enemy needs the Ho Chi Minh trail, which is on Laotian territory. But if South Vietnam survives, even then it will be a struggle, because the North Vietnamese Communists are greedy, and they will continue to prey on Laos.

Yet the country breeds a rugged kind of optimism, or so it seems. The American ambassador, Mac Godley, is energetic, exuberant, determined. It isn't an easy job. For one thing there is the language problem—more generally, the problem of communication. There is a total of 7,500 copies sold per day throughout Laos of all the daily newspapers combined. Very few Laotians speak English; indeed very few Laotians read Lao (75 percent are illiterate). So that one needs to start from the very bottom, which Americans have undertaken to do, helping, for instance, to train Laotians to fly airplanes, an indispensable accomplishment for any nation that desires to protect itself.

Incredibly, there are now over fifty Laotian pilots, some of them taken right from their water buffalo, who are now flying four or five sorties per day against the enemy. It requires eighteen months to train such a pilot, who first must be taught the rudiments of English so as to be able to perform simple acts of maintenance. It was after dinner, away down in Savannakatt, across the river from Thailand, when it occurred suddenly to a young intelligence officer that we could see for ourselves.

He telephoned; yes, a Laotian crew will be going out momentarily. All very informal, not to say anarchical, and we don parachutes not because we are instructed to do so—the pilots and crew are most permissive—but because they keep us a little warmer. But since we do have them on, the pilot leans over and shouts through the noise, "If I make long bell we crash," so that we know that if we hear long bell, we are to jump out the door, count slowly to two, and pull the handle appropriately perched over the heart.

But the pilot made only short bells, after each one of which a big flare was jettisoned, itself to parachute down toward the enemy. An hour or so of this, but no firing, then suddenly, off to the southeast, more flares, and suddenly the whole side of the plane becomes a machine gun, the three parallel beams describing, at a hundred rounds per second, a golden tracery to the ground.

Four, five bursts, and the nine thousand bullets have been fired, and it is time to return to the ground, which we greet with great reverence. The Laotian pilots are matter-of-fact about it, strolling into the little room with the radio. They expect to go out again that night, maybe even twice more. The passengers would sooner retire to where the water buffalo roam.

I do not know why heroism and stamina and simple determination in a just cause are so unexciting nowadays to so many who have never had to fight for the freedoms they so often abuse; certainly who have never had to fight against such awful odds as the Laotians, whose introduction to the wonders of the modern world takes them, late at night, out into the cold, foraging through the blackness for those who are bent on taking from them the very little that they have.

But the memory is indelible, and the sadness overpowering, because the laws of nature will not be suspended, and they speak as certainly as they spoke for the young pilots who volunteered to save Britain against the falling of the night, saying, surely, that one day, though maybe not tomorrow, the men we flew with will have to make a long, an endless bell.

—December 15, 1969

Solzhenitsyn at Bay

The new volume of Aleksandr Solzhenitsyn, *The Gulag Archipelago*, raises policy questions for the West which, if we answer them wrongly, will bring down upon us that curse of history reserved for those despicable men who, though knowing everything they needed to know, declined to act, thus contributing to a crucifixion. Solzhenitsyn is only an individual, but there was never in human history a clearer identification of an individual and a class. Martin Luther King as representative of the American Negro pales alongside the authority of Aleksandr Solzhenitsyn as representative of the 200 million people of Russia who have suffered, and continue to suffer, at the hands of the creed-ridden tormentors of that wretched country.

The Soviet government does not disguise its feelings about Solzhenitsyn, any more than the establishmentarians disguised theirs toward Jesus. Now, on the publication of *The Gulag Archipelago*, they have begun their offensive. It is clearly launched with a certain tentativeness—else they'd have simply yanked him from the streets and shipped him off directly to Siberia, or to a convenient room in the cellar of the Lubyanka, there to receive a little lead in his stupefying, awe-inspiring mind.

Though Solzhenitsyn is only one man, his elimination would amount to an act of genocide. It is as if, thirty-five years ago, Adolf Hitler had released, for the convenience of the next few editions of the *World Almanac*, the projections on the diminishing percentage of Jews alive and well in Germany. Would the West, in such circumstances, do anything about it? Or would that be to interrupt the rhythm of détente?

Permit a drastic truncation—in just a few sentences—of the experience of just one Soviet victim. This one is an American citizen who, incredibly, has been living in Maryland since 1971. It required that we should learn of his existence from Aleksandr Solzhenitsyn. His name is Alexander Dolgun. He was a clerk with the American embassy. He was seized on the streets of Moscow in 1948 and would spend eight years in Soviet camps, and another fifteen years in civilian detention. A cheerful representative of the Workers' Paradise named Ryumin, second in charge of Soviet security, called in young Dolgun, who had declined to confess to crimes he had not committed.

"'And so,' said Ryumin politely, stroking his rubber truncheon which was an inch and a half thick, 'you have survived trial by sleeplessness with honor. So now we will try the club. Prisoners don't last more than two or three sessions of this. Let down your trousers and lie on the runner.'

"The colonel sat down on the prisoner's back. Dolgun had intended to count the blows. He didn't know yet what a blow with a rubber truncheon is on the sciatic nerve. The effect is not in the place where the blow is delivered—it blows up inside the head. After the first blow the victim was insane with pain and broke his nails on the carpet. Ryumin beat away. After the beating the prisoner could not walk, and of course he was not carried. They just dragged him along the floor . . . [then] Ryumin went wild, and started to beat him in the stomach and broke through the intestinal wall, in the form of an enormous hernia where his intestines protruded. And the prisoner was taken off to the Butyrka hospital with a case of peritonitis, and for the time being the attempts to compel him to commit a foul deed were broken off."

~

The reason Brezhnev et al. are so much afraid of Solzhenitsyn is that his indictment isn't of the man Stalin, or even of the man Lenin, whose atrocities figure greatly in this book. His indictment is universal: an indictment of totalitarian society. Brezhnev can no more convincingly denounce Stalin than he can denounce his own aorta. The governors of the Soviet Union cannot break with their own past without walking, unmanacled, to Red Square, to set a torch upon themselves.

This is the moment not for bureaucratic response, but for gallant response, and those of us who know Henry Kissinger pray that he will take the initiative—no one could do it better. If a hair of the head of Solzhenitsyn is harmed:

1. The United States of America will suspend all cultural exchange with the Soviet Union beginning immediately.

2. An absolute embargo, for a mourning period of one year, will be imposed on commerce of any kind with the Soviet Union, and against any purchase of goods of any kind from the Soviet Union.

~

Perhaps Solzhenitsyn requires martyrdom, fully to anneal his work to the service of humanity. Perhaps, even, he desires it. But we cannot willingly play the role of Pontius Pilate.

—January 12, 1974

Endless Talk about Cambodia

I am quite serious: Why doesn't Congress authorize the money to finance an international military force to overrun Cambodia? That force should be made up primarily of Asians—Thais, notably, but also Malaysians, Filipinos, Taiwanese, Japanese. Detachments from North Vietnam and China should be permitted, and token representatives from voluntary units of other countries that are signatories to the Genocide Convention and to the various protocols on human rights. Our inactivity in respect of Cambodia is a sin as heinous as our inactivity to save the Jews from the holocaust. Worse, actually; because we did mobilize eventually to destroy Hitler. We are doing nothing to save the Cambodians. What is happening in Cambodia mocks every speech made by every politician in the United Nations and elsewhere about our common devotion to human rights.

The idea, in Cambodia, isn't to go there and set up a democratic state. It is to go there and take power away from one, two, three, perhaps as many as a half-dozen sadistic madmen who have brought on their country the worst suffering brought on any country in this bloody century.

Father François Ponchaud, who lived in Cambodia from 1965 to 1975, estimates that 800,000 Cambodians have died since the Khmer Rouge took over two years ago. And he is thought to be inaccurate on the low side. Richard Holbrooke, our assistant secretary of state for East Asian affairs, puts the figure as high as 1.2 million.

Hundreds of thousands of these deaths were by execution. The balance was worse: death mostly by starvation. We finally mustered the judicial energy to execute Gary Gilmore last January. We could not have found one American, short possibly of Son of Sam, who would have voted to starve him to death. Others die of malaria and other diseases. The Khmer Rouge disdains to accept medical aid from the West, or food.

As for the death figures, what do they mean to those for whom human life means nothing? Mr. Stéphane Groueff, of *France Soir*, went to within a dozen kilometers of Cambodia recently and talked with hundreds of refugees. It is the deepest mystery what actually is the composition of Cambodia's evil leadership, as no correspondent has been there in two years, and the eight diplomatic legations (seven Communist, plus Egypt), are house-bound, and denied permission to speak to any Cambodians. There is speculation that the energumen running the show is the forty-six-year-old French-educated Khieu Samphan, the head of the Presidium.

When you ask the refugees who is the authority behind the Khmer Rouge, they will tell you, presumably in whispers, "Angkar." What is Khieu Samphan to Angkar? What is the role of the prime minister, Pol Pot? Or of Ieng Sari, the Hanoi intellectual whose real name is Nguyen Sao Levy? Or the Communist Party secretary general, Saloth Sar? Mr. Groueff reports that there is only one known interview with Samphan. It was given to an Italian journalist at last summer's Colombo conference.

"'In five years of war,' Khieu Samphan told him, 'more than a million Cambodians died. The present population of the country is five million. Before the war it was seven million.'

"'What happened to the other million?' the journalist asked.

Samphan was annoyed. "'It's incredible,' he said, 'the way you Westerners worry about war criminals.'"

Two out of seven Cambodians already dead. That is the equivalent of 57 million Americans killed. Even Stalin might have shrunk from genocide on such a scale. And what are we doing about it? Waiting for Rolf Hochhuth to write a play? Is there no *practical* idealism left in this world? Only that endless talk, which desecrates the language, and atrophies the soul?

—September 10, 1977

What to Do about Poland?

It is the dream of every man who dreams that one day, over the rainbow, one incident in the Soviet empire will prove to be the cordite that will bring down the House of Lenin. It is the nightmare of the slavemasters of the House of Lenin that one day, one incident in the Soviet empire will be the cordite that will bring the emancipation of the dead souls they collect so avariciously. That is the reason why a mere labor-union strike in a remote corner of Poland causes the world to hold its breath.

The chances that we have come to the end of the rainbow are infinitesimally small. Far likelier that we have come to another of those periodic tests of will, at which the Soviet Union excels even as we flounder. At the same moment when the prospective next vice president of the United States is more or less assuring the largest totalitarian nation in the world that if elected the Reagan administration will do nothing to formalize our commitment to Taiwan's freedom, the Soviet Union, through its puppet Edward Gierek, is telling the Polish strikers that if they persist in their demands for economic and political freedom, what goes by the name of the Polish border will disappear. I.e., direct control by the Soviet Union, versus indirect.

Those who think this makes little difference have not experienced that difference. Ten years ago, after a week in the Soviet Union followed by a day in Warsaw, I wrote that if you have just come from Russia, everyone in Poland sounds like Lenny Bruce. It requires a special map to find in Poland anyone who approves of the current bondage or of those in Moscow who make it so. But the Poles, as a people, are realists and know that they are better off than they would be under a more fastidious domination by the Russians, which is why the explosion of frustration at Gdansk is a possible flash point.

What to do?

The autopsists still rage against one another endeavoring to answer the question of whether United States policy was responsible for the bloodbath in Budapest in 1956. The position of the United States government is that there is nowhere traceable any official suggestion that the United States would intervene to protect a Hungary that sought to detach itself from the Soviet empire. Still, in those days there were idealists who spoke occasionally about liberation; indeed, that galvanizing word was uttered by John Foster Dulles during the 1952 campaign that ended in his installation as secretary of state. And, in 1968, the gleeful international reception given to the Prague Spring unquestionably influenced the Russians in the direction of their massive suppression—which (again, an excruciating historical symbol) coincided with the massive dissolution of our will in Southeast Asia.

What hurts is that there is always a suspicion that the Carter administration—even though its national security advisor is a Polish-American, Zbigniew Brzezinski—rather wishes the crisis had not occurred. We are wallowing about in something that (fairly or unfairly) goes by the name of the Sonnenfeldt Doctrine, and what it says, essentially, is that we must avoid destabilization. Destabilization is a fancy word for: "Don't do anything that might upset the Soviet Union, either by taking from it something it already has, or by acquiring for your own account something you didn't use to have." Protections against destabilization were written into the Helsinki Accords, which, by a juridical sleight of hand, suggested that that over which the Soviet Union has control, it shall continue to have control over. The great compensator was the provision, signed by the Soviet Union, guaranteeing all kinds of freedoms. It went by the name of Basket III and was instantly celebrated by the Soviet Union by putting into jail anyone from whose lips the word "Helsinki" was uttered.

So, again, what do we do? Well, Radio Free Europe and the Voice of America are faithfully reporting events over their facilities—but, careful, all opinions are those of other entities; nothing provocative. Mr. Carter is likely to express his deep, deep concern, especially to Polish audiences, before whom he is unlikely to recall his glowing words about the goals of Polish Communist leadership, uttered in Warsaw early in his presidency.

There is always the United Nations. It is (a) a moral mess; and (b) primarily an anti-Israeli lobby. But when last heard from, we did occupy a seat on the Security Council, and we might just bestir ourselves to call a session in order to condemn Soviet violations of Articles 18, 19, 20, 21, and 23 of the Universal Declaration of Human Rights, Principle Seven of Basket I of the Helsinki Accords, and all of Basket III. That won't do very much for the Polish heroes, but it will do something for our own self-esteem.

—August 26, 1980

Missing the Point of Grenada

There is an upwardly mobile cliché going the rounds, to wit that we should not resort to force except as the last resort.

The trouble with that doctrine, if strictly applied, is that it can lead to a call for action at a moment when the objective has become very nearly impregnable. At that point either you proceed or you do not proceed. If you do, the cost can be very great. If you do not, then you end up accepting that of which you began by assuming the unacceptability.

Consider, for instance, Cuba. It is, quite simply, the one great strategic foothold of the Soviet enterprise in this hemisphere. It is a seven-hundred-mile-long staging base for Soviet operations in Latin America. But for Cuba, there would not now be the problem of Nicaragua, let alone Grenada. So when does it become relevant to take Cuba out by force? Twenty-two years ago we made a half-hearted attempt to move, and even then it was too late. Too late for the effort we were willing to put into it. To take out Cuba today, a senior military strategist reports, "would be on the order of taking out Okinawa in World War II." Assuming, of course, no nuclear interference.

The *New York Times*, which would have argued against using force to take Bunker Hill, expresses its dismay over the rationale for moving against Cuban-dominated Grenada by saying, "What, in any case, could Cubans have done from Grenada that they cannot do better from Cuba?" Quite apart from the military fatuity of the observation ("What, in fact, can Americans do from Guantanamo that they cannot do better from Miami?" "What, in fact, can the Russians do from Afghanistan that they cannot do better from Russia?"), what is precisely left unanswered is what we are going to do about Cuba. Unanswered, because the answer is unanimously affirmed.

What we are going to do about Cuba is nothing. Why? Because we waited until a resort to force would have required too much of it; and when that happens, the will to use force has a way of atrophying.

Notice also that critics of the Grenada operation are telling us that there was no indication that our students in Grenada were going to be detained. Well, there was no indication that our embassy staff in Iran was going to be detained. Suggesting that the detention of American personnel was a step General Austin was too civilized to resort to requires us to say that the same man who shot in cold blood his predecessor and most members of his cabinet would have been too squeamish to take five hundred Americans hostage. Thanks, but most of us prefer a commander in chief who doesn't run risks of that sort. We know that there were arms enough in Grenada to equip five divisions. Those arms were presumably designed to aim at people other than the Cubans who brought them in.

Why are they so appalled when the United States makes an intelligent move on the world scene? Would you believe the Harvard law professors who cabled the White House their protest against the rescue operation on the grounds that "it seems one more incident in the history of American suppression of progressive movements"? You tell me that it is progressive to stage a military coup, imprison, torture, and execute the opposition, turn the island into an armed fortress, and I'll send you to Harvard to teach law.

If we reflect on it, it is discouraging that so many voices are raised to say the most irrelevant things. Rather like asking whether the lifeguard who rescued the drowning swimmer was correctly attired. Yes, it is true that on the whole we want the press to cover our military operations. Yes, it is true that there is a presumption against the landing of the Marines to straighten out local messes. Yes, it is true that our students were not yet hostages. But surely the salient point is that with minimum loss of life we have rescued a little island in the Caribbean from a monstrous tyranny whose script was being written in Moscow and Havana; that we obliged that island's neighbors, who were obviously targeted for subversion; and that we have the manifest gratitude not only of the American students, but also of the population of Grenada. Isn't that, really, the point?

—November 5, 1983

For Moderation in Osculation

I want to know one very simple thing. It is this: Why do non-totalitarian leaders embrace totalitarian leaders? By "embrace" I do not intend a metaphor, as in, "During the Second World War, President Roosevelt embraced Josef Stalin." I mean the real thing. I am staring now at a picture of two men smiling at each other, their arms about each other, their noses not two inches separated. Any closer and they'd have skirted sodomy. The caption reads: "A Friendly Meeting—President Fidel Castro of Cuba, right, is greeted by Prime Minister Felipe González of Spain at Madrid's airport."

We all recognize that the business of diplomacy requires interpersonal contacts, as for instance between Neville Chamberlain and Adolf Hitler in the fall of 1938. But why is it that such meetings need to communicate a personal relationship that transcends politics? Felipe González and Fidel Castro managed to look like the Smith Brothers greeting each other after receiving Nobel Prizes for their cough drops.

Now the news story reveals two interesting data. One of them is that Felipe González is something of an old friend of Castro's. Most of Castro's old friends Castro has shot or imprisoned, so that one possible motive of González's embrace was to celebrate the fact that he is an exception.

The other datum of interest is that King Juan Carlos telephoned his greetings to Castro, whose stay in Spain was for a mere four hours (he was flying back from Andropov's funeral). King Juan Carlos evidently hopes to make a state visit to Havana, one knows not why, and was evidently anxious not to be left out of the celebration of Fidel Castro's very first visit to any country in Western Europe. Always before, he has overflown Western Europe en route to Moscow and the satellites. The Reuters dispatch records, "The gesture"—the royal phone call—"was a reflection of the enthusiasm in Madrid for Mr. González's action."

Why this enthusiasm? I mean, is there any reason anyone can think of why in a country in which Francisco Franco has become a dirty word because he imprisoned a dozen people every year and exercised a light political censorship in the press, Fidel Castro should be lionized? Fidel Castro, who exercises totalitarian power, imprisons priests, is an excommunicated Catholic who tortures poets, incites revolutions, protects terrorists, husbanded Soviet thermonuclear missiles: Why does a Socialist democrat wish to embrace Castro?

You will say: Ah, but don't you see, it is a part of the Mediterranean style. You cannot, if Spanish blood runs through your veins, greet another leader without embracing him. To do otherwise would be to offend him.

And it is true that President Carter bussed President Brezhnev when they signed SALT II. And true that although Richard Nixon was a little more platonic in Peking that first night, he did approach eight or ten individual survivors of the Cultural Revolution with sheer ardor in his eyes, a toasting glass in hand. Is this necessary to effective diplomacy?

So far as one can remember, if this is so, it is something new. There are no pictures easily recalled of President Roosevelt smooching with Josef Stalin. FDR did give Stalin a few countries, as souvenirs of their meetings, but he drew the line at a public embrace. Neville Chamberlain did not embrace Hitler (ugh!).

Why did Austria's Bruno Kreisky feel the need to embrace Yasser Arafat? And anyway, in our heart of hearts, don't we know perfectly well that there isn't a leader in the world who would kiss the prime minister of South Africa—unless he were black? We know this intuitively, and our knowing it intuitively makes all the more mischievous the promiscuous bussing against which I rail.

Because, you see, if we acknowledge that there are some people one simply will not embrace publicly, then one acknowledges that there are moral criteria that govern these matters. And then one asks, What moral criteria are drawn so loosely that Fidel Castro should not fall within their proscriptive range? What is the use of having any criteria, if Brezhnev is not excluded by them? If the Boston Strangler is a member of the club, what is the use in having an admissions committee?

Accordingly, herewith a proposal to be incorporated in the Republican platform: "No American president should embrace any world leader responsible for the death and/or torture and/or imprisonment of more than 0.01 percent of his people." For short, it can be called the Osculation Clause.

—February 16, 1984

What if They Were Nazis?

My colleague the syndicated columnist Joseph Sobran remarked, apropos of the whole Bitburg business, "What if Daniel Ortega and his Sandinistas were Nazis?"

It is a riveting observation. It informs us deeply about the moral scramble of our time, in which, as we struggle to remember how hideous was Hitler, we struggle equally to forget how hideous is Communism.

Consider, for instance, the calm revelations of the past few years concerning the Cultural Revolution in Mao's China.

When eighty top journalists went into Shanghai in 1972 with President Nixon, there was something on the order of elation: Here, finally, we all were. In the Middle Kingdom. Mao Tse-tung was a hero. True, he was a tough man, but you needed a tough man to create Mao men. En route to China we all read the glowing accounts of Mao's accomplishments, written by Ross Terrill of Harvard and published in *The Atlantic Monthly*. Theodore White, the distinguished American journalist and Sinologist who was an early enthusiast for Mao, nowadays shakes his head and says, "We did not recognize just how bad it was." Yes, it was that bad. Brutal killings, torture, categorical imprisonments of everyone associated with the old Communist Party, a despoliation of college life, burned books, anti-intellectualism rife.

All the details are painstakingly collected in the meticulous, resourceful book by Fox Butterfield of the *New York Times, China: Alive in the Bitter Sea.*

We welcome, of course, the regime of Deng Xiao-ping, who has studiedly attempted to institute reforms, economic and political: without, however, altering the totalitarian nature of life in China. But there is no sense of horror, detectable among Americans who visit there, either at what happened in China under the banner of Deng's old boss and mentor Mao Tse-tung, or of Deng's other boss, Chou En-lai. We treat it as, merely, an unpleasant episode, on which we do not choose to dwell. It is inconceivable that any American traveling in China would exhibit moral hesitation at fraternizing with surviving members of the Old Guard, those who had a hand in implementing the Bolshevik Revolution. All but inconceivable that any American staying at home would loudly protest such fraternization as a betrayal of the victims of the regime of Mao Tse-tung, the Great Helmsman.

But all this is also true, though perhaps a little less so, of the Soviet Union, is it not? Two rulers back, less than two years ago, the head of the Soviet Union had been the counterpart of Himmler in Nazi Germany. But about Mr. Andropov we were all tacitly urged to speak in civil accents, and of course there was considerable dismay when President Reagan elected not to attend his funeral, although he did drop by the Soviet embassy to write his signature into the official book of condolences.

How come this disparity in how we feel about evil regimes indistinguishable from one another?

Probably the difference is not much more complicated than that the Soviet Union has The Bomb. If the Soviet Union so elected, there would be a world war, conceivably the terminal experience of the planet Earth.

Well now, suppose that Hitler had got himself a bomb, which as a matter of fact he came very close to doing. Imagine that that bomb had exploded over Liverpool in the early spring of 1945: exit Liverpool and, by the way, four little baby Beatles. Suppose Hitler had then said that the next bomb would fall on London, and the third on Paris, unless we came to terms with him. What would have happened? Yes, precisely that. Just as Japan reacted to Hiroshima, so would London have reacted to Liverpool.

So Hitler lived on—in 1945 he was only 56 years old. Say that he lived on to approximately the same age as Churchill, and Mao, and Adenauer, dying a natural death in 1975. There were 300,000 Jews left in the concentration camps when Hitler's bomb ended World War II, so he polished them off, and of course continued to torture and kill and otherwise persecute any dissidents, even as Stalin did. But before he died, he had amassed in Germany the equivalent of the nuclear throw-weight amassed by the Soviet Union. Wouldn't our diplomats be attending anniversaries of Hitler's rise to power, even as they attend, in Moscow, anniversaries of the October Revolution?

One fears that that is the case. That considerations of self-concern govern our moral attitudes. Evidently we need to defeat a totalitarian power before we can settle down to despising it. If Daniel Ortega wore a swastika on his sleeve, the liberals in Congress would be calling for an American Expeditionary Force to crush him. As it stands, he is relatively safe.

—May 11, 1985

What Is Potism?

The capture, conviction, and sentencing of Pol Pot brings primarily to mind that "banality of evil" identified after the Eichmann trial in Israel thirty years ago. What was it that finally did Pol Pot in? A sudden recognition of the enormity of his deeds? No, he was apparently brought down by members of his own cadre who were shocked by his execution of one of his aides. Shocked!

Mentions of Pot over the past two months—when he first disappeared, then came to view, then was manacled and tried—vary on the matter of how many Cambodians he killed. Some say one million, some two million. Some put the population of Cambodia at five million, some at six million. Depending on these variables, he killed as little as 17 percent of the population or as much as 40 percent. Whatever figure one chooses, he killed a higher percentage of his country's population than Hitler or Stalin did of theirs.

As far as we know, if any mentions of the genocide were made at the trial, they were incidental. The mind pauses, as it did a year ago over Daniel J. Goldhagen's book, *Hitler's Willing Executioners*, on the killings in Germany under the Third Reich: How many people were involved, and why?

The Nazis had a palpable goal, the elimination of those not of the Aryan race. The Communists had, if only intermittently, the goal of eliminating the bourgeois and the kulaks. Mostly the Gulag slaughters were idiosyncratically motivated, an expression of the insecurity and malevolence of Stalin and his successors and their dependence on slave labor. The killings at the war front don't figure in this attempt at moral reckoning—they were simply what happens when Country A goes to war against Country B.

Here Goldhagen's point is worth revisiting: Namely, that in order to liquidate six million people you have to have a pretty extensive killing machine. There are the people who actually turn the valves to let out the toxic gas. But those, relatively few, stand on the shoulders of the guards who bring in the victims, who in turn stand on the shoulders of the army and police who bring the victims to the slaughterhouses. Goldhagen's estimate is that 250,000 Germans had to have been employed in the genocide.

The situation in Cambodia is in a sense even more dismaying. Pol Pot had no elaborate crematoria. The killings were, as far as we know, overwhelmingly the effect of a bullet entering the back of a person's head or, shot from a rifle, his chest. To kill one or two million people, so to speak without an assembly line at your disposal, is a quite extraordinary enterprise and very much labor-intensive. So we must assume that Pol Pot's executioners were—what? fifty thousand? two hundred thousand?

One wonders then: What motivated the killers? What is Potism, even as we refer to Hitlerism or Stalinism? The easy answer is that they simply did as they were told. But the intimate knowledge we have of the Cultural Revolution, from among others Fox Butterfield in *China: Alive in the Bitter Sea*, suggests that the killer orientation having been effected, a bloodlust of sorts tends to take over, as when the crowds in Havana cheered the public execution of Fidel Castro's enemies soon after he took over—aping the *tricoteuses* seated around the guillotine in Paris during the Terror. In China, sixteen-year-old girls could be got to give testimony that their mother was truly an enemy of the people and should be punished.

The designated enemy of Pol Pot was not counter-revolutionaries or bourgeois. He killed more people than there were bourgeois in Cambodia. Always reclusive, he nevertheless made clear his proscription in 1975: Everyone who knew how to read must be shot.

His idea can't be found in Marx, though Marx became his mentor when Pol Pot studied in Paris. It was a kind of nihilism, true-blue Orwellianism, grounded presumably in the suspicion that anyone who could read might learn enough to stand in the way of the Khmer Rouge's designs.

Designs to do what?

Again, there is no answer—to transform society, perhaps a votary might step forward to say. But how, and in order to do what?

That there is no rational answer to the question substantiates the melancholy point, which is that people do not need a major rationale to become accessories in mass criminal action.

It is here and there heard that Pol Pot is getting off lightly (a life sentence) for what he did. But then everyone is getting off lightly, in our failure to ponder, measure, and fathom what Pol Pot did.

Perhaps he is better left alive than executed, if we hope ever to get a lead from the premier killer in history.

—August 5, 1997

CULTURE AND POLICY

Who Killed Adam Smith?

It's *true* Adam Smith was wrong, but I'm the only person I ever heard of who knows why.

Curiously, his most astringent and shrewd critics have never quite put their talons on the Achilles' heel of economic individualism. A hundred years of experience and research notwithstanding, the socialist still intones the surplus-value theory, the polarity between "economic goals" and "social goals," the labor theory of value, the "mature economy," and the rest of it: adding up to a lot of sophisms and wasted time, and to not so much as the tiniest interstice in Adam's armor. And yet withal, Adam Smith was wrong.

He was wrong because he based his economic theories on the "enlightened self-interest" of man, in particular of the pivotal man of economic society, the entrepreneur.

Smith examined the world around him and drew conclusions about human nature. He generalized that man will always act in such a way as to maximize his own well-being with minimum effort. He then concluded that the juxtaposition of this human drive with the immutable laws of economics leads inexorably—assuming no political interference—to greater and greater wealth for everyone. An essential ingredient of this formula—enlightened self-interest plus economic law equals abundance—is the absence of political interference.

Thus, self-interested man is entrusted with the responsibility of holding the functions of the state to the barest essentials. This, Adam Smith clearly states, is *sine qua non* to the free, successful, and prosperous economy. In short, a careful reading of Adam Smith reveals that man must manifest his self-interest not only economically, but also politically. Economically, man will work for material self-aggrandizement. Politically, he will work to frustrate that prehensile element of every society, the power-hungry statists. If man is unsuccessful in the political activity, it must follow that he can never fully enjoy the freedom to indulge in the economic activity.

And today, even the most slavish disciples of the gaunt Scotsman must admit that there is little similarity between the self-interested merchant of *The Wealth of Nations* and the average American businessman.

Quite the contrary. The American businessman is possibly the most bizarre mutation in the evolution of social man. To a greater extent, possibly, than anyone save the Trappist monk, the capitalist is distinctly and manifestly *un*interested in himself, his fortunes, and his future. For, incredibly, he is hard at work nourishing the collectivist giant, who has yet to grow only a little before he wheels on his benefactor and swallows him in one mouthful. This is hardly the self-interest Smith was talking about.

~

A look at the world around us is enough to see that the self-interested entrepreneur Adam Smith wrote about is scarcely visible in our society:

— Far from working for himself, the businessman who earns over $20,000 a year works from 40 percent to 90 percent of the time—or from twenty to forty-five weeks per year—for the state. Some do better than this by volunteering their service to the state, painstakingly guiding it along its path to socialism, and all for a token fee.
— Politically, businessmen liberally support organizations that career about the country promising an end to "economic royalism," or a purge of "Wall Street wolves." (See 1944's Businessmen for Roosevelt, and counterpart organizations in 1948.)
— As a general rule, capitalists refuse to back a political party that seriously opposes state collectivism in all its forms. They will settle, instead, for a mildly dissident Dewey–Stassen–*Herald Tribune* type of organization, which is of course no opposition at all.
— Philosophically, the businessman has virtually abandoned the doctrine of natural rights and, most particularly, the insistence that private property occupy a pre-eminent position in any list of such rights. In consequence of this, there emerges the inevitably fatal pragmatism of his approach to government: his sanction of progressive income taxes, of government-controlled currency, of federal Social Security laws, of the inroads into the free economy.
— Consistently disregarding their long-term self-interest, businessmen are even more enthusiastic statists when there is temporary personal gain to be got by political manipulations of the sort that breed tariff barriers, TVAs, high ceiling prices, or such colossal pork barrels as the Marshall Plan.

— Businessmen refuse adequately to support or promote individualist publications, which might challenge the hegemony of collectivist periodicals. Thus, for example, the circulation and tenure of *The Nation* as compared with that of *The Freeman*; the continued publication of the *PM-Star-Compass* axis as opposed to the demise of the *Sun*.

— And business firms continue, through advertising, to infuse money—i.e., life—into magazines that hew hard to collectivism and that open their columns to Schlesingers and Bowleses and Commagers, as with *Harper's* or the *New York Times* or *Look*.

— Our most prominent businessmen proudly subsidize huge foundations that, in turn, pour their money into collectivist tills. It was not illogical that Alger Hiss should head a Carnegie foundation, or that Rockefeller money should finance the Marxist composer Hanns Eisler.

— And most important, though weary after a hard day's work accumulating money for the government, the businessman often sets about in his off hours to raise money for his alma mater, that the theories of Keynes and of Laski and of the Webbs may be articulated at greater and greater volume into the ears of the younger generation, the generation that will surely, once and for all, abolish capitalism.

∽

There we have it. As with most generalizations, there are exceptions, and there are some self-interested businessmen—just as there do exist some socialists who genuinely respect the individual.

But the mainstream of American capitalists—hard-working, industrious, and dedicated folk—are working toward their own destruction, certainly as an economic group, and just as certainly as free human beings. The political philosopher James Burnham calls it the Suicidal Mania of American Business. The industrialist Vivien Kellems calls it the phenomenon of the Golden Jacka$$. Whatever you call it, an indispensable component of economic individualism has withered away. The generous and relentless nurturing of the all-powerful, predatory state by the capitalist class makes the theories of Adam Smith as unworkable and ludicrous as if supply increased in inverse proportion to demand. So it is that Adam Smith is as dead as freedom.

In performing the murder of Adam Smith, the capitalists have incidentally done service to Karl Marx in an ideological way. They have resurrected and paid homage to a theory of his that had long lain dormant. They have given the followers of Marx something else to crow about. Marx declared that the capitalist class is driven relentlessly toward its destruction by historical necessity. The proletarian class, likewise propelled by the forces of history, cannot avoid its appointed goal, the dictatorship. Nothing any individual can do can prevent this process, which comes to rest only with the advent of socialism.

Now, it so happens that this prediction of Marx seems to be supported by events. Socialism is hard upon us. The evidence, however, does not prove the Marxist thesis of dialectic necessity. On the other hand, the rapid decline of capitalism has been attended with so many examples of it that we cannot but charge the class with suicidal intent. Credit for our progress toward socialism belongs to the bourgeoisie, without whose active cooperation the socialist might never have succeeded in hoisting the world on his shoulders. The proletariat had little to do with it. But, either way—no matter which class has made the most important contribution—Marx was right in proportion as Adam Smith was wrong.

~

Curiously, there isn't much attention being paid to the American kamikazes. Look at it the other way round: Suppose that tomorrow we saw Ludwig von Mises and Friedrich von Hayek hired out to the faculty of the Thomas Jefferson School; Walter Reuther and John L. Lewis raising funds to back Taft's candidacy for the presidency; *Human Events* counting on a budget as high as *The Nation*'s; the Americans for Democratic Action backing the proposed Twenty-Third Amendment, to set a ceiling on income and inheritance taxes—then we would have an equivalent situation, although, I'll warrant, one that wouldn't go unnoticed.

No, along with Adam Smith, justice died. The American businessman is the forgotten element of a society that prides itself on recognizing selflessness. When will the American people pay tribute to the Unknown Soldier in the war against individualism? And when will he be, appropriately, toasted and feted and enshrined as the most unstinting altruist of contemporary society—the man who is slaving to destroy the system that has given him freedom and prosperity?

Our society is not given to hagiolatry, but here there are grounds for an exception: Nothing less than beatification will do. Perhaps some day Justice will be aroused, and there will sprout up in the parks and gardens of our tidy, planned society statues in his image. And there he will stand, in all his glory—in a double-breasted suit and a fur-lined overcoat, his foot on a volume of *The Wealth of Nations*, a smile on his face as he tightens the noose about his neck.

—*Human Events*, October 24, 1951

Father Fullman's Assault

God, it appears, is not on my side. Or so Father Christopher E. Fullman, O.S.B., M.A., insists in his article for *The Catholic World* (May 1952), entitled "God and Man and Mr. Buckley." Not only have I offended God ("Mr. Buckley has created a cleavage between God and man. . . . God does not need Mr. Buckley to defend Him."), I have also offended man ("I feel sure that Mr. Buckley has done a signal disservice to the cause of religion and the good society by writing this book."). There is left the vegetable world, which is neutral on the issues raised in my book, *God and Man at Yale*.

Now, my book is divided into three sections. In the first, I discuss religion at Yale University; in the second, economics at Yale; and in the third, the nature of "academic freedom." Father Fullman approves my treatment of religion, though he is more inclined, as befits his calling, to "pity" than to "condemn" the evangelistic atheists who so largely staff the social-science departments of many of our schools and colleges that are ostensibly dedicated to furthering the ways of the Lord. About academic freedom he has nothing whatever to say. Hence it is in the remaining section of my book—where I deal with economics—that I lose both God and man.

And the reason I do, says Father Fullman, is that I set up a "cleavage between God and man, between religion and economics, between the individual and society. . . . It never seems to occur to him, or at least he gives no evidence of it in his book, that there is some point of juncture between religion and human affairs. He fails to demonstrate that religious values must enter into all of life."

～

This is the substance of Father Fullman's objections. He repeats these charges, changing only a comma here or an expletive there, a half-dozen times. In addition, he reads me a fatherly lecture alleging that (a) I am unacquainted with the excesses of nineteenth-century capitalism and the evils of depressions, (b) I am ignorant of the great social encyclicals of the recent popes, (c) I imply that all good Christians must be individualists, and (d) I am very young.

To the central charge—that I divorce religion from economics—I frankly plead an innocent and flabbergasted "Not guilty." Clearly, Father Fullman suffers from a suffocating methodological incompetence, as revealed by the statement that I refuse in any way to relate religious and marketplace behavior, fast followed by the charge that I imply that all good Christians must be individualists! Either I do, or I do not, in some way link God with man. If I do, then Father Fullman's case evaporates. If I do not, then he can hardly maintain that I consider individualist economics to bring with it a divine sanction. Yet Father Fullman would have it both ways.

~

To the extent, then, that his objections are intelligible, let me answer them with a candor that may, when all is said and done, serve to fortify his indictment of my book. I stated in the foreword (p. xvii) that I did not intend to write an apologia either for Christianity or for individualism; that I would "proceed on the assumption that Christianity and freedom are 'good' without ever worrying that by so doing, I am being presumptuous."

In other words, I did not deem it my concern, in this particular tract, to explain to my readers *why* I believe God exists and *why* I believe in the divinity of Christ, any more than I considered it relevant to explain *why* I believe economic freedom conduces to maximum prosperity, *why* I believe economic freedom is the foundation of political freedom, or even *why* prosperity and freedom are desirable. These were all assumptions—tacit, it is true, but perfectly evident.

Quite consistently, I think, I did not introduce theological justifications for the free marketplace; but it does violence to reasonableness to infer that because I did not do this, I insist on a rigid dichotomy between Christianity in church and Christianity on Wall Street. To put it the other way round, what evidence has Father Fullman that my stated belief in God and His Commandments is hypocritical and meaningless? Because nothing short of the most contemptible hypocrisy would cause me on the one hand to acknowledge a transcendent allegiance to the Christian God and, on the other, to avow a belief in an economic system that collides with His teachings. In short, it is more than gratuitous to assume that I have "created a cleavage" between God and man; it is an unreasonable, unwarranted, desperate interpolation.

Now, I am willing to believe that Father Fullman didn't mean to imply what he actually did imply. There are other causes for his fury. I believe these to be his personal predilection for a strong central government encharged with guaranteeing the blessings of security and equality for all members of society. Thus I interpret his attack on my book (which is certainly vulnerable; but not, in my opinion, to Father Fullman's particular criticisms) as manifesting nothing more than his highly sensitive allergy to any position that does not deem it a proper or desirable function of the state to regiment the lives of its citizens.

On this point, Father Fullman makes claims so extravagant as to shock those men whose afflatus is less vivid. For he implies that God is on the side of the New Deal. If this is so, then Father Fullman is quite right that, as an anti–New Dealer, I am working against the will of God. This is, I suppose, what Father Fullman and I have to talk about, the differences between us being that I consider God's attitude toward state welfarism to be conjectural, while Father Fullman does not, and that my relationship with God is one of unilateral admiration, while Father Fullman's is more democratic.

Let me begin by distinguishing very carefully between a divine sanction behind human behavior, and a divine sanction behind any particular economic system. In line with the popes' refusal to commit themselves to the virtues of any particular system of government, stressing that the good life can be led under a democracy, or a monarchy, or an aristocracy, I believe it is also true that the good life can be led in a variety of economic systems. We discard from our reckoning, of course, such patently unpalatable extremes as absolute totalitarianism or unrestrained majoritarianism in politics, and anarchism and doctrinaire socialism in economics.

I heartily agree, in other words, that religion must inform the individual in *all* his activities. I feel that religion must guide the individual when he faces such questions as what are honorable and what are dishonorable means of amassing wealth, and what are responsible and irresponsible means of disbursing this wealth. But I do not believe that God has passed judgment against the traditional adjustments that the American people have selected to arbitrate the universal conflict between the insatiable appetites of man and the scarcity of economic resources.

I believe that the great American adjustment—economic freedom— has presented highly convincing credentials as a basically humanitarian, dignified, and realistic system of economic behavior. What else can you say

of a system that has maximized individual freedom and individual prosperity? We can only condemn it if there is evidence that both prosperity
and freedom are contrary to the wishes of God, and the Church does not
take this position.

~

I am certainly aware of the "excesses" of nineteenth-century liberalism,
and I wonder why Father Fullman failed to note my acknowledgment of
them (p. 53). But I did note, in my book, that to classify the nineteenth
century as an era of ruthless, cutthroat monopolies is about as intelligent
as denouncing Lincoln as "that man who put his feet up on the desk and
told coarse stories." The power of monopolies has been largely broken by
antitrust laws, of which I approve, and cutthroatism has been adulterated
by a code of fair business practices, of which I also approve.

But it is not these modifications of nineteenth-century liberalism to
which I objected in my book; it is, rather, the hacking away at the basic
planks of that system by the enactment of egalitarian tax laws, by the
maintenance of gagging bureaucracies, by capitulation to the demands of
special-interest groups, by the increased power and centralization of the
government, and by inflation and fiscal skulduggery. It is these measures
that are leading us, inexorably—with the consent of Father Fullman, and
with my disapproval—away from the great adjustment that enabled this
country to get where it is.

I have further maintained that our march down the primrose path of
collectivism, far from alleviating the social evils of Manchesterism, will
ultimately aggravate them, and nail down the coffin-lid on individual
freedom besides.

It is quite correct that Popes Leo XIII, Pius XI, and Pius XII have exco-
riated nineteenth-century liberalism. It is also true that they have condemned socialism with unecclesiastical ferocity. Also, the Holy Fathers
have emphasized the importance of the institution of private property,
insisting that the right to possess property is "derived from nature." And,
of course, the popes have time and again spelled out the pre-eminence of
the family.

Now, I confess I cannot categorize the stand of the popes on the economics issues I discussed in my book, because the relevant encyclicals are
sometimes less than clear, and sometimes, I feel, perplexing. But I refuse
to believe that Pius XII should be so naïve as to believe that the right to
private property can long endure in a society that has abandoned natural

law and any meaningful concept of private ownership. And can the pre-eminence of the family and the primacy of Christianity long withstand a public educational system that is forbidden to teach religion, or a govern-ment that refuses on the one hand to aid the private schools, while bent, on the other hand, on razing incomes so as to make the maintenance of private schools a luxury impossible to indulge?

It's not likely that the institution of private property, on which economic freedom and political freedom sit, will long arrest the predatory impulses of the American people so long as such statements as "No enlightened society, no reputable philosopher can uphold the concept of the right of private property" set the tone of an entire economics department at one of our leading universities. Yet just such a statement was made by the most influential professor of economics at Yale University. It is supported by the attitudes of the textbooks I criticized. And, yes, these textbooks are used in some Catholic colleges and universities.

Father Fullman could, with profit, check the emphatic papal denun-ciation of centralization (in *Quadragesimo Anno*) against the trend in the United States today:

> . . . it is wrong to withdraw from the individual and commit to the community at large what private enterprise and industry can accomplish[;] so, too, it is an injustice, a grave evil and a disturbance of right order for a larger and higher organization to arrogate to itself functions which can be performed efficiently by smaller and lower bodies. This is a fundamental principle of social philosophy, unshaken and unchangeable, and it retains its full truth today.

Thus, while, as I state, I cannot believe the Holy Father could approve of the march of our government down a road that weakens the prestige of religion, the institution of the family, the institution of private property, and the principle of subsidiarity, I readily admit that I am confused by some of the statements that appear in the social encyclicals. And to the extent that I am, I suppose I am open to Father Fullman's censure. For example, I am filled with horror at the possible interpretations of Pius XII's statement (from *Summi Pontificatus*), "Hence, it is the noble pre-rogative and function of the State so to control, aid and direct the private and individual activities of national life that they converge harmoniously toward the common good."

Perhaps my qualms are founded on idiomatic misunderstandings; at any rate, I confess that I consider the genus State as "begotten of aggression and by aggression," and as "the common enemy of all well-disposed, industrious, and decent men"—hardly equipped, on the basis of its historical performance, to superintend the common good. Some of the several strictures against the state are to be found in the writings of the early Church Fathers.

Still, if these be differences between my attitude and the social edicts of the Holy Father, then I pray for a reconciliation, which, I am confident, would be forthcoming if we invited papal commentary on the brand of secularist welfarism that is overwhelming the United States, under the aegis of the state.

~

Father Fullman asks of me, "Where did he get the impression that the dissemination of the Christian ideology was a *fait accompli*? He seems to forget that the work of leavening society with the spirit of Christ has always been an uphill struggle. That there has never been a time when the Gospel has made its way into the hearts of vast majorities as an efficacious power for good."

I have never considered the dissemination of the Christian ideology a *fait accompli*. If I had, I should hardly have written a book exposing the anti-Christian bias of a great university. I am dedicated, as a layman, to assisting Father Fullman, and other spokesmen for Christ, as best I can in their uphill struggle.

I have concentrated my efforts on piercing what I believe to be the superstitions of the prevailing doctrine of "academic freedom." This is the doctrine that asserts that the parent, the alumnus, the supporter of the private school are not privileged to have a voice in giving a purpose to education. This is the doctrine, as it has worked out, that most successfully impedes the growth of Christianity in precisely that culture where it could most efficaciously take root and spread, the student mind. I can assure Father Fullman that this has been an uphill struggle.

But I am most disheartened, to be frank, by the note of desperation that is so inescapably evident in Father Fullman's article. His is the despondency of a man who has reflected upon the lack of success that Christianity has had in guiding the thinking of mankind, in "informing the marketplace," and who turns, then, for easy success, to what he terms "the only power big enough" to resist the abuses of man, the state. Christianity has largely failed in teaching man to be a humane employer; hence deprive him of the right to employ. Man has largely failed to spend his money wisely; hence take his money away from him. Man has neglected his responsibility to his fellow man; hence relieve him of that responsibility—give it to the state.

Then who will inform the state? What evidence has Father Fullman that the potentates of the present administration—or of the rival party, if you will—are more keenly attentive to the commandments of Christ? And how can virtue merit divine recognition if man's responsibility to society is extorted from him by a tax collector, backed by a police force?

The struggle is certainly uphill. But it won't do to leap on the nearest funicular. For all its appearances, it's not headed our way.

—*The Catholic World*, August 1952

Return to States' Rights

For a number of years, it has been an axiom of American political science that the issue of states' rights was settled almost a hundred years ago. It follows that the principal philosopher of the losing side, John C. Calhoun, goes virtually unnoticed; for brilliant though he admittedly was, History has adjudged him a political aberrant, and History speaks with finality.

And anyway, we have been reminded, modern defenders of states' rights speak with hollow voices. Their opportunism has betrayed them. They are for states' rights when the federal government agitates for compliance with policies with which they disagree. But when the federal government proposes to lavish its economic charms on a particular state, resistance vanishes—even though every little states-righter knows, in his heart of hearts, that the federal government can practice generosity to one state only by exercising a very proprietary relationship indeed toward the rights of other states. When a Tennessee Valley Authority is proposed, the talk is of the Commonweal, of the Union, of the essential brotherhood of the Delta cottonpicker and the Milwaukee brewer. When the subject is a federal anti-poll-tax law, the talk is of the Great Sovereign State of Tennessee, of its Inalienable Rights and Privileges.

The Supreme Court decision of May 1954 (classifying segregated schooling as unconstitutional), because it struck hard at traditions deeply rooted and very deeply cherished, may have the effect of shaking inchoate states-righters out of their opportunistic stupor. Perhaps it is too late; but political resistance in the South seems to be centering on the broad and—potentially—dynamic concept of decentralized political authority. There has been more talk, these past few months, about the meaning of federation, and about the significance of the Tenth Amendment to the Constitution, than there has been for a generation. The result is that many of the arguments and much of the rhetoric advanced with respect to issues besides that of segregation have taken on an immensely rejuvenating theoretical substance; so that they begin to sound, as they have not for years, reasoned, principled, and consistent.

States' rights figure in aspects of the fight over the federal treaty-making power. They are at issue in the Supreme Court's ruling last week that only the federal government has authority to enact anti-subversive legislation (upsetting laws in forty-one states). They are at issue in the bitterly contested question whether the federal government should have the power to regulate the price of gas at the wellhead. A congressman now suggests that the farm problem be solved by the individual states. Important struggles loom on federal aid to—and jurisdiction over—education, housing, and road-building.

We at *National Review* believe that if there is such a thing as a mechanical safeguard to freedom, it is political decentralization. We welcome, then, the return of serious discussion of states' rights; and we pray that those who today talk states' rights because of the proximate usefulness of the concept will not toss it back to the wolves after it has served them—or failed to serve them—in a single battle. For the war is long.

—*National Review*, April 18, 1956

A Retired Colonel Takes on the Educationists

In 1939 a quiet middle-aged man, who had for the time being retired from the Army and was living on Long Island, decided he would take on Harold Rugg. *There* was a fight for you. Harold Rugg was one of the Frontier Thinkers (as they styled themselves) who set out in the Twenties and Thirties to remake American society. Professor Rugg, who dispensed his tablets from Columbia Teachers College, where he sat at the feet of John Dewey, was the author, at the time Colonel Augustin G. Rudd moved in, of books and pamphlets no fewer than five million copies of which were circulating in the nation's schools.

Professor Rugg's books, the core of the so-called social-studies program in thousands of secondary schools, huffed and puffed in behalf of a New Social Order for America, any of whose similarities with the traditional order were strictly coincidental. A socialist (Rugg denies this), a pragmatist, a relativist, a social architect in the grand tradition, Rugg had come damn close to owning social science in secondary-school America when Colonel Rudd and a few associates published a small book called *Undermining Our Republic*, which analyzed Rugg's teachings. The book had a sensational success. Almost overnight the community examined—and rejected—the social order toward which Professor Rugg was ardently beckoning their children; and the tide turned. Today Harold Rugg's books are out of print.

But the battle against the New Education is by no means won, Colonel Rudd realizes, and he tells why in a wonderfully useful book, *Bending the Twig* (The Heritage Foundation, 121 West Wacker, Chicago, $3.95). Rugg is down, but progressive education is not out, not by any means. Columbia Teachers College is still the center of the educationists' patronage network, and it is still mesmerized by the superstitions of an educational philosophy that is partly responsible for the stupefying ignorance and indiscipline of a generation of Americans. Colonel Rudd devotes several chapters to identifying the political tendencies of progressive education and its most recent high priests. Beyond that, his book is concerned with the essential emptiness of progressive education as an educational philosophy.

Colonel Rudd demonstrates that PE doesn't even produce the goods—so that indulging progressive education is about as horrible a thought as nominating Mr. Eisenhower for president and then *not even getting any votes!* Colonel Rudd reminds us of the wonderfully ironic fact that the Communists put up with permissive education just long enough, which by Western standards was lightning fast, to convince themselves of its utter impracticality. At a time when PE was in the saddle and riding high in the United States, it was being summarily liquidated in the Soviet Union. In 1931 the Central Committee, prescribing a complete reorientation in Soviet educational methods, called attention to a "fundamental defect of our elementary and secondary education"—the schools' failure to send to "the higher institutions of learning persons fully literate and possessed of the fundamentals of knowledge (physics, chemistry, mathematics, literature, geography, etc.)." By 1934, content had been restored to the Soviet curriculum, and discipline to the Soviet classroom.

Bending the Twig is, above all things, a highly useful reference book that contains abundant information on the background, nature, and results of progressive education. But Colonel Rudd's book does more: implicitly he says that the primary responsibility for education lies with the parents. That is a bold position, for the corollary of it is that the parent must have a say as to what goes on in his child's school; and though there is elaborate machinery in this country for collecting a consensus of parents and alumni, their role, when all is said and done and the proper ritual observed, is like that of the Queen of England—sign the Parliament's legislation and keep her royal trap shut.

Considerable strides have been made in the past ten years in resisting some of the enormities of progressive education. Most people, nowadays, will go along in ridiculing the professor who several short years ago wrote in defense of illiteracy that after all there is no more reason to expect one student to learn to read proficiently than there is to expect another to be proficient in glassblowing. But no headway at all has been made in the essentially political fight to reassert the authority of the layman in matters of educational organization and direction. Occasionally, as in Pasadena in 1950, the laymen win by exercising, in a glorious moment of impulse, brute political power: but so severe are the consequences of victory against the educationist bureaucracy that conservatives tend to be discouraged by their successes. (People in Pasadena who had a hand in ousting the principal tend to clear their throats and change the subject when the matter is brought up these days. Rather, they should be telling their grandchildren about the day they booted out a snooty bureaucrat of the National Education Association.) The professionals, then, continue to maintain, in effect, that education is an expertise with respect to which only experts (i.e., them, not us) have anything relevant to say.

Colonel Rudd does an admirable jab in his admirable book of showing that by any standard, no one could have been further off than the noisiest experts of our times. He makes clear, too, that the educationists will not yield without a fight. That fight, though, is surely worth it. For those in doubt, it is only necessary to remember that the next disorderly ignoramus who graduates from PS 322 may be your own.

—*National Review*, July 13, 1957

The Economics of Illusion

1. More Houses

Governor Nelson Rockefeller has announced a grandiose plan for stimulating the construction of "middle-income" housing in the State of New York. It is not clear why the governor of New York should have proclaimed his program so many months before the New York legislature is due to reconvene, but it is very clear that a candidate for president has emerged as the man with a Solution to a national problem—living space for middle-income families (defined in Mr. Rockefeller's report as those in a position to pay $17 to $29 per room per month).

The plan is simplicity itself. The way to stimulate middle-income housing is, roughly speaking, the way to stimulate any other kind of economic activity. You (a) guarantee private capital a profit, and (b) relieve private capital of the burden of taxation. Mr. Rockefeller's plan: Let the State of New York, through a "little Federal Housing Administration," issue debentures, guaranteed by the State of New York, to private capital, in behalf of entrepreneurs who will use the money to construct middle-income housing. The projected 6 percent interest on these debentures will not be subject to state or federal taxation. Now open your eyes, ladies and gentlemen, and—whee!—you will see middle-income housing units sprouting up all over the Empire State.

It is quite literally that easy. By guaranteeing a loan against loss—and, moreover, by guaranteeing an artificially high rate of interest and exempting that interest from taxation—you will unquestionably lure capital in the direction you want. Governor Rockefeller is implementing the policy of Professor J. Kenneth Galbraith's *Affluent Society*, whose premise is that a central political intelligence knows best where to direct the flow of capital, and, fortunately, has available to it all the coercive devices necessary to divert capital anywhere it chooses. Politically, Mr. Rockefeller's plan is appetizing, because (a) there are a great many voters in the middle-income brackets, and (b) the plan calls—initially—for a mere $20-million capitalization for the little FHA.

Yet we are face to face with the economics of illusion, once again. For implicit in the scheme is a disguised levy first on the citizens of New York

State, secondarily on all taxpayers. Unspecified in the plan: (1) the amount of extra taxes that will have to be levied in order to compensate for the exemptions granted to the capital invested in the little FHA's debentures in lieu of, say, AT&T; (2) the decrease in available capital for other economic enterprises resulting from the great sums (an estimated $2 billion) that will be diverted to the construction business, and the concomitant increase in interest rates to individuals and businesses vying for capital; (3) the inflationary cost that is inherent in any loan guaranteed by government (productive capital should be risk capital; statutory elimination of the risk factor commits a society to the success of a particular kind of economic activity and thus adds, without economic justification, to the society's overhead).

It comes down very simply to this: Mr. Rockefeller is dissatisfied with the free-market allocation of capital. It is easy enough to regret the shortage of middle-income housing units. But to eliminate that shortage in this fashion involves the imposition of politically determined choices on the free marketplace.

Mr. Rockefeller would accomplish his objective more honestly if he were to call on the legislature to tax the people of New York to build his houses, and never mind the hocus-pocus.

He might even contribute to the availability of housing units by recommending laws against featherbedding and other artificial costs. It would be better still, of course, if the governor were to reduce state taxes, and join in a drive to reduce federal taxes, so that middle-income families would have at their disposal the funds, nowadays pre-empted by government, necessary to meet the cost of housing.

2. More Education

We have been informed by the president's Science Advisory Committee, headed by Mr. James Killian of MIT, that we need to spend more money on education—roughly twice as much as we are now spending. To this proposal Mr. Walter Lippmann has given his assent. So therefore let us assume that there is no room for further argument, and confine ourselves to the question: How should the money be raised?

"There is no escape from the conclusion," writes Mr. Lippmann, to whom the apodictic formulation comes so naturally, "that if the new and necessary costs are to be met, if they are not to be ignored and neglected, we shall have to raise some considerable part of them out of federal taxes. *This is bound to happen*, and the sooner we face up to the necessity, the more likely are we to be prepared to act with deliberation and with awareness of the hazards, and with wisdom."

Once again, the myth of the self-generating dollar, the economics of illusion. The mundane point, of course, is that the federal government has no money of its own, but must raise it by taxing—by taxing the very same people who can, in behalf of education, be taxed by the state governments; indeed, the same people who, in the light of their presumptive interest in education, could theoretically be counted upon to allocate voluntarily any extra money that is needed for the education of their children.

Consider the role of New York State in a federal-aid-to-education program. If we take the figures for the period 1951 to 1956, New York State can expect to put up 18.5 percent of any future national tax levy. However, the percentage of any federal aid New York is due to receive (using the same base) is 6.9 percent. In other words, New York senators and congressmen willing to spend, say, $100 million of "federal" money for education in their state will find themselves voting to tax New Yorkers about $275 million to make that expenditure possible. By contrast, Mississippi puts up 0.22 percent of the federal tax dollar—and gets back 2.07 percent. In other words, the Mississippi congressman can safely assume that for every million dollars of extra taxes he is instrumental in loading upon his fellow Mississippians for a federal-aid project, he can return to Mississippi $10 million. (Other figures: California pays in 7.4 percent, gets back 7.7 percent—i.e., about even on the deal. Illinois pays in 8.2 percent, gets back 4.1 percent. Montana pays in 0.10 percent, gets back 0.71 percent. South Dakota pays in 0.11 per cent, gets back 0.66 percent.)

A fair question: Do New Yorkers know what they are up to, when they support federal aid to education?

In a word, liberal economic theory, exemplified by Mr. Lippmann's recent venture in it, depends heavily on the hallucination of the spontaneously generated dollar: on the suppression of economic reality. There is considerable political sentiment in New York State in favor of federal aid to education. Indeed, there are residents of New York State who are concerned with the depressed level of education in Mississippi to the point, even, of wanting to contribute New York dollars to the advancement of Mississippi education. But how many such people are there? As many as one-tenth of 1 percent? Probably not. Yet the majority of New York's congressmen voted, in the 85th Congress, in favor of massive federal aid to education.

It comes down to the fact that the average New York voter is wholly unaware that the federal government, in order to disburse a billion dollars, needs to take in a billion dollars; that as a resident of one of the wealthiest states, per capita, in the Union, the New Yorker will find himself contributing three times the per-capita average to the educational pool—but receiving no more than the average in return; that therefore the net effect of the federal program on the New Yorker is to drain his state's resources. Federal-aid programs are, for New Yorkers, a form of foreign aid to depressed states of the Union.

These are some of the realities studiedly avoided by spokesmen for the economics of illusion.

3. And Then Some Sense

The White House, particularly in the period when Sherman Adams was chief of staff, has not been free of the economics of illusion. But somehow, at someone's instigation (or maybe his own), economic illumination has suddenly taken the place of illusion in President Eisenhower's pronouncements on money, debt, and budget matters.

It is as if a Samson had suddenly recovered, not merely his strength, but also his sight. Speaking to a Washington rally of Republicans the other day, the president, in a burst of inspired clarity, put the whole matter of inflation in its true human perspective. "This is not a fight to balance the budget as an end in itself," he told Republican diners. "This is a fight . . . to protect the worker as he earns his pension and the retired man who must live on it . . . to prevent prices from impoverishing every man, woman, and child in the nation . . . to promote an expanding economy and domestic prosperity."

For time almost out of mind—going back to the years in which Republican proponents of a sound dollar were traduced as unfeeling "gold bugs" bent on pressing a crown of thorns on the brow of labor—conservatives have allowed themselves to be jockeyed into the position that a concern for national solvency is to put "dollar values" ahead of "human values." The "human value" of a stable dollar, however, must become more and more apparent to an age that has gone all out for wrapping its future in the cotton batting of pensions, deferred wages, and other fringe benefits scheduled to take effect after retirement.

Now, at last, the conservative can convincingly base his case for financial orthodoxy on the needs of the human heart. The president, it seems to us, has struck political as well as fiscal gold in basing his case for a balanced budget on the purely human needs of an aging population.

On two other occasions during the past week, the president let it be known that his "economics of illumination" comes from a total personal commitment. Talking to the American Medical Association, he recurred to the plight of the elderly under inflation. And, speaking to some business-magazine editors, he hinted that the Treasury must cease to unload its securities on the banking system, where they become an engine of inflation as individual banks use them as the basis for extending credit. To prevent the inflationary use of government borrowing, Eisenhower suggested that Congress should authorize a sufficiently high interest rate on government bonds to attract individual buyers, who would, presumably, salt them away in deflationary strongboxes.

True enough, the president's unavoidable proposal that the legal debt ceiling should be raised is sad reading against his other recent pronouncements. But the ceiling has never been proof against "temporary" breach. If the president can move Congress to accept his economics of illumination in other matters, the actual debt would drop as a matter of course, however high its legal ceiling might be.

—*National Review*, June 20, 1959

God Bless the Rich

It was said in *The Saturday Evening Post* once upon a time about Nelson Rockefeller that, although it isn't known how rich he is, it is known that he is "stupendously, redundantly rich." All this was said rather amiably, indeed by an admirer of the governor, but of course the knife was there, and blood was drawn: Why should we countenance redundancies in wealth any more than in poetry? Henry Ford a while ago gave a party for one of his young daughters, and the estimate was that it cost Mr. Ford $500,000, which is concededly a lot of scratch to spend in order formally to announce the already obvious nubility of a dear young thing, but the oohs and the ahs were not all limited to the question of whether Henry Ford hadn't rather overdone the display of his affluence. No, the discussions, some of them public—those for instance in the journals explicitly favoring the redistribution of incomes—expressed shock at Mr. Ford's spending so much money at a time when people are in want. Others, members indeed of Mr. Ford's own social and economic class, whispered together about his extravagances and wondered whether the rich did not nowadays endanger their own future by such profligate consumption. A dozen years ago it was the ball in Venice of Carlos de Beistegui, at which the guests were instructed to appear in costumes appropriate to the time of Mozart, which the guests proceeded to do, some of them with facsimiles so exquisitely authentic as to cause one commentator to reflect that if the price of just one of those dresses had been available to mitigate the material misery of Mozart's life, he might have lived on another decade and left us another dozen symphonies. And again in Venice, a generation earlier, Cole Porter was the host, and the lights were out all over a world that wrestled with an international Depression. But not the lights at Cole Porter's *palazzo*. On that one evening 25,000 candles were consumed—just enough, Porter reckoned, to provide just the illumination he sought, and never mind the blackness of his conscience: he earned the money, didn't he? Tremors went out through the capitalist community, whose sense of history may be blurred, but whose knowledge of what happened to Marie Antoinette very soon after she suggested that the poor eat cake is a vivid part of their personal psychological equipment.

And then there is H. L. Hunt. Winston Churchill is reported to have said about a tedious socialist of unconventional sexual disposition that he had managed to "give sodomy a bad name." Mr. Hunt has done his share to give capitalism a bad name, not, goodness knows, by frenzies of extravagance but by his eccentric understanding of public affairs, his yahoo bigotry, and his appallingly bad manners. It is especially ironic that Mr. Hunt, who may be the richest man in the world, has in the course of time employed any number of people professionally devoted to the capitalist ideal, almost all of whom found that their exposure to Mr. Hunt turned out to be the greatest test of their ideological devotion. But it isn't Mr. Hunt's behavior so much that rankles the socialist or the dogmatic redistributionist, it is the fact that he is so very rich, so stupendously, redundantly rich. Mr. Norman Thomas, for instance, gets utterly carried away by the subject. One time, when I was exchanging views with him at the Bronx High School of Science, he almost lost his voice in indignation at the recently announced calculation that Mr. Hunt was worth two billion dollars (give or take a hundred million, as they say in Texas). Mr. Thomas roared, and fumed, and pawed the ground, and tore at the lapels of his jacket, and belched forth such indignation as the fires of Vesuvius showered upon the people of Pompeii.

It is the fashion, after asserting that H. L. Hunt is the richest man in the world, to say that on the other hand there is Paul Getty, and maybe he is the richer of the two—we'll never know for sure until probate time. Mr. Getty has distinguished *himself* by reporting that he personally examines every single request for funds addressed to him by every single applicant;

that he has been doing this, week in and week out, ever since the word got round in the late Thirties that he was stupendously, redundantly rich, and that only twice has he yielded to a written entreaty. Mr. Getty does not give us any indication of the especially efficacious flavor of these two appeals, even though it is probably the single most interesting piece of information he is in a position to communicate to those of us who might one day ask him for money. As it stands, we know only as much about Mr. Getty's internal motives as the court was able to wrench from Shylock on asking him why he should prefer a pound of flesh over repayment of his loan. "It is my humor," he replied, refusing another syllable's amplification. It was, obviously, Mr. Getty's pleasure to gratify two supplicants in the course of a generation of supplication, even as it was his pleasure to deny the applications of thousands during the same period. So? *Epatez le bourgeois?*

Well, well, well. We can work ourselves up—can we not?—into a considerable lather against the rich. Not only can we, we do. I confess that I myself, who am if anything oversold on the capitalist system, get more exasperated by rich people than ever I do by poor people, for the obvious reasons (the rich should know better) and the less obvious reasons (the rich should know better how to enjoy themselves). But even so, what isn't most needed nowadays is a stupendous, redundant excoriation of the rich, but rather a defense of the rich—and the sooner the better, before they are made to disappear, which would be very bad news indeed.

The most far-out defense of the rich has been made by that most austere economist F. A. Hayek. In *The Constitution of Liberty*, he makes an empirical defense of liberty and therefore of capitalism, and he reasons the progressive feature of the income tax out of intellectual existence. He even goes so far as to say that if the rich did not exist, they should, quite literally, be invented. A society has an enormous stake in its rich—so much so that, assuming a society were starting from scratch, everyone equally poor, you would do well to pick a hundred citizens and give them each $10 million. Because the rich are uniquely situated: Hayek explains what is obvious, yet what is obviously unrecognized—e.g., by Mr. Norman Thomas—namely that the rich, because they are rich, are free to turn their attentions to other matters than getting and spending. Sometimes the rich will spend their money not to buy themselves the redundant wife (like Tommy Manville), or to distribute silly books (like H. L. Hunt), or to pay the bills of misanthropic revolutionists (like Friedrich Engels), but to commission another symphony from Mozart (like Lichnowsky), give money for medical research (like Roy Cullen), or pay the school bills of talented students (like Solomon Guggenheim).

The function of the rich as risk capitalists is so childishly easy to understand as to escape the attention of people who can think only in ideologized ellipses. The whole process of capital accumulation begins by the conception of the surplus. If there is to be civilization, there must be a surplus, and someone must have control of it. It comes down to the individual, or the state. In Russia it is (mostly) the state. In America it is (mostly) the individual. The way of life in Russia, and the way of life in America, are pretty rigorous inferences from the respective preferences for the one, or the other, means of acquiring and distributing capital accumulations.

And then I found myself saying to Norman Thomas, in defense of H. L. Hunt The Institution: What if it could be demonstrated that Mr. H. L. Hunt had by his own exertions reduced the price of a gallon of gasoline by a single penny? Isn't that an immense benefaction, considering the average family's consumption rate—worth at least the two billion he has accumulated? And isn't the existence of that accumulated two billion itself a part of the national patrimony, inasmuch as it is constantly at work, supplying credit, employing people, paying tax bills? As a matter of fact, didn't Cole Porter, in order to burn 25,000 candles, need to purchase them from candlemakers? And, in economic terms, would he have left Venice that much better off if he had given the money to the poor, rather than employed the poor? Not to mention Cole Porter's satisfactions, which just possibly were involved in fueling his creativity? Could he have written *In the Still of the Night* without candlelight?

But the arguments in defense of the rich are almost by nature defensive. Let the rich be, is my motto. It is no more my burden to defend the rich than to excuse the poor. Some people *will* be rich. Some people *will* be poor. I have found myself in the past wishing that Mr. Rockefeller were not quite so rich as to assault me as frequently as he does with the cosmic imperative of electing him to public office, but I do not propose to do anything about it. Nobody goes around talking about the excesses of poor people as a *political* problem, or rather, nobody goes around saying that the poor should be forbidden their excesses as a *political* matter. (Could you imagine a law forbidding ghetto dwellers to drink whiskey or conceive illegitimate children? The Javits-Kennedy Act?) So why pick on the rich?

As a matter of fact, if one wanted to go to the trouble of collecting the accomplishments of the rich as a class, they would be considerable—in education, in art, in philanthropy, in continence, in modesty, in devotion to duty and to country and to God. But that shouldn't be the point; what *should* be the point is that the rich are a natural state of affairs, a healthy state of affairs, and we should carefully scrutinize our deeper motives when we talk about the buffoonery of H. L. Hunt or the Medician gall of Nelson Rockefeller. Surely if we can survive free speech, which means Wayne Morse, and a free press, which means *New York Times* editorials, we can survive Mr. Hunt's self-subsidized utopianism, and Mr. Rockefeller's flotillas of self-concern, which bombard our political defenses from time to time.

The rich are by no means entitled to a presumptive respect, though some of them who seem least respectable usually have hold of a very special skill. G. K. Chesterton said that he never understood the compunction to honor a man simply because at some point in his life he had contrived to corner the soybean market. On the other hand, there isn't any reason to disdain the particular skill and daring it takes to corner the soybean market. My guess is that the last man to corner the soybean market, whoever he was, put at least as much time and creative energy into the cornering of it as, say, Norman Mailer put into his latest novel, and produced something far more bearable—better a rise in the price of soybeans than *Why Are We in Vietnam?* As long as the rich don't try to exact from us any special respect, we should give them such respect as, in each case, is the individual's due. There are the deserving rich, and the undeserving rich, and we should as individuals treat them individually rather than as a class. But what we should do collectively is leave them alone, stop scolding every time they give an expensive bash, tell them that the pressure on them will be social and moral and intellectual, not political, not coercive. Let them alone. They are valuable people. And they have their own problems. One of them is us. Let's relieve them of that.

—*The Saturday Evening Post*, December 30, 1967

The End of the Public Schools

There is in the air a sense of great excitement among American conservatives, who have reason to believe that their time is coming. In the past few years any number of ideas developed in the garrets of conservative scriveners, and roundly dismissed as radical and irrelevant, have suddenly begun to appear in the classiest political shopwindows. Four years ago they laughed themselves silly at Barry Goldwater's proposal that they sell the TVA. Now the Democratic postmaster general proposes selling off the Post Office (to a public corporation).

Twenty years ago, Lord Keynes's fiscal policies were written into the economics textbooks as holy writ; and now the monetary policies of Milton Friedman are beginning to displace the obsession with fiscal policy. There are other examples—the sudden perception of the metaphysical limitations of government action, the slow understanding of the derivative limitations of wars on poverty and urban-renewal programs. But the most exciting of the lot is the emergence from the fever swamps of the idea of private schools, in preference to public schools.

Seventeen years ago, Mr. James Conant, then president of Harvard University, delivered a speech in which he called for the formal abolition of the private schools. Formal, because in any case the private schools had diminished to a mere 5 percent of the whole. But Mr. Conant's brief against them was that they were "divisive," his reasoning, which I do believe that he would at this point gracefully repudiate, being that all Americans should have a shared experience, and that the place to have that is at school.

Now the private schools are proliferating. It is generally supposed that the reason why is the racist prejudices of so many white people. That answer is superficial. The real reason why is that an increasing number of parents believe that their children can be better educated in private schools, removed from the pressures of overwrought communities that are at least as much concerned with making agreeable politics as with producing literate children; and also that there is increasing dissatisfaction, among rich and poor, among white and black, with the whole idea of a central school authority specifying textbooks, curricula, standards, and the rest of it—a dissatisfaction mirrored in the Bundy Report presented to Mayor Lindsay of New York a couple of months ago, calling for virtually autonomous school districts.

No one now doubts that what keeps the majority of American students in the public schools in the major cities is economic pressure. Let us admit that if the state were to give each child a voucher, on the order of what is given to veterans under the G.I. Bill of Rights, cashable for sum X at any accredited school, there would be massive redeployments of children in all the major centers of the United States. And not only the children of the upper middle class. Also poor Negro children, for instance—to private schools specially designed to give special assistance to meet special needs.

Once admit that such movements would occur, and the mind focuses on the coercive nature of existing arrangements. Libertarian philosophers have been interested in the question for years. But now it isn't merely a matter of the liberty of the parents to select their own children's schools: America isn't given to the pursuit of abstractionist freedoms at the expense of politically profitable egalitarian principles.

It is the dawning realization that everybody would be better off under a mixed system in which public schools remained—for those who chose to patronize them. It is even suggested now by pedagogues of great reputation that it might be sound for the public schools to employ private contractors to teach the art of reading to individual students aged four and five and six. Indeed, the day may not be far away when it becomes possible— one is breathless at the prospect—to advocate the voucher system, and take education away from the bureaucrats and the egalitarians and the politicians and return it to the teachers and to the parents.

There are many first-rate public schools in America. But most of these have the characteristics of the private school. They are mostly in exurban areas, and are supervised by committees of teachers and parents, reflecting ambitious community standards. The students are well-disciplined, academic standards are high. The preternatural advantages that inure to them are the ultimate affront on democracy. So that even people whose primary interest is in what they call democracy are beginning to understand the relevance of the idea of the private school.

—January 13, 1968

Is There a Last Straw?

It is increasingly difficult to work up public indignation over outrage, as long as it is committed by a labor union. In the past few years in New York City labor unions have closed down newspapers and killed off three of them. Labor unions have shut down the ships at sea, closing off passenger and freight traffic. Labor unions have grounded the airlines, or most of them, leaving passengers the option of flying either to Toronto or to Detroit, but nowhere else. The labor unions have shut down New York City's schools, all the schools, in violation of the laws which it is the supposed purpose of the schools to preach obedience to. The labor unions have shut down public transportation, causing something very like a closing of the entire city. The labor unions struck the taxis, and violence was inflicted on the independent operators who declined to join in the strike. New York's severest retaliation against these strikes—some of them illegal, others merely convulsive, economically, socially, and culturally— was three and one-half days in jail during the Christmas holidays for Mr. Albert Shanker, the leader of the teachers' union, during which he is said to have run out of tea and crumpets on the third day, resulting in a loss of weight of three and one-half ounces.

I remember three years ago arriving at a television station and meeting at the elevator Professor John Kenneth Galbraith, all six feet five of that eminent intelligence, who always gives the impression that he is on very temporary leave of absence from Mount Olympus, where he holds classes on the maintenance of divine standards. We rode up the elevator and met Billy Rose, the impresario, rich, famous, a little cranky; and (if my memory serves) Dick Gregory, the amiable but extremely touchy Negro comedian. It was opening night for a new talk show hosted by David Susskind, and the gimmick was a small television, set on a swivel, which would face which-ever member of the panel the questioner—who was a half mile away, in Grand Central Station—was addressing his question to.

Now gentlemen, Mr. Susskind explained, there has been a jurisdictional question between the unions here on the question of which union has the responsibility for turning the knob in the control booth that swivels the television set toward the guest being questioned. So, when a question is asked, the person the question is directed to should get up from his chair and run quickly to the chair opposite the television, exchanging places with whoever was sitting there.

To this day I cannot believe it. We all received our instructions as duti-fully as if we had met at the foot of Mount Sinai to receive from our trans-figured Maker eternal commandments concerning our future behavior. I dimly remember an evening spent jumping up from my chair and passing Mr. Galbraith running at sprint speed from his chair to occupy mine, diving into the empty chair, panting, and attempting a suave answer to the lady or the gentleman at Grand Central Station who little knew what heroic physical exertions were involved in situating the guest in front of the little screen.

I do solemnly believe that if the Queen of England had asked Mr. Gal-braith or Mr. Rose or Mr. Gregory or myself to make such asses of our-selves in order to indulge her imperial pleasure, we'd every one of us have said: Madam, go jump in the royal lake. But not so the labor unions. You treat them as fatalistically as a fog, a drought, or a hurricane.

The other day a colleague of mine, a lady of bright disposition and middle years, went to her garage to fetch her car, only to find the garage doors closed and her car interred inside. A strike. She asked the doorman of the apartment building to raise the garage door, but he informed her that the striking garage attendants had removed a critical part from the machine that hoists the doors, so that there was no feasible way to lift them. I spoke of "her garage" intending to be precise. She owns her apartment and, accordingly, a part of the garage, which is a part of the building. So that *her* car is being detained in *her* garage against *her* will, and if you think that big brave courageous law-abiding people-loving John Lindsay is going to utter one word of reproach to the labor unions, let alone dispatch a unit of policemen to wrench open that garage door and restore a citizen's rights, you are a romantic, and a patriot, and out, out of this crazy world.

—February 6, 1968

Papal Gaucherie

Pope Paul VI has released an unfortunate encyclical (*Populorum Progressio*), particularly unfortunate because its naïveté in economic and other secular matters drowns out passages of eloquence which, had they gone unencumbered by confused and confusing ideological detritus, might have served to remind the responsible community of the inspiring ardor of the pope's passion for human reconciliation and the exercise of charity on a universal scale.

One wishes one might dwell on these passages. But it is not they, unfortunately, that are newsworthy. Around the world the press has elected to feature passages in which the pope seems to be calling attention to the limitations of capitalism, the need for the further redistribution of wealth between the "rich nations and the poor nations," and another passage acknowledging that the control of the birth rate (by "moral means") is desirable.

Those who are unfamiliar with the style of papal encyclicals are naturally baffled at their failure to specify. That, however, is the papal mode, and often it is useful in that it encourages a universalist diction that frees itself of the parochial quality of specific references. On the other hand, it runs the risk that in the mind's eye of the pope as he writes, he is seeing a very particular situation, concerning which he intones generalities that appear to apply—most irrelevantly—to other situations.

The most specific of the encyclical's passages seem to be directed at the Latin American *latifundia*, the landed estates sometimes owned by an absentee millionaire and operated primarily by peasant sharecroppers. "If certain landed estates," he writes, "impede the general prosperity because they are extensive, unused, or poorly used, or because they bring hardship to peoples or are detrimental to the interests of the country, the common good sometimes demands their expropriation." Even so. But further: "It is unacceptable that citizens with abundant incomes from the resources and activity of their country should transfer a considerable part of this income abroad purely for their own advantage, without care for the manifest wrong they inflict on their country by doing this."

The difficulty with this generality is that if it is kneaded for meaning, it can be made to say a good many things that obviously were not intended, such as that the pharaoh was quite right in resenting the exodus of Moses and all the Jews from Egypt. There are a lot of selfish Latin American millionaires with bank accounts in Switzerland. On the other hand, there are a lot of Latin American ex-millionaires who stuck around and were impoverished—and maybe shot—by demagogues who justified themselves by using the kind of language the pope uses. Any Brazilian or Argentinian—or Indonesian—who took his money to Switzerland before Goulart or Perón or Sukarno took over the management of those countries contributed more to social well-being by investing his capital via Switzerland in productive enterprises than he would have done by leaving it around to be squandered by the three left-wingers who in the name of human progress reduced the economic structures of their nations to ashes and set back by a generation any hope for improvement in the material condition of their people.

Once again a matter of emphasis. To discuss the obligation of the rich to stretch their necks out over the guillotine without exhortation to the politicians to maintain order and stability, to reduce their appetites sufficiently to encourage organic economic growth, is advice in the name of charity and good conscience which, if followed, would add to, not subtract from, the sum total of human misery.

It is nothing more than a repetition of elementary Biblical injunctions to urge the rich to share what they have with the poor. It is another thing to urge that this process be executed primarily through the taxing or expropriating power of the state. "We must repeat once more that the superfluous wealth of rich countries should be placed at the service of poor nations. The rule which up to now held good for the benefit of those nearest us, must today be applied to all the needy of this world." This has been interpreted as a call for more foreign aid. In fact the richest nation in the world, the United States, though giving in direct foreign aid only one-half of 1 percent of her gross national product, is even now having serious difficulty in balancing her gold accounts, a final failure to do which would result in the devaluation of the dollar and the impoverishment of a score of poor and semi-poor nations which hold billions of dollars as their principal reserves.

History has repeatedly shown that the most durable benefactions are not those that are mulcted from the people by their government to be sent disorientedly abroad, but those that flow abroad in enlightened search of opportunities, providing capital, jobs, and productive activity. There have been two forms of aid to Latin America by the United States during the past thirty years: direct financial grants of the kind the pope presumably favors, and investment by Americans and American companies in Latin America. The results of the former are to say the least exiguous. The results of the latter have been to furnish jobs for 20 percent of the Latin American labor force.

And so it goes. Indeed the pope sometimes reads like a simplistic Barbara Ward, than whom there are few writers more simplistic. He enjoins upon "government officials" "above all"—would you believe it?—"to make [your peoples] accept the necessary taxes on their luxuries and their wasteful expenditure in order to bring about development and to save the peace." The terrible congestion of misinformation in that sentence! Tax *all* the luxuries of the rich and you still wouldn't have enough money to buy all the Vatican treasures—it is the middle class and the lower middle class who are shouldering the great economic load today, for the simple reason that the rich, if you took away everything they had, could not relieve the world's poor for a single week. The peace is not most usually disturbed by the poor, but by the power-hungry, rich or poor: the great peace breakers of this century, Russia, Japan, and Germany, were not poor nations by common standards. It all reminds one of St. Thomas Aquinas's warning that, outside the field of morals and doctrine, the Church is quite capable of erring, "*propter falsos testes*"—on account of bad information. Those who have worked hardest and most productively for the diminution of human misery and know that the preconditions are (1) political stability and (2) economic freedom will be disappointed not by the goals, exquisitely described by the pope, but by the suggested means, illusory and self-defeating, which if followed would have the contrary effect to that desired by this intense and holy man.

—August 4, 1967

Mr. Nixon and Inflation

Mr. Nixon has stood up very resolutely against wage and price controls in, however, an address that combined, and not so very harmoniously, the analysis and the rhetoric of the free market with that of *dirigisme*. What Mr. Nixon said (good) was that we intend to go forward with a free economy in which the principal economic decisions will be made by the consumer through the mechanisms of the marketplace. All of which, he added (bad), will work provided people exercise a proper restraint—provided that they understand the threat of inflation, and govern themselves accordingly. What, under this analysis, ever happened to the doctrine of the Invisible Hand?

That was the doctrine of Adam Smith, who wrote the charter of economic liberty two hundred years ago by arguing that the invisible hand of the marketplace transforms into social usefulness that which was determined by the individual merely to be privately useful. For instance, the farmer who decides for altogether selfish reasons to increase his productivity by investing in, say, a tractor ends by lowering the cost of the food, which is publicly useful; and so on.

During the Johnson years, before the war in Vietnam reached its full pitch, the idea was to keep down inflation by persuading people to limit their demands: by persuading corporations to keep down their profits, and labor to keep down its wages. The movement had its more or less world premiere when John F. Kennedy in 1962 decided publicly to castigate the head of United States Steel for announcing a price rise. Mr. Roger Blough instantly capitulated, giving rise to an editorial in *National Review* entitled, "Roger Blah, President, U.S. Putty." The editorial writer was making more than an *ad hominem* point. He was saying that if there had been good economic reason for the projected rise in the price of steel, then the steel company was being governed by necessity, not by greed: and had no business allowing the president to bully it out of that decision. If the rise in the price of steel was truly capricious, then what was needed was tougher anti-monopoly laws, but who was proposing these?

Still, the policy seemed to work for a while, during which, as John Kenneth Galbraith put it, "enforcement was hortatory." That it could not work over the long term seemed obvious, as inflationary fires were stoked by budget deficit after budget deficit. Prices had to rise, and did. Meanwhile, across the sea in England, the socialists met their economic crisis—inflation, and a deficit in the balance of payments—with rigorous measures, including price controls, such as Mr. Galbraith and the Democrats are heartily urging for us at this moment.

A summary of the effect of price controls on inflation in England was recently done by Enoch Powell. "From the end of 1964, when the government secured a 'Declaration of Intent' from the employers and the unions, to the end of 1969, when the attempt to regulate prices and wages by statute was virtually abandoned, the positive effect was exactly nil. Indeed it might more plausibly be argued that the policy was counterproductive: inflation accelerated, and was faster than during the previous period." With price controls, England's price level rose from 108.2 in 1965 (1963 equals 100) to 127.2 in 1969. The rise here was from 103 to 119.7.

What solved the problem in England was the devaluation of the pound, followed by the revaluation upward of the mark. What has not been solved in England is the problem of price inflation, although it is interesting that a socialist government has abandoned price controls, even as the Galbraiths in this country are advancing price controls as the truly sophisticated way of dealing with the problem of economic freedom. Their argument comes down to this: Look, certain corporations and labor unions are powerful enough to proceed toward inflationary levels. So, since the prices and wages they command are arbitrarily fixed in the first instance, why not fix them arbitrarily in the public interest?

The reasoning is, in context, plausible. What Galbraith et al. fail to suggest is what Mr. Nixon also failed to suggest, namely that true regulation is done by competition. And that the only way to regulate socially—to restore the Invisible Hand, if you will—is to apply anti-monopoly legislation. And since such legislation already exists against business, it follows that what is primarily needed is the extension of such legislation to the monopoly unions. But that is not the kind of talk we will hear from Republicans during election year, or from liberal intellectuals ever.

—June 20, 1970

Are You against the Handicapped?

The reaction to Richard Nixon's veto of the aid-to-the-handicapped bill brilliantly illustrates a difference between the Democratic and the Republican modes of operation; indeed, a difference between the always-elusive "liberal" and "conservative" ways of looking at things.

Never mind for a moment any structural defect in the proposed law. Consider it simply as a means of helping the handicapped by voting federal dollars for their use.

Senator Hubert Humphrey emerged as the best, i.e. the quintessential, spokesman for the Democratic approach to such questions. For Senator Humphrey it was very simply this: Do you or do you not believe in helping handicapped children? Pure and simple. The senator went so far as to personalize the argument going even beyond his abstract identification with the cause of the handicapped. He spoke his rage over Nixon's veto on the floor of the Senate, saying, "I am the grandfather of a mentally retarded child. Our family can afford to take care of that child, but many families can't. I ask every senator here to search his own conscience. I don't believe the president of the United States knew what he was doing. If he did, he ought to be ashamed of himself." Such language is highly volatile. It spreads like wildfire through the college campuses.

From such an onslaught the conservative reels. If the critic will listen, the conservatives can patiently ask a few questions.

1. Do the Democrats believe that there is as much public money available as there are worthy causes in the world on which it might be spent?

No one, on reflection—not even Teddy Kennedy—would answer that question with a categorical yes.

2. Do the Democrats acknowledge that we have at this moment in American history strained the safe level of government spending?

No one, on reflection, can safely say that we have not. To do so would mean to interrupt his own criticism of the high price of meat, for one thing. All Democrats deplore the effects of inflation, and all Democrats recognize that the dollar's humiliation in the money markets abroad is the direct result of inflation at home.

3. Did the Democrats suggest that the billion-dollar aid-to-the-handicapped bill take the place of a billion dollars already appropriated for another social service? Did Senator Humphrey propose that Congress reduce by a billion dollars appropriations for medical aid to the elderly? For education for the young? For the purification of our water and our air?

We nudge up against the argument that we should commensurately reduce the military budget.

4. As a matter of fact, the military budget has been reduced. In constant dollars we would need to spend $105 billion to maintain the same level of spending the Democratic Congress judged necessary when Mr. Nixon assumed office, subtracting the cost of the Vietnamese operation. Now, spending on defense is what a society, resolved to maintain its sovereignty, begins with, even as you begin a house by building a foundation. To economize by pouring more sand and less cement into the concrete is to be compared with economizing by offering the sick man a half million units of penicillin when the doctor has prescribed one million.

5. Since approximately one half of the states of the Union send pay more money for social expenditures to Washington than they receive for social expenditures from Washington, what is to keep these states from appropriating their own funds for the help of the handicapped? Senator Javits, for instance, who voted to override President Nixon's veto, comes from a state that sends to Washington $1.60 for every dollar it gets back. Why doesn't Senator Javits satisfy himself to recommend to New York State that it look after its own handicapped?

In his classic book, *Economics in One Lesson*, Mr. Henry Hazlitt remarks that it is distinctively the conservative who looks beyond the immediate effect of any particular expenditure; that the liberal foreshortens his perspective, so that he is able to talk only in terms of, Are you or aren't you in favor of helping invalids? It is an onerous responsibility that the conservative needs to bear under the pressure of such demagogy, and we can only be grateful that Mr. Nixon and a few senators have had the courage to think in strategic terms.

—April 7, 1973

How to Argue about Abortion

There is room for passion in almost every argument, but there is room, too, for dispassion, and those arguments overfreighted with passion tend only to polarize the combatants, and tune out those who do not care.

The arguments over abortion have been in this category, and it is a pity. Indeed it may very well be more than a pity, a tragedy: if the moral analysis of the anti-abortionists finally prevails upon the national ethos. The arguments over slavery used to be full of passion, and resulted in a civil war. Even so, there were those who were patiently making the rational points on the basis of which the great insight was finally established. Lincoln, debating with Douglas, for instance. And in due course we came to know not only that man was born to be free, but that men with black skins brought over in ships from Africa were also men: and born to be free. The Civil War settled the political issue. The arguments of Lincoln and others, resting on a distinguished moral and philosophical patrimony, clinched the moral case.

I have seen, I think, the very first attempt to talk about abortion that manages to avoid every one of the blood-curdling clichés used both by those who believe in abortion, and those who oppose it. It is a most remarkable essay by John T. Noonan Jr., and it is simply entitled, "How to Argue about Abortion."

John Noonan is a professor of philosophy and of law at the University of California at Berkeley, and he shows us here how a subject as sundering as abortion *can* be discussed. What to look for. What the relevant perceptions are. What at all costs to avoid. What are the implications of certain modes of arguments. It is not only a distinguished performance, it is a beautiful performance, and although the pamphlet sells for one dollar, I'll send it for nothing to anyone who wants it, if you will write me at Box 574, Murray Hill Station, New York, 10016. Just say: "Please send me Noonan pamphlet."

Professor Noonan does some truly marvelous things in a few thousand words. He examines, for instance, the role of perception in the controversy in question. I have myself gagged over the anti-abortion material that features pictures of fetuses. I have also gagged at pictures of war that feature mangled corpses. I have always assumed that the reaction of horror and disgust was philosophically irrelevant. Noonan shows, without drawing the same analogy, why in fact it is not. Why in fact perception means so very much in modern intercourse.

"Perception of fetuses is possible with not substantially greater effort than that required to pierce the physical or psychological barriers to recognizing other human beings. The main difficulty is everyone's reluctance to accept the extra burdens of care imposed by an expansion of the numbers in whom humanity is recognized. It is generally more convenient to have to consider only one's kin, one's peers, one's country, one's race. Seeing requires personal attention and personal response. The emotion generated by identification with a human form is necessary to overcome the inertia which is protected by a vision restricted to a convenient group.

"If one is willing to undertake the risk that more will be required in one's action, fetuses may be seen in multiple ways—circumstantially, by the observation of a pregnant woman; photographically, by pictures of life in the womb; scientifically, in accounts written by investigators of prenatal life and child psychologists; visually, by observing a blood transfusion or an abortion while the fetus is alive or by examination of a fetal corpse after death. The proponent of abortion is invited to consider the organism kicking the mother, swimming peacefully in amniotic fluid, responding to the prick of an instrument, being extracted from the womb, sleeping in death. Is the kicker or swimmer similar to him or to her? Is the response to pain like his or hers? Will his or her own face look much different in death?"

There is something close to moral and psychological poetry in this passage, and throughout the pamphlet, which friends and foes of abortion will join in acclaiming.

—July 14, 1974

Thinking about Crime

The conventional wisdom is that one needs to spend one's time in probing the cause of our social maladies. A few very bright men (e.g., James Q. Wilson, Ernest van den Haag) have been trying to tell us, particularly in the field of penology, that it would be splendid if we were to discover the causes of crime, or the techniques of rehabilitation, but it is our absorption with these pursuits that distracts us from coping with crime. Weeks after the looting and rioting during the blackout in New York City, the talk still tends to dwell on the causes of it. But what should be done?

Herewith a few propositions:

1. More people than are now in jail ought to be in jail.

2. The objection that there are not enough jails is an insufficient one. There are two ways of dealing with the problem. The first would be to build more jails. The second would be to release from jail prisoners who have been sent there as punishment for committing nonviolent crimes. In federal institutions, only 25 percent of the inmates are there for having murdered, kidnapped, raped, or mugged. In New York State prisons, 30 percent of the inhabitants are not guilty of violent crimes. These people could be punished in different ways, outside jail.

3. There being no way to make parents responsible for the behavior of their children when there are no parents (it is estimated that over 50 percent of black teenagers in New York City live with just one parent, or in foster care) legal distinctions between children and adults should be abolished where there are no parents; and where there are parents, they should be abolished after repeated offenses.

4. Judges or parole boards who release a prisoner of whatever age before he is 25 years old, if he has been convicted three times of Class A misdemeanors, or twice of Class E felonies, should be subject to impeachment proceedings.

5. The community should acknowledge responsibility for failures to grant adequate protection to a member of that community. Victims of violent crimes should be compensated; so also should victims of theft, under reasonable regulations.

Now none of this is to suggest that thought should cease to be given to the causes of every kind of misbehavior. If the future holds for us some thaumaturgical medication that will transform the Son of Sam into St. Francis of Assisi, we should by all means do our best to get it past the Food and Drug Administration. But the methodological breakthrough is overdue: We must reason from the particular back toward the general, rather than the other way around. It is nice to see old Spencer Tracy movies with Father Flanagan saying such things as: "There's no such thing as a bad boy." But the broken arm, the ravished girl, the tortured old man are the concrete realities. It does not preclude any kind of inventive ministrations to bad boys to rule that these should be given inside prison walls.

Going after the symptom of the disease (a cognate cliché) is unreasonable only when it is known how to treat the disease. Since we do not know how to treat the disease, lacking—for instance—the authority to require people to procreate children only in wedlock, then we must ask whether dealing with the symptom isn't to be preferred to doing nothing at all.

The answer should be plain. But of course it isn't; and that is why no reform movement has grown out of the awful events of the past weeks, and years.

—August 11, 1977

Three-Martini Lunch?

One has to conclude that Jimmy Carter's crusade is, really, against martinis, not against the revenue lost to the government by their deductibility in certain circumstances. The martini, let's face it, has become a code word. References to the "three-martini lunch" are designed not so much to evoke anger at the prospect of a dollar per martini lost in revenue to the government. They are designed to point to a lifestyle against which all the complicated glands in Jimmy Carter's body boil in protest.

I'm not a betting man, and neither is Jimmy, but I'd bet you on this, that if JC were given a lie-detector test, I know what his answer would be to the question: "Mr. President, if you could outlaw the drinking of martinis at lunch, or merely outlaw their tax deductibility, which would you do?"

Now the reason the "three-martini lunch" is evocative in a sense that, say, a "three-Scotch lunch" or even a "three-whiskey lunch" is not, is that the martini is thought to be the quintessentially alcoholic drink. And, really, it is. And the drier you insist the martini be, the closer you come to the essence of alcohol: straight gin. Indeed, there are those who go all the way, ordering straight gin on the rocks. Though, come to think of it, they will not really have gone all the way until they order straight gin without any rocks. Which is what the Dutch do, by the way.

But martinis have a special appeal for certain people. Bernard de Voto, who wrote a book about spirits, dubbed it one of the two genuinely creative American contributions to the repertoire of strong drink (the other: bourbon and water). I know an elderly man who has said that immediately on entering St. Peter's Gates, he intends to seek out the man who invented the dry martini. He tells you why in devout tones: "I just want to say to him 'Thanks.'" But the consensus is that a dry martini in the evening is a straightforward invitation for instant relief from the vicissitudes of a long day. And that a martini at lunch is a quick invitation first to exhilaration but then—very quickly—to torpor.

Now Mr. Carter clearly faces emotional difficulties here. He cannot, for instance, outlaw the deductibility of a martini at lunch without also outlawing the deductibility of, say champagne. Would he attempt to outlaw the deductibility only of alcoholic beverages? There are restaurants in New York at which for food alone at lunch you can run up a bill of fifty dollars. Is it proposed that the food be deductible but not the booze? That would appeal to the prohibitionist vote, but not very much to the libertarian vote. Will they try to put a limit to the price you can deduct for any lunch? But how would they attempt to mete out impartial justice for those who live in New York, say, and those who live in Cedar Rapids?

Ah! our bureaucrats have come up with an approach. Why not exclude from deductibility the price of the host's lunch, acknowledging as a legitimate business expense only the cost of his guest's? But this is one of those solutions bred in the hygienic laboratories of the bureaucracy, unrelated to experience. If the idea is to take the potential customer to a fancy restaurant to help induce a commercially compliant mood, how can the boss expect his employee to pay for his own fancy lunch? Or should he, having reserved a table at 21, arrive with his lunch box, and order pheasant for the guest? My guess is there would result a certain social uneasiness not conducive to commerce.

It is, of course, one more example of the age-old truth of the proposition that tax laws are never successful when they try to effect justice. The answer is: Of course, martinis should not be deductible, nor should lunches, nor should Tabs. What would there be to deduct from? Nothing: because, of course, there should be no tax on business.

—December 10, 1977

The Failure of Ronald Reagan

Mr. Reagan's proposals—an across-the-board 10 percent per year tax cut going over a period of three years—came as partial relief after persistent news stories to the effect that he would not propose to Congress reduced taxes at the highest brackets. To cut taxes on the rich, his advisors are quoted as having finally persuaded him, would be to bring on political damage and jeopardize tax cuts altogether.

But President Reagan was true to his commitment to endorse the Kemp-Roth principle. Unhappily, what he did not do was to stress the critical point, the thing primarily to remember about the Laffer curve and the point made with such comprehensive brilliance in George Gilder's new book, *Wealth and Poverty*: It is that relief is most important at the higher tax rates. What is the marginal rate of taxation? is the single most relevant question to ask if you are an economic physician probing an anemic patient. The pity is that the greatest living political communicator did not take the opportunity to confront such arguments as those Senator Kennedy and Mr. Mondale used to bring down the house at Madison Square Garden last summer during the Democratic Convention. There must have been fifty references to "rich men's" tax bills. There were none directed at the question: Is it sound public policy to overtax the rich if by doing so (a) you reduce the prospects of the nonrich, and (b) you reduce total revenues?

Because that is what has been happening, and Mr. Reagan should take an early opportunity to spread those figures before the public. The *Wall Street Journal* recently poked about various studies of the effect of the 1979 reduction in the capital-gains tax (from 49 to 28 percent). Opponents of the proposed reduction did everything except commit satyagraha to stop Congress. Among other things, they claimed that the measure would cost the government, in lost revenues, $1.7 billion.

What in fact happened? The Treasury collected $1.1 billion *more* in taxes under the lower rate than under the higher rate.

But that isn't all. In 1969, the last year of an earlier lower capital-gains tax rate, 698 new stock offerings went out, issued by companies whose net worth was less than $5 billion. Five years later a total of four new issues were floated. In 1977, the figure was thirteen; 1979—the year of the sub-stantial decrease in the capital-gains tax—forty-six; in the first ten months of 1980, eighty-nine. In other words, although we are a long way from the level of entrepreneurial activity by small business we were at in 1969, we are pointed in the right direction. The importance of such activity is merely suggested by the following data, drawn together by the economist for the W. R. Grace Company. Between 1969 and 1976, over 80 percent of all new jobs were created by companies with fewer than one hundred employees. So that the approximately 11 million Americans added to the work force during the past decade owe their jobs to the disposition of fellow Americans to take risks. Will they, under Reagan's plan, do so at a more intensive level?

Kemp-Roth is good stuff, though it would be sounder if the lesser rates held and the top rates were instantly reduced. But consider: The average security is now held for 7.2 years. Assuming the current maximum rate of taxation on capital gains and 14 percent inflation, this means that if during that period you doubled your money, you would pocket after paying taxes 67 percent of your original investment. Reduce the inflation rate to 10 percent: that means that an apparent 200 percent return translates to a real return of 87 percent—better, but still less than you had seven years earlier.

"Probably no one in the current Administration," says a *Wall Street Journal* editorial, "disputes the economic rationale" for an instant reduction of the maximum rate on unearned income to 50 percent—the maximum rate on earned income. "The problem is purely political"—notwithstanding that history shows the "rich" would actually be paying more, appearances suggest they are being favored. But surely Mr. Reagan's skill is in demonstrating the fallacy of so many populist assumptions. Why not use that skill for that purpose?

—February 10, 1981

Gentlemen, Please

Gentlemen, gentlemen—please. Quiet—just a minute—let me speak now, OK? Thank you, thank you. Thank you very much.

Now, I was born with a balanced-budget spoon in my mouth. I was for a balanced budget when I was sixteen, and if I had been precocious, I'd have been for a balanced budget when I was six. But that it was in my blood is my point, and in due course it trickled to the brain, notwithstanding that I majored in Keynesianism at Yale. So please don't proceed as if I were indifferent to the ramifications of an unbalanced budget. In fact, I'm in favor of a balanced-budget constitutional amendment, so my orthodoxy is absolutely straight.

And yes, I know that Ronald Reagan criticized the hell out of Jimmy Carter for having run a budget deficit of $160 billion in the course of his four years in office, and yes, I know our deficit this year is going to be in excess of that figure.

What was that, Mr. Mitterrand? Our deficit is endangering the French economy? But when you ran for office, you complained that the principal danger to the European economy was the U.S. inflation rate. It was 13 percent then and is down now to 4 percent.

—What's that? Interest rates?

Well, our interest rates were running at over 20 percent when Reagan took office, and they are half of that now. What's that? They're going to head back up because of our deficit?

Yes, I think that's true. Only not as much as is widely held. It is true that credit is finite, and that to the extent the unbalanced budget eats up that credit, there is less of it left for other needs, and it's true that scarcity breeds price increases. It's also true that the feds, if they step in to mitigate the credit shortage by creating a lot of money, will bring inflation back. So that it would appear we are headed either for (a) higher interest or (b) higher inflation. I think that is correct. But you people—yes, Fritz, I'm looking at you, and Alan, and John (how does political campaigning compare with weightlessness, John?), and also the neo-Rockefellerites, if that's what you want to call Bob Dole, John Chafee, Mac Mathias—are suggesting two things. They are (a) cut down on defense expenditures and (b) raise taxes.

Now the Constitution vests the president with the responsibilities of commander in chief. That doesn't mean it vests him with infallibility. It does mean that his evaluation of the defense needs of the country becomes a grave statistic. And remember that if we were to go the freeze route, and the no-nuclear route, we'd have to double, maybe triple, our defense spending.

On the matter of taxation, what's the quickest way of saying it? How about this: During the Second World War, when nothing counted except victory, when 15 million Americans were drafted, we were taxing the American people 29 percent of the gross national product. Right now we're taxing 39 percent of the GNP. Colin Clark, the Oxford economist, cautioned a generation ago against taxing more than 25 percent of the GNP.

Does that mean, you ask, that I'm resigned to a big deficit and what it portends?

You're asking a political question, and I'll give you a political answer. We have an election coming up, as God knows this group knows. Military spending accounts for 23 percent of total federal spending. What spending program has Reagan initiated, other than in defense? When last, before

1980, was either house of Congress controlled by Republicans? That's right, 1954. So that every dollar being spent, creating the huge deficit, is a dollar voted to be spent by Democratic Congresses, and authorized in most cases by Democratic presidents. Reagan has no authority to repeal entitlement programs.

So Congress needs to take the blame for the deficit. That part of the deficit that represents increased defense spending, Reagan can take the blame for, if that's the right word for the culpability of mounting our defense. Take what Carter wanted to spend on defense—$138 billion—and what Reagan proposes to spend—$170 billion. A difference of $32 billion. Assign Reagan the blame for that much of the deficit. The rest is a Democratic responsibility.

OK, go ahead and boo me. But I got under your skin, didn't I? OK, OK, I'm leaving. Just wanted one word. Pluralistic society, remember? Ask the ACLU. They'll be here any minute now. They're all home praying.

—May 26, 1983

The Thatcher Curve

Ten years ago on television I asked Mr. Denis Healey, at the time the reigning economic intelligence in Britain's Labour Party, whether he didn't think that a tax of 93 percent—at that time the going tax on incremental earnings in Great Britain—was too high. He said well, yes, 93 percent is high. But, he explained, Britain has high military expenditures, which expenditures, ho ho ho, are in part the result of American influence, and what can you do? If you have high expenditures, you have high taxes, right?

We got a measure of how far we have come in ten years when, on Tuesday, the government of Margaret Thatcher announced her tax and budget policies for the coming year. The income tax, which under Mrs. Thatcher has gradually been reduced to a top rate of 60 percent, is coming down again. Indeed, Mrs. Thatcher is aping the approach of Reaganomics. Under her penultimate reform, the tax rates were 27 percent, 40, 45, 50, 55, and 60 percent. Under the new law (remember: What Mrs. Thatcher sends over to Parliament becomes law, under the British system), there will be only two tax rates. The first tax rate will be reduced from 27 percent to

25 percent. The second is 40 percent. If you earn $35,700, you will begin paying 40 percent tax.

In passing, one rotes that that is too high a rate, not quite as enlightened as the United States' high rate of 33 percent; but then, a little culture lag is understandable. It was much further back than ten years ago that we had a rate of 93 percent.

But how strange to recall the analysis of a man as bright as Denis Healey: You need to make heavy expenditures on weapons, and therefore you need taxes at 93 percent. Mrs. Thatcher has been cutting taxes and reducing inflation (to the present level of 3.3 percent—lower than our own). And, last year, Britain had a balanced budget, its first in almost two decades. The pound has been soaring on the market, and one would be tempted to suspect, save that the honor of the chancellor of the exchequer, Nigel Lawson, is as solid as Mrs. Thatcher's popularity, that this had something to do with expectations that this radical tax reform was in prospect.

What Mr. Healey and the Labour Party are embarrassed to learn is that excessive income-tax rates yield less revenue. For many years, supply-side economics and the Laffer Curve have been the laughingstock of the redistributionist economic fraternity. But the figures accumulate now with devastating impact, year after year, in category after category. When, in 1979, capital-gains taxes were reduced from 49 percent to 28 percent, the Treasury Department's official prediction was that the measure would cost nearly $2 billion annually in lost revenue.

When President Carter was informed that such a tax reduction was in prospect, only two years after he had advised the Democratic Convention that nominated him that our tax policies were "a disgrace to the human race" (his verbal formulation must have been a wink at Jesse Jackson), he reacted as if all Ten Commandments were scheduled to be violated in the Rose Garden at high noon. One year after the reform was written into law, revenues from capital gains, which had been $8 billion, far from reducing to $6 billion, increased to nearly $12 billion.

Can we hope that such knowledge, painfully accumulated, which Mrs. Thatcher is now putting to use, will spread, little by little, to other countries devastated by high marginal tax rates? We know that it has happened radically in parts of the world once thought invincibly ignorant when up against any plank of dogmatic socialism. Perhaps the worst offender this side of the Scandinavian countries, whose tax rates have led to the most extensive underground economy in Europe, is Ireland, where a tax rate of 58 percent is imposed on income above $17,000. The result is low growth, high unemployment, and massive emigration. With the new economic reforms, Northern Ireland will seem all the more desirable to Irish nationalists, save for the paradox that they tend for the most part to be socialists.

The United States, history will surely record, led the way under Ronald Reagan to the universalization of elementary knowledge about tax policy—though one should also give credit to Taiwan and Singapore and Hong Kong. The *Wall Street Journal* recently called attention to a surviving contradiction, the high capital-gains rate. In the United States it is still 33 percent. The United Kingdom: 30 percent; Sweden: 18 percent; Canada: 17.5 percent; France: 16 percent; West Germany, Belgium, Italy, Japan, the Netherlands, Hong Kong, Singapore, South Korea, Taiwan, Malaysia: zero.

But the sun begins to shine, and Mrs. Thatcher and her brilliant collaborator Nigel Lawson are doing much for Great Britain, and for economic window-shoppers.

—March 17, 1988

"Justice" and the Iran-Contra Trial

Will Ronald Reagan pardon the Iran-Contra defendants? The answer to that question, transcribed by press secretary Marlin Fitzwater, is: "We do not talk about pardons. Period." This will not deter the prurient, or the morally inquisitive, from asking the question: Ought the president to pardon them?

The public's knowledge of the case is pretty well limited to the television extravaganza of last summer. On the basis of what one saw there, the impulse (let us focus on Colonel Oliver North and Admiral John Poindexter; the other two are more complicated) would clearly be: Yes, he should pardon them. But there is a complication. It is this: Did their misrepresentations spring from a plausible understanding of their duty to presidential foreign-spolicy vectors? The initial impression is that this was so. Why? Because Mr. Reagan many months ago said that he thought of Colonel North as a "hero." And second, because as recently as a week ago, Mr. Reagan said that he knew of "no crime" committed by either of the two men.

This doesn't mean that they didn't commit a crime (Mr. Reagan cannot be expected to be fully familiar with what North-Poindexter said under oath to prosecutor Lawrence Walsh). The most that we can safely infer from apparent relationships is that although Mr. Reagan did not know that surplus funds from a covert operation in Iran were being used to help to subsidize the Contra operation, the success of that operation was dear to his heart, and the tangle in Congress (yes to Contra help on Monday, no on Tuesday, yes on Wednesday) was responsible for the presumption that the executive branch was never actually defying the settled will of Congress.

At some point, if his subordinates are convicted, Mr. Reagan will need to concentrate on the question whether they were acting in defiance of the law. And, most important, whether their acting in defiance of the law is the principal criterion he needs to consult. After all, the whole idea of granting the president the right to pardon acknowledges that the president's judgment is, on his own initiative, permitted to transcend the law.

Pride! Here is how this observer, who has published eight novels attempting to probe the mind-breaking problems of a democracy that seeks to be governed by the law and to engage in certain kinds of covert activity, views the political implications of the prosecution. Reagan's opponents—who tend to be anti-Contra, for various reasons—are good and sore about the popular triumph of Oliver North while on the stand. His appeals to patriotism, duty, and the cause of anti-Communism struck these observers as fundamentalist, and corrosive of the majesty of the law. It is for that reason that for every million viewers North won over, a hundred thousand viewers were determined that, ultimately, he should be punished for his contumacious bravura.

That passion was married to the passion of Walsh. Inevitably, pride here also plays a part. It is professionally embarrassing to lead a team of twenty-nine lawyers on a $4 million paper chase and not come up with something. So he has done so: enough counts, if North were found guilty of all of them and given the maximum sentence for each, to send him to jail for eighty-five years. Walsh recognizes that there is always the threat that the entire case will be thrown out on the grounds that the immunities granted by Congress to North and Poindexter would only be exercised if the government came up with a jury that spent last year in a Trappist monastery in Tierra del Fuego. Everybody else (it will be argued) would proceed to pass judgment with some reference to his pre-exposure to the arguments in the case.

But, of course, egging on the prosecution, especially on the matter of scheduling, is the entire Democratic political engine. If a jury can be persuaded to pronounce North and Poindexter guilty—of fraud, perjury, obstruction of justice—then, it is hoped, the toxic exhaust from the episode will recontaminate the Reagan administration and, especially, the second most important figure in it, George Bush, candidate for president. One can imagine the boon to the Democrats if the campaign and the trial ran concurrently, permitting reporters at every press conference to ask candidate Bush his opinion of the preceding day's developments. Never mind that he will have the packaged (and proper) answer, that he cannot comment on a trial in motion. The audience is there, heard the question, was reminded of its embarrassing implications.

If defense counsel's motions fail and the case goes to trial, and if Reagan concludes that a pardon is in order, would he then give it preemptively? No. That would be psychologically impossible. It is appalling, and humiliating to contemplate, but it is true that the next occupant of the White House might bounce off this fascinating (but historically trivial) legal carnival.

—March 25, 1988

The Health Paradigm

The emanations from President Clinton about the new health program understandably baffle many who try to materialize from what he said the exact shape of the program he will endorse.

We know about it only that the idea is to universalize health care, and to make employers responsible for paying the cost of it, and to impose some kind of managed system on suppliers, in order to keep costs down; and, yes, there will be a role there for the individual states to play; and, no, the burden on business will not be overwhelming or instantaneous inasmuch as the program will phase in over a period of five to seven years, and we mustn't make this a partisan struggle, and so's your old man.

It's understandable, in the circumstances, that early commentary on the Clinton prolegomena wanders hither and thither, seeking to get to the bony tissue of the Clinton plan. What follows is one man's version of the basic structure that ought to govern thought on this problem:

1. The American people have decided that they will not tolerate a society in which individuals who run into costly medical problems will find themselves either incapable of paying the costs of their treatment, or destitute after paying such costs.

2. That is where insurance comes in. It is no different, really, from what you do to protect yourself in case your house burns down. Instead of facing, suddenly, a $150,000 loss, you go to a company that is taking in money from a thousand other homeowners, and the representative tells you that if you pay $525 every year, the company will insure your house against fire loss.

You run your eyes down the Yellow Pages and find another insurance broker who tells you that his company will write an identical policy for $500, so you give your business to him. The broker who lost out alerts his company to the loss of the policy, and efforts are made to tighten up so that, the following year, the company can be competitive against the lower bidder.

3. Now the company that agrees to insure you for $500 lays out options. If you will agree to a $5,000 deductible—only your garage burned down, maybe, not the house—the company will agree to reduce your premium from $500 per year to $425 per year. You sit down and do some calculations.

What is decided depends on a million variables, and no one can satisfactorily anticipate what will be the decision of Mr. and Mrs. Jones applying their own variables to the question with reference to their own disposition to run risks. They decide to take the risk; to save the extra premium. Their neighbors, Mr. and Mrs. Smith, decide: No way! They want the full insurance, so they pay the extra premium.

4. The insurance company then says: Look, some fires do more damage than other fires, depending on precautions that are taken. If your electric wiring is out of date, if you live more than five miles from the nearest fire station, if you don't have enough fire extinguishers in your house, then the risks mount. If you will agree to an annual examination of your house by our expert, we'll reduce your premium by another $25.

The expert will then make recommendations. If you act on those recommendations, then, depending on the gravity of the exposure, we'll reduce your premium by anywhere from still another $25 to $75. This idea appeals a lot to the Smiths, whose house is pretty new, but not much to the Joneses, whose house is quite old and might require a fair amount of rewiring. One couple says yes, the other couple says no.

5. A third couple resists the entire plan. The hell with it, Mr. Lucky says, I am a gambling man. Ah, but Mr. and Mrs. Lucky run into The Law. The law in their state says: All residents of this state have to take out insurance against a fire that totally ravages their home. Unless you can show an insurance policy that protects you against a 100 percent loss, the state will take out a policy for you and send the bill to your town clerk, who will add the premium to your property tax.

6. Meanwhile, no company has stepped forward to offer a fire policy for $50—which is all that 10 percent of the homeowners can afford. So those who are paying for fire insurance agree to share the cost of those who simply can't afford any policy. That means a 10 percent surcharge, so that now the basic policy is going to cost $550—$500 to the company that supplies the coverage, $50 in taxes that go to the state capital, and are then forwarded to the insurance companies to underwrite coverage for the poor.

This is the schema against which Clinton's plan should be judged.
—August 19, 1993

Up from Witchcraft

It is hard to believe that the whole of justice-minded America stood by breathlessly wondering whether the judge in Los Angeles would actually throw out as admissible evidence the bloodied glove apparently belonging to the person who killed Nicole Simpson and her visitor. Commentary the night before by Fourth Amendment cultists crowed over what they anticipated as a victory. A victory for what, exactly?

"It is as simple as this," lawyer William Kunstler announced on the Larry King program, in words to this effect. "Either you believe in the

Fourth Amendment or you do not believe in the Fourth Amendment."
Well, there are those who both believe in the Fourth Amendment and
believe that a bloodied glove discarded near the murder site is licitly used
as evidence against an accused. It is odd how inattentively commentators
referred to the Fourth Amendment, which guarantees against "unreasonable searches and seizures." The operative word surely is "unreasonable,"
and while the detectives who spotted the glove might be reproached for
not routinely calling a judge to get a warrant to search, this would be on
the order of upbraiding a combat soldier for forgetting to shine his shoes.
To suggest they were violating a constitutional right is voodoo constitu-
tionalism. When William Kunstler takes such a position he should appear
on television with warpaint on his face and a ring through his nose designating him as a tribal believer in Fourth Amendment witchcraft.

One might quote from a former chief justice of California. Roger
Traynor wrote in 1955 (*People* v. *Cahan*): "The rules of evidence are designed
to enable the court to reach the truth and, in criminal cases, to secure a fair
trial to those accused of crime. Evidence obtained by an illegal search and
seizure is ordinarily just as true and reliable as evidence lawfully obtained.
The court needs all reliable evidence material to the issue before it: the
guilt or innocence of the accused. How such evidence is obtained is immaterial to that issue. It should not be excluded unless strong considerations
of public policy demand it."

What happened after 1955 is of course the evolution of the exclusionary
rule. One observer of American judicial practice after the Warren Court
decisions remarked, "Only a system with limitless patience with irrationality could tolerate the fact that where there has been one wrong, the
defendant's, he will be punished, but where there have been two wrongs—
the defendant's and the [police] officer's—both will go free."

The utter confusion of some of the Warren Court rulings is nicely
exemplified by *Coolidge* v. *New Hampshire* (1971). Get this: The police, suspecting Coolidge of a brutal murder, went to interrogate his wife. Outside the house sat a car answering the description of the murderer's car.
The police opened the door to take a look. They pulled out evidence of
Coolidge's guilt. Everyone conceded that if a magistrate had been there,
he'd have issued a warrant to search the car.

Well, Coolidge was convicted. But then citing as inadmissible the
evidence taken from the car, the Supreme Court reversed. The plurality
opinion of Justice Potter Stewart referred to the constitutional provision
on the subject as an "uncertain mandate." The Warren Court had overruled itself twenty-seven times in its own decisions on search and seizure.

In *Coolidge*, a dissenting opinion by Justice Byron White criticized the plurality opinion not merely as "unexplained," but as "inexplicable." Justice Stewart described Justice White's opinion, in turn, as "nonsense." Separate opinions by Justices Hugo Black and John Marshall Harlan disagreed with the fundamental rationale of the plurality opinion, Justice Harlan noting that the law on search and seizure needed an "overhauling."

It is into that degree of confusion that the defense lawyers sought to sink Kathleen Judge Kennedy-Powell. She resisted by using everyday language based on common experience, common reflexes. The notion that the two detectives were storm-trooping their way into the private residence of O. J. Simpson is insanely inappropriate under the circumstances. The planted axiom of the defense is that any search is unreasonable if a warrant hasn't been issued. To give such sacramental meaning to a magistrate's warrant is, once again, to engage in legal sophistry. Anyone who thinks O. J. Simpson is not getting a fair hearing is out of this world.

—July 8, 1994

Oh, What a Beautiful Morning

Senator Dole said that Republicans must not gloat. On the other hand Tom Wolfe, shortly after the Soviet Union capitulated, addressed an assembly of lifelong Cold Warriors and said—Why not gloat? To gloat is to express great pleasure, "often malicious." The particular temptation to gloat last Tuesday as the returns floated in and Democrat after Democrat glugged down under the tidal wave was generated by the nature of the rhetoric of the losers. Bill Clinton cannot say "John hit the baseball," without insinuating a moral sentiment into the datum. John hit the baseball, which is testimony to John's fine health and to the rigors of exercise and to the joys of a great sport in which millions of Americans engage with such evident pleasure. . . . Snore time indeed, and so help me the impulse arises (we are human) to worry about the baseball.

Has no one given any thought to how you'd feel if you were a baseball? It's all very well to talk about John hitting the baseball, but baseballs represent an ecological asset and there has to be husbandry in dissipating such assets. Snore. I mean, that's how Bill Clinton sounds, and he sounds all the time, everywhere, on every issue, and when he will stop knoweth not the listener and, one began to suspect toward midnight on Tuesday, a lot of voters.

Okay, so a decent interval to gloat, to express great pleasure and a touch of malice directed at those who always represent themselves as speaking for the people, while us-types speak only for special interests. Special interests like, it transpires, the majority of the American people.

Now Newt Gingrich has made the question, Where do we go from here? wonderfully explicit. He has that agenda to which he and all Republican congressional aspirants subscribed in September. Democratic pundits oohed with pleasure at the Contract with America when it was enunciated. Their reasoning was that the mere enumeration of the ten goals gave the Democrats something to chew on, a great relief over the alternative of defending Clinton, which was proving a sweaty exercise with exiguous benefits. Gingrich was undismayed by the criticism and reiterated the legislative, and in some cases constitutional, goals.

The parliamentary situation is this: Assuming that every Republican voted one by one in favor of the agenda, both in the House and in the Senate, all the items on the agenda would be passed. If President Clinton vetoed every measure and every Democrat in the House and in the Senate voted against the agenda, the Republicans would be without sufficient votes to override the vetoes. But it is by no means predictable either that every single Republican senator will go along with every item on the agenda (the Contract was made with members of the House of Representatives and contenders for House seats); nor is it by any means to be supposed that every Democrat will reject the agenda.

Then too there is piquancy in the provision that would give to the president a line-item veto. Congress could pass the line-item number, the president could veto it, Congress could override: and the president could thenceforward decline to exercise the privilege given him.

And of course a term-limitation amendment is a constitutional question, and constitutional initiatives don't stop at the White House for confirmation. They go directly to the states. The question of term limitation is complicated by varying views on its constitutionality. There is the school that says it is absolutely up to the states, and already twenty-two states have voted in favor of term limitation. A second school says it is up to Congress, since Congress sets its own rules. A third school insists that not even Congress can deny to the voters of any congressional district the right to send whomever they wish to Congress, provided he/she is 25 years old. To be sure, Congress—but here we get into constitutional fine-tuning that, for the most part, should be exercised only in law-school seminars—could refuse to seat a congressman if he had already served the proposed limit of twelve years.

Mr. Gingrich is definitely the man of the hour, and for those who have an occasional taste for political grand opera, it is simply too gratifying for words to know that he will replace as Speaker of the House the man who only a little over a year ago when the budget bill was passed announced that finally we had come to the end of the era of Ronald Reagan.

—November 12, 1994

Kemplore

There is talk that Jack Kemp will not run for president. Not necessarily to be credited, because there is also talk that, on Super Bowl Sunday—that is the day Kemp gives his big annual party—he'll say, Count me in.

These words are not designed to give him, or the voters in Iowa and New Hampshire, authoritative advice on the question. They are intended to salute a wonder of the world, which is Jack Kemp's polemical gifts.

A few days ago I was exposed to him on four consecutive television programs, two of them dealing with the Federal Reserve Board's interest-rate policies, the others with tax reform proposals floating about. Other panelists were distinguished analysts, and there were many points of disagreement, but it isn't unfair to say that the preternatural enthusiasm of Jack Kemp for his positions and his quite extraordinary resourcefulness were the most memorable deposit of the four hours.

Presidential candidate Phil Gramm confided to a friend that Jack Kemp was wonderful, but there was this problem: Kemp attached all his hopes to growth. Gramm meant by this that Kemp's soaring optimism about what would happen—most emphatically to the underclass—as a result of getting the government off the back of its citizens is a wholesale increase in the standard of living. When asked to compare the merits of the Clinton tax plan, the Gephardt plan, and the Gingrich and the Gramm plans, Kemp asked, Why were we not considering the Armey plan, which appeals to him most?

The Armey plan is the flat-tax plan. Well, says Kemp, suggesting that he is embarrassed by his forthcoming capitulation to populist disposition, maybe we can't begin it at 17 percent. But why not 18 percent? Or even 19 percent?

The flat-tax proposal would exempt a family of four earning $36,800 or less from paying any federal income tax. After that, everyone would pay 17 percent (Armey's proposal). All other hedges and exemptions would disappear, whence "flat" tax. The money that would then accumulate as federal revenue would equal what is now brought in under a tax law that fills seven volumes with its regulations, exemptions, immunities, and myriad complications.

The advantages are manifest and reach beyond merely the prospective joy of making out one's income-tax return on a single sheet of paper. The advantage, Kemp reminds us, is the lubrication of the entire economy and the disappearance of progressive rates of taxation, which have the effect of dulling enterprise or directing investment policies toward tax avoidance, rather than productivity.

It all sounds very much, one panelist observed, like supply-side economics.

Look, said Kemp eagerly, you were in favor of GATT, weren't you?

Well, yes, sure, of course.

Well, Lloyd Bentsen was secretary of the treasury when the GATT vote came around, and what he said was, Lower the tariffs, and we will have more, not less, trade, export as well as import. And early figures tend to confirm that, right?

Well now, a tariff is a tax, isn't it? So here was Clinton's secretary of the treasury saying, Lower that tax and revenues will increase, not decrease. What's the difference between that tax and other taxes?

If you believe in free trade, don't you believe in supply side on that front? Why is that sound thought on trade but unsound thought on other issues?

The night before, Kemp had been in Jerusalem. He reported on the hunger of young Israelis for relief from the heavy load of taxation. He visited, en route, with President Vaclav Havel of the Czech Republic. He asked Havel whether that republic, enjoying mounting prosperity, unlike its sister states with their sclerotic tax laws, would promulgate a capital-gains tax.

Havel smiled and said to Kemp that no, he did not desire to imitate those practices of the United States that were bad. "And Asia?—no capital-gains tax."

As for the Fed, it is habituated to thinking in terms of set patterns of activity, and is wrong in imposing interest rates that will prevent economic energy from rising to a higher level.

Yes, Kemp talks too much. Walter Mondale once quipped: "What comes after a speech by Hubert Humphrey on Saturday night? Sunday." At least as much can be said of Clinton, the man who almost stopped the Democratic convention in Atlanta in 1988 by his longwindedness.

But when Kemp does it, one isn't left with the feeling that megalomania is out running around the track. He communicates an enthusiasm for his enterprise that is nourished by hard application of his mind to the factual and theoretical bases of freedom, no less. Jack Kemp is himself a wonderfully nourishing experience.

—January 13, 1995

Big Day for Federalism

I begin with a solemn pledge to undertake 750 words without any partisan whoops or sneers. The design is to celebrate Tuesday's promulgation of the new welfare measure.

To jog the memory, the federal government began welfare disbursements about sixty years ago. There were three parties to the transaction. To personalize the schematic, John in Oklahoma paid $$ in taxes to Washington to enable Washington to pay $$ in benefits to James in Oklahoma. Pay James to do what? Pay James to be less poor.

Under the new system, John in Oklahoma pays $$ in taxes to Washington to enable Washington to pay $$ to Oklahoma City to pay James to do what? Oklahoma City will decide what.

Question: Why the round trip? Why not get Oklahoma City to tax John in order to pay James whatever it is Oklahoma City wants James to have, at the expense of John? Answer: That reform, maybe, is for tomorrow.

For those curious about net transactions: In 1994 Oklahoma paid 82 cents to Washington for every $1 that Washington paid to Oklahoma. Oklahoma therefore has been getting a little bit of a free ride from wealthier states.

But concentrate on the electric development of the new law. What it does is permit the exercise of state muscles, which is the basis of the entire federal idea. Listen, for instance (with thanks to Dana Milbank of the *Wall Street Journal* for the research), to what some states have already planned to do with their newfound liberty to design their own welfare programs.

Until the American Civil Liberties Union finds out about it, Michigan intends to get the Salvation Army to connect welfare mothers with religious families who will help with child care, transportation, and the like.

Florida doesn't really want to encourage more immigration and so will cut aid to aliens, sending welfare balances to others in different kinds of distress. Maine, by contrast, isn't suffering from swollen immigration and therefore will continue to help aliens at current levels.

Oregon will subsidize the wages of welfare recipients.

Here is a cool one: Ohio will exercise the most powerful stick available in the United States. An Ohio father who does not pay his child support will lose his driver's license.

New Hampshire will concentrate on poverty reduction by tackling school dropouts and teenage pregnancy. Next-door Vermont, meanwhile, will continue its swagger, allowing single parents to receive benefits for thirty months before they have to work. If they are students, they will need to work only seven hours a week to hang onto their benefits.

So it goes. There are first-year anomalies. Michigan will receive $150 million more than it got under the previous schedule. Florida, Texas, and Massachusetts will gain considerably. But much of this will settle down as the books consolidate and practices are revised.

Meanwhile, private enterprise is getting into the act. Lockheed Martin Corp.'s Information Management Services is available to administer states' welfare plans. Texas wants to privatize the whole business, putting the money it saves back into the welfare pool.

One notes the exciting potential here for medical-welfare experimentation. There are already states (Hawaii most conspicuous among them) that have devised their own medical plans and are sailing along with them. The new approach should encourage a proliferation of such plans.

Five years ago Harris Wofford was elected senator from Pennsylvania pledging to go to Washington with a national health plan. Hillary Rodham Clinton's health plan was defeated, but why should that stop the residents of Pennsylvania, whose payments to Washington almost exactly equal Washington's payments to Pennsylvania? The point does suggest itself, doesn't it: Why get Washington into the act at all, except to broker aid to states in distress?

It is very exciting for those who have always been enthusiastic about the federal idea. Exploit the resources of federalism. If Vermont, sitting cheek by jowl with New Hampshire, wants very different social-welfare programs from its neighbor, what better means of observing their relative effects than to encourage experimentation?

I have made it so far without partisan emphasis, but am required to quote a passage from a speech.

"How can indiscriminate redistribution accommodate the emphases of individual states? Florida is for obvious reasons more concerned with the older generation. Massachusetts with its density of colleges has to worry more about education costs than Utah, where educational needs are stable. Why not let them define their own welfare programs?"

Yes, that was yours truly, in 1967.

—October 1, 1996

Cleaning Up Social Security

Senator Thomas Daschle (D., S.D.) has embarrassed some of his Democratic colleagues by his exchange with columnist Robert Novak on the matter of the Social Security trust fund, and all of this in a season in which privatization is in the air.

To focus on the question, we'll use round numbers.

—Say sixty people are receiving Social Security payments.

—One hundred eighty are paying Social Security taxes.

The result is that more people are paying into the Social Security pool than are drawing from it. The result is a surplus of X. We call that the Social Security trust fund.

But as you would expect, X burns a hole in the pocket of Uncle Sam, and he can't resist borrowing it to pay the projected current deficit, which without help would be 4X. So he spends the money in the trust fund and leaves a calling card: "IOU X. Many thanks, Sam."

The government, having acquired X and spent it on aircraft carriers and interest on outstanding loans and champagne for foreign visitors, can report that its annual deficit is reduced. If it had been necessary to borrow the money other than from itself, it would have been acknowledged as a plain debt. But since it is a kind of in-house arrangement, the accountants don't put it quite in that corner, if you see what I mean—which isn't easy to do, in part because I don't know quite know how to say it.

Here is how it was handled in Novak's exchange with the Senate Democratic leader: "Senator, do you believe there is a Social Security trust fund?"

"Ah, yes, I do."

"What's in it? Can you tell me what's in it?"

"Legally, there is a requirement that that money can be invested, and you could call that a fund, yes."

"But there is no such fund?"

"No, there is no such fund per se."

To go now to the other end of the economic cycle, the year is 2012. Now there are one hundred people getting Social Security (the baby boomers are beginning to retire), and only one hundred twenty paying into Social Security. The result is that the "fund" is drawn down, and by the year 2039, it has disappeared.

What, exactly, has disappeared? Answer: The government's fictitious obligation to an abstraction. The only thing that has been accomplished by that flurry of computer bytes is the illusion that we have spent $50 billion less, per year, than in fact we have.

The panel set up to investigate the future of Social Security is divided on what should be done. Five of its thirteen members believe that at least one part of the money taken in every time a paycheck is issued should revert to an account for the benefit of the payer, to be invested in stocks and bonds. This would mean (a) that income to the participant would grow (in every ten-year interval, stocks have done better than government bonds), and (b) that the individual would have personal control over a part of what has become a U.S. pension fund (he could decide to retire early or late), and (c) that a capital pool would materialize (dollars going not into the phony trust fund, but to sure-enough enterprises that hire people, pay taxes, and pay dividends).

The Chilean government has been doing this since 1983, and the results, so far, are gratifying, giving Chilean participants five times the return on their savings accumulated under Social Security.

What if a great economic blight were to descend over us, freezing us into a depression as severe as that of the Thirties but much longer? In Chile, a government guarantee kicks in, and whatever happened to the portfolio of the Chilean pensioner, he would be guaranteed a 3 percent return.

It wasn't designed in that way, Social Security "insurance" having first been thought of as insurance against destitution. As a general pension plan it has side effects not fully parsed, among them the question: How responsible is this general pension for the low rate of savings? And then if savings are abnormally low, when contrasted with the savings of other industrial societies, what effect is hyperconsumption having on inflation? On interest rates?

Questions to ponder, but to ponder usefully requires a little hygiene in the language, and this could logically begin by forbidding the use of "trust fund" to describe the IOU from Uncle Sam to Uncle Sam.

—December 6, 1996

Illegalizing Illegals

The new intelligence law, courtesy of 9/11, is mystifying because it does not face directly what is the most prominent threat to homeland security. And that is: inimical action by non-Americans. All the people who participated in 9/11 were foreigners, here under various auspices. And yet the bill that has evolved from the findings of the 9/11 commission reads like an elocutionary exercise by a national committee to avoid saying anything unpleasant about unpleasant people born abroad.

Specifically, the threat at this moment is from foreign terrorism. The day may come when there are native-born Americans who join in such a threat, such as the Weather Underground types we experienced during the Seventies.

But at this point, the terrorists come from abroad. "Last May," writes *National Interest* editor John O'Sullivan, "illegal aliens from Malaysia, Pakistan, Morocco, Uganda, and India were released without bond. They are now at large in the U.S."

What happened is that as the intelligence bill crystallized, a fear developed that it might be construed as xenophobic. Somewhere along the line the word came down from the White House that for President Bush to be able to sign the bill, it had to be plucked clean of any suggestion that an illegal Muslim fundamentalist should be treated at all differently from an illegal Christian evangelist. Remember the odd deportment of

Norman Mineta, who has been reappointed as transportation secretary? He went to extraordinary lengths several years ago to insist that security personnel at airports should pay no greater attention to thirty-year-old Near Eastern Muslims called Mohammed than they would to Shirley Temple.

The immigration problem is the primary unmet challenge of modern times. It is so because the whole of our political establishment cringes at any suggestion that the United States is inhospitable to immigration. We do have laws on the books, but they are apparently made for the sole purpose of allowing people to flout them. *Time* magazine published the most florid essay on the question, estimating the annual flow of illegal immigration at more than two million persons.

There are two questions on the table. The first deals with raw immigration: How many people beyond those formally welcome under existing laws should we admit into the United States? The second, What are the risks to security in being as offhanded as we have been?

In the age of terrorism, it is obvious that the enemy will seek to do damage operating within U.S. territory. That, of course, was the story of the 9/11 hijackers, nineteen Muslim terrorists who took advantage of loose laws to practice flying accurately into U.S. skyscrapers.

But the movements of such folk are not of primary concern to the U.S. government, to judge from the record. Mr. O'Sullivan reports that the Transportation Department has launched several lawsuits against airlines because pilots had banned passengers they thought were security risks.

Asa Hutchinson, an official in the Department of Homeland Security, recently cut down a Border Patrol initiative to catch illegal aliens. The reason? It was catching too many illegal aliens.

We have the piquant problem of what to do with illegals. It approaches the problem of what to do with drinkers during Prohibition. You couldn't put them all in jail because there weren't enough jails. Illegals remain largely undisturbed, and the main reason for it isn't U.S. sentimentality toward aspirant Americans. It is the market contribution to the dilemma: There are jobs only illegals are willing to perform, e.g., serving as nannies for the children of New York Police Commissioner Bernard Kerik. Much of the menial and agricultural work done in the southwestern states is done by illegals.

The result of the combined forces—the need for cheap labor and the passion to avoid any appearance of ethnic or religious discrimination—is an open frontier. Yes, a few illegals are deported. These should get a parade, signaling such distinction as attaches to so rare an event. And perhaps a parade when they come through the next time, often through the same gap in the southwestern frontier.

A subsidiary but not uninteresting question is: Where do our deportees gather? What help is available to them to reassemble? Perhaps to return to Arizona in time for high-school reunions?

It's a tough one politically, but Congress should bear down on the subject, intimately related to concerns for homeland security.

—December 14, 2004

What We Lost at the Astor

This is a morality tale, springing from the old saying, "I lost it at the Astor." For the benefit of the newborn (age seventy or younger), the Astor was a hotel with a famous bar popular with the young, at which seductions were frequently initiated, resulting in the loss of virginity.

The Astor, reconceived in formal economic terms, usefully summons John Maynard Keynes as the great seducer. What we lost was the innate sense of national husbandry, which taught us that deficit spending was wrong. Why? Because it was simply wrong—not right, not moral—to spend money you hadn't set aside.

Keynes taught us, of course, that deficit spending is morally neutral. It is simply an instrument of economic policy, useful—indeed, invaluable—in correcting maladjustments. If there is great unemployment, and the impulse to spend is anaesthetized, you get things like national depressions. To avoid these you need to deploy hot cash into the economy, such as will revitalize consumption, induce production, and restore full employment.

Say's Law (Jean-Baptiste Say, 1767–1832) taught that there can't really be overproduction, because the appetite of man is infinite. If, therefore, there is unemployment, that's because something has got in the way of the impulse to satisfy the appetite. In Keynesian doctrine, what got in the way was an imbalance between production and consumption, which is mitigated by federal spending.

Of course Keynes was absolutely right on that score, and for sixty years deficit spending has been approved even by people who thought themselves impregnable to the lures of misbehavior at the Astor.

But what crept into the act, with the acceptance of deficit spending as required for national economic policy, was an attitude of detachment toward the old principle that you should not spend what you do not have. And this detachment is degenerate, as witness popular political attitudes on the matter of Social Security.

President Bush didn't attack the Social Security problem in moral terms. He'd have been laughed out of town if he had attempted this, but that doesn't bar others from attempting it. What Mr. Bush said wasn't that, pure and simple, Social Security payments on the present schedule were unearned. What he said was that beginning in the year 2017, there wouldn't be enough money in the "bank" to pay them out as prescribed. The kind of money he was talking about could not simply be issued as a Keynesian infusion into the economy. The federal government can't just write checks for $300 billion, because money on that scale transcends Keynesian instrumentation, becoming simply huge ventures into national inflation.

What Mr. Bush might have said, summoning the moral authority of lost norms, was that Social Security payments correctly do two things. The first is to repay the American sixty-five-year-old the money taken from him during his working life, plus interest. The second, to provide insurance against such emergencies as bring on destitution.

Before losing it at the Astor, an American listening to this explanation would have found it entirely reasonable. But in the effusive economic pattern of welfare-state thinking, he has come to accept Society Security as a kind of bonanza. Combining Social Security with longevity, we anticipate, with the present scheduling, welfare payments to millions and then tens of millions of Americans. And there is no movement by any organized body of American consumers that is prepared to say: Just give us back what you borrowed from us, and we'll call it quits.

You can't, in these days, successfully appeal to Americans to reason in that way. If the accounting goes forward as it now threatens to do, Social Security will give the retired American who lives to age eighty twice or three times what he invested in the Social Security program.

Mr. Bush didn't make an appeal based on these moral maxims. But he took a huge first step by saying simply that there wasn't the money there to pursue the program as conceived and elaborated over the years. He also took the extraordinary step of proposing reduced payments to middle- and upper-income beneficiaries. And most of them (as witness the pronouncements of AARP) are ready to fight to the death for their benefits/extortions.

Bush may not win this through remedial legislation. He has the alternative of letting the impact of inflation make its own way, and if that happens, we'll have lost it all at the Astor, including any pride we take in responsible self-government.

—May 3, 2005

Post-Katrina Doublethought

The war against stable thought blazes on, the objective being to put the blame on the Bush administration for what happened in New Orleans.

Thomas Friedman of the *New York Times* goes far in personalizing the whole thing. The administration has a "tax policy . . . dominated by the toweringly selfish Grover Norquist—who has been quoted as saying: 'I don't want to abolish government. I simply want to reduce it to the size where I can drag it into the bathroom and drown it in the bathtub.'"

You would think that Mr. Friedman would leave a little place in life for hyperbole—what would he do with the political poets who speak of the "end" of hunger and disease? But he hangs onto the metaphor: "Mr. Norquist is the only person about whom I would say this: I hope he owns property around the New Orleans levee that was never properly finished because of a lack of tax dollars. I hope his basement got flooded." Planted axiom: The unrepaired levee in New Orleans is the result of a shortage of federal dollars.

Across the editorial page we have the argument put a little differently. Not that Maureen Dowd will neglect an opportunity to personalize Katrina. No, she explains, the tragedy was the result of the Bush political family, Dick Cheney being the next in line. What was he doing when Katrina struck? He was "reportedly . . . shopping for a $2.9 million waterfront estate in St. Michael's," which is a "retreat in the Chesapeake Bay, where Rummy"—the secretary of defense, Donald Rumsfeld—"has a weekend home."

"As the water recedes," Dowd explains, "more and more decaying bodies will testify to the callous and stumblebum administration response to Katrina's rout of 90,000 square miles of the South." Another planted axiom: The Bush administration, to return to the language of Mr. Friedman, "has engaged in a tax giveaway since 9/11 that has had one underlying assumption: There will never be another rainy day."

The gravamen against Bush becomes plain: The Bush administration insisted "on cutting more taxes, even when that has contributed to incomplete levees and too small an army to deal with Katrina, Osama, and Saddam at the same time."

The proposition that the federal government under George W. Bush has been shortchanging welfare is in astonishing conflict with the figures. Under Bush, federal spending has increased at the fastest rate in thirty years. Non-defense discretionary spending under Bush has grown by 35.7 percent, the highest rate of federal-government growth since the presidencies of Richard Nixon and Lyndon Johnson.

Again, the planted axiom is that the New Orleans levee has been for years a national pustule that President Bush refused to lance because he didn't want to drain the money needed by Dick Cheney to buy his waterfront estate. If New Orleans was conspicuous for its vulnerability, why hadn't the city's articulate mayor, or his fellow Democrat the articulate governor, said something about it? Why did it not figure in the demands of the Democratic Party at its convention in Boston? How to explain the silence on the subject by candidate John Kerry?

It is tempting to weigh directly the cost of repairing the levee and the size of the tax cuts. But what is going to pay for all the ounces of prevention we could contingently use on all the frontiers of national vulnerability? To single out the levee is on the order of blaming the destruction of the Twin Towers on the architects who situated them where they were. The first-level threat to America is a nuclear bomb, then biological and chemical weapons. What pre-emptive precautions should be taken against the development of such weaponry? Which Republicans are objecting to federal expenditures on those fronts?

We have been promised reports on Katrina from almost every official body, legislative and executive. It diminishes confidence in purposive thought to lose oneself in polemical theater. Grover Norquist uses his own language. But he could equally have used that of John Adams, who warned that the government seeks to turn every contingency into an excuse for enhancing power in itself. Or that of Woodrow Wilson, who said that the history of liberalism is the history of man's efforts to restrain the growth of government. If New Orleans is a land doomed by nature, then nature's reach needs to be tamed, or else yielded to. The critics have not yet charged that movement away from New Orleans was prohibited by George W. Bush.

—September 9, 2005

THE COLD WAR AT HOME

The Colossal Flunk

Just as priests go to confession, and presidents to the polls, and distinguished men of letters to the critics, just so the professors ought to turn to the American people for an occasional report card. As a layman, one of the signatures on the report card will be mine. For those professors who have dealt with issues of immediate and vital interest to the welfare and integrity of the United States, I vote a resounding flunk.

And the failure of the intellectuals is serious indeed in consideration of the nature of their relationship to the American people, who are a busy lot of folk. Too busy, in fact, to do as much contemplating as they ought to; too busy to do very much original research.

But just as the American people are in the habit of overcoming most of the technical obstacles that stand between them and prosperous and efficient lives, they long ago hit upon a solution to the problem of where to go for expert intellectual guidance: They would turn over a share of their revenues to the professors, who would not only teach their children but also spend many hours in the dusty stacks of the university libraries (which the citizens would stock), additional hours in thinking hard about the practical and theoretical problems that constantly beset the community, the nation, and the world—and then they would publish and preach their findings, to which the people would look for counsel.

Most people know that in 1936 Lord Keynes merely put into first-class English what the world has known time out of mind, that "The ideas of economists and political philosophers . . . are . . . powerful. . . . Indeed the world is ruled by little else. Practical men . . . are usually the slaves of some defunct economist. Madmen in authority, who hear voices in the air, are distilling their frenzy from some academic scribbler of a few years back. . . . The power of vested interests is usually exaggerated when compared with the gradual encroachment of ideas."

The people also know that the virtual monopoly exercised by the intellectuals in discovering new ideas, or in fortifying old ones, is no grievous reflection on the people's own sovereignty. Not even the most fervent democrat bases his faith in representative government on the expectation that every voter will be an independent political philosopher. And after all, the professors must defer to the people to review their findings. It is for the people to accept those they see fit to accept, and to reject those they see fit to reject.

Still and all, nobody questions that the intellectuals have a major responsibility to make recommendations which will help harmoniously to regulate social life, and which will guide our congressmen, statesmen, and executives wisely to formulate national and community policies. History is very clear in revealing that no social movement has ever made significant headway unless it has intellectual support.

The success of this democratic adjustment depends, of course, on the integrity of the professors, on their devotion to truth at any cost, and, not least, on their perspicacity.

And in all these respects—one, two, three—the intellectuals as a whole have failed the American people, who, in return for their faith, are left today looking, at point-blank range, at a catastrophic international situation, a staggering and martial economy, a looming era of domestic tyranny, and with it all, an arrogant and impenitent intellectual class.

~

What better start than to review the course of our relationship with the Soviet Union since that day in November 1933 when the president of the United States, after quoting from a letter by Thomas Jefferson written in 1809 to the effect that Russia and the United States were "in character and practice essentially pacific, with a common interest in the rights of peaceful nations," clasped the hand of Maxim Litvinov and extended full diplomatic recognition to the Soviet Union. In return, Roosevelt received a promise that Russia would refrain from any act "liable in any way whatsoever to injure the tranquility, prosperity, order, or security of the whole or any part of the United States . . . or any agitation or propaganda having as an aim the violation of the territorial integrity of the United States . . . or to bring about a change in the political or social order of the United States."

Now whose responsibility was it to confront Franklin Roosevelt with the available and overwhelming evidence that his capricious act was nothing more than an invitation to the Comintern to set up in the United States hemispheric headquarters for a violent revolutionary movement historically consecrated to the encouragement of class warfare and racial tension, to violence, slander, infiltration, and sabotage, and even to assassination to bring about the only honorable goal in the Communist code: total subjugation of the free world to the Kremlin?

By 1933, abundant, conclusive evidence about the nature of Stalinism was available to any dispassionate researcher. By that time, the Soviet Union had ruthlessly destroyed a whole class of her own people in pursuit of her doctrinaire goals. In prosecuting the personal and political enemies of her dictator, she had flagrantly scorned those fundamental principles of justice and decency long ago recognized as indispensable to civilized society. She had fostered and directed revolutionary movements in Germany, Poland, Austria, and Italy, in Argentina, Uruguay, Cuba, and Mexico. It was known to the student of Communism that Commissar Zinoviev had written to his Comintern representative in Argentina that Mexican recognition of the Soviet Union had opened up "the brightest vista for the future, the greatest possibilities for international expansion, and the source of possible difficulties for the United States . . . ," and that the secretary of the Communist International, R. Tomasov, had written in February of 1932 that "The examination of reports from our commissars in Latin America during the last three months of 1931 leads us to decide to begin a period of concentrated revolutionary action. The lower classes of Argentina, Brazil, Chile, Peru, and Uruguay are ready to fight and bring down the established governments."

In short, there was evidence aplenty for whoever looked for it that Communist behavior was hewing close to Communist theory, that world revolution, directed by Moscow and backed by all the resources of the Soviet Union, was a central drive which no petit-bourgeois considerations of decency or justice or humanitarianism, or even of promises to FDR, would be allowed to deflect.

The question remains, of course: Whose was the foremost responsibility to bring to light, insistently and diligently, the intellectual ammunition that the American people needed to repudiate the irresponsible and ignorant act of their chief executive? It was clearly not the factory worker or the housewife who was in a position to assemble relevant data about the Communist conspiracy and thrust them in the face of the electorate. No, the responsibility sat squarely on the shoulders of the academic community—to turn on the Communists and their activities a withering spotlight, and to do the same to any government, most especially our own, whose policies tended to enhance the estate of international Communism.

Yet a survey of the literature of the day reveals hardly a dissenting wave length originating from the nation's ivory towers. The reverse, in fact, was the case: the academic journals of the period treated compassionately and even encouragingly American recognition, which served immeasurably to fortify Stalin's then-faltering domestic position, and brought with it a reverberating international impact in its implications of American faith in the good intentions of the Soviet state. And it meant, for the United States, diplomatic immunity for hundreds of Soviet saboteurs well armed with funds and propaganda and the know-how to fashion American foreign policy, which only recently—after irreparable damage—has begun to shrug off the influence of the Comintern.

The academic betrayal of 1933 was only the precursor of consistent soft-headedness toward the Soviet Union which reached its peak in 1946. For during this era Russia was spoken of in countless classrooms throughout the country as the land of the great social experiment, very likely destined some day to present the world with the long-sought-for formula for solving the world's nagging social and economic ills. These were the days of flourishing student John Reed Clubs and Young Communist Leagues, whose members found themselves willing or unwitting participants in the Soviet conspiracy, clearly reflecting the behavior and ideals of their professors, so many of whom manned the mastheads of so many Communist fronts.

It was during this period that Earl Browder, head of the American Communist Party, made frequent appearances on campuses. It was during this period that fellow-traveler J. B. Matthews made 250 talks in forty-eight states until he renounced Stalin and turned investigator for the Dies Committee. Matthews's apostasy abruptly ended all academic speaking invitations; yet Comintern operative Gerhart Eisler continued to address college groups while awaiting deportation.

And the Dies Committee, of course, had to cope not only with the distilled calumny of countless politicians and journalists, but also with almost daily denunciations from the college lecture platform, just as its successor, the Thomas Committee, was assailed in the public press by almost the entire staff of the Yale Law School nine years later.

~

There was no stopping the intellectual accolades for the Soviet Union, which bore fruit during the war in the tragic attitude of the administration toward China, our ally in the East. The brief popular flurry against the Soviet Union when she attacked Finland lasted not much longer than the refrains from a few Finnish relief balls. The episodic insight of the people soon ended, and they turned back to uncritical adulation of Soviet Russia. How desolate and isolated were the few academic voices that warned against the drift of our international policies during wartime, and how deafening and assured, by comparison, the clamor of approbation as

Roosevelt glibly went about his business of preparing for the enslavement of millions of free men and a third world war.

The casual attitude of the intellectuals toward the truth was nowhere better typified than in their tolerance of Ambassador Joseph E. Davies's absurd and palpably dishonest *Mission to Moscow*, and their subsequent refusal to rally to the support of W. L. White's *Report on the Russians*.

The whole book-reviewing trend, in point of fact, gave evidence of an unconscionable intellectual contempt for truth combined with an astounding absence of perspicacity, and it reached its peak with the alert reception, between 1943 and 1948, of books that dealt with Communist China. Far from insisting that the truth about China be spelled out to the citizenry, the academicians (with a few notable exceptions), led by such men as Harvard's John Fairbank, Johns Hopkins's Owen Lattimore, and Columbia's Nathaniel Peffer, waged a constant battle to becloud the issues. Their efforts—taking into consideration what it was in their power to do—sealed the fate of four hundred million Chinese, doubled the circumference of the Iron Curtain, and opened the dikes of the 38th Parallel in Korea.

∼

Handicapped for years by the expert academic guidance they had so long confided in, the American people, enlightened primarily by shrewd and devoted newspapermen, finally broke through the fog. The month of July 1948 will probably live as the turning point. The brilliant exposés in *Time* and *Life* and *Newsweek* of the Progressive Party Convention, what it meant, what it was, and where it was going, threw light on our worsening crisis. And whereas there was abundant evidence—over a year old—that the Wallace candidacy was an instrument of Soviet foreign policy, it was not the college professors, the shrewd professional truth-seekers, who warned the American people what the Communists were about; it was most noticeably *Newsweek* (viz. its notable issue of September 1947), the maligned editors of *Counterattack*, Fred Woltman of the *New York World-Telegram*, and various other journalists who apprehended the truth, showed the courage to cling to it, and had the dedication to circularize it.

So the tide turned. But many academicians (a diminishing number, it is true), cloaked in "academic freedom" and swinging Diogenes' lantern whenever there was one other person in the room, stubbornly clung to falsehoods, deception, and intransigence. To such a point that when the notorious Cultural and Scientific Congress for World Peace raised its curtain at the Waldorf-Astoria a year later—even amidst almost universal public awareness of its constitution and aims—we saw that it was chaired by a professor, that several college presidents had originally consented to sponsor it, and that the list of those in attendance was weighted down with academicians who thereby served notice to the American people that they would be the last to face up to their responsibilities as intelligent and honest men.

The tide, though, was not to be turned again, and although the Communist peace movement still finds notable support from the academicians, the American people, with their customary gentleness and occasional firmness, are teaching the professors the facts of life about the Communist conspiracy. And with such marked success that in July of 1949, an extraordinarily illustrative event at last served to graduate the professors from political kindergarten. The National Education Association—the most powerful educational organization in the United States, one of the oldest, and manned exclusively by academicians—came rallying forth to the aid of God and country. Meeting in Boston, our blue-ribbon educators announced that membership in the Communist Party and its "accompanying surrender of intellectual integrity, render an individual unfit to discharge the duties of a teacher in this country."

It had taken our most venerable educational group thirty years of digging to hit pay dirt which had stared them in the face all the while; but hit it they did, though their pronouncement struck their disciples, the American people, as being about as timely and valuable as would have been a resolution by the American Medical Association, meeting at about the same time, to the effect that men who believed all illnesses could be cured by staring into a kaleidoscope and muttering the Hippocratic oath would not make adequate doctors.

～

The failure of the professors to direct American thought and action into fruitful channels at times of crisis has been perhaps the most flamboyant academic characteristic of the recent past. But this is not the extent of the great intellectual travesty. Necessary to their total self-esteem is a friendly posterity. To that end, they set about to domesticate history. There is no better illustration of this than the academic reception of revisionism.

It is no longer a controversial fact that Franklin Roosevelt's foreign policy between 1939 and 1941 was conducted independently of the wishes of the majority of the American people, and, further, that he was not sincere when he publicly expressed his intentions to keep the United States out of war.

We must remember that for the purposes of this discussion it is altogether immaterial whether or not the American people have cause to be grateful to Roosevelt for his transcendent vision, for those actions which earned for him Professor Basil Rauch's encomium, the "architect of our happiness." The question is rather whether history books will chronicle events and attitudes as they took place or as the dominant political party of the day would have had them take place. The question, of course, is not entirely academic, for lessons are to be learned from experience. If the American people know it as a historical fact that one president, with the aid of influential factions, friends, and jobholders, was able by personal diplomacy to commit a pacifist and articulate nation to a world war, why then perhaps the Constitution should be amended to modify more specifically the chief executive's monopoly on making foreign policy.

But the people are not destined to know the particulars of Roosevelt's foreign policy because the intellectuals have banded together to short-circuit any attempt by a truth-seeker to reveal the truth.

Even Charles Beard, the most respected American historian of the past thirty years, was not trusted enough to penetrate the iron curtain that surrounds Roosevelt's activities during the period in question. His last book, *President Roosevelt and the Coming of the War*, invited the concentrated wrath of the Ph.D. apologists for the New Deal, and earned for the last work of this titanic and objective thinker such epithets from his colleagues as "distorted," "petty," "vulgar," "perverted," "amateurish," "personal," "cheap journalism," "mythology," and so on. After the initial blast, calculated to discredit Beard once and for all, the vigilantes of Roosevelt's reputation have sat hack to write their own "histories," satisfied with occasional oblique and evasive thrusts, as for example Louis Hacker's parenthetical remark in a review in the Winter 1951 issue of the *Yale Review* that Beard "did so many wise things and one foolish one."

While Beard's reputation entitled him to a frontal attack, most of the other revisionists met up with the tested silent treatment. Except for a few explosive and well-placed parries, the works of George Morgenstern, John Flynn, William Henry Chamberlin, and Frederick Osborn were simply ignored or treated to token reviews. And almost always—where reviews appeared—the same group of hatchet-men were called in to preside over the assassination. Samuel Morison, Arthur Schlesinger Jr., Harvey De Weerd, Oron Hale, Lewis Mumford, Harry Gideonse, Walter Millis, Charles Griffin, Samuel Bemis, James Minifie, Robert Sherwood, Henry

Commager, Paul Douglas, Thomas Bailey, Basil Rauch, Edward Earle, and Allan Nevins—i.e., our ruling cadre of historians and publicists—can he counted on to step in and save Franklin Roosevelt from detached historical scrutiny.

The conspiracy against giving the American people the facts goes a great deal further than vicious attacks or total neglect of published revisionist books. Professor Harry Elmer Barnes, the solitary and neglected leader of the "struggle against a historical blackout," of the movement to "bring history into accord with facts," reports that sources of material vital to informed and exhaustive research into pre-war foreign policy are closed to objective researchers. Public documents of a sensitive nature are displayed only to hired hands who can be trusted to come through with the Court Interpretation of history. Another major obstacle to the researcher interested in exposing facts as they occurred is where to find a publisher. Were it not for two small publishing houses, the Devin-Adair Company and the Henry Regnery Company, and for one sally by the Yale University Press, no revisionist literature would have reached the public. In fact, Charles Beard was so effectively smeared after his Roosevelt book that a leading publisher, committed to bringing out a memorial volume after Beard's death, paying tribute to his contributions, refused to honor his agreement.

Notice has been served, in short, that the prevailing political-historical orthodoxy is not to be challenged. It has been accepted by the majority of American intellectuals, and that, and that alone, is sufficient reason for its uncritical acceptance by the masses.

Let it be perfectly clear, though, that the professors can speak up like nobody's business when they're offended, and in fact, they constantly do. Available to them are the columns of almost every influential periodical in the United States, and also the radio, and now television. Editors cry for their copy, and resolutions by the National Education Association or by the American Association of University Professors have no difficulty reaching the news columns. Additionally, hundreds of thousands of Americans hear from them in lecture and commencement halls throughout the country.

Take the California Loyalty Oath as an example. The academic class, broadly speaking, decided they were opposed to it. Almost immediately, millions upon millions of Americans were unable to turn around without reading or hearing about the tyrannical regents of the University of California. Books, magazine articles, reviews, radio talks, forums, and inaugural addresses poured it on, till the American people began to think of the startled and well-meaning educators as worse than the Communists themselves, who never suffered from quite the equivalent tirade.

When the spirit moves the professors to pass along their opinions, they do it, and they are heard.

So why, we're entitled to ask, haven't the professors passed better advice along in the past? Why don't they insist that the truth be circulated, the consequences notwithstanding? Why, for example, don't the professors once and for all put the kibosh on the crazy notion that Madison and Jefferson and Hamilton, in insisting on separation of Church and State, implied that no courses in religion could be taught in the public schools? Why don't they point out that whatever their opinion of McCarthy, his charges were unfairly handled by the Tydings Committee? Why don't they publicly condemn the persecution of anti-Communists all over the United States, and rally to their defense as glibly and consistently as they do for those members of the fraternity of the Left whom they consider occasionally short-cut on their civil rights?

The answer, of course, is appalling; but there is no reason why the American people should be as afraid of the truth as the professors. The answer is that generally speaking, the academicians have at best lost their perspicacity; it is more likely that they have lost their appetite for truth and their integrity. And the outlook is all the gloomier for the knowledge that it's this same group that has educated the new generation with their concepts of truth and integrity and reason.

—*The American Mercury,* March 1952

The End of McCarthy

In the same week that Senator McCarthy fell fatally ill, the Penguin publishing company brought out a *Dictionary of Politics,* by two Oxford scholars, which defines "McCarthyism" as "Intolerance of liberalism." The book was laid to rest by Mr. William Schlamm in *National Review*'s issue of May 4. It is certainly believable, on Mr. Schlamm's showing, that its authors are Communists; and if that is the case, the perverted definition, of course, is neither here nor there. Such a definition of the movement to which Senator McCarthy gave his name is, however, accepted by men who are not Communist or insane, and there is the awful truth. The Labour Party of Great Britain is not Communist, but its mouthpiece, the

Daily Herald, identified Senator McCarthy last week as the man who had "used his position to hound men whose only crime was love of freedom of thought." There are no Communists or, that we know of, neurotics on the Conservative *Daily Sketch,* which last week wrote that it was with justice that "McCarthy became the world's most hated man." The Liberal *News Chronicle* was not moved by a Communist's bloodlust to conclude its obituary notice on the senator by saying "America was the cleaner by his fall, and is cleaner by his death."

That kind of savagery was not aroused in the hearts and minds of Europeans by Communist propaganda. Communism rails, with varying intensity, against all who are not with it: against Senator McCarthy and President Eisenhower—and even Herbert Lehman. In the Communist demonology Senator McCarthy and William Fulbright are alike men to be hated and opposed, for they have both rejected the revolution. McCarthy, as a day-to-day matter, was due to be resisted more ferociously than Fulbright, to be sure; for by temperament and understanding he was the kind of man Fulbright will never be, the kind that fires a whole people's resolution. A McCarthy might fire the Western will; and that is the single development the Communists have to fear.

But it is unrealistic to suppose that in Europe, any more than in America, the superstitions about the nature of McCarthy and McCarthyism that seized the minds of rational and decent men were concocted by Communist sorcerers. In McCarthy-baiting, the Communists always ran second. The superstitions were brewed by liberal intellectuals. These intellectuals had a considerable success in imposing the myths of McCarthyism on their own country. In Europe they bewitched entire populations. Why? Because there was so eager a disposition to believe that ours is the kind of country where scoundrel-demagogues make such great public headway? Because, in its flatulence, Europe was dismayed at the kind of toughness that was discernible in some of McCarthy's words and deeds? Because there did not happen to be, in Europe, those who were well enough informed to expose the wandering American scholars and journalists who sang of the blackness that had shrouded their native land, now become the preserve of a young primitive from Wisconsin? We do not know what happened: but we do know that by 1953 it had become possible for Bertrand Russell to inform fellow members of the British intelligentsia that America was the land where one could no longer read Thomas Jefferson; and that by 1957 the editors of the *Daily Herald* could seriously identify the aim of McCarthy, and those who supported him, as that of "hound[ing] men whose only crime was love of freedom of thought."

We have been very skeptical, for a number of years, about the future of Europe. Not more skeptical than many Europeans have been, and are. It is worth noting, in passing, that only the gravest intellectual sickness can explain the collective suspension of the critical faculties of an entire continent. It was irrationalism on the grand scale that licensed the prevailing myth of McCarthyism. But it is not Europe's mind and morals, but our own, that we pause to reflect upon on the day McCarthy is buried. For the intellectual virus that ravaged Europe was not native grown. It was, in this case, an American export; and the nation that spawned it is sick. It is America—if we may be permitted a nostalgic relapse into an area of concern which nowadays is denounced as Isolationist—that we are concerned with. And America—we speak of her leaders, and her intellectual elite—(a) refused to understand the man McCarthy or the phenomenon McCarthyism, and (b) acted brutally toward him, and unreasoningly toward it.

There is no reason to hope that the fact that McCarthy is no longer in a position to inconvenience them, or prevent them from reading Thomas Jefferson, will so weaken the defenses of the Liberals as to persuade them to go back, now that it is all over, and look at what really happened. That intellectual voyage they may, heeding the warnings of a subconscious solicitude for their self-esteem, put off forever. It would be a frightening journey, for it would involve reflecting on the data, and who was responsible for them, that led a renowned British logician to conclude that freedom in America had perished; there would be a visit to a crowded Senate chamber where an elderly and prudish senator from Vermont dutifully read from a script prepared by an organization backed by the nation's mighty, alleging that an unnatural relationship between Senator McCarthy and his counsel could explain their behavior; the voyager would pause over the hysterical frivolities of the scholars who saw McCarthyism as consisting in weird comings and goings, up and down, eastward and westward, of Catholics and Baptists and rich men and poor men and anti–Ivy Leaguers and Nebraskans who couldn't get into Hotchkiss; at least a day would be spent pondering the virtual absence of serious literature on McCarthy, and the violent hostility to the few efforts that were made to understand what was going on; and, finally, an embarrassed hour with anti-McCarthy confidence man Paul Hughes, who would describe how he took in, and spent, by the thousands of dollars, the money of senior members of the Democratic Party, of Americans for Democratic Action, of the *Washington Post*, by simply pretending to spy on McCarthy's staff and feeding them, day after day, provocative and salacious accounts of a day in the iniquitous life of Senator Joe McCarthy.

Such a journey would be long, and hard, and humiliating. Far easier to continue, doggedly, to complain that McCarthy had hounded men whose only concern was with free speech; that he labeled all his critics pro-Communist; that he was no more than a profiteer of the distress of the West. The legends of the McCarthy the liberals have memorialized in the journalism of the past half decade must not be destroyed, even now that their subject is destroyed. But as long as those myths survive, our country's record is unclean, and dirty nations deserve dirty ends.

—*National Review, May 18, 1957*

The Breakdown of the Intellectuals in Public Affairs

I contend that the principal responsibility of the thinking man is to make distinctions. Physics primers remind us that "all of the progress of mankind to date has resulted from the making of careful measurements." That is a way of saying that distinctions are necessary to purposive thought. Evidence that distinctions are not consistently being made is at least a prima-facie indication that thinking men are not exercising their primary responsibility; and so long as they do not, civilization cannot profit from what man has to offer: and the nation's problems do not get solved.

That the nation's problems are not being solved is plain, and there is nothing to be gained by a lurid demonstration of the fact. We should bear in mind that the major problems that beset us are not the result of importunate demands on destiny; nor do our demands go against the grain of history and human nature. We want security for our country, and peace and freedom and security for our people. If ever the collective ambitions of a people were licit, ours surely are; and this fact, if one bears in mind that we are the most powerful people in the world, makes it all the more extraordinary that fortune does not indulge our moderate demands. Yet things are *not* going our way, as anyone knows who will reflect on the overarching reality of our day, the growth of the Soviet Empire. Communism—with its unnatural, primitive, total appetite—is on the march, and the West yields before it.

The question is why. There is, of course, no more complex question than that one, and I do not pretend to begin to answer it. I merely assert that one reason why we are losing is that the nation's intellectual leaders, because they have other commitments, are taking imprecise measurements, and, in the confusion, progress is not possible.

Let me give a couple of examples, drawn from contemporary and recent history, of the failure to make distinctions, after which I shall put forward a hypothesis.

1. *Were Sacco and Vanzetti guilty?* It is a part of the American creed that they were not. Yet what happened is that for failure to distinguish, many of those who felt that Sacco and Vanzetti were unfairly tried (as I do) transmuted this belief into an affirmation of Sacco and Vanzetti's innocence of the crime for which they were executed. And that is something else again.

Most students of law appear to agree that in the proceedings against Sacco and Vanzetti, there was reversible error; therefore, Sacco and Vanzetti should not have been executed—at least not as the result of that trial. Very well. But may we not explore the question whether they were actually guilty of the murder? Speculation on the point is not encouraged; for as I say, it has become a part of the American creed that they were *martyrs.* "The momentum of the established order required execution of Sacco and Vanzetti," reminisced the editor of the *Boston Herald.* And yet I *believe* the evidence points strongly to the guilt of Sacco and Vanzetti, and I *know* I could prove from an examination of the rhetoric used in the typical account of the case—for example, in Mr. Schlesinger's first volume on the *Age of Roosevelt*—that the relevant distinction is *not* kept in mind. But is this important? Yes, for two reasons. The commitment of the intellectual community to the innocence of Sacco and Vanzetti profoundly affects the current mood, particularly respecting the problem of internal security. And belief in the martyrdom of Sacco and Vanzetti is a part of the syndrome I am attempting to identify. Sacco-Vanzetti, like Dreyfus, like Galileo, cast long shadows.

2. *Was Owen Lattimore a Communist?* Certainly not, one is told by the majority of the academicians. The charges against him were dropped by the court, were they not?

They were. And one repeats, Was Owen Lattimore a Communist? The decision of the court of appeals to set aside the indictment of Mr. Lattimore had nothing whatever to do with the question whether, during the period when he directed the policies of the Institute of Pacific Relations, he worked—as an investigating committee of the Senate put it—as a "conscious, articulate instrument of the Soviet conspiracy." The case against Lattimore was dropped on a technicality that shed no light on the central problem involved. Yet Johns Hopkins University—and the academic community in general—pounced on the technicality as constituting total exoneration of Lattimore. Academic communities are usually asking that they be allowed to police their own personnel; they assert that it is their business, not that of congressional committees, or vigilante groups, or, worse, alumni, to decide whether a teacher has abused his profession— but here they joyfully consigned to a totally incompetent court of law the responsibility of deciding in their behalf not merely the *legal* merits of the Lattimore case, over which the court did have competence, but other questions as well, over which only Johns Hopkins and Mr. Lattimore's professional peers had competence. I believe that a study of the thirteen-volume investigation of the Institute of Pacific Relations not only affirms the conclusion of the Senate committee but does it so conclusively as to render dissent from it (there was none in the committee—eleven out of eleven senators concurred) positively perverse.

I have a letter from the president's office at the Massachusetts Institute of Technology addressed to an alumnus who had written in to question the reinstatement last year of Professor Dirk Struik. Answered Mr. James G. Kelso, executive assistant to Dr. Killian, "Upon the dropping of all charges against Professor Dirk Struik by the Commonwealth of Massachusetts, he was restored to teaching duties at the Institute. We are not a legal body with powers of trying or conducting a case. If the authorities cannot find suitable charges, it seems hardly our role to do so."

Now if Professor Struik were to begin teaching that far from the apple's falling down on Newton, Newton fell up on the apple; and that the shortest airplane route between Atlanta, Georgia, and Washington, D.C., is via Phoenix, Arizona, the Commonwealth of Massachusetts would not find, in its statute books, grounds for action against Mr. Struik. But would MIT? For the Commonwealth of Massachusetts there is no mechanism by which to judge whether Professor Struik is a competent teacher of physics, and, let us hope, there never will be. But does this relieve MIT of the responsibility of setting up its own standards of professional behavior? The question for MIT is not whether being a concealed Communist is against the laws of Massachusetts, but whether, to qualify to teach at MIT, one must meet rather more fastidious requirements than merely staying out of Massachusetts jails.

But MIT and Johns Hopkins—and just about the entire academic fraternity—which one might have expected to be startled by the evidence of Mr. Lattimore's and Mr. Struik's abuse of their calling, and resolved to settle for nothing less than an exhaustive examination, *conducted by themselves,* have allowed, respectively, a court and a legislature to bail them out. They have slurred over a distinction that one might have expected even men of lesser critical faculties to observe.

What happened to the mission of the intellectuals, so perfectly defined seven hundred years ago by Albertus Magnus? That mission, he said, "is to tell whether an action is good or bad, not by passing sentence, as do the judges, but according to the truth, as do the sages; and to do this truly, whoever may be the author of the action, and whatever his position, be it above, or below, our own."

If I had merely singled out aberrational lapses of judgment, my contention could be rejected that there is here a national affliction; but I have not. I draw attention not to the sins of commission, but to those of omission. It is not the enormities of Arthur Schlesinger, or Owen Lattimore, or Dirk Struik that arrest me: what matters is that the MITs and the Johns Hopkinses fail to so classify them. Whether they fail to do so because they fail to understand that that is what they are, or whether they have transcending commitments which keep them silent, is essentially a psychological question, one which I shall not go into any more than is necessary. The point is the effective critical apparatus of America has broken down in matters of urgent national concern. The intellectual class has developed the capacity to suspend virtually *en masse* the critical judgment on those occasions where a rigorous application of standards, the careful drawing of distinctions, leads to inconvenient conclusions. That is a major breakdown.

Our nation is primarily imperiled by the march of international Communism. That threat—which costs us $45 billion a year, pre-empts the creative energies of some of our most talented scientific minds, and forces upon us the abhorrent institution of conscription—is a threat which, had it been properly assessed a generation ago, might have been disposed of by the strategic use of a few dozen manacles. Even ten years ago, the problem, though much more difficult, was, relative to today's, easy to solve. Perhaps a better way to put it is that ten years ago it was a problem one could afford to postpone addressing only at the price of seeing the enemy develop hydrogen bombs and intercontinental rockets. But consistently, a generation ago, ten years ago, and now, down to and including the present moment, our policy has reflected our failure to think rigorously. There is always with us the desire—never entirely excreted—to think well of the Soviet experiment; there is the desire to believe that time and tide will draw Communism's teeth; there is the selective obsession with peace— I say selective, because today's pacifism contrasts sharply with the bellicosity shown by the intellectuals toward Hitler. All these contribute to the intellectual breakdown. On account of that breakdown we fail to take the measure of the enemy, and it is from that failure—not, I like to think, from the fact that the moral resources are simply not there—that our lack of will derives. What does this lead to? "I believe," said President Eisenhower in Geneva in 1955, in an effusion heard round the world, "that the Soviet Union wants peace every bit as much as we do."

Who is really to blame for so egregious a misestimate as this (and all that it means coming from the man who writes American foreign policy)? What have the distinction-makers done, that the president should, by their counsel, avoid such an error? "You people"—Eisenhower might say in self-defense—"haven't yet spotted Owen Lattimore as a fellow-traveler—what are you getting after me for if I think Marshal Zhukov is a man of peaceful intentions?"

The question has not been asked—and as things are going will not be, until the Apocalypse. And it is not easily answered. Meanwhile our governors, who are not for the most part men of independent critical resources, draw, as they must, on the thinking community for counsel; and, on account of the thinking community's failure, themselves fail in their job.

The commitment by the intellectuals to democracy has proved, I think, to be inordinate, obsessive, and fetishistic. It is part of their larger absorption with *method*, and *method* is the fleshpot of those who live in metaphysical deserts. Democracy, Erik von Kuehnelt-Leddihn rightly observes, is the lubricant of relativism. Democracy (like the United Nations) is a procedure, not a policy; yet in it all the hopes of an intellectual epoch were vested. Many intellectuals tend to look upon democracy as an extension of the scientific method—as the scientific method applied to social problems. In an age of relativism, one tends to look for flexible devices for measuring this morning's truth. Such a device is democracy; and indeed, democracy becomes epistemology. Democracy will render reliable political truths just as surely as the marketplace sets negotiable economic values. If democracy certifies Harry Truman, who are we to call him down? And since we are prepared to believe, *a priori*, that democracy simply could not punish a God-fearing people as, some people suggest, they were indeed punished when Mr. Truman became president—then is not Truman really like Lincoln?

"Truth will emerge victorious in the free contest of ideas"—there is the root superstition of today's intellectuals. Do they believe in it? Yes, in that they carry it to its theoretical extreme in establishing academic policy. No, in that they do not (could not), in their own behavior, practice what they preach. It is established doctrine, under academic freedom, that a school may not consciously (even via released time for religious instruction) further one point of view over against another. "A university does not take sides on the questions that are discussed in its halls," a committee of scholars and alumni of Yale reported in 1952. "In the ideal university all sides of any issue are presented as impartially as possible." To do otherwise is to violate the neutrality of a teaching institution, to give advantage to one idea over against another, thus prejudicing the race which, if all the contestants were let strictly alone, truth is bound to win.

That is the distilled voodoo of academic freedom—and it could be taken seriously only in an age when people will move mountains rather than believe, when the nightmare of academic theorists is that someone will apprehend one of those truths the university is allegedly chasing after all the time. What a horrifying dilemma! For the university would then be face to face with those consequences of finding the truth that one is always told we are bravely prepared to accept. But *what* consequence is theoretically permissible? The rejection of the truth's opposite as error? No: that is a presumption not permitted under academic freedom. What then? Nothing—except the repudiation of that truth; or else, on better thought, the reclassification of it as untruth or—*always* good—partial truth.

The notion that, in education, all ideas should start out, so to speak, even in the race (*Who can say with absolute confidence that Communism is in error? It has not lost many races lately.*) is, in my judgment, sheer caricature. It is relativism (*See what happens when you have orthodoxy? Before you know it, Sacco and Vanzetti are lying there dead.*)—relativism gone mad, the final rout of reason (*Just what laws did Professor Struik break?*) at the hands of sophistry, the denial of the validity of three millennia of purposive thought.

The modern intellectual has gone absolutist where he should be relativist, and relativist where he should be absolutist. It is an immutable fact that Communism, because its premises contradict the nature of man, is wrong: and it should be treated as wrong, absolutely. It is a fact that academic freedom and democracy must be judged by their works, and hence one's enthusiasm for them must be tempered by time and place and circumstances; must, in a word, be relative. It is a fact that the exertions of the human mind and spirit have left us with an intellectual patrimony that were we to live one thousand years, we could not fully absorb, or adequately cherish: and yet the theory of higher education seeks primarily to sate the god *method*: with the emphasis on the search for new truths, rather than the apprehension of old ones. And so as regards truths, we are become like the girls of Randall Jarrell's novel, whose capacity for tolerance was so industriously stimulated by the faculty of Benton College that the girls "yearned for the discovery of life on the moon, so that they could prove that *they* weren't prejudiced against moon men."

So diverse are the problems that plague man that it is unwise to speculate as to their central cause. No cause more elaborated than original sin seems adequate. Even so, let me venture this: The principal problems that face the world are the making of governments in action; for only governments can exercise the leverage necessary to transform individual vices into universal affliction. It took government to translate *Das Kapital* into concentration camps; it takes positive action by government to preserve many of the imbalances in our economic system; only government, with its monopoly of force, can perpetuate injustices that individuals, given the freedom to do so, would redress. It was long ago understood, in the evolution of political theory, that just about the only *in*tolerable answer to big government is *no* government. Government there must be, this side of paradise, so that the challenge is, and always will be, how to restrain and direct that government without which we cannot get on. The facile answer of the nineteenth century, when the body of the world's progressive social theorists seized intoxicatingly upon literacy and self-rule as the bases of the enlightened and domesticated state, has proved naïve. The insufficiency of democracy as a guarantor of enlightened public action is now perceptible. The only defense against the shortcomings and abuses of the state is concerted resistance by individuals. That resistance can only issue from an undamaged critical faculty, and moral sense. If the entire thinking class indulges itself in the suppression of the intellect and the conscience, anything can happen: Wars that should not be fought are fought, and wars that should be fought are not fought; human impulses that should be restrained are not restrained, and human impulses that should not be restrained are restrained; and great nations are humbled.

—Speech first given at St. John's University in Queens, New York, April 21, 1958

Peace and Pacifism

I am much interested in the phenomenon of student pacifism, and make bold to suggest that others should be too. My most memorable brush with it was at Dartmouth College a few months ago, where I lectured in connection with the Great Issues Course. The experience was unusual because the entire senior class is required to attend the Great Issues lectures, which constitute the text of the course. It is only every now and then that university authorities compel students to listen to my words; and so it is not often that I, or other marauding publicists, meet with a truly representative portion of the student body. Generally you find yourself speaking only to those who are politically responsive: who demonstrate a degree of political curiosity by the very act of having come to hear you, and hence are not typical. But at Dartmouth it was everyone, and I learned that pacifism is everywhere. Pacifism's fallout has got into the bones even of those who do not voluntarily give a moment's thought to the issues of our time.

There at Dartmouth one student walked up in the heat of the question period to within a foot of me, and as he began to question me, his voice broke with emotion, and the silence in the hall was his chorus. He began again, "Do you mean to say"—he whispered, struggling to keep his voice even—"that there are circumstances under which you would make war if it meant death for a hundred million men, women, and children?"

"Yes," I said.

The audience gasped. I gasped too, but they didn't hear me, and that is one of the difficulties. Students know nothing of, have no intimation of, the horrors of pacifism.

The distinction is between peace and pacifism. All civilized men want peace. And all truly civilized men must despise pacifism. It is everywhere implied that anyone who is in favor of peace must be a pacifist, and that anyone who is not a pacifist has no love for peace. The Communists, for whom language is so servile an instrument, have very little trouble with the classifications: In the Western world there are only pacifists and warmongers. But however greatly the Communists, by their tireless offensive on distinctions, have contributed to the confusion, American students could not have been rendered as helpless as many of them are except by the cooperation of their teachers.

Pacifism is a Christian heresy that springs from critical misunderstandings. *Peace on earth* is a plea for those conditions on earth—love, charity, temperance—which make peace thinkable. Peace is unthinkable in a community in which plunderers have hold of the city at night; and the prayer for peace is not a prayer that the elders of the community maintain the peace by yielding every night to plunderers: rather it is a prayer that men be helped in finding the strength to suppress their acquisitive and aggressive instincts sufficiently to make unnecessary armed resistance to man by man. In praying for peace, we pray that grace will settle in the hearts and minds of those bellicose people in the world who are critically situated, and cause them to exercise that restraint which makes peace possible. If peace were the first goal of man, you would not have to pray for it: you could have it. The price is to yield. If you are prepared to yield your family, your property—your honor—it is generally safe to assume that you will be ceded your life: that you will have gained "peace."

Why is youth pacifist? There are the commonplace reasons, and there are others unique to our time. It is probably correct that youth have the keenest sensual appreciation of life, having so recently discovered their own appetites and the earth's reciprocating pleasures, and that out of that infatuation idolatrous passions arise, of pacifist tendency. We know all about that. But we know also that the hot blood of youth since the dawn of history has been readily fired by the call for suprapersonal service to an ideal. In almost all ages men have voluntarily risked their precious lives to relieve the misery of others, or to bring reverence to their God, honor to their nation, glory to their families and themselves. Idealism of this kind, it is widely supposed, has been locked in by the dimensions of modern warfare: one's role in modern war is too infinitesimal, too infinitely mechanized to yield personal satisfaction, yes except to those whose hearts go out to the distress of the West, who know how acute is the West's condition, and take satisfaction from service to it in whatever capacity. And here is the cause of student pacifism—not the cinemascopic horror stories of nuclear death (does death sting more now than it did then?) but a diluted loyalty to the West, which the prevailing philosophy (some of us call it liberalism) has engendered.

Today's student pacifists trade mostly in nuclear luridities in justifying their pacifism; but without reflecting on the meaning of what they say. Is it human suffering they are really concerned about? But the awful tribulation of Nagasaki and Hiroshima cannot compare with the workaday agony of the enslaved world—which in the name of humanity the students are prepared to leave forever enslaved, to spare themselves an increase in the radioactivity in the atmosphere, and the hazard of provoking the Soviet Union. They do not know that the conditions under which peace is thinkable for the Westerner do not now exist: that the West is besieged, and the world tyrannized over. And that the lack of perception which made possible the advances of the enemy even now prevents us from turning the battle to our favor, which we could do by bold and singlepurposed action if only we could unload the freight that sentimental pacifism has put on our shoulders. We must try to win without war: but we must above all try to win, and for the sake of humanity, whose first concern is for the quality of human existence, rather than for life biologically defined.

—*National Review*, October 24, 1959

What Happened?

This much at least should be said in behalf of Henry Kissinger in the matter of Vietnam:

The treaties he initialed he would not have initialed if he had had any intimation that Congress would, in the months ahead, pull back from discharging its implicit obligations.

It should be recalled that in January 1973, Richard Nixon was triumphant. He had won the largest political victory in the history of the United States. Congress, duly chastened by the successes of the Christmas bombing, was at his feet. Vietnamization was in effect. Our prisoners of war were about to be returned. Who can doubt that if, instead of presenting the Paris Accords along with their implicit obligations, the president had asked Congress to bind itself by the Accords, they would have sailed through both houses?

Kissinger did not doubt it, and he gave an assurance to Thieu in good faith. Thieu accepted that assurance, and this was his tragic mistake. Chiefs of state cannot afford to make such mistakes. But who could have anticipated Watergate?

A recent issue of *New York* magazine features a close analysis of the behavior of Richard Nixon during 1973 and 1974 by John Osborne. He is the well-respected writer, associated with *The New Republic*, who developed a feature that became famous, called The Nixon Watch. Osborne concludes, in words of one syllable, that Richard Nixon, sometime early in 1973, went—nuts.

This analysis sounds cruel, said about anybody. It is hard to understand why, when said about Richard Nixon. Is there a more charitable explanation for his behavior during 1973 and 1974 when Watergate closed in than that he was not in possession of his faculties? If, during those eighteen months, he had been hypnotized by Tom Wicker, making statements and reaching decisions calculated to ensure the destruction of his presidency, could he have acted more brilliantly to achieve that end? Why should conservatives shrink from reaching a conclusion merely because it has been advanced by a political liberal? John Osborne could very easily be correct, and if he is, the judgment of Nixon, far from becoming more severe, becomes more charitable. One does not expect responsible conduct from people who have lost effective control of their faculties.

All of which reminds us that for all we know about Watergate, in fact the great story has not been told. It is this: What would Nixon, under Kissinger's prodding, have done, if his reactions had been healthy, when only a few weeks after the Paris Accords were executed the North began its blatant disregard of them?

My own information is that it was planned, sometime in April 1973, to pulverize Hanoi and Haiphong. If that had been done, not only would the North Vietnamese juggernaut have disintegrated, an entirely new meaning would have attached to the concept of détente.

Remember, we are talking about a treaty that was initialed by the other two great superpowers, China and the Soviet Union, and which was broken only as a result of their active collaboration. Thus to have acted decisively would have had the effect not only of saving South Vietnam, but also of warning the Soviet Union and China that détente is what we have always insisted it is: an invitation to our two principal antagonists to cooperate with us. Not an invitation to them to fish in troubled waters, to repeat the phrase President Ford used thumpingly when last he addressed Congress. When he uttered those words, they were bereft of meaning. What Soviet general or Chinese theorist has any reason, at this point, to believe that détente is in fact anything other than that—an invitation to profiteer from America's unilateral attachment to a will-o'-the-wisp?

This does not bring South Vietnam back to life. But it gives one an idea of the incredible reaches of Watergate. It very probably drove Nixon out of his mind, and the result is a disequilibrium in world politics. There is nothing here to explain the strange, perverse failure of Congress, or to lessen the pain our allies must feel. But if Henry Kissinger is ever free to tell it all, we can hope that he will say something on this order. And that he will remember that Congress must not ever again be taken for granted.

—April 26, 1975

Who Is the Ugliest of Them All?

When Lillian Hellman's *Scoundrel Time* (Little, Brown, $7.95) was first published, in the spring of 1976, only the cooing of reviewers was heard. Up front, in the most prominent seats, they applauded so resolutely, so methodically, the overtone of the metronome teased the ear. Solzhenitsyn, in the first *Gulag* book, writes about how, during one of the terrors, Stalin's agents would fan out from Moscow to give speeches to the satellite brass, hastily convened in crowded theaters in the outlying cities to receive the details of Stalin's hectic afflatus. After the speaker was done, the subjects would break into applause, and the clapping would go on and on, because no one dared be the first to sit down, lest he be thought insufficiently servile. Indeed, rather than wait for the speaker finally to beckon the whole assembly back to its seats, on one occasion someone did it—stopped clapping, though only after a boisterous while. That man was spotted, given ten years, and shipped off to a prison camp—where, perhaps, he was given to read selections from the anti-fascist *opera* of Lillian Hellman. . . .

It seemed for a while the reviewers would be that way all around the town—the *New York Times*, the *Washington Post*, *Commonweal*, *America*, the *Chicago Tribune*. Then . . . then, in *The New York Review of Books*, Murray Kempton interrupted his own paean to Miss Hellman to make a comment or two which, however gentle, quite ruptured the trance. It was as if, in Paris during the occupation, an anonymous arranger had, by fugitive notation, insinuated the motif of the *"Marseillaise"* into a great Speer-like orchestration of *"Deutschland über Alles."* Others, after that, came rushing in. It would never be quite the same again for Miss Lillian.

Even so, one has to hand it to her. Though the book is slender, the design is grandly staged, in self-esteem as in presumption. To begin with, here is someone described in the introduction to her own book as the greatest woman playwright in American history. Now this is probably true. But (a) Isn't that on the order of celebrating the tallest building in Wichita, Kansas? and (b) Doesn't an introduction to oneself in such terms, in one's own book, by one's own chosen introducer, interfere with the desired perception of oneself as a hardworking artist ignorant, indeed disdainful, of the outside world of power-plays and flackery? and (c) Aren't the auspices the most alien for making sexual distinctions? I mean, Garry Wills, the Last Kid, talking about the Greatest Woman Playwright as one would talk about the downhill champion on the one-legged ski team?

And here is a writer (Wills) introducing an autobiographical book by a woman who is publicizing now her complaint against an America that, as she might put it, victimized her because of her alleged championship of the regime of Josef Stalin. And what, then, does Wills go and do in his introduction? Quote from the author's pre-McCarthy works, to demonstrate the impartiality of her opposition to tyranny? Not at all. He goes on (and on and on—Mr. Wills consumes thirty-four pages with his introduction, one-fifth of the book), blithely—offhandedly—describing the era of Miss Hellman's travail as the era in U.S.-Soviet relations during which horrible old us, led by Harry Truman, promulgated a Cold War against reasonable old them, the startled, innocent Communists, led by Josef Stalin. In *Commentary*, Nathan Glazer quoted from Wills's introduction: "*A newly aggressive Truman had launched the Cold War in the spring of 1947, with his plan to 'rescue' Greece and Turkey. . . . We had still a world to save, with just those plans—from NATO to the Korean War . . .*" Glazer commented: "One reads such passages—and many others—in astonishment. Garry Wills [evidently] believes that Greece and Turkey did not need to be rescued, that one of America's 'plans' was the Korean War. It seems that he prefers the political condition of, say, Bulgaria and North Korea to that of Greece and Turkey." That introduction, which might have been written in the Lenin Institute, introducing that book, under the circumstances of Miss Hellman's apologia, was a venture either in dumb innocence (inconsistent with Hellman's persona), or in matchless cheek, on the order of Mohandas Gandhi writing his autobiography and asking General Patton to introduce it.

But the difficulties had only just begun for her. Is Miss Hellman a nice guy? In a way, it shouldn't matter. A sentence from her book, much quoted, asks, "*Since when do you have to agree with people to defend them from injustice?*" By the same token, we shouldn't require that someone be endearing as a prerequisite to indignation at unfair treatment of her. But Miss Hellman, author of *The Little Foxes*, is quickly spotted as being no less guileful than one of her characters. It's like the case of Germaine Greer, filibustering against male chauvinism, while stripteasing her sexual biography across the magazine rack. Miss Hellman, affecting only a disinterested concern for justice, twanging the heartstrings—with, however, more sleight of hand than craft. She had to sell her country house! She had to fire her cook and gardener! She had to give up a million-dollar contract! She had to take a part-time job in a department store! Her lover had to go to jail! If, unlike the earlier reviewers, you finish the book believing that you have read something less than an episode in the life of Thomas More, either you are callous—or else her art has failed her.

She takes awful risks, entirely unnecessary. For instance, she exhibits hit-and-run contempt for Lionel and Diana Trilling—for the sin of believing in the sincerity of Whittaker Chambers. Nice people would have handled that differently. James Wechsler of the *New York Post* is denounced for being a "*friendly witness*" before the House Committee on Un-American Activities (he never appeared before HUAC; it was McCarthy's subcommittee, and Wechsler was hostile). Theodore White is dismissed contemptuously as a "*jolly quarter-historian*"—because he once wrote a book saying that Nixon was a complicated man (Lillian Hellman finds nothing complicated in evil incarnate). Elia Kazan, struggling to appease his conscience, in revolt now against his earlier complicity with the Communist movement, took a full page in the *New York Times* to run his palinode—characterized by Miss Hellman as "*pious shit.*"

All in all, her performance is about as ingratiating as a post-Watergate speech by Richard Nixon, and so we quite understand it when Murray Kempton is driven to saying, in concluding his review, that, really, he would not want Lillian Hellman "overmuch as a comrade." Indeed, the scaffolding of the book is pretty shaky. It is, after all, implicitly entitled, "*The Heroism of Lillian Hellman during the Darkest Days of the Republic*, by Lillian Hellman." It would have been a little seemlier if her book had gone out as: "*Scoundrel Time*, by Lillian Hellman, as told to Garry Wills." Or—why not just "*Scoundrel Time: How Lillian Hellman Held Her Finger in the Dike and Saved American Freedom and Self-Respect*, by Garry Wills"? He would not have needed to increase the size of his contribution by that much. In any event—an artistic point, and with apologies to Burke—this martyr, to be loved, should be lovelier.

~

Then there is the problem of factual accuracy, best captured in the author's unguarded reference to Whittaker Chambers and the pumpkin papers.

Here is what Miss Hellman wrote: "*Facts are facts—and one of them is that a pumpkin in which Chambers claimed to have hidden the damaging evidence against Hiss, deteriorates.*"

Now here is a sentence that might have been written by Eleanor Roosevelt. It sounds strange coming from greatest woman playwright in American history, and is incredible when proffered in support of the proposition that facts are facts.

Yes, it is a fact that pumpkins deteriorate. But they do not deteriorate appreciably overnight, which is how long the Hiss films reposed in the pumpkin.

As for "*in which Chambers claimed to have hidden,*" nobody questions that Chambers hid the films there, not even Alger Hiss. Not even Stalin. Nor could she have intended to write, "*in which Chambers hid the allegedly damaging evidence.*" Because it wasn't *allegedly* damaging, it was just plain damaging, which indeed is why all the fuss. The films went a long way toward establishing Chambers's credibility, and therefore the guilt of Hiss. What she presumably *meant* to write was, "*in which Chambers hid the damaging but, it now turns out, meaningless evidence.*" Earlier in the book she had constructed an explanatory footnote from which the sentence in question coasted, to wit: "*In 1975 the secret pumpkin papers were found to contain nothing secret, nothing confidential. They were, in fact, non-classified, which is Washington's way of saying anybody who says please can have them.*"

~

Facts are indeed facts. But Miss Hellman's rendition of the facts caught the attention of one of her fans, Congressman Edward Koch of Manhattan. He read her book, and wrote the author a letter of fawning praise reciting his own sustained effort to kill the House Committee on Un-American Activities. But Edward Koch has a streak of Yankee inquisitiveness, even as it is advertised about Miss Hellman that she is curious. John Hersey has written about her—his dear friend—"Miss Hellman's powers of invention are fed by her remarkable memory and her ravenous curiosity. Her father once said she lived 'within a question mark.' She defines culture as 'applied curiosity.' She is always on what she calls 'the find-out kick.'" Well, not quite always. Not on those occasions when she begins a paragraph with the phrase, "Facts are facts." (Like the *Daily World*'s ritual introduction of a lie: "As is well known . . .")

Congressman Koch wrote to the Library of Congress to ask about Miss Hellman's description of the pumpkin papers, and simultaneously wrote to Miss Hellman asking for an elucidation. The lady who lives within a question mark didn't reply. But the lady at the Library of Congress did. As follows: "The footnote statement is inaccurate. On July 31, 1975, Alger Hiss was permitted to see the 'pumpkin papers,' which consist of five rolls of microfilm. One roll, as Mr. Kelly reports, was 'completely light-fogged.' Two other rolls were pages from apparently unclassified Navy technical manuals. The other two rolls, however, contained Government documents 'relating to U.S.-German relations before World War II and cables from U.S. observers in China.' Documents in these two rolls were marked highly confidential. Of the five rolls of microfilm, only these latter two had been used as evidence against Hiss in the trial which led to his conviction for perjury in 1950."

Miss Hellman's reputation as a literary precisionist (she is said to write and rewrite her plays four, six, ten, twelve times) leads one to expect a cognate precision in those of her books and articles that bid for the moral attention of the Republic; so that one is inclined to take literally such a statement by her as, "*Certainly nobody in their* [sic] *right mind could have believed that the China experts, charged and fired by the State Department, did any more than recognize that Chiang Kai-shek was losing.*"

But whom is she referring to? Who is it who was "*charged and fired*" by the State Department for such an offense? The controversial John Carter Vincent was three times *cleared* by the State Department's Loyalty Security Board, and when the Civil Service Loyalty Review Board found against him, Dulles *overruled* that Board, though accepting Vincent's resignation. McCarthy's target John Paton Davies was *cleared* by the State Department. John Stewart Service was, granted, finally dropped by the State Department, but only because the Civil Service Loyalty Review Board ruled against him, not the State Department's board, which repeatedly cleared him. And Service was otherwise engaged than merely as a diplomatic technician predicting the ascendancy of Mao. His emotions in the matter were hardly concealed. He had provided his superiors, from the field in China, such information as this: "Politically, any orientation which the Chinese Communists may once have had toward the Soviet Union seems to be a thing of the past . . . they are carrying out democratic policies which they expect the United States to approve and sympathetically support." And Service's case was further complicated when he was arrested for passing along classified documents to the editor of *Amerasia*, a Communist-front publication. But of course the principal architect of our China policy, singled out by the Senate Internal Security Subcommittee, hadn't even been a member of the State Department, exercising his influence on policy through the Institute for Pacific Relations. The blurb printed on Owen Lattimore's book *Solution in Asia* went further than merely to predict the downfall of the Kuomintang. "He showed," the book's editors compressed the author's story, "that all the Asiatic people are more interested in actual democratic practices such as the ones they can see in action across the Russian border, than they are in the fine theories of Anglo-Saxon democracies which come coupled with ruthless imperialism. He inclines to support American newspapermen who report that the only real democracy in China is found in Communist areas."

~

We learned about democracy in the Communist world. What have we learned about Miss Hellman's credibility?

Nor is she entirely candid in describing the nature or extent of her own involvement with the Soviet Union. She vouchsafes, in a subordinate clause that could be interpreted as contritional, only this much: "*Many* [American intellectuals] *found in the sins of Stalin Communism—and there were plenty of sins and plenty that for a long time I mistakenly denied—the excuse to join those who should have been their hereditary enemies.*" (Interesting, that one. Is she talking about American Jewish socialist anti-Communists? Who else?) Later she says, "*I thought that in the end Russia, having achieved a state socialism, would stop its infringements on personal liberty. . . I was wrong.*" Isn't there something there on the order of, "I thought that, on obtaining the services of Mickey Mantle, the Yankees would go on to win the World Series. I was wrong."? But the ritualistic apology was not enough to satisfy. Soon after Mr. Kempton broke the spell, one began to notice the misgivings of others. William Phillips in *Partisan Review*, Melvin Lasky in *Encounter*, Nathan Glazer in *Commentary*, most notably Hilton Kramer in the *New York Times* (ardently defended by Arthur Schlesinger Jr. in the letters section), and even Irving Howe, in *Dissent*.

Forsooth, Lillian Hellman's involvement in the Communist movement was not comprehensively divulged in her offhanded remarks about her concern for justice and peace, and her stated disinclination for politics. Miss Hellman went to Russia for the first time in 1937, where her ravenous curiosity caused her to learn enough about the Soviet system to return to the United States confidently to defend Stalin's purges and denounce John Dewey and his commission for finding Stalin guilty of staging the show trials during the great purge. She devoted much of her professional career during that period to dramatizing the evil of brown fascism. *Watch on the Rhine*, staged in 1941, is devoted to the proposition that *"the death of fascism is more desirable than the lives and well-being of the people who hate it."* When, a quarter-century later, in 1969, she criticized, in a letter to the *New York Times*, the novelist Kuznetsov for fleeing Russia and seeking asylum in England, having first secured an exit visa by "cooperating" with the Soviet Union by giving an obviously fabricated and useless deposition against fellow dissidents, Kuznetsov replied that Miss Hellman's attack on him, "like that of a few others," was "prompted by some surviving illusions about Russia." "The Soviet Union," he explained to Miss Hellman, "is a fascist country. What is more, its fascism is much more dangerous than Hitler's. It is a country which is living in Orwellian times. . . . Tens of millions of bloody victims, a culture destroyed, fascist antisemitism, the genocide of small nations, the transformation of the individual into a hypocritical cipher, Hungary, Czechoslovakia. In literature—nothing but murder, suicides, persecution, trials, lunatic asylums, an unbroken series of tragedies from Gumilev to Solzhenitsyn. Is that really not enough?" There is no recorded reaction from Miss Hellman.

During the war, she traveled to the Soviet Union and was received there as a celebrity. She returned the hospitality in first-rate mint: an article in *Collier's* magazine about the heroism of the Russian people and the Russian soldiers. In that article there is a passage of triumphant irony. She has been implored by her guide to ask more questions. She records her reply: "*I said, 'The first week I was in the Soviet Union I found out that if I did not ask questions, I always got answers. . . . Tell your people to tell me what they want to. I will learn more that way.'*" (Life within a question mark.) And, indeed, she learned everything Stalin and his agents wanted her to learn, and came back to America to share her knowledge, and to despise those of her fellow Americans who insisted on asking questions.

In 1948 and 1949 she was, for a non-politician, very active. She backed Henry Wallace's bid for the presidency on the Progressive Party ticket, and was visibly amused on being asked privately by poor old Mortimer Snerd if it were true that there were Communists in positions of power in his party. "*It was such a surprising question that I laughed and said most certainly it was true.*" She then put in a call, convening the top Communists in the Progressive Party, and said to them at that meeting, Look, why don't you go paddle your own canoe in your own party? There cannot have been such dumb amazement in Christendom since Lady Astor asked Stalin when would he stop killing people.

A few months later, Lillian Hellman played a big role in the famous Waldorf Conference—the Cultural and Scientific Congress for World Peace. In her book, her running guard Mr. Wills treats most fiercely those who attended the meeting for the purpose of "disrupting" it—such redbaiters as Mary McCarthy and Dwight Macdonald, and officials of the Americans for Democratic Action who, at a press conference, raised with the wretched Russian superpawn, Dmitri Shostakovich, head of the Soviet delegation, questions about the fate of his cultural and scientific colleagues back home, Russian writers, intellectuals, and musicians who had disappeared from sight after the most recent choler of Josef Stalin. Miss Hellman does not allude to any of this. Her quarrel with American intellectuals is over their failure to devote the whole of their time to criticizing the chairman of HUAC, J. Parnell Thomas. Presumably, criticism of Stalin could wait until Miss Hellman was personally satisfied that now that he had established state socialism, he had in fact failed to introduce human freedom.

Indeed, her attitude is ferocious toward those who, looking back on their complicity with Communism, wondered more inventively than she how to make amends. By writing books? (Koestler.) Cooperating with congressional committees? (Kazan.) Doing both? (Chambers.) Miss Hellman, who wrote about how the cause of anti-fascism was bigger than anything, seemed to have lost interest in tyranny, preoccupied now with her material well-being, and that of Dashiell Hammett, her relation with whom is jovially described by one reviewer—"She was then and had long been a friend of Dashiell Hammett—more than a friend: a wife, off and on, but for the paperwork." In that spirit one could say that thus had been Lillian Hellman's relations with the Communist movement—a marriage, but for the paperwork. If one feels that paperwork, the formal exchange of vows, is essential to a sacramentally complete union, then perhaps Lillian Hellman was not married to the Communist movement any more than she was married to Dashiell Hammett. But the investigating committees, like Miss Hellman's reviewers, were interested in de facto relations.

So off she went to Washington, for her great moment before the congressional committee. There has not been such a prologue since the *Queen Mary* weighed anchor in Manhattan in order to move to Brooklyn. Her device was simple. She wrote to the committee to say she would not answer questions about anybody's activities other than her own, and unless the committee agreed not to ask such questions, she would take the Fifth Amendment. Implicit in her position was her sacred right to be the sole judge of whether her acquaintances in the Communist world were engaged in innocent activity. The committee of course declined to permit her to define the committee's mandate, so she took the Fifth, and wants us to celebrate her wit and courage every twenty-five years. The committee treated her with civility, did not ask Congress to hold her in contempt, and is hardly responsible for the decline in her commercial fortunes. She, not the committee, dictated the script that got her into trouble with Hollywood.

Yet the lady is obsessed with the fancy that she and her common-law husband were specific victims of the terror. "Dash" floats in and out of the book disembodiedly, but always we are reminded that he actually spent time in jail—for refusing to divulge the names of the financial patrons of the Civil Rights Congress, a Communist front (Dashiell Hammett was not a dupe, at least not in the conventional sense: he was a Communist). Miss Hellman makes a great deal of his victimization. Murray Kempton, who would not send Caligula to prison, at this point has had enough. He writes, "We do not diminish the final admiration we feel owed to Dashiell Hammett when we wonder what he might have said to Miss Hellman on the night he came home from the meeting of the board of the Civil Rights Congress which voted to refuse its support to the cause of James Kutcher, a paraplegic veteran who had been discharged as a government clerk because he belonged to the Trotskyite Socialist Workers Party. But then Hammett was a Communist and it was an article of the Party faith that Leon Trotsky, having worked for the Emperor of Japan since 1904, had then improved his social standing by taking employment with the Nazis in 1934. Thus any member of the Socialist Workers Party could be considered by extension to be no more than an agent of Hitler's ghost. Given that interpretation of history, Paul Robeson spoke from principle when a proposal to assist the Trotskyite Kutcher was raised at a public meeting of the Civil Rights Congress. Robeson drove it from the floor with a declaration to the effect that you don't ask Jews to help a Nazi or Negroes to help the KKK." The voice of Paul Robeson lives on, speaking from the same principle: "Oct. 7, 1976, Lillian Hellman, author and dramatist, will receive the third annual Paul Robeson Award tomorrow at 12:30. The award is presented by the Paul Robeson Citation Committee of Actors' Equity for concern for and service to fellow humans.'"

The self-pity reaches paranoia. Edmund Wilson once wrote an entire book the thesis of which silts up as suggesting that we went to war in Vietnam for the sole purpose of increasing his income tax. Miss Hellman is vaguer on the subject of motivation, but denies her reader any explanation for bringing the matter up at all, leaving us to suppose that Somebody in Washington singled her and Dash out for Special Treatment. Thus Hammett goes to jail for contempt of Congress (for six months). *"That was a tough spring, 1952. There were not alone the arrangements for my appearance before the Committee, there were other kinds of trouble. Hammett owed the Internal Revenue a great deal of back taxes: two days after he went to jail they attached all income from books, radio, or television, from anything. He was, therefore, to have no income for the remaining ten years of his life. . . . That made me sad."* And again, *"Never in the ten years since the Internal Revenue cut off his income—two days after he went to jail—did he ever buy a suit or even a tie."* As for herself, *"Money was beginning to go and go fast. I had gone from earning a hundred and forty thousand a year (before the movie blacklist) to fifty and then twenty and then ten, almost all of which was taken from me* [note, "taken from me"] *by the Internal Revenue Department, which had come forward with its claim on the sale of a play that the previous Administration had seemingly agreed to."*

La Précisionniste rides again. (a) It is, of course, the Internal Revenue *Service*, not Department; (b) if she means to say that her companion Dashiell Hammett should have been excused from paying the same taxes other people pay on equivalent income (perhaps because, as a Communist, he was entitled to preferential treatment?), then let her say that; (c) the IRS doesn't "agree" to the sale of a play, but might have agreed to accept a taxation base: in any event, the tax levied by the IRS was on profit; to say nothing of the fact that (d) Lillian Hellman is not Vivien Kellems's sister. The latter was the authentic American Poujadiste, and when she complained about taxes, she spoke from the bowels of principle. When Lillian Hellman complains about high taxes, she is complaining about the monster she suckled.

~

What does one go on to say about a book so disorderly, so tasteless, guileful, self-enraptured? The disposition to adore her, feel sorry for her, glow in the vicarious thrill of her courage and decency (her favorite word, "decency": she is apolitical now, she says, desiring only "decency") runs into hurdle after hurdle in the obstacle course of this little book. Consider. It is 1952, and she is living in her townhouse in New York, and the buzzer rings. *"An overrespectable-looking black man . . . stood in the elevator, his hat politely removed. He asked me if I was Lillian Hellman. I agreed to that and asked who he was. He handed me an envelope and said he was there to serve a subpoena from the House Un-American Activities Committee. I opened the envelope and read the subpoena. I said, 'Smart to choose a black man for this job. You like it?' and slammed the door."*

Ah, the decent of this earth. The same lady who in her book tells us that she will not style her life to political fashion, now refers to her visitor, back in 1952, as "black," when of course that word was unused in 1952. Miss Hellman was brought up in New Orleans where, paradoxical though it may seem, the same class of people who institutionalized Jim Crow never (I speak of the decent members of that class) humiliated individual members of the Negro race. It is difficult to imagine suggesting to a Negro bureaucrat who has merely performed a job assigned to him that he is collusively engaged in anti-Negro activity; impossible to understand a civilized woman slamming the door in the face of someone— a messenger—executing a clerical duty. Truly, the lady's emotions are ungoverned, and perhaps ungovernable. She seems to like to advertise this. "*I have a temper and it is triggered at odd times by odd matters and is then out of my control.*" And, elsewhere, talking about her "black" nanny, she reveals that she was given "*anger—an uncomfortable, dangerous, and often useful gift.*" To be used against black messengers bearing instructions from Washington, but on no account against white messengers bearing instructions from Moscow.

The author, though she attempts to project a moral for our time out of her own travail, does this less avidly than most of her critics, who seized greedily on this mincing tale of self-pity as the matrix of a passion play. It doesn't work. The heart of her failure beats in a single sentence: ". . . whatever our mistakes, I do not believe we did our country any harm." "Dear Lillian Hellman," the socialist Irving Howe writes, "you could not be more mistaken! Those who supported Stalinism and its political enterprises, either here or abroad, helped befoul the cultural atmosphere, helped bring totalitarian methods into trade unions, helped perpetuate one of the great lies of the century, helped destroy whatever possibilities there might have been for a resurgence of serious radicalism in America. Isn't that harm enough?"

What were we supposed to defend? asks William Phillips of *Partisan Review*, himself an ex-Communist. "Some *were* Communists, and what one was asked to defend was their right to lie about it." The message of Lillian Hellman, says Hilton Kramer of the *New York Times*, is rendered in "*soigné* prose," causing one to wonder if one ought to be less sensitive than Khrushchev in denouncing the work of his predecessor.

But it was Providence that provided the epilogue, the ironic master-stroke. When Miss Hellman finally brought herself to criticize the Soviet Union, she singled out for special scorn Soviet censorship: *"The semi-lit-erate bureaucrats, who suppress and alter manuscripts, who dictate who can and cannot be published, perform a disgusting business."* And lo! the pub-lishers of Miss Hellman's book, Little, Brown, instruct Diana Trilling to alter an essay on Miss Hellman in *her* manuscript. Mrs. Trilling declines, and Little, Brown breaks the contract—does its best, in effect, to suppress her book. "Miss Hellman is one of our leading successful authors," said Arthur Thornhill, president of Little, Brown. "She's not one of the big so-called money makers, but she's up there where we enjoy the revenue." The principled Miss Hellman, who condemns Hollywood for its base concern for profit, has not severed her relations with Little, Brown, never mind that they sought to suppress and alter a manuscript—in deference to *her*! But, don't you see, the vertebral column of her thought finally emerges. *She* can do no wrong. *"There is nothing in my life of which I am ashamed,"* she wrote to the chairman of the House Committee on Un-American Activities, set-ting herself, by that sentence, in a class apart from her fellow mortals. Well, it took a long time for her to learn about Communism. She is elderly, but there is time yet, time to recognize that she should be ashamed of this awful book.

—*National Review,* January 21, 1977

On Right and Wrong

A casual line, thoughtlessly dropped in *Newsweek* in a report on stalled SALT negotiations, gives us a clue to the principal moral responsibility of the Reagan administration, which is persuasively to reassert certain truths that distinguish us from those we seek to protect ourselves against. In citing the dangers of a nuclear buildup, *Newsweek*'s correspondents conclude: "At best, the extra billions of dollars for defense would severely drain both countries' economies. At worst, the pell-mell, action-reaction cycle would produce a temporary advantage for one side that it might be tempted to exploit."

One side, the other side . . . Who began that stuff? Probably the worst expression of it was in a speech given at Yale by Senator William Fulbright in the Sixties. George Kennan, when he gets clinical, oversterilizes his vocabulary, and before long you see the Soviet Union as the A team and the United States as the B team, all very simple.

Probably the worst of the lot, both because he spoke always from an august pedestal, and because he spoke augustly, was Charles de Gaulle. Above all because his statements were taken to be informed by a distinctive historical sweep, and guided by right reason. He referred, on several occasions, to *"les deux hégémonies"*—"the two hegemonies." He would have been altogether dumbfounded if Winston Churchill had referred to the Vichy government, dominated by the Nazis, and the government in exile, dominated by de Gaulle, as "France's two contending governments."

The nadir in our self-abuse came during the Vietnam War, when such as Noam Chomsky of MIT, and others mostly forgotten but whose moral reasoning continues its extraordinary resonance in the academies and in the press, denounced America. It became altogether routine to make comparisons between Americans and North Vietnamese, to the disadvantage of the Americans. For Soviet propagandists to construe the United States as the aggressor nation is routine stuff.

It ought not to be routine stuff for Americans to accept lackadaisically the most significant triumph of the Communist aggressors, which is to persuade so many that there are, as between the Soviet Union and the United States, merely historical-cultural differences. The difference between us isn't that we are saints, and they are sinners. It is that we seek to be saints, and they seek to be sinners. Sainthood here defined as the acceptance of the individual human being as a man born to be free; sin here defined as the de-divinization of man in pursuit of secular ideology.

What's the matter with *Newsweek?* For twenty years the United States had conclusive military and nuclear superiority. I don't know a single public figure who proposed that we should use it to dispose pre-emptively of the creeping Soviet menace. At the end of 1945 we occupied Germany, Japan, Italy, and a dozen peripheral countries. We could, had we been so disposed, have colonized Great Britain and France. Instead we got out of all those countries, gave the Philippines their independence, and, after a generation's entreaty, agreed to annex Hawaii and Alaska as sovereign states.

Newsweek secured an interview with Rubin Zamora, who is emerging as the principal spokesman for the revolutionaries in El Salvador. Question: "Why did the American government release its so-called white paper claiming [note: "claiming," not "demonstrating"] outside meddling in El Salvador?"

Answer: "The United States is up to its neck in support for a genocidal government. . . . It's so similar to what the United States was saying just before its 1965 intervention in the Dominican Republic. My personal feeling is great sorrow."

My personal feeling is that talking with Mr. Zamora other than behind bars is a waste of time. Find me a member of the Reagan administration interested in genocide. Why did the overwhelming majority of the Organization of American States support President Johnson's intervention in the Dominican Republic? How long did U.S. troops stay there? Who backed democratic practices there during the last election?

Newsweek's reporters reveal that "according to intelligence sources, most of the rebels are between 15 and 18 years old, and their youth consistently betrays them in actual combat." Their youth consistently betrays their awful manipulability by such as Zamora. The government of El Salvador is a mess. It has gone through thirty upheavals since 1932.

The notion that the clouds would part, and posies spring up in the pavements of San Salvador if only the junta redistributed the land, is as naïve as that we are intervening in El Salvador because we like to support people engaged in killing other people. Reagan is right: The distinction between the Duartes of this world and the Zamoras of this world is a distinction within which we need to maneuver.

But let us be morally assertive. It is not chauvinistic to announce that the United States will not tolerate another Soviet-dominated abscess in the Western hemisphere, and if people don't understand why, then they are moral idiots.

—March 7, 1981

What Did You Know? When?

A student at Swarthmore College sends around a notice from the college bulletin board. It serves as a stake in the heart of memory, reminding us that the philosopher was right when he said that just as there are no permanent defeats, so there are no permanent victories.

The student notice prompted us that it was time to reread the galvanizing essay by Professor Eugene D. Genovese, published last summer in the socialist quarterly *Dissent*.

He called the essay "The Question." It was the same question Senator Howard Baker hauntingly enunciated about Richard Nixon and Watergate when the investigating committee began its work: "What did he know, and when did he know it?"

Genovese, whose important work is on the pre-Civil War South, was a Communist from very early on. At age 15, he tells us. By the time he was teaching at Rutgers in the 1960s, he was so conspicuously pro-Communist that a Republican candidate for governor of New Jersey publicly demanded that Genovese be expelled from the state university system.

Although Genovese believes profoundly in academic freedom, he would not now deny any charge leveled against him by Nixon, even while rejecting Nixon's recommendation. Genovese did indeed follow the Communist Party line. He did indeed excuse the massive killings undertaken by Stalin, his predecessors, and his successors. He excused the Soviet foreign policy line. And then, one day, it stopped.

Genovese read widely, of course; he always did and does. But he stumbled on Roy Medvedev's charge that the Soviet Union had executed more human beings than the Nazi and Fascist regimes combined.

Genovese concedes that he thought the brave Medvedev had probably taken to drink, and so, however clumsy his own arithmetic, he undertook a personally researched calculation.

He learned that it was true. But what most deeply upset him, and moves us, is his acknowledgment that he really did know it before he launched his systematic inquiry.

When did he know it? How much of it did he know? That is what essayist Genovese calls The Question in his essay. Because he wishes to confront something other than ignorance. He is telling us that he had every reason to suspect that all the talk about the torture, death, and rot of systematic socialism was true, but he could not command the moral courage to face the problem when he had every empirical reason to do so.

What he now asks members of the socialist fraternity to do is to ask themselves the same question, and to make the going tough for themselves by acknowledging that what was wrong with Communism wasn't aberrant leadership, it was Communism.

There is no such thing as democratic socialism. To the extent it is democratic, it is less than socialist. Socialism attempts to refigure the human soul and brain, and ends by disfiguring it. And all the norms so carefully accumulated over centuries pointing to right conduct are lost, most decisively with the abandonment of religion—in the United States, "bolstered by the monstrous lie that the constitutional separation of church and state was meant to separate religion from society."

Genovese is sixty-four years old, and he has learned pari passu with the passage of time in the bloodiest century in history. Is this learning to be compared with "learning" that the Earth is round, not flat? No, because the physical features of the Earth are not deniable. But it is different in the social sciences. Everything can be denied, or ignored.

The note on the Swarthmore bulletin board reads: "A group of students interested in rafting to Cuba is emerging at Swarthmore and other colleges and universities around the country. We have three goals: 1. To successfully navigate the 90-mile stretch from Miami to Cuba. 2. To volunteer to work for the summer wherever the revolution needs us. 3. To gain a better understanding of Socialist Cuba (particularly community participation). 4. To return to the United States with the hopes of re-educating our fellow students and peoples around the country. If anyone is interested, please call . . ."

Could it be a hoax? Oh no, my correspondent writes me. Not at Swarthmore.

Genovese in his essay begs the historical and moral fraternity of scholars to ask themselves in public direct questions about their behavior over the years. "Am I wrong in believing that unless the left reopens these fundamental questions it will have no future and deserve none . . . no matter how many pyrrhic victories it piles up on deranged and degraded college campuses?"

The only reason to raft to Cuba is to give succor to the multitudes who raft from Cuba because they have learned about socialism under socialism.

—June 23, 1995

Alger Hiss, R.I.P.

Those of us involved, however indirectly, in the Hiss case waited with some curiosity to see how his death would be handled in the paper of record, the

New York Times. The story was written by Janny Scott, and curiosity was justified. The headline on page 1:

Alger Hiss, Divisive Icon of Cold War, Dies at 92

And, on the jump page, border to border,

Alger Hiss, whose spy case became a symbol of the cold war, is dead at 92

The reader had to wait until the sixth paragraph to be informed that Hiss "was convicted of perjury." The ensuing sixty-eight paragraphs were given over to detailing both sides of the question on Alger Hiss. The writer did record the brief appearances on the scene of the Soviet general (Volkogonov) whose nonchalant statement (prompted by a Hiss devotee) to the effect that the KGB files had no evidence that Hiss had served as a Soviet agent had done an overnight facelift on the tatterdemalion Hiss loyalists. The general went on to divulge a few weeks later that he hadn't examined all the files. And yes, the *Times* story recorded all the legal appeals Hiss had made and lost; it informed the readers that biographer Allen Weinstein had begun his scholarly book on the case thinking Hiss innocent, but then changed his views as his research progressively undermined, and then collapsed, the Hiss case.

But the reader is left to conclude, after reading the long article, that in fact what we have here is nothing more than that some say tomato, some say tomahto. Indeed, we were specifically invited to think of it as in the category of the assassination of Kennedy and the murder of O. J. Simpson's wife and her friend. Some people say Oswald did it, and did it alone. Some people think O.J. did it; some, including the jurors, think he didn't do it. One wonders how the headlines would have read in 1935. "Alfred Dreyfus, Divisive Icon of Pre-War France, Dies at 76"? "Alfred Dreyfus, Whose Spy Case Became a Symbol of French Confusion, Is Dead at 76"?

The final paragraphs in the long story read: "Looking back, those who believe that Mr. Hiss was not guilty insisted he would never have accepted their support all those years had he not been telling the truth. In his long insistence, they found final proof. They said he had lived his life like an innocent man.

"As William F. Buckley Jr., the founder of *National Review*, who viewed Whittaker Chambers as a moral hero and never doubted Hiss's guilt, put it recently: 'It's probably understandable that he would feel that he had let too many people down.'"

When Hiss was released from prison in 1954, the counteroffensive came in full thunder—legal appeals, books by his own hand, others by his sympathizers. The appeals failed, one after another, and the books were, one after another, overwhelmed. The forthcoming biography of Chambers by Sam Tanenhaus (a main selection of the Book-of-the-Month Club for April) will quiet anyone who has a remaining doubt.

Should there be such?

No, not really. Miss Scott of the *New York Times* was right to wonder why Mr. Hiss persisted in affirming his innocence. His supporters had the most obvious answer: To affirm one's innocence is what an innocent person does. My observation to the *New York Times* was to the effect that there is the other explanation, namely that Alger Hiss didn't want to let down his old dogged, loyal followers.

But there is a third explanation for his surviving followers, which is that, in silence, they came first to doubt, then to disbelieve; but pride kept them in the Hiss camp. To have crossed that aisle would have been to acknowledge a weakness of mind or of character. Some years ago, exasperated by yet one more curtain call taken by a Hiss trouper in a magazine edited by an acquaintance of mine, I wrote to the editor and told him I would send him or his charity one thousand simoleons if he would submit to a truth test whose findings documented that he truly believed Hiss innocent. He changed the subject.

Pride could account for the loyalty of the followers. But what, other than reciprocal loyalty, might account for Hiss's persistence?

There remains the reasoning of Nikolai Bukharin. In 1957, Chambers wrote me that he had been pondering two quotations. The second "is from Bukharin's last words [in 1938] to the court which condemned him to death. I do not understand how men, knowing that, in our own lifetime, another man spoke these words at such a moment, can read them and fail to be rent apart by their meanings. Yet these words are scarcely known. I would print them bold and hang them at the front of college classrooms, not to be explained as a text, but to be seen often and quietly reflected on. Bukharin, it must be remembered, is literally innocent [of the crimes imputed to him by Stalin]. . . . It is his uncommitted crime that he pleads guilty to. He said: 'I shall now speak of myself, of the reasons for my repentance. . . . For when you ask yourself: If you must die, what are you dying for?—an absolutely black vacuity suddenly rises before you with startling vividness. There was

nothing to die for if one wanted to die unrepentant. This, in the end, disarmed me completely and led me to bend my knees before the Party and
the country. . . . At such moments, Citizen Judges, everything personal, all
personal incrustation, all rancor, pride, and a number of other things, fall
away, disappear. I am about to finish. . . . I am perhaps speaking for the last
time in my life.'

"Is there not a stillness in the room," Chambers closed, "where you
read this? That is the passing of the wings of tragedy."

I have from time to time thought that one measure of Alger Hiss as a
man should never be overlooked. It is that he won the devotion of Whittaker Chambers, who knew him as friend and fellow conspirator. By continuing to plead not guilty, Alger Hiss was performing for his faith the
same sacrifice Bukharin made by pleading guilty.

—*National Review*, December 9, 1996

Howard Fast, R.I.P.

The caller, some years ago, identified himself as Howard Fast. We are representatives, he said, you and I, of different faiths, and I would like to
dine with you. We did this, and some weeks later he joined the editors
of *National Review* for dinner. The friendship did not blossom—we were
indeed apostles of different faiths. I was candid enough to tell him at lunch
that if he hadn't left the Communist Party I would not have sat at table with
him, inasmuch as the faith I belonged to demurred at social consort with
active Communists. He smiled, nodded his head, and told me about when
he had resigned.

The famous author of best-selling historical fiction, including *Citizen
Tom Paine* and *Spartacus*, had been, no less, the managing editor of the
Communist *Daily Worker*. His work for the party was recognized by,
among others, Josef Stalin, who awarded him the Stalin International
Peace Prize the very year that Stalin died. Fast's engrossing story was that
when Khrushchev gave his famous Twentieth Congress speech in 1956,
renouncing Stalin and his works, a copy of that speech reached the *Daily
Worker* immediately before the CIA got hold of it. It was released to the

press, which would give this revolutionary speech, or perhaps better, this counterrevolutionary speech, front-page attention, even as the historians have done. "There was a dispute in the *Daily Worker* on whether we should publish a report of Khrushchev's speech," Fast said. "The editor complained that if the *Worker* went with it, the Communist Party of America would lose 10 percent of its membership. I corrected him. We'll lose 90 percent, I predicted.

"And I was right."

Howard Fast too left the Communist Party. But when he died on March 12, the long obituary in the *New York Times* referred (paragraph 1) to "the blacklisting of the 1950s," to his proclivity for unpopular causes (paragraph 4), to the interruption in his writing caused "by the blacklisting he endured in the 1950s, after it became known that he had been a member of the Communist party and then refused to cooperate with the House Un-American Activities Committee." It was finally (paragraph 9) noted that he had joined the party in 1943 "because of the poverty he experienced as a child growing up in Upper Manhattan," and that he had left it in 1956.

Paragraph 18 recounts that "because of the blacklist," Fast's book *Spartacus* was turned down by various publishers, but that (paragraph 19) "the stigma of the blacklist gradually faded after Mr. Fast's repudiation of Communism."

The lesson here is that obituary writers for the *New York Times* proceed on the cultural assumption that blacklists were undeserved, and that what is worth writing about in the Howard Fast situation is the blacklisting of him, rather than the poison Mr. Fast spread around, during his years of servitude to the criminality of Stalin. Until, that is, Khrushchev enlightened him that Stalin was a terrible man who brought death to twenty million Russians and decades of servitude to the captive nations, which lived on in captivity because Stalin's reach greatly outlasted his own lifespan.

A suitable lead for Howard Fast's obituary might have read, "Howard Fast, best-selling historical novelist, brought on his blacklisting when the public sought to draw attention to his activities as a prominent advocate of Stalin. Mr. Fast went on to write many best-sellers . . ."

If a writer who had been an active pro-Nazi until ten years after the Nuremberg trials were to die tomorrow, that part of his life would merit some attention, and would get it.

I liked Howard Fast, and hope that he will rest in not entirely untroubled peace.

—*National Review*, April 7, 2003

FRIENDS AND ADVERSARIES, HEROES AND VILLAINS

Wanda Landowska, R.I.P.

During the same period when the world of art lurched forward in flight from form and substance and idealism, Wanda Landowska discovered the majestic order of Johann Sebastian Bach. She was not only an artist but a scholar, and so brought to her ceaseless efforts to know the music of Bach not only her ample and fiery spirit but the considerable resources of a trained and inquisitive mind. She turned away from the piano to a more suitable instrument for rendering the genius of Bach, and revived the harpsichord, on which she concertized for forty years; and the gentle little clavichord, which she played for her friends. One of them, himself a master, has said that in our time, no one has dominated a musical instrument as Madame Landowska did the clavichord.

She had her detractors. Some of the purists liked to say that what she played was not Bach but Landowska; and indeed, there is no authority on the shelves for some of the embellishments, some of the liberties with tempo that she took with his music: but she took them always with a decisiveness that overpowered all but her most unmusical critics; for she played Bach with a serene suggestion of a smile on her face, as though *she* knew definitely what he wanted, and didn't the sounds that came forth validate her communion with Bach?

Wanda Landowska is dead. The musical world has lost an anchor cast to windward so many years ago, on which it has much depended to relate the wildness and egomania and solipsism of so much of modern art to Bach's heavenly world of order and beauty—the world to which Wanda Landowska, five feet tall, head barely reaching to the upper console, devoted her reverential life.

—National Review, August 29, 1959

Lindsay, Lincoln, and the GOP

"It seemed to me," John Lindsay advised his biographer, D. E. Button, "that it was important that this was the party of the individual—as I saw it, and as I still see it. It's the party of Lincoln, of civil rights, the protection of the person and his liberties against the majority, even against big business or the federal bureaucracy."

Again: "I am a Lincolnian, in that I believe when an individual or a locality can't help itself, it is the function of the federal government to help it . . . to live in dignity and to live decently as human beings. This is the ancient tradition . . . of Republican thought."

"When he talks about his 'Republican heritage,'" Button summarizes, "he means intellectually rather than by family tradition. He says, 'I can't imagine being anything other than a Republican.' Clearly his belief in Lincoln's Republican Party is substantial, not really shaken even by the trauma of 1964, and one of his great tasks as a promising leader and spokesman for that party is to convey the basis of his faith to a growing number of not necessarily convinced voters."

Granted that Lindsay has no greater difficulties in identifying himself with Abraham Lincoln than a modern Democrat has in identifying himself with Thomas Jefferson—historical name-dropping is standard practice among politicians, and one becomes resigned to these arbitrary co-options. But serious students of politics will want, if only for the academic exercise, to go beyond political opportunism to probe the nexus that allegedly binds the old hero and his presumptive heir.

Abraham Lincoln was an infinitely complicated figure, and learned debate still rages about the exact nature of his contributions to the formulation of American political philosophy. It is worth a moment to meditate on the shadow of Lincoln in midcentury politics. But the preliminary point needs to be made that the obligation is heavy on the modern politician who represents himself as the carrier of the Lincoln tradition to explain just what it is that he means by this tradition, especially insofar as it is separable from the Democratic tradition.

It isn't as if Lincoln were a figure, whether profound or simple, whose thought, at whatever moment in history it is consulted, immediately suggests an appropriate approach to a contemporary problem. If a man proclaims himself, to use a simple example, a "Couéist," he is instantly understood to be someone whose optimism is the distinguishing point of his political philosophy, who expects that every day, in every way, things will get better and better. If he calls himself, say, a Comptian positivist, people know instinctively something about the character and tendency of his thought. If he calls himself a Marxist, once again he communicates something about his thought, and his values.

But if he calls himself a "Lincolnian," he can, by the expert testimony of equally informed scholars, be different and even conflicting things; the question, among scholars, being moot as to which is the authentic Lincoln tradition, at least as regards some very important particulars. At a negative level, the designation is more useful: One thing a self-professed Lincolnian cannot be is a defender of slavery. But what of the contemporary order of politics? One of the nation's best Lincoln scholars and most ardent admirers of him, Professor Harry Jaffa of Claremont Men's College, was a supporter of Barry Goldwater—who is held, by such as Lindsay, to be the very antithesis of a Lincoln Republican. On what authority? To make matters even more complicated, an able theoretician of modern conservatism, Mr. Frank Meyer, deplores Lincoln as a champion of executive and statist arbitrariness, i.e., an anti-conservative. If the modern politician's invocation of Lincoln is to be taken as other than opportunistic and saprophytic, the invoker must describe what it is about Lincoln that he understands to be the quintessential Lincoln, toward whose ideas he gravitates in the course of waging modern Republicanism.

Lindsay, so far as I am able to discern, has not done this. His references to Lincoln tend to be proprietary, historically snobbish, diffuse, and sentimentalized (*and whashmore, I wanna toast the* gray-test *mother-in-law who ever lived*), not a little evasive, intellectually incoherent. Lincoln's party is not the party of civil rights, according to the modern understanding of civil rights—the Democratic Party clearly deserves the title. Lincoln's executive highhandedness during the Civil War is generally frowned upon by those who, for instance, believe that he had no right to suspend, unnecessarily, the citizen's recourse to the writ of habeas corpus; or, for that matter, who question the means by which he freed the slaves, without either compensation or due process. (Lincoln, himself, a year before he signed the Emancipation Proclamation, expressed doubts that he had the constitutional right to free the slaves; and when, finally, he acted, he readily admitted that he was moved to do so not by doctrinal imperatives but by military expediency.) Lincoln was not, in any modern sense, an avid protector of the person and his liberties against the majority (though he was perhaps the most powerful advocate in history of human equality as the necessary basis for self-government). Lincoln simply didn't have the time or the opportunity to concern himself with the existing, or potential, threat of big business, or, in any systematic way, with the federal bureaucracy and its bearing on human rights. And certainly Lincoln had no opportunity to weigh, say, the rights of individuals over against those of labor-union monopolies—though Lindsay has had such opportunities, and has, almost uniformly, upheld "the majority" over against "the liberties," or "the protection," of the "individual."

The search for points of contact between Lindsay and Lincoln is, to say the least, a romantic pursuit. Lincoln too, in his political lifetime, was asked to run as a "fusion candidate"—with a Southerner as vice president. And he replied: "As to the matter of fusion, I am for it, if it can be had on Republican grounds: and I am not for it on any other terms. A fusion on any other terms would be as foolish as unprincipled . . . I am against letting down the Republican standard a hair's breadth."

Lindsay complained, after the 1964 campaign, that ". . . [for] the first time in history a major party has failed to find a major ground. . . . It is essential that the [Republican] party assume proper direction, think of itself as the party of Lincoln."

"Let us be diverted," Lindsay's mentor, Abraham Lincoln, said at Cooper Union, "by none of those sophistical contrivances wherewith we are so industriously plied and belabored—contrivances such as groping for some middle ground between the right and the wrong."

Lindsay's consistent support of federal poverty programs, of deficit financing, of redistributionism, of compulsory welfarism, are, one would think, at least in arguable disharmony with Lincoln's famous homiletic, "You cannot bring prosperity by discouraging thrift. You cannot strengthen the weak by weakening the strong. You cannot help the poor by destroying the rich. You cannot establish sound security on borrowed money. You cannot keep out of trouble by spending more than you earn. You cannot build character and courage by taking away man's initiative and independence. You cannot help men permanently by doing for them what they can and should do for themselves."

On the question of civil rights—again, as currently understood—Lincoln must be an embarrassing memory to Lindsay. As a defender of the metaphysical proposition that men are equal, Lincoln was the greatest post-Biblical political philosopher. However, concerning the big contemporary issues, Lincoln was not only, according to current terminology, a segregationist but also a racist. 'The Republican Party," said Nelson Rockefeller—Lindsay's co-adjutor in New York modern Republicanism—in the summer of 1963, "is the party of Lincoln. It was founded to make men free and equal in opportunity. It is the party of all men, the only national party in America. For that party to turn its back on its heritage and its birthright would be an act of political immorality rarely equaled in human history."

"I have no purpose," Lincoln said in the summer of 1858, "to introduce political and social equality between the white and black races. There is a physical difference between the two, which in my judgment, will probably forever forbid their living together upon the footing of perfect equality;

and inasmuch as it becomes a necessity that there must be a difference, I am in favor of the race to which I belong having the superior position." The Republican Party that Lindsay exhorted at the San Francisco Convention in 1964 to emulate the tradition of its founder did not—most fortunately—ever even consider attempting to harmonize its platform with that of the august Republican Party that nominated Abraham Lincoln for the presidency in 1860. That platform averred "that the maintenance inviolate of the rights of the states, and especially the right of each State to order and control its own domestic institutions according to its own judgment exclusively, is essential to that balance of power on which the perfection and endurance of our political fabric depends." The Republican candidate so widely deplored by Lindsay as standing outside the Lincoln tradition, Barry Goldwater, wrote in 1960: "It so happens that I am in agreement with the objectives of the Supreme Court as stated in the *Brown* decision. I believe that it is both wise and just for Negro children to attend the same schools as whites, and that to deny them this opportunity carries with it strong implications of inferiority. I am not prepared, however, to impose that judgment of mine on the people of Mississippi or South Carolina, or to tell them what methods should be adopted and what pace should be kept in striving towards that goal." Who was in the tradition of Lincoln's Republican Party?

It may be contended that Abraham Lincoln would surely have changed his views between 1860 and 1960. Contended, yes: presumed, no. Neither the Goldwaters nor the Lindsays of today would accept Lincoln's pessimistic generalities based on presumed differences of a congenital nature between the races, differences of a kind that would bind them together forever—not as slavemasters and slaves, to be sure; but as governors and governed. But if tradition means anything at all, the Lincoln tradition on the related question of segregation clearly suggests that the states should retain a measure of authority respecting at least some of the questions nowadays pre-empted in the various civil-rights bills enacted by the federal government. So that the credentials of, for instance, the Goldwaters are historically superior to those of the Lindsays or the Rockefellers on the matter of the "Lincoln tradition," in dealing with race relations. It is rather in the Democratic tradition, one would think, than in the Republican tradition gradually to erode the ancient and, to Lincoln, venerable, allocations of power within the federal community.

At the profoundest level, Lincoln was a moralist, and as such altogether outside the positivist and relativist tradition of present-day social thought and jurisprudence, the jurisprudence, for instance, of Oliver

Wendell Holmes and Earl Warren, heroes of Mr. Lindsay. Lincoln's principal metapolitical insight was that for *transcendent* reasons logically expli-
cable, men cannot be considered *other* than equal. From this proposition
many others derive having to do with the rule of law and the philosophy of
jurisprudence—propositions that are utterly inimical to the most popular
philosophical attachments inculcated in the major law schools and departments of philosophy and social science (behaviorism, the movement is,
most loosely, called), to which one has yet to hear any objections from
people like Lindsay. True, as Professor Jaffa says, "Lincoln was the least
doctrinaire man who ever lived." Meaning that Lincoln was not merely a
philosopher but a statesman. Accordingly, Lincoln the statesman could
write to Horace Greeley, halfway through the Civil War, that he meant,
by the war, not to abolish slavery, but to save the Union; still, Lincoln the
philosopher meant to save the Union in order to abolish slavery. The unity
of statesmanship and philosophy prompted Professor Richard Weaver,
surveying Lincoln's career, to conclude that, at the margin, he "reasoned
from definition," rather than from "circumstance"; and as such fell in the
tradition of the natural law, rather than of the positivism that modern liberalism absolutely depends upon.

Beyond that towering point, Lincoln is up for grabs and has been
claimed as a patron by any number of ideological opportunists. The co-
option of Lincoln by those who praise the present Supreme Court; who
believe that Communists have "rights"; who look to the federal government to prescribe not only the mores but also the folkways of our race
relations, to the federal government to formulate our anti-poverty and
social-welfare programs; who are forever working to centripetalize our
social and political energies—that co-option is at best shallow; at worst,
nakedly blasphemous; in most cases, merely ignorant. A present-day
liberal Republican of limited imagination would, if wholly honest, more
likely find himself saying that he is a Republican notwithstanding many of
the utterances and attitudes of Abraham Lincoln. A conservative Republican of wider imagination would defend the proposition that Lincoln was
a great political philosopher, though inept, at times, in statesmanship and
ill-advised in some of his utterances. The safest position would be that
of the ideological outsider, the man who, wisely, does not seek wholly to
synchronize his own and Lincoln's positions; who would agree to go no
further than to say that Lincoln was one of the last great teachers of the
natural law, but that in matters of practical policy, at a level below that of
his major affirmation about human equality, he was sometimes confused
and confusing, an eclectic, the most superb rhetorician of his century; and

that modern exercises in posthumous political reconciliation at the precinct level of political controversy are either playful, arbitrary, or vulgar.

—Excerpt from *The Unmaking of a Mayor*, 1966

Thinking Back on Eleanor Roosevelt

I have been sharply reminded that I have not written about Mrs. Roosevelt and that only a coward would use the excuse that when she died he was in Africa. There there are lions and tigers and *apartheid*. Here there was Mrs. Roosevelt to write about. Africa was the safer place.

People get very sore when you knock the old lady. And it isn't just the widow who thinks of Mrs. Roosevelt as the goddess who saved her children from getting rickets during the Depression. It is also the Left intellectuals. "When are you going to stop picking on Mrs. Roosevelt?" a very learned writer asked me at a reception a few years ago after one of my books was published. (I had a sentence in it that annoyed him, something like: "Following Mrs. Roosevelt in search of irrationality is like following a lighted fuse in search of an explosion: One never has to wait very long.") I answered: "When you *begin* picking on her." I meant by that that people are best reformed by those they will listen to. Westbrook Pegler could never reform Mrs. Roosevelt or her legend. But Adlai Stevenson or Max Lerner might have.

The obituary notices on Mrs. Roosevelt were as one in granting her desire to do good—she treated all the world as her own personal slum project, and all the papers, of course, remarked on that fabulous energy; surely she was the very first example of the peacetime use of atomic energy. But some publications, I think especially of *Time*, went so far as to say she had a great mind. Now is the time for all good men to come to the aid of Euclid.

Does it matter? Alas, it happens to matter very much. For Mrs. Roosevelt stamped on her age a mode. Or, it might be said by those who prefer to put it that way, in Mrs. Roosevelt the age developed its perfect symbol. Hers is the age of undifferentiated goodness, of permissive egalitarianism. Mrs. Roosevelt's approach to human problems, so charming in its Franciscan naïveté, was simply: Do away with them—by the most obvious means. The way to cope with Russia is to negotiate. . . . The way for everyone to be free in the world is to tell the U.N. to free everyone. . . . The way to eliminate poverty in Latin America is to give the Latin American countries money. . . . The way to solve the housing shortage is for the government to build more houses. . . .

All that is more than Mrs. Roosevelt writing a column. It is a way of life. Based, essentially, on unreason, on the leaving out of the concrete, complex factor, which is why it is *undifferentiated* goodness. Negotiation with Russia, you see, implies there is something we are or should be prepared to yield. . . . And everyone in the world cannot be free so long as freedoms are used by whole nations to abuse the peoples of other nations or the freedoms of their own people. . . . Latin American poverty is something that grows out of the pores of Latin American institutions and appetites and cannot be seriously ameliorated by mere transfusions of U.S. cash. . . . And the way to get houses built is to reduce their cost, so that people can buy them without paying crippling wages to monopoly labor unions or crippling prices to manufacturing concerns that have to pay the taxes levied by a government which, among other things, decides it needs to get into the housing business. . . .

Mrs. Roosevelt's principal bequest, her most enduring bequest, was the capacity to so oversimplify problems as to give encouragement to those who wish to pitch the nation and the world into humanitarian crusades which, because they fail to take reality into account, end up plunging people into misery (as Wilson's idealistic imperialism plunged Europe into misery for years and spawned Hitler) and messing up the world in general (under whose statecraft did Stalin prosper?) Above all, it was Mrs. Roosevelt who, on account of her passion for the non sequitur, deeply wounded the processes of purposeful political thought. "Over whatever subject, plan, or issue Mrs. Roosevelt touches," Professor James Burnham once wrote, "she spreads a squidlike ink of directionless feeling. All distinctions are blurred, all analysis fouled, and in the murk clear thought is forever impossible."

Someday in the future a liberal scholar will write a definitive thesis exploring the cast of Mrs. Roosevelt's mind by a textual analysis of her thought, and then history will be able to distinguish between a great woman with a great heart and a woman of perilous intellectual habit. "With all my heart and soul," her epitaph should read, "I fought the syllogism." And with that energy and force, she wounded it, almost irretrievably—

how often lately have you seen the syllogism checking in at the office for a full day's work?

—December 29, 1962

JFK, the Morning After

Norman Mailer, reviewing Victor Lasky's book on John Kennedy several weeks ago for the *New York Herald Tribune*, remarked that Kennedy's political genius rested in his apprehension of the main point in American politics toward the close of the Fifties: namely, that the American people were ready, in Mailer's words, to turn away from the father image (Eisenhower) and accept as ruler someone cast in the role of the young hero—someone in the Hollywood image, as Mailer put it.

Mailer seems to have been right, as he very often is. What happened, two and one-half weeks ago, was the *morte d'Arthur*. The grief was that of a nation that had lost a young king, a young king whose own fairytale rise to power recapitulated the national experience, whose personal radiance warmed the whole nation—and whose great fiascoes were charitably disregarded, for were we not, really, forgiving ourselves? And are we not, really, grieving for ourselves? "A part of me has gone with him," one orator said, and a great chorus responds to the theme, and they all are exactly correct—they *have* lost a part of themselves. Much of America, the intelligentsia especially, succeeded in casting itself in the image of John Kennedy, whereon it had to follow that when he lay bleeding, they lay bleeding, and that the great ache, the anxiety expressed so effusively, lay in the numbing realization that though their king was dead, they were still alive and would have to learn again to act for themselves. And, God help us, to think for themselves.

For it gives one the grues. The assassination itself, yes, obviously. We know what death is and what evil is in the twentieth century. We live with violence, and apocalypse is camped just over the horizon. We have lived with violent endings, for individuals, and for nations, and for races. We know the unyielding finality of death and one's helplessness before recurrent acts of individual and collective depravity. But what is this other thing that seems to be going on? Pay the man all the many compliments to which he is entitled, and sing the praises he is due. But not all this, no, indeed, and for the reason, first among the others, that it tends to undermine those qualities in national life that John Kennedy at his best exemplified: courage, dignity, fortitude, tough-mindedness, independence.

The rhetoric has gone quite out of control. The symbol of our emotional, if not neurotic, excess is the Eternal Flame at Arlington, a few hundred yards from the shrines we built to the memories of George Washington (85 years after he died), Thomas Jefferson (117 years), and Abraham Lincoln (57 years), who have no eternal flames. The lovely and tormented Mrs. Kennedy needs a gentle hand, lest in her understandable grief she give the air of the Pharaoh, specifying his own magnitude.

John F. Kennedy lived a life of tough controversy, and while it is correct that an individual's weaknesses should be buried with him, it is not ever possible to bury the public issues on which a public figure committed himself. Mr. Kennedy told us the fight would last beyond his lifetime, and his successor has pledged himself on the same side of those policies. It is sobering to recall that there was great dissension, left and right, in respect of John Kennedy's policies, up until the very moment he died. The issue of *Time* magazine dated the awful day of the assassination carried the news of a growing campus "disenchantment" with President Kennedy's policies, "now spread far and wide." "At conservative Georgia Tech," said *Time*, "the complaint is that 'he's interfering with my personal life' through Big Government. At liberal Reed, where 'he doesn't inspire respect as Stevenson did,' the gripe is Kennedy's caution on the civil rights bill. At exuberant Wisconsin, 'he's liked in a negative way,' faulted for lack of political conviction." The restlessness, as we see, was not partisan, not only from the right.

Are we now being emotionally stampeded into believing that Kennedy was the Incarnation and that respect for him requires that we treat his program like the laws of the Medes and the Persians?

What we need is a period of dignified mourning for a graceful human being, who passed through our midst with style and energy, a mourning more intense in virtue of the treachery of his end, but less intense than that which degenerates into abject pity for ourselves or that which asks that we place our personal grief above the best interests of our country as we understand them, which best interests many people thought of as calling for the retirement of Mr. Kennedy from public life one year from now. Jack Kennedy wouldn't want a caterwauling public besotted by its tears for its own self or accepting his program for sentimentality's sake. He asked us to keep the torch lit. And that means to work, each one of us according to his own lights, to keep this country at least as strong and as free, stronger, we can hope, and freer, by acting on his own idealism than it was when John Kennedy last knew it.

—December 7, 1963

Douglas MacArthur, Missing but Well Accounted For

The sad news has come in from Walter Reed Hospital. There never seemed really to be any doubt that this time General MacArthur would die. But the news has shocked the public just the same, because we are once again reminded that even the imperishable perish.

MacArthur was the last of the great Americans. It isn't at all certain that America is capable of producing another man of MacArthur's caste. Such men spring from the loins of nations in whose blood courage runs: and we are grown anemic. That is why so many have spoken of an age that would die with MacArthur. An age where, occasionally, heroes arose, acknowledging as their imperatives that Duty, Honor, and Country which MacArthur cherished, but which the nation that rejected him has no stomach for, preferring the adulterated substitutes of our age of Modulation.

I have often thought that it is a key to the understanding of what has happened to this country that Dwight Eisenhower became president, rather than Douglas MacArthur. This is not the time to slight Mr. Eisenhower, whose principal fault, after all, lies in his being quintessentially a part of his age: the age is at fault, not Eisenhower; the age was not imaginative enough for MacArthur. The age was afraid of MacArthur, and well might it have been, because he stood above it, as de Gaulle stands above his own time. In France they turned, at last, to de Gaulle, but only because the monstrous inefficiency of the French finally prevented recourse to yet one more mediocrity. We in America, being more efficient, more conservative, than the French, never felt the need to reach beyond a mediocrity, so we elected the affable Eisenhower, and let MacArthur go to his Colombey-les-Deux-Eglises at the Waldorf Towers, there to fade away.

Even while he did that, he managed to retain his grandeur. It is an unfortunate image—fade away—as if, as the years went by, the general had grown paler and paler, ending up in a pastel insipidity from which all the vital colors of his manhood had drained. He grew, eventually, physically weak, but his powers were undiminished, his august presence unmistakable. When, as recently as a year ago, he walked into the meeting of the jaded celebrities from all over the world that *Time* magazine had convoked to celebrate an anniversary, he, and only he, produced that throat-catching sense of excitement which Henry Luce, subsequently introducing him, was prepared, honestly and boyishly, to acknowledge, as an almost metaphysical property of that man.

It did not matter that he lived as a recluse in the Waldorf Towers, his presence was felt right up until the last minute, when messages of grief stormed the Walter Reed Hospital, on a scale that overwhelmed hospital officials, who had never seen the like of it. A lot of us felt that for so long as he lived, the nation drew, somehow, from his great strength. And now they are, we are, sad, and lonely; and grateful. If we as a nation must die, we can find no better words to die by, this side of Scripture, than his, given at his last public appearance at West Point:

> The shadows are lengthening for me. The twilight is here. My days of old have vanished—tone and tint. They have gone glimmering through the dreams of things that were. Their memory is one of wondrous beauty, watered by tears and coaxed and caressed by the smiles of yesterday. I listen vainly, but with thirsty ear, for the witching melody of faint bugles blowing reveille, of far drums beating the long roll . . . But in the evening of my memory . . . always there echoes and re-echoes: Duty, honor, country.
>
> —April 5, 1964

Churchill in the Balance

For as long as heroes are written about, Winston Churchill will be written about. The proportions are all abundantly there. He was everything. The soldier who loved poetry. The historian who loved to paint. The diplomat who thrived on indiscretion. The patriot with international vision. The

orderly man given to electric spontaneities. The man who flunked everything at school and then kept a generation of scholars busy interpreting
his work and his words. The loyal party man who could cross the aisle and
join the opposition when principle called. The Tory traditionalist revered
in his old age by the neoteric levelers.

He was a very great man, and it is the crowning pity under the circumstances that he did not have that final ounce of strength to deliver
Europe from the mess in which he left it after the great war to which he,
as much as anyone else, committed the entire world. It is ungrateful to
say of the dead, particularly of those few among the dead who were so
distinguished in their lifetime, that they owed us more than they gave us.
But Churchill is as much responsible as anyone else in our time for calling
forth exacting judgments. The nobility of his utterances galvanized us to
believe in the final possibilities of individual human beings, of statesmen,
and of nations. His great orations during the war which he told us he was
waging, and believed that he waged, in behalf of righteousness require the
observer to apply the highest standards to his life and goals.

All those men who were moved by the martial rhetoric of Winston
Churchill to go out and die also figure in any obituary notice of Winston
Churchill, and they are not appeased by glossing over the final imperfec-
tion of Churchill's life.

It was Churchill who pledged a restored Europe, indeed a restored
world order after the great war. He did not deliver us such a world. No
one else could so have stirred the world's imagination as he, at that critical point in world history, to press for the final goal the war was fought
to achieve—the elimination of the source of aggressive evil that finds
us today, on Churchill's death, living not only in a world in which more
people are slaves than were slaves in the darkest hours of the Battle of
Britain, but in a world that cares infinitely less about the wretchedness of
these peoples than cared about such things even during the lackadaisical,
disorganized Thirties. At least during that period Churchill was there to
bellow his indignation at the depravities of Adolf Hitler. Now, a generation
later, it has become uncouth, dislocative, warmongering, to bellow against
injustice even on a vastly magnified scale.

Churchill suggested, in his autobiography, that after all he could
not be held responsible for the incomplete peacemaking inasmuch as
power was suddenly taken from him in the surprise election of 1945.
But Churchill had been in power, was almost omnipotent, at Yalta, and
at Teheran, where the great statesmen of the West took some steps and

failed to take others, and together these acts of commission and omission ensured the consolidation of Stalin's power in the territories he had overrun during the war, and ensured also the expansion of the Communist system over whole continents. During those days Churchill the diplomat overwhelmed Churchill the statesman, the practitioner of justice. During those days Churchill found himself in the House of Commons delivering eulogies on the person of the abominable Stalin—a man whose evil he had years before remarked, representative of an evil whom no one had better analyzed than Churchill in the Twenties. During those days he stood still for such disastrous fatuities as Franklin Roosevelt's impetuous call for unconditional surrender, a rhetorical fillip which in the analysis of some military experts may have cost us the unnecessary deaths of several hundred thousand men, and which most certainly was responsible for the supine condition of much of Europe at the moment when Stalin's legions came rolling in.

Is Winston Churchill a hero to the Polish people who were betrayed by the West? To the Yugoslavs? To the Hungarians and Rumanians and Czechs, whose plight under Nazism Churchill had so effectively dramatized as to mobilize all the forces of moral concern the world over into a war that began as a war for their liberation from the evil Nazis, and ended as a war for their perpetual imprisonment by the evil Communists? It is true that at Fulton, Missouri, in 1946, Churchill focused the attention of the world, as again only he had the power to do, on the deteriorating situation. But he seemed thereafter to have lost the great engine that had fired him ten years earlier to force the recognition of reality. Thenceforward he seemed concerned only to complete his literary and historical masterpieces, and to regain power from the Labour Party almost only for the sake of regaining power.

He turned over the leadership of the world to the faltering hands of Americans who were manifestly his inferiors in the understanding of history and the management of human affairs, and contented himself to write dramatically about decisive battles won for freedom on the soil of England centuries ago, battles whose victory he celebrated vicariously, having no appetite left to fight real enemies, enemies whose health he had, God save him, nourished by that fateful shortage of vision which, in the end, left him, and the world, incapable of seeing that everything he had said and fought for applied alike to the Russian as to the German virus. May he sleep more peacefully than some of those who depended on him.

—January 21, 1965

Kenneth Tynan Says a Naughty Word

A few weeks ago on the BBC, no less, an unmentionable word was mentioned by, no less, the literary manager of England's National Theatre, and, once again, Kenneth Tynan was in the news. He has been newsworthy for a good many years in dramatic circles because he is, if not a first-rate critic (he is impeded from being that by his world view, which is materialist and egoistic), at least a very, very good one, in that he is a shrewd observer and expert verbalizer who disposes of a pyrotechnical vocabulary and abundant wit and is, therefore, fun to read, whatever one thinks of him, of drama, or, indeed, of the universe itself.

He is extremely interesting to theater folk because of his exemplary technical skills as a critic; but it is, alas, not these but other exhibitions which have caused him to become an international figure, recognized as such by the *New York Times Magazine*, which has devoted an admiring spread to him, triggered—o sweetest of ironies!—precisely by the commotion that resulted from his violation of a taboo for the maintenance of which the *New York Times* would go to the electric chair.

Mr. Tynan is interesting to us ordinary folks, we learn, because of his freewheeling iconoclasm and because he is, thereby, a part of that wave of the future which good gray editors dutifully cover on the grounds that in due course it must inundate us all, and we may as well be good sports about it when the time comes.

The philosophy of Kenneth Tynan is not by any means original, although he depicts it refreshingly in his quite ungovernable effluvia, most of them published in this country in the cleavages of *Playboy* magazine. It is the usual kind of business. Man is born to enjoy himself. The acutest pleasures in life are cultural and sexual, or maybe sexual and cultural. From the time he was a schoolboy, Tynan was onto the instant scandal value of manifestos in favor of sexual permissiveness, and it is recorded that he resigned as an independent candidate for a school election when the headmaster denied him permission to make his stand in favor of free homosexuality. Unlike some of his friends and admirers, he himself is not a practitioner of the freedom he advocates, but he finds it a constant source of amusement to toy with the subject.

A few years ago he wrote a piece for the highbrow English periodical *Encounter* in which he took great delight, a delight he apparently believed was communicable to his readers, in recounting an episode with a tailor whom he visited to hire a costume for the annual affair given by the Lord Mayor of London and before whom he declined to undress on the ground that he (Tynan) was a homosexual. That, believe it or not, was the punch line of his long essay, which suggests that as a critic, he has his own second-act problems.

In the United States he made great publicity for himself a few years ago by signing the Fair Play for Cuba Committee's manifesto to the effect that we were being beastly toward Fidel Castro and then writing a whimpering piece of self-pity when Senator Thomas Dodd of the Senate Internal Security Subcommittee had the nerve to question him about his knowledge of where the funds were collected to pay for the publication of the manifesto. For a man who was so brave with his tailor, it was disappointing that he was so unbrave with Senator Dodd, whom he esteems less than his tailor and over whose impending questions he worried greatly, wondering even whether the result of Senator Dodd's interrogation might be that he would never, ever be able to earn a living again ("economic fears welled up," he wrote. ". . . would my American earnings be jeopardized?"). It didn't hurt him, of course, and he has been too busy ever since to apologize to Senator Dodd, whose pertinacity absolutely established that the money for that particular Communist front had indeed been provided by a Communist—no less a man than Fidel Castro's own ambassador to the United Nations.

But Tynan went back to England and continued his chatter about sex and revolution, calling, among other things, for capitulating to the Soviet Union at the time of the Berlin crisis, lest he should die in the holocaust that would result if we stood firm. ("I would rather live on my knees than die on my knees.")

In England he lives contentedly among the literati, available to all interesting people, save only for his reservation that he "couldn't be friendly with a convinced Tory . . . all the people I know and like are Liberal or Socialist."

The syndrome is complete when we learn that he can't be friendly with God either, which is, one hopes, an unrequited attitude and, in any case, an especially sad one, considering that Mr. Tynan was exposed to the most persuasive Christian scholar of his generation, C. S. Lewis, at Oxford. "I hope," says Mr. Tynan, "I never need to believe in God. It would be an

awful confession of failure." Rather like a show that closes after the first
week, which is the dramatist's idea of hell.

—January 13, 1966

Evelyn Waugh, R.I.P.

I once encountered a very angry lady in Dallas, Texas, who announced
herself as head of a vigilance committee to keep dirty books out of the local
libraries, and we talked a bit. I forget just how the conversation moved,
but at one point I said that to pull out all the salacious passages from
modern literature would require the end of individual reading. All of us
would have to have private readers, like the old eccentric in the novel by
Evelyn Waugh who forced his prisoner to read to him the works of Charles
Dickens. Who, asked the lady book-critic, is Evelyn Waugh? The greatest
English novelist of this century, I ventured; but on ascertaining that he was
not a dirty writer, she lost all interest, and went off to look for more dirty
books to rail against.

I wrote to Waugh and told him about the episode. My letter did not
include any reference to any business matter, so I knew he would not
reply to it; but I knew the little story would appeal to his sense of satire, so
strongly developed as to make him, in the judgment of the critic Edmund
Wilson, the "only first-rate comic genius the English have produced since
George Bernard Shaw." (Waugh's reply, several years later, to an interviewer who asked what was *his* opinion of Edmund Wilson: "Is he American?" End comment.) But Waugh was much more than that, though
millions of his readers who read only *A Handful of Dust*, and *Scoop*, and
The Loved One, did not know about the other dimensions; did not know
that Evelyn Waugh the great satirist was a conservative, a traditionalist,
a passionately convinced and convincing Christian, a master stylist routinely acknowledged, during the last decade, as the most finished writer
of English prose.

He died at sixty-two, having completed only one volume of a long autobiography. In it he recorded, dispassionately, the impressions of his early
years; something of the lives of his ancestors, many of them eccentric; and
something of the chaos of his undergraduate career at Oxford, from which

he was duly expelled, as so many interesting Englishmen are expected to be. He decided, in his mid-twenties, that the thing to do was to commit suicide, and he describes, as he would in a novel, his own venture in this dramatic activity—leaving the verse from Euripides about water washing away the stains of the earth neatly exposed where it could not be missed by grieving relatives and meticulous coroners; wading out into the ocean, thinking diapasonal thoughts; then running into a school of jellyfish and racing back to the beach, putting on his clothes, tearing up Euripides, and resuming his career, for which we thank God's little jellyfish.

He was an impossible man, in many respects. At least as far as the public was concerned. Like J. D. Salinger and James Gould Cozzens, he simply refused to join the world of flackery and televised literature. On one occasion when he did consent to grant an interview to a young correspondent from the *Paris Review*, because he was related to an old friend, Waugh thoroughly disconcerted the interviewer by arriving at his hotel suite, taking off his clothes, getting into bed, lighting a huge cigar, breaking open a bottle of champagne, and then uttering: "Proceed."

Rather than live a public life, he situated himself in a large old house in the country, surrounding himself with a moat that was proof against all but his closest friends, and the vicar. The piranhas made a specialty of devouring all first-class mail asking for interviews, comments, suggestions, whatever. I confess to having successfully swum across that moat, after several fruitless assaults. I discovered that the squire felt an obligation to reply to all letters concerning questions of commerce; so that if you wanted a comment or two on a matter of literature or philosophy or politics, you could hope to get it by dropping into your letter a trivial question relating to business.

But he was a man of charity, personal generosity, and, above all, understanding. He knew people, he knew his century, and, having come to know it, he had faith only in the will of God, and in individual man's latent capacity to strive toward it. He acknowledged the need to live in this century, because the jellyfish will not have it otherwise; but never, ever, to acclimate yourself to it. Mr. Scott-King, the classics teacher, after his tour through Evelyn Waugh's *Modern Europe*, comes back to school, and there the headmaster suggests that he teach some popular subject, in addition to the classics—economic history, perhaps, for the classics are not popular. "I'm a Greats man myself," the headmaster says. "I deplore it as much as you do. But what can we do? Parents are not interested in producing the 'complete man' any more. They want to qualify their boys for jobs in the modern world. You can hardly blame them, can you?"

"Oh yes," Scott-King replies, "I can and do." And, deaf to the head-master's entreaties, he declares, shyly but firmly, "I think it would be very wicked indeed to do anything to fit a boy for the modern world."

Waugh got the best of the modern world, but paid a high price for it: he gave it his genius.

—April 14, 1966

Frank Chodorov, R.I.P.

Most of you know, some of you better than I, the biography. He was born in New York, poor, the son of Russian immigrants, and he lived on the lower West Side, even as it was slowly becoming fashionable. "They painted the fronts white and the shutters green," he wrote fifty years later, "and invested the section with profitable romance by reviving its ancient name of Greenwich Village."

He finished high school and enrolled at Columbia University, where, during his first year, his principal interest was football, and he made the varsity squad. He graduated, and married, and went out to make his way in commerce, "having," as he wrote, "given up as hopeless for a Jew the ambition of becoming a professor of English." He worked, and made a modest living, for himself, his wife, and his two children. And then, in the Thirties, his children grown, he turned one day to his wife, Celia, and asked her permission to leave his job and the little security it had given him in order to teach. Up until then, like Paul Gauguin, he had mostly seen, and now, like Gauguin, he wanted to express himself. Her consent, to that as to every request he ever made, was instantly given. And he began the career, quietly, studiously, passionately, which made him friends among so many people who never laid eyes on him.

During all the years he had worked as a salesman and in advertising he had continued to read, and early in his postgraduate career he had fas-tened on Henry George as the object of his primary fascination. At first he was drawn to George because of the literary style. "Here," he once recalled, "was something of the cameo clarity of Matthew Arnold, a little of the parallel structure of Macaulay, the periods of Edmund Burke. I know I was more interested in how this man Henry George—some fellow who, I had heard, had run for mayor of New York—said it than in what he had to say. Probably a nineteenth-century essayist, I surmised, whom I had missed, and the deficiency had to be made up. I borrowed [*Progress and Poverty*] for a week or two."

Now, having for many years cultivated what he grew to believe was the unique social vision of George, he became the director of the Henry George School. But in due course there was a falling out, and he resigned. One cannot truly understand Henry George, he once remarked, without understanding his antipathy toward socialism. But most of George's modern exegetes, he feared, were disposed to traduce George, to put his social philosophy at the service of the state. And it was the centralized state that Frank Chodorov was born, and lived, to oppose.

He had a go at journalism. During those years he had met Albert Jay Nock. Once again, in his admiration for Nock, he could unite his passion for prose and for a philosopher of the individual. Nock, the stunning belletrist, the author of *Our Enemy, the State*, the founder of the renowned journal *The Freeman*. The two of them had a go—unsuccessful—at reviving the old *Freeman*. He turned then to individual journalism, rented a dingy little office downtown near where he grew up, and founded a personal monthly four-page journal, which he called *analysis*. I met him there, where he wrote, edited, copyread, published, distributed, and merchandised the little journal, which got under the skin of those, comparatively few, who recognized that seemingly all of America, in a fit of opportunism, had lost hold of the ancient moorings. *analysis* was the testimony of a single man against the spirit of an age that had become infatuated with the possibilities of the central solution for the problems of society. In *analysis* the old fires burned, or rather were kept flickering. "Lenin," John Chamberlain wrote in 1952, "said it long ago: to make collectivism stick in a land that has known the blessings of individualism, you must catch a whole generation in the cradle and forcibly deprive it of tutors who have learned the bourgeois alphabet at their mothers' knees. In a land of republican law this is impossible; no matter how clever or omnipresent the collectivist propaganda may be, a few culture-carriers of the old tradition will escape. They may be reduced to publishing broadsheets like *analysis* instead of books; they may be compelled to conduct their straggling classes in dingy rooms in old brownstone fronts. Certainly they will have a hard time getting posts on a university faculty. But they will be still hanging around—and still talking—when the tinsel begins to wear off the latest Five-Year Plan or government-sponsored Greenbelt colonization scheme. Their books and pamphlets, ready for the chance encounter that sparks all revolutions or 'reactions,' will fan the revival of the old tradition that perdiodically displaces the callow presumptions of the 'new.'"

The sparks were struck. He accepted a post with *Human Events*, which in those days was four pages of sparkling news commentary by Frank Hanighen and four pages of philosophy by him, alternating with Bertrand de Jouvenel, with William Henry Chamberlin, and, on the fourth week, with a guest. From there he went to the once again resurrected *Freeman*, which he served as editor, in association with Leonard Read. He left it to freelance, joining the staff of *National Review*, and then, in rapid succession, the tragedies struck.

Celia died, shortly after they celebrated their fiftieth wedding anniversary. He was inconsolable, lost; a mild rebuke, this individual powerlessness, some would say, to the spirit of total individualism—some, but only those who misunderstand the nature of the individualism he believed in, which called for aloofness from remote and synthetic and involuntary associations, but which flowered in the giving of oneself to one's family, and friends, and philosophical soulmates. He went to Europe, for the first time, and was able to report exultantly on the collapse of rigid Marxism in Germany, the end of that demonic ideology that had elevated to religious faith the necessity to subordinate the individual. He returned to New York happy to conclude that dogmatic socialism was on the wane, but pessimistic, in his gentle, yet obdurate, way, believing that the forms would outlive the substance and that the inertia of statism would continue to erode the individual and the free society. And he kept on preaching.

And then, at the Freedom School in Colorado, he was struck down. His daughter, Grace, went to him, and he was barely able, after the stroke, to talk. But he did, in near delirium, mention that his faith in Henry George was whole, that George, above all others, understood.

Grace brought him back to New York, and he recovered his powers of speech. But he could not write again, and as he grew worse, he could not read, and not to write, not to read were consignments to an insanity from which he was saved only by his devotion to Grace and her husband, Herbert, and to his grandchildren, Lisa, and Erik, and Francine. After a while he needed professional nursing care. That first summer he stayed in the country, near Grace. I saw him there, and puffing his fugitive pipe, he leaned over to me and said grumpily: "You know what this place is? It's a die-in." His eyes twinkled, but he was not greatly amused—without his typewriter, without his books, without even, for long hours of the day, his family. But he was resigned. He had been resigned ever since Celia died.

That fall he returned to New York City, to the Mary Manning Walsh home, run by Catholic sisters, and there was nursed first by Sister Fidelis, then—when she was transferred to Boston on the grounds that her miraculous attentions could not be monopolized by a single city—by Sister Bernadette Mary, who gave him attention and love. And always Grace, and Herbert, and the children. And the forbidden cigarette lighters, sneaked in to him like hacksaw blades to men in a death house, and the wicked gleam of appreciation at this final defiance of authority. Individualism to the end. And finally, last Wednesday, a crisis, and a merciful death.

~

After I met him at *analysis*, we were frequently together. He came to Yale to speak while I was still an undergraduate. His manner was diffident, slightly didactic, firm, gentle—always gentle. Edmund Opitz reviewed one of his books and remarked that an extraordinary feature of it was that he united a polemical passion with an apparent incapacity to utter any meanness toward anyone, dead or alive. He spoke from a heart full of belief, enlightened by a mind keen and observant and understanding. He spoke thus, in a style resolutely undemagogic, on every occasion. He thought it somehow profane to seduce, by the force of oratory, any listener toward positions with which he wasn't, somehow, organically oriented. "The purpose of teaching individualism," he wrote, "is not to *make* individualists but to *find* them. Rather, to help them find *themselves*. If a student takes readily to such values as the primacy of the individual, the free market place, or the immorality of taxation, he is an individualist; if he swallows hard, he must be counted a recruit for the other side." There are those, he was saying—and he took his thought from the Book of Job and later from the immortal essay of Albert Jay Nock on the Remnant—who are latently capable of understanding. Those who aren't—well, they aren't. But do what you can for those who are.

Whether a point of view so morose about the political redeemability of the non-Remnant is realistic doesn't much seem to matter somehow. It is quite enough for any man to do to stir the sentiments and thought of those who are predisposed to listen. And so at a relatively late age he swung into high gear. Among the enterprises he started was, in 1953, the Intercollegiate Society of Individualists, whose goal it is to undo the damage done a half century earlier by the Intercollegiate Socialist Society. I was ISI's first president, but I was purely a figurehead, as I was soon reminded. In short order I had a letter from him: "Am removing you as president. Making myself pres. Easier to raise money if a Jew is president. You can be V-P. Love. Frank."

And then he started to write his books, his wonderful books of essays, innocent—and that was their strength—of the entangling complexities of modern life. It simply didn't matter that there had been an Industrial Revolution, that economists had made finicky examinations of the business cycle, that E had been discovered to be equal to mc squared. Because he dealt in personal and social truisms in his books, and he did not ever entertain the possibility that the world, whatever its conceits and effronteries, would conceivably presume to justify the subordination of the individual.

During the years immediately after he left Columbia, he was greatly infatuated with atheism. Then, on reading and rereading Henry George, he abandoned his faith in nonfaith, though he never joined a religion; indeed, he ordained that no service said over his grave should be religious. He came to believe in "transcendence," a confession he wrote into an essay which he entitled "How a Jew Came to God." Many people, he penetrated, are unwitting believers. "Even the ultra-materialistic socialists," he wrote, "in their doctrine of historical inevitability, are guilty of transcendentalism. Admittedly, I reasoned, this is a flight of the finite mind from its own limitations; it is a search for security in an invariable; it is mining for bedrock in the infinite." As for him, he could only bring himself to say that religion, the kind of religion he believed in, is a "faith in the possibility of an explanatory pattern of constancies." John Chamberlain called him a mystic—"but only," said Chamberlain, "in the sense that all men of insight are mystics. His mystical assumption is that men are born as individuals possessing inalienable rights."

"These rights of man," his daughter, Grace, wrote me yesterday, "stem from a source higher than man and must not be violated. To him this *was* a religion. It was a belief handed down to his son and daughter as a religious concept—even though he did not consciously mean it thus. . . . He refused to think about spiritual freedom or the freedom gained through the spiritual life; but in his concept of man's right to himself he unknowingly carried and tried to spread a message from the spiritual world."

~

We are gathered here today to affirm that knowing Frank Chodorov or even knowing his works was a spiritual experience. We weep at the loss of a father and a grandfather, a personal friend and teacher to those who knew him and his writings, a friend of the human race, whose faith in it—and love for its individual members—ennobles mankind. As a Christian, I postulate that today he is happy and serene in the company of the angels and the saints and his Celia. We who have time left to serve on earth rejoice in the memory of our friend and teacher, a benefactor to us all, living and unborn. May he rest eternally in peace.

—Eulogy delivered on December 31, 1966

A Relaxing View of Ronald Reagan

In this here neck of the woods there is some uneasiness in the air, and the reason why is Ronald Reagan. Here is how the nightmare goes. Romney does so-so in New Hampshire, not well enough to give him a solid lead, not poorly enough to dispose of him once and for all and leave time to build up another liberal. Nixon does poorly, maybe not so poorly as to make him withdraw either, but poorly enough to prevent the bandwagon's forming. On to Wisconsin. Same sort of thing. Then in Oregon and Nebraska, Reagan supporters submit his name, and without campaigning Reagan wins decisively. On to the convention. A bitter fight, but once again the liberals are disunited. George Romney has had a divine visitation telling him to stay in the fight, and he does: through the first and second ballots, fracturing the liberals. And—big difference from 1964—somehow the disparagement of the Reagan forces hasn't had the desirable effect of weakening the Republican Party so as to guarantee, at least, its ultimate defeat in November. Add to that the ecumenical goo that Ronald Reagan is so good at extruding—why, you would think, sometimes, that Senator Kuchel was his best friend. So Reagan gets nominated, and then we all rush off to our artillery pieces, aim, pull the triggers, and—typical nightmare—nothing happens, so that, smiling that confounding smile of his, he rides his horse right onto the front lawn of the White House, dismounts, hands the reins over to the benumbed editor of the *Washington Post*, and proceeds to the throne, whence he judges over us all.

The nightmare peters out at this point, for one thing because it never is absolutely clear just how a political conservative is actually going to succeed in destroying the country. It is better for nightmares to end with such details unspecified (a haunted house should never be entered—no bad can come of it). Presumably, what he would do that is undesirable is a projection of what he has done that is undesirable in California. And concerning what he has done in California, there is thoroughly mystifying disagreement in many quarters.

There is the opinion, for instance, of Hale Champion. Mr. Champion, who is now uncoiling at Harvard at what has been called the Center for the Advancement of the Kennedy Family, served Governor Pat Brown as state finance director (one thinks of serving President Kubitschek of Brazil as budget balancer). Mr. Champion undeniably earned a period of repose in the groves of academe, or even in a sanatorium. He suggested an appropriate structure for the criticism of the Reagan administration in *West* magazine (April 23), in which he commented on the new governor's first hundred days in office. Governor Reagan, said Mr. Champion, (a) is "in deepening trouble with the legislature and with the public"; (b) has a "completely negative and destructive attitude [toward] higher education"; (c) has "accomplished" almost nothing "except the dismissal of Clark Kerr"; (d) is likely to be swamped by "the future consequences of [his] failure to work out solutions to problems"; and (e) is aesthetically offensive, as witness "the loose bundle of social and moral pronouncements that constitute the governor's vague, historically inaccurate, philosophically sloppy, and verbally undistinguished inaugural address."

From this criticism we all were to infer that Mr. Reagan is quite as bad as it was feared by the most fearful that he would be. Well, perhaps not *quite* as bad as some of Governor Brown's campaign rhetoric predicted. After all, at one point in the campaign, Governor Brown, addressing a group of schoolchildren in a widely played television spot, reminded them that Ronald Reagan was an actor and that it was an actor who had shot Abraham Lincoln—a sorites that Mr. Champion did not, at the time, identify as philosophically sloppy or even verbally undistinguished. On the other hand, Mr. Champion is in a position to point out that Reagan hasn't had the opportunity to assassinate Abraham Lincoln, and how can we know that, given the opportunity, he would not seize it?

But then, having prepared ourselves to think about Mr. Reagan the way Mr. Champion thinks about him, one is confused by the contradictory analyses of another very liberal critic of Mr. Reagan, Andrew Kopkind, who has kept in very close touch with Reagan over the years and disapproves of him every bit as much as Mr. Champion—but for different reasons. He thinks that Mr. Reagan is a phony—that he isn't really conservative at all, just talks that way. Whereas Mr. Champion warned that Mr. Reagan's difficulty is precisely his genuine commitment to his atavistic ideas (a "surprising number of state employees, educators, and members of mental health organizations . . . didn't really believe he meant what he said in the years before 1966"), Kopkind quotes an anonymous observer as remarking that "Reagan plays Pat Brown better than Pat Brown." "Reagan," he begins his recent analysis, "is selling out. . . . He rationalizes his own position by calling himself a pragmatist, and may even believe that he is working from the inside. But he is out for himself alone." Once again Kopkind finds a useful anonymous observer to quote: "There are three big phonies in politics in this state—Sam Yorty, Max Rafferty, and Ronald Reagan."

Granted, there are people on the Right who also believe that Reagan has sold out. California has a state senator, John G. Schmitz, who is a member of the John Birch Society, and he says that Reagan is "a tragic end to the brightest hope on the American political scene today. Many of the best of our citizens may never again be willing to trust the word of a seeker or holder of high political office." On the other hand, there have been no complaints from the conservative Californians who helped finance the Reagan movement and who would presumably feel most deeply the weals of ideological infidelity—no complaints from Henry Salvatori, Holmes Tuttle, William Knowland. Moreover, they contend, and Mr. Kopkind would go along, that if the election were held again tomorrow, Reagan would win against Brown as triumphantly (one million votes) as he did last November.

All this is very confusing to non-Californians. There are the liberals (e.g., Champion) who say he has done the state irreparable damage—and liberals (e.g., Kopkind) who say that he has, as a matter of fact, administered a stoutly liberal government. How can you cause irreparable damage—in the liberal view of things—by taking militantly liberal action? There are those (e.g., Champion) who say he is losing popularity and those (e.g., Kopkind) who say he is gaining popularity. Some say he is true to his conservative faith; others that he isn't. Some that he is sincere, that's his trouble; others that he is insincere, *that* is his trouble. There are the Birchers (e.g., Schmitz), who are greatly disillusioned, and the conservatives (e.g., Salvatori), who are by and large elated.

What's he like personally? Ask Evans and Novak: "Naturally aloof. The thing Reagan needs to do [they quote an unnamed "Republican leader"] is to ask the legislators over to his house to play poker and drink some booze. But that's not going to happen any time soon." Fascinating. But—oops—*Time* magazine quotes Assembly Republican Caucus Chairman Don Mulford: "I don't think there is a single legislator who doesn't like Governor

Reagan as an individual." *Time* commented on Reagan's "success" at the end of his first session, which he accomplished "by holding frequent meetings with the lawmakers, infect[ing] them with his straightforward, purposeful approach." Champion insisted on the diminishing prestige. Now William S. White observes that "no one who has recently been in California with eyes and ears open can doubt that Reagan is going from strength to strength. By every ordinary measurement he is both a popular and an effective state executive."

⁓

As far as the outer world can see, there have been three significant confrontations between California and Reaganism. They had to do with (1) education, (2) mental health, and (3) taxes.

The first was in two parts. There was, to begin with, the firing of Clark Kerr as president of the University of California. The second was over the proposal to charge tuition in the UC and state-college systems.

In fact, Reagan's role in the dismissal of Kerr, while it could be held to have been psychologically critical, was insubstantial. It is true that the regents, execution-bound, addressed the freshly inaugurated governor at the regents' meeting in January and said to him: If it would be greatly embarrassing to you for us to proceed with the business at hand—which is to ask Clark Kerr for his resignation—we are willing to put off doing so for a few months. Reagan's answer was: Don't mind me, go right ahead, and God bless you. What happened then is instructive. In the first place, Reagan's siding with the majority of the regents—who after all had been named as such by his celebratedly liberal predecessors Pat Brown, Goodie Knight, and Earl Warren—ended him up carrying the onus of the entire majority. Thus, Mr. Champion, relaxing in the scholarly detachment of Harvard University, refers to Mr. Reagan's having "accomplished" the "dismissal of Clark Kerr." In fact, if Reagan had voted against Kerr's dismissal, Kerr would nevertheless have been fired (the vote was 14 to 8)—unless one assumes that Reagan controlled the marginal votes, which why should one assume it, considering that only a single voter directly owed his status as a voter to the governor? Never mind, Reagan was widely held to be responsible.

One learns ever more about the powers of the Educational Establishment, and they are, of course, formidable. The rule of thumb is: Never disagree with the educators; never give them less than anything they want; and never act other than as a postulant at their shrine. It is all neatly put

by Professor James Q. Wilson of Harvard University, who wrote recently
a "Guide to Reagan Country" for the academically chic *Commentary* in
which he ventured a number of observations not entirely congenial to
orthodox anti-Reaganism, and thought to protect himself winsomely by
acknowledging: "I do not intend here to write an apology for Reagan; even
if I thought like that, which I don't, I would never write it down anywhere
my colleagues at Harvard might read it." No indeed: academic freedom is
very broad-minded, but it stops short of defending the position of Ronald
Reagan.

Actually, there is among the Academic Establishment a great deal of
potential support available to a right-bent public figure, but he must know
how to discharge the correct vibrations to shake it out. Governor Reagan
didn't know how to do that in January 1967, and does not—and here is his
most baffling dereliction of the moment—know how to do so even now.
It isn't really all that difficult. One has only to meditate on the silent vote
against Clark Kerr among the chancellors of the individual UC campuses,
who for years have deeply resented his importunate ways. And there are
others who recoil against the anti-intellectualist spirit of the Berkeley dis-
orders and even against the anti-personalist impulses of macroeducation.

But those folk need to be approached in just the right way, and it may
be the single lesson that Governor Reagan has not learned. So that when
Reagan simultaneously voted with the majority to dismiss Kerr and came
out (via a subordinate who spoke ahead of schedule) in favor of uniform
reductions (10 percent) in state spending and in favor of charging tuition
at the University of California and the state colleges, all the educators felt a
tug of class solidarity that Karl Marx, Eugene Debs, and James Hoffa never
succeeded in eliciting from the proletarian classes. It was a field day for
the professors and the students, who delightedly burned their governor in
effigy. The canny and brilliant Jesse Unruh, lord of all he diminishingly
surveys in the evenly divided state Assembly, quickly took his advantage.
Only months before, because he had seen the necessity to deplore the
excesses at the Berkeley campus, he too had been burned in effigy; but
now, in gratitude for his scornful resistance of the governor's position that
students should contribute to the cost of their own education, the plac-
ardists bore signs: JESSE SAVES. The speaker was vastly amused and vastly
instructed: He knows, he knows, the strength of the Harvard vote.

And then Governor Reagan made probably the principal verbal *faux
pas* of his career, a remark to the effect that the state of California has no
business "subsidizing intellectual curiosity." The difference, Mark Twain
reminded us, between the right word and almost the right word "is the

difference between the lightning-bug and the lightning." Intellectual curiosity is a very good thing; intellectual frivolity is not. When asked to document his case against educational excesses Governor Reagan brightly observed that he did not see why the state should need to support courses in "how to burn the governor in effigy." An amusing response, the kind of riposte that an Adlai Stevenson or a John F. Kennedy would make with pleasure and profit. But Ronald Reagan needs to remember that he is a Republican and a conservative and does not have the ordinary man's license to exaggerate. In fact, industrious reporters discovered, the course in question was being offered by an organization adjacent to the state university, which teaches the theory of nonviolent resistance, and though to be sure the university was extending credit to students who took the course, it was technically untrue to say that the taxpayers were spending money to finance the burning of their governor in effigy. Just a little research would have armed the governor with copious examples of the abuse of education. Reagan could have split the university community and got going a very useful debate by asking whether in fact all the gentlemen and scholars in the university system were prepared to defend the notion that courses in home economics and fly fishing and hotel hygiene and life adjustment are a part of the life of the mind, to the advancement of which the voters of California are dedicated.

And then, too, Reagan should raise the question: Granted the desirability of more and more education, what are the practical limits that even an idealistic community should observe? Over the past decade, enrollment in California state colleges is up 397 percent, operating costs are up 260 percent, capital expenditures are up 260 percent—whereas the state's population and hence ability to pay are up only 39 percent. Question: How much further? Here is a very serious question, which Governor Reagan has an excellent opportunity to probe. The society would be ideal in which everyone with a velleity to become a doctor of philosophy could proceed to stroll through the years of his early manhood in order to become one, at no expense to himself. But—as Professor Ernest van den Haag of New York University tartly pointed out a few years ago—isn't it a fact that professors will earn more money than plumbers and taxi drivers and that, therefore, to tax plumbers and taxi drivers to subsidize the education of professors is a form of regressive taxation, and therefore anti-liberal, by a definition with which both Mr. Champion *and* Mr. Kopkind could agree?

Such questions as these Mr. Reagan has not asked as yet, and, indeed, he has not perfected any line of communication to the academics. However, heuristic questions have been raised—questions that should have been raised before; questions that properly relate state-funded higher education to the total resources and needs of a community. The exact formulation of the ultimate questions neither Governor Reagan nor anyone else is ever likely to come up with. But Reagan has naysayed the superstition that any spending in the name of higher education ought to be exempt from public scrutiny. And that, perverse though it may sound, is a contribution to public education.

~

Concerning mental health, it was widely disseminated that Reagan's superficiality caused him to ignore the salient point. True, the in-patient population had been reduced from 34,000 to 20,000, and true, the state budget for the maintenance of the mentally ill had not been reduced at all. Why not, asked Reagan, reduce it *pro tanto*? Because, his critics leaped, the fact of the diminution of the number of in-patients is testimony to the effectiveness of the entire working force of the mental hospitals, and precisely the wrong thing to do under the circumstances is to reduce their total firepower. Reagan countered that that was supposition, and that he was quite prepared to reverse his recommendations in the event of a decline in the rate of the cured.

Sounds reasonable, one would suppose. But the point, of course, is that economies are never easily effected and just about never effected when the emotional instrument at the disposal of the spenders is, no less, the mentally ill. Take the incidence of stricken mothers-in-law, and multiply it by the prospect of their repatriation, and you have an idea of the size of the political problem. If President Eisenhower was unsuccessful, even during his relatively brief period of militant frugality, in eliminating the Rural Electrification Administration because of the lobbies available to agitate for its survival, one can imagine the difficulties in paring a state's mental-health agencies. So Reagan yielded. But again he had made a public point. And as in the case of education, the point will yield dividends, or should at any rate, when the time comes, as routinely it always has, to augment the budget for mental health. Reagan's position is after all distinguishable from the position that the state should ignore its mentally ill. His is a position that says: If modern psychiatric advances, e.g., through the use of tranquilizers, permit a diminution of the problem, even as the Salk vaccine has diminished the problem of polio, oughtn't the states to adjust their budgets accordingly?

~

And then, of course, there is the general question of the budget. It is a matter of universal hilarity. The most economy-minded governor since the inauguration of J. Bracken Lee as governor of Utah in 1953 forwards to the legislature the highest budget in state history! Loud guffaws. Not utterly wholesome guffaws, to be sure. Nelson Rockefeller, who at least noticed, though he did not precisely run against, the extravagances of his prede-cessor, Averell Harriman, in New York, also proceeded to submit a higher budget than that of the Democratic Mr. Harriman. But in Rockefeller's case, that was considered an act of statesmanship, or at least it was consid-ered such by the same kind of people who have reacted so ardently against Ronald Reagan.

Reagan's reasoning can, of course, be made to sound disingenuous. He claims to have discovered only *after* achieving office the programmed deficit of Governor Pat Brown. Casper Weinberger, chairman of Reagan's Little Hoover Commission, likes to tell the story: "Hale Champion, out-going director of the department of finance, cheerfully walked into the conference room, greeted [us] affably, and announced that while there would be a surplus available on June 30, 1967 (when the last of Governor Brown's eight fiscal years ended), there was going to be a problem starting in January, 1968.

"The department's best estimates showed, he said, that there would be a cash-flow shortage in January, February, and March of 1968 amounting to $740,000,000. Champion added that approximately $340,000,000 could be borrowed from other state funds, leaving the state's bank accounts short by $400,000,000 of the amount needed to write checks covering the state's daily bills during those months. When the new tax monies came in April, 1968, most of the cash-flow problems would be behind us, added Champion, but, of course there would be quite a big deficit by June, 1968, if present rates of revenue and expenditure continued. In fact, the deficit by then would probably amount to over $350,000,000.

"After a moment's silence," Mr. Weinberger recalls, "somebody asked, 'Hale, what would you have done about this if you had been reelected?' 'Well,' he answered with a slow smile, 'we've been telling you Republi-cans we needed withholding and more taxes, but you've always defeated them.'"

"We knew there would be a deficit during the campaign," Reagan remi-nisced. "But we didn't know how large it would be. Accountants told us there simply wasn't any way of ascertaining how much. Brown kept borrowing all over the place. The civil service people said there was a bare chance we could make it without raising taxes. As we got closer to the election, it began to look as though there wasn't any chance. I said during the campaign that there would have to be new taxes. The Constitution requires that you submit a budget right after you take office. I did. But the research hadn't been completed. And soon it became clear that even if we could effect $250,000,000 in economies, there wasn't a chance for a balanced budget. We just didn't know the extent of the problem. We had no way of knowing that Brown was spending most of the contingency funds. I've now recommended that in the future, independent auditing firms be given a crack at the figures, so that how the state stands financially can be a part of the public knowledge."

He paused to wave back cheerfully at four college types, who had pulled their sedan alongside, driving 55 mph in tandem with the state trooper who was chauffeuring the governor and exactly observing the speed limit. A honey-blonde leaned, smiling, out of the open window, hoisting a cardboard square hastily improvised from a grocery box or whatever when the party spotted the governor's license plates. Scrawled on it with lipstick was NO TUITION! Reagan laughed as the collegians pulled away. "The faculties are mostly responsible for that," he said. "They tell you one thing, and then they tell the press another." He gave examples. "The no-tuition bit is a local superstition. Even Brown said years before the election that tuition was 'inevitable.' Did they jump him? But it'll take time. Right now the point is to save money where we can. I'm a *good* person for people to trust their money with. I'm a good *manager*, and I'll treat their money as though it were mine. When we suggested 10 percent across the board, we knew some departments would have to expand, though others could trim back even more than 10 percent. We won't make 10 percent, but we will make about $8^{1}/_{2}$ percent. And remember, that's $8^{1}/_{2}$ percent of the spending we have control over. Two-thirds of the spending in California is fixed by the Constitution or by statute, and we can't do anything about it. It's bad enough to try to make economies when you need the help of a legislature that's controlled by the opposition party. We can't very well tackle the Constitution at the same time. But what we're doing will take hold.

"What makes me mad is obstructionism that's clearly intended to screw up your program. For instance, I said no more new hiring. If one department needs another secretary, pull her from a department where there are surplus secretaries. So some of the civil-service people got together, and when you need a secretary for the most urgent job, they tell you sorry, there isn't one available in the whole goddam state of California. You know there is, of course; but it's a problem of locating her, and that takes time. It isn't any different from what you would expect. Why should the bureaucracy behave any different from the way I always said it did—protectively toward its own authority and vested interests?

"A governor can't do everything; he hasn't got that much authority, and maybe he shouldn't have that authority. I have only a psychological authority, because the politicians know that the people are with me, that they see a lot of waste, and they resent the taxes and the inflation, and they'll support me. There are lots of things I just can't do, at least not for a while. Take judicial reform. You know how many judges Brown appointed as a lame duck? Four hundred! I must be the only governor in the U.S. who can't fix a parking ticket. But in time there will be vacancies. You've got to be patient, and you've got to make a start. I'll be around for a while."

So the budget went finally to the legislature, a $5-billion budget, 8 percent higher than his predecessor's. (By contrast, Rockefeller's first budget was 11 percent higher than *his* predecessor's.) Up went the income tax, the sales tax, and the so-called sin taxes. And on the issue of withholding, he was against it because, he said, "taxes ought to be out in the open. They should hurt, so that people know the price of what they're getting." Jesse Unruh was as determined that taxes should be painlessly withheld drop by drop as Reagan was that they should be collected in one painful annual extraction. Reagan held out; Unruh held out. But, finally, on July 28, the legislature approved almost exactly the figure Reagan asked for, and without withholding. "All in all," Jesse Unruh, concluded obviously taking another look at Reagan, "he did very well."

~

The critics of Ronald Reagan are fond of quoting from his autobiography, *Where's the Rest of Me?* It is an unfortunate book, not at all for what it says, which is wholesome and intelligent, but for the way it is said. There is no doubting that it is primarily responsible for the insiders' assumption that the governor is a hopeless cornball. The opening passage of the book (it is Mr. Kopkind's favorite) is, well, disastrous. "The story begins with the close-up of a bottom. My face was blue . . . my bottom was red . . . and my father claimed afterward that he was white. . . . Ever since . . . I have been particularly fond of the colors that were exhibited—red, white, and blue."

I suspend the narrative in order to allow a minute for derision.

Now, in the first place, the book was co-authored, and co-authored "autobiographies" are, as a general rule, the stylistic work of the other guy. The fact of the matter is that Reagan is not that way. "John Jones," I observed recently to him about a controversial public figure, "has the face of a bank teller." "Bank teller, hell, he has the face of the neighborhood child molester." One cannot be as banal as (a) and as mordant as (b), and the circumstances clearly argue that the second, not the first, is the real-life Ronald Reagan. "Stand in front of the asparagus counter today," he told a political gathering, "and you discover that it's cheaper to eat money." That kind of crack, Made in America, unmakable anywhere else, is a pretty big industry in California. But—good. "Keeping up with Governor Brown's promises," he said during the campaign, "is like reading *Playboy* magazine while your wife turns the pages." Good. Very good. And they come effortlessly. They are a function of his vision. The perspectives are very good; the mind very quick.

I met him seven or eight years ago. He was to introduce me at a lecture that night in Beverly Hills. He arrived at the school auditorium to find consternation. The house was full and the crowd impatient, but the microphone was dead; the student who was to have shown up at the control room to turn on the current hadn't. Reagan quickly took over. He instructed an assistant to call the principal and see if he could get a key. He then bounded onto the stage and shouted as loud as he could to make himself heard. In a very few minutes the audience was greatly enjoying itself. Then word came to him: no answer at the principal's telephone. Reagan went offstage and looked out the window. There was a ledge, a foot wide, two stories above street level, running along the side of the building back to the locked control room. Hollywoodwise, he climbed out onto the ledge and sidestepped carefully, arms stretched out to help him balance, until he had gone the long way to the control-room window, which he broke with his elbow, lifting it open from the inside and jumping into the darkness. In a moment the lights were on, the amplifying knobs turned up, the speaker introduced.

During those days he was busy delivering his own speech. *The* speech, it came to be called—probably the most frequently uttered since William Jennings Bryan's on the golden crucifixion. All over the land, to hundreds of audiences, a deft and rollicking indictment of overweening government. And then the speech became the most galvanizing fundraiser in political history. Reagan televised it during the Goldwater campaign for statewide showing in California. "And then, an hour before it was scheduled to go on, word came from Goldwater's headquarters to hold it—the boys at HQ had heard it rumored that it was 'too extreme.' I remember I went to the nearest pay booth, just by a gas station, and called Goldwater. There were only minutes to go. Luckily, he was on the ground. I reached him in Arizona. 'Barry,' I said, 'I don't have time to tell you everything that's in that speech, but you can take it from me, buddy, there isn't a kooky line in it.' Goldwater said: 'I'll take your word for it,' and I called the studio in the nick of time."

If Goldwater hadn't been at the other end of the telephone, Reagan would not have become governor. Because the speech was an incomparable success, statewide and subsequently nationwide. (It is said to have elicited almost $8 million in dollar-bill contributions.) It was on account of that speech that the Reagan-for-governor talk began.

I saw him during a long evening a few weeks after Goldwater's defeat, when the Reagan movement was just beginning to stir. We talked about the national calamity for the conservative movement and how it bore on his own situation. He was then quite positive that the Republican Party of California would not want him, especially not in the aftermath of so definitive a loss. But, he said, he wasn't going to say anything Shermanesque. He talked about the problems of California. The discussion was in generalities, very different from a second conversation a year later, in December 1965, on the eve of his campaign. The change was striking. He knew a great deal about specific problems of California. And he had grown, too, in other ways. I remember being especially impressed when, looking out over Los Angeles from the elevation of Pacific Palisades, he remarked: "You know, it's probable that the cost of eliminating the smog is a cost the people who want the smog to be eliminated aren't, when it comes to it, willing to pay."

Still later, on a half-dozen occasions, I noticed the ongoing improvement in his personal style, particularly in his handling of the press. Last June in Omaha, after a press conference before his speech to the Young Republicans, the *New York Times* correspondent blurted out to a young correspondent he hardly knew: "I've never seen anything like it. I've been covering them since Truman. There isn't anybody who can touch Reagan."

It's something people are going to have to get used to as long as Reagan's star is on the ascendancy. "To those unfamiliar with Reagan's big-league savvy," *Newsweek*, pained, dutifully pointed out last May after observing Ronald Reagan and Bobby Kennedy in a joint appearance answering student questions on Vietnam, "the ease with which [Reagan] fielded questions about Vietnam may come as a revelation. . . . Political rookie Reagan left old campaigner Kennedy blinking when the session ended."

I mean, it is more than flesh and blood can bear. Reagan, the moderately successful actor, the man ignorant of foreign affairs, outwitting

Bobby *Kennedy* in a political contest. It's the kind of thing that brings on those nightmares.

Richard Nixon was in the room. Who, someone asked, would the Republican Party consider as eligible in 1968? Nixon gave the usual names: and added Ronald Reagan's. I objected. It strikes me, I said, as inconceivable. "Why?" Nixon asked. "Suppose he makes a very good record as governor of California?" (This was in December, just after Reagan's election.)

Because, I said, he is very simply an implausible president. Anyone would be whose career was in Hollywood. People won't get used to the notion of a former actor being president. People are very stuffy about presidential candidates. Remember what Raymond Moley said when someone asked him how to account for Kefauver's beating Adlai Stevenson in the Minnesota primary in 1956—"Did *you* ever try to tell a joke in Minneapolis?"

And then—I added, carried away by my conviction—how does one go about being a good governor in an age when the major moves are, after all, up to the federal government? Who last—I asked Nixon—can we remember whose record as governor propelled him to the first ranks of presidential hopefuls?

Dewey, Nixon ventured—then corrected himself: Dewey became famous as a prosecutor, not as governor. Rockefeller was projected by the fact of being a Rockefeller, being personally able, being wealthy, and being governor of New York: not because New York had become a model state under his administration.

During the next year the California state government will spend $5 billion. During the next year the federal government will spend approximately $140 billion. Well over 17 billion of these dollars will be spent in California. But more important, it is the federal government that will decide how many California boys are drafted into the Army, how much inflation there is going to be, how far the monopoly labor unions can go, whether there will be any praying in the schools, whether Californians can sell their property as they choose, where the main highways will come from and where they will go, how the water flowing in from nature will be allocated, how large Social Security payments will be. Are there interstices within which, nowadays, a governor can move, sufficiently to keep himself in focus and establish his special competence?

Reagan clearly thinks so. After all, he has brought almost everyone's attention to the problems of California, even to some of California's problems over which, as in the matter of tuition, he has no control. Always there is *some* room. "To live," Whittaker Chambers wrote, "is to maneuver. The choices of maneuver are now visibly narrow. . . . [But] those who remain in the world, if they will not surrender on its terms, must maneuver within its terms."

The knowledge of that is what causes Mr. Kopkind to call Reagan a hypocrite, a phony. Brings the Birch Society senator to consider him an impostor. Brings George Wallace to call him a lightweight. What did they expect? That Governor Reagan would padlock the state treasury and give speeches on the Liberty Amendment? They say that his accomplishments are few, that it is only the rhetoric that is conservative. But the rhetoric is the principal thing. It precedes all action. All thoughtful action. Reagan's rhetoric is that of someone who is profoundly committed, *mutatis mutandis*, to the ancient ways. His perspectives are essentially undoubting. Mr. Kopkind has recently written that the United States' venture in Vietnam is "the most barbaric imperialistic war of this century." If that is so, there are phonies in America by the scores of millions. Reagan would never get the Kopkind vote; Reagan is more inscrutable to Kopkind than the Aztec calendar. For the Kopkinds, America itself is inscrutable. Reagan is indisputably a part of America. And he may become a part of American history.

—*West,* November 28, 1967

John Dos Passos, R.I.P.

I have come back from the funeral of John Dos Passos. It was in a way typical of him to die a few minutes after Nasser, who of course swamped the obituary headlines, so much so that Dos Passos's own stepson, away at law school, who reads the papers lackadaisically and listens not at all to the radio or TV, was not aware of the death until a few hours before the funeral, to which he hastened, registering the grief felt by everyone who had known Dos Passos, let alone been brought up by him. There was no way to keep his death off the front page (geniuses have a pre-emptive right to die on the front page), but the reader felt that the editorial handling was somehow harassed. Nasser had died, and the chancelleries of the world were in turmoil, and the death of mere literary giants doesn't substantially occupy the front page (nor should it: front pages are correctly devoted to news of immediate and transitory significance. Never mind that few people can now remember who reigned over England and Spain during the week that Shakespeare and Cervantes died.)

On the other hand it is worth noting that Dos Passos did not suffer the pains that torture those artists who cry over the neglect of them by their contemporaries. The only reason he did not treat the literary press with the total aloofness of, say, an Edmund Wilson or a Charles Lindbergh is that he was too good-natured. He could not bring himself to say no to the tenacious literary reporter who wanted to interview him and write a profile of him.

Mr. Dan Wakefield, himself a novelist and a most conscientious journalist, wrote a considerable profile of Dos Passos a few years ago. I remember asking Dos Passos what his opinion of it was, to which he replied, with a shyness which he could not—nor could David Garrick—have feigned, that in fact he hadn't read it. "I find," he said, with a self-effacing giggle that his friends knew as his conversational signature, "that when I start reading those things"—by which he meant profiles of himself, or reviews of his books—"my eyes just dribble off the page, so I just don't look at them."

Did this mean that he had no self-esteem? No, that would be inaccurate. It means that he was a genuine artist, who did the very best he could every time he sat down to write a novel, or a book of history; but that since there was absolutely nothing he could contribute to the improvement of a book after it was published, what was the point in reading reviews of his books? Or—for heaven's sake—reviews of himself, as author of said books? "If I had to describe him in a single sentence," his next-door neighbor told me after the funeral, "I would say that he was a modest man; the most modest man I ever met."

We are talking about someone who stupefied the literary generation of the Twenties. Critics as disparate as Jean-Paul Sartre and Whittaker Chambers remarked matter-of-factly that he was the greatest novelist in America. At the time he was an ardent sympathizer of left-wing political movements. But then, after the Spanish Civil War, all that changed. He identified the Communists as the great evildoers of his time, an insight that caused him to do that which pained him most, namely to break off a friendship: in this case, with Ernest Hemingway. But he pursued his conviction, that man was best off untrammeled by political authority, and when he died, the obituarists merely repeated what had been said about him so often before, namely that his literary work was at the service of political reactionaries.

Translation: JDP had become a political conservative, and the rules of the game being that no one can simultaneously be a literary genius and a political conservative, you must draw your own conclusions about his work. In the event that you are slow at doing that kind of thing, here is the key: JDP was a genius during his left-wing period. After that, he was pedestrian, a time-server. (It was an open secret that he was scorned by the Nobel Prize committee because of his political sympathies.) Never mind the two dozen books he wrote, the extraordinary histories of Jefferson, of Brazil, of Portugal; the novel *Mid-Century*. Forget them. If you can.

The answer is that no one can forget Dos Passos, and the working press, somehow, sensed it. The reporters and the television people were at his funeral. I was accosted by one, who asked me to assess the literary work of JDP. I was at that moment in the company of John Chamberlain, whom William Lyon Phelps once called the principal literary critic of his generation, and to open my mouth on Dos Passos in Chamberlain's presence would have been doubly to profane the situation inasmuch as what I wanted to say was simply that I would have been present, here at the Episcopal Church of Towson, Maryland, as sorrowfully if JDP had never written a word, because I knew him primarily as a friend; but if literary taxonomy was what the press wanted, why didn't they ask Chamberlain? The widow, firm, tall, beautiful, moved serenely through the vague confusion, the result of an uneasy apprehension that the death of this modest man who came closest to explaining America to the world might just turn out to be a historical event the neglect of which would above all proclaim the philistinism of the country he loved so very much more than his literary detractors love it.

It was all so very hard to sort out, because the historical meaning of the occasion was clearly secondary to all who were there except the press. I traveled to Baltimore with an extraordinarily self-disciplined attorney who (it was his seventieth birthday) had known JDP for fifty years, and on three occasions, my traveling companion had to turn away from a conversation, overcome by tears at the awful prospect of facing life without the friendship of John Dos Passos. If the great political cartoonist C. D. Batchelor were still active, he'd have done a drawing of the Statue of Liberty weeping over America's loss; this irreparable loss.

—October 6, 1970

Lyndon Johnson, R.I.P.

SAN ANTONIO—The lady is middle-aged, shrewd, politically active, impeccably kind, civic-minded, born in Texas and raised here, and she spoke as if she were facing such a problem for the very first time in her life. Well, obviously not the first time: when acknowledged monsters like Hitler and Stalin died, people did not, for the most part, scratch about to find something redeeming to say about them. LBJ was clearly of another category, but the lady now remarked, "What am I supposed to say? I didn't like what I knew about him personally. I didn't admire his domestic programs. And I thought his foreign policy was a mess. So what am I supposed to say?"

I counseled her to say nothing, absolutely nothing at all. Having done so, I regretfully acknowledge that my advice is only one part discretion, nine parts funk. Accordingly, into the breach. . . .

Even if history justifies Lyndon Johnson's determination to stand by South Vietnam, it is very difficult to believe that history will applaud his conduct of the war. We set out, in Vietnam, to make a resonant point. We did not make it resonantly. In international affairs as in domestic affairs, crime is deterred by the predictability of decisive and conclusive retaliation. The Soviet Union knows that it can count on a dozen years between uprisings in its empire because when it moves, it moves conclusively. If the Soviet Union had sent a few battalions into Hungary, and a dozen years later into Czechoslovakia, the Soviet Union would not have made its point.

Johnson, reminiscing in the White House a year before he was evicted, told two reporters that there was no way he might have avoided a showdown in Indochina, that not only John Kennedy (who told him shortly before leaving for Dallas that he intended to make a stand there) but also Dwight Eisenhower (who told him in the early Sixties that Southeast Asia would be the principal challenge of his presidency) agreed on the strategic point. But what, one wonders, has been achieved under the circumstances?

To begin with, nobody can predict that, a year or two from now, South Vietnam will still be free. But of greater importance than that, no one in his right mind will predict that the United States, facing a comparable challenge a year or two from now, would respond with military decisiveness. If, in that part of the world, the decision is to gobble up Thailand, what are we going to do about it? Exactly. And if, in another part of the world, they decide to go after Yugoslavia, or even Greece—what would we do about it?

It was the strangest aspect of this strange man that, once having decided on a course of action, he did not pursue it characteristically—i.e., with exclusive concern for its success. By his failure to do so, he undermined the very purpose of the intervention. And if the great Communist superpowers exercise restraint at this point, it will not be because they have learned the lesson of Vietnam, in the way that Stalin learned the lesson of Greece and Iran. It will be merely because of the coincidence of their mutual hostility and their desire for American economic aid.

So what of his great domestic accomplishments? *What* great domestic accomplishments? He sought a Great Society. He ushered in bitterness and resentment. He sought to educate the whole population of America, and he bred a swaggering illiteracy, and a cultural bias in favor of a college education so adamant and so preposterous that if John Milton applied for a job with Chock Full o' Nuts, they would demand first to see his college diploma. The rhetoric of LBJ was in the disastrous tradition of JFK—encouraging the popular superstition that the state could change the quality, no less, of American life. This led necessarily to disappointment, and the more presumptuous the rhetoric, the more bitter the disappointment.

The Great Society did not lead us into eudaemonia. It led us into frustration—and to the lowest recorded confidence vote in the basic institutions of this country since the birth of George Gallup. But: he was a patriot, who cared for his country, who was unsparing of himself, and who acquired at least a certain public dignity which lifted him from buffoonery, into tragedy. And he was the object of probably the greatest sustained vituperation in American political history. He paid a very high price for the office he discharged. And his detractors, as it happened, are America's worst friends, if that was any consolation.

—January 24, 1973

Frank S. Meyer, R.I.P.

I called him from Peking (which I knew would give him a kick), and he told me that the cause of the pains that had begun seriously to hamper him in December was not yet diagnosed, that the culture sent out a few weeks earlier to discern whether he was suffering from tuberculosis had not yet matured, that meanwhile he had no appetite, but was getting on with his work as usual. "I never guessed I would sit here hoping I had tuberculosis," he said, and quickly got on to the subject of Nixon's mission in Peking, which he had been following closely, very closely, even as he had been observing the international chess tournament, his son Gene's progress as a freshman at Yale, his son John's preoccupation with his law paper, the awful behavior of the *New York Times*, the erratic habits of one of the book reviewers for *National Review*, the absolute inability of the young to spell even the *simplest* words, the developing congressional sentiment against the Family Assistance Plan, the meteorological low coming down from Canada which would bring yet more snow—and who should review Garry Wills's new book about modern Catholicism? By Frank Meyer's standards, it wasn't a long conversation, though I assured him that telephone rates from Peking were quite modest thanks to the satellite we had situated high over the Pacific to accommodate the press, but I caught a quiver in his voice which when I spoke to him next, from Switzerland, had acquired amplitude, and then on Monday, the day after I returned to New York, the news came in. Cancer. Inoperable. He would return from the hospital to his house on Wednesday, to die there, in a month or two (he believed); within two weeks (his wife, Elsie, confided to Brent Bozell). On Thursday morning he spoke over the telephone for the first time in ten days—there was not such a stillness since quiet came to the Western Front. He asked Priscilla if the book section was all right, and she told me, moistly, after he hung up, she doubted he would last for two weeks.

I arrived the afternoon of Good Friday, tense with the pain of knowing that never before had I visited with someone when the lifesaving dissimulations ("The doctor says you'll be fine in just a couple of weeks") were simply out of the question, but his instinctive consideration saved me. Otherwise he was wonderfully querulous, shouting at the top of what was left of his lungs for Elsie (*Elsie! Elllsie!!*) every two minutes, wanting this leg moved or that pillow adjusted or the oxygen cap refitted—but mostly what he wanted was for her to sit there holding his hand, as she had done hour after hour, day after day, since the plunge of March 11.

But then he asked her to leave the room, and also his son, and the nurse, and he said to me did I know that "Gene" (the Very Reverend Monsignor Eugene V. Clark, the young, learned, buoyant, and devoted unofficial chaplain to New York conservatives, secretary to Cardinals Spellman and Cooke) had been there the afternoon before? Yes, I said. Well, said Frank, he wanted to join the Church, but he had declined yesterday to be baptized because he did not believe that the Church's position on suicide was convincing. Frank was not going to give up arguing merely to expedite death. I said, Frank, do you mean it isn't convincing, or do you mean that you do not propose to observe the Church's prohibition? His mind wandered a bit, and he told me that Gene had said he would return on the next day, and I said that I was no scholar on the subject but that it was my impression that the self-knowledge that one will transgress in the future, and even that one will seek to justify one's transgression, is not sacramentally disqualifying, and he nodded.

Did I know, he asked, that his son John quite coincidentally was thinking of joining the Church? No I didn't, I said, recalling, years ago when I knew him only over the telephone, back when he was writing the book reviews for *The American Mercury*, his telling me that he believed, and that if only he could figure out a way of taking the collectivism out of the Church (the emphasis of Vatican II on collegiality set Frank back ten years), he would come into it, though there was the problem—"I'm a Jew," he said, "and it's always harder, especially if there's persecution going on. Maybe I'd better hurry up, because usually there's persecution but right this second [this was 1954] there isn't much that I can think of."

He was small, with grey-white crewcut hair, baggy clothes, smoke-stained teeth, cigarette in hand, whiskey voice, solemn mien; he was a pacer, with an athletic gait, though I doubt that in his lifetime he exerted any other muscle more vigorously than necessary to move a pawn on the chessboard. I thought, my arm on his bed, which he let his own arm fall upon when he took a second's doze, that now he didn't have the strength to do even that, lying on his bed in his study. Looking past his emaciated features I could see three volumes immediately behind him: *The History of Ancient Sicily*, *The History of Mediaeval Sicily*, *The History of Modern Sicily*. Three of the twenty thousand books that came to the little house on Ohayo Mountain Road during the last fifteen years which he didn't send out to review, didn't give away, which he "skimmed," storing something in his mind from them.

Elsie called me out of the room, and told me the nurse would give him now, for the first time, a shot of Demerol; that the doctors had delayed beginning it because he'd need a lot of it toward the end. *El-*sie!!—she went in with the nurse, and he submitted, they turned him over, and I left. The next day he was worse, much worse. That afternoon he saw Father Clark, and made the great submission, and a few hours later I was called to the telephone. It was his son Gene. I told him the truth, that his father was a great man, and hung up.

—National Review, April 28, 1972

Sadat and the People

It is sad to read accounts of the relative indifference of the body of Egyptians to the death of Sadat. No doubt such reports are exaggerated or, more accurately, they are juxtaposed with the kind of hysterical emotional pitches to which the Moslem community is accustomed. The comparison is made with the public grief shown over the death of Nasser. One might add to this the high pitch of enthusiasm shown for Khomeini, and the vituperative mob scenes of which the shah and the United States were jointly and severally the objects. What one learns about people—Egyptians, Iranians, and, one ruefully supposes, Americans under certain kinds of stress—is saddening; and most painfully interesting.

Nasser was a cruel man, a despicable fomenter of hatred. He cared about war and about the destruction of Israel. He thought nothing of wooing Moscow, never mind Communism's explicit hostility to any kind of religion. His radio stations blared out the need for a holy war against Israel, in accents not substantially different from those of Qaddafi. He knew, as Qaddafi probably doesn't, how to behave when kings and queens drop in for tea. But he stood for war, for absolute despotism at home, and for the consecration of Mohammad to the cause of anti-Semitism. And, when he died, the Egyptian people went mad with grief.

Last week Iranian authorities officially gave out the figure of 1,356 executions since June 1. One reasonably supposes that the actual figure is greater. These are done under the sponsorship of a man who calls himself a religious leader, and whose representatives cheered the assassination of Anwar Sadat. The mobs in Iran, it is said, are still led emotionally by Khomeini.

One edges, however regretfully, to the conclusion that the meek are unlikely to inherit the earth. Anwar Sadat was not a weak man. One judges that his meekness was biblical in its sincerity, that his personal irradiation of benignity was utterly genuine. True, he had apprenticed under Nasser. But somehow he succeeded in excreting all of Nasser's ways.

He fought honorably but concluded a ceasefire. And then he gave voice to the single most resonant statement of the postwar period, when, standing before the ancient enemy in Jerusalem, he said, "I renounce my past." He then sought peace with honor.

A few years earlier, recognizing the subversive disposition of his Soviet allies, he booted them out of the country. In the past months he endured many humiliations at the hands of Mr. Begin, whose sincerity in the matter of autonomy for the West Bank became more and more difficult to aver: but Sadat did so, insisting that Begin was a man of honorable intentions, and with that fatalism with which he treated his own life, he treated a historical process which he helped more than any man in the recent history of the region to shape.

At home, he insisted on being the undisputed ruler. But his resolution was not sufficient unto the task, because his leadership was disputed. By the Left, by the Moslem fundamentalists, by the Israel-haters.

There was never any doubt that, if challenged publicly, he would call out the police, and if necessary the military. And yet when he was killed, the most concentrated aggregation of world leaders came to pay tribute to him since the assassination of John F. Kennedy, president not of a single Near Eastern power but of the most important and powerful country in the world. Anyone who, particularly in the past six months, has labored over the question whether there is a difference between authoritarian and totalitarian need only consider the differences between Sadat and Qaddafi, or Sadat and Brezhnev, to know instantly the truth.

There remain the people. It is unfair to say of them all that they were unaffected. But it is true that the character of Sadat moved them less than the character of Nasser, and this of course is the reason why, in so much of the world, authoritarianism necessarily prevails.

—October 15, 1981

Princess Grace, R.I.P.

When Grace Kelly arrived in Monaco to marry the reigning member of one of the oldest royal families in Europe, the prenuptial festivities included a seemingly endless parade of ships that slipped by the royal yacht where, alongside her prince, she stood, watched by what was at the time one of the largest television audiences in history. One reporter remarked that she waved her right hand with apparent spontaneity, with delight, at the endless line of well-wishers, struck by the theatrical magic of it all—America's most beautiful woman (they said with some reason) marrying Europe's most eligible prince. But the reporter noted that her left hand gripped the railing of the ship with a tension unnoticed by the crowds who gathered, but undisguisable—one could see the muscles in that arm, taut, pulsating even. And it was so, this reporter remarked, for the entire four hours of the physical ordeal.

Grace Kelly had been most recently trained to perform professionally as an actress. But before that she had been trained by her family to perform as a human being: to control herself, and to strive for perfection. The hard effort she put in, that afternoon, requiring of her so much strength—all but hidden from the audience, because she had been trained to hide pain, to disguise effort—all that was a part of her character.

It would not have been easy for anyone to live the role she lived; to master a foreign tongue, foreign habits; to mix easily with a class brought up to be offhandedly conscious of occupying a station to which, in Europe, it isn't generally supposed that mere commoners can attain. One of the triumphs of Grace Kelly was the apparent effortlessness of this achievement, what proved to be her lifelong work: half her life spent in being a princess, while giving the impression that she had become one the moment she and the prince exchanged their vows.

Those who knew her, as Princess Grace, and simply as Grace, never ceased to marvel at the mysterious combination. On the one hand Venus herself was not more naturally cast than Grace as a goddess. On the other, no one privately worked harder to achieve a natural regality. It wasn't that of a spoiled princeling, taking for granted the high perquisites of life. It was rather an act of submission. There are those who knew her well, one of whom commented last week that if she had decided to become a nun rather than a princess, there would not have been a distinctive difference in her approach to her vocation. She would have struggled, in the knowledge of the generality of human weakness, to be a nun of whom God and her fellow sisters would be proud. Even as she struggled to be a princess of whom God and her prince, and her family, and her people, would be proud.

She was, formally, an expatriate. But here she was not entirely convincing. She would have given anything for her little principality. But she was never other than an American. In her frequent visits to Philadelphia, and to other parts of America, she could not conceal her love for her native land, nor her concern for its tribulations. Her natural capacity to laugh permitted her to enjoy the ironies, to be indulgent about human excesses, to understand fatalistically that there is no inquiry that takes one further than that which seeks to conform with the will of God, even if that will is never fully understood. When last spring what seemed like all of Philadelphia came together to rejoice in its most illustrious citizen, she called me to say nervously that she was at a loss how exactly to express her appreciation at the forthcoming ceremony. I counseled her to look at a videotape of a former colleague, Fred Astaire, who only one year earlier had with mesmerizing grace turned quietly aside the accumulated compliments of ninety minutes of tributes by the high and mighty of Hollywood. She looked at the program, and responded, as was no surprise, that she could not seek to duplicate the art of Astaire: which, however, she proceeded to do.

Two years ago we went to Rome to participate in a documentary filmed in the Sistine Chapel based on the parables of the prodigal son and the good Samaritan. (For various reasons it was never completed and shown.) On that occasion, standing only a few feet from where Pope John Paul was seated when proclaimed Vicar of Christ on earth, she spoke of her faith in the continuing reach of the parables, electing to describe the venture into organized charity of the founder of the Red Cross, the good Samaritan of the industrial age. She said then that nothing changes in respect of the opportunities, which are always there, for the individual Christian to attempt to do good, and, in doing good, to repay the great munificence of the Providence that gave us life: that gave her life, and, on September 14, took it from her, so very abruptly; took her from us, leaving so many disconsolate. There are no princesses where she is bound, but the secular imagination must at least suppose that wherever she is, a special light will irradiate, even as it did here on earth, which mourns her so grievously.

—*National Review*, October 15, 1982

Morrie Ryskind, R.I.P.

In 1960, Senator Wayne Morse of Oregon was the *ne plus ultra* liberal in Washington. He announced that he was a candidate for the Democratic Party's presidential nomination. The big question—could Morse win?—was to be settled in an all-important primary on May 3. *National Review* asked Morrie Ryskind to cover the campaign and the contest.

His article began with an extensive account of the Morse platform, which incorporated every policy plank opposed by Morrie Ryskind. He went on to recount his heightened tension on the evening of primary day:

The night of May 3, as I sat in my living room nervously twisting both radio and TV dials while awaiting news of the returns of the Washington primary, I was well fortified with jars of vitamins, aspirin, Bufferin, anti-acids, tranquilizers, and smelling-salts. I hadn't shaved because my wife had apparently mislaid my razor blades in her weekly clean-up, so I was slightly embarrassed when two strangers, in white uniforms, came in. My wife explained that they were new members of her PTA board and she had asked them over for a cup of coffee. Why they carried that straitjacket I'll never know, but then I don't try to keep up with all my wife's committees. My doctor, passing by, happened to drop in in time for coffee: He had apparently just operated on somebody in the neighborhood, because he was still toting some chloroform and a jar of blood plasma. Luckily he knew the men in white, so I didn't have to waste any time in social chit-chat and could stay with the dials.

As the returns began to come in, I unbelievingly kept switching knobs from station to station: but one and all carried the same blessed story. Not only was Humphrey bashing Morse's brains out, but even Adlai, unlisted on the ballot, was pulling a bigger vote. I remember the rest of that night only vaguely: I know only that I chased the PTA boys out of the house, hurling Morsian epithets and all my vitamins, tranquilizers, etc., after them; I hazily recall that we had only one bottle of Napoleon brandy left, but there were several bottles of Scotch and bourbon, and, when they ran out, the doc graciously donated his chloroform; and that, since then, my ulcer is gone.

That was the same man who wrote *Animal Crackers* for the Marx Brothers, and *A Night at the Opera*, and who won the Pulitzer Prize in 1933 for *Of Thee I Sing*. His picture appeared last week on the front page of the *New York Times*, whose account of Morrie Ryskind's life noted that after the Second World War he stopped writing comedies and screenplays and devoted himself substantially to politics and political writing. It was not widely known (although Morrie Ryskind often recited it as a fact) that after the war the Left was in such thorough control of Hollywood that an anti-Communist activist had trouble finding work. One of the great superstitions of the century is that there was only the one, anti-Communist blacklist during the Forties and Fifties. There were two: and the anti-anti-Communist blacklist was by far the more pervasive.

It is in one sense good that Morrie Ryskind was otherwise unengaged during 1954 and 1955, because without him it is doubtful that this journal would ever have been launched. Morrie and Mary Ryskind gave no fewer than twenty receptions for the young man from the East Coast who was trying to raise the capital necessary to found *National Review*. They came, a half-dozen or a dozen potential stockholders, largely because Morrie asked them to: He was difficult to turn down, because of his humor, the frantic intensity of his opinions, his universal kindness. He would then write or call his guests, and wrest from them pledges that, dollar by dollar, crawled up toward the magic figure that brought life to *National Review* in November of 1955. Morrie Ryskind wrote a piece for the first issue. He was a director of *NR* from the first day. We mourn him as a friend, are bereft as fellow Americans, and wish for his wife and children the consolation they must feel in having known so long and been loved so much by so good and talented an American.

—National Review, September 20, 1985

Theodore White, R.I.P.

It is so with very few people who are discreetly hospitalized, but when Theodore H. White was struck down at his desk on Friday afternoon, by Sunday morning it seemed as if half of America knew of it, even though there had been no notice in the press. Friends, friends of friends, and friends of theirs relayed the news, because everyone cared so deeply who had read his books, and especially those who knew him. The sensation was on the order of hearing that fire threatened the library at Byzantium, storehouse of great deposits of national self-knowledge, a source of national pride.

But it was not long after hearing the first news that those made aware of his condition prayed he would not recover. The image of Teddy White sitting up, mute and mindless, was unbearable. Not Henry Mencken all over again! Because the stroke—word had got out—was of just that nature, deep, malevolent, voracious; a brain-eater.

In White there was much brain to feed on. He had revolutionized the art of political reporting, the obituarists all agree. And in doing so he broadened the understanding, because his were the eyes of a journalist who could convey the inclinations of a small gathering of Americans who convened to hear a candidate by noting how much effort they put into wiping their own hands clean before accepting the politician's proffered hand. The voters spoke their intimate thoughts to him, his colleagues spoke theirs to him, presidents and presidential candidates sought him out. It was to him that Jackie Kennedy turned after Dallas.

Theodore H. White made one grave strategic mistake in his journalistic lifetime. Like so many disgusted with Chiang Kai-shek, he imputed to the opposition to Chiang thaumaturgical social and political powers. He overrated the revolutionists' ideals, and underrated their capacity for totalitarian sadism. Those who traveled to China in President Nixon's entourage in 1972, when White first revisited the desolation at the hands of the man for whom he had shown so great an enthusiasm, viewed the bitter confusion he felt. It was as if Mao had committed an act of personal disloyalty, a vice alien to White's nature. He saw in his own country a wildly successful, if aberrant and eccentric, march toward general enlightenment; and he had seen in Yenan something that he thought would o'erleap the tenacious traditions of a China immersed in its anachronisms. He wrote *Thunder Out of China* in 1946, and twenty-six years later he learned firsthand that the nature of the thunder that had hit China was not exuberant, rather it was convulsive. As was his custom, he integrated his new knowledge into his writing, and all his readers profited from the quality of revised insights.

When in 1965 he had completed the second of his magisterial series on the making of American presidents, this one on the contest between Lyndon Johnson and Barry Goldwater, he dared to say that Goldwater had galvanized dissatisfactions in America that would not be put down by the facile rhetoric and quick-fix social legislation of Lyndon Johnson. For daring to say this about the ideas of a man who had been devastated by a thunderous New Dealer, Theodore White was widely derided. Since then, only one Democratic president has sneaked into office, and one Democratic presidential contender managed to lose forty-four states; another, forty-nine states. Teddy White had seen into the future, but his skills in reporting on the future made it very nearly, if never quite, palatable to some of the most disappointed ideologues.

He came to me late one morning in October of 1965. We had never met, and he was writing a piece for *Life* magazine on the mayoralty contest in New York City, in which I was engaged as the candidate of the Conservative Party. In my little office he began to ask questions, and to take those copious notes of his, neat save for the cigarette ashes that spilt on them. I was feeling saucy and answered two or three of his questions with a levity not entirely appropriate to sober analytical interrogation. He would suppress a smile, even as his eyes would twinkle.

Finally, he put down his pencil and said: "Look, Mr. Buckley. I am doing business now. We will make friends later."

That was Theodore White's mode, and, conjoined with his fine mind, his artist's talent, his prodigious curiosity, and his genuine affection for the best in humankind, it made for a transcendent wholesomeness. It is quite awful to know we will not see him again alive, altogether consoling for those who believe we will experience him again in a life to come.

—May 22, 1986

Malcolm Muggeridge, R.I.P.

Ten years ago Malcolm Muggeridge and I shared the job of commentator for two programs filmed in the Sistine Chapel. Two weeks before we got to Rome he telephoned. "Do you know," he said, "I have met, I suppose, all the important men and women in my lifetime, and on the whole I think them an awful bore—but I want to meet the present pope. Could you arrange it?"

I laughed. One always—inevitably—laughed in his company, which is one reason why one so looked forward to it.

When Pope John Paul approached Muggeridge, he looked over benevolently and said to him: "Ah. You are radio!" It is very difficult to answer that question coherently, so Muggeridge simply smiled a response. The pope turned to the next guest in line at the private audience and said to David Niven, "Ah, you were the great friend of my predecessor." David Niven mumbled something about having had great admiration for Pope Paul VI, whom he never knew, and probably hadn't given five minutes' thought to. The poor, dear pope was confused about the composition of the group he was meeting.

After our blessing, Malcolm could not get over his amusement; but then, years later, visiting with him in his little country house, I saw neatly framed in a corner of his living room a photograph. Him and the pope.

When Malcolm Muggeridge died a week ago the commentators listed his affiliation with Christianity rather as if it had been the next post, after editor of *Punch*. They did not seem to know that he had become the foremost evangelist of Christianity in the English language.

When we did a television program together in 1980, at his suggestion the hour was called, "Why I Am Not a Catholic." It was off to a wonderful start when he recounted his disillusion with the Catholic chaplain at the University of Edinburgh. Muggeridge had just been installed as rector of the university, and the student newspaper called for giving the students free contraceptives. Rector Muggeridge refused, expecting that at least the Catholics at the university would back him up. Instead, the Catholic chaplain wrote a letter to *The Scotsman* saying what a monstrous thing he had done.

WFB: Excuse me, but why was it monstrous?

Muggeridge: It was monstrous, according to him, because it accused the students of wanting to be promiscuous. But in a letter I wrote in answer to it, I said I wondered what the Reverend Father thought they wanted the contraceptives for. Was it to save up for their wedding day?

That was *Muggeridge vitale*, the mordant clairvoyance that taught him to see through Communism in the early Thirties and brought him as high a reputation as a journalist as has been achieved by anyone in this century. He was everywhere, doing everything, but his odyssey was not without purpose. He was moving toward Christianity.

"Why did this longing for faith assail me? Insofar as I can point to anything, it has to do with this profession which both you and I have followed of observing what's going on in the world and attempting to report and comment thereon, because that particular occupation gives one a very heightened sense of the sheer fantasy of human affairs—the sheer fantasy of power and of the structures that men construct out of power—and therefore gives one an intense, overwhelming longing to be in contact with reality. And so you look for reality and ultimately you arrive at the conclusion that reality is a mystery."

Why did he relish the mystery?

"Because it leads you to God. . . . It's exactly like—Bill, it's exactly like falling in love. You see another human being and for some extraordinary reason you're in a state of joy and ecstasy over that person, but the driving force which enables you to express that and to bring it into your life is love. Without love, it's nothing; it passes. It's the same with seeking reality, and there the driving force we call faith. It's a very difficult thing to define, actually."

He never did define grace, which is not definable, but in due course he and his wife, Kitty, joined the Catholic Church, and he pursued his writing and his lecturing, now as an explicit Christian, of the best kind, the kind whose second greatest pleasure in life is laughter. After his stroke three months ago, his brother wrote to say that Malcolm still enjoyed hearing from his friends, but could on no account acknowledge his mail.

He yearned then to die, and hoped only that his beloved Kitty would go first. She survives him, reinforcing his belief in what it is that teaches us most. "As an old man, Bill, looking back on one's life, it's one of the things that strikes you most forcibly—that the only thing that's taught one anything is suffering. Not success, not happiness, not anything like that. The only thing that really teaches one what life's about—the joy of understanding, the joy of coming in contact with what life really signifies—is suffering, affliction."

He suffered, at the end. But throughout his lifetime, he diminished the suffering of others, at first simply by his wit and intelligence; finally, by his own serenity, which brought serene moments to those graced by his presence.

—November 22, 1990

Richard Nixon, R.I.P.

Clare Boothe Luce once remarked that all public figures come to be associated with a single achievement, never mind how complex their careers. And, true, we can say about Lincoln that he won the Civil War, about Edison that he harnessed electricity, about FDR that he created the New Deal. But with what achievement will Richard Nixon be associated, a generation from now? A negative achievement: He is the only American president in history to be kicked out of office. Even so, in America and in much of the world, he was the dominant political figure. It can happen only to a man who takes very large strides in history, that he could win re-election with a runaway majority, and in less than two years leave the White House in greater ignominy than was ever before suffered by a departing American president.

His excommunication from public life was so decisive that his subsequent return has to be credited to him alone, the most spectacular reopening in contemporary political history. Remarkable not only because he came back, so to speak, into power, but that he did so notwithstanding the implacability of those who were hostile to him. In the darkest days of August 1974, it looked unlikely that a single member of the press corps could ever again be persuaded to be civil to Richard Nixon. Ten years later, after he addressed their convention in Washington, he was given a standing ovation.

It is an important part of his singular story that, really, he disposed of no spectacular personal talent. He was not a great orator, nor a great writer. He had only the force of his extraordinary personality, his unswerving determination to succeed, and his mastery of the political craft. He competed during his career in forty state political primaries. He lost one.

Alexander Haig was his chief of staff when Nixon left the White House. "As you'd have guessed," General Haig reminisced a few years ago, "when Nixon got to Casa Pacifica in California late that afternoon in August, his White House line was still connected. He was in a daze: president of the United States until noon; one minute later—nothing. He was master of a villa which, without a president to preside over it, was simply a big house on the Pacific Ocean. But when Nixon got there, he used the telephone to the White House exactly as he'd been doing for six years. He must have called ten, fifteen times a day, and of course the White House operators didn't want to be responsible for breaking the trance, so they'd put him straight through to me, as though I were still his chief of staff."

How did he get the message that it was all over?

"On the fifth day I recognized that reality had to get to him. So when he called the next morning, I told the operator to put him on hold . . . It had the magical effect, the necessary effect. Suddenly he realized he wasn't president."

But Mr. Nixon didn't abandon his sense of priorities, the first being to tell his story and to make a living for his family. A day or so later he reached by telephone, in Geneva, Irving Lazar. The exchange was as follows.

"Mr. Lazar, you are known as the number-one agent in America."

"Well, thank you very much, Mr. President. Yes, I suppose I'd have to own up to that reputation."

"Well, I'd like to see you tomorrow morning here in California."

"Mr. President! I have five days' appointments backed up here in Europe, appointments made weeks and months ago!"

"I take it you do not want to handle my memoirs? I have been told by someone who knows his way around in the publishing world that my memoirs may be worth as much as a million dollars . . ."

"Of course I'd be glad to handle your memoirs, but there simply is no way I can get to you by tomorrow."

"Well then, make it the day after tomorrow."

Swifty Lazar finally succeeded, so to speak, in putting President Nixon on hold, but by the time he got to Casa Pacifica a week later, he arrived with a contract for two and one-half million dollars.

Nixon had begun the return journey. Retirement suited him singularly well. Henry Kissinger, in his own memoirs, remarked on how little Nixon actually enjoyed the life he had struggled so hard to achieve in the White House. He hated meeting with the press, hated state functions. He engaged in much that chiefs of state engage in with a visible detestation of ceremony and light talk.

That now was all gone, and he had only his tiny staff, his yellow pads, and the publishers, waiting for book after book. He resumed those travels he did enjoy—briefing foreigners, being briefed by them; renewing the company of men and women he had met when he was Sun King.

Gradually the agents of power everywhere in the world acknowledged that Richard Nixon's prestige did not derive exclusively from the office of president. He had a feeling for the American political scene invaluable to those who needed a confident grasp of it. And although meetings with Mr. Nixon would (except for two, perhaps three of his closest friends) never be confused with going down to the club and having a drink with old Tricky Dick, his company was thought rewarding by the men and women who ran the affairs of Europe, the Soviet Union, and Asia. He did not deceive them about what to expect from America, or indeed from Richard Nixon. When most recently he visited Moscow and Yeltsin canceled an appointment, indignant because Nixon had given interviews to Russian rivals, the sympathy was immediately with Nixon, rather than with his host: Nixon was being Nixon, and that, after all, was why he continued to be so eminent a figure. It did not surprise the diplomatic community that Yeltsin backed down, and that one of the earliest tributes logged by the hospital in New York, bidding Nixon adieu, was from Boris Yeltsin.

In America, Nixon was always thought of as a towering figure of the conservative camp, yet this was so only when the perspectives were narrowly confined. At the earliest conspicuous moment in his career, he had been spotted as the man who believed Whittaker Chambers, and disbelieved Alger Hiss. During the Fifties, the anti-Communists mobilized against the anti-anti-Communists, and when Eisenhower permitted himself to reveal that he had not yet decided whether to put Nixon back on the ticket in 1956, the American Right spoke threateningly to General Eisenhower, who had learned all about *force majeure* at West Point; and Nixon stayed on. During the Goldwater upheaval, Nixon was the loyalist, but he had learned in 1962, in California, the lesson he never forgot. He was driving through Central Park in 1967 after taping a television program and told his companion, "I learned in 1962 that you can't do without the support of conservatives. But I learned also that you can't win with just the conservatives."

One year later he won the presidency. During those ill-fated years he lost the Vietnam War, pulled out of the Bretton Woods alliance, declared wage and price controls, and traveled to China, where he toasted the achievements of Mao Tse-tung. Not exactly a majestic roll for a right-wing American president. For all the talk about the triumphant resumption of diplomatic relations with China, it has never been clear just what was achieved by going to Peking in 1972, instead of waiting another few years until Mao, and the Cultural Revolution, had run their course. Indeed, one more remarkable achievement of Richard Nixon is how he earned the special affection and admiration of U.S. conservatives without ever significantly advancing their cause.

In the final analysis, he was a heroic, intensely personal figure, whose life was lived on the public stage. He was at once the weakest of men, and the strongest; a master of self-abuse, and of self-recovery. Stained by worldliness, and driven by the hunger to serve. For Americans under seventy, there never was a world without Richard Nixon. Not many people can pitch whole generations into loneliness, as he has now done. R.I.P.

—National Review, May 16, 1994

John Chamberlain, R.I.P.

Late one afternoon in the fall of 1955, on the eve of the appearance of the first issue of *National Review*, something people more loftily situated would have called a "summit conference" was to be held in New York City, for which purpose a tiny suite in the Commodore Hotel was engaged. Tensions—ideological and personal—had arisen, and the fleeting presence in New York of Whittaker Chambers, who had dangled before us in an altogether self-effacing way the prospect that he might come out of retirement to join the fledgling enterprise, prompted me to bring the principals together for a meeting that had no specific agenda, being designed primarily to reaffirm the common purpose. As I think back on it, two of the five people present were born troublemakers. To say this about someone is not to dismiss him as merely that: Socrates was a troublemaker, so was Thomas Edison. But troublemaking was not what was primarily needed to distill unity, and so, one half hour after the meeting began, things were not going smoothly.

And then, when it was nearly six o'clock and I thought I detected on Chambers's face a look of terminal exasperation, John Chamberlain showed up, briefcase in one hand, a pair of figure skates in the other. He mumbled (he almost always mumbled) his apology. He had already booked the practice time at the ice rink for himself and his daughters . . . The early-afternoon editorial meeting had been protracted, the traffic difficult . . . No thanks, he didn't want anything to drink—was there any iced tea? He stole a second or two to catch up on Whittaker's family, and then sat back to participate in the conference—which had been transformed by his presence at it. When a few days later Chambers wrote, he remarked the sheer "goodness" of John Chamberlain, a quality that no man or woman, living or dead, has ever to my knowledge disputed.

At the time a sharp difference had arisen, not between me and John Chamberlain, but between Willi Schlamm and John's wife, Peggy (R.I.P.). Schlamm viewed the projected magazine as a magnetic field, professional affiliation with which could no more be denied by the few to whom the call was tendered than a call to serve as one of the Twelve Apostles. Poor Peggy would not stand for it: John was then serving as an editor of *Barron's* magazine and as a writer for the *Wall Street Journal*. Before that, he had been with *The Freeman*, before that with *Life*, before that *Fortune*, before that the *New York Times*. In each of these enterprises he had achieved singularity. He had two daughters not yet grown up. How could anyone reasonably ask that now, in middle age, he detach himself from a secure position to throw in with *National Review*—an enterprise whose working capital would not have seen *Life* magazine through a single issue, or *Barron's* through a dozen, and whose editor-in-chief was not long out of school?

I like to remind myself that I did not figure even indirectly in the protracted negotiation, respecting, as I did, not only the eminence of John Chamberlain, but also the altogether understandable desire of his wife for just a little economic security. But Willi was very nearly (nothing ever proved so conclusively shocking to Willi) struck dumb with shock, at the thought that *National Review* might be created without John Chamberlain as a senior editor. That was one of the clouds that hung over that late-afternoon discussion, in which Willmoore Kendall exploited every opportunity to add fuel to the fire, principally by the device of suggesting that for some people security means everything; the kind of thing John did not wish to hear, among other reasons because it so inexactly reflected his own priorities—he was concerned not with security, but with domestic tranquillity.

So it went, and in one form or another the tensions continued, though they never proved crippling. John settled the problem by moonlighting as lead reviewer for *National Review*. But I learned then, during that tense afternoon, the joy of a definitively pacific presence. Ours might have been a meeting to discuss whether to dump the bomb on Hiroshima; and John Chamberlain's presence would have brought to such a meeting, whatever its outcome, a sense of inner peace, manliness, and self-confidence.

There are stories John never told, even in his memoirs published a dozen years ago. That was characteristic. Bertrand de Jouvenel once told me, in a luncheon devoted to discussing our common friend Willmoore Kendall, that any subject at all is more interesting than oneself. I am not absolutely convinced that this is so—because some people know no other subject so thoroughly as themselves. But with John Chamberlain self-neglect was an attribute not of manners, but of personality. When *National Review* started up, six weeks after our Commodore summit, he would come in to the office every week (the magazine was then a weekly), sit down at whatever typewriter was free, and type out the lead book review with that quiet confidence exhibited by sea captains when they extricate their huge liners from their hectic municipal slips to begin an ocean voyage. After forty-five minutes or so a definitive book review was done; and John would, quietly, leave, lest he disrupt the office.

In those days the office consisted of six or seven cubicles, each one with desk and typewriter. Most of *NR*'s top editorial staffers—James Burnham, Willi Schlamm, Willmoore Kendall, Whittaker Chambers, Frank Meyer— from the beginning on, served only part time, so that at any given moment at least one cubicle was unoccupied, though seldom the same one. Four or five months into the magazine's life a young graduate of Smith, age twenty-four, serving in the circulation department, complained to her classmate, my sister Maureen, that the repairman who came once a week to check the typewriters had not once serviced her own. We couldn't wait to tell John Chamberlain, the delinquent typewriter repairman, when he came in the following Tuesday. He laughed heartily, then sat down to write an illuminating review of the entire fictional work of Mary McCarthy.

I never saw him, during the 1930s, slide into his chair at the *New York Times* to write his daily book reviews, many of them masterpieces of the form. Nor at *Fortune*, where he would return from two weeks on the road to write what he called a "long piece," which would prove the definitive article on this or that intricate problem of management or labor. Nor at *Life*, where he presided over the editorial page that was Henry Luce's personal cockpit, from which he spoke out, through John, to God and man in authoritative, not to say authoritarian, accents. But I decline to believe that in any of these roles, or in any of the myriad others he filled—as professor at Columbia, as dean of journalism at Troy State University in Alabama, as book writer and columnist—John Chamberlain ever did anything more disruptive than merely greet whoever stood in the way, and amble over to wherever the nearest typewriter was, there to execute his craft: maintaining standards as high as any set by any critical contemporary.

Because John Chamberlain could not sing off key. And the combination of a gentle nature and a hard Yankee mind brought forth prose pure and lasting. His was a voice of reason, from an affable man, unacquainted with affectation, deeply committed to the cause of his country and to liberty. He believed the fate of his country co-extensive with that of civilization; and, certainly, with that of his two daughters from his first marriage, and of his son—a young poet—from his second, to the enchanting Ernestine, to whom he went soon after Peggy's untimely death.

John Chamberlain's memoirs were surely the most soft-throated in the literature of men who took passionate political positions. As a young man who had demonstrated his prowess as a critic (William Lyon Phelps called him the "finest critic of his generation"), and as a political thinker addicted to progress, he wrote his book *A Farewell to Reform*, in which he seemed to give up on organic change, suggesting the advantages of radical alternatives. But his idealism was never superordinated to his intelligence, and in the balance of that decade of the Thirties, and then in that of the Forties, Chamberlain never ceased to look at the data, which carefully he integrated in his productive mind. Along the line (he tells us) he read three books, so to speak at one gulp—and the refractory little tumblers closed, after which he became what is now denominated a "conservative." The books in question, by the three furies of modern libertarianism—Isabel Paterson, Rose Wilder Lane, and Ayn Rand—provided the needed cement. After that, he ceased to be surprised by evidence, now become redundant—evidence that the marketplace really works, really performs social functions, really helps live human beings with live problems.

His writings told the story of his journey through this century. His calmness and lucidity, his acquiescent handling of experience, free of ideological entanglement, provoked in the reader the kind of confidence that John Chamberlain throughout his long life provoked in his friends. But his friendships would never run any risk of corrupting the purity of his ongoing search, through poetry, fiction, economic texts, corporate reports, and—yes—seed catalogues, for just the right formulation of what may be acknowledged as the American proposition. He sought an equilibrium of forces that would foster the best that could be got out of the jealous, contentious, self-indulgent, uproarious breed of men and women that have made so exciting a world here, giving issue, in one of America's finest moments, to a splendid man.

I last saw him at a little party given in a noisy New York hotel to celebrate his ninetieth birthday. My sister Priscilla sat next to him, and I was with the proud and lovely Ernestine. I reflected on my first meeting with him. He came to the little house in which I had written *God and Man at Yale*, the manuscript of which had been sent him by the publisher, Henry Regnery. It was inconceivable to me that he would consent to write an introduction to a book so disruptive in the circles in which he lived. The purpose of his call—he was then the editorial-page editor of *Life*—was to say, Yes, he would write the introduction. We were friends for 45 years, during all of which we knew his goodness. The staff of *National Review* joins in extending our sympathy to his wife and family.

—*National Review*, May 1, 1995

Remembering Russell Kirk

The death of Russell Kirk on April 29, 1994, left the conservative community desolate. He had been omnipresent, coming at us from every direction. He wrote a seminal book, *The Conservative Mind*, and, for many years, a syndicated column. He lectured, gave speeches, wrote ghost stories and histories, and edited anthologies. Through it all he maintained a lovely presence ever so marginally bohemian. He was the orthodox husband of a beautiful wife, father of four daughters, obdurately professorial in demeanor; yet those who paid special notice never needed to wait too long before catching a wink, in what he said, and how he said it.

My own association with him—and here I clutch, with your permission, into the personal mode—preceded the birth of *National Review*. I had of course read his important book, and we had the same publisher. But we had not met. The publication of *National Review* was now anticipated to begin about a year later, and I judged that it was time to come to terms with Russell Kirk.

It was in the fall of 1954. I made the date, flew to Detroit, and rented a car. I had a single objective, and greatly feared that I would fail in it. I hoped ardently that Professor Kirk would consent to contribute, beginning with the opening issue, a regular column to *National Review* on the educational scene in America.

I confess I was very nervous. Although Russell was only a few years older than I, at 28 I felt that an entire world separated us, so wide a gulf was there between his learning and my own. Arriving in Mecosta in the late afternoon, after two hours on the road, I went to the public telephone at the post office to tell him of my arrival. Could I have the number for Dr. Russell Kirk? I asked the operator who came on the line. She replied, "You looking for Russell? He's at the store right now." Well, I might as well ask her for driving instructions. I killed time for fifteen minutes to allow him to get back from the store, and drove to Piety Hill.

Professor Kirk was then a bachelor, and shortly after I arrived to stay overnight as a guest at his house, he motioned me out the door, got into my car, and directed me to a neighborhood restaurant, where he sat down and promptly ordered two—"t-two"—Tom Collinses. Emboldened by that always slightly aloof warmness, which was his social trademark, I put it to him directly: I wanted him for a conservative national magazine. He replied instantly: Yes. He would undertake to write a weekly column for my prospective journal.

I was so elated by his spontaneous and generous willingness to associate his august name with that of a wizened ex-schoolboy known mostly for an iconoclastic screed directed at his alma mater that I took to ordering more Tom Collinses, but in every case, one for each of us. The evening proceeded toward a pitch of such genial exuberance that, at nearly midnight, I was barely able to drive back to Piety Hill. My host led me to the guest room, opposite the lighted study to which he told me he would now repair, and bade me goodnight. I collapsed into my bed, was asleep in five minutes, and rose seven hours later. I opened the door and bumped into Russell Kirk emerging from his study.

He had, in the interval since dinner, written a chapter of his history of St. Andrews University, and would catch a little sleep after he served me breakfast.

In the ensuing twenty-five years he never missed a deadline. He covered the educational scene nationwide, as a philosopher of education and an observer of college life and teaching. He did not shrink from polemics and came up with dispositive characterizations of educators he didn't esteem. These included the president of the University of Michigan, where Professor Kirk had once taught. The president had a degree in agricultural economics. Russell Kirk regularly referred to him as a "chickenologist."

He strode on, and at his wedding a few years later—to the woman his readers became accustomed to his identifying as "the beauteous Annette"—I deliberated that possibly the most useful gift I might make him would be a honeymoon's-length moratorium from his column, inasmuch as he was off to Scotland for six weeks. I stammered out my bounty to him moments before he walked to the altar at the little church at Idlewild Airport. He acknowledged my gesture by reaching into the pocket of his morning coat and presenting me with . . . three columns. Perfectly typed. Perfectly edited. Perfectly executed. Not many contemporaries could rival Russell Kirk's extraordinary professionalism, ranking him with Samuel Johnson and G. K. Chesterton.

He served us notice, a few months before our twenty-fifth anniversary, in 1980, that he planned to discontinue his column at that point. He gave no reason for doing so and, after twenty-five years of loyal service, questions weren't asked. A. J. Nock, I remember, recalled in one of his essays that Thoreau abandoned his pencil factory after he had achieved the definitive pencil. What was there left for Russell to do in *National Review*, as definitive education editor?

∼

In the ensuing fourteen years he wrote many books and a hundred essays, gave a thousand speeches, and influenced the thought of two generations.

He enunciated at one point the ten principles by which a conservatism of thought and imagination should be guided—ten canons which, according as we were faithful to them, would qualify us to term ourselves conservatives.

Conservatives, he said, must believe in an enduring moral order—to which he himself subscribed as a wholehearted Christian.

On that matter of his faith he was absolutely explicit. He was not to be confused with a metaphorical Christian. "It is no wonder," he wrote me ten years ago, "that the Pharisees regarded with suspicion, nay, horror, the Nazarene who advised them to resist evil. But the Resurrection in the flesh—which some now hint was bound up with nuclear disintegration and reintegration, our solid flesh being known now to consist of innumerable electrical particles held in coherence by means of which we know nothing—proved that indeed Jesus the son had transcended matter and was divine. The Resurrection," he explained, "is critical both to my personal faith and to the whole elaborate edifice called Christianity. It is now more rationally possible to believe in the Resurrection than it was in Saint Paul's time."

The conservative of whatever religious faith—he went on, in listing his ten commandments—must acknowledge custom, convention, and continuity. We must believe in the principle of prescription. That, of course, relieves us of the daily autodidactic chore of evolving rules of personal and civic behavior.

The conservative must be guided by prudence and an acceptance of variety, and, always, a denial of any notion of perfectibility on earth. Russell Kirk argued with increasing vehemence the link between freedom and property, and pleaded the importance of community, which he exemplified in his total commitment to Mecosta, Michigan.

And so on, through the rest of the canon. Finally—standing in the way of the inclination of some critics to think of Kirk as bound by the horizons of Burke—he pronounced his tenth principle: "The thinking conservative understands that permanence and change must be reconciled in a vigorous society." Kirk was rooted in Burke, but not confined by him.

~

He lived his life as he prescribed it, working long days, traveling incessantly, reading day and night, tending to his family. On that last day on earth, in a life which we are here to commemorate, he awoke at Piety Hill, exchanged words with his wife and two of his daughters, closed his eyes, and died. Few have so extravagantly made offerings, or repaid debts, to their family, to their country, and to their faith.

—Remarks given at a White House tribute, October 24, 2003

The Ongoing Reagan

We are told that 960 books have been written about Ronald Reagan, which registers that he continues to be an object of consuming historical curiosity, ninety-five years after he was born. That emanation confounds liberal critics, who assessed him many years ago as a bumpkin with oratorical gifts pandering to American self-esteem.

But Reagan alive prevailed over that stereotype, and Reagan dead is airborne as never before. One recent book, *President Reagan: The Triumph of Imagination*, is by Richard Reeves, a skillful historian who got onto an enormously interesting device in his books on Nixon and Kennedy. He would take you to opening day of their presidential terms and recount what his subject did on that day, which of course was an opening to political, social, and personal adventures, ending, for Nixon, as, arms thrust skyward, he mounted the helicopter to avoid impeachment; for JFK, it ended in Dallas.

Reagan ended his eight years as president snug in the White House, though biographer Reeves judges him to have been less, in 1989, than the Reagan who took office in 1981, which is okay by Reeves, as, on the whole, he prefers a diminished Reagan to a Reagan in his prime, who might have succeeded with his right-wing agenda.

Reeves concedes that in foreign policy Reagan did succeed. He did so by "scrapping containment and détente and making the world believe it when he rejected the old Cold War strategies in favor of his own, which he articulated to his first national security advisor, Richard Allen." Reagan said to Allen, "My idea of American policy toward the Soviet Union is simple, and some would say simplistic. It is this: We win, and they lose. What do you think of that?"

Lance Morrow, in a stunning collection of essays (*Second Drafts of History*), remembers Reagan in the 1984 campaign for re-election, battling Walter

Mondale. Their first debate, in Louisville, was perilous; Reagan was off his form, and Mondale did well. But "the voters came to absorb Ronald Reagan in an entirely different and subjective manner. They internalized him. In later months, Reagan found his way onto a different plane of the American mind, a mythic plane. He became not just a politician, not just a president, but very nearly an American apotheosis. The Gipper as Sun King."

It is this mythogenic quality of Reagan that continues to attract attention to his memory and to his reign. "Partly by an accident of timing, partly by a simple genius of his being, Reagan managed to return to Americans something extremely precious to them: a sense of their own virtue. Reagan—completely American, uncomplicated, forward-looking, honest, self-deprecating—became American innocence in a seventy-three-year-old body."

It was never unanimous, though of course Reagan won in forty-nine states, losing to Mondale only Mondale's home state of Minnesota. This loss recalled a quip by historian-journalist Raymond Moley, who began his official life as a confidant of the young President Franklin Delano Roosevelt. He stayed on the scene for many years after his defection from the New Deal, always proffering his views on political developments, sometimes with acid humor. When the pedestrian Estes Kefauver upset the witty and glamorous Adlai Stevenson in the 1956 presidential primary in Minnesota, Moley cracked, "Did *you* ever try to tell a joke in Minneapolis?" That witticism perfectly applied to Reagan vs. Mondale in 1984.

The evolving understanding of Reagan was hugely affected by the publication of his letters. There was not a trace of sham in those thousands of letters, written to motley people who had engaged his interest or his concern, or who had aroused his curiosity. The letters revealed a man whose concern was always for others, and whose intelligence was literate and active. His eyes might have closed while the pope was speaking to him, but such moments had no historical hangover. No gaucheries on any scale were traceable to lapses of attention or even of memory.

One regrets that Reeves, in his assessment of Reagan, is too resolute in his commitment as a backbencher on the other side to indulge the buoyancy of the Reagan years, honestly and industriously though he surveys them. Morrow, addressing many themes and many people in his book, never goes overboard, but he senses what it is that moved so many people to act so decisively on the one occasion—1984—when Reagan was standing there waiting for a national plebiscite after four years in the White House.

—February 7, 2006

John Kenneth Galbraith, R.I.P.

It pleases me that John Kenneth Galbraith knew the value I placed on his friendship, which here impels something of a corruption of my duties.

The public Galbraith I knew and contended with for many years is captured in the first paragraph of my review of his 1992 book, *The Culture of Contentment*. I wrote then:

"It is fortunate for Professor Galbraith that he was born with singular gifts as a writer. It is a pity he hasn't used these skills in other ways than to try year after year to bail out his sinking ships. Granted, one can take satisfaction from his anti-historical exertions, and wholesome pleasure from his yeomanry as a sump-pumper. Indeed, his rhythm and grace recall the skills we remember having been developed by Ben-Hur, the model galley slave, whose only request of the quartermaster was that he be allowed every month to move to the other side of the boat, to ensure a parallel development in the musculature of his arms and legs. I for one hope that the next time a nation experimenting with socialism or Communism fails, which will happen the next time a nation experiments with socialism or Communism, Ken Galbraith will feel the need to explain what happened. It's great fun to read. It helps, of course, to suppress wistful thought about those who endured, or died trying, the passage toward collective living to which Professor Galbraith has beckoned us for over forty years, beguiling the subliterate world, here defined as those whose knowledge of what makes the world work is undeveloped, never mind that many of them have Ph.D.s."

So it is said, for the record; and yet we grieve, those of us who knew him. We looked to his writings not for his social indenture to a progressive state, but for the work of a penetrating mind who turned his talent to the service of his ideals. Unfortunately, this involved waging war against men and women who had, under capitalism, made strides in the practice of industry and in promoting the common good. Galbraith denied them the tribute to which they were entitled. It was bad enough, for him, that some Americans contributed to the commonweal the fruit of their industry. When they went further and offered their intellectual insights, Galbraith was unforgiving. Professor Arthur Laffer, the idiomatic godfather of supply-side economics, Galbraith dismissed as if his work were of zero interest. His appraisal of such intellectual dissenters from his ideas of the common good derived from the psaltery of his moral vision, cataloguing the persistence of poverty, the awful taste of the successful classes, and the wastefulness of the corporate and military establishments.

He dismisses conflicting notions with a wonderful contempt. "It is not clear that anyone of sober mentality took Professor Laffer's curve and conclusions seriously," Galbraith writes. Watch now the moral dig: "He must have credit, nonetheless, for showing that justifying contrivance, however transparent, could be of high practical service." Where Mr. Galbraith is not easily excusable is in his search for disingenuousness in such as Charles Murray, a meticulous scholar of liberal background, whose *Losing Ground* is among the social landmarks of the postwar era. "In the mid 1980s," Galbraith writes, "the requisite doctrine needed by the culture of contentment to justify their policies became available. Dr. Charles A. Murray provided the nearly perfect prescription. . . . Its essence was that the poor are impoverished and are kept in poverty by the public measures, particularly the welfare payments, that are meant to rescue them from their plight." Whatever qualifications Murray made, "the basic purpose of his argument would be served. The poor would be off the conscience of the comfortable, and, a point of greater importance, off the federal budget and tax system."

One needs to brush this aside and dwell on the private life of John Kenneth Galbraith. I know something of that life, and of the lengths to which he went in utter privacy to help those in need. He was a truly generous friend. The mighty engine of his intelligence could be marshaled to serve the needs of individual students, students manqué, people who had a problem. Where he would not yield was in intellectual and social perspective. I had a letter from him a week before he died, pressing a point he had made orally when we last visited a few weeks earlier. He added: "Nothing, of course, gives me more pleasure than lecturing you on the nature of true conservatism."

Two or three weeks ago he sent me a copy of a poll taken among academic economists. He was voted the third most influential economist of the twentieth century, after Keynes and Schumpeter. I think that ranking tells us more about the economics profession than we have any grounds to celebrate, but that isn't the point I made in acknowledging his letter. I had just received a book about the new prime minister of Canada, Stephen Harper, in which *National Review* and its founder are cited as the primary influences in his own development as a conservative leader. But I did not mention this to Galbraith either. He was ailing, and this old adversary kept from him loose combative data that would have vexed him.

I was one of the speakers at his huge eighty-fifth-birthday party at the Boston Public Library. My talk was interrupted halfway through by the master of ceremonies. "*Is there a doctor in the house?*" The acoustics at the library were bad, and the next day I sent Galbraith the text of my talk. A week later I had his acknowledgment. It read: "Dear Bill: That was a very pleasant talk you gave about me. If I had known it would be so, I would not have instructed my friend to pretend, in the middle of your speech, to need the attention of a doctor."

Forget the whole thing, the getting and spending, and the Nobel Prize nominations, and the economists' tributes. What cannot be forgotten by those exposed to them are the amiable, generous, witty interventions of this man, with his singular wife and three remarkable sons, and that is why there are among his friends those who weep that he is now gone.

—*National Review*, May 22, 2006

Patricia Taylor Buckley, R.I.P.

By any standards, she was extraordinary. She shared a suite with my sister Trish and two other girls at Vassar, and I was, that spring evening in 1949, the blind date she had never met. When I walked into the drawing room the four students shared, I found her hard pressed. She was mostly ready but was now hurriedly involved in attendant arrangements on the telephone. I offered to paint her fingernails, and she immediately extended her hand. The day before, she had broken the sad news to her roommates that she would not be returning to Vassar for her junior and senior years. She was needed at home, in Vancouver, to help her mother care for a dying family member.

My parents had gone to their place in South Carolina for the winter and had not yet returned to Sharon, Connecticut, but I would dart over from Yale for an occasional weekend in the huge empty house, and Trish brought Pat there after the prom, and we laughed all weekend long, and Trish promised to visit her in Vancouver during the summer.

I had a summer job in Calgary working for my father in the oil business, and from there happily flew over to Vancouver to join Trish and Pat for a weekend. Her father's vast house occupied an entire city block, but that did not dampen our spirits, on the contrary. The tempo of our congeniality heightened, and on the third day I asked Pat if she would marry me. She hastened upstairs to tell her mother, and I waited at the bottom of the huge staircase intending to get the temper of her proud mother's reaction (her father was out of town), and soon I heard peals of laughter. I waited apprehensively for Pat to advise me what that was all about. The laughter, she revealed, was generated by her mother's taking the occasion to recall that eight times in the past, Pat had reported her betrothal.

One year later, in the company of about a thousand guests, we exchanged vows. Two months after that, we rented a modest house in the neighborhood of New Haven. Pat resolved to learn how to cook. Her taste was advanced and ambitions exigent, so she commuted to New York City and learned cooking from experts, becoming one herself. Meanwhile, I taught a class in Spanish to undergraduates, and wrote *God and Man at Yale.*

I joined the CIA, primarily to avoid exposure to further duty as an infantry officer, and we went to live in Mexico City, buying a lovely house in the district of San Angel Inn. Pat was radiant and hyperactive in decorating the house and working in its little garden. She resolutely failed to learn the language, even though, until the end, the staff was Spanish-speaking, but intercommunication was electrically effective.

~

Her solicitude was such that she opposed any venture by me which she thought might adversely affect me. She opposed the founding of *National Review,* my signing up with a lecture agency, my non-fiction books and then my fiction books, the winters in Switzerland, my decision to run for mayor of New York, and other enterprises which, once they were undertaken, she took part in enthusiastically. It was she who located the exquisite house, every inch of which she decorated, that we shared for fifty-five years. We had only one child, Christopher, of whom she was understandably proud. And it was she—all but uniquely she—who brought into our home the legion of guests, of all ages, professions, and interests, whose company filled her lively life.

Her infirmities dated back to a skiing accident in 1965. She went through four hip replacements over the years, and then last summer came the accident that seriously injured several toes, which would not heal, requiring finally an amputation, from the aftermath of which she never really recovered. When she went for what proved the final time to the hospital, she had not been able to walk for six weeks. But there was no thought of any terminal engagement. Yet following an infection, on the seventh day, she died, in the arms of her son.

Friends from everywhere were quick to record their grief. One of them was especially expressive. "Allow a mere acquaintance of your wife to sense the magnitude of your loss. As surely as she physically towered over her surroundings [she was six feet tall], she must have mentally, spiritually, and luminously surpassed ordinary mortals. She certainly was in every sense of the term *une grande dame*, a distinction she wore as lightly as a T-shirt—not that one can imagine her in anything so plebeian. The only consolation one may offer is that the greatness of a loss is the measure of its antecedent gain. And perhaps also that Pat's memory will be second only to her presence. For as long as you live, people will share with you happy reminiscences that, in their profusion, you may have forgotten or not even known.

"I am a confirmed nonbeliever, but for once I would like to be mistaken, and hope that, for you, this is not good-bye, but *hasta luego*."

No alternative thought would make continuing life, for me, tolerable.

—*National Review*, May 14, 2007

LOOKING OUTWARD

Israel to the Rescue of the United States

Perhaps we should sign that mutual defense pact with Israel—if only for our own self-protection. Let's face it, that was a blood-stirring show she put on against the Egyptian swaggerer with all his Communist tanks and airplanes, and all his jingoistic rodomontade. One can hardly imagine a better military machine to help us out of a jam than Israel's. There is courage, tenacity, single-mindedness, skill—all of them put to essentially non-imperialist uses, if you grant the legitimacy of the Balfour Declaration, which at this stage you might just as well do.

Nasser declared that the Mideast was too small an area for the Arabs and the Israelis, to which the Israelis' only possible response—always assuming they were not prepared neatly to dismantle their nation and march into the sea—was that under the circumstances, the Arabs would have to move over. After thirty-six hours of an Israeli blitzkrieg, the Arab braves have stopped war-dancing long enough to discover that they are surrounded by Israelis, and that their great brothers in the Soviet Union were off at the United Nations jawing about ceasefires, and never mind the old borders, the new ones would be perfectly satisfactory.

Not only might Israel be of great military help to the United States in any future emergency: there is absolutely no limit to the psychological help she can be. Who else but Israel could have turned our doviest doves into tiger sharks? Who but Israel could, for instance, have persuaded Dwight Macdonald, that eminent pacifist, who walks out of the room rather than listen to Hubert Humphrey because Hubert Humphrey is committed to the proposition that the United States has to help small nations around the world when threatened by aggression: who else but Israel could have transformed Macdonald into the very image of Long John Silver, patch over his eye, dagger between his teeth, napalm grenades in his rucksack, boarding the enemy's ship shouting lustily: Murder! Loot! Rapine! Come one, come all!

Difficult to believe? My friends, Gamal Abdel Nasser accomplished the impossible. We are being told to go out and defend the security and the survival of Israel and its people (which we should certainly do under the existing circumstances) in order to "uphold our own honor." That is the statement actually signed by Dwight Macdonald, who dismisses as mad anyone who applies the same reasoning to South Vietnam. And it isn't only Macdonald. It is the whole clutch of them, who could not have cared less if it had been the South Vietnamese whose territory was threatened, or whose ports were closed.

A single advertisement sponsored by "Americans for Democracy in the Middle East," whose text I myself heartily endorse, is signed by Theodore Draper, critic of LBJ; Michael Harrington, also a pacifist of sorts; Robert Heilbroner, the economist and critic of LBJ; Irving Howe, the critic and editor of *Dissent*, which is to the American Left what the John Birch Society's *American Opinion* is to the American Right; H. Stuart Hughes, who so loveth man that he would have had the U.S. disarm unilaterally years ago—leaving us, Sir Stuart, with what means of implementing the action you call for now in Israel?; Norman Podhoretz of *Commentary*; Joe Rauh of the ADA; and so forth and so on.

Any nation with the strength to compel such men as these to start talking in terms of international obligations, the demands of honor, and the necessity for the use of force thousands of miles from home is a priceless asset, quite apart from the sentimental value of the country. Indeed, one should consider giving to Israel a few square miles of territory in South Vietnam, in West Berlin, in the Strait of Formosa, and at other pressure points where East and West are likely to meet on unfriendly terms.

The big question of course is what will have happened to the bridge-building program with the Soviet Union. The balance of power in the Mideast has been shattered. It is unfortunately true that the stunning victories of the Israelis are not likely to lead to any strategic tranquillity. Israel will not settle for the old frontiers, and why indeed should she so long as the Arab determination persists to wipe out the Israeli state? Why not frontiers more easily defended in tomorrow's war? The Arabs will be only temporarily chastened. The battle-cry against Israel—that "foreign body" in the Arabic system—will be as galvanizing as ever, probably the single reliable means of effecting unity among a people atomized by myriad differences.

New frontiers take years and years to consolidate, and during those years the Soviet Union will see itself as de facto defender of the Arab position, the U.S. as de facto defender of the Israeli position, though both sides will feign a certain neutrality and, even, urge restraint upon their protégés. But the fact that the area is in flux will greatly interfere with that tri-continental serenity which has been advertised as the *mise en scène* for a true détente between East and West, the great stage for what has been described as the big kissing conference LBJ wanted to put on with the Soviet Union via trade, treaties, disarmament, and the like. Johnson's difficulties with

Russia will now increase. But for a while, anyhow, he has most of the critics of our policy in Vietnam on the run.

—June 10, 1967

De Gaulle on America

I have it from a friend who has it from a friend of Charles de Gaulle: what is bugging the general. De Gaulle has for several years now greatly vexed us. He has destroyed alliances, upset balances of power, spoken about us contemptuously as one of "the two hegemonies," as if there were left no grounds for distinguishing between our own historical mission (which is to resist), and the Soviet Union's (which is to conquer). And his attitude has been all the more puzzling because de Gaulle would appear to be the quintessential conservative, loving God, country, and family. How could he, then, fail to love the United States?

Here is the answer. De Gaulle's misgivings about the United States had already begun, but when John F. Kennedy was shot down by Lee Harvey Oswald, de Gaulle began confiding to his friends that, in his estimate, the erosion of values in America had gone to landslide levels; that the rifle shot fired in Dallas was heard in the heavenly spheres and was just the beginning, the beginning of an age that would see the destruction of the United States by violence.

It is needless to note that the anarchy of the past few months tends to confirm the general's thesis. And it is no good asking de Gaulle why one demented assassin whose aim was true in Dallas means something about the United States at large, whereas the several not-so-demented assassins *manqués* who three times ambushed but failed to kill President de Gaulle a few years ago say nothing at all about France, not to mention the *plasti-queurs*. One does not debate with Charles de Gaulle, and in any case what concerns us here is not whether de Gaulle's estimate of America is correct, but, rather, what *is* de Gaulle's estimate of America.

The way it is in America, de Gaulle tells his intimates, is that we are through. Our society has broken down. It has broken down because of a confluential collapse of family (see the divorce rate, see the rate of illegitimacy, see the broken homes), of church (see the new skepticism, the playboyism of American theologians), and of patriotism (see the growing popular resistance to the war in Vietnam, resistance that is traceable less to a specific opposition to the war in Vietnam than to a general unwillingness to exert oneself greatly for a country one doesn't particularly love).

For Lyndon Johnson, de Gaulle has little respect, believing that Mr. Johnson has got his country hopelessly involved in an area in which we cannot impose our will, in part because of the practical problem of subduing a tenacious bunch of Orientals, in part because our own will is lacking in credibility, hence in force.

And de Gaulle believes—most painful blow of all—that the probabilities are against our finding a solution to our racial problem, or even a modus vivendi. Once again he cites the collapse of the family. A recent dispatch in Le Monde, believed to have fortified de Gaulle's convictions, cites American ideologues' refusal to listen to the arguments raised by the Moynihan Report pointing to the dissolution of the Negro family as being the center of the problem. Le Monde's correspondent observes that even Daniel Patrick Moynihan was dismissed as a racist in influential quarters, suggesting the continuing pre-eminence of abstraction over reality—which is the crux of the American difficulty.

De Gaulle believes that our obsessive concern with ideal democracy will prove the likeliest cause of our demise as a great nation; certainly it will prevent us from making advances on the racial problem.

Our prodigious gross national product, de Gaulle reasons, our fancy technology, cannot overcome the disease America suffers from. Thus viewing us, de Gaulle has formulated his foreign policy accordingly. If that's the way we are, then indeed France should not bank on us.

Of course, it isn't the way we are. And one would think that André Malraux, his closest consultant, would look around and report back to de Gaulle. If he looked, he would detect as much heroism among Negro and white Americans in Vietnam, and in the ghetto areas, and even in the academies, as he celebrated in a novel—Man's Fate—which, for all the penumbral gloom of it, stirred the optimism of a generation of intellectuals, and caused Whittaker Chambers to write about the revolutionary who is tossed into the boiler of a steam locomotive, "Il faut supposer Katow heureux": one must suppose that, in dying even thus, Katow was happy. So also, in that sense, America remains a nation of high morale, a nation that will bury Charles de Gaulle.

—September 23, 1967

Israeli Notes

JERUSALEM—I asked Prime Minister Golda Meir why she does not call more pointedly to the attention of world Jewry the threat posed by the relative military weakening of the United States and by the post-Vietnam nonchalance with which we are being urged to regard our mutual-defense treaties. She replied that although it was unquestionably her own conviction that these trends were threatening, nevertheless it would be unfitting for her to presume to speak to all the Jews of the world concerning political matters. But, I said, you are the chief of government of Israel, and Israel is more than merely a state, is it not?

"It is and it isn't," Mrs. Meir explained; vexedly, because she wrestles, every day, with the two Israels.

There is Israel the formal state. She is the head of its government, and as such she must observe the conventional protocols, and one of them is that you do not permit yourself to instruct people in other countries, whatever their ties to your own, on how to analyze the international political situation.

On the other hand, of course, modern Israel was conceived by its most conspicuous founders as something more than merely another state. More, even, than a homeland for the Jewish people who had been bereft for so many centuries "through a historical catastrophe—the destruction of Jerusalem by the Emperor of Rome," as author S. Y. Agnon put it on accepting the Nobel Prize for literature in 1966.

The founders, in the words of journalist Amos Elon, sought "a safe haven for Jews, and a new paradise to boot. A kingdom of saints, a new world purged of suffering and sin. . . .

"In this," Elon sighs, "they would fail. . . . Modern Israelis are motivated by self-interest and the brutal realities of power. The early pioneers were dreamers: their innocence gave them great strength; courage came from inexperience. Modern Israelis are likely to be weakened by hindsight."

What then is Israel? The question is eternally disputed—what is it that defines a Jew? To which question the accepted answer has come to be: To believe oneself to be one. By the same token, Israel is whatever the individual Israeli believes it to be. Some continue to think of it as the crucible for a truly just and egalitarian society. Others think of it primarily as the most exciting contemporary example of the historical reaches of human willpower. (Murray Kempton muses that for all that we are supposed to have entered the age of superpowers after the Second World War, historians of the future will spend most of their time talking about Israel and North Vietnam.) Still others think of Israel as having lapsed altogether into conventionality.

The founders were mostly socialists, but socialism is not a fighting faith here. I have not heard it put better than by Mr. Shimon Peres, the talented minister of transportation and communications. "By and large, those in the world who placed freedom above equality have done better by equality than those who placed equality above freedom have done by freedom."

This is a statist country, but I expect that any country would be, which came into being under such duress as Israel did, and which needs, in order to defend its sovereignty, to continue, into the indefinite future, as a garrison state. But one does not run into the kind of faith in socialism that was matter-of-factly accepted a generation ago. Even the spirit of the kibbutz flickers, and it is hard to attract young people to them.

Whatever happens, Israel is the home of shrines. Secular and political—what is there to compare with Israel's singlemindedness since 1947? And, of course, the religious shrines. The Western Wall, where the pilgrims from every country in the world come to weep.

I saw one day two dozen American Negro women, in the subterranean cave in the Church of the Nativity. Their preacher spontaneously delivered a little homily, and led them, then, into song. I remembered Whittaker Chambers's words about the rise of the spiritual among the Negro people, "the most God-obsessed (and man-despised) [people] since the ancient Hebrews. Grief, like a tuning fork, gave the tone, and the Sorrow Songs were uttered." There, at Bethlehem, holding each other's hands, they sang "Little David, Play on Your Harp," and one senses why the term Judaeo-Christian came to be used.

—February 5, 1972

So What *Is* Wrong with Great Britain?

Well, to begin with, it is uncharacteristic, not to say unthinkable, for Englishmen to wonder just what it is that foreigners may he thinking is wrong with them, and unheard of formally to solicit their opinions on the matter.

That kind of thing has for generations been an American copyright. We have begged non-Americans to tell us what is wrong with us for more than a century. And we consider that they have earned their keep only if they tell us how thoroughly unsatisfactory we are. Oscar Wilde and George Bernard Shaw would have spoken to empty houses in America if they had arrived with the whispered news that America's achievements, rather than her derelictions, were compulsively the subject of any discussion about America.

The trouble with Britain, I suppose, is that too much is expected of her—why should any country continue forever to be "Great"? I remember a dazzling moment with Harold Macmillan when a student panelist on a television program asked him whether it might not sadly be concluded of Great Britain that she no longer was generating great leaders.

He turned on the young lady (rather than to her) and in a few sentences huffily-avuncularly reminded her that England was an island of barely three million people when she defeated the Armada and began, over a period of three centuries, to put three-quarters of the globe under her flag.

But always during those years, Macmillan said, there was talk, talk, talk of the imminent end of British greatness. Indeed, as a young man he remembered being at White's the day Bonar Law died, listening to an elder statesman at the bar bemoan the loss of indispensable and irreplaceable Great Englishmen. "Bonar Law gone . . . Lloyd George . . . Asquith . . . now," he shook his head sadly, "there are only a few of us left."

Macmillan's serenity was electrifying, and you could hear the strains of "Amazing Grace" in the studio. He was testifying, so to speak, as an Old Boy from British History; cocksure that when the williwaws were done, the air, so preternaturally clear in the sceptered isle, would breathe fresh life into this remarkable breed. As it had done—one of the great prodigalities of history—when simultaneously producing men who could defeat the Armada, and poets who could enshrine St. Crispin's Day. That afternoon I'd have followed Macmillan anywhere—except to the sanctuary of his thesis.

What's wrong with Great Britain is its class structure. The conventional criticism of it is that it keeps Britons separated, frustrates mobility, and encourages an abjectness of the spirit. I view the problem differently. The class structure in Great Britain is a tropism, the obsession with which draws Britain to internecine war with itself.

Socialism, that hoary vision of a factitious fraternity which gave theoretical respectability to an untutored generation's superstitions (collective
ownership will breed collective satisfaction), fired its enthusiasts only in
part because they were seduced by its eschatological pretensions. It didn't
take very long to establish that in socialized industries dissatisfied workers
produce inferior products at high prices.

You can get a smile even at Brighton—maybe even from Barbara Castle,
if the sun is shining—by quoting *Krokodil*'s charming little heresy about
socialism: "What happens when the Soviet Union takes over the Sahara
Desert?" Answer: "Nothing for fifty years. After that, there is a shortage
of sand."

It isn't that the socialists desire, really, to own the steel companies; it
is that they desire that the people who owned the steel companies should
cease to own them. One part is envy, but a much more important part
is resentment, and the fury of that emotion is, I think, magnified at the
polls precisely by virtue of that docility which a tradition of good manners
enjoins at home and at work.

The character in fiction who, on his day off as fawning valet to "Milord,"
marches with the most radical pickets demanding an end to wealth and
privilege isn't a character from Shaw. He is Colonel Blimp's stepson.

The guide who took my son and me a few years ago around Copen-
hagen rattled on about the accomplishments of his remarkable little state
and, arriving at the peroration, said rather breathlessly: "Here we have
a 99 percent tax on the highest brackets of income." He beamed with
pleasure, as if no one could now deny that Denmark had achieved the
high-water mark of Western civilization. I remarked that Britain was not
far behind, and he said patronizingly that, yes, Britain with its 85 percent
tax was doing pretty well.

But of course Britain is not doing pretty well, and it isn't only the ravages of a tax rate so preposterously high as to encourage economic stupidity. It is the implicit mandate behind such plutophobic tax rates.

A rate of 85 percent against the most productive members of society,
quite apart from what it does to discourage savings, investment, and the
intelligent allocation of resources, (a) abrogates any plausible theory of
equal rights under the law (we are *not* all Englishmen; we are, in an involuntary way, servants and masters); (b) stimulates a sense of bitterness in
the victimized class; (c) robs Britons of the morale that makes partnership
of endeavor an act of spontaneity (the genius of Switzerland); (d) encourages outright defiance of parliamentary authority, thus undermining

political democracy; and (e) causes a few sensitive and important Britons to feel that their only defense is to take residence outside Britain.

Anthony Burgess is not moved primarily by materialist emotions. He feels it an indignity to live in a country that does not need his paltry surplus, but declines to let him have it.

Something is wrong with any society a significant number of whose luminaries feel that, Procrustes having taken their measurement, they are found guilty of being too tall; and so, tiptoeing past the immigration authorities, they leave the country, lest they rouse Harold Macmillan from his reverie.

—May 9, 1976

Reflections on the Departure of the Shah

The shah's ejection is certainly the great event, as advertised. Nothing, as the saying goes, will ever be the same again. In the perspective of a fortnight, a few thoughts come to mind.

The first is that it was a grand event viewed purely as testimony to the human spirit. The thought of dislodging a despot who superintends the whole modern apparatus of suppression is—*eo ipso*—exciting. The very thought of its being doable seems almost reactionary. We are trained to believe that totalist governments cannot be overthrown by the people, only by *coups d'état*. Yet here was a single individual, Ayatollah Khomeini, who, playing the role of the prophet and leader, found that his words had electric effect a thousand miles away among millions of people who did exactly as he bade them to do. Electronic communications, which are the century's gift to totalitarian states, played paradoxically into the hands of the insurgents. If ever in the history of the world there was a popular revolt, the one against the shah was it. Which teaches us a great deal about the limited vision of popular revolts.

Two generations ago it happened in the Soviet Union, only there it began as a popular revolt, and ended as a coup. Still, those were days that shook the world. But Lenin had working for him the excitement not only of throwing over a dynasty, but of remaking a state around an ideological paradigm that electrified everyone by its call to equality.

The ayatollah's revolt is more negative in nature. The people knew what they did *not* want, which was a continuation of rule by the shah. They do not really know exactly what it is that they do want. "An Islamic republic" conjures up a departure from secular concerns, from that modernization of which the shah was the symbol. Those Iranians whose enthusiasm is for the return of orthodoxy will presumably get what they want. But after the return of orthodoxy, what else will they be looking for? It was insufficiently stressed during the upheavals that the shah's violations of Islamic practices were on the order of allowing commerce on Sundays in a Christian country. The shah himself worshipped at Islam's shrines.

But the state was not run as a theocracy, and one wonders therefore exactly what it is that the ayatollah has in mind when he speaks of an Islamic republic. Probably he bothers to use the word "republic" only in the symbolic sense of assuring his followers that the dynasty will be overthrown. But to depose a king is not to institute a republic. A republic—the kind of thing devised in Philadelphia two hundred years ago—is far from what is in the mind of the ayatollah, however inscrutable his pronouncements.

The people of Iran are, therefore, almost certainly in for great disillusions. Not, one hopes, on the scale of the disillusions practiced on the wretched Russians by the wretched Lenin. But the people of Iran have seen Paree, and monasticism almost by definition appeals only to the very few. The notion of imposing it on an entire state is the stuff of dreams, of ideology. The Iranians, after they have done with the rituals of execration, are going to want that which is universally popular. Cars, rock music, Bloomingdale's. This is not in prospect.

There was talk, during the convulsive days of demonstrations and riots, of dismantling the military. But the problem isn't the military, the problem is the threat the military has guarded against. If the Soviet Union turned its army into sheep grazers and threw its missiles into the sea, the Iranians could concentrate entirely on the good life, spiritual and material. But Iran presents the most tempting contiguous country on the borders of the most avaricious superpower in history. To disarm is, in effect, to sue for annexation. In the event matters take that turn, Iranians will discover that their new Soviet rulers are, on the whole, unmarked by the dictates of Islam. There were plenty of Russians who, early into Leninism, dreamed about life under the czars. Perhaps the destiny of the shah will be to lead a guerrilla war for the return of his country's sovereignty.

Still, there is no denying the sheer thrill of the experience viewed discretely. Imagine if there were other ayatollahs around, one each for Bulgaria, Rumania, Czechoslovakia, Poland, the Baltics. For the republics within the

Soviet Union. A general strike in Moscow! The raising of the portcullis in Gulag! The ayatollah has demonstrated the strength of the people, even if he is unlikely to demonstrate the superiority of the alternative.

—January 27, 1979

Margaret Is My Darling

Not that I am prejudiced. Though the day before the election, I wired the lady: "I AND WHAT'S LEFT OF THE FREE WORLD ROOTING FOR YOU, LOVE." From now on, inasmuch as she is prime minister, I shall have to address her more formally. I am practicing. It has narrowed to two choices: "Command, madam, your devoted servant," or "*Persevera proeliari, Margarita*," which is an ancient Latin saying, roughly translated as "Keep swinging, Maggie."

Let us acknowledge the cliché: "This is the most important election of a generation." That statement is made about every election. Let us acknowledge the cliché's secondary form: "It is said about almost every election that it is the most important in a generation, but this one truly is."

I venture into a third version: Notwithstanding the usual cant, this one *was* truly vital, and everyone who voted for Thatcher should be as proud as if he had fought on St. Crispin's Day.

Here is why the British experience is important to all of us: For over a generation we have been assaulted—castrated, is probably closer to the right word—by the notion that socialism is the wave of the future. That explanation is given us, sometimes patiently, sometimes impatiently, in those accents of ineluctability that tend to drown out dissent. It is a statement that has indulged those little oscillations between Social Democratic and Christian Democratic in Europe, Tory and Labour in Great Britain, Republican and Democratic in the United States. But it has always been possible for the leftward party to say about the rightward party that its platform is roughly identical to the platform of the leftward party one or two elections back. There is no doubting the truth of the observation. Roosevelt would have considered the Republican Party platform of Richard Nixon as radical beyond the dreams of his braintrusters.

British socialism, it is widely accepted in the critical world, had no place left to go short of a quantum leap into the ethereal world of the Tribune group, of the Tony Benns, whose défi extends, really, to root concepts about human liberty. We had in Great Britain a government that had turned over effective power to a few militants who dominated a single institution, the trade unions. The trade-union leadership represented the best interests of British workers in the same sense that Carnegie-Morgan-Vanderbilt represented the best interests of American enterprise three generations ago. In Britain, a handful of men constructed a theology around the paramount rights of labor unions. Under their aegis, the mother of parliaments began to surrender what had been the distinctive feature of political life since the Glorious Revolution in the seventeenth century: the supremacy of Parliament.

Under the government of Mr. Callaghan, postal workers were permitted to refuse to deliver the mail to a small company being struck. That was bad enough as political pusillanimity. That it was defended in serious journals was intolerable. The only thing worse than Hitler on the loose is someone who defends Hitler using the vocabulary of reason.

The British had reached the point where all the conventional nostrums of socialism had been explored. All the relevant industries had been nationalized, producing enduring discontent within those industries. A respect for the immutable rights of individuals was eroding. The cultivation of envy had become institutionalized in bills of attainder against ingenuity, industry, and husbandry.

The nation would have been as bankrupt as Uganda save for the discovery—by non-socialist entrepreneurs—of oil in the North Sea. Britain's foreign policy was as disheveled as a continuing dialogue between David Owen and Andy Young. The only way to go, if Callaghan had won, would have been gradually to yield power to those arrantly disposed to use it for the sake of transmuting society toward one of those ideological visions that have pockmarked the century in Germany, Russia, and China.

There was nothing demagogic about the campaign of Margaret Thatcher.

She has to deal now with tacky little things like ending secondary boycotts, repealing sclerotic tax laws, bringing order to jurisdictional disputes, controlling inflation, acknowledging that Brezhnev is a greater threat than Rhodesia's Ian Smith. But behind it all is a commitment to an idea. Here is how she put it on one occasion: "It seems to me that our Christian tradition has bequeathed to politics two great and permanently important ideas, and that almost the whole of political wisdom consists in getting these two ideas into the right relationship with each other. The first is defined as the notion that we are all members one of another, and from it the importance of interdependence is learned; the second and equally important Christian contribution to political thinking is that the individual is an end in himself, a responsible moral being endowed with the ability to choose between good and evil."

Evelyn Waugh complained that the trouble with our century is that we never succeeded in turning the clock back a single second. The voters may now have proved him wrong.

—May 8, 1979

Kennan's Bomb

Tucked deep in a story that features one part of George Kennan's testimony before the Senate Foreign Relations Committee is an account of what he thinks we should have done when the Iranians took our embassy personnel hostage. To reproduce the effect the testimony must have had on the senators, the context is necessary. Mr. Kennan had been talking about Afghanistan: we overreacted most awfully. The author of the doctrine of containment believes that the military conquest of Afghanistan by the Soviet Union, though of course deplorable, is not to be interpreted as a first salient toward the Persian Gulf; we should not have retaliated as we did, exhausting our non-military resources; we shouldn't aid the resistance movement with arms; and so on. Mr. Keenan in late years has had a vision concerning the vector of Soviet leadership, and if he turns out to be correct, I would give him the Nobel Prize, make him emperor of Siam, turn over the keys to Fort Knox, and—perhaps the greatest gift of all—resign my profession as a political commentator. So much for Afghanistan, and picture now the smiles of contentment on the faces of those senators who, whenever they hear the warbling of a dove, will coo along with delight.

Then somebody raised the question of Iran. Ah well, said Professor Kennan, the United States should have declared war against Iran.

The United States should have *what?*

Declared war against Iran, said Professor Kennan.

I wasn't there, but I can imagine that the senators stared at him as if he had just been entered by an incubus. Dr. Strangelove.

Professor Kennan continued with his characteristic calm. Yes, we should have declared war, and then instantly interned all Iranians living in this country, holding them hostage against the safe return of our own citizens. We should, moreover, have prepared to take such military measures as might seem advisable in the event our people were harmed.

Holy caterpillar! To declare war in this country would require a researcher to inform the president and Congress on just how to go about doing it. Declaring war is totally out of style, the post-Hiroshima assumption being that the declaration of war brings with it the tacit determination to use every weapon necessary in order to win that war. Thus we didn't go to war against North Korea, North Vietnam, or Cuba.

But George Kennan made a striking point, namely that a declaration of war invoked the correct relationship between a power whose citizens have been officially detained and a country which has refused petitions for their release. A call by the president for a declaration of war last November would have passed Congress overwhelmingly and, you betcha, with Senator Kennedy voting in favor. The declaration having passed, the juridical house is now in order. Not only the impounding of funds, which the president managed under an old law, but much more. Specifically, the internment of the Iranian population in this country, most of them students. It is never pleasant to punish those who are personally guiltless, but that happens necessarily when reason and diplomacy break down. Our hostages are innocent too. Fifty thousand interned Iranians, held in a revivified army fort, and the commander-in-chief licensed by the Congress of the United States to pursue the war against Iran by any means he thought applicable would have had some influence not only on Iran, but also on other fractious members of the world community, not excluding the Soviet Union.

How would the Soviet Union have reacted? No doubt by contriving some means of siding with Iran. But at huge risk. Except for the Communist bloc and Grenada, if we can any longer distinguish between the two, the United Nations registered their protest against Iran, denouncing an action which at any time in the history of warfare would have been accepted as a *casus belli*. To declare war is not necessarily to dispatch troops, let alone atom bombs. It is to recognize a juridically altered relationship and to license such action as is deemed appropriate. It is a wonderful demystifier, sucking up the smoke from the room, so that you are left there with your objective in very plain view. That such a recommendation should have been made by a man once dubbed one of the principal ambiguists among the American intelligentsia reminds us that purposeful thought is still possible; and causes us to wonder, wonder, why our leaders, surrounded by all those expensively trained brains, can't come up with something that now appears so obvious.

—March 11, 1980

Mrs. Thatcher Stays the Course

The joy should not be confined to Great Britain, if there is joy to be got from the exercise by a plurality of mature political sense. The reverberations of Mrs. Thatcher's victory will be heard in great and small echo chambers up and down the chancelleries of Europe and the United States. What happened on Thursday is by no means of parochial interest.

You remember Anthony Wedgwood Benn, Viscount Stansgate? He is the highly educated gentleman who was in the forefront of the left wing of the Labour Party. Over the years he did a kind of aristocratic striptease, in his effort to achieve an adamite austerity. First he dropped the title. Then he dropped Wedgwood. Then he shortened his Christian name and was no longer Anthony, just plain Tony. Somewhere along the line I remarked that his march toward proletarianization had left out only the elimination of the second "n" in his surname. Well, on Thursday, the voters took Tony Benn's seat away from him, after thirty-three years.

Oh, how certain the dashing Benn was that socialism was the way of the future for England.

"It is widely predicted that in the next few years there might be three parties, of which yours—or what's left of yours—would be a kind of left-split, a trade-union party, devoted to the repristination of socialism. Is this a fair analysis of the trend in British politics?"

I was in London, on television, exchanging views with Mr. Benn. It was September 1980. The leader of the left forces of the Labour Party replied: "The Labour Party will never split, and it won't split because it is held together by the commitment to seek to represent the interests of working people, so that all these predictions about its splitting are wholly false. I feel absolutely confident about that." In fact, just six months after our exchange, a group of moderate Labourites, disaffected from the far-left leadership of the party, formed a new Social Democratic Party, which joined forces with the Liberal Party

He was then asked whether the hard left turn of the Labour Party might not reduce its constituency, even as membership in the trade unions had recently diminished. He replied: "The Labour Party is a socialist party, it always has been, and its socialism has been renewed. The fall in membership occurred at a time when the Labour Party was swinging sharply to the right. The biggest votes we've ever had is when we had the most radical programs—1945, 1964, 1973."

Although the Labour Party has more seats than the SDP-Liberal Alliance, and retains enclaves of power here and there in Britain, two great mandates have been given by the voters, and they have to do with unemployment and with sovereignty.

Unemployment in Great Britain is at 13 percent, a frighteningly high figure. But how does one define frightening, without a context? Although the word "unemployed" has not changed its formal meaning in the past generation, it has greatly changed its substantive meaning. To be unemployed in Great Britain continues to be a severe hardship. But its severity is of the spirit more than of the pocketbook. In England people do not starve or lack for lodging or for medical attention if they are out of work. Accordingly, the voters are not moved by exclusive consideration of the one datum: How many people are unemployed?

The alternatives offered by Labour were, in effect, to put all unemployed workers on the payroll of the government. The effect of this would have been to isolate Great Britain economically; because a nation that solves its economic problems in that way does so by means of inflation, and serfdom. The road to serfdom was being paved by the program of the Labour Party. The voters said they would rather endure unemployment, and a gradual economic recovery, than surrender to the inflationists, pull out of the Common Market, and sink like Albania into an autarkic isolationism.

And then, at a critical moment in European history, the British voters resolved that they would not progressively surrender their independence to the Soviet Union by unilaterally disarming. Mrs. Thatcher's decisive movements in the Falkland Islands captured a spirit in England thought to be flagging. The same spirit that was captured by Winston Churchill. And, while we are at it, the same spirit that was captured by Queen Victoria and Queen Elizabeth I, with whom, with all justice, Margaret Thatcher is being compared.

—June 14, 1983

Self-Mutilation

One important irritant is a new ruling by the Department of the Treasury's Office of Foreign Assets Control (OFAC). It has ordained that Cuban-Americans may not visit their families in Cuba more often than once every three years, that they may not spend more than $50 per day there, that they may not stay in Cuba for more than two weeks (this is Uncle Sam talking, not Fidel Castro), and that contributions to Cuban family members must be limited to $1,200 per household per year.

Nobody who keeps political tallies will doubt that these initiatives are politically based. This conclusion derives from a general knowledge of the impotence of boycotts, and a particular knowledge of Castro's indomitability. So the pinpricks are not going to derail Castro—but will they deliver Florida to Bush? That of course is the idea. If it's anti-Castro, the Cuban-American community is for it, right?

But not all Cuban-Americans will cheer. For one thing, the law is designed to prevent them from doing what some of them would otherwise do. Regulations of the kind promulgated by OFAC have no effect on people who do not plan to travel to Cuba or to send money for Cuban relief. It can be held that the measures affect everyone concerned with a free Cuba—if it could be established in which way they would tilt the Cuban scene. If they weakened Castro, the world would benefit. If they strengthened him, then we would have bad politics bringing on worse policy.

Some Cuban-Americans, who no longer have family ties to Cuba (Castro took power forty-five years ago), have expressed resentment of those who feel free to travel to Havana. There are Cuban-Americans who believe that any traffic of any kind with Castro weakens the solidarity of U.S. policy.

But that policy hasn't brought on reforms. No reform in Cuba is going to be effective except as it brings on the death or retirement of Castro. He is a monument of socialist dogma. In the early 1960s he chided Khrushchev for exhibiting less ideological rectitude than Mao Tse-tung. There isn't anything this side of a volcanic eruption while he is nesting in the volcano's crater that is going to get him to loosen up. The papal visit in 1998, to which so much hope was attached, had no permanent effect. Even the American Library Association simply gave up on a movement to gain liberty for jailed Cuban librarians.

There is a very high cost to Castro's obduracy. But the cost is being paid by Cubans. It is odd that a government that recognizes the government of Vietnam, and is ready and willing to send aid to Sudan and the Congo, should engage, for spite and politics, in denying to Cuban-Americans the right to gratify their own impulses.

There is resistance to this initiative of OFAC. Congressman Jeff Flake of Arizona has for three years sponsored an amendment (the Flake Amendment) which seeks to forbid the use of federal funds to enforce the United States' anti-travel regulations. He recently succeeded in getting the Senate's endorsement of it. But that is still this side of the horsepower required to write the provisions into law. His own view is that the new OFAC regulations will net damage Republican political interests in November.

The final irony is that Fidel Castro is being permitted, by Americans, to impinge on the freedom of Americans. That, at least, should please Castro, and he can ride about the country proclaiming his success in imposing on the lives of yet more Cubans, who hoped to be living in the land of the free.

—July 6, 2004

French Despair

Jean-Philippe Cotis is the chief economist of the OECD, the Organization for Economic Cooperation and Development, based in Paris. His views, as one would expect, have been solicited in the matter of the extraordinary French paralysis that has resulted from the passage, by the Villepin government, of a law instituting what they call the "CPE"—which translates loosely as the First Employment Contract. What this reform says is that people hired in France who are under twenty-six years old can be dismissed by their employers within two years. For specific causes? No, without the need to state any cause.

There are laws in France, as in the United States, that prohibit a refusal to hire, or a decision to fire, based on religious, ethnic, or sexual prejudice. But the CPE says that, those prohibitions to one side, the McDonald's hamburger stand can dismiss a (young) employee without the need to file encyclopedic papers with various French ministries.

Everyone knows what then happened. A strike. At first, it was hoped that it would be a localized strike, young people contingently affected by the new law demanding protection from it. But oh no, the French these days like to strike on a grand scale. In 1968, one of those strikes immobilized the great Charles de Gaulle, and though he survived the immediate event, he was so weakened by it that not much later he resigned his office. President Jacques Chirac is already so weakened by policy confusion and personal corruption as to be something on the order of a lame-duck president. The principal political figure today is Prime Minister Dominique de Villepin, who plans to succeed Chirac in 2007, unless Interior Minister Nicolas Sarkozy, the tough challenger, beats him in a primary fight.

What the OECD chief economist said was that the embattled CPE would actually benefit the majority of French workers because it would lend stability to the sickly French economy. Mr. Cotis announced grandly that he hoped that French unemployment would reduce from 9.6 percent to something under that, but that such an improvement would depend on fortifying the structural economic scene in France. To do this, one needs to give the market a freer play than it has when tied down by regulations that prevent production from adjusting to seasonal demands.

Cotis pointed out what one would hope would have been acknowledged intuitively, namely that inflexible employment contracts diminish productivity and augment genuine insecurity, especially for workers temporarily needed, who are not being hired because prospective employers can't make commitments that would jeopardize the future.

A staggering 30 percent of the French are not active in the job market. This is outré welfarism. It is not diplomatic to make comparison with the United States, but Cotis did so, advising his European constituency that there are two models that work, the first being the U.S. model, where firing is easy and where "spontaneous" return to work is achieved. By that is meant that an American who loses his job finds another job within a reasonable length of time.

In 1982, during the economic slowdown in the United States, President Reagan professed dissatisfaction with the weekly reports he was being given by the Labor Department. He was being told, let us say, that 1.2 million people were out of work. He instructed his staff that he wished to be advised how many people, in the period under observation, had been hired. If 1.2 million have been out of work for six months, the picture is dire. If the figures for the month reveal that 100,000 lost their jobs and 100,000 were hired, then the question to ask is: How long were the afflicted without employment? A vigorous economy will accept losses if compensated by hirings. As the overall situation improves, periods of joblessness diminish.

The second model cited by Cotis is the Nordic model, in which the government leaps in when a worker loses a job and helps him find another job. Cotis, without saying so in as many words, was arguing the benefits of the U.S. model.

A striking observation on the entire question was made by a student leader. He said, with reference to the flexibility factor that the CPE reform sought to achieve, that he had no interest whatever in economic flexibility— and went back to expressing himself on the streets with his picket sign.

There is little economic impact on Americans from French economic lethargy. Granted that nations less wealthy than they might otherwise be generate less demand—including demand for exported U.S. products. But that is small time, under the aspect of the heavens. What is big time is the sheer ignorance by a civilized nation of the rudiments of free and wealth-generating economic policies. Resorting to a strike in order to protest fundamental economic reform taxes the intellectual and spiritual vitality of freedom.

—March 31, 2006

THE RAGING SIXTIES

Hate America

On the question, Who are the new pro-Communists? there is further evidence that the new breed is negatively defined. They are not so much pro-Communist as anti-American. But since they work at anti-Americanism feverishly and at anti-Communism not at all, the vector of their analysis and passion is pro-Communist.

The current issue of *Partisan Review*, the quarterly omnium gatherum of literate leftists, features a symposium simply called "America," which might better have been called "Hate America." To give you an idea, *The New Yorker*'s arch-liberal Richard Rovere is, in that company, the voice of Smug Reaction.

Just about everyone in the symposium seems to be agreed that the United States is irredeemably a racist country. "As some Negroes begin to move beyond civil rights into the need for radical changes in education, housing, and employment policies," writes the critic Nat Hentoff, voicing the views of the majority, "the fundamentally racist character of the majority of the white adult population is unmistakably revealed. In September 1966, Senator Eastland observed: 'The sentiment of the entire country now stands with the Southern people.' There wasn't much hyperbole in his satisfaction." Mr. Hentoff wants to run Dr. Benjamin Spock for President. (If they'd let babies vote, Spock might do well.)

Boy do they hate LBJ. Paul Jacobs, the labor writer, urges American youth as their highest duty to let it be known "that the America of President Johnson is not the only America there is." Jack Newfield, the *Village Voice*'s most agonized conscience, says that LBJ's "egotism, deceitfulness, pettiness, vindictiveness, provincialism are poisoning the country. To see the President on the 7 o'clock news each night, and know he is lying again, does more damage to us than any specific policy."

And always, right after a criticism of LBJ, there follows, as inexorably as the day follows the night, the friendly reference to Bobby—"I don't know whether Robert Kennedy would end the war, wage a more grassrootsy War on Poverty, or send more federal registrars into the rural South, but I do think his intelligence, candor, wit, and activism would have a beneficial effect. His style and character could unify, inspire, energize people, rather than disgust, alienate, and embarrass them."

And then there is the critic and novelist Miss Susan Sontag, a sweet young thing who puts it this way: "When (and if) the man in the White House who paws people and scratches [himself] in public is replaced by the man who dislikes being touched and finds Yevtushenko 'an interesting fellow,' American intellectuals won't be so disheartened."

The said Miss Sontag is the most expressive of the spokesmen of discontent. "Today's America, with Ronald Reagan the new daddy of California and John Wayne chewing spareribs in the White House, is pretty much the same Yahooland that Mencken was describing. . . . The quality of American life is an insult to the possibilities of human growth. . . . If the Bill of Rights were put to a national referendum as a new piece of legislation, it would meet the same fate as New York City's Civilian Review Board. Most of the people in this country believe what Goldwater believes, and always have. But most of them don't know it. Let's hope they don't find out."

Is it just America that they hate? No, not really. It is the West. "The truth is that Mozart, Pascal, Boolean algebra, Shakespeare, parliamentary government, baroque churches, Newton, the emancipation of women, Kant, Marx, Balanchine ballets, et al., don't redeem what this particular civilization has wrought upon the world. The white race is the cancer of human history . . ."

Miss Sontag, whose sense of humor is about as well developed as King Kong's, unguardedly concedes that American culture is "making grey neurotics of most of us" (she means most of us who write for *Partisan Review*), to which the appropriate answer is alas not altogether reassuring for a sane American. Because *PR*'s zoo are an influential lot. "Americans know," Miss Sontag informs us, "[that] their backs are against the wall, that 'they' want to take it away from 'us.' And I must say America deserves to have it taken away." An authentic voice of the new pro-Communism.

—March 18, 1967

Are the Rioters Racists?

Add to the judgment of Governor Richard J. Hughes of New Jersey that the riots are unrelated to civil rights the judgment of Mayor Jerome P.

Cavanagh of Detroit, also a Democrat, that of Governor George Romney of Michigan, a Republican, and that of Governor Ronald Reagan of California, ditto. It is easy enough to see what these gentlemen mean. A man who breaks into a store to hijack himself a case of whiskey can hardly be said to be engaged in the advancement of colored people. And it is certainly true that most of those who are roaming the streets like drunken janissaries pillaging and razing our cities are not engaged in the forwarding of any certified ideals.

Even so the riots are, in a critical sense, related to civil rights broadly understood—i.e., they are politically motivated. The point is that those who have succeeded in transforming local disturbances into wholesale insurrections seem to have been motivated by racial animosities which rise, or are said to rise, from a concern for the distribution of power.

Most obviously, there is H. Rap Brown, successor, as chairman of the Student Nonviolent Coordinating Committee, to Stokely Carmichael (who is nowadays in Havana giving the Communists a postgraduate course in the art of revolution). Mr. Brown lectured on Tuesday in Cambridge, Maryland, and urged his listeners to "burn this town down. . . . Don't tear down your own stuff," he cautioned. "When you tear down the white man, brother, you are hitting him in the money. Don't love him to death. Shoot him to death. . . . You better get yourselves some guns. . . . This town is ready to explode." And explode it promptly did—though ironically it was the Negro section of town that was demolished, not the white section.

The volunteer firemen declined to move their fire engines into streets manned by snipers acting on Mr. Brown's injunction to shoot whitey to death, the position of the firemen being that they had volunteered for fire duty, not combat duty. Here, in other words, was a pretty clear case of civil-rights involvement, if one is still prepared to think of Mr. Brown and SNCC as related to civil rights.

The snipers played a critical role elsewhere as well, for instance in Newark. *Life* magazine reported an extraordinary interview held with several of the snipers during mid-fighting. These were no more routine looters than Danton and Robespierre were routine executioners. They calmly explained that their purpose in sniping was not to kill the police (you may have noticed that in fact very few policemen were killed) but rather to exacerbate the situation so as to hone the revolutionary spirit and, while at it, to permit an effective redistribution of goods. How else, one sniper asked, can you get color TV into the hands of those who do not have it? (An interesting note for the International Revolutionary Bulletin Board: Man is born free, but everywhere he is without color TV.)

Once again, these gentlemen are related to the civil-rights movement, even as Malcolm X and the Black Muslims are related to the civil-rights movement, however much it can be said that they perverted that movement. In other words, a hard taxonomic look at the riots places them other than in the category of wanton crime. They are racist and political in character, even if most of the participants can be said to have been moved only by a concern for free liquor and color TV. How many of those who stormed the Bastille or the Winter Palace were true idealists? Yet no one doubts that those assaults were revolutionary in their final meaning, even if panty raiding was the spirit of the mob.

In short, if one subtracts from the situation those who were motivated by malevolent racism, you have pretty well defused the riots, which without the snipers document nothing very much more than the tiresome commonplaces that there are reserves of anarchy in all of us and that demagogy, especially if armed by a righteous rhetoric, can bring those reserves to violent life.

Well, the FBI has now issued a bulletin on riot control for use by local police forces, and we can assume that the FBI will penetrate the racist organizations and abort some of the riots planned for the future. But there is work for the moralizers to do, and in order to speak effectively, they will have to speak the truth. The truth is that some of the civil rights rhetoric of recent years has provided the phony justifications for violence which the Carmichaels and the Browns and, yes, some of our principal journalists have leaned on in explaining the disasters they are partly responsible for creating.

—July 29, 1967

The End of Martin Luther King

It is curious, and melancholy, that hours after the death of the Reverend Martin Luther King, and one hundred thousand words after the doleful announcement of his murder, not a single commentator on radio or on television has mentioned what one would suppose is a critical datum, namely that Mr. King was an ordained minister of the Christian faith, and that those who believe that that ministry is other than merely symbolic servitude to God must hope, and pray, that he is today happier than he was yesterday, united with his Maker, with the angels and the saints, and with the prophets whose words of inspiration he quoted with such telling effect in his hot pursuit of a secular millenarianism.

Those who take seriously Dr. King's calling are obliged above all to comment on this aspect of his martyrdom, and to rejoice in the divine warranty that eyes have not seen, nor have ears heard of, the glories that God has prepared for those who love Him.

No, it is the secular aspects of his death that obsess us; very well then, let us in his memory make a few observations:

1. Whatever his virtues, and whatever his faults, he did not deserve assassination. There are the special few—one thinks of Joan of Arc—whose careers dictate, as a matter of theatrical necessity, a violent end, early in life. Dr. King was not of that cast. His virtues were considerable, most notably his extraordinary capacity to inspire. But although the dream he had seemed to many Americans—particularly the black militants, but not excluding many orthodox liberals—less and less useful (freedom now, in the sense he understood it, *was* a dream, mischievously deceptive), it simply wasn't ever required that, in order to reify that vision, he should surrender his own life. In that sense his martyrdom was simply not useful. Because it is plainly impossible that, on account of his death, things are going to change. The martyrdom he seemed sometimes almost to be seeking may commend him to history and to God, but not likely to Scarsdale, New York: which has never credited the charge that the white community of America conspires to ensure the wretchedness of the brothers of Martin Luther King.

2. And concerning his weaknesses, it would take a lunatic (his murderer has not at this point been apprehended, but he is sure to be one) to reason that Dr. King's faults justified assassination. The theory to which most of us subscribe is that there is no vice so hideous as to justify private murder. Even so, we tend emotionally to waive that categorical imperative every now and then. If someone had shot down Adolf Eichmann in a motel, the chances are that our deploring of the assassin's means would have been ritualistic. The only people who were genuinely annoyed by Jack

Ruby's assassination of Lee Harvey Oswald were those who maintained a fastidious interest in the survival of Oswald, for the sake of the record.

Dr. King's faults, and they most surely existed, were far from the category of the faults of those whose assassination is more or less tolerated, as we all of us more or less tolerated the assassination of George Lincoln Rockwell. Principal among those faults was a terribly mistaken judgment. A year ago King accused the United States of committing crimes equal in horror to those committed by the Nazis in Germany. One could only gasp at the profanation. Ten days ago, in his penultimate speech, delivered at the National Cathedral in Washington, D.C., he accused the United States of waging a war as indefensible as any war committed during the twentieth century. Several years ago, on the way back from Oslo, where he received the Nobel Peace Prize, he conspicuously declined to criticize the Gbenye movement in the northern Congo, which was even then engaged in slaughtering, as brutally as Dr. King would be slaughtered, his brothers in Christ. But for such transgressions in logic and in judgment, one does not deserve the death sentence.

3. The sickening observation of the commentators is therefore particularly inapposite. The commentators (most of them) said: How can we now defend non-violence? Surely the answer is: More perfervidly than ever before. It was, need we remark, violence that killed Dr. King. Should we therefore abandon non-violence?

Those who mourn Dr. King because they were his closest followers should meditate the implications of the deed of the wildman who killed him. That deed should bring to mind not (for God's sake) the irrelevance of non-violence, but the sternest necessity of reaffirming non-violence. An aspect of non-violence is submission to the law.

The last public speech of Martin Luther King described his intention of violating the law in Memphis, where an injunction had been handed down against the resumption of a march which only a week ago had resulted in the death of one human being and the wounding of fifty others.

Dr. King's flouting of the law does not justify the flouting by others of the law, but it is a terrifying thought that, most likely, the cretin who leveled his rifle at the head of Martin Luther King, may have absorbed the talk, so freely available, about the supremacy of the individual conscience, such talk as Martin Luther King, God rest his troubled soul, had so widely, and so indiscriminately, indulged in.

—April 9, 1968

The Kids in Chicago

I dare say that the resentment and bitterness at Chicago last week had something to do with the public's philosophical unwillingness to decide, really, how to deal with rioters.

The outrage, so lavishly displayed on television, was only one part ideological. There are those who are always against the cops, on the traditionalist grounds that associate policemen with the repressive establishments of history. But even those who have worked their way out of that emotional snare were horrified at what they saw, because what they saw included the redundant blow of the nightstick, at the head or shoulder or rump of a victim already incapacitated; included, on one notorious occasion, policemen calling for the vacating of a street at a speed with which, literally, those who were not practiced sprinters could not comply.

But then the police and their supporters counterattacked, and their general case was compelling. They began by boldly challenging the terminological myths—on the one hand the big sadistic Gestapo-minded policemen, on the other the sun-speckled, gentle-minded young idealists; Otto Preminger versus Harvey. That didn't take too long, what with the (belated) revelation that the gentle folk had taken intensive training in the arts of public disturbance, featuring, among other select disciplines, how to capture public sympathy by provoking police into the use of unnecessary force.

The avowed intention of the high command of the rioters was to paralyze the convention. Most of those who expressed themselves on the question dismissed the strategic objective as palpably idealistic and, therefore, unrelated to any justification for what the police did. Still, the confidence of the Anti's was shattered. At this point the convention was adjourned, leaving questions unanswered.

1. Do we really desire to enforce police regulations adamantly, or do too many people suspect that such regulations, promulgated under pressure, are arbitrary and constricting, and therefore lacking in sufficient moral authority to justify automatic acceptance? There were those in Chicago who

were saying, in effect: Was it worth the bloodshed to hold the line at Avenue A when, after all, there were all those avenues in between it and Avenue X? Question: Can the public be persuaded to grant the police the right to designate, from their command posts, their own Verduns, beyond which rioters will not pass? Or must the police announce these boundaries well in advance, in order to attempt to persuade the doubters of their plausibility?

2. Do the excesses of policemen reflect the tendencies of their superiors? We were hotly urged to this conclusion in Chicago, and it required an ice-cold shower in the realities to bring us out of it. On Sunday night, Mayor Daley having declined to endorse Humphrey, he was on his way to becoming a hero. If on Wednesday he had announced his support for Gene McCarthy, the flower children, so help me, would have been graven into history as the modern counterparts of the Hitler Youth by 6 P.M., CBS news time, Thursday. I kept wondering why no one meditated on the event of last spring, when Super-Impeccable Mayor Lindsay gave orders to Super-Impeccable Commissioner Leary to super-impeccably bust Columbia, nevertheless resulting in howls and screams about police brutality which are even now the roar at Columbia. Suggesting,

3. That Americans really haven't made up their minds concerning aspects of the problem which absolutely require attention before we can handle such phenomena as the Chicago riots with any sense of self-assurance. But our minds are not disposed to seek resolution. What it comes down to, I think, is that the opinion makers prefer a highly plastic line between the law and the defiers of the law, believing as they do that salients struck across the line by the defiers of it are matters that require urgent democratic attention; that if young rioters in Chicago throw themselves into police lines, they are saying to us things which we ought to hear. I suspect that if Thomas A. Edison were to appear on the scene tomorrow with an anti-riot weapon which would totally immobilize rioters without causing them as much pain as a minor sunburn or an editorial in the New York Times, Mr. Edison and his machine would be quickly proscribed by law, in the company of that long list of unpopular riot-controlling weapons which have been serenely pounced upon, from fire hoses, to cattle prods, to tear gas, to mace.

The initiative, at this point, is with the intellectuals, who should tell us-folk how to square off to these problems.

—September 5, 1968

The Neglected Notebooks of Sirhan Sirhan

The newsletter *Combat* has performed a signal service by publishing three pages from the notebooks of Sirhan Sirhan, most of which were ignored by the press at the time of his trial. They are nevertheless instructive for those who desire to understand the crime of Sirhan Sirhan, which, it transpires, was more than merely a homicidal paroxysm of a young man deranged.

Last fall I wrote in *Esquire* magazine that Sirhan was "neither de jure nor de facto American." Legally, I observed, he was "a Jordanian citizen, [whose] loyalties were clearly to Jordan."

Shortly before his trial, in an interview with a writer for *Life* magazine, Sirhan angrily quoted this observation. "'What does he mean?' asks Sirhan, his eyes blazing. 'Not American?' Later he told me," the *Life* reporter continues, "'I feel like an American. If I went back to Jordan I would be a foreigner.'"

If we can assume that Sirhan's rage was sincere (certainly it has proved unsafe to get in the way of that rage), it repays one's attention, in the context of his deed, to reflect on his belief that he was in fact an American. That he shot Senator Kennedy not in his capacity as a Jordanian, seeking to remove a prominent political figure who was siding with Israel, but as an American seeking to adjust American policy into other directions. What other directions? Besides revising our Mideastern policies?

The opinion makers have been as reluctant to draw conclusions based on Sirhan's ideological inclinations as they would have been anxious to draw such conclusions if it had proved that Sirhan was, say, a member of the John Birch Society. Thus also it was with Oswald, whose objection to President Kennedy had no ideological foundation whatever except for the obvious one, namely that Oswald was a Communist, and President Kennedy was the leader of the great anti-Communist world power. But for every line reflecting on the possible nexus between Oswald's Communism and Oswald's deed, twenty have been written probing illusory by-ways leading to the CIA, or the oil interests, or the fascist subculture of Dallas, or just about anything at all, rather than the reality: an amply documented history of relentless pro-Sovietism.

Here is Sirhan Sirhan writing in his notebook: "I advocate the over-throw of the current president of the [obscenity] United States of America. The U.S. says that life in Russia is bad. Why? [underlined three times] Sup-posedly no average American has ever lived in a Slavic society so how can he tell if it is good or bad—isn't his gov't putting words in his mouth?"

And, finally, the Sirhan Manifesto: "I firmly support the Communist cause and its people—wether [sic] Russian, Chinese, Albanian, Hungarian or whoever—Workers of the world unite, You have nothing to loose [sic] but your chains, and a world to win."

The temptation to dismiss these passages as illiterate rubbish, the rant-ings of a madman, was specifically rejected by the jury asked to consider them. Notwithstanding the sloppiness of the syntax, the thought is not incoherent, nor the writing illiterate. One page later, Sirhan wrote a sen-tence of a sort that does not issue from illiterates. "My line of thought in this presentation is not steady in flow—due to the multiplicity of griev-ances and charged emotions that generate within me."

One concludes that Sirhan understood himself to be acting not merely as an anti-Zionist, a Pasadena-based fedayeen: but as an American, aroused by, God save us, the rhetoric of the Communist Manifesto to strike down a prominent American bound for the presidency. It is a mistake to suppose that Robert Kennedy alone was his target. Kennedy was a target of oppor-tunity. "Sirhan Sirhan," he wrote in his notebook, "must begin to work on solving the problems and difficulties of assassinating the 36th president of the glorious United States." The 36th president was Lyndon Johnson. The moral is that the 35th president and the man who might have been the 37th president were removed from this world by men indoctrinated in Commu-nism. Even though George Kennan no longer knows what Communism is, some people do who also know how to aim firearms.

—May 24, 1969

Calley

The reaction to the conviction of Lieutenant William Calley has greatly sur-prised everyone, and is directly responsible for President Nixon's sudden intervention, ordering Calley removed from the stockade to house arrest, and promising personally to review the case. It appears that the mail is altogether lopsided, 100 to 1 in favor of Calley, and that is a vexing datum, inasmuch as Americans do not usually rally to the cause of someone who, it has been determined, aimed a rifle at old ladies and little children, and killed them.

A few observations:

1. The American people are very well aware that a diligent effort is being made to discredit the military. They sense, moreover, that the effort springs from other than mere technical dissatisfaction with the performance of the military. It is one thing to say that General Westmoreland is incompetent because he assured us over and over again that the Vietnam War was on the verge of being won, dozens of thousands of casualties ago. It is another to scoff at the military in what amounts to generic terms, and that is the kind of criticism that is being leveled.

It is the fruit of a cultural assault, of which *Dr. Strangelove* was a historic landmark, and CBS's "The Selling of the Pentagon" a recent expression. In between is the running contumely, the closing down of ROTC chapters at the fashionable colleges, the decline in re-enlistment, the chaos surrounding the draft laws.

All of this is not merely the derogation of an American institution: it is the derogation of the institution that is supposed to defend the Republic against foreign enemies. So that without exactly realizing why, many Americans view the conviction of Lieutenant Calley as an elaboration of the attack on the military. And they view the attack on the military as a vote of no-confidence in the society the military is supposed to defend.

2. It is, moreover, widely suspected that Calley is a "scapegoat." The word is being used loosely: too loosely. Properly speaking, a scapegoat is an innocent who is singled out to receive the punishment that should properly be visited elsewhere. Calley's situation is not such. In the first place, there is apparently no doubt that he did kill twenty-two people whom he had no reason to kill. But the court martial is not over: his immediate superior is about to be tried, and so is the immediate superior of his superior. Whether it will reach on above the brigade level one cannot at this point be certain, but already, there is hardly evidence that the case is being ended with Calley as scapegoat.

3. To the extent that the public is outraged that Calley should be singled out for court martial, one needs to urge reflection. It is true that only one

man out of perhaps five hundred is stopped on the highway for speeding. It is the luck of the draw, and one feels a twinge of bitterness when it happens to oneself, knowing of all the others who got away.

But are we really prepared to believe that what Calley did in South Vietnam was routine? I do not doubt that there are other living and unnoticed American soldiers who have taken innocent lives illegally. But surely one should await the evidence, before presuming that the American military has become so callous and cruel and irresponsible as to make My Lai massacres altogether workaday phenomena?

The point about surely is that My Lai is an aberration—an atrocity. Not that the court martial is the victimization of only a single man who happened to be caught speeding. Those Americans who protest the Calley verdict thus indiscriminately are unwittingly allied with others who are desirous to believe that Calley is a typical product of the American womb.

4. As regards the question of ultimate responsibility, the public is entitled to be confused. We hanged General Yamashita after the Second World War, and if we applied rigorously the logic of that execution, we would have a case for hanging General Westmoreland. That would be preposterous and cruel. So that we learn, gradually, what some people knew and warned against in 1945: the dangers of victors' justice.

We are overdue for shame in our complicity in the Nuremberg-Tokyo trials. But whatever we do to amend these doctrines, it is inconceivable that we should come up with new rules of war that would permit to go unpunished such an act as Lieutenant Calley was found guilty of, and I for one am proud of a country that makes such activity punishable by imprisonment or death.

—April 6, 1971

Impeach Justice Douglas?

The Democratic congressman who demanded of Republican leader Gerald Ford that he be specific on the matter of why Justice William O. Douglas should be impeached makes a good point—although it is as much his responsibility as Mr. Ford's to concern himself with whether Mr. Douglas

has destroyed his usefulness, and Mr. Douglas's book is as easily available to Democrats as to Republicans. And anyway, a précis of Mr. Douglas's book appears in the current issue of a pornographic monthly readily
available.

There, nestled among the pudenda, is an article by Justice Douglas entitled "Redress the Revolution," which is an excerpt from his book, *Points of
Rebellion*. Mr. Douglas begins by talking about the generally unsatisfactory
state of affairs in America today, including the recent elimination of his
favorite trout stream. Then suddenly he finds himself talking about violence, which he concedes "has no constitutional sanctions." This he would
appear to regret, because he adds immediately, "but where grievances pile
high and most of the elected spokesmen represent the establishment, violence may be the only effective response."

Mr. Douglas reaches abroad for illustrations. He recites tales of horror
about life in Guatemala as related by two priests and a nun—ex-nun and
ex-priests being perhaps more accurate, since post-Guatemala, they got
married. Anyway, Mr. Douglas, who is supposed to be an expert on the
rules of evidence, passes along the extraordinary news that the Maryknoll
priests, "between 1966 and 1967, . . . saw more than 2,800 intellectuals,
students, labor leaders, and peasants assassinated by right-wing groups
because they were trying to combat the ills of Guatemalan society." An
altogether astounding story, as I say. First, that there should have been
2,800 assassinations in tiny Guatemala over a one-year period without
anybody knowing about it; second that the assassinations should have
been directed against those who sought to combat rather than promote
evil; but most extraordinary of all, that Guatemalan authorities should
have summoned two priests and one nun to witness each and every one of
said assassinations.

Mr. Douglas has at this point picked up a lot of steam, and he reports
gleefully that the priests advised Guatemalan peasants who approached
them that under the circumstances, it is okay by God to use violence.
Under the circumstances . . .

Mr. Douglas moves now to America. Here, he concedes, we do not turn
so readily to violence. However, we do run the risk of violence—because the
young generation doesn't like the way things are run in America, believing
that the entire governing class is run by the special interests.

Now, he explains, the situation was very similar back in 1776. Then,
Americans demanded a restructuring of our institutions. "That restructuring was not forthcoming and there was revolution."

And then, explicitly, the climax: "You must realize that today's establishment is the new King George III. Whether it will continue, we do not know. If it does, the redress, honored in tradition, is also revolution."

Now what Mr. Douglas has said very simply is that such conditions as legitimized revolution in 1776, now exist in America in 1970. He seems to be saying that George III—the establishment—might well be given, for a little longer, a chance to reverse itself. But that is one man's judgment. Those who—for instance the Chicago Seven—believe that America has been given long enough to change its ways, and therefore advocate instant revolution, disagree with Mr. Douglas only on a matter of timing. What they advocate—violent revolution—is, in Mr. Douglas's view, very simply, honored by tradition.

If that is not sufficient cause for impeaching an official of the U.S. government who has sworn to defend the Constitution, then nothing justifies impeachment. It is quite extraordinary that Congress should have got lathered up over the nickel-and-dime malversations of Justice Fortas, while sleeping on this one. If Mr. Douglas is not impeached, he may have proven, by other means than he intended, that indeed American society is irretrievably corrupt.

—April 21, 1970

MANNERS AND MORALS

Reflections on the Failure of *National Review* to Live Up to Liberal Expectations

The current (July) issue of *The Progressive* features a full-dress assessment of *National Review* in which we are charged with all manner of offenses against the light and the truth. It arrived on the heels of a very long and very involved attack in *Commentary,* in the April issue; and *Commentary*'s article followed, by only two months, an extended analysis, or rather psychoanalysis, of *National Review* in *Harper's Magazine.* All three journals seem to resent the mere existence of *National Review*—not, understand, because they are intolerant of dissent (there is nothing-they-would-welcome-more-than-genuine-dissent); but because it pains them to be bored by it, and when they are not being bored by it they are being affronted by its vulgarity, appalled by its insouciance, or dismayed by its ignorance. Nothing, absolutely nothing, is more urgently needed than a real conservative magazine; but, alas, ours is not such a thing, and they must, accordingly, continue to scan the heavens for it.

One often hears it said that one should ignore criticism. I do not agree that it is *always* wise to ignore criticism of oneself and one's endeavors, even when the criticism is ill-natured, exhibitionistic, and predictable. For even when that is the character of the criticism, there is sometimes something to be learned from it not only about oneself and one's critics, but about the world we live in. Dwight Macdonald, the author of the onslaught published in *Commentary,* agrees with me, I have reason to believe; in any event, he certainly has never doubted the usefulness of *his* criticism. A couple of weeks after his article appeared, he wrote me, on the flimsiest pretext (would I send his subscription to another address?) to ask coyly—or, come to think of it, perhaps nervously—"Don't you think my article was full of Useful Advice to the Editor?" Indeed I do. And some of that advice to the editor, as transmitted in *Commentary* and elsewhere, brings me to discuss the three attacks, to identify the men who made them, and to say a word or two about *National Review*'s more settled judgment of its task now that we have completed a half-year's publication of what should apparently be known as the country's only non-conservative conservative weekly journal of opinion. Regrettably, the nature of the criticism demands that I devote more space than I should normally be inclined to, to examining the critics rather than the criticism. They have left me no other course.

Mr. Fischer

John Fischer, who devoted what amounts to the entire editorial section of *Harper's* to *National Review*, is the editor of *Harper's*. He is, in a sense, the least interesting of the three critics we are discussing; for he had very little public reputation, and no public personality, at the moment when he succeeded Frederick Lewis Allen as editor. He was known primarily, if not exclusively, for a book called *Why They Behave like Russians* (written while serving as a public-relations official for the United Nations Relief and Rehabilitation Administration), which is a competent, though not distinctive, report on the Soviet Union. Fischer succeeded to the editorship of *Harper's* for rather accidental reasons. On Allen's death, there were on hand two logical contenders for the position of editor. Both of them were so clearly entitled to the job that they ended up, given the diplomatic exigencies of the situation, mutually disqualifying each other.

Perhaps this is the reason why Mr. Fischer communicates the feeling of personal uneasiness in his administration of *Harper's*. Whatever he does, he seems to do nervously. (His single venture in audacity—an invitation to a Southern editor to set down the segregationist point of view—was hedged in by an introductory editorial note of such near-hysterical disavowals, and waterlogged by so many embarrassingly dutiful obeisances to the shrine of interracial amity, as to sap from the project every drop of courage, or verve, or justification.) It is safe to say, about Mr. Fischer, that he is very anxious to ingratiate himself with a clientele unbendingly liberal; hence he hews close to the liberal position, which is that such pariahs as write for *National Review* cannot have anything relevant to say. With it all, Mr. Fischer (and in this respect he is typical of the whole class of liberal publicists) sees himself caught up, within the pages of his magazine, in exhilarating controversy involving alternatives of cosmic moment. In fact he presides, as editor of *Harper's*, over endless discussions which added together do not generate enough noise to wake an ex-urbanite suffering from insomnia. A magazine like *National Review* is, in short, foredoomed to horrify such a man, whose idea of a chiller is a gladiatorial contest to the death between, say, Arthur Schlesinger Jr. and Richard Rovere on the Challenge of Our Times.

And horrify him we do. Mr. Fischer's attack on *National Review* is of the encyclopedic type. What is wrong with *National Review* is, simply, everything.

Including, mark you, its format, which, in its austerity, "exhibits all the classic stigmata of extremist journalism." Then, too, we are "dedicated to the Conspiracy Theory of politics." (Other than that Mr. Fischer could be expected to level against us any accusation commonly leveled by liberals against conservatives, where did he pick this one up? *National Review*'s position is that our society behaves the way it does because the majority of its opinion makers, for various reasons, respond to social stimuli in a particular way—spontaneously, not in compliance with a continuously imposed discipline; there is no conspiracy involved.) Moreover, we are "dreadfully earnest"—our editorial tone is one of "humorless indignation." We reveal ourselves as having "grave doubts about freedom"; we "yearn for discipline—often with heavy clerical overtones." Why? Perhaps because we suffer from "a persecution complex." We are "emotional" folk who throw ourselves "frantically into a cause," undoubtedly to "make up for some kind of frustration in [our] private lives." To sum up—you guessed it—we "are in fact the very opposite of conservatives."

Mr. Macdonald

Anybody ambitious to please Dwight Macdonald had better be prepared to devote full time to it, given the fact that one cannot count on pleasing him tomorrow by adhering to the position that pleases him today. Verily, Dwight Macdonald is the Tommy Manville of American politics; he has been married to just about every political faith. Ideologically, one finds him, particularly in recent years, exultantly unattached, some might even say, deracinated; he is never quite sure where he is, let alone where he is going. Yet at any given moment, he is privy to the very last word—on any matter—and it is death to question him, whether on his reading of Simone Weil, or on his (most recent) judgment on the attorney general's list of subversive organizations. It is very much to his credit that, because of his chronic nonconformity and intellectual restlessness, he is, as a liberal, a security risk. He will call Henry Wallace a dupe of the Communists (in a wonderfully lively and topical book) in 1947, and Owen Lattimore an "energetic pro-Communist" in 1954, and, in the circles in which he moves, that takes courage.

But after a while, he leaves the impression less of independence than of perverseness, and at that point his aimlessness, combined with his dogmatism, begins to grate hard. A humbler—a more realistic—man would have taken stock of his temperament and made the necessary adjustments. But vanity did Dwight Macdonald in. Now he mostly resents—I have the impression, and I used to know him—other people's serenity. He was born, I think, with an infinite capacity for wonderment which must once have been stimulating and useful. Others with similar curiosity stride purposively, coming, slowly and painfully, to a series of conclusions and, ultimately, to a position. But not Macdonald, who cannot understand why, so long as he doubts, others should dare to believe. And, as the years went by, the disparity between his very prodigious self-esteem and the esteem in which the world holds him became painfully evident to him, whereupon he turned to a sort of wisecracking misanthropy, to tireless denigration, showing himself, in many of his writings, to be bitterly resentful of anyone else's peace of mind, and cruelly reproachful. It is painfully clear why he indulges, with unique constancy, his fetishistic devotion to the cause of pacifism. It is for him a psychic necessity. Dwight Macdonald, who is against Suffering, is, himself, often brutal.

Macdonald's first major revolt took place in the early Thirties, when he emancipated himself noisily from the thralldom of Time, Inc., declaring war on just about everything except the Working Class and French poetry. He fled into the arms of Trotsky, where he nestled for several years. But in due course, they parted company, Trotsky having branded Macdonald— with undue severity, I think—a totally ineffectual man, "who can neither think nor write." Macdonald went hither and yon, in the ensuing years. From 1937 to 1943 he was editor of *Partisan Review*. In 1944, he founded a magazine called *Politics*, in which he interspersed anarchism, benevolent pacifism, bellicose attacks on American institutions and public officials, adamant socialism, and an obsessive Francophilia (Macdonald reads French). By 1946, even Macdonald's indulgent former colleagues at *Partisan Review* were moved to write *Politics* off as a "peculiar hodgepodge" (to which criticism Macdonald replied by insisting—in a churlish and largely incoherent counterblast—that the word hodgepodge really should be written "hotchpotch").

Macdonald's capacity to bore finally triumphed over his other qualities, and, the magazine having progressed from a monthly to a bimonthly to a quarterly, his messages finally reduced to episodic oral monologues to his friends, and Dwight Macdonald chalked up another grievance against society. Add to it the fact that in 1952 he was unable to raise $80,000 with which to capitalize yet another magazine, for which Arthur Schlesinger Jr., Richard Rovere, Hannah Arendt, and Mary McCarthy (all of them choked for outlets for their prose) were to serve as co-editors, and the Philistinism of the society into which fortune had cast him became intolerable; whereupon, cursing the commonplace like Miniver Cheevy, Macdonald wept that he was ever born.

At exactly this point Senator McCarthy entered the national scene, and Dwight Macdonald went almost berserk. Some of his friends quite literally feared for his stability. A mere mention of the senator's name brought on a reaction almost epileptic in nature. Discourse became impossible; I lost touch with him. He wrung out his spleen all over me and Brent Bozell and our book, *McCarthy and His Enemies*, in seven or eight pages of *Partisan Review*, trying hard for his old urbanity, but failing badly, in this and other respects, so taken up was he with fuming.

In the past five years, Dwight Macdonald has more or less retired. He is employed now—a degrading fate for one who, from youth through middle age, fought bitterly against the society of the leisure class—by *The New Yorker*, the most conspicuously parasitic organ of that class. There Macdonald spends his days, churning out yard after yard of epicene and stylized prose to fill those interminable columns between the perfume and jewelry ads (e.g., three hundred–odd pages on the Ford Foundation). It is perhaps understandable that, in the moments when he comes out of the stupor generated by that magazine, frustration should well up within him and overflow, as it did in his article on *National Review*, in an uncontrolled torrent of spite.

As late as 1948, Macdonald classified himself, in print, as a pacifist and a socialist. Although it is certainly safe to assume that his position is different from what it was in 1948—1948 being, for Dwight Macdonald, several intellectual epochs ago—it is not safe to say just what his position is, except that it is not that of *National Review*. *National Review*, being militantly anti-socialist and belligerently anti-pacifist, never hoped to please Dwight Macdonald. But we did expect that, as a professional controversialist professionally interested in developments along the ideological front, he would show himself as being at least passingly familiar with what has been going on in conservative circles in the last decade.

Mr. Macdonald's ignorance turns out to be astonishing. Moreover, as so often is the case with the ignorant, he cheerfully exhibits it. There he was, writing for *Commentary* an authoritative piece on *National Review* and the state of affairs in the right-wing camp, and early in the piece he writes, "the first issue [of *National Review*] . . . announced sixteen 'Associates and Contributors' of whom I recognize the names of only seven, although I have been around journalistic circles a good many years. Obscurity is no crime—we all have to start somewhere—but, judging from the product, I should guess the obscurity here is deserved."

Macdonald proceeds to list those writers he has heard of, and it turns out that until *National Review* came his way he was not aware of the existence of the following: (1) Frank Chodorov—a former director of the Henry George School, an editor of *Human Events* and *The Freeman*, and the author of two widely read books (in order not to have heard of Chodorov it is necessary not to have read a single issue of *The Freeman* during the period when it was the only right-wing magazine in existence); (2) Forrest Davis—for years Washington editor of *The Saturday Evening Post*, author of the best-seller *How War Came*, and also a former editor of *The Freeman*; (3) Professor Medford Evans—whose book *Secret War for the A-Bomb* caused a deep split in the American Committee for Cultural Freedom, of which Mr. Macdonald is a (evidently inactive) member; (4) Professor E. Merrill Root—author of several books of distinguished poetry and of a study of *Collectivism on the Campus*, which drew the attention—that is to say, the fire—of dozens of Macdonald's fellow critics as recently as a year ago; (5) Professor Richard M. Weaver—of the University of Chicago, whose *Ideas Have Consequences* and *The Ethics of Rhetoric* are conceded even by their critics to be books of fundamental intellectual importance; (6) F. A. Voigt—former editor of *The Nineteenth Century and After* and an eminent British journalist; (7) Eudocio Ravines—the Peruvian intellectual who helped organize the Popular Front movement in South America in the Thirties, author of the widely quoted best-seller *The Yenan Way*; (8) John C. Caldwell—author of three well-known books on the Far East; (9) Professor Erik von Kuehnelt-Leddihn—the Austrian political philosopher, author of *Liberty or Equality*; and finally (and perhaps most incredibly) (10) Professor Wilhelm Roepke—dean of the neo-liberal movement in Europe, author of *Civitas Humana*, etc., mentor of Ludwig Erhard, certainly one of the world's four or five most important economists.

Of these men Dwight Macdonald had never heard, and, characteristically, the fact that he has never heard of them means that they are "obscure." Now, one can live a normal and ordered life in ignorance of the existence of any or all of these men. But one would hesitate, under the circumstances, to pass oneself off as an informed critic. Rip Van Winkle still had a dance or two in him when be awoke from his slumbers, but he did not offer his services as a historian of the preceding twenty years.

What is it that accounts for Mr. Macdonald's extraordinary professional carelessness? He will say, without blinking, "the editors of *National Review* feel themselves excluded from a world they believe is ruled by Liberals (or eggheads—the terms are, significantly, interchangeable in *NR*)"—yet they are not; the word "egghead" is hardly ever used (does it follow, Mr. Macdonald, that *that* is significant?). He will (on purpose?) characterize a humorous account ("I Raised Money for the Ivy League," Nov. 11, 1955) of the stereotyped response of outraged alumnae as a "bitter" complaint against conservative failures. He will refer to the conservatism of *The Freeman* of Albert Jay Nock as being "the real thing" (*The Freeman* in those days was a pro–Soviet Revolution, radical, single-tax weekly—and a joy to read). And so on, in matters important and unimportant.

The article itself depends almost entirely on the use of a variety of descriptive adjectives, sent out to offset any claim, however modest, that *National Review* might conceivably put forward. The adjectives are not there as auxiliaries to analysis or description; they are used to *avoid* the necessity of analysis. They are instruments of sheer affirmation.

NR is backed by responsible persons, is it not, concerned to put forward a certain view? (one might ask Mr. Macdonald). *No: those who surround it are "the lumpen bourgeoisie, the half-educated, half-successful provincials."*

Well, then, they are surely normal, healthy, well-adjusted folk? *Decidedly not. They are "anxious, embittered, resentful . . . and they have the slightly paranoiac suspiciousness of an isolated minority group."*

Well, they are intelligent . . .? *Far from it—"these are men from underground, the intellectually underprivileged."*

Is *National Review*'s editor capable of doing a good job? *"Yes, he would be an excellent journalist [—] if he had a little more humor, common sense, and intellectual curiosity; also if he knew how to write. [As I say, Yes]."*

Well, certainly *National Review* has got hold of a good staff of editors. . . .

James Burnham?—*"a spectacular backslider from Trotskyism . . . whose intellectual horizon has steadily narrowed to a kind of anti-Communism as sterile and doctrinaire as the ideology he fights."*

Willmoore Kendall?—*"a wild Yale don of extreme, eccentric, and very abstract views."*

Suzanne La Follette?—*"a boiling point even lower than Kendall's."*

William S. Schlamm?—*"vulgar, philistine, chauvinist—in a word, lowbrow."*

Editorials any good?—*"as elegant as a poke in the nose, as cultivated as a camp meeting, as witty as a pratfall."*

Journalistically effective?—*"actually manages to be duller than the liberal weeklies. It is even more predictable, much more long-winded, and a good deal less competent."*

Professional?—*"considering that its editors are by no means journalistic neophytes, it is a remarkably amateurish job."*

Lively?—*"especially painful are the 'light efforts' . . ."*

Would he sum up? *NR* is characterized by (the following are subheads in his article) *"Opacity," "Brutality," "Banality," "Vulgarity."* (Mr. Macdonald ought to try his hand at writing lyrics for Danny Kaye.)

And yes: "they call themselves conservatives, but that surely is a misnomer." And in case you don't dig that the first time, Mr. Macdonald says it again, three different times: *National Review* is "pseudo-conservative," *National Review* is "neither good nor conservative," *National Review* represents not conservatism, but merely "a crude patchwork of special interests."

Chacun à sa nausée!

Mr. Kempton

Murray Kempton spends very little time reproaching us for not being "truly conservative," for his position (at odds with that of Fischer and Macdonald) is in effect that conservatism doesn't really exist—not in flesh and blood, anyhow—except as a set of very anachronistic abstractions, hardly the stuff a successful weekly is made of. "The New American Right," he has written, "is most conspicuous these days for its advanced state of wither"—and how can one reasonably expect a magazine, written and edited by mortals, to arrest something far gone in putrefaction, and bring it back to life?

Kempton does not, any more than Fischer or Macdonald, come to grips with any central political or philosophical stand *National Review* has taken in order to contest it, to discredit it, or even to hold it up to scorn. In the last paragraph but one of his lengthy review, evidently a little conscience-stricken on this score, he confesses, "I have come this far, and I have failed my assignment; I have not explained what a deplorably unenlightened view [*National Review*] takes of, say, the World Health Organization." And that is all one gets to hear—not only about the World Health Organization, but about any issue on which the magazine has spoken.

His complaints are desultory, and he sets them down desultorily. Kempton (who draws his paycheck from the *New York Post!*) complains that *National Review* exhibits "bad taste," and he cites the occasional use by our Washington correspondent, Mr. Sam M. Jones, of "Ave," "Estes," and "Adlai"—"a vulgarism only to be explained as the sort of thing Buckley thinks one has to give one's troops." Our reviewer Robert Phelps should not have made certain references to prefabricated homes. Our effort to co-opt Mencken as a conservative hero was obscene (we made no such effort; Mr. Schlamm specifically disowned him). Senator McCarthy should not have been selected to write the review of Dean Acheson's book. We publish awkward sentences which, though an "awful . . . affront to . . . literary sensibilities," we "feel no compulsion to rewrite." (A few paragraphs later, Mr. Kempton gives birth to the following: "If only all of us could understand that way to just how much of the essential part of ourselves our allies are enemies.") That kind of thing.

But mostly, Kempton complains, we are just plain boring. He entitles his critique "Buckley's National Bore," thus qualifying it for extensive treatment in *The Progressive*. Kempton's indictment, as he goes on to specify it, is more interesting than the collected complaints of Mr. Fischer and Mr. Macdonald. One gets the feeling, he writes, "that nobody on *National Review* has yet felt the compulsion to go out and look at the face of, say, George Meany or Walter Reuther . . ." "I have no right to enforce upon *National Review* my own peculiar notions of what is the stuff of journalism; but it is saddest of all to read [*NR's*] commentary on American life and find that so little happened with any juice and blood in it." In fact a great deal happened during this period, he writes. Adlai Stevenson fought and won a "terrible battle to preserve his own high concept of public purpose," and "Autherine Lucy was stoned from the campus of the University of Alabama. . . . But persons possessed by ideology are simply uninterested in that sort of thing; to them there are only ideas and no conflicts of the heart."

In my judgment, Murray Kempton is capable of discerning and appreciating and communicating distinctions of considerable subtlety. He is endowed with the eyes, the mind, and the pen which together can produce moving and important social criticism. Sometimes—not often, unfortunately—he appears, in a sentence or two, to be about to take advantage of the generous dispensations he is granted by the Establishment in recognition of his particular talent: sometimes he peers over into prohibited territory, and for a moment or two seems to be staring, horrified, at the metaphysical desert in which he and his friends are living out their lives. But undisciplined in every other respect—he writes, analyzes, and muses, the latter being what he does most of, unevenly—here he always pulls himself back, and ends up well within the boundaries of the reservation.

Murray Kempton can be counted upon to do his duty. As regards his calling, he is all professional. He is a soldier militant in the cause of what (for lack of a better term) the editors of *National Review* call "liberalism." Ultimately life is, for Murray Kempton, an Assignment. Uncommonly resourceful, he is able to embellish his work with considerable wit and force; but he is on a mission, and there is no foolishness about it, and if you look up from reading his column to take notice of the world around us, you realize that, when all is said and done, he is nothing more than a wordy tractarian.

That explains why a man as manifestly sensitive as he can associate himself with a newspaper that feeds on brutality and prurience. It explains why a man as absorbed as he by the anomalies of our age should select with such monotonous predictability the subjects he covers. It explains his long silence in the case of Paul Hughes. It explains the nature of his attack on—and maybe even his feelings about—*National Review.*

For Murray Kempton, even victims, to be victims, must be cast in a tendentious mold. Kempton, who sees us possessed by ideology, can shed copious tears over the persecution of Ammon Hennacy or James Kutcher or Autherine Lucy, but remain impassive in the face of the unique suffering of those helpless before the glacial advance of Murray Kempton's world.

What does it take to qualify for victimization—and the sympathy of Murray Kempton? Autherine Lucy, Ammon Hennacy, and James Kutcher have been pushed around, and Kempton is there with the agonized protest, for the battle is against White Supremacy, the Selective Service Act, and the Smith Act.

Now let me confess to a singular admiration for J. Bracken Lee, the Republican governor of Utah. Governor Lee, it seems to me, is an unusual man and an extraordinary politician. Having arrived at a set of principles of government, he announced them and succeeded in persuading the electorate to name him governor. On becoming governor, he turned out to be as good as his word, never moving from his position.

Which position is, notoriously, out of favor not only with all liberals, but also with the dominant members of his own party; so that Governor Lee ends up fighting Utah's Democrats, many of Utah's Republicans, all the nation's liberals, many of the nation's Republicans, and virtually all the nation's prominent Republicans; and yet Governor Lee proceeds about his business without demagoguery, without rancor (I have read three of his public speeches and I am dumbfounded by his good nature), always aware, in his heart of hearts, that he is on the wrong end of history, and that, ultimately, he will have to pay, with his career, for electing to align himself with the losing side.

Murray Kempton makes four references to Governor Lee (to whom *National Review* has devoted only a single page). Here they are, and in context:

1. "Professor John Abbot Clark can frame a heavy but somehow affecting piece about the decline of humanism in the United States,

which [*National Review*] . . . will accept gratefully and then surround with quotations from Senators Bricker and Knowland and Jones's pilgrimage to Georgia to examine the promise of Herman Talmadge or to Arizona to witness the achievement of J. Bracken Lee."

2. "[Imagine] Henry Mencken displaying sample copies of *The American Mercury* to a gathering of the Minute Women of America or dispatching his political correspondent to a motor court in Arizona for a raptured confrontation of Gov. J. Bracken Lee."

3. "Schlamm can quote with approval Mencken's dictum, 'A government is at bottom nothing more than a gang of men, and as a practical matter, most of them are inferior men.' . . . Now this may not be a totally accurate estimate; but a man who holds it can function with it. What cannot function is a magazine which approves the notion and then offers J. Bracken Lee for our study and admiration."

4. "No one who knows the persons [*National Review*] . . . writes about—whether with affection or distaste—could recognize any of them in its pages; what is wanting is their intricate humanity. It is as though even the paper in their lives had been transcribed by an inferior carbon; India is only Nehru; Georgia is only Talmadge; Arizona is only a motor court that is a way station for J. Bracken Lee."

J. Bracken Lee is obviously singularly useful to Murray Kempton; he serves him as a symbol of more or less self-evidently colorless mediocrity. Thus is J. Bracken Lee written off.

Having explored his intricate humanity? Having looked, hard and long, at his face? Having contemplated the terrible loneliness of the professional politician abhorred by his own party?

Is Ammon Hennacy so much more courageous—or so much more forlorn—than J. Bracken Lee?

I put it to Mr. Kempton: if you want to attain to the status of an authentic critic, rather than to that of executioner for sectarian interests, cut it out. If you're short on faces to look at, have a look, when Autherine Lucy gives out, at the men in Kohler, Wisconsin, who want to work, or at the millions behind the Iron Curtain who want to live. If you have any trouble finding them, *National Review* can tell you where they are. Now, be off with you.

National Review's Offense

The kind of criticism leveled at *National Review* by Messrs. Fischer, Macdonald, and Kempton leaves little doubt, it seems to me, as to the nature of our offense. *National Review* is neither supine nor irrelevant. It does not consult Arthur Schlesinger Jr., to determine the limits of tolerable conservative behavior, nor does it subsist on mimeographed clichés describing The Plot to Destroy America. It has gathered together men of competence and sanity who have, quietly and with precision, gone to work on the problems of the day and turned over many stones, to expose much cant and ugliness and intellectual corruption. It is to be expected that They should set the hounds on us.

For several years, the dominant intellectual agitators in the United States have got away with the fiction that those who substantially disagree with them do so because they suffer from serious diseases of one kind or another. The theory holds that not intellection but social or psychic difficulties are responsible for the perversity of right-wing dissent. That theory—which after all makes everything so easy for the Fischers, Macdonalds, and Kemptons—fascinates the great social diagnosticians. Many have had a go at it. It is the most recent enthusiasm of Peter Viereck, Richard Hofstadter, David Riesman, and Daniel Bell. The theory attained its academic apogee in the work of T. W. Adorno et al. on *The Authoritarian Personality*, in which it was "discovered"—via laboratory techniques, no less—that conservatives of the tough variety are, at heart, little dictators. Tactically, the theory is wonderfully useful, and the liberals will continue to live off it as long as they can get away with it. *National Review*, in that its neuroses are not so very easy to identify—witness the failure of three of the liberals' most expensive assassins—inconveniences that thesis, and hence becomes a high-priority target.

So be it. The magazine suffers from many imperfections, which we hope, little by little, to move in on. We shall continue to be grateful for counsel from our allies. Liberals, however, should submit their recommendations in self-addressed, stamped envelopes.

—*National Review*, August 1, 1956

Freedom to Cross Central Park

"NEW YORK, SEPT. 17—The Ambassador of Nepal, Rishikesh Shaha, was mugged, robbed, and stabbed this evening while walking in Central Park."

New York City's Central Park and Harlem and the Bronx, and parts of Brooklyn and central Manhattan as well, have become playgrounds for gangs of youthful marauders whom we must not confuse with the problem adolescents of the past. There is something altogether new in the super-brutality and super-abandon of these delinquents, and talk about the problem begins to reflect genuine desperation.

The police power of the municipality should, clearly, do what is necessary, in New York or San Francisco or Butte or wherever, to make life safe for the man of peace and unsafe for the marauder. But what is it we are actually fighting? What is it that makes the fourteen-year-old thief, sadist, or murderer? Some explain it by pointing to the disintegration of the family unit in our time. Some argue heatedly that the American Cult of Youth is yielding its harvest of unruly, undisciplined wildmen.

Some say the cause of delinquency is an excess of academic or social permissiveness. Others argue, contrariwise, that the hyper-regimentation of life, here as in the Soviet Union (which also has its delinquents), brings youths to indulge their normal instincts for self-assertion in anti-social ways. Still others speak of boredom, and how it drives men to terrible lengths in search of sensation and distraction.

Neither the youth cult nor overindulgence nor boredom, together or singly, accounts for the phenomenon. The detonator of this kind of human explosion is surely something else. It is the failure to *perceive* good and evil, and the difference between them; and the failure to respect the sanctions, temporal and otherworldly, against breaking the natural law. That confusion issues from the reigning disease of our time, which is relativism. A relativist who is mature and self-disciplined may recognize that compliance with the mores of one's society irrespective of one's feelings about them is necessary to avoid anarchy. That same relativist may dedicate his life to persuading others that their society is no "better" than any other society, for the reason that nothing is demonstrably "good" or "bad"—but he will not, chances are, wander about Central Park at night looking for people to roll.

Also, however, he is in a poor position to lay down the law, in any sense-making fashion, to his sons and daughters. When they ask him why they should obey the law, he has—and can have—no satisfactory answer, and if they are, for whatever reason, inclined to be predatory, inhibitions are brushed aside, and suppressed desire becomes overt act. Relativism does away with standards; standards indicate what is, and is not, permissible.

In a word, our juvenile delinquents are perplexed, and for good reason. We cannot, of course, permit them to vent their perplexity on us; but we can intensify our fight against the intellectual and moral disease whose victims range from whole civilizations to strollers in Central Park.

—*National Review*, September 28, 1957

What to Do about Sloppy Dress? Forbid It.

From a question-and-answer booklet issued by the Alumni Council of Princeton University, June 1, 1958:

QUESTION: *Why don't Princeton undergraduates look as glossy as they used to? Is it because the admissions people frown on well-dressed, social-looking young men?*

ANSWER: *Certainly not. Since the war, Princeton undergraduates, like those in other colleges, have gone out of their way to wear beat-up clothes. It's a fad the GI's started.*

If I had been permitted to butt in with the next question, I'd have asked, "What would you do if the next fad called on the students to go about naked?" The answer would presumably have been as evasive as the first, probably something like, "My dear sir, there are laws against indecent exposure." To be sure, and there are none against wearing sweatshirts in a venerable university's dining hall, or in a classroom where the lecture that morning may be on the age of elegance; none, even, governing dress in fraternity houses, where, it is commonly supposed, it is the elite who meet to eat. The reason? Rules affecting a student's dress are . . .

But let me relate an experience. At Yale, ten years ago, there gadded about a distinguished professor of philosophy with a mania for equalitarianism. Notwithstanding, he was himself a man of personal taste, of imposing countenance and erect bearing, and one day he decided it would be reasonable to expect members of his college (undergraduate Yale is quartered in ten colleges) to come to dinner at the college dining hall dressed in coat and tie. Accordingly, he laid down the edict. Hours later, a student had summoned fellow members of the college student council in extraordinary session to devise appropriate means of resisting the act of tyranny. In due course the president of the council appeared before the guileless master and announced that it was the consensus of the student council that the ordinance he had passed was undemocratic. The master did not reply (such a reply would not have occurred to him, even as a lascivious possibility), "Tell the student council to go—eat democratically someplace else." No, our professor of philosophy simply rescinded his order, aghast at the revelation that, albeit subconsciously, he had entertained an Undemocratic Thought.

It is the knout of Democracy that is most generally used to flail those who believe the administrators of a college are entitled to specify, nay should specify, norms of undergraduate dress. The economic argument, implausible though it increasingly becomes, is still widely used. It holds that coats and ties are expensive, that therefore the uniform requirement that they be worn daily, and hence worn out prematurely, is a form of regressive taxation. The argument is unrealistic because in point of fact ties do not cost very much, and coats made out of a tough material will outlive even a pauper's inclination to wear them.

It is something else, really, that prevents the deans and masters from acting. They fear, in an age of permissiveness, the howl of protest. The dean of the graduate school at Yale said recently, "The attire of students is incredibly sloppy. It would be fine if we could get away with a rule requiring ties at all meals. A good thing to press for in my retiring years."

Must we wait until the dean retires? Let us hope not. Meanwhile, I make a few observations. The first: Does not insistence on a minimal standard of dress reflect a decent respect for the opinions of mankind? The same community that insists that one pay at least a procedural respect to the opinions of ideological aberrants can hardly be expected to shrink from deferring to society on the appropriate means of clothing one's nakedness. Even in the world of getting and spending, for whose coarseness a considerable contempt is stimulated on many campuses, coat-and-tie is a prerequisite to participation. The Beats who indulge their sloppiness as a symbol of their individualism can take the measure of their hypocrisy by reflecting on their imminent surrender—effective on the day they graduate into the world of commerce, in which, almost to a man, they fully intend to spend their lives. The young graduate who informs Merrill Lynch, Pierce, Fenner & Beane that to require coat and tie is undemocratic can expect a most unphilosophical reply. I doubt, going further, that there is a Princeton undergraduate who would presume to call on Jack Kerouac without coat and tie. If disorderly attire is a genuine symbol of personal independence, then the college generation should stick by their symbol at least a few decorous weeks after the ink is dry on their baccalaureate degrees. If it is not that, then dishevelment is what it is: a blend of affectation and laziness.

The second point for the academic community to think over is the matter of authority. Is it theirs to stipulate a minimal standard of dress? Professor Joseph T. Curtiss of Yale said recently, "Respectful or respectable dressing is a characteristic of adult society. Some people are born gentlemen, other people acquire gentility during life, still others must have it forced on them." The tendency is to depreciate the beneficence of externally imposed norms of civilized behavior. There are many who, like myself, would, if left alone, permit our personal standards of dress to deteriorate to the level of the downright offensive. Conscientious members of society—and I include here, intending no offense, administrators of our colleges and universities—should not permit us to indulge our disintegrative proclivities. Coat-and-tie is merely a symbol. It could be courtesy; deference; reverence; humility; moderation: and are these not, all, the proper concern of a college administration? Is there a relationship between a faculty's weakmindedness, and a student body's disorderliness?

—*National Review*, January 17, 1959

Do They Really Hate to Hate?

On matters where legal guilt is not the issue, people tend to draw their passionate conclusions snap-shut; quite as if they were standing under the great sycamore tree tugging on the rope bound to the neck of the victim they hate.

Hate. How many times we have heard that word during the weeks since the tragic assassination of President Kennedy. And against whom has it been almost universally directed? Not against the Communists, of whom Lee Harvey Oswald considered himself one. Moments after the assassination some of the most influential—and self-righteous—opinion makers in this country jumped to the conclusion that an Extreme Rightist did it. In a matter of hours a Communist was apprehended, and it transpired that it was he who had done the job.

That disappointing reversal meant only a change in tactic. It could no longer be said that a rightist assassinated President Kennedy; but lynchers do not give up easily. The story then became that the Right had (1) created an "atmosphere of hatred" which (2) generated the impulse which (3) galvanized the trigger-finger of (4) a Communist assassin. ("Mommy," the remark was made, "is it true that John Wilkes Booth was a member of the John Birch Society?") The argument—may I speak my mind?—is not in any moral sense different from the argument used by the Nazi genocidalists who excused the extermination of the Jews on the grounds that they had, by their alleged venality, created an atmosphere that required their extermination.

In the hours immediately after the assassination I meditated on the sickest right-wing literature I have ever read; and, my friends, that literature is very sick indeed. But these are not calls to violence—not so much because of any scruple on the demented authors' part; but because, for them, The Enemy is so legion that one might just as well go and train one's rifle on Original Sin. According to such persons one must eliminate all the Jews; or all the Bankers; or all the Internationalists; or all the Socialists; or whoever—and they are very numerous—serve in the particular paranoiac's demonology. So that even the sickest "right" extremists cannot be held guilty for the atrocity of Dallas.

And yet people who fancy themselves as responsible—I think for instance of Bishop Pike, of Senator Douglas, of Ralph Bunche, of Earl Warren—have flatly suggested that the right wing, because the Right's opposition to their policies has been emphatic, and even uproarious, can be blamed for the hideous assassination. Consider the danger of such techniques of defamation. I could find in the rhetoric of Walter Reuther whole paragraphs that would seem to be more galvanic of direct action against actual, or fancied, oppressors than anything Robert Welch has written. Can it then be said that the CIO was responsible for Dallas? What about the extremist prose of the pacifists? By these standards, Thomas Paine was an assassin's Muse.

Who, in the last period, has defied law and order, has called for direct opposition to the law—if we are going to take the position that lawlessness leads to assassination? Is it just the universally contemned segregationists like Ross Barnett? Let us look at others of the law-defiers.

— Martin Luther King. He has said that certain laws are immoral laws, and therefore are not really laws at all; and under his leadership, and that of his many followers, Americans have directly flouted the law. They have moved into government offices and made transit in and out all but impossible.
— There are the Black Muslims, who though they do not call overtly for direct action, have said that violent action under certain circumstances means justice.

— There are the peace-marchers, and assorted left-activists, e.g., the heroes of Berkeley, who by physical and vocal obstructionism tried to halt the legal activities of the House Committee on Un-American Activities.

— There are those Americans who cheered the violence of Ben Bella against the French, or the violence of the generals in Vietnam against the Diem government.

— Above all, there are the Communists, for whom violence is a militant instrument, to be used under certain circumstances in furtherance of the goal of world revolution. There is the branch of Communist anarchism founded by the bloody-minded Nechayev, whose star was high in Europe toward the end of the nineteenth century, and has not completely set; and for him, or any of his legion of followers, the assassination of an American president would simply be the business of a productive day.

What does Earl Warren mean to accomplish by suggesting, as he did in the Rotunda of the Capitol, within a few yards of the president's bier, that the hatred of the American Right was responsible for this heinous deed? What the chief justice was doing was to indulge a hatred of his own for his most adamant opponents. How can he hope to stop what he understands as hatred by hating so glaringly under the most solemn auspices? If you were a member of the so-called extremist Right, whose ambitions vis-à-vis Warren never went further than to hope to impeach him by strict adherence to constitutional procedure—how would you feel if, in reply, you were accused of having a psychological hand in the assassination of the president of the United States?

You would not be drawn toward love. You would be driven toward the hatred in which so many alleged friends of the memory of John F. Kennedy are trafficking.

—December 14, 1963

Boys Will Be Heroes

The very best explanation I ever heard for man's compulsive race to get to the moon was offered by a shrewd and attractive lady, wife of a law-school don at the University of Indiana. "Don't you understand?" she asked, after the company had worn one another down with elaborate scientific explanations. They wheeled toward her: "Boys will be boys."

The rhetoric, of course, can be escalated without difficulty, making the statement to read, "Men will be men." That takes the hint of mischief out of it all; but it is much better with the mischief left in. Because there is a bit of mischief in adventure, and men who go off grandiloquently to meet their destiny often feel a trace of the excitement a boy feels when he goes out for the first time on an overnight hike. There is, of course, no fun at all in the pursuit of adventure if, as so often is the case, you die en route. No fun at all, when you feel fear, and loneliness, and helplessness. It is man's capacity to expose himself to the certainty that he will be lonely and afraid that makes possible great adventures of the human spirit.

And it takes a boyish zest for adventure for staid and middle-aged men to engage in such a dazzling adventure as Mr. Robert Manry's aboard *Tinkerbelle*, the thirteen-and-a-half-foot converted dinghy in which he crossed the Atlantic Ocean, covering 3,200 miles in eighty days. The chances of surviving such a voyage were less than the chance that our astronauts will survive their orbits around the planet, covering, in one-tenth the time, a distance one thousand times as long. The astronauts are to prove to us that heavenly rendezvous are possible between assorted flying objects, and that man's body can endure eight days of weightlessness and immobility. Mr. Manry proved that a few planks of wood, none of them over thirteen and half feet long, and strips of cloth, put together by a single carpenter of moderate skill, can, using only nature's power, transport a man across the most treacherous ocean in the world.

One feels nothing but admiration for the astronauts. Theirs is above all a mission to press their fragile bodies against the unknown, and in an experiment so mechanized that they are left with little to do except to obey the signals they hear. It must put a special tax on the spirit to be left with so little latitude. Mr. Manry, by contrast, had great latitude. He could point the nose of his boat in any direction he chose, except in the direction the wind was coming from; and he could leave both sails up, or take down one of them, or take down both of them, or trim one or both, or drag his sea anchor. An almost infinite number of possibilities. And if he made a serious mistake, he would drown. And he might have drowned anyway, because a truly determined sea will not respect the right of so frail a challenger to claim safe passage across the haunted area.

Mr. Manry, who is almost fifty, and makes his living as a copyreader in Cleveland, knew enough of the literature of the sea to know that, for every sailor, the sea is the enemy, that it must be treated as the enemy, and that the enemy is formidable enough to have wrecked whole navies in her time. And the astronauts know that nothing in the world is more mysterious than science, that the most fastidious preparations, projections, and calculations are sometimes confounded by utterly inexplicable scientific backtalk; or because someone didn't turn the screwdriver hard enough.

Even so, boys will be boys, and some boys have the makings of heroes. Astronaut Gordon Cooper has reported that "once, in the middle of the night, at an altitude of over 150 miles, over the middle of the Indian Ocean," he prayed. Mr. Manry may have had room in his cluttered dinghy for the Thirty-Third Psalm: By the word of the Lord, the heavens were established, and all the powers of them by the spirit of His mouth. He gathers together the waters of the sea as in a vessel, laying up the depths in storehouses.

—August 24, 1965

How I Discovered That Rock Is Here to Stay

I speak for those who have had difficulty cultivating a convincing admiration for the popular culture of the rockers, foremost among them, of course, the Beatles.

Those who were not born into the movement can usually remember their first experience with it. Mine is vivid. I remember first engaging rock on learning years ago that a Mr. Alan Freed (1) was very famous; (2) was generally credited with launching the new musical form; and (3) had bought the house a couple of dwellings down from my own in the country; whence (4) he was broadcasting three hours daily as a network disc jockey.

He and his wife came calling one day. It was late on a summer afternoon, and I had been up the night before, and my mind wandered as he talked about this and that and whatever. My watchful wife managed, unnoticed, to nudge me. I jerked back into consciousness and, fumbling for something apposite to say, ventured, "Tell me, Mr. Freed, do you know Elvis Presley?" This elicited from my wife a shaft of social despair such as to make me feel that I had just asked Mr. Gilbert whether he had ever heard of Mr. Sullivan. Alan Freed, upon recovering, explained to me that he had *discovered* Elvis. I couldn't think what was appropriate to say under the circumstances, but, having to say something, I asked, "Is he nice?"

"Is he nice!" Freed responded, clearly indicating that I had moved from ignorance into idiocy. "Why, do you know, he makes *ten times* as much as I make, and *he* calls *me* sir!"—he slapped me on the knee, so that I might share with him the full force of the paradoxes of life.

I had, by that time, come to and was now a working member of the band. I knew—I have a sense, baby, for that kind of thing, only just warm me up—I knew where to go from there, and all those bits and pieces of information I had run across in years of traversing the newspapers and magazines since first the phenomenon had begun focused into the question that was totally to redeem my previous ineptitudes: "But will the rock-and-roll movement last?"

My guest was made a happy man. He answered that question as lustily as the evangelist being asked whether God exists. Will it last! Why, he said, I must have appeared on one million panel discussions where they asked me just that question, and I told them all, I told them, rock and roll is here not just for a month or two, not like Davy Crockett and hula hoops, it's here *forever*. What was my opinion? he asked dutifully. I don't know, I said, I've never heard it. He told me numbly that the next day he was giving a party, down the road at his house, celebrating an anniversary, and Fats Domino and his orchestra were going to play, and would I like to hear some real rock. Indeed I would, I said; and we strolled over, my wife and I, not at the hour of seven, as suggested, but at ten, knowing the likely length of the preliminaries; but when we got there, we found Fats and his entire group, fully clothed, in the swimming pool, their instruments somehow unavailing.

But Mr. Freed, still shaken by my question of the night before, was clearly concerned that I should not arrive at the impression that here was a sign of the deliquescence of the art: "Don't you forget it," he said—only a few months before being indicted for provoking to riot by musical orgy, and a very few years before his sad, unrhythmical death—"Rock is here to stay." He was, of course, right.

And he had persuaded me to make a serious effort. I spent an evening—a very short evening—listening to one part of my son's collection. I found the noise quite scandalous. I remember a critic, writing for *National Review* after seeing Mr. Presley writhe his way through one of Ed Sullivan's shows, remarking that an extrapolation from the demure bumps and grinds of Frank Sinatra, on to the orgiastic b's and g's of Elvis Presley, suggested that future entertainers would have to wrestle with live octopuses in order to entertain a mass American audience. The Beatles don't in fact do this, I observed at the end of that brain-rattling evening, but how one wishes they did, and how this listener wishes the octopus would win. I proceeded to write a most unfortunate judgment. "Let me say as evidence of my final measure of devotion to the truth," said I in a newspaper column, "that the Beatles are not merely awful: I would consider it sacrilegious to say anything less than that they are God-awful. They are so unbelievably horrible, so appallingly unmusical, so dogmatically insensitive to the magic of the art, that they qualify as the crowned heads of antimusic."

The response was, to say the least, emphatic. I received more than five hundred letters denouncing not my lack of musical judgment, or my stodginess, or my Philistinism, but my infidelity. To manifest truth and beauty. I picked out one letter to reply to, because I found it so wonderfully direct and eloquent. "Dear Mr. Buckley," the young lady wrote from San Francisco, "you are a ratty, lousy, stinky, crummy idiot. P.S. You are too crummy to be called a person." After an exchange of four or five progressively more amiable letters, I came upon the final effusiveness of the human spirit. It was Christmastime, and my new girlfriend sent me, by registered mail, a square inch of white cloth. She explained that it was exactly 50 percent of her entire holdings in life, since she had sold or mortgaged everything in order to participate in a public auction the week before. She had been able to bid for only two square inches of the sheet on which Ringo Starr had slept while at the St. Francis Hotel. Thus did the Lord melt the heart of the pharaoh.

I mean, how can one prevail against them? The answer is: One cannot. And even if they are hard to listen to, there is an exuberance there that is quite unmatched anywhere else in the world. Imagine a group calling itself the Peanut Butter Conspiracy! You figure it can't ever be beaten, and the next day you run into the Strawberry Alarm Clock. And then you see the peace feelers: Truman Capote in *Playboy*, telling us that the young popular musicians are the most creative people around. Ditto, of course, such youth watchers as Jack Newfield. *Time* magazine, relenting, puts the Beatles on the cover. Suddenly one day, riding in the back of the car, you look up, startled. That was *music* you just heard, blaring out of the radio. It's gone now, but not long after, you hear it again. And soon, as in the ordeal of Gilbert Pinfold, it is coming in regularly, from everywhere. And you realize, finally, that, indeed, rock is here to stay.

—*The Saturday Evening Post, August 24, 1968*

Arthur Schlesinger Jr. at Camelot

The boys who gave us the Freedom of Information Act have showered us with unexpected blessings. For instance, we begin to get a real feel for how the Knights of the Round Table addressed King John, back in Camelot. Truly King John was a fine and graceful man, who inspired copious draughts of homage from his knights. Here, for instance, is a secret memorandum from Sir Arthur Schlesinger, addressed to the king, on the subject of how to handle PR during and after the impending engagement against Cuba in 1961. It shows that the courtly style of communication has not changed substantially since the days when Sir Lancelot addressed King Arthur.

"In the days since January 20," wrote Sir Arthur to his sire, "your Administration has changed the face of American foreign policy. The soberness of style, the absence of cold-war clichés, the lack of self-righteousness and sermonizing, the impressive combination of reasonableness and firmness, the generosity to new ideas, the dedication to social progress, the tough-minded idealism of purpose ["Fill Sir Arthur's glass," I can hear the gentle king saying to the steward]—all these factors have transformed the 'image' of the United States before the world."

Since this memorandum was written on April 10, ten weeks after the Kennedy administration had taken power, you would think the new court would have got over the awful monster Eisenhower who preceded them. But Sir Arthur would make sure, even though there were pressing matters to discuss—the Bay of Pigs was only one week away—that King John should know how happy was the contrast. "People around the world have forgotten the muddling and moralizing conservatism of the Eisenhower period with surprising speed." Indeed. And with surprising speed the world was soon to forget what it was like, under Ike, not to be fighting wars.

Eventually Sir Arthur got down to business. The Bay of Pigs was planned, and Sir Arthur feared it might boomerang. *Very* important to prepare the PR. "If Castro [wins the engagement and] flies a group of captured Cubans to New York to testify that they were organized and trained by CIA, we will have to be prepared to show that the alleged CIA personnel were errant idealists or soldiers-of-fortune working on their own." In later years, a successor courtier would call that stonewalling. And the very same errant idealists, a decade later, pried their way into Watergate.

Sir Arthur suggested the need for diversionary action on some other front. "Could not something be done against the Dominican Republic in the next few days?—some new call for action against the Trujillo tyranny?" Why not? Wish we had thought of that.

King John was not *himself* to be caught lying. "When lies must be told," Sir Arthur wrote, "they should be told by subordinate officials." That's chivalry, if ever we saw it! In fact, maybe King John should arrange to be out at Chevy Chase playing golf when the invasion actually began? "There seems to be merit in [the] suggestion that someone other than the President make the final decision and do so in his absence—someone whose head can later be placed on the block if things go terribly wrong." King John, feeling his throat tenderly, must have been especially grateful for the solicitude and loyalty and fraternity of his humble servant, Sir Arthur.

In my next dispatch, I shall reproduce a press conference as recommended by Arthur Schlesinger to John F. Kennedy in the event the Bay of Pigs went sour. On no account miss it. If Nixon had had Sir Arthur at his side, giving such top-quality advice, Nixon would still be president. Sir Arthur would have figured out a way to repeal the two-term amendment, so that the world might continue to enjoy the soberness of style, the absence of cold-war clichés, the lack of self-righteousness and sermonizing, the impressive combination of reasonableness and firmness, the generosity to new ideas, the dedication to social progress, the tough-minded idealism of purpose. Gee. Where was Arthur when King Richard needed him so badly?

—April 30, 1977

Lying: A Quick Lesson

Schlesinger, days before the Bay of Pigs invasion, is troubled that Kennedy's direct sponsorship of it may be discovered by the Woodwards and Bernsteins of 1961. Early in the memorandum he discusses the merits of having someone else actually trigger the invasion, "—someone whose head can later be placed on the block if things go terribly wrong." Some Gordon Liddy, or Howard Hunt, or even John Ehrlichman, or John Mitchell. Then Mr. Schlesinger writes out the kind of press conference President Kennedy might expect, supplying the most appropriate answers to the most embarrassing questions for his boss:

"Q. Mr. President, can you tell us about the reported invasion of Cuba this morning?

"A. We are doing our best to get the exact facts. So far as I can tell at present, a number of opponents of the Castro regime have landed on Cuba. I understand that the Revolutionary Council is trying to make contact with these people."

(How're we doing? Could Nixon have improved on that one? No sir, this is Grade A, Harvard B.A., Harvard Ph.D. Quality Lying. There is more:)

"Q. Sir, according to the newspapers the rebel forces were trained in American camps and supplied by American agencies.

"A. There have been many thousands of Cuban refugees in Florida in these last months. I have no doubt that many of them have been determined to do what they can at the earliest possible moment to restore freedom to their homeland. . . . I suppose that, just as the Castro forces got money and arms from sources in the United States, these rebels may well have too. But, so far as I can tell, this is a purely Cuban operation. I doubt whether Cuba's patriots in exile would have to be stimulated and organized by the United States in order to persuade them to liberate their nation from a Communist dictator."

(Can you imagine what the Watergate Committee, or John Doar's Impeachment Committee, would have done with that one?)

"Q. Mr. President, is the CIA involved in this affair?

"A. As I said a moment ago, I imagine that elements in the United States helped these opponents of Castro, as they helped Castro himself in 1958. I can assure you that the United States government has no intention of using force to overthrow the Castro regime or contributing force to that purpose unless compelled to do so in the interest of self-defense."

That is what one might call a Smoking Gun. But hark! Arthur Schlesinger was worried about it because he added in brackets, "[hardly satisfactory: it is imperative that a better formula be worked out before your next press conference]." It would of course have been better still if, before the next press conference, a better invasion had been worked out.

"Q. Mr. President, would you say that, so far as Cuba is concerned, the U.S. has been faithful to its Treaty pledges against intervention in other countries? Would you say that it has resolutely enforced the laws forbidding the use of U.S. territory to prepare revolutionary action against another state?"

Guess what answer Arthur Schlesinger supplied to that question in his memo to the boss? I quote it exactly as it appears in the secret document: "A. ????"

Even Mr. Schlesinger had exhausted his reserves of artifice. He had coached the president on how to lie about everything involving the U.S. sponsorship of the Bay of Pigs invasion. But he got stuck on that one point, how to answer that one tricky question. Would that exchange have served as a candidate for eighteen and a half minutes of erased recording tape?

Well, we all know what happened. Kennedy launched the Bay of Pigs, and it became obvious that the invaders had been trained and directed by the U.S. government. He then went to the people—and told them the truth; and survived. If he had gone to the people and given such a speech as Schlesinger recommended in his memo, he'd have been as guilty as Nixon. But such memos as in the public mind are identified with the kind of people attracted to Nixon, we see now were quite routinely written by the kind of people attracted to—JFK. My, how history repeats itself, especially at the hands of historians.

—May 3, 1977

Fun and Games

LOS ANGELES—It is Merv Griffin time, and guess who is scheduled on his show? Routine, no fuss; just another guest. We have already had Mr. and Mrs. Arthur Murray, who although they may have taught us dancing in a hurry, didn't do so because *they* were in any particular hurry: they are in splendid shape, having recently celebrated their fifty-third wedding anniversary. A second guest is a ballad singer, envelopingly warm, talented, who sings songs about father-son relationships. There is a smart-aleck author type there to sell his new book. And . . . and . . .

What's her line? Well, she produces and directs porno flicks. The hard stuff. She looks rather like Kay Kendall. How old are you, dear? Twenty-three. What religion were you brought up in? Catholic. Still practice your religion? Well—tee-hee—no, not really, don't go to church much. Did you go to college? Yes, Michigan State. Graduate? Yes. Major? Phys. Ed. What made you go into—porn movies? Wanted to get into the business, and worked for a while as a cashier at a movie house that featured X-rated movies, so got interested in the business, asked around, and went to Hollywood. Do you make . . . all . . . kinds of . . . films? No, we don't go into, well, bestiality, sadomasochism, that sort of thing. Just, you know, the regular stuff, only, in a way, you know, we try to experiment, new positions, that sort of thing.

The singer came in and said he thought it was all a pretty good idea. He and his wife had an X-rated film which they showed regularly on their home videocassette system, and he thought it was very healthy, after all we're part animal, and we have animal instincts, and what's wrong with recognizing anything that obvious?

The author mumbled something about its also being an animal instinct to eat other animals, but we don't make movies about people eating other people; but the audience didn't like that. And Merv said to the author: Have you ever seen a pornographic film? Sure, the author said, I've done a lot of reprehensible things.

Well, that did it—what was so reprehensible about it? I mean, here's a sweet young thing, twenty-three, Phys. Ed. from Michigan State, making the kind of movies that the singer and his wife showed in the privacy of their living room, and what's so bad about that?

At this point the author tried to take the offensive, but he sounded awfully stuffy. He said that the whole situation reminded him of the point Irving Kristol had made in one of his essays for the *Wall Street Journal*, that such was the inversion of values in America that an eighteen-year-old-girl could legally have intercourse live on a stage in New York provided she was paid the minimum wage. Are you—the author directed his question to the singer—in favor of permitting people to make snuff films?

What are snuff films?

Well, snuff films are where a guy (or a gal) is actually killed in the film, the victim being a masochist inclined to go all the way, and the executioner being a sadist inclined ditto. Is that okay?

The porn director shook her head, as did Mr. and Mrs. Arthur Murray, as did the singer, as did Merv Griffin.

Merv asked the lady how much she had spent on her current porn movie, and she said about $116,000.

How much money have you grossed from it?

So far this year? Oh, about a million dollars. But we can go on and on selling it, it will last for years, she reassured Merv.

What happens, the author asked, when you run out of positions? The lady laughed, Merv laughed, Mr. and Mrs. Arthur Murray laughed, the singer laughed, and the time was up and everybody went home, just as if they had heard from someone who had made a success starting up a chain of doughnut shops.

On the way home the author tried to remember a couple of lines from Hilaire Belloc, but couldn't. The next day he found them. "We sit by and watch the Barbarian, we tolerate him; in the long stretches of peace we are not afraid. We are tickled by his irreverence; his comic inversion of our old certitudes and our fixed creeds refreshes us; we laugh. But as we laugh we are watched by large and awful faces from beyond; and on these faces there is no smile."

—October 28, 1978

Black Thought, Black Talk

Listen carefully, I beg you, to these two or three sentences written by an English teacher (C. Webster Wheelock) and published in an essay in the *New York Times* on "Our Incredible Shrinking Language." They teach more than most of the rhetoricians you will hear from now to the end of the year.

"I recently sat through," the teacher begins, "a graduation ceremony in which one of the speakers used the adjective 'incredible' four times and its synonym 'unbelievable' once. Why did he appear to suggest by his choice of language that the accomplishments in question went beyond the laudable to the improbable? And why did all of us listening to him easily and automatically discount the value of the expressions he had selected? The answer lies in the steady erosion of power in an important part of our language over recent decades."

The English teacher is concerned over implausible raves. They are the treacly counterpart of their opposite, which are implausible negatives—except that these do more damage because they are made of bile. What Senator Edward Kennedy said last week about the nomination of Robert Bork as an associate justice of the Supreme Court should drum him out of the councils of civilized men engaged in democratic exchange. It will take more than just one book by Arthur Schlesinger Jr. to clean up this act.

"Robert Bork's America," said Senator Kennedy, quoted in large type in the issue of the *New York Times* published the day before the lesson from the English teacher, "is a land in which women would be forced into back-alley abortions, blacks would sit at segregated lunch counters, rogue police could break down citizens' doors in midnight raids . . ."

Now either Senator Kennedy was drunk when he uttered these lines, in which case he should not drink before he orates, or else he has proved as irresponsible as any demagogue in the recent history of the United States. It is hard to imagine anyone in this century—Bilbo, Smith, McCarthy, Coughlin—coming up with charges so withered in distortion and malice.

Consider the question of abortion. If Bork voted to reverse *Roe* v. *Wade*, he would need four other judges whose consciences instructed them that it was a bad constitutional decision. Does it then follow that women would be forced into back-alley abortions? Only if a solid majority of the American people went on to write anti-abortion laws. Kennedy knows as well as Planned Parenthood that that would not happen. To withdraw the license of *Roe* v. *Wade* is not to illegalize abortion.

And why would blacks sit at segregated lunch counters? Where has Robert Bork defended Jim Crow? He was always opposed to state laws enforcing racial segregation, which is different from upholding the right of the states to prescribe conduct—though even on this point, libertarian Bork is at one these days with the overwhelming majority of the voters, who would kick out of office anyone suggesting any return to Jim Crow even privately administered at one's own hot-dog stand.

What has Bork said that would give to rogue police the right to break down citizens' doors in midnight raids? And while we are at it, when police do break down citizens' doors in midnight raids, what is there inherently to convince us that they are rogue police? Might they be answering a woman's cry against a rapist or a murderer? And what other four Supreme Court justices, and what fifty state legislatures, are going to start a campaign to give license to rogue police?

But this is heady business, this victimology by which some irresponsible men and women prosper. Benjamin Hooks, the head of the National Association for the Advancement of Colored People, who fancies himself engaged in the promotion of toleration in America, proclaims that Bork "would in effect wipe out all of our gains of the past thirty years."

That would be an extraordinary commission. Somebody should inform Teddy Kennedy and Ben Hooks that Bork is not being nominated as dictator of a brand-new country; that the Supreme Court has not overturned a single one of the hundred decisions Bork has written in his five years as a federal judge; and that if, in their nightmare, he were nominated and approved as dictator, Robert Bork would not wish to transform the face of America in the image of Hieronymus Bosch. The voters should be reminded that such as Kennedy and Hooks are heavily engaged in attempting to transform a land of civil and vigorous discourse into a republic of slander. And that slander, which includes the abdication of reason and conscience, is, as Orwell taught, a step on the road to totalitarianism. Kennedy's vituperation of Bork is in a class with Goebbels's vituperation of the Jews.

—July 9, 1987

On Learning from Other Cultures

The prime minister of Pakistan has announced to the legislature, over which he rules supreme, that it is his intention to make the Koran the law of the land, subjecting all aspects of life, from social behavior to civil liberties, to Islamic tenets. If any of the gang at Stanford University who a year ago marched through the campus with Jesse Jackson shouting, "Hey, hey, ho, ho/Western Culture's got to go," wants to pull up roots and move to an Eastern culture, I herewith undertake to raise the plane fare.

Dinesh D'Souza, the talented young critic whose book *Illiberal Education* is causing campus-watchers to stop, look, and listen, has written an illuminating essay for *Policy Review*, the quarterly of the Heritage Foundation. It is called "Multiculturalism 101," and its purpose is to try to help the multiculture hounds out a little bit in their anxiety to reach beyond Western culture for true learning.

He concludes his essay, by the way, by recommending a dozen non-Western texts that are faithful to indigenous foreign cultures and helpful to Westerners who are anxious to cosmopolitanize their knowledge.

Take, for instance, the Koran, which the prime minister has proposed to elevate to Pakistan's equivalent of our Constitution. The Koran stipulates that "Men have authority over women, because Allah has made the one superior to the other." Do the boys and girls at Stanford—and at Michigan, and Brown, and Yale—really wish that the Koran be studied while, oh, British common law be slighted?

D'Souza quotes a renowned Islamic scholar, Ibn Taymiyya, who advises, "When a husband beats his wife for misbehavior, he should not exceed ten lashes." Ten lashes is about what some of us had in mind as appropriate for those at Stanford who succeeded in abolishing the theretofore compulsory courses in Western Culture that are deemed too "Eurocentric." It has yielded to a required course called Cultures, Ideas, and Values.

Having dealt with Islamic codes on women, the pilgrims in search of better ideas than those of our own culture can study the attitudes of others toward homosexuality, since "homophobia" is one of the central targets of the multicentrists.

It would not be wise to study the cultural role of homosexuality in Marxist Cuba, where practitioners are jailed and sometimes executed; in Mao's China, the problem of homosexuality is summarily dealt with by a firing squad.

What the protestors against Western values really have in mind, D'Souza confirms, is to induce a dislike for our own culture. To this end, different cultures are more or less assumed to be superior, but it is very hard to use the term "superior" unless one has a scale of values. For instance, if socialist practice is "superior" to liberalism, then it becomes safe to adduce Marxism as a superior means of social organization.

D'Souza (himself an Indian-American) explains: "Multicultural curricula at Stanford and elsewhere generally reflect little interest in the most enduring, influential, or aesthetically powerful products of non-Western cultures. 'The protestors here weren't interested in building up the anthropology department or immersing themselves in foreign languages,' comments Stanford philosophy instructor Walter Lammi. Alejandro Sweet-Cordero, spokesman for a Chicano group on campus, told the Chronicle of Higher Education, 'We're not saying we need to study Tibetan philosophy. We're arguing that we need to understand what made our society what it is.' Black activist William King says, 'Forget Confucius. We are trying to prepare ourselves for the multicultural challenge we will face in the future. I don't want to study China. I want to study myself.'" William King 101.

A widely used textbook by the hate-Western-ideas folk is called Multicultural Literacy—a book that "devotes virtually no space to the philosophical, religious, and literary classics of China, Japan, Indonesia, India, Persia, the Arab world, Africa, or Latin America. . . . Instead the book includes 13 protest essays, including Michele Wallace's autobiographical 'Invisibility Blues' and Paula Gunn Allen's 'Who Is Your Mother? Red Roots of White Feminism.'"

It is a pity, the whole messy thing, among other reasons because we could all learn from reading classics of other cultures, of which D'Souza mentions a few, beginning with the Hindu scriptures, written in Sanskrit, especially the Upanishads and the Bhagavad Gita, the burden of which is that God must not be sought as a being separate from us, but rather as a sublime force within us, enabling us to rise above our moral limitations.

There are many such works in the realm of multiculturalism, but unless they condemn everything from IQ tests to Reaganomics, they will not satisfy those whose principal aim is to rage, rage against the longevity of the West.

—April 12, 1991

Causing Tears

I very much fear that the joke makers will very quickly make fun of President Bush's performance before the Southern Baptists on Thursday.

It is considered high sport to make fun of a man who breaks into tears, especially if he is a politician. It is generally assumed, and not without reason, that the performance is synthetic. One should begin any reflection on Bush's evidencing tears when he spoke of praying in January, before pulling the final lever on war, that he is not a Huey Long, who could cry on the shortest notice.

(It is somewhere recorded that, reciting a speech written for him by one of his entourage, which speech he had not even read over before delivering it, Long reached a line in which he thought the trace of a tear theatrically appropriate. He engineered that tear without any difficulty, and later on casually commented on his proficiency in these dramaturgical matters.)

George Bush was stunningly eloquent in what he said. It is worth noting here that someone not given to rhetorical virtuosity is potentially more moving than the most finished orator. Li'l Abner, saying just the right thing in just the right way in extraordinary circumstances, might move in ways that even Cato, Henry V, Abraham Lincoln, and Martin Luther King could not. What reaches the listener is the raw agony of the effort to communicate emotion.

What the president of the United States told his audience was that he and his wife prayed together before he made the final decision to send Americans into battle, and in some cases to their deaths. As he recalled that on that evening in January he had broken into tears, tears came freshly to his face. Quickly he disposed of them—but, questioned on the airplane later, he did not deny them. He said that the decision had been one that tore at his emotions, and (he said this clumsily, which was reassuring) in describing his feelings on that historic night, once again he was moved to tears.

Whittaker Chambers wrote to me in 1959, "American men, who weep in droves in movie houses, over the woes of lovestruck shopgirls, hold that weeping in men is unmanly. I have found most men in whom there was depth of experience, or capacity for compassion, singularly apt to tears. How can it be otherwise? One looks and sees; and it would be a kind of impotence to be incapable of, or to grudge, the comment of tears, even while you struggle against them. I am immune to soap opera. But I cannot listen for any length of time to the speaking voice of Kirsten Flagstad, for example, without being done in by that magnificence of tone that seems to speak from the center of sorrow, even from the center of the earth."

When, during the presidential primary campaign in 1972, Senator Edmund Muskie broke into tears in frustration over an ugly libel against his wife and was then and there judged unfit for presidential office by the taste makers, I sent him that passage from Chambers, so blindingly beautiful, so incandescently true (though never having heard Kirsten Flagstad speak, I can say only that hearing her singing voice was a tremulous experience).

It is recorded that the night that Harry Truman authorized the *Enola Gay* to drop an atomic bomb on Hiroshima, he had his usual hearty dinner and went calmly to bed. It is admirable that Truman weighed the considerations and (characteristically) moved decisively, without any compunction about wrongdoing. But one must suppose that Abraham Lincoln—and George Bush—would have spent the night less calmly.

I am required to confess that the above is in part self-serving. I have never condemned soldiers to action and possible death, but I have sometimes been given the assignment of eulogist, and I remember two occasions when I was not able to finish words I had myself crafted, summoning as they did to the author of those words the palpable images of the men whose death I was mourning. I admire, but could not imitate, a man whose lachrymal glands could stand up against a eulogy over a departed child.

Milton wrote an elegy to a young man dead, and Bach wrote music searingly beautiful, his own tribute to a departed brother. One must suppose that Milton wept over his poetry, and Bach over his music.

George Bush's tears lent that special gravity that properly attaches to the act of condemning human beings to death. I can't believe that those soldiers who, on the following day, would march in triumph in Washington and, later, in New York would think any less of their president, who was willing to recall the devout experience on the night he acted as commander in chief, speaking from the center of sorrow.

—June 7, 1991

Chins Up! Be Personly!

Perhaps it is a Freudian effort to block out the news from Bosnia, Cambodia, and Haiti, but one does occasionally focus on the little oppressions. It may seem trivial in a genocidal season to bring it up, but there are some of us who are being driven nuts by the feminist assault on the language.

To the question, "Do you prefer to retain the beauty of the language? Or do you want to go the last inning on women's rights?" one is tempted to use Jack Benny's reply: "I'm thinking."

There is of course no reason the integrity of the language and women's rights should be mutually exclusive, and there is no reason to doubt that the majority of women who have ears themselves deeply resent what is being demanded in their name. But as is so often the case, the most strident get the attention, and people who like to think of themselves as sensitive to human rights are quick to yield. They do so without giving any serious thought to what they are doing. What they are doing is, pure and simple, helping to ruin the language.

When two years ago I first happened upon a directive from the editors of the *Yale Daily News* to the effect that henceforward first-year students would be referred to as "freshpersons," I concluded that some pubescent fanatic had got hold of the editor's chair, but that he was bound to grow up in a month or two.

But last weekend I discovered, reading the commencement issue, that "freshpersons" is now standard usage in the paper, though I caught one lapse into "freshpeople." One would be tempted to say that boys will be boys, but that is of course excluded under the current protocols, leaving us with what? Young persons will be young persons? The flavor of that will get you a diet Popsicle.

The day before, at a forum on race relations, attention focused on the master of ceremonies. Charles Ogletree is a distinguished black professor of law at Harvard, whose skills as a parliamentarian and moderator put him in great demand on the circuit to protect the audience from discursive speakers. He was introducing one of the participants, William Gray, president of the United Negro College Fund, and until recently a senior member of Congress.

So Professor Ogletree introduces Mr. Gray as a "prominent spokesperson for the Afro-American community." But you look at Mr. Gray, and listen to Mr. Gray. He is a perfectly normal, virile, middle-aged male, a foundation executive and a doctor of divinity. Why suddenly does he have to be a "spokesperson"?

It has got to be because Professor Ogletree fears that to introduce him as a "spokesman" would offend. Would offend whom? Mr. Gray didn't come in drag, so what would he be trying to conceal that requires him to be designated as a "person" in order to avoid the word "man"?

The tyranny offends at all levels. The *Wall Street Journal* recently attracted attention to a proposed new English version of the Bible. Luke 17:33 has for a few hundred years read, "He who seeks to save his life will lose it, but he who loses his life will save it." To replace that lustrous sentence the new barbarians have come up with, "Those who try to make their life secure will lose it, but those who lose their life will keep it."

That whole thing, for the sole purpose of burying the word "his." It would be preferable to substitute "her" for "his" and let the poetry go on.

Or we go to Genesis 9:6: "Whoever sheds the blood of man, by man shall his blood be shed; for God made man in his own image." Brace yourself. That now reads, "Whoever sheds the blood of a human, by a human shall that person's blood be shed; for in his own image, God made humankind." It must have required a summit meeting of church leaders to consent to use the word "his" before image, which would suggest that it's still OK to refer to God as "him."

And then there is the "him or her" business, which is increasingly hard to avoid. "The new law authorizes the DEA to confiscate his car." Oh no. "Confiscate his or her car." Either you do that, or you avoid pronouns altogether, and come up with something like, "The new law authorizes the DEA to confiscate the cars of drug offenders." Som distinguished stylists are going the his/her route, though it convulses the brain to try to understand why people should take offense at the inclusive "his" or "man."

"Man was born free, but everywhere he is in chains." You can say that again. These are the chains of the Lilliputian Amazons of verbal correctness, who have besieged and threaten to corrupt the English language, one of the great glories of personkind.

—May 27, 1993

Life in the Nineties

I long ago noted an article by James Michener in the *New York Times* making the point that longevity would become the primary social problem of the twentieth century, let alone the twenty-first.

We became friends, and walking together the ten-block distance from the press hotel in Beijing to the Great Hall of the People on a cold day in February 1972, to witness President Nixon's celebratory opening of the gates to China, I asked Michener how old he was. Sixty-five, he said.

Twenty-four years later—last week—I have a card from him. It is a printed message. It says merely that he would not wish his friends to think he had forgotten about them.

It is so with the very old, the problem of staying in touch. I was encouraged by his family to telephone Malcolm Muggeridge on his eighty-fifth birthday. He acknowledged in a light, hoarse voice his pleasure at my calling, and then said: "You know, I will not write to you. I am too old."

What are we to make of the diehards? In the last short season I have been closely in touch with four men and women who are more than ninety years old.

One of them was for twenty years the editor of the weekly with the largest circulation in the world. I dined with him in Paris a fortnight ago, and he reiterated his single sorrow, that his (beloved) wife had died before him.

The most touching of all the Greek legends tells of Philemon and Baucis, who though old and destitute admitted into their cottage and nourished a god who came to their door posing as a beggar. In due course Zeus revealed himself, irradiating sparks of Olympian divinity, and announced that in return for their disinterested charity they could request of him any favor they chose.

There was one only wish, said Philemon: that when the time came, they should die simultaneously. With a gentle stroke of his caduceus, the god transformed the aged couple into two trees, whose branches fondled one another in winter, their leaves nestling in the spring.

That is not a solution—simultaneous deaths—we can easily handle. A few years ago Arthur Koestler and his wife, Cynthia, twenty years his junior, were found sitting upright in their living room in London, dead from self-administered poison. They had decided, a document they had left revealed, that neither wished to survive the other. When Koestler got his negative reading from the doctor, with its conclusive prognosis, they enacted their vow. I pause to recall the evening of their wedding day, spent with me and their best man, James Burnham, aboard my little sailboat in the Hudson River.

Such thoughts bring to mind, of course, the Kevorkian alternative. The Koestlers took it; James Michener has not. Nor has my editor friend in Paris, or my retired lawyer in Connecticut, or my retired secretary in San Francisco, or my retired music teacher in Katonah, N.Y. It is a swelling statistic, the surviving ninety-year-old.

My mother died on the eve of her ninetieth birthday, and senility had set in. She was quite content in her spacious quarters at the old people's home. (She was under the impression that she owned the whole establishment.)

No such mental lapse has afflicted my four ninety-year-old friends who, although they lament the biological corollaries of old age, cannot complain about any deterioration in their minds.

Well, yes. My lawyer had to reach, on a recent visit, to recall a relevant Supreme Court decision in 1914. My music teacher can't manipulate her fingers as once she did to create her magical improvisations. My secretary tells me she uses the typewriter only to write to me, but hasn't the physical strength to use it regularly, let alone to take her long, habitual walks.

My friend in Paris is jubilant about his material arrangements: He has what they term a reverse mortgage. You deed your house/apartment to a bank. That bank pays your taxes, maintains your property, pays the maid and the cleaning woman. When you die, the house is the bank's. The bank wins if you pull out early; it loses if you go on and on. My friend told me about a Parisian woman who had made such an arrangement at age seventy-six and lived to age 121, having impoverished her late banker.

There are those who believe that suicide—euthanasia—is not the right answer, tempting though it can be. How much of life did Cynthia Koestler deprive herself of, in her act of love?

But James Michener's premonition is correct. Old age is the looming problem of the civilization that has discovered the keys to longevity.

—*March 19, 1996*

The People Aren't Always Right

We ought to be a little careful on the matter of the popularity ratings of President Clinton. In almost any match between the people and their intellectual leaders, it is wise to bet with the former. But the temptation to make a rule out of this preference is dangerous, and something of that order is happening when you hear it said (increasingly) that the approval ratings of Mr. Clinton are dispositive: If the people don't care—what business do *you* have caring?

The majority, in democratic practice, is powerful enough to tell us who will serve in the White House and in Congress. The founders of course recognized the dangers of impulsive democracy, which is why it takes a lot of agitation to amend the Constitution. Now, on the matter of the behavior of the president, two questions are asked. The first, Do the people believe he is not guilty, or do they just not care? The second, How grave is the offense with which he is charged?

Under oath, Mr. Clinton contradicted his 1992 statement affirming his innocence of an affair with Gennifer Flowers. Yes, he now says, he did it: once. The popular assumption is I think correct, namely that if a president is re-elected, something on the order of a plenary indulgence is effected, which holds him harmless, as of the day of the election, from responsibility for previous crimes and misdemeanors. The Paula Jones lawsuit isn't disturbed by this assumption, inasmuch as hers is a civil suit. What now happens becomes a matter of congressional concern only if the jury finds for Jones, the result of which is a perjury count for Clinton.

But here, surely, a reservation should be indulged. Peter Galbraith, retiring ambassador to Croatia, shrewdly pointed out in January that it is careless to distinguish between the offense of adultery and the offense of lying about it, inasmuch as the second offense goes hand in hand with the first. Anyone who commits adultery is expected to lie about it. Indeed, the point can be made persuasively that it is dishonorable not to lie about it.

But what is happening around the president transcends one (or one hundred) nights out with Gennifer Flowers, or a wild bout of exhibitionism with Paula Jones. The architecture of his defense betrays his weakness and demeans democratic practice. He refuses for weeks on end to discuss his entanglement with Monica Lewinsky—other than to deny it, and leave the world wondering why she visited with him thirty-seven times. Now he has pleaded executive privilege to hide from the scrutiny of justice such testimony as members of his staff might provide. The Supreme Court will overrule him, but the effort, in the light of the precedent of Richard Nixon, is itself contumacious, a sign of contempt for the law and its processes.

Now at what point do the people inform, or cease to inform, Congress in these matters? Suppose the people, sending signals to their representatives and to their senators, tell them: No matter what he does, don't impeach Mr. Clinton. Then the question becomes, Should Congress be governed by those signals?

It is always relevant to ask what the moral perspective is in any situation. It is presumptuous to assume that we are keener moral spirits than the men who wrote the Constitution just because unlike them we would not tolerate slavery. The key is perspective: In a world in which slavery was commonplace, it was the prophet who cried out against it, not the people or their institutions. It required a civil war with more than half a million dead to change that perspective, and even then what changed at first was the law, not the moral understanding of the obligations of equality, given that we are all creatures of God.

It is not inconceivable, at some point ahead, that we will be asking ourselves: What is the matter with the general public? Why does it not understand the gravity of what is happening? W. B. Yeats wrote a letter, back in the Thirties, to a Dublin daily that had published serial criticisms of the mayor of Dublin, the most recent of which had asked, "What has the Lord Mayor of Dublin recently done to commend himself to the people of Dublin?"

Yeats's letter read, "What have the people of Dublin recently done to commend themselves to the Lord Mayor?"

The impending situation is not to be compared with the popular approval given in our time to such as Hitler, Mussolini, and Perón. But we are properly reminded by those data that from time to time it is appropriate to wonder about the judgment of the people.

—March 24, 1998

Royal Pastimes

The talk of the wedding planned by the Prince of Wales and Camilla Parker Bowles seems mostly genial. For a while, some observers thought it would not come off; but they were wrong, it seems. After April 8, when the wedding takes place (it would be provincial to say, after the wedding is "consummated"), the Prince of Wales will get on with his duties, married to Her Royal Highness the Duchess of Cornwall.

But when he ascends the throne, he will be Defender of the Faith ("Fidei Defensor"), like his mother, the present queen. And indeed like every British monarch dating back to 1521, when the title was conferred by Pope Leo X on King Henry VIII, in appreciation of the king's rejection of Martin Luther's schism. Little did the pope know what the Defender of the Faith would go on to do, but the honorific stayed on through the Protestantization of Great Britain. The full title of the British sovereign once included Emperor of India. The time came, after the Second World War, when decolonization set in. King George VI had to abandon India, but he did not abandon the Faith.

There are temporal responsibilities held formally by the Crown. Prince Charles will, like his mother, be the head of the Church of England. His prospective ascendancy has been troubling because of the marital situation.

In brief, Charles was captivated, in 1970, by Camilla. On meeting him, she said, "My great-grandmother was your great-great-grandfather's mistress." But three years later she married Major Andrew Parker Bowles. They had children, but to make it clear that the close friendship survived, the son of that union was christened with Prince Charles serving as godfather. Parker Bowles even accepted the title (if you can bear it) of Silver Stick in Waiting to the prince. Anybody who will do that for the prince will do anything, and indeed Major Parker Bowles was quickly cuckolded, without apparent objection, though he and Camilla eventually got divorced.

Meanwhile, Charles had married Diana, who was soon complaining about her husband's double life. But she of course died in 1997, so that the decks were partly cleared. But Major Parker Bowles didn't die, so that Camilla is a divorced woman with a living husband, and the rules had been for a very long time rather firm. Kings could sleep around, but not marry divorcees, as Edward VIII discovered, forfeiting his crown.

Now there lingers the problem of the auspices of the forthcoming wedding. Well, it will be a civil ceremony. Queen Elizabeth is not about to exercise her power to simply repeal the prohibition against marriage to a divorced person. But the surrounding benignity of the whole scene incorporates the archbishop of Canterbury. He has to deny his premises to the couple, but he will have a special Christian service of "prayer and dedication" at St. George's Chapel in Windsor.

The two princelings have joined the chorus of well-wishers, issuing a joint statement: "We are both very happy for our father and Camilla and we wish them all the luck in the future." That's the kind of send-off one might have expected if Charles and Camilla had had an entry in the Derby.

But "luck" replaces other forms of equipoise, when princes take mistresses, mistresses shed families, queens dither in the matter of royal respectability, titles are contrived—Princess of Wales, no; Duchess of Cornwall, OK—and life goes on.

Is it jerky to ask, What article of faith is the Crown in the business of defending? If the solemnity of marriage isn't an article of faith, what is? Granted that British sovereigns have indulged in wayward romance. It is striking that Henry VIII declined this alternative to marital union. His way of doing it was simply to discard a wife (retire her, or execute her) and take on another wife. So that at least one could maintain that he defended the faith by having only one queen at a time.

The evanescence of the practice of Christianity in Europe is in contrast to the huge enrolments in the faith in the Third World. If present trends continue, author Philip Jenkins calculates in his recent book, *The Next Christendom*, by 2025 there will be 633 million Christians in Africa, 640 million in South America, and 460 million in Asia.

Whether faith in the Third World will flower in orthodoxy isn't predictable, though we had a flavor of doctrinal contention in 1998 when, at the Lambeth Conference of the world's Anglican bishops, the powerful bishop of Nigeria and other Third World bishops flatly refused to condone homosexual ordinations. That defiance was met by Episcopal Bishop John Shelby Spong of Newark, who explained that African Christianity had "moved out of animism into a very superstitious kind of Christianity," warning against "irrational Pentecostal hysteria." Yes, but how to explain the hysterical doctrines of Abraham and Moses and Christ?

—February 11, 2005

KO by Michael

The reaction was different from the reaction to the bizarre exoneration of O. J. Simpson in 1995. In the matter of O.J., the jury hardly paused before entering a verdict of not guilty. This time around, with Michael Jackson, it was seven days of deliberation, though the final result did not suggest any schismatic bodies holding out for a guilty verdict.

And—truly important—the race question wasn't a factor. Incredibly, there was not, seated, a single black juror. Those who followed the trial only by hearing the occasional radio bleat while driving were surprised that racial prejudice wasn't brought up more insistently by Michael Jackson's supporters. One can only imagine the hue and cry on this subject if Jackson had been found guilty. The defense of O.J. was based blatantly on alleged racial discrimination. A useful concise view of it is that if O.J. had been white, he almost certainly would have been convicted.

Now a big difficulty with Michael Jackson has to do with what the jurors were being asked to convict him for doing. One of his first hit songs at the superstar level, twenty-six years ago, was called, "Don't Stop 'til You Get Enough." Nice young men would not utter such sentiments except in smokers. Certainly they would not bid for market approval with a song so titled. Jackson not only did so, he was awarded a Grammy for it. Such data persuaded the jury that Jackson had to be thought of as a man whose life was of another culture.

As to this, there was evidence writ large on the public screen. Jackson has lived as extravagantly as any sheik. His palace is a great extravaganza fashioned after children's dreams. He managed to marry twice, but those who heard him discuss home life with Lisa Marie Presley quickly and accurately predicted that that wedding had been one more act in a serial drama. The marriage lasted eighteen months, slightly longer than the subsequent marriage, which resulted in two children and divorce. A television interviewer scratched around the subject of conjugal life, but was easily disposed of by Michael and Lisa Marie, whose onstage affection was so ardent, there were those who wondered whether their managers had instructed them to give viewers a little public copulation.

But the Jackson jury was not asked to inquire deeply into what kind of life is expected of a forty-six-year-old superstar who at age twenty enjoined his listeners, "Don't Stop 'til You Get Enough." Some people, we know, tend to behave differently from other people. The point the poor prosecutor was trying to make was that this is indeed so, but unorthodox behavior can became aberrant behavior and, in the case of Michael Jackson, did so when he invited young boys into his bed, which is where aberrant behavior usually happens.

The Jackson team brought in a few boys and their families who insisted that overnight in Michael's bed was like overnight in a laundromat. This proposition suffered from Michael's experience of 1993. What happened then was that an outraged mother filed a suit alleging felonious pedophilia. But before any jurors were canvassed on that charge, the case disappeared from the dockets. There had been a settlement. Different figures were cited. Most recently, in the *New York Times*, it was reported that Jackson Inc. paid $20 million to the plaintiff, who agreed never to mention the case again under any circumstances; so that when the prosecutor in this trial tried to get the mother or her son to talk about past life in close quarters with Michael, there was a stone wall there.

But although that story counted against Michael's credibility, the prosecution was hampered by a complementary aspect of life in that culture. Growing up as a plaything of Michael at Neverland suddenly opened up the possibility of $20 million. The jurors could certainly understand that the moment had to come when Michael's team said no—no more payoffs. But though such thinking argued for the integrity of Michael, it also provoked legitimate curiosity as to why the suits were brought in the first place.

And—finally—the kind of horror aroused within cultural orthodoxy by tales of dirty old men taking the innocence of little boys didn't seem to have the iron hold on the jury that would have been expected even a few years ago. There is at least one organization that pleads publicly for permitting man-boy love. What is indisputably happening is that child prostitution has become all but a Yellow Pages item. And these jurors, while by no means identifying themselves with this particular new age, were apparently never stirred to the point of feeling any responsibility to do their bit to discourage it.

—June 14, 2005

So Help Us Darwin

An intimidatingly learned colleague has written to a few friends to deplore the latest bulletin on Senator John McCain, who is of course running for president. The news is that McCain has agreed to speak at a luncheon hosted by the Discovery Institute in Seattle. What offends my friend is that the think tank in question supports the concept of intelligent design. And the question raised—believe it or not—is whether someone so latitudinarian as to associate with such an organization should be thought qualified to be president of the United States.

It seems an ancient controversy, and of course it is. Fifteen minutes after Charles Darwin explained his theory of evolution, his disciples—apostles—ruled out any heresy on the subject of the naturalist explanation for human life. Young people are educated to think of the question in the grammar of the Scopes trial, Clarence Darrow vs. William Jennings Bryan. That trial made for great naturalist theater. Mr. Bryan was not born either to become president or to explain how God could tolerate chicken pox, so Clarence Darrow ground him into dust.

But the contention continued, and has been explored from time to time under heavy lights. My own forensic involvement took place nine years ago as host of *Firing Line*. The two-hour, nationally televised debate on the topic "Resolved: The evolutionists should acknowledge creation" featured seven professors. Four of them took the establishmentarian scientific position. It is, essentially, that not only is naturalism established as verified science, but any interposition into the picture—of inquisitiveness, let alone conviction that there might have been design in the evolution of our world—is excluded.

But that was a tough night for those who hoped that the lunacy of creationist thought would prove self-evident. The evolutionists had to contend with, for instance, Phillip E. Johnson, professor emeritus of law at the University of California at Berkeley, who wrote the book *Darwin on Trial* and then *Defeating Darwinism by Opening Minds*.

In outlining epochal events in this quarrel, Johnson quoted the official directive on teaching evolution as it appeared in the 1995 position statement of the National Association of Biology Teachers. "The diversity of life on earth is the outcome of evolution: an unsupervised, impersonal, unpredictable and natural process."

Please note, said Professor Johnson, that two years later the board of that association dropped the words "unsupervised" and "impersonal." The meaning of it being that hard scientific research has taken from the evolutionary position not its authenticity—no one can argue with much of its description of what happened in the development of man—but its title to exclusivity. To prove absolutely that an apple, dropped from above Johnny's head, will fall down on it is not the equivalent of proving that no extrinsic force had a hand in setting up that gravitational exercise.

Johnson's objections have to do with separating real science from the materialist philosophy that provides "the only support for Darwinist theory."

The questions are profound, and the arguments subtle. It is not reasonably expected of Senator McCain, or any other contender for the presidency, that in his public appearances he will explicate all the conundrums.

But the intelligent liberal community should not impose on anyone a requirement of believing that there is only the single, materialist word on the subject, and that only contempt is merited by those who consent to appear at think tanks composed of men and women prepared to explore ultimate questions, which certainly include the question, Did God have a hand in creating all of this? Including the great messes we live with?

Representing the affirmative that night on television, one debater closed with this: "I'm taken with the reply of an elderly scientific scholar to an exuberant young skeptic: 'I find it easier to believe in God than to believe that Hamlet was deduced from the molecular structure of a mutton chop.'"

—February 16, 2007

FAITH AND THE FAITHFUL

The Catholic in the Modern World: A Conservative View

O*pening statement from a debate with William Clancy, former editor of* Commonweal

I am not aware what point of departure Mr. Clancy will take in getting into the subject of this debate, nor is he aware what will be my point of departure. We simply took it as an act of faith that we would end up disagreeing with each other, and both Mr. Clancy's faith and my own are strong; with perhaps the difference that I go so far as to have faith that Mr. Clancy will one day be liberated from the superstitions of liberalism, whereas he doesn't believe I shall ever be saved from the truths of conservatism—so that perhaps it can be said my faith is stronger than his.

We must necessarily be arbitrary. The problems of the modern world cannot be enumerated, let alone analyzed, in twenty minutes. I am the student who is asked to write a ten-minute paper on the results of the French Revolution; and must, necessarily, fail the test. I can do no better, I suggest, than simply to speak out loud some of the thoughts that crowd the mind of one American Catholic conservative as he faces an evening by the fireside with Mr. Clancy.

Let us try to understand what lies behind the human and organizational associations of liberal Catholics in this country. Why is it that the liberal Catholic is on easy terms with everybody in America on his left, saving only the Communists? Go through one hundred issues of *Commonweal*—to name a single but wholly representative journal of liberal Catholic opinion—and you are not likely to find a sustained criticism of any left American or left proposal. If the figure on the left is a Catholic, he is almost sure to be immune—as Dorothy Day, for instance, is. I am not suggesting that *Commonweal* is secretly sympathetic to the grotesqueries that go into making up the Catholic Worker movement: but I am struck by the significance of the fact that *Commonweal* does not criticize, let alone anathematize, the slovenly, reckless, intellectually chaotic, anti-Catholic doctrines of this good-hearted woman—who, did she have her way in shaping national policy, would test the promise of Christ Himself, that the gates of Hell shall not prevail against us. Miss Day is off to the left almost out of sight, granted; but between her and the editors of *Commonweal* are multitudinous others who would the seas incarnadine: socialists, pacifists, fellow-travelers, secularists, utopians, positivists, freethinkers: and it is their company in which the Catholic liberal—or perhaps better, the liberal Catholic—moves with such disturbing ease.

For those on the right it is a very different matter. I should not want to name, and perhaps embarrass, those eminent men who have suffered the smart and the indignities that the disfavor of the American Catholic Left brings. I think of one man whom I cannot embarrass, for he is dead. It is well known that the liberal Catholic community is engaged in a fervent effort to forget the existence of Father James Gillis, an effort in which his own order is sedulously cooperating.

The hard opposition, the contempt, the bitterness, is directed—usually covertly, sometimes openly—at members of the American Right. I think of Mr. William Shannon as an expressive symbol: Here is a bright and learned and articulate Catholic who, from the togetherness of the *New York Post*, where he sits with secular socialists, with Freudians, determinists, and pacifists, looses his thunderbolts at the McCarthys, McCarrans, and Manions of the contemporary scene. Here is a man who visits his blistering animadversions upon almost every member of the Right, while the devil's ragbaby himself, assuming he came up from the Left—which he would—could get close enough to pour sand in his typewriter before engaging the unfriendly attention of William Shannon.

Why? For profound reasons. I think a study of the habits and attitudes, social and polemical, of many liberal Catholic intellectuals reveals an intellectual and social insecurity; a sense of embarrassment with the insufficiency of the Church and its laity to work out an adequate social experience. That uneasiness is primarily a reflection of our society's general ignorance of the Catholic tradition. It is widely held that when the civilized world was mostly Catholic, there was only darkness. We know that is not so. But I venture to say that the devil-view of Catholic history has ended up influencing not merely fundamentalist Baptists, but also highly intelligent Catholics, who, though they themselves know the raw facts of history, tend to lose their perspective, and so are conditioned to construct the facts upon an alien paradigm; just as it has become almost impossible in our country for even those who know the facts of the controversy surrounding Senator McCarthy to escape altogether the construction of them that history is inexorably imposing upon us. I have the impression that many of my friends on the Catholic Left are worn haggard by the ghost of the Inquisition; that they cannot forget that the metaphorical meaning of such words as "jesuitical" and "inquisitorial" has now, through centuries of usage as metaphor, come to be the prime meaning of the words. These men grope for reassurance by seeking a symbiotic relationship with the Left, and by propitiating the liberals with an imprudent and incontinent enthusiasm for progressive nostrums, for radical social experimentation, of the kind that wins for them (they think) that long-sought-for recognition as men identified with the Future, not the past; with Progress, not reaction.

One has to rely very heavily of course on impression. In suggesting that typical liberal Catholic intellectuals suffer from an inferiority complex that impels them to do and say strange things, I cannot promise a case that will satisfy Mr. Clancy; any more than one can prove to the wallflower that she is not enjoying herself. In suggesting that the liberal Catholic intellectuals have surrendered the leadership of the City of God to secular millenarians because these Catholics are ignorant of, or afraid to canvass, the great internal resources of their own Church, I say things that cannot go on a blackboard; but which are nevertheless so. About certain types of things one does not tend to talk out loud. In searching out a person's prejudices, let us cock our ear to the casual, unguarded inflection, rather than seek out rigid externalization. It is easier to judge whether a Catholic is ill at ease intellectually or politically or socially in a non-Catholic society by observing his mannerisms, his rhetoric, his style, than by analyzing the arguments he makes.

I suggest that leading American Catholic intellectuals are embarrassed, as I have said, by the understanding of the Church's history that is a part of the patrimony of our Protestant society; by the commonplace identification of Catholicism with reaction; by recurrent political phenomena such as the conspicuous support extended in this country by the Catholic population to such men as General MacArthur, Senator McCarthy, and Senator McCarran; and by the fact that there has not developed in America a Catholic intellectual or social aristocracy influential enough to earn the admiration of the whole society. (Though we are probably not, alas, more than a few days away from the inauguration of a Catholic political aristocracy.)

This embarrassment manifests itself in several ways. There is the grouchy ill humor shown not only to rightist Catholics, but also to distinctively Catholic social conventions. Members of the Catholic Left shy away from many forms of organized Catholic activity, regarding them as totemist, and vulgar. They do not gravitate easily, for instance, to Communion breakfasts (though, in all fairness, Communion breakfasts do not gravitate easily to them). Instead of attempting to enrich the cultural forms that have grown out of the experience of their religion within the American culture, they shrink from them. That insecurity manifests itself in an abrupt impatience with a particular set of political positions, most especially those that, through the facile drawing of false parallels, permit the enemies of Catholicism to emphasize the social dangers of our religion. In the years since the war, we have all been touched, in some way or another, by the controversy, sometimes violent, over the question of the national security. Opponents of a tough federal security program were quick to label virtually any effort to pursue such a program as "inquisitorial." Every time that word was used, Mr. Clancy would wince. To escape having to wince, some of our friends fell thoughtlessly into line, and began dispensing alarmist clichés about our Reign of Terror and waning liberties.

Let me be clearly understood: There is good reason to deplore the fact of the Inquisition; but there is no reason that I can see for crediting the notion, so sedulously advanced in recent years, that there is a kinship that reaches out over the centuries to link the activities of a Torquemada with the activities of a Senator McCarran. Thus, in judging the activities of Senator McCarran, it was not necessary to do so under the shadow of the Inquisition.

The complex I speak of manifests itself in a deep sensitivity to charges of social or intellectual conformity. Thus, these Catholics can be heard inveighing with unsettling vehemence against any effort to exact, by the use of social or intellectual sanction, a consensus of values, a conformity however broad—even a conformity tight enough to exclude Communism.

The Catholics I speak of are, it seems to me, so frightened that the society in which they live should find grounds for plausibly suggesting that the Catholics seek, ultimately, to wed Church and State that they put up, in opposition to secular education, only a token resistance. I do not know of a greater injustice than that which Catholics at large seem willing forever to tolerate: the taxation of Catholics for the support of schools in which it is forbidden, by a most tortuous judicial invention woven around the First Amendment, to teach religion. These Catholics—again, I am certain, because of their anxiety to abate the suspicions of the liberal intellectuals—are much more easily mobilized by the issue of racial segregation in the schools in the South. They are prepared to smite Jim Crow hip and thigh—while allowing to go virtually undisputed the central challenge to freedom involved in forbidding a family to insist upon religious instruction for its children in a tax-supported public school.

The complex manifests itself, finally, in an irresistible fascination with "forward-looking" social schemes and grand designs for remaking the world. The uncritical acceptance, by some Catholic men and women, of the dizzier postulates of world government and the redistribution of wealth sometimes appears to stem from that obsessive anxiety to please. What is more, a prodigious and perhaps even sacrilegious effort is made to bring the authority of the Church behind such programs. Father George Dunne will tell you that Leo XIII meant to condemn not programmatic socialism, but merely philosophical socialism; that the political and economic program of Christian Socialism is, mutatis mutandis, the Word of the Lord. Donald MacDonald, a febrile Catholic liberal, will tell you with apodictical finality that the Church believes in world government, and disbelieves in Senator McCarthy.

I have a feeling that in the course of uttering some of the more florid passages advocating guaranteed annual wages, and world government, and water fluoridation, and one hundred years of foreign aid, and the repeal of the Smith Act, liberal Catholic intellectuals have half an eye trained over there in the direction of Paul Blanshard, to whom they are saying, wistfully, "See, Mr. Blanshard, we're really not that bad. We are progressive liberals. We are, to be sure, fellow communicants with the editors of the Brooklyn *Tablet*, but ours is necessarily a universal Church. Forgive them, for they know not what they do. And bear in mind, although we are Catholics, we are politically and socially assimilable within a democratic society. Pray, do not misunderstand us."

If what I say is true, the Catholics in question are among other things wasting a lot of time. Their first mistake stems from the notion that Paul Blanshard—I use him, of course, as a symbol—is a human being, and hence persuadable and, by the grace of God, mortal. He is not. Paul Blanshard is an institution. He is simply the latest and most talkative practitioner of the ancient profession of anti-Catholicism; the representative of the New Nativism. Anti-Catholicism is the anti-Semitism of the highbrow, Peter Viereck reminds us. Such men as Paul Blanshard are always with us. And they will not be satisfied by political or economic concessions. They are satisfied only by the surrender of dogma (and this the Catholics of whom I speak of course have no intention of doing). For them the only good Catholic is the ex-Catholic. Paul Blanshard may speak about Father Dunne with a certain tolerance he would not show in speaking of Father Gillis; but deep within him he feels that Father Dunne is as inextricably caught up in philosophical and authoritarian benightedness as is Father Gillis, and hence, when all is said and done, is—like Father Gillis—an enemy of a good democratic, secular society. And Blanshard is correct. Father Dunne is a learned and civilized man, and a minister of the Faith. Such a man has difficulty, at the margin, coexisting with Mr. Blanshard.

~

I do not mean to imply that it becomes the Catholic to move about his society with a sense of personal infallibility which itself more surely than anything else would undermine the whole meaning of the Catholic faith. He must be quick to acknowledge error, and he must be personally humble, and personally kind, and personally tolerant. But he should not take up a position for any reason other than that he finds the position itself valid, and compelling. And he should, I believe, train himself to show more toleration for his co-religionists than he sometimes tends to show. I have not seen more bitter criticism of certain Catholics than by other Catholics. And I don't mean criticism focused on a Catholic's failure to do his duty as a Catholic; I mean criticism of a Catholic in his political or economic life, in an area where controversy and differences of opinion are possible within the framework of Christian principles. It is the responsibility of the Catholic, it would appear to me, to be tolerant not only toward Protestants and Jews, but also toward Catholics; even Catholics on the right.

And so I ask:

— Do we really need to rely on the thinking of the Fund for the Republic and Arden House to guide us toward a solution to modern problems? Or can we look into our own vast resources, which reject, root and branch, the animating prejudices of our secular scholarship?

— It is suggested that we must be prepared to coexist with the Soviet Union. That certainly is the position of our secular political leadership. Is it the position—to the extent that there can ever be "a" position—of the Catholic laity? I say it is our principal responsibility to search out means by which to hasten the dissolution of Communist society.

— It is suggested that our principal responsibility with respect to the Negro is to bring him civil rights. Should civil rights, political rights, be the object of our primary concern? I say it is not established that the promulgation of the Negro's civil rights at the recommended speed will help him to save his soul. Are the two enterprises, indeed, related? If so, how?

— Are we so sure that the free market has been anachronized by our industrialized society? It is widely held by the liberal Catholics that the concept of the just price as described by the Scholastics is the theological authority behind the welfare state. I venture to say that the scholarship of those who make this contention turns out to be defective, and that it is established that the principles of the free market were endorsed by a preponderance of the thought of Scholasticism.

— Are we so sure that the development of the labor-union movement in the United States is in harmony with the ideal of community enunciated by the recent popes; that the labor unions are the modern counterparts of the ancient guilds, which allegedly spared the Middle Ages the ravages of capitalism and monopoly (though in fact they served a different function entirely)? I suggest that the labor-union movement is nowadays feeding on the common good; that in fact there appears to be an apprehension of this in the Vatican; that labor unions, or many of them, show dehumanizing tendencies which bring into question whether, in their present form, they are a social force we should encourage.

— What is the proper authority of the popes and the bishops? Is it, as Senator Kennedy would have us believe, virtually nonexistent in political matters? The bishops of Ohio came out against right-to-work laws in 1958. Did they have the right to do so? Were they prudent in doing so? What is the force of their authority—on us, or on Senator Kennedy? Were the bishops of Puerto Rico correct in coming out against the election of Muñoz Marín? Is the manifesto of the 166 American Catholic intellectuals published some weeks ago—in the drafting of which my learned adversary, Mr. Clancy, played a prominent role—correct in suggesting that interference by the Church with Senator Kennedy's freedom of movement as president is inconceivable? Is Jacques Maritain correct in saying it is intolerable for any Catholic to "claim to speak in the name of Catholicism and imply that all Catholics as such should follow their road"? Or are the writers of *Commonweal, America,* and *The Catholic World* right in telling me, as so many of them are so fond of doing, what to think?

— Are we so certain that there is a consensus among theologians on the true nature of the state? Is it indeed primarily the seat of justice? It is held nowadays that the state must exercise almost infinite authority, that being what it takes to do the work that is needed, to cope with the problems of the day. I say that in forwarding the statist solution we have not adequately reflected on the history of man's experience with the state; nor have we pondered the classic and dissenting definitions and analyses of St. Augustine and Cardinal Newman, each in his day the principal Catholic thinker of the age.

I suggest, in closing, that Mr. Clancy and the school he represents have latched onto a fundamentally alien movement. They will never Catholicize it, alas, and it remains to ask, What will it do to them? *Oremus.*

—*Commonweal*, December 16, 1960

The End of the Latin Mass

In January of this year my sister died, age forty-nine, the eldest of ten children, and mother of ten children, the lot of us catapulted into a dumb grief whence we sought relief by many means, principal among them the conviction, now reified by desire, that our separation from her is impermanent. It was the moment to recall not merely the promises of Christ, but their magical cogency; the moment to remind ourselves as forcefully as we knew how of the depths of the Christian experience, of the Christian mystery; so that when one of us communicated with her priest, we asked if he would consent to a funeral mass in the manner of the days gone by, which request he gladly granted. And so, on January 18, in the sub-zero weather of a little town in northwestern Connecticut, in the ugly little church we all grew up in, the priest recited the Mass of the Dead, and the organist accompanied the soloist who sang the Gregorian dirge in words the mourners did not clearly discern, words which had we discerned them we would not have been able exactly to translate; and yet we experienced, not only her family but also her friends, not alone the Catholics among us but also the Protestants and the Jews, something akin to that synaesthesia which nowadays most spiritually restless folk find it necessary to discover in drugs or from a guru in mysterious India.

Six months later my sister's oldest daughter was to be married. With some hesitation (one must not be overbearing) her father asked the same priest (of noble mien and great heart) whether this happy ritual might also be performed in the Latin. He replied with understanding and grace that that would not be possible, inasmuch as he would be performing on this occasion not in a remote corner of Connecticut but in West Hartford, practically within earshot of the bishop. We felt very wicked at having attempted anything so audacious within the walls of the episcopacy, and so the wedding took place according to the current cant, with everybody popping up, and kneeling down, and responding, more or less, to the stream of objurgations that issued from the nervous and tone-deaf young commentator, all together now, Who Do We Appreciate? Jesus! Jesus! Jesus! —Je-*zus* it was awful. My beloved wife—to whom I have been beholden for seventeen years, and who has borne with me through countless weddings of my countless relations; who was with me and clutched my hand during the funeral a few months earlier; whom I had not invited to my church since the vulgarizations of 1964, so anxious was I that, as a member of the Anglican Communion, she should continue to remember our services as she had known them, in their inscrutable majesty—turned to me early in the ritual in utter incredulity, wondering whether something was especially awry. Hypersensitive, I rebuked her, muttering something to the effect that she had no right to be so ignorant of what had been going on for three years, and she withdrew in anger. She was right; I was utterly wrong. How could she, an innocent Protestant, begin to conceive of the liturgical disfigurations of the past few years? My own reaction was the protective reaction of the son whose father, the chronic drunkard, is first espied unsteady on his feet by someone from whom one has greatly cared to conceal the fact.

Let it be objected that the essential fact of the matter is that the sacrament of matrimony was duly conferred, and what else is it that matters? My sensibilities, that's what.

They do not matter, of course, in any Benthamite reckoning of the success of the new liturgy. Concerning this point, I yield completely, or rather almost completely. It is absolutely right that the vernacular should displace the Latin if by doing so, the rituals of Catholic Christianity bring a greater satisfaction to the laity and a deeper comprehension of their religion. There oughtn't to be any argument on this point, and there certainly isn't any from me. Indeed, when a most learned and attractive young priest from my own parish asked me to serve as a lector in the new mass, I acquiesced, read all the relevant literature, and, to be sure warily, hoped that something was about to unfold before me which would vindicate the progressives.

I hung on doggedly for three years, until a month ago, when I wrote my pastor that I no longer thought it appropriate regularly to serve as lector. During those three years I observed the evolution of the new mass and the reaction to it of the congregation (the largest, by the way, in Connecticut). The church holds 1,000 people, and at first, four hymns were prescribed. They were subsequently reduced to three, even as, in the course of the experiment, the commentator absorbed the duties of the lector, or vice versa, depending on whether you are the ex-commentator or the ex-lector. At our church three years ago perhaps a dozen people out of 1,000 sang the hymn. Now perhaps three dozen out of 1,000 sing the hymn. (It is not much different with the prayers.) That is atypical, to be sure; the church is large and overawing to the uncertain group singer— *i.e.*, to most non-Protestant Americans. In other Catholic churches, I have noted, the congregations tend to join a little bit more firmly in the song. In none that I have been to is there anything like the joyous unison that the bards of the new liturgy thrummed about in the anticipatory literature, the only exception being the highly regimented school my son attends, at which the reverend headmaster has means to induce cooperation in whatever enterprise strikes his fancy. (I have noticed that my son does not join in the hymn singing when he is home, though the reason why is not necessarily indifference, is almost surely not recalcitrance, is most likely a realistic appreciation of his inability to contribute to the musical story line.)

I must, of course, judge primarily on the basis of my own experience; but it is conclusive at my own church, and I venture to say without fear of contradiction that the joint singing and prayers are a fiasco, which is all right, I suppose—the Christian martyrs endured worse exasperations and profited more from them than we endure from or are likely to benefit from the singing of the hymns at St. Mary's Church. What is troublesome is the difficulty one has in dogging one's own spiritual pursuits in the random cacophony. Really, the new liturgists should have offered training in yoga or whatever else Mother Church in her resourcefulness might baptize as a distinctively Catholic means by which we might tune out the fascistic static of the contemporary mass, during which one is either attempting to sing, totally neglecting the prayers at the foot of the altar which suddenly we are told are irrelevant; or attempting to read the missal at one's own syncopated pace, which we must now do athwart the obtrusive rhythm of the priest or the commentator; or attempting to meditate on this or the other prayer or sentiment or analysis in the ordinary or in the proper of the mass, only to find that such meditation is sheer outlawry, which stands in the way of the liturgical calisthenics devised by the central coach, who apparently judges it an act of neglect if the churchgoer is permitted more than two minutes and forty-six seconds without being made to stand if he was kneeling, or kneel if he was standing, or sit—or sing—or chant—or *anything* if perchance he was praying, from which anarchism he must at all costs be rescued: "LET US NOW RECITE THE INTROIT PRAYER," says the commentator, to which exhortation I find myself aching to reply in that "loud and clear and reverential voice" the manual for lectors prescribes: "LET US NOT!" Must we say the introit prayer together? I have been reading the introit prayer since I was thirteen years old, and I continue unaware that I missed something—e.g., at the Jesuit school in England, where at daily mass we read the introit prayer all by our little selves, beginning it perhaps as much as five seconds before, or five seconds after, the priest, who, enjoying the privacy granted him at Trent, pursued his prayers in his own way, at his own speed, ungoverned by the metronomic discipline of the parishioners or of the commentator.

Ah, but now the parish *understands* the introit prayer! But, my beloved friends, the parish does not understand. Neither does the commentator. Neither does the lector. Neither, if you want the truth of the matter, does the priest—in most cases. If clarity is the purpose of the liturgical reform— the reason for going into the vernacular—then the reforms of the liturgy are simply incomplete. If clarity is the desideratum, or however you say the word in English, then the thing to do is to jettison, just to begin with, most of St. Paul, whose epistles are in some respects inscrutable to some of the people some of the time and in most respects inscrutable to most of the people most of the time. The translation of them from archaic grandeur to Dick-and-Jane contemporese simply doesn't do the trick, particularly if one is expected to say them in unison. And those prayers which are not exacting or recondite—are even they more galvanizing when spoken in unison? LET US NOW RECITE THE INTROIT PRAYER. *Judge me, O God, and distinguish my cause from the nation that is not holy; deliver me from the unjust and deceitful man.* Judge-me-O-God/And-distinguish-my-cause-from-the-nation-that-is-not-holy/Deliver-me-from-the-unjust-and-deceitful-man. —Why? How come? Whose idea? —that such words as these are better understood, better appreciated, when rendered metrically in forced marches with the congregation? Who, thinking to read these holy and inspired words reverentially, would submit to the iron rhythm of a joint reading? It is one thing to chant together a refrain—Lord deliver us/Lord save us/Grant us peace. But the extended prayer in unison is a metallic Procrusteanism which absolutely defies the rationale of the whole business, which is the communication of *meaning*. The rote saying of anything is the enemy of understanding. To reduce to unison prayers whose meaning is unfamiliar is virtually to guarantee that they will mean nothing to the sayer. *"Brethren: Everything that was written in times past was written for our instruction, that through the patience and encouragement afforded by the Scriptures we might have hope. I say that Christ exercised his ministry to the circumcised to show God's fidelity in fulfilling His promises to the fathers, whereas the Gentiles glorify God for His mercy, as it is written: 'Therefore will I proclaim you among the nations, and I will sing praise to your name.'"* These were the words with which I first accosted my fellow parishioners from the lector's pulpit. I do not even now understand them well enough to explain them with any confidence. And yet, the instruction manual informs me, I am to communicate their meaning "clearly" and "confidently." And together the congregation will repeat such sentences in the gradual.

Our beloved Mother Church. How sadly, how innocently, how—sometimes—strangely she is sometimes directed by her devoted disciples! *Hail Mary, full of grace, the Lord is with you* . . . The Lord is with *who? Thee to you, buster,* I found myself thinking during the retreat when first I learned that it is a part of the current edification to strip the Lord, His Mother, and the saints of the honorific with which the simple Quakers even now address their children and their servants. And the translations! *"Happy the humble—they shall inherit* . . ." One cannot read on without the same sense of outrage one would feel on entering the cathedral of Chartres and finding that the windows had been replaced with pop-art figures of Christ sitting in against the slumlords of Milwaukee. One's heart is filled with such passions of resentment and odium as only Hilaire Belloc could adequately have voiced. O God O God O God, why hast thou forsaken us!

My faith, I note on their taking from us even the canon of the mass in that mysterious universal which soothed and inspired the low and the mighty—a part of the mass, as Evelyn Waugh recalled, "for whose restoration the Elizabethan martyrs had gone to the scaffold, [and in which] St. Augustine, St. Thomas à Becket, St. Thomas More, Challoner, and Newman would have been perfectly at their ease among us"—is secure. I pray the sacrifice will yield a rich harvest of informed Christians. But to suppose that it will is the most difficult act of faith I have ever been called on to make, because it tears against the perceptions of all my senses. My faith is a congeries of dogmatical certitudes, one of which is that the new liturgy is the triumph, yea the resurrection, of the Philistines.

—*Commonweal*, November 10, 1967

Guru-Bound

LONDON—The doings of the Beatles are minutely recorded here in England and, as a matter of fact, elsewhere, inasmuch as it is true, what one of the Beatle gentlemen said a year or so ago, that they are more popular than Jesus Christ. It is a matter of considerable public interest that all four of the Beatles have gone off to a place called Rishikesh to commune with one Maharishi Mahesh Yogi.

Rishikesh is in India, and the reigning chic stipulates that Mysterious India is where one goes to Have a Spiritual Experience. Accordingly, the Beatles are there, as also Mia Farrow, who, having left Frank Sinatra, is understandably in need of spiritual therapy; and assorted other types, including, the press reports, a space physicist who works for General Motors. It isn't altogether clear what is the drill at Rishikesh, except that—and this visibly disturbed a couple of the business managers of the Beatles—a postulant at the shrine of Mr. Yogi is expected to contribute a week's salary as an initiation fee. A week's salary may not be very much for thee and me, but it is a whole lot of sterling for a Beatle, and one gathers from the press that the business managers thought this a bit much and rather wish that the Beatles could find their spiritual experience a little less dearly.

The wisdom of Maharishi Mahesh Yogi is not rendered in easily communicable tender. It is recorded by one disciple that he aroused himself from a trance sufficiently to divulge the sunburst, "Ours is an age of science, not faith," a seizure of spiritual exertion which apparently left him speechless with exhaustion; I mean, wouldn't you be exhausted if you came up with that? It is reported that the Beatles were especially transfigured when the Maharishi divulged, solemnly, that "Speech is just the progression of thought." One can assume that the apogee of their experience was reached upon learning, from the guru's own mouth, that "Anything that comes from direct experience can be called science." It is a wonder that the entire population of the world has not gravitated toward the cynosure capable of such incandescent insights.

I am not broke, but I think that if I were, I would repair to India and haul up a guru's flag, and—I guarantee it—I would be the most successful guru of modern times. I would take the Beatles' weekly salary, and Mia Farrow's, and the lot of them, and I would come up with things like: "Put on, therefore, as the elect of God, holy and beloved, bowels of mercies, kindness, humbleness of mind, meekness, long-suffering; forbearing one another, and forgiving one another, if any man have a quarrel against any; even as Christ forgave you, so also do ye. And above all these things put on charity, which is the bond of perfectness. And let the peace of God rule in your hearts, to the which also ye are called in one body; and be ye thankful."

To the especially worldly, I would say: "Walk in wisdom toward them that are without, redeeming the time. Let your speech be alway with grace, seasoned with salt, that ye may know how ye ought to answer every man." Can it be imagined that I would be less successful, quoting these lines from a single letter of St. Paul, than Maharishi Mahesh Fakir has been? The truly extraordinary feature of our time isn't the faithlessness of the Western people; it is their utter, total ignorance of the Christian religion. They travel to Rishikesh to listen to pallid seventh-hand imitations of thoughts and words they never knew existed. They will go anywhere to experience spirituality—except next door. An Englishman need go no farther than to hear Evensong at King's College at Cambridge, or to attend high mass at Chartres cathedral; or to read St. Paul, or St. John, or the psalmists. Read a volume by Chesterton— *The Everlasting Man, Orthodoxy, The Dumb Ox*—and the spiritual juices begin to run, but no, Christianity is, well—well, what? Well, unknown.

The Beatles know more about carburetors than they know about Christianity, which is why they, like so many others, make such asses of themselves in pursuit of Mr. Gaga Yogi. Their impulse is correct, and they reaffirm, as man always has and always will, the truism that man is a religious animal. If only they knew what is waiting there, available to them, right there in Jollie Olde Englande, no costlier than two shillings sixpence at the local bookstore. It is too easy nowadays to found new religions, though the vogue is not new. Voltaire was once abashed at the inordinate iconoclasm of one of his young disciples, who asked the master how might he go about founding a new religion. "Well," Voltaire said, "begin by getting yourself killed. Then rise again on the third day."

—February 29, 1968

The Bishops and the War

Garry Wills begins a long paean to the Berrigan brothers in the current *Playboy* by citing two sentences from Fidel Castro, spoken in 1967. "The

United States shouldn't worry about the Soviets in Latin America because they are not revolutionaries any more. But they should worry about the Catholic revolutionaries, who are."

The words are apt, appearing in print a few weeks before the Catholic bishops—who earlier in the month opposed an amendment to the Constitution that would have permitted non-denominational prayer in the schools—passed a resolution denouncing the continuation of the Vietnam War. It is left only for the bishops to proclaim that American soldiers have no business fighting for a country that wants to permit prayer in its public schools.

Whatever the bishops are up to, let us not permit ourselves to think of them categorically—to think of them as if they were all alike, all united behind the effronteries of what Auberon Waugh, surveying the post-Conciliar wreckage, calls the "silly season" of the Catholic Church. But a statement was issued in the bishops' name, and they must answer for it. It is kindest to say of it that it did attempt to reason. "At this point in history," said the bishops, "it seems clear to us that whatever good we hope to achieve through continued involvement in this war is now outweighed by the destruction of human life and of moral values which it inflicts."

One bishop, from Detroit, drew from this resolution the breathtaking inference that anyone who agrees with the "Catholic position" "may not participate in this war." This startled Archbishop Philip Hannan of New Orleans, who snapped that he did not "agree with that conclusion."

The bishops' resolution must be considered abstractly, and concretely. Abstractly, the bishops appear to be saying that the maintenance of our treaty obligations in South Vietnam is wrong, because it is now "clear" that our maintenance of these commitments causes more harm than good. But the good that the administrators of our Vietnam policies, both Democratic and Republican, pursue is the maintenance of public confidence in our network of treaties, a collapse of which could bring on a world war.

The political meaning of the bishops' resolution is surely that they are dissatisfied with President Nixon's rate of withdrawal.

Fewer Americans are dying per week in Vietnam than in the streets of New York City, and the projections are that we will have fewer men in Vietnam than in Korea within one year, and that South Vietnam will survive. A precipitate withdrawal at this point would change all that; would result in thousands upon thousands—hundreds of thousands, some say, to whom the situation is at least as clear as to the bishop of Detroit—slain by a vindictive aggressor. What was the point of the bishops' resolution, if not to undermine the president's program for withdrawal?

"True religion does not look upon as sinful those wars that are waged not for motives of aggrandizement, or cruelty, but with the object of securing peace, of punishing evildoers, and of uplifting the good." Those words, of St. Augustine, are quoted by St. Thomas Aquinas in his passage on the just war. And he went on to write, "Those who wage war justly aim at peace, and so they are not opposed to peace, except to *the evil peace, which Our Lord came not to send upon earth* (Matt. 10.34)."

One wonders how long we can hold out, in America. Garry Wills, in an age when priests are tortured by two of the world's major powers, writes about the "hysterical repression" of the Fathers Berrigan in America; and the Catholic bishops—when twenty Americans per week are giving their lives to guard a frontier linked by a network of treaties to the critical frontier that separates us from a race of madmen who in a single century have slaughtered many times the number of men who gave their lives for their faith during the first two millennia of Christendom—rail against our military policies.

Such is our moral paralysis. Thus do we go whimpering for the approval of the underground Catholics, whose transfiguration teaches them that the enemy is J. Edgar Hoover and Richard Nixon, in a world that gave us Josef Stalin and Mao Tse-tung. What overwhelms one is the historical frivolity of these confused, confusing men.

—November 25, 1971

Chuck Colson and Christianity

I have been interested by the leers that greet the news of Charles Colson's conversion to Christianity. They are variously expressed. Those among us who consider themselves most worldly—Mr. Pete Hamill, for instance, or the writers for the *Village Voice*—treat the whole thing as a huge joke, as if W. C. Fields had come out for the Temperance Union. They are waiting for the second act, when the resolution comes, and W. C. Fields is toasting his rediscovery of booze, and Colson is back practicing calisthenics on his grandmother's grave.

It says a great deal about the meaning of Christianity in our culture. Traditionally, it has been those who have sinned the most who are the special objects of providential grace. The prodigal son is welcomed most by Heaven precisely because he has the most to atone for.

Ah, but does that mean that we shouldn't be most surprised by the most drastic alterations in known attitudes? If Al Capone had become a Franciscan monk, there is no doubting that that operation would have exhausted huge storage banks of heavenly grace. Or if Anthony Lewis uttered a compassionate word about Richard Nixon, one would certainly take notice, though indeed there are those who would suspect guile: *reculer pour mieux sauter*, as the French say, who know how to step back a little in order to leap forward a lot. But it does not matter who it is, it is possible to suspect guile, as in the case of Charles Colson. If one of the president's conversations had in it, "Let's figure out what our duty is and do it," most people would have suspected that those words were uttered for the sake of the record, maybe after calling in the Secret Service to dust off the hidden microphones. It has all become so twisted that we tend to be particularly skeptical when we detect someone doing something that is right, even though it is something that is tactically damaging.

Concerning Chuck Colson, it seems to me less implausible than it apparently does to others that he should have found Christ. His weakness, as generally identified, has been his heliocentric concern for one person—Richard Nixon. When he told the court that it did not occur to him to challenge Mr. Nixon when told to go out and do something, are we asked to disbelieve that? Not by the critics of Colson, or those of Nixon; indeed, that is what they most desire to believe: that everything Colson did that was disreputable, he did at the bidding of someone he treated as commander-in-chief. Whether he'd have served Richard Nixon if Nixon had been not the president of the United States, but chairman of the board of Murder, Inc., we have no way of knowing: no way of knowing whether Colson carried about within himself springs of resistance the devil himself could not overcome.

But now he says that he has discovered Christ. To say you have discovered Christ, in our secular society, is to say something that causes most people to wince with embarrassment. Christ is to be discovered only between the hours of ten and noon on Sunday morning by Billy Graham, before or after a golf game, or by a bearded young man on the corner of Hollywood and Vine for whom Christ-freaking is a way station between college sociology and Timothy Leary. Or the sort of thing that caused cruel wars in the Dark and Middle Ages because one set of people said Christ had six toes, the other that He had five. For Charles Colson to say that he has found Jesus Christ is like Coca-Cola announcing it has discovered

Pepsi-Cola: J. Walter Thompson has to be impeached before that kind of thing is credible.

So much for the *stupor mundi*. And just when we need Him most. "I see it as one of the greatest ironies of this ironical time," writes Malcolm Muggeridge, "that the Christian message renouncing the world should be withdrawn from consideration just when it is most desperately needed to save men's reason, if not their souls. It is as though a Salvation Army band, valiantly and patiently waiting through the long years for Judgment Day, should, when it comes at last, and the heavens do veritably begin to unfold like a scroll, throw away their instruments and flee in terror."

—June 24, 1974

Death of a Christian

A day or two before Thanksgiving, Charles Pinckney Luckey, pastor of the Congregational Church of Middlebury, Connecticut, was making his ministerial rounds, as usual on his motorcycle, when suddenly, rounding a corner, he lost his balance and fell. He arrived home to his three vacationing sons—two from college, one from nearby Taft School—a little bedraggled. But this didn't matter much—he was always a conspicuously informal dresser, though never affectedly so; in fact there was no trace of affectation in him, which is one reason why he was so greatly, and quietly, popular with his congregation, even as he had been at Yale, and at Taft.

What vexed him was that he should have lost his balance. A perfect physical specimen at fifty, tall and rangy and handsome, with the face of a thirty-year-old and the physique of a long-distance runner. So he went to the doctor suspecting he had something wrong with his ears, knowing like the rest of us only Boy Scout medicine, which tells you that when your balance is off, something is wrong in your ear canal. The doctor examined him, couldn't find anything, and everyone hoped whatever it was would go away.

It didn't. Within a week or two he began to lose his vision, at an alarming rate. In three weeks he was blind, and was beginning to lose motor control on his left side. A legion of specialists had by that time surveyed his wilting frame, and a name was spoken which squirts ice water even among hardened doctors, because there are only a half-dozen recorded cases of it and it is most gruesomely and implacably lethal. They call it Creutzfeldt-Jakob disease. Something about a galloping attrition of the nerve endings. Prognosis: one to three months. Cause? Nobody knows, though there was much speculation. Could he have got it eating strange fish in the Yukon on his camping trip last summer with the boys?

They took him to Columbia-Presbyterian in New York City, to "confirm" the diagnosis. One suspects the altogether understandable reason for the trip was to give the medical students a chance to examine someone suffering from such an exotic disease, rather like the gathering of the astronomers to gaze at a once-in-a-lifetime comet. It was only there that he yielded to depression, as they poked about and asked him questions, to measure, scientifically, the physical and intellectual deteriorations. Before, and after, he was obstinately cheerful and affectionate, dictating to his secretary every day letters of farewell to his friends, letters exalted by a curious dignity that attached to him even as a teenager. He preached his last sermon, propped up by his seventeen-year-old son at the lectern, on the Sunday before Christmas to a congregation wracked with pain and admiration.

The crisis came shortly after. He called his secretary and dictated a paragraph which he sent to a few friends, and which was pronounced by the retired, aged chaplain of Yale University "the most moving credo to the Christian faith written in my lifetime."

"What"—Charlie dictated—"does the Christian do when he stands over the abyss of his own death and the doctors have told him that his disease is ravaging his brain and that his whole personality may be warped, twisted, changed? *Then* does the Christian have any right to self-destruction, especially when the Christian knows that the changed personality may bring out the horrible beast in himself? Well, after 48 hours of self-searching study it comes to me that ultimately and finally the Christian has to always view life as a gift from God, and every precious drop of life was not earned but was a grace, lovingly bestowed upon the individual by his Creator and so it is not his to pick up and smash. And so I find the position of suicide untenable, not because I lack the courage to blow out my brains but rather because of my deep, abiding faith in the Creator who put the brains there in the first place. And now the result is that I lie here blind on my bed and trust in the succeeding, loving power of that great Creator who knew and loved me before I was fashioned in my mother's womb. But I do not think it is wrong to pray for an early release from this diseased, ravaged carcass.

"Lovingly given," he closed the statement, diffidently, "to my congregation and to my friends if it seems in good taste."

It seems to me in very good taste, and I pass it along, with the good
news that at least that final prayer was answered. The coma began two
weeks later, and on January 21, he died. There had been no personality
change. That, all the dreadful powers of Creutzfeldt-Jakob couldn't do to
Charles Luckey.

—January 22, 1975

The Prophet

The pope has come and gone, and what will the Polish people do now?
And the Polish state? What, as Western instrumentalists like to put it, has
been "accomplished"?

One strains for prophetic help. It is a coincidence so bizarre as to defy
credence. But halfway through John Paul's pilgrimage to his own country
I had reason to forage in old files. I came upon a letter from Whittaker
Chambers which, because it had been misplaced, was not published in the
volume *Odyssey of a Friend* (1970) and therefore has never been seen other
than by the writer and the addressee, twenty-two years ago.

Chambers wrote in April 1957, six months after the Russians had qui-
eted the Poles by appointing the tough-minded Communist Gomulka as
their Polish satrap. Cardinal Wyszynski—then as now—was primate of
Poland's Catholics. And Cardinal Wyszynski, who shaped the present
pope's political development, launched Poland on a controversial course,
dramatically at odds with that of his counterpart in Hungary, the tortured, heroic, ascetic Cardinal Mindszenty, who, having languished in
Communist dungeons, was freed for a few glorious days in 1956 by the
freedom fighters, only to take refuge in the American embassy in Budapest, where he would live for fifteen years until he became an embarrassment to détente. The two cardinals, one of them breathing a kind
of coffined defiance, the other going about the streets of Polish towns
attending shrewdly to his workaday chores as minister to the spiritual
needs of his countrymen.

"Those Poles and Hungarians," Chambers wrote, "stand looking at us from the fastness of that difference which is rooted in a simpler experience of sweat, blood, filth, death. . . . I have been a Wyszynski man *ab initio*. I have argued that his course was right because no other course was possible. I am afraid that I have deeply disappointed (perhaps even estranged) certain Catholic friends by my unbudgeability on this point. I point [to] . . . the contrasting attitudes of their Cardinals. No one who has not suffered so much may judge Cardinal Mindszenty, even if he were stupid enough to incline to. But contrasting policy results can be appreciated; I hold that the contrast favors the results in Poland. Early in the crisis, I took part in a private group discussion on these contrasting policies; a discussion that under its formal courtesy constantly threatened to flare, in part, I believe, because one faction was astonished to find me pro-Wyszynski, and took it as a defection. It is nothing of the kind. With the knife at your throat (the situation of the Poles and of their Cardinal), there are only two choices: to maneuver, *knowing fully the chances of failure*, but remembering that Hope is one of the Virtues; or to hold your neck still to the knife in the name of martyrdom.

"But just here is the crux. We are not talking about the Church Triumphant. We are talking about the Church in this world, the world of Warsaw and of Budapest, whose streets are of a drabness that squeezes the blood from the heart. In that sad light, the figure of the Polish Cardinal is a figure of hope. I say: we know nothing about these things. I say that what makes us all sick with a sickness we cannot diagnose is that, in the current crisis, the West has gained the world (or thinks it has), but has lost its own soul. I say: the Poles and the Hungarians have lost the world (or whatever makes it bearable—they live in Hell), but they have gained their own souls. What price, power without purpose? Dulles mouthing moralities while on the streets of Budapest children patrolled the shattered house-fronts, with slung rifles and tormented faces. I say those children, whatever their politics, will have grown to men while Dulles and his tribe lie howling. . . .

"That is why I keep beside Wyszynski. That is why Gomulka keeps beside him and he beside Gomulka. In each other they recognize men; they are scarce enough. How lonely these two men must be. Was ever such loneliness endured, and not made less by the knowledge, clear to both, that, under necessity, Gomulka may destroy the Cardinal before he is destroyed himself. But these men at least acted: I think we must see this clearly."

It is difficult to see clearly through to the meaning of Wyszynski's successor, now the bishop of Rome, in Poland, dealing with the successor to Gomulka. But who can deny that those of us who thought Mindszenty right, Wyszynski wrong, lacked the prophetic insight of Whittaker Chambers?

—June 14, 1979

Is There a God behind Religion?

Most public discussion of religion has to do with earnest constitutional and political quarrels. Does the First Amendment prohibit the recitation of a public prayer in the public schools? The display of a creche at Christmas? The display of the Ten Commandments?

Then there are the derivative issues: Is the Christian Coalition dominating GOP politics? Do Pat Robertson and Ralph Reed have a stranglehold on the Republican platform on the question of abortion? Of homosexual marriages? Of euthanasia?

Odd, but almost never does the discussion turn on religion itself: i.e., what is the excitement all about? If students heard a prayer in the public schools, or if religious sentiment crystallized against abortion, what is it all about?

The public schools, for two generations, have proceeded without any notice being taken of religion, as the Supreme Court has decreed. What about non-public schools?

Interesting question. Obviously one begins by excluding schools that are explicitly religious in orientation. One would expect that in Catholic schools, Orthodox Jewish schools, Episcopal schools, religion is an explicit factor.

But what about others? There are 240 private boarding schools in America. What do they do? The Supreme Court isn't going to tell them what to do. They can worship the god Pan, if that's what the trustees decree.

One doesn't know where to turn for an answer to the question: How does religion fare in the private non-denominational schools? But the mere inquiry provokes the curious mind to ask what is, one supposes, the primary question. Why?

A recent visitor remarks that attendance at her Episcopal church has, in the past half-dozen years, increased by 100 percent. Why? Is there, as we are here and there told, a religious "revival" in the offing?

Again, why?

The anthropologists are there to tell us that it is in human nature to aspire for a spiritual life, even as it is in human nature to wish to exercise sexual appetites, and of course it is biologically necessary to appease hunger. The idea of the sociological set is, in effect, to say: There, there, Mrs. Jones, we quite understand why you believe in God, etc., but kindly do so in a way that doesn't get in the way of public affairs. You know, like bicycle paths, or the diminishing supply of buffaloes.

What surprises is the relative reticence of the religious community— in the United States, overwhelmingly, the Christian community. A politician running for office is prepared to say that he believes in school prayer because he insists that the Constitution does not prohibit school prayer. But ambient folkways prevent him from saying, "I think Jesus Christ was divine and therefore I find the lessons He taught us illuminating and vital in affecting our lives."

Wow!

Does that make him an anti-Semite? No, no, madam. He is an anti-Semite only in the sense that a fan of the Yankees is anti–Red Sox. Never mind the difference in the order of gravity; the point is that a Christian exercises his faith without believing that others' faiths are wrong or misled.

The Christian owes absolutely nothing more to other religions than a respectful toleration of them. The wonderful old saw about the inter-religious conference in Tokyo fifty years ago is amusingly relevant. After the ecumenical blessing at the banquet, one participant turns to the pilgrim on his right. "My miserable superstition is Buddhism. What is your religion?"

It would be grand to hear a public figure, in the course of discussing this or that public or private question, say, "Well, on this matter, I am instructed, or try to be, by the New Testament, which, you know, tells us that greed is wrong. So is adultery. . . . I don't say I live up to the Christian calling; all I say is that I wish I did because I recognize it as truth."

There is no reason at all for the listener, whose god speaks a different tongue, to object to the superordination of Christ over, say, Buddha. But the question before the house is: Why don't people say, more often, Yes, I love my country and my flag and my God, but let me tell you who my God is, and why what He has told me for years and years has given me comfort and fortitude and stimulated my love for—yes, you, madam?

—January 19, 1996

Buggery in Church

I rode in a car for an hour with an FBI agent, a man in his late thirties, trained as a lawyer, and he spoke (we were en route to a distant airport) of his profession, which included recruitment.

"There are so many people who want to join the bureau we don't have to go scouting for them. But when they do apply, it takes six or seven months before they're checked out."

The final barrier is a truth test. The applicant is wired up and asked, in sequence, "Have you in your life smoked marijuana more than fifteen times?" And then, "Have you smoked in the last three years?" Fifty percent of the applicants either plead guilty or else lie and are detected; in either case, they are dismissed.

The news items on priests and child abuse all but paralyze one's sensibilities: How can such a thing be? In Ireland, a seventy-year-old who abused boys for more than thirty years. In Canada, a similar, if less protracted, case. Most highly publicized is the affair in Dallas involving the Reverend Rudolph Kos, remarkable for several reasons.

The first is that the jury awarded the eleven plaintiffs the sum of $120 million. The second, that there was considerable exploration, during the nine-week trial, of the circumstances of the crimes, and a marked division among parishioners about how the bishop had handled the situation. He was manifestly horrified and apologetic, but onlookers were not all of them satisfied that sufficient care had been taken.

The lawyer for the diocese told the jury that everything had been done to determine whether the offender was a pedophile, but that the diocese had been duped. To that, plaintiff lawyer Sylvia Demarest replied, "The lives of children cannot continue to be sacrificed so the bishop of the Diocese of Dallas can continue to conceal the perversions of the priests of the diocese." The reference was to other priests also charged with pedophilia.

Another plaintiff lawyer said that out of seven candidates admitted to Catholic seminary in Dallas in 1980, three (including Kos) later were charged with pedophilia.

One pauses to meditate on the bitter affront to decency. The montage is gruesomely perfected—as if painted by Hieronymus Bosch—by the knowledge that the plaintiffs were serving, when abused, as altar boys. The debasement invokes the words of Christ, that for those who offend little children it would be better if they were drowned in the sea.

But the same Christ enjoined forgiveness, after genuine repentance. The criminal and civil penalties should be severe and unrelenting, but if contrition is true, the priests wearing prison garb are welcome at the altar.

The civil judgment is the obligation of the diocese. One hundred twenty million dollars, added to the pain of the sacrilege, and the hurt and contempt engendered by the crime. One reporter on the scene predicts that many Catholics will simply refuse to contribute money to help pay the judgment, a gesture of disgust over the maladministration of the bishop.

One wonders, in respect of that bishop in Dallas, and the two bishops in Ireland and Canada, whether public mortification isn't appropriate. Resignation, or at least a leave of absence of several years spent in a monastery, would be a sign of pain felt and forgiveness merited.

Most directly needed, clearly, is a sharp revision of supervisory practices. Psychologists tell us that pedophilia is the most persistent of all sexual deviations. The data (or so I am advised) tell of the recurrence of the crime even after terms spent in jail.

Crank up the polygraph, FBI style, and then ask the postulant: "Have you ever, with sexual motive, fondled a boy?" Or, perhaps more advisedly, to guard against the risk of transforming a thirteen-year-old crush into life-long disqualification, "Have you fondled a boy at any time since reaching sixteen?"

But most important is to remember to detach the sinner from the faith. On that subject, the Reverend Andrew Greeley once wrote, "The question is not whether the Catholic leadership is enlightened, but whether Catholicism is true. A whole College of Cardinals filled with psychopathic tyrants provides no answer one way or another to that question."

And then a killer of a closing line: "Search for the perfect church if you will; when you find it, join it, and realize that on that day it becomes something less than perfect."

—August 1, 1997

Bloody Passion

The film by Mel Gibson is moving because of its central contention, namely that an innocent man of high moral purpose was tortured and killed. It happens that the man in question, Jesus of Nazareth, is an object of worship, and that harm done unto Him, in the perspective of those (myself included) who regard Him as divine is especially keen because it is not only inhuman, it is blasphemous.

But suppose that a similar travail had been filmed involving not a Nazarene carpenter Who taught the duty of love for others but, say, an attempted regicide. In 1757, Robert-François Damiens set out to assassinate Louis XV. The failed assassin was apprehended, and the king was quickly restored to health from his minor wound. The court nonetheless resolved to make an enduring public spectacle of what awaits attempted regicides, to which end were gathered together in Paris the half-dozen most renowned torturers of Europe, who, in the presence of many spectators, including Casanova, managed to keep Damiens alive for six hours of pain ever so artfully inflicted, before he was finally drawn and quartered. What kind of audience could Mel Gibson get for a depiction of the last hours of Robert-François Damiens?

The film depends, then, on the victim's being Jesus of Nazareth; but even then, the story it tells is a gross elaboration of what the Bible yields.

Consider Matthew: "And when [Pilate] had scourged Jesus, he delivered him to be crucified. . . . Then they [the soldiers] spit upon him, and took the reed, and smote him on the head." Luke: "I will therefore chastise him and let him go"—Luke records that the soldiers "mocked" him. And John: "So then Pilate therefore took Jesus and scourged him. . . . And they [the soldiers] smote him with their hands."

What Gibson gives us in *The Passion of the Christ* is the most prolonged human torture ever seen on the screen. It is without reason, and by no means necessarily derivative from the grand hypothesis that, after all, the crucifixion was without reason, as Pontius Pilate kept on observing. One sees for dozens of minutes soldiers apparently determined to flog to death the man the irresolute procurator had consented merely to "chastise." There are records of British mariners who were literally flogged to death, receiving four hundred strokes of the cat-o'-nine-tails, delivered on separate vessels, lest any sailor in the fleet be deprived of witnessing the informative exercise.

It isn't only the interminable scourging, which is done with endless inventories of instruments. The Bible has Christ suffering the weight of the cross as he climbs to Golgotha, but that is not enough for Gibson. He has stray soldiers impeding Christ every step of the way, bringing down their clubs and whips and scourges in something that cannot be understood as less than sadistic frenzy.

This kind of improvisation is headlong in Gibson's *Passion*. Still, the film cannot help moving the viewer, shaking the viewer, even as he would be moved and shaken by seeing a re-creation of the end of Robert-François Damiens or one of those British sailors flogged to death. The suffering of Jesus isn't intensified by inflicting the one-thousandth blow: that is the Gibson/*Braveheart* contribution to an agony that was overwhelmingly spiritual in character and perfectly and definitively caught by Johann Sebastian Bach in his "Passion of Christ According to St. Matthew." There beauty and genius sublimate a passion that Gibson celebrates by raw bloodshed. The only serious question left in the viewer's mind is: Should God have exempted this gang from His comprehensive mercy? But that is because we are human, God otherwise.

—March 9, 2004

A Farewell

A lot of people—roughly speaking, everybody—saw the pope alive at least once on television. It is estimated that tens of millions of people laid eyes on him in the flesh. All of us have our own memories. The keenest in my own mind was his appearance twelve years ago in Colorado. Why Colorado? One never really pondered the question; but there he was.

The wonder of it to this viewer, watching from two thousand miles away, was the crowd that surrounded him as he celebrated mass: the expression on the faces of the ten thousand people the cameras skated about, giving close-ups of hundreds of them. They were young people, in their late teens, their early twenties. And they were finding the scene—finding the pope—riveting. They were drawn into a true and resonant silence. How did this come about?

Well, for one thing, John Paul had been on the center of the international stage for more than a dozen years. He did not command an air force or any bark larger than that commanded by the Founder when he stilled the storm. Where did this old Pole get that magic?

No doubt many who watched him that day in Colorado believed themselves to be viewing the successor of Christ himself, though the pope's title is as simple as "Bishop of Rome." But probably the majority thought him, simply, a singular figure as they stared and stared, and remained quiet for the hour.

The phenomenon occurred not only in Colorado. He had such an effect on men and women of all races, of all ages, though it was in particular his impact on young people that arrested attention. And then there was the cloud hovering over him in later years, the Parkinson's disease that finally made even simple speech problematic.

I watched him in Havana at relatively close quarters, being civil, even benign, to the unworthiest of hosts. I saw John Paul cope with the problem, and transfigure the scene. There were, in the estimate of journalists present, one million people in the Plaza de la Revolución. The auspices were memorable at several levels, beginning with the invitation itself. But on that Sunday, a sign had been hung at one end of the famous plaza, a mere hundred yards from where Castro sat detachedly in front of the altar. The sign was the size of a tennis court, and it read, "JESUCRISTO EN TI CONFIO" ("Jesus Christ in Thee I Trust"), as concentrated a repudiation of Castro and his works as four words could manage.

There being no way to shield the host from that resplendent defiance, one wondered what protection would be furnished against nature. Happily there was cloud cover, which shielded the crowd from the sun, as also a brisk wind that mitigated the ambient heat generated by one million fellow creatures crowded closely together.

We heard then the quaking voice of the pope. Not very expressive, but the Spanish he spoke was well turned and clearly enunciated. In a matter of seconds he communicated his penetrating, transcendent warmth. Intending to see better, I walked to a television set. His face was mostly hangdog in expressionlessness. We saw the result of his affliction and his age, and his gunshot wound. The pope had traveled at that point to more than eighty countries. Observers were dumbfounded by the sixteen-hour-a-day schedule he regularly imposed on himself.

There was the stoop and the listless face. But then intermittently the great light within flashed, and one saw the most radiant face on the public scene, a presence so commanding as to have arrested a generation of humankind, who wondered whether the Lord Himself had a hand in shaping the special charisma of this servant of the servants of God, as the pope styled himself, his death leaving a most awful void, and a disconsolate world.

—April 5, 2005

END OF THE COLD WAR; NEW DANGERS

Hallelujah!

When the news came in, President Bush sat quietly in his large chair in the Oval Office and said in grave tones that we must not overreact. He is absolutely right about this. *Jingle bells! Jingle bells! Jingle all the waaaay!* It is proper to deem it a historical development, but its significance must not affect our judgment. *Oh, what a beautiful mor-ning! Oh, what a beautiful day!!!* After all, there is tomorrow to think about in Germany, *Germany?!?! What do you mean, "Germany"? You mean West Germany or you mean East Germany?* and the score allows for many variations. Calmness is in order.

I remember the day in 1973 when, as a delegate to the General Assembly of the United Nations, occupying the chair, I had to sit there and listen to the ambassador from the German Democratic Republic lecturing to the Third Committee (Human Rights Committee) on the differences between his own country, where the pastures of the people were evergreen and life was pleasant, and just, and equable, in contrast to "elsewhere" in Europe, dominated by strife and competition and all the vexations of bourgeois life. I interrupted the speaker to make some reference or another to the Wall that obscured the view of the Communists' green pastures, but all the professional diplomats of course knew all about the Wall and about Communist rhetoric. I learned early during my brief service at the United Nations that the thing to remember is that nobody pays any attention whatever to anything anybody says at the United Nations, which is one up for sanity. But the insolence of the East German diplomat stayed with me, as a freshman diplomat, who never graduated.

And so I wrote a book about the United Nations, and made reference to the special hypocrisies of totalitarian states, which, instead of isolating in such secrecy as is possible what goes on there, actually go about the world boasting about their civil depravity. But the Wall and what it represented stuck in the mind, as it did with so many people—the antipodes of the Statue of Liberty; the great symbol of Gulag life—and a few years later I wrote a novel based on a young idealist's determination in 1952 to attempt to reunite Germany, a political effort finally frustrated by the assassination of the young, upward-bound idealist. By the GPU? No, by my hero, Blackford Oakes, under orders from Washington, because Stalin had said the alternative was a Third World War. I dramatized that novel (*Stained Glass*) and in March of this year, on Good Friday, it was splendidly produced by the Actors Theatre in Louisville, Kentucky.

Still, the ugliness of divided Germany hadn't left me, and in 1978 I went to Berlin actually to look. It is hard to describe the impacted loathsomeness of it. Every season, the Communists added one more obstacle to stand in the way of the occasional Houdini who managed to get through. That was the winter they added the dogs. It had begun with a concrete wall. Then barbed wire. Then watchtowers with machine-gunners. Then huge spotlights. Then land mines. Then mountains of shards of glass. It is a comment on the limited resources of the Communist imagination that they forgot to plant poison ivy alongside the Wall.

And so I wrote a novel about another young German idealist, determined to prevent the construction of the Wall, when on August 13, 1961, all of a sudden it began to materialize. My young German, who as a Jewish child had been spirited to England for safety, his parents being left to die in a Nazi camp, had his contact in East Berlin, a secretary to the monster Ulbricht. And the word from the secretary was that if three NATO tanks charged through the Wall that first day during its flimsy stage, the East Germans, backed by the Russians, would make a great show of opposition, but actually they would yield, as Khrushchev did not want a showdown with the West—not in August 1961, a full year before the missile crisis in Cuba. But the U.S. military, under orders, seized the little column of tanks that had been secretly pulled out from the U.S. armory by young resistance Germans—and so we never knew what would have happened if we had asserted our rights to co-governing East Berlin. My young German hero, Henri Tod, did not live to see the sun set on the growing Wall.

It was a great day, November 9, 1989, and one day it must be nominated for international celebration. *Joshua fit the battle of Jericho, Jericho, Jericho! Joshua fit the battle of Jericho! And the wall came tumblin' down!*

—November 10, 1989

The End of the Cold War

Mikhail Gorbachev survived in power through 1990, but his empire was crumbling, and he was losing interest in its outer reaches. East German spymaster Markus Wolf quotes in his memoirs from a reproachful letter he addressed to Gorbachev in October of that year: "We were your friends. We wear a lot of your country's decorations on our breasts. We were said to have made a great contribution to your security. Now, in our hour of need, I assume that you will not deny us your help." What Wolf wanted from Gorbachev was straightforward: to make his signing the end-of-occupation papers dependent on an amnesty for East German spies. Gorbachev didn't even raise the question in his talks with Chancellor Kohl. "It was the Soviets' ultimate betrayal of their East German friends, whose work for over four decades had strengthened Soviet influence in Europe," Wolf wrote.

The year 1991 began with Soviet troops attacking protestors in Lithuania. Fifteen civilians were killed. That deed led to the usual criticisms from around the world, but also to one unusual criticism. Comrade Boris Yeltsin, president of the Russian Federation, called on Russian soldiers to disobey any such order in the future. He then mutinously pondered establishing a Russian "defense force," to protect the Federation from the Kremlin.

This led to an intensification of the battle between Gorbachev and Yeltsin, which included calls for each other's resignation. Gorbachev also took a turn on the international stage, requesting to be invited to the Group of Seven meeting in London that July. "I am already thinking over what I will say," he told a news conference in Moscow. "And if I am not there, I will say it anyway." After appeals by French president François Mitterrand and Chancellor Kohl, President Bush agreed that Gorbachev should be invited to the meeting as an observer. Gorbachev duly attended, and he succeeded in getting various forms of technical assistance; but he did not get the direct aid he was really after. Before returning home, he arranged for Kohl and the new British prime minister, John Major, to visit him in Moscow later in the year. He did not foresee the problem, later in the year, he would have receiving official visitors.

On August 5, Gorbachev left for his usual summer vacation at his dacha in the Crimea. He planned to return to Moscow on August 20 to sign a freshly negotiated "union treaty," devolving certain powers in the Union of Soviet Socialist Republics from the Kremlin to the constituent republics. At 6:00 A.M. on Monday, August 19, TASS, the official Soviet news agency, announced that Gorbachev was incapacitated by illness and that something called the "State Committee for the State of Emergency" was exercising power in his place.

For the world abroad, this turning point was different from the Hungarian Revolution, the building of the Berlin Wall, or the crushing of the Prague Spring. Different even from the recent opening of the Berlin Wall. This was a very great moment that we in the West could watch live, minute by minute, on CNN. The images we saw were great wrenches from Marxist history and Soviet nationalism. There were the Soviet tanks rumbling through the streets of Moscow on missions unknown, and civilians pulling up paving stones to use as weapons. At 11:00 A.M. on August 19, just five hours after the TASS announcement, a burly white-haired man in a business suit appeared on screen. He was standing on a Soviet tank and addressing the crowd around him. Boris Yeltsin had acted heroically, and within two days the hardliners' coup had been frustrated.

At the end of eleven delirious days in August, the Supreme Soviet voted to suspend all activity done in the name of the Communist Party. In December, the Union of Soviet Socialist Republics was officially re-designated. It was now the Commonwealth of Independent States. The great Communist monolith that had dominated international life was dead, a wreck from within.

Reactions were national, corporate, public, individual. I record my own summary, given at a celebration of National Review, which had been founded in substantial measure to urge on the struggle against the Soviet Union. "I was nineteen years old at the time the Yalta conference was held. Soon after that came Potsdam, and the West lost Eastern Europe to the Communists. The Cold War had begun. On the last day of August, one month ago, the Communist Party was banned in the Soviet Union. Coincidentally, I am sixty-five years old. I passed from teenage to senior citizenship, coinciding with the duration of the Cold War.

"We can sleep better for knowing that our cousins have regained their freedom. But we can't bring back those who lost their lives, nor bring back lifetimes in freedom to those who spent theirs without it."

Might millions of those people have been spared the heavy hand of Soviet repression if the Allies, led by the United States, had taken direct counteraction at various turning points in the Cold War? Say, in 1948, when the Soviets applied their salami tactics to the countries of Eastern Europe? Or in 1953, during the East Berlin riots? Or in 1956, 1961, 1968? When change finally did come in those countries, it came most directly from resistance done by their own people—to be sure, with moral support from the West, plus some direct initiatives from sympathetic leaders, notably Ronald Reagan, Margaret Thatcher, and Pope John Paul II.

But the rise and fall of the Berlin Wall were great moments. It stood more than twice as many years as Hitler ruled Germany, yet finally it yielded, to a human spirit that took nearly a half century but, finally, effected the liberation of that part of Germany that made its way from the Democratic Republic of Germany, to the democratic republic of Germany.

—Excerpt from *The Fall of the Berlin Wall,* 2004

The Abandonment of the Kurds

The events of the past two weeks have been as destructive of Western morale as anything that might have been conceived of during the ecstasy of early March, short of a midnight raid by Iraq's Republican Guard that carried off General Norman Schwarzkopf and his principal aides.

The dissipation of the moral satisfaction earned by George Bush merits careful examination, because it teaches us that rigid geopolitical formulas have to yield, in special circumstances, to moral considerations when these achieve transcendent importance.

The view of the Bush administration going in was that having effected the evacuation of the Iraqi army from Kuwait, we had done our job. Moreover, that it would be critically important not to pursue the enemy to Baghdad, because to do that would be (a) to exceed our franchise, as written by the United Nations; (b) to raise suspicions among Arab nations that we were back in the imperialist business, telling other countries what to do and what not to do; and (c) to run the specific geopolitical risk of upsetting a balance of power in the area whose stability depended on an unfragmented Iraq, in the absence of which, to use the much-misused term, we would have the Lebanonization of a country that shares borders with Iran, Turkey, Syria, and Jordan.

That was the schematic that guided U.S. policy. It is textbook stuff which, left standing on its own, could competently defend itself in any seminar.

But it was overwhelmed by events of the kind that influence Western thought. We do not know the casualty figures, but the context of them is one and a half million Kurds destroyed by Iraq during the past eight years and, in the south, the excuse for the ruling Sunnis to mobilize against the

Shiites. These were the catapult that might have flung Saddam Hussein out of office.

Suddenly, all that the world could see was little Kuwait, slowly trying to put its house in order, well protected in the south by Saudi Arabia, in the north by the diminishing ranks of the great coalition. And everywhere to the north of Kuwait, bloodshed and torture and threatened starvation for every enemy of Saddam Hussein.

If Schwarzkopf had been retained to destroy the opposition to Saddam Hussein, he could not have done better than he has been ordered to do, standing immobile while in some cases within the sight of his legions we witness attack helicopters manned by agents of Saddam Hussein shooting and killing the freedom fighters.

Is it too late? Probably. But Representative Stephen Solarz, whose voice was critical in the days when Congress debated whether to back Bush's military operation, is at it again. In the winter months he pleaded with his colleagues to heed political realities and back military opposition to Saddam Hussein. He did so as a politician who had opposed the Vietnam War with his special gift for omnipresence. (When Solarz decides to take on a cause, you read about it in the *New York Times* and *The New Republic*, view him pleading on the Sunday talk shows and on *Crossfire*, and hear him on the radio.) It was not possible, under the circumstances, for his critics to dismiss him as a perennial hawk.

Solarz plans now to call on the U.N. Security Council to consider a resolution that would instruct the government of Iraq to stop instantly the genocidal war against the Kurds and the rebels in the south. The failure to comply with such an order would constitute a call on the coalition to renew its military operations against Iraq.

It will not prove easy for those countries that voted in favor of the liberation of Kuwait to cavil at the Solarz resolution. No doubt it will be argued that to kill one's own citizens is an internal affair, by which standard the United Nations could not have interfered with Adolf Hitler, so long as his death camps were confined to the territorial boundaries of Germany.

Spokesmen for relief can argue that renewing the military operation would be merely to complete what was begun in January: that the repulsion of the Iraqi forces from Kuwait served only to chop off a few tentacles of the monster that continues to wage aggressive war.

On Monday, European Community leaders called on the United Nations to establish, in effect, a new country out of a chunk of Iraq, a Kurdish enclave. If these statesmen find that action consistent with the U.N. charter, they should have no trouble with the Solarz resolution.

The best thing Bush could do would be on his own authority to destroy the destroyers, because time has very nearly run out; failing that, to back the Solarz resolution; failing that, to abandon any claim to the triumphant act of statesmanship we have all applauded.

—April 11, 1991

It's the Other Things Too, Stupid!

Except that he hasn't quite earned it, one is tempted to feel sorry for Bill Clinton. He gives the air these days of the college student elected president for a day by his classmates who then wakes to find himself actually occupying the Oval Office.

Now when, during the campaign, George Bush kept stressing that we live in a dangerous world, and what his experience in maneuvering about in such a world was, one could not deduce exactly how Bush would have handled, mishandled, or finessed some of the crises of the day. To say that the world is complicated isn't to reveal that one knows how to handle a complicated world. But it is a step in the right direction—the acknowledgment that we are a superpower in a very complicated world, and that the definition of our responsibilities is probably best done by someone who has had training in the art.

One single day's newspaper, the *International Herald Tribune*, offers a chamber of horrors on the subject of the world we live in. The main headline: "Clinton Weighs Signal/On New Trade Battle/Brewing with Europe."

The administration's decision to levy huge tariffs against the importation of steel products was a shot heard round the world. Clinton evidently understood himself to have pledged, during the campaign, to move along protectionist lines, and already it had been announced that we will raise by 1,000 percent the tariff on minivans, even though this violates our pledge to GATT.

To move toward protectionism at a time when we are attempting to mobilize international opinion against the French farm lobby is an invitation to Smoot-Hawleyism, which is not what one associates with people who were Rhodes scholars and presumably urban sophisticates.

"Now, Tokyo Takes Its Turn/To Yell 'Foul' on Dumping." Japan is aiming at China, but the tuning fork—tariffs—was sounded by Washington. Searching for relief on the front page, the eye turns to a picture. The caption: "Rubble from a destroyed sluice gate in a spillway of the Peruca dam in Croatia that was blasted by Serbian forces." And the headline: "Blasted by Serbs, Dam May Collapse." Twenty thousand people are being moved out of the way.

Elsewhere we learned that British Foreign Secretary David Owen and American Secretary of State Cyrus Vance have said the hell with it—after five months trying to impose a peace plan on the former Yugoslavia, they are heading back and throwing the whole thing at the United Nations. Any impulse by the United States to take an active military lead is, to say the least, doused by Russian cold water, the foreign minister having announced that Russia does not wish the United States to go any further than it has done.

Meanwhile, Germany, France, and Great Britain have made it clear that their military good offices are available only as auxiliaries to an American military initiative. The careless newspaper reader is left with the impression that any decision involving the military will have to wait six months, pending a crystallization of the question whether announced homosexuals can reasonably be expected to advance on an enemy arm in arm with heterosexuals; or vice versa; or something.

One looks for relief at the bottom of the page. "For 2 African States, Breakdown Is Nearly Total." The French ambassador has been shot and killed in Zaïre, along with forty-five lesser mortals, and foreigners are crossing the river to Brazzaville in the Congo, while chaos sets in. This is the fruit of thirty years under "Marshall" Mobutu, whom this world-watcher, serving for a season as a delegate to the United Nations in 1973, remembers regaling the General Assembly with the scorn Mobutu felt for less civilized countries than his own, like the United States. (He traveled to the United Nations aboard the French superliner *France* with a hundred equerries, including his wife's hairdresser and his private photographer.)

Another dispatch speaks of another African country, a few hundred miles south: "Angola 'Worse Than It's Ever Been.'" Eighteen years after the Portuguese were thrown out, and a year or two after the Communists were thrown out.

Well, where in Africa is the news good? South Africa? "De Klerk Sees Civil War if Negotiations Fail."

It almost has the effect of orienting us toward the Middle East in search of tranquillity. But there, there is the matter of the four hundred deported

Palestinians, and the impending vote by the U.N. Security Council calling for sanctions against Israel. Clinton can veto that. All he has to do is surrender what good will we have with the Arabs.

On page 3 of the paper we see, "Dialing the White House: Busy, Busy, Busy, Click." Could it be the voters calling? To say, "It's not just the economy, stupid"?

—February 2, 1993

Is Multiculturalism the Answer?

The sensation seekers have been amply satisfied lately, and every day leaves the betting man in the quandary of not knowing whether the number of people who tried to blow up Manhattan a few weeks ago will match or exceed the number of prostitutes murdered there by Joel Rifkin.

Of course, there are precedents for both crimes—massacres in the pursuit of jihad are historically commonplace, and Jack the Ripper is the stuff of legend.

But suddenly we are up against something we have no cultural training for. When during Reconstruction the Ku Klux Klan emerged, we were so to speak ready to contend with it. By this I mean that what the KKK sought to do was generally recognized as (1) illegal and (2) immoral. Whatever the laxities of the law in the South during Reconstruction, there was never such a condition of anarchy as to authorize lynching Negro dissenters or flogging white suspects.

Moreover, there was the ultimate appeal to the Southerner, namely the word of the Christian God: The sanctions of the culture of the South were available to the critics of such behavior. Martin Luther King Jr. appealed to the higher law of Americans when he invoked the teachings of Christ as dispositive.

But we are dealing now with that creature, the Muslim fundamentalist, which we have all along comfortably thought to be a problem of other cultures. We knew that the Algerians recently decided to forgo democracy for a spell, when a democratic exercise brought in Muslim fundamentalists in a general election. We knew that the assassination of Anwar Sadat in Cairo was the act of Muslim fundamentalists who were protesting his civilized attitude toward Israel; and, again, we reasoned that this was a regional problem.

When Ayatollah Khomeini locked up American diplomats, the suggestion was made in this column that an appeal to the ayatollah using Koranic language having to do with justice might be the best available weapon. And such an attempt was made, but Khomeini wasn't somebody to whom it was easy to lecture on the more benevolent strictures of the Koran.

We are, after all, face to face with something very different from the religion that has dominated our own culture. Even in the most theocratic of times, St. Thomas Aquinas rejected the idea that the state is obliged to tailor its laws exactly to those of the divine by, e.g., compelling conversion. But that is not so in Islam, where The Law as put forth in Scripture (the Koran) and Tradition (Sunnah) is to be reflected exactly not only in the personal lives of believers, but in the laws of the state as well.

The word "*islam*" means "submission." The government of a Muslim state is explicitly an institution of God. Moreover, such governments are to irradiate Islam not merely by the example of their rulers, but by the institution of *jihad*.

Again, that word literally means "to struggle," or to endeavor, and it can be used to describe personal self-discipline. But it is most notoriously used to describe the holy war that Islam is engaged in to expand its reach over the whole world.

There was a period in Christian history when the same impulses were felt, but it has been centuries since Christians excused spreading the word by shedding blood. Chapter 2, Verse 193, of the Koran enjoins the faithful to "fight in the way of God against those who fight against you, but do not commit aggression. Fight against them until sedition is no more and allegiance is rendered to God alone; but if they make amend, then make no aggression except against evildoers." That seems to say that there is no need to blow up Manhattan after Manhattanites all make their allegiance to Islam.

The current enthusiasm in academic circles for multiculturalism has got to face some difficult problems. The Koran, for instance, informs us (2: 228), "The husband is one degree higher than the wife, because he earns by his strength and expends on his wife." The institutional implications of this superordination of the man over the woman we are all familiar with: From all appearances, the only time men and women get together socially in Muslim countries is when they copulate. Somewhere along the line, the feminist movement in America is going to have to give up either feminism or multiculturalist egalitarianism.

And we are all going to have to take explicit notice of the incompatibility of our own culture and that of the fundamentalist Muslim, and we need to organize our immigration laws with some reference to this problem. The idea of welcoming the alien doesn't include inviting him to blow up Ellis Island en route to citizenship.

—July 6, 1993

Defend America?

Representative Henry Hyde of Illinois has introduced a measure titled the Defend America Act of 1995. He is joined by a fellow Republican, Representative Martin Hoke of Ohio, in coming up with an idea strange to the imagination: namely, that the defense of America depends to some extent on the freedom to act, and that the freedom to act was substantially forfeited in the ABM Treaty.

We are talking about that legendary bone of contention, an outgrowth of the 1972 treaty, which allegedly forbids certain kinds of experiments in antimissile technology, and flatly forbids deployment in more than one site.

For a long time, a technical argument engaged legislatures and diplomats on whether experiments focused on the "brilliant pebble" were precluded under the terms of the 1972 agreement. The idea has been to arm satellites with slingshots that would destroy atmosphere-bound missiles. But the more interesting question is: Why don't we simply pull away from the 1972 treaty?

When Caspar Weinberger was defense secretary under Ronald Reagan, he argued the legitimacy of experimentation, but Congress was not convinced, and all the forces of appeasement all over the world argued against rescinding—in effect—any treaty the Soviet Union had agreed to.

Reagan, although the proud author of the original insight into anti-missile missiles (the Strategic Defense Initiative), never got around to serving the six-month notice required by the treaty to announce its rescission.

Out of office, Weinberger publicly argued in favor of rescission, but his voice and other voices were drowned out by those afraid of any initiative the Soviet Union would frown on.

But of course now there is no Soviet Union, and although we have a treaty, there is a question whether the entity with which we entered into that arrangement still exists. The government of "Russia" is not the legitimate heir to the government of the Soviet Union, any more than the government of Lenin was the heir to the government of Nicholas II.

Still, it is argued, it does no particular harm to proceed as if the treaty were alive. The thing to do is to rescind it.

Now this can hardly be interpreted as a provocative act, given that the doctrine of mutual assured destruction is no longer operative, since Russia and America are no longer at war with each other. But the Senate of the United States, on September 6, reached a "bipartisan compromise" on the matter of missile defense.

The senators who produced that compromise claimed to have been guided by their concern for missile defense. But what they proceeded to do was to authorize future deployment only on behalf of America's allies and of American forces abroad.

The important question, which has to do with research and deployment for the defense of America itself, is therefore skirted—leaving us, in the phrase of defense strategist Frank Gaffney, in a state of "abject vulnerability" to nuclear attack by missiles of a rogue state.

The senators who framed the great evasion of September 6 acknowledge all the correct things: "The threat that is posed to the national security of the United States by the proliferation of ballistic and cruise missiles is significant and growing, both quantitatively and qualitatively. . . . There is a danger that determined countries will acquire intercontinental ballistic missiles in the near future and with little warning by means other than indigenous development."

The senators even acknowledge that "the concept of mutual assured destruction, which was one of the major philosophical rationales for the ABM Treaty, is now questionable as the basis for stability in a multipolar world."

So? So—do nothing. That is, nothing that contributes to the national defense.

Hyde, with his keen nose for the quick of a question, acknowledges that the shadow of the 1972 treaty has the effect of dimming strategic and tactical vision, and should be disposed of once and for all. Accordingly, the Hyde-Hoke measure would direct the president to notify the Russian Federation that the United States intends to exercise its right under the treaty's Article XV to withdraw from the accord.

One has to hope that an enlightened debate will ensue. There aren't really many questions that need answering.

1. Does rescission of the treaty in any conceivable way endanger Russia? No.

2. Can research and deployment of new anti-missile systems help us to shore up our defenses? Yes.

3. Are there other nations that might benefit from a vigorous anti-missile program? Yes. All nations that wish protection from missiles.

—September 19, 1995

Finding Honor in Abu Ghraib

Several voices, trying, if not exactly to overlook the grim events, at least to put them in an anaesthetic perspective, are saying: "So's your old man." And there is no questioning the truth of it, which is that the people to whom President Bush has extended an apology are people who have spent very little time deploring the atrocities of the enemy we face. They are, then, hypocrites.

But what does that do for us, to label them as such? Nothing very much, because our concern is over the behavior of British and American troops, not the behavior of Baathists. Having apologized to the enemy and to the Arab community, what else is in order?

Senator Tom Harkin of Iowa was quick to ask for the dismissal of Secretary of Defense Donald Rumsfeld. Senator Harkin, just a few months ago, was counseling the election of Howard Dean as president of the United States, which tells us something of his own judgment. He is part of a little group of Left toughies who are calling for Rumsfeld's dismissal—Nancy Pelosi and Charles Rangel and other solons. The trouble with leaving it to such folk to prescribe the norms of behavior in the Abu Ghraib prison is, according to one commentator, "that one ends up blowing opportunities to effect true reforms."

But we do not need any reforms. Reforms are something we need in Guantánamo, where we have isolated a new species not previously known in the taxonomic order, the man who is not a prisoner of war, not a traitor, but an enemy combatant. If there is reason to be vexed by Rumsfeld, it is surely that he has not encouraged a table of organization that deals with that phenomenon other than simply by sticking him in a corner of Cuba without any avenue of hope or resolution.

But there are no reforms indicated in the treatment of prisoners in Abu Ghraib. What was done was against (1) regulations, (2) Army convention, and (3) civilized tradition. What do the reformers want? Pre-induction courses for U.S. soldiers in which they are told not to strip and torture captives and photograph them naked?

The Democratic offensive has to limit itself to the failure to keep superiors informed. The lieutenant in charge of the delinquent soldiers should have done more than he did—should have passed word about what happened on to battalion headquarters, which should have passed word to regiment, to division, to corps, to Army, to the Pentagon, to Rumsfeld, and to the president. Rumsfeld held back for several weeks telling Bush about it, and he has been reprimanded. We reasonably assume that Rumsfeld thought the delay would give Army investigators time to trace the special rot that infected the perpetrators. Something a little different from just plain original sin.

Everybody suffers from that, but not everybody ties strings to prisoners' genitalia and simulates electrocution.

The singularity of this offense—precisely its failure to be routine—puts it on a plane with the singularity of those Arabs in Fallujah who hacked Americans to pieces and hung the pieces up on a bridge. We swore to avenge that crime and are bent on doing so. But we have distinguished between those Arabs, and others who do not engage in such conduct.

Our singling out the men—and women—at Abu Ghraib as different, as criminals to be distinguished from non-criminals, is all the perspective we need in handling this case. No reforms are needed. What is needed is the re-energizing of codes of conduct. After the My Lai massacre in 1968, we needed not fresh rules, but the reaffirmation of existing rules, and the vindication of American honor came in the corporate feeling of revulsion over what was done.

The corporate sense of revulsion over what was done at Abu Ghraib is what regenerates Western honor now.

—May 14, 2004

Bushspeak in Europe

The debate was quickly framed as follows: Did President Bush, by his remarks, contribute to the stability of democracy in Russia, or did he enhance the prospects of destabilization?

The question is serious and attracts immediate concern. A reductionist formulation of the criticism that has been directed at Bush would remind us that territorial Russia stretches across eleven time zones, and that however bedraggled the Russian military is at this point, Russia is still the second-largest nuclear power in the world—by some reckonings, the premier nuclear power, since the old, wicked USSR hid and lied about its nuclear production. Add to this that democracy is not a fixed component of the Russian DNA, and we're left with the question: Did President Bush make a mistake in provoking Putin, and the Russian people?

It was a great weekend for major-power politics. On Sunday we had *60 Minutes*, with Mike Wallace doing his unique act with a Putin who was driven, by Wallace's prosecutorial questioning, to demand, in effect, to know about the Negro situation in the South. Old Cold Warriors will remember that cliché of the Fifties, when the Communist apologist would reply to the American who documented charges of Soviet aggression, imperialism, concentration camps, and genocide by denouncing the United States for Jim Crow. Mike Wallace observed that the Russian *nomenklatura* controls the media and that democratic accounting simply did not prevail, to which Putin replied (finding his Jim Crow) that it wasn't democracy but a judicial court that decided the Bush-Gore election in 2000.

It transpires that Mr. Putin is curious about world affairs and reads the foreign press diligently. But to hang in there with a non sequitur when replying to charges of non-democratic practices must have made him wistful for the old days, when simple assertions of Soviet rectitude were all that was needed, or expected.

What President Bush did, meanwhile, was wonderfully bracing. To begin with, he apologized for our own complicity in postwar arrangements authorized at Yalta. When he spoke in Latvia, he made no attempt to elide the events of 1945, when Communist aggression simply replaced Nazi aggression, and the long period began when the little Baltic republics were merely vassal states of Russia. The president applauded the evolution of democracy in Ukraine and Georgia and even pitched for freedom for Belarus. After Bush's two hours with Putin at the presidential dacha outside Moscow, Secretary of State Condoleezza Rice reported that the president had spoken of the rule of law, a free press. and a political opposition as constituent elements in a democracy.

Mr. Putin in due course got it said that Russia was its own master and needed no help from foreign ideologues in making its way into a democratic future. As much was expected. National pride almost always prevails.

But what was special about the scene was the all-American direct-ness of Mr. Bush's commentary. Sometimes it matters when, in dealings with leaders of foreign powers, there are exchanges of social intimacies. When President Eisenhower greeted Premier Khrushchev in 1959, he was meeting for the first time on American soil with a Soviet leader, and he passed on the word to the photographers that he would not smile. His countenance would be that of an official doing his duty. When, thirteen years later, President Nixon consorted with the leaders of Communist China, there were those who felt dismay at the bonhomie of a shared repast with men actively engaged in the pursuit of bloody tyranny.

Bush brings a hygiene that shields him from criticisms that would be engendered by others who are thought fatalistic, or indifferent, to the slights to human freedom. He is certain to be criticized in Europe by those who don't like spontaneous approaches to diplomatic affairs, who don't like Bush, and who in their present mood don't like America.

Bush knows that there are such problems, and it would be wrong to suppose that he is indifferent to them. But he is bound by the dictates of his own nature, and these encouraged him, over the weekend, to say candid things to President Putin, to acknowledge historical failings of his own country, to remark the doleful decades in the Baltic nations, and to exude a cheerful feel for the whole situation. What he did was, if not exactly made in America, very American. And the next time he comes to town, if he sets down in Berlin or Paris, he is certain to say pleasant and cheerful things to the leaders of our allies.

—May 10, 2005

Next-Day Thoughts in Britain

EDINBURGH—Some critics of Tony Blair have pounded on the point that one of the four London Transit bombers had been identified by the secu-rity people as mischievously connected with aggressive elements of the Muslim community.

So why had they not brought him in?

The innocence of the question recalls the questioning, in 1964, of J. Edgar Hoover by the Warren Commission, inquiring into the assassination of President Kennedy. Was it not known to the FBI that Lee Harvey Oswald had been active in a pro-Castro political organization in New Orleans? Yes, we knew that. Didn't we know that he had left the U.S. Marines and declared himself a Communist, marrying a Russian girl and setting out to live in the Soviet Union before returning home? Yes, we knew that. Wasn't it known that he had traveled to Mexico City, where he might have conspired with Fidelistas to break U.S. laws? Yes, we knew he had been there. Well, how come, on November 22, 1963, he was squatting there in the Texas School Book Depository, a Mannlicher-Carcano rifle in his hands, at liberty to assassinate the president of the United States?

Mr. Hoover said that if everyone in America at the security-risk level of Lee Harvey Oswald were secluded when the president passed by, we would have a politically intolerable situation. He gave the number of people in Chicago whom, if we applied to them a hypothetical Oswald security meter, we would have to segregate, and that number (was it two thousand?) sobered the house, and the commission moved on to the challenge of protecting a president other than by identifying and removing from the scene everyone who might wish him dead.

Hot critics of the vulnerability of London on July 7 edged into a different question: Hadn't the government encouraged the bombers by the PM's endorsement of U.S. policy in the Iraq war? Chatham House, a British think tank, encouraged such thought by observing that the British were now riding as a "pillion passenger" in the U.S. war tank, incurring enemies while abandoning freedom of movement. Mr. Blair replied that Britain is engaged in counterterrorist activity, and that it was several times singled out for al-Qaeda violence before the Iraq war even began.

The detailed examination of the movements of the four bombers tells of their awesome coordination, calling to mind the nineteen Arabs who coordinated their movements so as to take control only a few minutes apart of four airliners, which they then reoriented to plunge into buildings in New York and Washington. The British terrorists even seemed to pause, flukily, to appear on the camera screen at King's Cross station, each one carrying a rucksack with explosives, just before three of them descended into the underground system, one headed west, one south, one east, to detonate their bombs at 8:50 A.M., the fourth one heading for a bus to do the same an hour later. That kind of coordination is not effected by random encounters, and we are required to think about the nature of the challenge: four very young men, resolutely set on death for themselves, provided only that there be at least ten deaths of innocent British citizens for each of their own.

Mr. Blair, whether riding as pillion passenger or serving as guide, needs to contend against such persons at whatever scale they present themselves—riding in the Tube below London streets, or flying high over the skies of Manhattan or Washington, or working in a laboratory to coordinate biological, chemical, or nuclear horror. We have to hope that sanity will break through. What Islamic voice—we are entitled to ask over and over—can break through to those consciences awry, to tell them they cannot accomplish the end of the Western world? And that in pursuit of that goal, they are committing their own suicide, and enhancing the kind of impatience toward Islam which could doom their co-religionists by the tens of thousands, to deaths as bloody as they are bent on inflicting on others?

—July 19, 2005

Hitting Iran

A sane and studious observer of the international scene addressed the dinner guests and concluded his optimistic analysis of our Iraqi venture with an arresting afterthought: "What we will not be seeing, when President Bush leaves office, is an Iran with a nuclear bomb."

Almost all discussion of pressing strategic concerns touches down on Iran. The drum rolling on nuclear Iran makes it retrospectively incredible that when Pakistan joined the nuclear club, we simply heard about it, roughly speaking, the day after it exploded its first weapon. By contrast, Iran is almost every week in the news on the matter of its determination to have a bomb. Most recently there was a setback, when Moscow declined to provide some of the help that Iran had asked for. It was this development, in the opinion of some analysts, that caused Teheran to agree to send a mission to Baghdad to confer with our ambassador, Zalmay Khalilzad.

This hardly means that Iran is ready to negotiate an end to its nuclear development. Stephen Hadley, national security advisor to President Bush, caught the spirit of U.S. reaction to this development: "We're talking to Iran all the time. We make statements, they make statements."

But repeated statements by the president on the matter of U.S. concern over a nuclear-armed Iran bring up the question: What do we intend to do about it if Iran, departing from its bluster, adopts the Pakistani mode and proceeds noiselessly to nuclear armament?

The conversation turns to military intervention. A year ago, *The New Yorker* ran an extensive essay on the subject by Seymour Hersh, the salient finding of which was that to bring off an interdictory operation is very nearly impossible:

Item No. 1: The Israeli air force does not have airplanes with a range sufficient to complete a round trip to Iranian targets. Israeli culture does not sanction suicide missions; it is inconceivable that planes would fly from Israel on such missions.

Item No. 2: Nuclear sites in Iran are spread about, so that what the Israelis did in the 1981 bombing of Osirak, aborting the whole Iraqi nuclear operation, cannot be reproduced in Iran. An air strike superior to anything the Israelis could mount would be required.

And Item No. 3: Getting on with such an operation, requiring aircraft carriers and strategically useful bases on the perimeter of the target area, could not conceivably be done stealthily. The whole world would be ongoing witness to the impending operation, and pacifist anti-American capitulationist forces would rise to put almost impassable diplomatic obstacles in the way.

Well, then, can we get on with sanctions? These would seem to be in order, with the reiterated threat to call to the attention of the U.N. Security Council the illegality of Iran's program, as a signer of the Nuclear Non-Proliferation Treaty. But, again, there are obstacles.

In the first place, Moscow, in its anfractuous way, would probably veto sanctions. But what if it didn't? A determined international effort would hurt Iranians and Iranian interests, but how decisively? We aren't going to refuse to consume Iranian oil. Economic boycotts mostly do not work, and if and when they do (e.g., against Rhodesia), they require great stretches of time to generate real pain, and time is what we do not have.

The point insufficiently pressed is this: Why does the United States need to shoulder the critical burden here? If Iran gets the bomb, a new set of strategic relationships would arise. Saudi Arabia and Egypt would clamor for the bomb, perhaps also Turkey. Perilous regional pressures would mount hugely. What it comes down to is that the United States would be critically affected, but other nations would be more directly affected, and the question frames itself: Why do they not take on the responsibility of intervening in Iran?

Why should France not interrupt its August holiday to participate in a military mission? The interests of Germany and India are clearly affected. Where is U.S. diplomacy going with all of this? It's one thing that the United States is the ultimate deterrent power, but we act as if there were no others, and this is both emasculating and psychologically subversive.

Ideally, the initiative would be taken elsewhere, with a forceful European or Middle Eastern leader mobilizing continental and Asian concern.

But failing that, the need to take the initiative would necessarily fall on us, and the question then becomes: Is it something Mr. Bush is going to handle before the end of his term in office?

—March 17, 2006

Duty, Honor, Country

While no historical event exactly replicates another, it is certainly the case that what happened in Vietnam in 1972–75 bears very closely on the current situation in Iraq.

To truncate the story drastically, what happened back then was the result of the correlation of four strategic factors:

1. Hanoi's resolution to conquer the South. The North Vietnamese were held back by the failure of their spring offensive in 1972. That offensive was weakened by U.S. mining of the harbors and by the reluctance of China, in the swoon of the Nixon visit to Mao, to give full-bodied support to an invasion. But Hanoi simply bided its time.
2. The withdrawal by the United States, ending in March 1973, of a combative military presence. Only a few hundred U.S. advisors were left in South Vietnam.
3. The growing stability of the South Vietnamese government, which was assumed competent to carry out the terms of the Paris agreements of 1973. These agreements had been negotiated in dozens and dozens of meetings between Le Duc Tho and Henry Kissinger. The agreements called for the removal of U.S. forces, the cessation of North Vietnamese offensives, and recognition of the Saigon government as the ruling political entity in the South.

4. The progressive disunity of the United States government. Here we had the antiwar movement as a continuing force. But that movement attained dominance *pari passu* with the weakening of President Nixon. As Watergate metastasized from a "second-rate burglary" into grounds for the removal of a president, U.S. support for success in Vietnam wilted.

The parallels in the current situation are plain, beginning with the nature of the United States' participation. What we have right now is a progressively immobilized executive and a dissenting legislature, leading—inevitably—to an impotent military.

The question immediately posed is: Do we feel responsibility for what happens in the period ahead? The Iraqi government resembles the government of South Vietnam in 1973–74 in that Baghdad is fighting, as Saigon fought, for a political system free of hostile foreign elements. But Saigon could not hold out in the long run without U.S. military support, and neither can Baghdad.

If the parallels hold, i.e., if the result of failure in the Middle East is equivalent to the result of failure in Indochina, then we would expect to see the collapse of the Maliki government in Baghdad, some kind of bloody vengeance against Iraqis who had supported that government, and a people subjugated by a regime that sits on 1 percent of the world's supply of oil and is unlikely to proceed indifferent to the march, by Iraq's eastern neighbor, to becoming a nuclear power.

In the currency of human deaths, it is unlikely that they would match in Iraq what we stood by for in Vietnam. The statistics aren't even there to count accurately the casualties of defeat in that theater. But the most graphic symbol is the picture of Vietnamese, young and old, clinging to a U.S. helicopter in the desperate, final hope to be taken away from those waiting to torture and kill them. As stated, the statistics are not exact, but somewhere between a quarter-million and two million or even three million Vietnamese suffered from our flight from the burden we first had undertaken, and then abandoned.

Henry Kissinger has said that the use of the American fleet to contain the invasion of 1975 could have saved the day. What could save the day in Iraq? Nothing short of public revulsion toward those Democrats who are measuring these days the political value of honor. In the election ahead, all the world will be looking over our shoulders, including the ghosts of Vietnam.

—June 1, 2007

GRACE NOTES

Beethoven's Two-Hundredth

This being Election Day, it occurs to me that it is the two-hundredth anniversary of the birth of Ludwig van Beethoven. And that I have not paid my tribute, which is all right because the line is very long, and anyway my flowers are pretty inconspicuous alongside those of the stellar figures of the musical world.

But I am provoked by my old friend William F. Rickenbacker (yes, son of Captain Eddie), writer, sportsman, stock analyst, linguist, musician: and, first and foremost, provocateur. Mr. Rickenbacker has written in *National Review* acknowledging that much of Beethoven's later music is "impossible to overrate," but maintaining that most of the early stuff is merely "manipulative bangbang." The appreciation of any particular piece of music is of course a subjective matter, as everyone knows, especially Mr. Rickenbacker, though he attempts what sounds like an objective demonstration. Beethoven, he says, is easy to imitate. "Mrs. Brown, the English mystic who claims to receive music dictated directly from dead masters, has 'introduced' some music she says Liszt gave her, but it doesn't sound like Liszt; the things she says Schubert gave her don't sound like Schubert; her Beethoven sounds exactly like Beethoven in his early, i.e., awful, period." Now all that that story suggests to me is that Beethoven is cooperating with Mrs. Brown while Liszt and Schubert are not.

So what does Mr. Rickenbacker propose? A "Beethoven Suppression Society whose purpose will be to stamp out all the master's works up through Opus 52." ("And all the goddamn operas.") (He means *Fidelio.*) Mr. Rickenbacker, wise beyond his years in extra-musical matters, ends his article, "I will not answer any letters from anyone on this subject, unless it be the editor's letter accompanying the check." Well, I have sent the check. This is my letter.

By the time Beethoven came around to Opus 52 (eight songs), he was thirty-four years old. He had composed two of his symphonies, three of his piano concertos—indeed, over one-third of his entire production. Never mind the symphonies, or the concertos, but concentrate for a minute on what Mr. Rickenbacker would have us exclude from among the piano sonatas.

There are thirty-two of them, and he would ban the first twenty-one, right up to the "Waldstein." Interestingly enough, he does not ban the "Appassionata," while passing along about it (and exaggerating) the recent slurs of Glenn Gould. Consider the carnage. Name one or two of the better-known sonatas. Take the most famous of them all, the "Moonlight Sonata."

Now what is the matter with the "Moonlight Sonata" is that people play it who shouldn't play it, because the first movement is technically easy. I had a teacher who solved in one stroke The Problem of the "Moonlight Sonata": She would not permit any of her students to take on the first movement who had not developed the skill to perform the third movement. That kept all but the top 5 percent from playing that sonata, and by the time you get so you can play the last movement, you probably have enough sophistication to play the first without ruining it.

Now, you cannot keep music students from permanently ruining the reputation of, say, the "Minuet in G": though when it is played by, say, Myra Hess, one is reminded of the simple beauty of it, like one of the pastoral poems of Wordsworth. The third movement of the "Moonlight" is a little junky, so what? It is perfectly agreeable, and in any case it is a foundation for some of the exploits so perfectly consummated in the later sonatas.

The very first sonata, in F minor, is wonderfully pleasant; really, what a bore it is to say that having tasted the great vintages, you can never enjoy table wine. Can Mr. Rickenbacker seriously maintain that the adagio movement of the C major sonata (number 3) is less than sublime? The "Pathétique Sonata" is grand and exciting, though to be sure one can skip the last movement, even though music boxes are also worth listening to every now and then.

I tell you what. Here is my propitiation to Beethoven. There is a splendid artist whose name is Alfred Brendel, a Viennese who teaches in Mexico and performs everywhere. He has recorded all of Beethoven's piano music, in stereo, for Vox. And a wonderfully enterprising company, The Dollar Record Plan, Inc., at P.O. Box 86, Pearl River, N.Y. 10965, has brought out these records at the astonishing price of one dollar ($1) apiece. You can buy all the sonatas for $12. If you have caught the Rickenbacker virus, you can buy all the later sonatas (volumes 2 and 3) for $6.

Now, my offer is this: Buy the lot. If you don't like the first half, send them to me and I'll reimburse you your $6, and transship the records to a hospital, as the anonymous gift of someone who went deaf. And when next I ask Bill Rickenbacker to write for *National Review*, I shall ask him please to refrain from using the early letters of the alphabet.

—November 3, 1970

Reflections on Skiing

GSTAAD—Having been invited by the editors of *Travel and Leisure* to discuss, opposite John Kenneth Galbraith, a subject concerning which I know less than almost anybody, more only than, say, Professor Galbraith, I begin with that Full Disclosure which is among the reforms of the New Deal most generally celebrated.

1. I am not a very good skier. If you were to rank skiing ability on a scale of 1 to 20, I would rank approximately 12. By comparison, you should think in terms of ski teachers at 20, a first-day novice at 1, Professor Galbraith at 8.

2. The aptitude for learning how to ski is something that is primarily a function of age. By this I mean: If you are five years old and learning how to ski, you will almost surely, by the time you are six, ski better than I can ski, having begun at age thirty, and persevered to the age of forty-six.

3. The older you are, the more necessary it becomes to intellectualize skiing. For instance, there are those who, very early, discover that leaning uphill in order to avoid falling downhill doesn't work, and they tend therefore to do the right thing instinctively. Older debutantes (as the European ski teachers persist in calling us) need to knead this datum (forgive the homonym; in fact, it should cause the reader to knit his brow in contemplation of the point, even as we middle-aged skiers need to concentrate on the delicate distinctions we are handed down by our instructors). The young skiers simply take it for granted, and lean downhill quite naturally after the first day or two.

4. The ski teachers are always ahead of you intellectually. So that even if you develop instantaneous docility, such as to cause you to do exactly what the teacher tells you to do, you tend to founder on: paradox.

For instance, they are nowadays telling you that it is extremely important to make your turns *slowly*. My teacher has a sexy way of saying this: *Caressez la neige*. She takes her ski pole and, leeringly, moves it in front of you down the fall line and e-v-e-r so gradually to the right, or of course to the left, if that is the direction in which you want to turn, assuming you are so mature a skier as actually to command such great decisions. And then the teacher tells you that you must never be ambiguous on the point of where your weight is. In other words, you must move your weight *decisively*. Now, how to move your weight decisively, when at the same time you are engaged in so subtly seducing your skis across the fall line into the new direction, becomes one of those philosophical problems about which you meditate long into the evening. You find yourself having very highfalutin thoughts about such philosophical concepts as complementarity, which thoughts, typically, are unresolved when you find yourself, the next morning, instructing your muscles in contradictory imperatives which have been abstractly warring against each other in your sleepless mind.

5. Skiing is a capitalist's paradise, and I do not mean the cost of ski lifts and hamburgers and hotels. The sport is so much the object of a great many people's passion, that they are always finding new ways to improve you, and this means (a) ever-different equipment, and (b) ever-different techniques.

Concerning (a), I remember that for the first six years I skied, my instructor would look at me the first day of the season, behold my ski poles, look up despairingly at the sky, then down to my shriven face, and say condescendingly: "Who told you to buy ski poles that are six centimeters too short for you?" You would mumble something about last year's instructor, and then go buy ski poles six centimeters longer. Next season: "Who—who conceivably?—recommended ski poles six centimeters longer than they should be?" After six years it doesn't much matter, because you own a full inventory of ski poles, and merely bring out the re-anointed pair.

Concerning (b), the problem is much more difficult. When I first "learned," I was told by my teacher that when I made a turn, I should suppose in my mind that I was picking up a pail of water from my left side and moving it to my right side. I had just managed to perfect that discipline when it was discovered (I think they called it the Austrian system) that it was *exactly* wrong—that when you turn you should keep your shoulders *facing downhill*, rather than moving them from left to right, or right to left. Okay. I was once young and resilient. Now—now, they tell me that shoulders-downhill, down-knees, up-knees, is *quite wrong*, that you should be structurally immobile, with only the ankles moving, the weight way way back on your skis—and I find myself telling my instructor that I have given up aspiring to Olympic perfection. I found that, on saying so, I came close to hurting her feelings, so I reached for a way to say it satisfactorily, which way I here publicly divulge for the first time.

Look, I said to Anita, the science people have discovered a way to resituate the keys on the typewriter so as to speed up one's typing by 30 percent. But do you understand my declining to relearn how to use the typewriter? She agrees to understand, though I know that when I face downhill bravely and bob down before each turn, and up, triumphantly, after completing the turn, on those happy occasions when I succeed in completing a turn, she is a little embarrassed, looking around at the fancy company that is witness to her pupil's recalcitrance.

6. Skiing is becoming very expensive, particularly in America, and I suppose it won't be too long before the Democratic National Committee decides that the only thing to do is to nationalize the sport. Professor Galbraith, no doubt, could be got to write a touching declaration to that effect.

7. Skiing manages, somehow, to retain a sense of privacy notwithstanding that it is the fastest-growing sport in the world. And it has economic and hedonistic advantages over, say, ocean racing. Ocean racing, a bitter participant once wrote, "is like standing under an ice-cold shower, tearing up thousand-dollar bills." Skiing is less expensive than that, and—as a rule—less painful. Sure, sometimes skiing manages to be sublimely sadistic. I think of my friend the publisher, who, rounding a bend in the trail a few years ago took a forward fall that left him immobilized, rear end skyward, at which point a swinger zapped around the bend, managing to slice his ski edge (the uphill edge, let the purists relax) right across both of my friend's Achilles' tendons, severing them as neatly as a surgeon would have done at an exhibition, the whole freshman class looking on. The executioner, appalled, braked and climbed back to confront a victim whose morale was sustained only by a vindictive passion to turn his lawyer loose on his assailant, whereupon they instantly recognized each other, the tortfeasor being the closest personal friend and personal lawyer of the (now legless) publisher.

Notwithstanding such experiences, skiing manages to be, primarily, a *private* preoccupation, sharply to be distinguished from all those Chinese, Russian, and Nazi gymnasts who coordinate together in great public spectacles for the delectation of their slavemasters and visiting chiefs of state. It has to do, I think, with the natural rhythm of the sport, whose animating force is—gravity; which was there, free, even before the New Deal discovered it was a human right, even as the wind that propels the sailboat is the gift of nature, rather than of distributive justice, as also the thermal current that lifts the sailplane—the three great sports: natural, related, individualized, divine.

—*Travel and Leisure*, Fall 1972

The Ocean Race of William Snaith

There are sublime uses for the cliché. An example was Westbrook Pegler's, reminiscing about the fascist demagogues of the Thirties. He came to Gerald L. K. Smith. "It was Smith," Pegler wrote, "who said about Franklin Delano Roosevelt: 'That liar, that scoundrel, that thief!'" You could hear Pegler pausing on the page before going on to write, with a sigh, "I wish I had said that." It is a cliché that sunsets-at-sea-are-beautiful, as also that crossing the ocean in a small sailing boat is a dangerous and exhilarating experience, and that the sea is the enemy but a seductive enemy. And there are many books about crossing the ocean in sailing boats, some of them as overindulgent as a banana split, some as telegraphically dull as the log of a Coast Guard cutter. Both extremes have, however, yielded classics in the literature, Joshua Slocum's at the Apollonian end, Joseph Conrad's at the other. In *On the Wind's Way*, William Snaith has produced a classic. It combines the steadfast narrative energy of Slocum and the discursive verbal fecundity of Conrad. Snaith hasn't Conrad's overlay of quiet tragedy, but he has its counterpart, a ribald, self-skewering sense of hilarity, and the result (for all that the writing is uneven) is the most exuberant reading experience of the season. (How I wish I could have written it!) If there is a human impulse it does not satisfy, that is an impulse to be veiled with shame. It nearly ruined Apollo XI for me when I overheard someone say, "Imagine how many housing projects might have been built instead!"

Yes yes. And William Snaith, president of (I guess) the most famous industrial designing firm in the world, might have used his money to plant more soybeans. Instead, this liberal Democrat subsidizes his recreational passion: ocean racing yachts. On the occasion here recorded he slipped his boat out of Bermuda and headed it, against a competitive field of a dozen and a half other boats, toward Skagen Lightship off Sweden, 3,500 miles away. He had with him his oldest son and six experienced friends, some younger, some older, each of them marvelously integrated into the engrossing narrative. Under him, a forty-six-foot yawl designed by the restlessly perfectionist team of Sparkman & Stephens, but altered and burnished and fussed over by Snaith with a concentration that brings to mind the demi-lifetimes high-strung men have spent on single enterprises, great and small. Snaith is a scientist who can read the lines of a hull as Henry Ford read the lineaments of an automobile engine. He is also an architect and artist, whose eye for line and color has got his work hung in New York galleries. He is also the most infuriating, exacting, hedonistic, sadistic, competitive, engaging captain in the Atlantic fleet, and I can imagine that if a huge wave were to carry him overboard, any member of his crew would first hesitate for a luxurious, fugitive moment, and only then throw himself ardently overboard to rescue him at any cost. True devotion, in contrast to automatic heroism, requires, when risking one's life for another, that split second of hesitation.

You are at sea; the conditions are grandly awful. Only yesterday the crew discovered that an eccentric leak had voided the tanks of all but a few gallons of drinking water. But there are 3,000 miles of open ocean yet to go. The grim decision (one of the few collective decisions reached aboard the autocratic *Figaro*) was to go ahead—to add dehydration to the risks of dismasting, knockdown, fire, man-overboard, not to enumerate the routine discomforts of racing at sea, which need to be experienced to be believed.

There is a supreme pleasure on such passages, and it is—sleep. It is the obligation of someone going off duty to awaken those who are going on duty; and the only civilized way to do it is with a dry, matter-of-fact, faintly compassionate resignation, lint-free, God help us, of bonhomie. Here is Snaith performing this function:

"I call the off-watch with a rousing solo, an *a capella* selection from the Cantata 'Sleepers Awake,' which I think not only beautiful but apt. As always any attempt to keep the cultural level of this voyage up to the mark is greeted with complaint. I am disheartened. It is disheartening for one who believes in the uplifting and healing properties of art to find such a level of response from grumpy, disheveled auditors. They quench all thought of evangelism as they stagger about in their baggy-kneed long johns. In their unfeeling responses they are concerned with niggling plaints of being done out of five more minutes of sleep. These are difficult companions at times, but my very own."

The crew, in particular the younger members, show just the right blend of dutifulness and irreverence, and during the endless hours on deck, when the skipper is below, they play at awarding themselves points as the helmsman succeeds in tilting the boat in just such a way as to cause a torrent of water to tear down the lee deck to serve sometimes a useful purpose, such as washing the dishes, but most often malevolent purposes. The highest score registered by midpassage was fifty points. The captain, after presiding over a body- and spirit-breaking watch in ice-cold and tumultuous weather, requiring untold changes in rig, hours of sail patching, trips to the masthead, and public séances on inscrutable meteorological developments, is finally off duty, exhausted, and dead asleep. When, "by some freak of timing, *Figaro* rolled to leeward at the moment of meeting a wave, took on a boarding sea which came roaring up the waterway, hit the cabin house like a breaker hitting a cliff, broke high in the air, poured over the cabin house, and shot down the companionway. Most incredibly it found me in my *bunk*, some distance from the opening. It came over me like a firehose. The shock was indescribable. The gasp which normally comes with a sudden cold immersion was choked off by water in my nose and mouth. I coughed and sputtered. I could hardly grasp what had happened. But the cause of that spreading wet and cold was not long in making itself known. All peace and contentment gave way to rage. I crawled from the berth, mad as a wet captain, shouting my wrath, trying in some way to release the outrage that flooded my being, only to hear my first-born, Cleody, my son, carrier of my name, the staff and rod to comfort me in my declining years, shouting, '*I get a thousand points! I get a thousand points!*'"

William Snaith's complex understanding of such an episode in this race across the Atlantic is suggestive in every relevant field. He has a literary gift for technical description I have not seen equaled this side (curiously) of the critic Hugh Kenner, who can describe a solenoid with an airborne precision Sir Isaac Newton would have envied. The spinnaker halyard suddenly gives way. "The trouble and its cause were simple enough. The fitting was made of bronze when it should have been made of stainless steel. In the two days' wear of go-go swiveling, added to earlier erosion, the soft flange at the bottom of the spindle had worn down until it slipped through the barrel of the cylinder like bath soap through a wet hand." Is this the engineer talking, or the artist?

Or the sailor? It is all three who execute Snaith's unparalleled description (pages 121–122) of the helmsman's role in maneuvering the ship in a following wind, or his analysis of the circumstances that produced the lowering menace slowly catching his little yawl in midpassage. "Now the horizon was black, Dylan Thomas's Bible-black. It arched up [and] joined the gray in knife-edged resolution. Underneath, the gray sea took on a pale ophidian flecking without shine. The flat highlighting of the breaking wave tops was dull and lusterless. . . ."

Figaro survived that one, and worse, and in between the crises there was hilarity; a doggedly voluptuous cuisine; fitful, blurted-out confidences, during the long night watches, by young men of their secret cares, fears, and ambitions; musings by the author on old romances and tribulations— but all of it under the metronomic lash of the competition: they meant, in this pretty, stalwart, silly little boat, to finish the race, to survive sleet and storm and calm and fog and maelstroms off the Orkney Islands: and to win. They did win, but the trophy is this numinous book, so vibrant with adventure and spirit and beauty.

—*New York Times Book Review*, November 18, 1973

David Niven Recreates Hollywood

Bring On the Empty Horses is a book about Hollywood and incidentally a masterly self-portrait. Inasmuch as what David Niven recalls is mostly what he saw, smelled, and tasted, you wonder, after putting it down, how he managed to bring it off without making it sound like a book starring David Niven, produced by David Niven, and directed by David Niven from an original screenplay by David Niven. This does not happen because of a talent for self-effacement which is one of the many things Niven did not learn in Hollywood, the others being a resolute amiability and thoughtfulness. That talent serves him now as a pillar supporting what must easily be the best book ever written about Hollywood. A volume, moreover, that is not likely to be challenged on its own terms, because there is no other survivor of the scene from 1935 to 1960 (a) who knew everybody Niven knew and (b) who can write the way Niven writes. He is a fine actor and comedian. He is an even better writer.

How does he manage to keep the focus away from himself? Watch. "One Fourth of July he [Douglas Fairbanks] and Sylvia chartered a motor cruiser and invited a small group, including Norma Shearer and Irving Thalberg, to sail with them to Catalina. The idea was to anchor on arrival alongside Cecil B. DeMille's sleek white three-masted schooner. Our captain had an ominous name—Jack Puke . . ." *Our* captain! Is there a neater way to all but inflect oneself right out of an episode?

Yet in ghosting himself out he limns, unconsciously, a portrait that superbly complements the hilarious autobiography of his youth, *The Moon's a Balloon*. One comes to know David Niven as one might one's brother; so to speak, by feel. Hear him again, writing this time about Cary Grant: "Through the years to come he made generous efforts to straighten out my private life by warning me of the quirks and peculiarities of various ladies, by giving me complicated advice on how to play a part in a film I was making with him, by telling me which stocks to buy when I could not afford a phone call to a broker, and by promising that he could cure my liking for Scotch by hypnotizing me." We have learned something about Cary Grant, and at least as much about David Niven.

~

A book for grown-ups about Hollywood and the lives of Hollywood stars? But the skepticism ends with the first chapter. There is a narrative tension from the beginning, and an ear for piquancy, an eye for the amusing and absurd and the poignant. The compulsion of the entertainer, in Niven's case a blend of exuberance, skill, and good manners (it is after all rude to be dull, if one knows how not to be), keeps the book moving like an Olsen and Johnson production. He will now and then defer to meticulous and illuminating detail: "He [Edmund Lowe] . . . drove me around the cozily named 'Back Lot'—a 200-acre spread upon which stood the permanent sets, including New York streets, New England, French, and Spanish villages, medieval castles, a railroad station complete with rolling stock, lakes with wave-making machines and rustic bridges, a university campus, an airliner, a section of jungle and another of pine forest, a Mississippi steamboat, a three-masted schooner, native canoes, a submarine, a stretch of desert with ruined fort and, in case anything was missing, several acres of carefully dismantled, docketed and stored streets, villages, cathedrals, mud huts, dance halls, skating rinks, ball parks, theaters, vineyards, slums, Southern plantations, and Oriental palaces."

Thus the paraphernalia of Hollywood. There is much more about the beast. A two-part chapter—he calls it "Our Little Girl," withholding from the reader, for once, the identity of the principal—describes the physical and psychic torture of stardom by giving two days in the life of one star, hour by hour, compressing a decade's exhilaration and decomposition as imaginatively and evocatively as Robert Nathan describing the evolution of a young girl in his *Portrait of Jennie*. David Niven has no illusions about the Hollywood that died in the late Fifties, even if he has not quite yet compounded an antidote to paganism. "[It] was hardly a nursery for intellectuals, it was a hotbed of false values, it harbored an unattractive percentage of small-time crooks and con artists, and the chances of being successful there were minimal, but it was fascinating, and IF YOU WERE LUCKY, it was fun." In a curious sense, David Niven continues to be starstruck, but the reader finds himself—caring. Not because the reader is involved in mankind, but because he actually finds himself involved in Errol Flynn! That makes David Niven something of a sorcerer.

Douglas Fairbanks furtively revealed to Niven him his fear of growing old. George Sanders confided in 1937, when he was thirty-one, that at age sixty-five he would commit suicide, which he did. Errol Flynn suggested the uses of just a touch of cocaine on the tip of the penis. Greta Garbo swam naked in his pool. (Their enduring friendship Niven is required modestly to concede, even as he describes her pathological fear of friendship, recalling Robert Montgomery's acid remark on being snubbed only weeks after co-starring with her, that "making a film with Garbo does not constitute an introduction.") Ronald Colman, noblesse oblige, speeded to his side in his launch and narrowly rescued him from a shark. Clark Gable began by giving him his catch to clean when Niven, broke, was working as a sport-fisherman's assistant—and was soon agitating to get him a screen test. Fred Astaire, a clumsy social dancer, ripped off a wild routine in his living room. Tyrone Power dressed as Santa Claus for his children. Miriam Hopkins acknowledged a Christmas gift of two handkerchiefs by giving him a Studebaker. Charlie Chaplin described in a throwaway paragraph how to contrive to make truly comic a fat lady approaching a banana peel. Charles MacArthur, resentful over the second-class status given by the big producers to writers, took revenge by elaborating to L. B. Mayer the fictitious talents of a London garage mechanic who happened to be entirely illiterate, and landing a thousand-dollar-a-week contract for him. Scott Fitzgerald was numb with gratitude when Niven matter-of-factly offered him the use of his refrigerator for the Coca-Colas Fitzgerald briefly besotted himself with while trying to exorcise demon rum . . .

The book teems with that kind of thing, but the incidents are not carelessly catalogued, like a book of jokes by Bennett Cerf. Some of the portraits—of Clemence Dane, for instance, and Errol Flynn—approach art, and easily surpass entertainment. The sentiment, which abounds, stops (usually) short of sentimentality. The descriptions are agile, terse or profuse as the situation demands. And all this the work of an *undertaker*. Because although David Niven is still acting, and hit movies are still being made, the phenomenon of Hollywood has passed, and David Niven has no desire to resurrect it, though in fact he has done so.

—*New York Times Book Review*, July 21, 1975

Just to Say Thanks

For many years I have labored under the burden of an unrequited passion. What have I done for it, in return for all it has done for me? Nothing. But I have wondered what I could use as what journalists call a "peg."

I have found one. This may strike some of the literal-minded as attenuated, but it goes as follows: This is the centennial year of the Tuskegee Institute, which was founded on the Fourth of July, 1881, by Booker T. Washington. Tuskegee continues to be a remarkable institution, and former Secretary of Defense Donald Rumsfeld is the head of a committee of illustrious men and women who are devoting themselves to raising $20 million to encourage it in its noble work.

What noble work? We have arrived at step two. It was, among other things, the principal academic home of George Washington Carver, and it was G. W. Carver who to all intents and purposes invented the peanut. What he did, more specifically, was to document that the cultivation of the peanut despoiled the land far less than the cultivation of cotton, and then he set out to merchandise the peanut in order that there might be a market for it.

He discovered an estimated three hundred uses for it, many of them entirely removed from the peanut's food value. But it is this, of course, that is the wonder of the peanut. The *Encyclopaedia Britannica* informs us that "pound for pound peanuts have more protein, minerals, and vitamins than beef liver, more fat than heavy cream, and more food energy (calories) than sugar." And George Washington Carver discovered—peanut butter.

I have never composed poetry, but if I did, my very first couplet would be:

I know that I shall never see
A poem lovely as Skippy's peanut butter.

When I was first married and made plain to my wife that I expected peanut butter for breakfast every day of my life, including Ash Wednesday, she thought me quite mad (for the wrong reasons). She has not come round, really, and this is a source of great sadness to me, because one wants to share one's pleasures.

I was hardened very young to the skeptics. When I was twelve I was packed off to a British boarding school by my father, who dispatched every fortnight a survival package comprising a case of grapefruit and a large jar of peanut butter. I offered to share my tuck with the other boys at my table. They grabbed instinctively for the grapefruit—but one after another actually spat out the peanut butter, which they had never before seen and which only that very year (1938) had become available for sale in London. No wonder they needed American help to win the war.

You can find it now in specialty shops in Europe, but I have yet to see it in anyone's home. And it is outrageously difficult to get even in the typical American hotel. My profession requires me to spend forty or fifty nights on the road every year, and when it comes time to order breakfast over the telephone I summon my resolution—it helps to think about peanut butter when you need moral strength—and add, after the orange juice, coffee, skim milk, and whole-wheat toast, "Do you have any peanut butter?"

Sometimes the room-service operator will actually break out laughing when the request is put in, at which point my voice becomes stern and unsmiling. Often the operator will say, "Just a minute," and then she will turn, I suppose to the chef, but I can hear right through the hand she has put over the receiver—"Hey Jack. We got any peanut butter? Room 322 wants some peanut butter!" This furtive Philistinism is then regularly followed by giggles all around. One lady recently asked, "How old is your little boy and does he want a peanut-butter sandwich?" To which I replied, "My little boy is twenty-eight and is never without peanut butter, because he phones ahead before he confirms hotel reservations."

I introduced Auberon Waugh to cashew butter ten years ago when he first visited America, and although I think it inferior to peanut butter, Auberon was quite simply overwhelmed. You can't find it in Great Britain, so I sent him a case from the Farmer's Market. It quite changed his writing

style: For about ten months he was at peace with the world. I think that was
the time he said something pleasant about Harold Wilson. In the eleventh
month, it was easy to tell that he had run out. It quite changes your disposition and your view of the world if you cannot have peanut butter every day.

So here is yet another reason for contributing money to the Tuskegee
Institute. For all we know, but for it we'd never have tasted peanut butter.
There'd be no Planter's, no Jif, no Peter Pan—that terrible thought reminds
us of our indebtedness to George Washington Carver.

—March 26, 1981

Goldberg Divined

Some years ago, as the word was getting around that he would soon die from
leukemia, Dinu Lipatti played a concert in France that was rumored would
be his last, as indeed it proved to he. It was recorded, and it is not merely the
act of a morbid imagination that causes one, listening to the Bach and the
Chopin, to detect in it a strain of poignant yet somehow exultant fatalism.

When, in the fall of 1980, the harpsichordist Fernando Valenti surmised
from what his doctors said that he would not survive the cancer detected in
his throat, he was practicing to record Bach's *Goldberg Variations*. He had
played them before, as a very young man; then he buried them, devoting
the thirty-five years after his graduation from college to giving recitals and
making recordings (over eighty records)—of Bach, to be sure, but his specialty has always been Scarlatti (in rendering Scarlatti he has no peer). But
the itch to do the *Goldberg* came, and would not go. And now it appeared
that if he made the recording, it would be his valedictory.

It happened that the season was full of *Goldbergs*. A generation ago if
one wanted to hear the *Goldberg Variations*, one needed to buy the recording
of Wanda Landowska, and then, a little later, Rosalyn Tureck's on the piano,
and Ralph Kirkpatrick's (one of Valenti's teachers) on the harpsichord.
Then, of course, Glenn Gould came along, and his convulsive rendition
swept the attention of the musical world. The critics were carried away
by the sheer effrontery of his conception, so that whether one thought
it a musical epiphany or sheer travesty, his interpretation was for twenty
years the center of attention of what is arguably the supreme achievement

of the baroque keyboard. In 1982 two events coincided ironically: Glenn Gould, age fifty, died, and Fernando Valenti, age fifty-five, did not die. And, at about the same time, they had recorded the *Goldberg*, Gould again to an uproarious reception.

A casualty was Fernando Valenti's *Goldberg Variations* (*sine qua non*), scarcely noticed when it was first released. He had repaired to a studio in New Jersey, and there, in three days, he did the aria and thirty variations, written in 1742 at the behest of Count Kayserling for his friend Johann Gottlieb Goldberg.

Although Bach stipulated that all the variations should be repeated, Valenti repeats none of them, and inevitably—for those who knew he was uncertain whether he would survive the season—there is something of the sense of his rushing forward to arrive at the final aria before the grim reaper cut him off. But that said, one finds in the performance an absolutely secure sense of tempo. One very quickly discerns, on hearing Valenti, that he is technically capable of taking any of the movements at the speed of Glenn Gould or Andras Schiff, but generally he elects not to, and the result is that sense of ultimate composure that perfect music, perfectly executed, brings. After variation 30, before the last reiteration of the aria, there is a pause of (by Valenti's standards) melodramatic length: it lasts perhaps five, six seconds. And then the aria proceeds, stately as a winged chariot, until, six bars before the end, there is, in the slight rubato, just a hint of that reluctance to conclude anything so nearly divine: the artist expressing his reluctance to conclude life itself, and in so doing, giving life so noble a sound.

—*Esquire*, March 1986

Praiseworthiness

In this season we are encouraged to express our reverences. Not as specifically as on the Fourth of July, or on the birthdays of national leaders passed on. It is something of the human disposition, if not exactly to doubt, at least to be patient of doubt. Skepticism, it is sometimes called, and we are urged to reflect that skepticism brings on curiosity; curiosity, an alteration of accepted ways and of accepted solutions. It was dissatisfaction with the heavy traction of sled over ground that brought the wheel.

Continued impatience with physical actualities harnesses man's efforts to overcome them. We accepted the immutability of the laws of gravity even when we discovered means of defying them in flight. But we do not attempt to repeal gravity, to which—this being the lesson of the season— we liken patriotism. The love of country. Patriotism can attenuate, and defective patriotism isn't instantly punished. But we can, and should, detect it when it rises to the level of a challenge to the great moorings of life, as when one hesitates, on our country's holy days, to pay obeisance to what we have.

Piety also suffers from the sting of skepticism. A recent issue of *Time* magazine contains iconoclasm on the subject of Joseph of Nazareth. What do we "know" about him, never mind that we revere him as the husband of Mary and the custodian of the Christ child? Not much, is the answer to that question. Columnist Bill Toland plays it out further: "Joseph's appearance in the New Testament was practically a cameo walk-on: His death was never recorded, his age was never certain, and John's gospel barely mentions him. Our knowledge of the carpenter father is so limited that we are not certain whether he even attended the birth of Jesus or, as some artists have imagined it, whether he napped through the whole event."

The language here betrays the lure of impiety. And there is a cognate temptation, in dealing with figures in the secular world. Sometimes there are cameras on hand to egg skepticism on. No one can ever deny the truth of it, that sometimes President Reagan's eyes closed at high theatrical moments in history. We cannot deny that Thomas Jefferson wrote the great pieties expressed in the Declaration of Independence, and died owning slaves.

What irks, and even grieves, is when the motives of the commentator are detectable as agents of greater designs than merely to touch on amiable eccentricities. The writer who wonders out loud whether Joseph slept through the birth of Christ is fondling a skepticism that seeks not so much humanizing, as desanctifying. The author reports on the shifting views of Joseph over time. He was initially seen as "the chaste caretaker," but it was not long before he was portrayed as "the alienated cuckold." In the late Middle Ages he became "the adoring protector . . . the paternal model for what would eventually be called the nuclear family," and now he is the "modern-day evangel," a "lunch-pail hero not born to holiness but who, by his hard-won and steadfast belief, finds a role in salvation."

It has to be true that reverence discourages trivialization, and that such as has recently been retailed about Joseph encourages an exploration of the meaning of impiety. In some societies, impiety was punishable by death. The thinking, most directly expressed, was that the society's god would take offense at slights and punish them by corporate displeasure, for instance the visitation of a plague.

Socrates was condemned to death for impiety, for putatively disregarding or offending the Athenian gods, whose displeasure the judges would not court. It is rather a pity that Socrates gave impiety a good name, Socrates being Socrates, his accusers being Philistines. (A respectable case can be made justifying the sentence given to Socrates.)

But impiety is not merely the violation of the command against taking in vain the name of Our Lord. It is also the denigration of holy things, and not only those which are housed with altars and organs. To mention the saints of modern liberty without any sign of appreciation is an impiety that casts doubt on one's care about freedom, and about the deference owed to man because he is God's creature.

A retreat from the lure of doctrinal skepticism tells us about the long, effective reach of grace. The scholar Howard Edington, who is also a Presbyterian minister, is quoted at the end of *Time* magazine's feature on Joseph. Edington wrote, "Joseph took God's son into his heart, thus discovering a purpose for his own life within the greater purposes of God." Then Edington concludes, in words many Christians might echo, "My prayer is that you will do the same."

—December 30, 2005

ENVOI

The Patrimony and Civic Obligation

We are accustomed to hearing it said that criminals ought to repay their "debt" to society. The term of obligation is used too narrowly. Those who do not murder, rape, or steal also owe a debt to their society, if only because it pauses to distinguish between those who rape, murder, and steal and those who do not. Call it, broadly, a debt to civilization; more distinctly, a debt to the "fatherland"—the nation-state into which we were born, or to which we repaired.

The debt we owe our civilizational patrimony is impossible to define if we set out to particularize it. If you listen, in Bethlehem, Pennsylvania, in May of every year, to four hundred musicians performing the *St. Matthew Passion* by J. S. Bach, it becomes numbingly plain that there is simply no way in which one can "repay" the musical patrimony we have inherited. I speak of Bethlehem's annual festival, but one needn't make the pilgrimage, not at all. I first heard the *St. Matthew Passion* at age fifteen at school on 78-rpm shellac records. To hear the entire *Passion* required listening to about fifty records. By the time I graduated from college I could have it all on four long-playing records. One year after graduating I heard Leonard Bernstein on television announcing that the performance he was about to conduct of the *Passion* (or was it the B-Minor Mass?—it doesn't matter) would be heard that afternoon by more human beings than had heard it cumulatively since its composition in the 1720s. Twenty years later I could have the *Passion* on a half-dozen cassettes. And now it comes on four compact disks. They tell me that before I die it will occupy a very small part of a single disk, the rest of it presumably being given over to the balance of the hundreds of hours of music that Bach wrote.

All that I need to do, as a mechanical matter, to repay everyone from Bach to the piccolo player is to shell out fifteen or twenty dollars for the four hours of music that can realize sublimity for the ear and—an important point in this context—for the mind, if the experience, appealing at once to all the senses, is synaesthetic. One correctly *struggles* to distinguish between reveling in the *Passion* and rejoicing in it, because the latter sensation awakens an extrapersonal sense of obligation for the pleasures received.

Or consider the *Oxford English Dictionary*. It is sensually pleasurable even to write about *that* miracle—not simply the dictionary, but its astonishing new accessibility, the lexicographical equivalent of the *Passion* on compact disk. It is expensive today, but will be less so tomorrow, I warrant; currently the whole of the *O.E.D.* (the original edition) can be had for nine hundred fifty dollars on a single disk. This accomplishment permits you not merely to avoid the indignity of having to pick up a volume and hunt down the word you are looking for, but also to mobilize disparate energies of an entirely different kind in order to pursue allied or entirely different interests. You can ask your computer etymological questions, or historical or literary questions, causing it to dispatch millions of bytes to scurry about several million words in order to assemble, in any sequence that suits your curiosity, and present to you, neatly collated, anything you wish to put together that lies within the pages of the dictionary. (How long would it take you, manually, to establish how frequently citations from the book of Isaiah had been used?) How do you "repay" the debt you owe to those mostly anonymous lexicographers who labored, and indeed continue to do so, to give us, at the touch of a finger, access to information electronically delivered that a battalion of monks working several lifetimes could not accumulate?

Access. Freedom. I think back to an afternoon in 1955 when I visited the University of Salamanca and was taken to its original library. Salamanca is the second-oldest university in Europe, and in one of its rooms, not much larger than a barbershop, reposes the entire known literature of the West, as of the thirteenth century. The scholars and the monks could enter the library to do their studying. But a Big Bertha was there, a really big cannon to discourage them from removing from that little room any of its all but irreplaceable treasures. The ultimate weapon continues to hang over the arched doorway, a few lines of calligraphy, modestly framed: *A bull of excommunication, signed by Pope Gregory IX.* Remove a book from that library, and you go to Hell.

It goes on. I am a sailor who does his own navigation. Stored inside a two-hundred-dollar instrument about the size of my hand I have the exact location of fifty-seven navigational stars, six planets, the sun, and the moon, for every second of every day between now and 2010. This instrument isn't, for me, a toy. By consulting it I have known how to nudge slightly the wheel of my sailing vessel to come upon remote little islands in obscure parts of the world. The market answer to the question, How do I repay those who made this possible? is easy: I pay the merchandiser two hundred dollars.

I am less than satisfied that I have requited that debt. Or perhaps the point is that I ought to be less than satisfied.

Yes, there are the utilitarians who will tell you that we owe nothing at all beyond whatever it is we are ready to give, in exchange for what we see displayed in the market. In a biography of Salvador Dali it is recorded that, quarreling with his father when a young man, the hot-blooded artist set out in a fury to dispose once and for all of the question, "What do I owe my father?" He sought to answer the question by withdrawing during a night of passion and collecting his ejaculate, which he sent to his father in an envelope marked *Paid in Full*. That was a high-wire act of reductionism, but philosophically bulletproof: The debt to one's father, repaid by the biological reciprocal. In the implicit social philosophy of too many of our contemporaries one finds little that helps to explain why this is less than an appropriate, let alone tasteful, return: this discharge of one's total obligation to one's father.

No fatherhood, no brotherhood was Nelson Rockefeller's social philosophy as he expressed it in public (some called it BOMFOG—the Brotherhood of Man, the Fatherhood of God). Other attempts to express collateral relations in the shared patrimony are found here and there. Tocqueville lamented that while "aristocracy had made a chain of all the members of the community, from the peasant to the king . . . democracy breaks that chain and severs every link of it. Thus, not only does democracy induce to make every man forget his ancestors, it hides his descendants and separates his contemporaries from him; it throws him back forever upon himself alone, and threatens in the end to confine him utterly within the solitude of his own heart." An arresting indictment of a democratic peril: That which makes a man a stranger to his father makes him also a stranger to his brother—and what severs the cords binding the generations also snaps the web that unites contemporaries. The orphan. Solitary, estranged from tradition and therefore from communion: He is the figure of modern alienation, the making of the mass-man. Ortega y Gasset anatomized this avatar of modernity. Three decades ago I set out to write a book to remark the thirtieth anniversary of the appearance of his classic, *The Revolt of the Masses*. I intended to call my little book *The Revolt Against the Masses*, because I thought I saw on the social horizon in America signs of a disposition to reject the nescient aimlessness Ortega had diagnosed. The antinomian explosion that followed—we speak sometimes of the "Vietnam years," sometimes of the "kid years," or, simply, of "the Sixties"—proved I had profoundly misread the auguries.

Ortega's analysis of the mass-man is timelier today, in the rubble of the ensuing social explosion, than when he wrote it, or when I first thought to respond. I very much wish that the meaning of the word "masses" was not so fixed in the Anglo-Saxon world as the aptest word to describe what Ortega was declaiming against, because the word as we use it has either Marxist or plutocratic connotations. True, the "masses" about whom Marx wrote weren't the huddled masses welcomed by the Statue of Liberty: The masses of Emma Lazarus were merely the numerous poor. The masses of Marx were the proletariat, the hollow men of the Industrial Revolution.

Not Ortega's masses. Ortega was talking about a quality of mind unrelated to factors of wealth or poverty—or, indeed, of erudition. He was talking about the disposition of modern man *to take for granted* everything he enjoys, without any sense of incurring an obligation, either to repay the old woman from whose larder he has helped himself, or even to share with others what the larder contains.

A handy analogue is the challenge of conservation. The insight has gradually crystallized in the common consciousness that a man who cuts down a tree owes the planet one (1) seedling. In the first decades of the twentieth century, that obligation was institutionalized in the United States by various laws generally associated with the presidency of Theodore Roosevelt. The question became subtler as, with more polished instruments at hand, we developed skills to measure more impalpable abrasions against the planet than the missing tree. We began to ponder endangered species. And the finite supply of fossil fuels. And then the invisible particulates that attack the human lung and the ozone layer over the earth.

About our debt to the planet there is nowadays a considerable consciousness. A thriving social movement is concerned with conservation in the widest sense. As with almost every movement, there are advocates who go to extremes. (Admire as I did President Kennedy's secretary of the interior, Stewart Udall, I remember writing at the high tide of his influence that Mr. Udall sometimes left the impression that he would have arrested the development of the West rather than risk getting in the way of one meandering buffalo.) But forget fanaticism; the consolidation of a social insight is what matters.

In politics and social philosophy there is a movement that shares with conservation an etymology that is also a perception. This perception is that the past is alive in the present, and that all the effects of action and thought are amplified by concentric rings of consequence which the utilitarian's Benthamite calculus is too crude to record. The movement, in politics, that has ramified from that radical perception is, I maintain, conservatism. The conservative movement perceives connections between the individual and the community beyond those that relate either to the state or to the market-place. That is the point, the primary rationale, of this essay. And one need not be a conservative in other particulars to respect it.

It was this essentially conservative insight that the liberal John Stuart Mill expressed when he wrote that "though society is not founded on a contract, and though no good purpose is answered by inventing a contract in order to deduce social obligations from it, every one who receives the protection of society owes a return for the benefit, and the fact of living in a society renders it indispensable that each should be bound to observe a certain line of conduct toward the rest."

The difficulty lies in defining the appropriate "return" for the benefit. That we should answer a formal call to arms when the state is in danger is all but universally acknowledged as one of those returns we owe to society. A second return is taxation. And the nexus between that which absorbs the single largest slice of our taxes (education) and the return we are giving society raises militantly relevant questions. If a citizen is expressing a "return" to his society by consenting to be taxed for the purpose of providing education, he is presumed to care that the society's children are taught and to care what it is that the society's children are going to be taught. His concern is that the children will be taught to understand the philosophical reasoning by which that seasoned citizen was himself governed years ago when he made no objection to the draft that called him to military service, and is governed today when he makes no objection to the tax collector who comes to get from him his share of the cost of running the schools. The schools, then, become vessels for preserving the principles that generated the disposition to sacrifice in order to make this return to society.

What preserves the idea beyond mere schooling? A formal attempt at requital, the citizen to the nation. The new challenge is to suggest an appropriate form, one that doesn't violate the libertarian presumption against rendering to Caesar any power Caesar does not need, and in any case ought not to want. We need to seek out the form, and to frame a policy whose ground is sunk deep in the ethos. If we succeed, democratic legitimacy comes with progressive public acceptance. This acceptance one can anticipate as the fruit of that policy become palpable, and the sense of duty in the citizen is stimulated, evolving into a sense of gratitude, and is fulfilled. The citizen serene as the debtor returning from the lending insti-tution, canceled mortgage in hand.

—Excerpt from *Gratitude*, 1990

INDEX